ANNUAL REVIEW OF IRISH LAW 2006

UNITED KINGDOM
Sweet & Maxwell Ltd
London

AUSTRALIA
Law Book Co.
Sydney

CANADA AND THE USA
Carswell
Toronto

HONG KONG
Sweet & Maxwell Asia

NEW ZEALAND
Brookers
Wellington

SINGAPORE AND MALAYSIA
Sweet & Maxwell Asia
Singapore and Kuala Lumpur

Annual Review
of Irish Law 2006

Raymond Byrne

B.C.L., LL.M., Barrister-at-Law
Director of Research, Law Reform Commission
Lecturer in Law, Dublin City University

William Binchy

B.A., B.C.L., LL.M., F.T.C.D., Barrister-at-Law
Regius Professor of Laws, Trinity College, Dublin

Thomson Round Hall
2007

Published in 2007 by
Thomson Round Hall
43 Fitzwilliam Place,
Dublin 2, Ireland

Typeset by
Gough Typesetting Services
Dublin

Printed by
MPG Cornwall

ISBN 978-1-85800-469-3
ISSN 0791-1084

A catalogue record for this book
is available from the British Library

Table of Contents

Table of Contents

Preface

This is the twentieth volume in the Annual Review series, and as with previous volumes, our purpose continues to be to provide a review of legal developments, judicial and statutory, that occurred in 2006.

We are conscious of the many changes that have occurred in the 20 years since the first Annual Review was published, notably in the increasing volume of legislation enacted by the Oireachtas and the consequent increase in secondary legislation. We are equally aware of the increasing volume of case law that emerges each year from the courts and which we assess in each annual volume. Accessibility to this increasing volume of material has changed beyond recognition in recent years, in particular with the advent of electronic sources for both legislation and case law. We appreciate that this will remain an issue requiring constant attention in the years ahead and we merely note here the importance that legal researchers, practitioners and the general public attach to this. We must also record here our particular thanks to the many specialist contributors who have added their particular insights to the various chapters of the Annual Review volumes in recent years and also to our many colleagues whose assistance in ways too numerous to note, have eased the burden of analysing the legislation and case law discussed here.

Returning to this volume, in terms of legislation, we endeavour to discuss those Acts and statutory instruments enacted and made during the year. In terms of case law, this includes those judgments delivered in 2006, regardless of whether they have been (or will be) reported and which were available to us and our contributors by mid-2007.

Once again it is a pleasure to thank those who made the task of completing this volume less onerous. For this 20th volume of the Annual Review series, we are delighted to have had the benefit of specialist contributions on Asylum and Immigration Law, Company Law, Constitutional Law, Contract Law, Information Law and the Ombudsman, Legislation, Planning Law, Practice and Procedure, Probate and Succession Law, Social Welfare and Sports law included in this volume. We continue to take final responsibility for the overall text as in the past, but are especially grateful for the contributions of Nuala Egan and Patricia Brazil in Asylum and Immigration Law, Gráinne Callanan in Company Law, Oran Doyle and Estelle Feldman in Constitutional Law, Fergus Ryan in Contract Law, Estelle Feldman in Information Law and the Ombudsman, Brian Hunt in Legislation, Garrett Simons in Planning and Development Law, Melody Buckley in Practice and Procedure, Albert Keating in Probate and Succession Law, Gerry Whyte in Social Welfare and Neville Cox in Sports law

Finally, we are very grateful to Thomson Round Hall, in particular Nicola Barrett, Suzanna Henry and Susan Rossney, and to Gough Typesetting Services, whose professionalism ensures the continued production of this series.

Raymond Byrne and William Binchy,
Dublin

October 2007

Table of Cases

IRELAND

EUROPEAN CASE LAW

European Court of Human Rights

European Court of Justice

UNITED KINGDOM CASE LAW

INTERNATIONAL CASE LAW

Australia

Canada

Table of Legislation

TABLE OF STATUTES

STATUTORY INSTRUMENTS

EUROPEAN LEGISLATION

UK STATUTES

NEW ZEALAND STATUTES

INTERNATIONAL TREATIES AND CONVENTIONS

Table of Legislation lxi

Administrative Law

APPROPRIATION

The Appropriation Act 2006 provided as follows. For the year ended December 31, 2006, the amount of supply grants in accordance with the Central Fund (Permanent Provisions) Act 1965 was €40,189,155,000. Under the Public Accounts and Charges Act 1891, the sum for appropriations-in-aid was €4,023,439,000. The 2006 Act also provided, in accordance with s.91 of the Finance Act 2004, for carrying over into the year ending December 31, 2006 undischarged appropriations for capital supply services totalling €159,135,000. This, in effect, allowed this amount, which had not been spent on, for example, large infrastructure projects in 2006, to be carried over into 2007. The 2006 Act also provided that the financial resolutions passed by Dáil Éireann on December 6, 2006 (after the 2006 Budget) would have legal effect provided that, in accordance with s.4 of the Provisional Collection of Taxes Act 1927, legislation was enacted in 2007 (in the Finance Act 2007) to give full effect to the resolutions. The 2006 Act came into effect on its signature by the President on December 19, 2006.

FREEDOM OF INFORMATION

Prescribed public bodies   The Freedom of Information Act 1997 (Prescribed Bodies) Regulations 2006 (S.I. No. 297 of 2006) prescribe each of the long list of bodies in the Schedule as a public body for the purpose of the Freedom of Information Act 1997 by their inclusion in Sch.1, para.1(5) of the 1997 Act. They came into force on May 31, 2006.

JUDICIAL REVIEW

Much of the case law under Ord.84 of the Rules of the Superior Courts 1986 that arose in 2006 is discussed in the various chapters in this *Annual Review* where the substantive subjects arising are detailed, notably in the Immigration and Planning Law chapters. Further reference may also be obtained through the Table of Statutory Instruments under the entry for the Rules of the Superior Courts 1986. The case law referred to here deals with remaining matters concerning judicial review where other substantive issues did not arise.

Discovery: DPP   In *Cunningham v President of Circuit Court and DPP*
[2006] I.E.S.C. 440; Supreme Court, July 26, 2006, the Supreme Court ordered
the Director of Public Prosecutions (DPP) or his agent to make an affidavit of
discovery against the following background. In July 2003, the applicant had
been charged with seven offences contrary to s.23 of the Offences Against the
Person Act 1861 (administration of a noxious substance, since replaced by
offences in the Non-Fatal Offences against the Person Act 1997), arising from
her handling of Anti-D Immunogloblin while she was a biochemist employed
by the National Blood Transfusion Service. Three of the alleged offences were
said to have taken place in 1991 or 1992 and four in 1977. After these charges
had been brought, the applicant brought judicial review proceedings seeking
injunctive relief on the grounds of delay. In the course of these proceedings
she sought an order for discovery and the High Court granted discovery of
some of the categories of documents sought, but refused discovery of: "(a) All
correspondence between the office of the DPP and the Gardaí in respect of the
progress of the criminal investigation into the applicant ...". On appeal, the
applicant submitted that one of the issues for resolution in the judicial review
proceedings was whether the prosecution proceeded with due expedition. The
DPP had put forward, amongst the reasons for the long delay, the ongoing
correspondence between his office and stated persons mentioned in affidavits
filed on his behalf. The correspondence was not exhibited and the subject-matter
of it was, for the most part, not fully identified. The DPP contended that the
proper approach of the question of prosecutorial delay was not to conduct a
"micro analysis" of every step taken and every direction given, or to conduct a
complete documentary review. Rather, there should be "a more general analysis
of the broad periods of time in question and the general steps that were being
taken in the investigation." It was submitted that, if the applicant were to
succeed in her application, this would undermine the special protection of the
DPP, recently acknowledged by the Supreme Court in *Dunphy v DPP* [2006]
1 I.L.R.M. 241. Counsel for the DPP argued that, although the applicant stated
that she was not seeking the reasons for her prosecution, her application had
the same effect.

    As indicated, the Supreme Court held that the DPP or his agent should
make an affidavit of discovery. Citing the decisions in *Dunphy v DPP* [2006]
1 I.L.R.M. 241 and *Hannigan v DPP* [2001] 1 I.R. 379, the court stated that
this finding "in no way removes, reduces, or limits the special position" of the
DPP as to giving reasons for his decisions to prosecute or not to do so. The
court noted that the file on the applicant was in the DPP's office for over six
years and it considered that this was, prima facie, indicative of prosecutorial
delay, especially in the context of the enormous volume of material already
available at the start of the DPP's consideration of the file. The court accepted
that the period of time may turn out to be quite justified, but it required it to
be justified. The court concluded that the applicant must have the opportunity
of satisfying herself that what the DPP had chosen to refer to represented the

whole of the material relevant to the issue in question, and had been accurately characterised. The DPP had the fullest entitlement to claim privilege over any document, over all documents, or any portion of any document as he may be advised or think fit, but the court held that he must list every document, whether he is willing to disclose it or not.

NATIONAL ECONOMIC AND SOCIAL DEVELOPMENT OFFICE

The National Economic and Social Development Office Act 2006 established the National Economic and Social Development Office (NESDO) on a statutory basis. NESDO incorporates three existing bodies, the National Economic and Social Council (NESC), the National Economic and Social Forum (NESF) and the National Centre for Partnership and Performance (NCPP). Both the NESC and the NESF have been in existence on their own for some time but the more recently established NCPP—successor to the National Centre for Partnership—arises from the commitment in the social partnership agreement, the *Programme for Prosperity and Fairness* (PPF), that it be located with the NESC and the NESF, within the National Economic and Social Development Office, where it would work with IBEC and ICTU in supporting the deepening of the partnership. All three bodies have been operating on a non-statutory basis since their establishment. The 2006 Act places them, for the first time, on a statutory basis. The NESDO came into effect on January 1, 2007 through the National Economic and Social Development Office Act 2006 (Establishment Day) Order 2006 (S.I. No. 606 of 2006).

The National Economic and Social Council (NESC) was established in 1973 as an advisory body to the Government on the development of the national economy and the achievement of social justice. The council also provides a forum in which views can be exchanged between people who have a common interest in the development of the economy and the pursuit of social justice. The council is representative of the major economic and social interests in our society and this fact is reflected in its membership. Many of its strategy reports have provided the framework for negotiation of the national agreements between Government and the social partners since 1987.

The National Economic and Social Forum (NESF) was originally set up by the Government in 1993 for the purpose of widening the social partnership process and of achieving consensus on as wide a basis as possible on major economic and social policy issues. Since 1998, the forum's work has focused on evaluating the implementation of policies dealing with equality and social inclusion. The main tasks of the forum are as follows: to monitor and analyse the implementation of specific measures and programmes identified, especially those concerned with the achievement of equality and social inclusion; to do so through consideration of reports prepared by teams comprising the social

partners, with appropriate expertise and representatives of relevant Departments
and agencies and its own secretariat; to prepare reports to be published by
the forum with such comments as may be considered appropriate; and to
ensure that the teams compiling such reports take account of the experience
of implementing bodies, customers and clients, including regional variations,
in such experience. The forum may consider such policy issues on its own
initiative or at the request of the Government.

The National Centre for Partnership and Performance (NCPP) was
established by the Government in 2002. Its purpose is to support and drive
change in the Irish workplace. It enables organisations in the private and
public sectors to respond to change, to build capability and to improve
performance through partnership. The NCPP's mission is to support and
facilitate organisational change, based on partnership, to bring about improved
performance and mutual gains. This contributes to national competitiveness,
better public services, higher living standards, a better quality of work life
and the development of the workplace of the future. The centre will carry out
this role by conducting research, identifying past practice and developing new
national strategies and new models for partnership in the workplace.

It was pointed out during the debate on the 2006 Act that these distinct bodies
will come together to operate as the National Economic and Social Development
Office (NESDO). Their own roles are separate yet complementary, and the 2006
Act established NESDO as a means of supporting the three constituent bodies
and providing administrative and logistical support on a cost-effective basis. It
will also act as the employer of staff, and so provide a better career structure
for the secretariat of the three bodies.

PUBLIC SERVICE RECRUITMENT AND APPOINTMENTS

Commission for Public Service Appointments   A number of important
orders were made in 2006 under the Public Service Management (Recruitment
and Appointment) Act 2004 (*Annual Review of Irish Law 2004*, pp.18–21).
The Commission for Public Service Appointments (Additional Function)
Order 2006 (S.I. No. 599 of 2006) provides for the following additional
function to be conferred on the Commission for Public Service Appointments:
making codes of practice relating to recruitment and selection processes for
unestablished civil servants. The Commission for Public Service Appointments
(Additional Function) (No.2) Order 2006 (S.I. No. 600 of 2006) provides for
the following additional function to be conferred on the Commission for Public
Service Appointments: making codes of practice relating to recruitment and
selection processes for those persons with a disability within the meaning of
the Disability Act 2005 (*Annual Review of Irish Law 2005*, pp.313–21). The
Commission for Public Service Appointments (Additional Function) (No.3)

Order 2006 (S.I. No. 601 of 2006) provides for the following additional function to be conferred on the Commission for Public Service Appointments: making codes of practice relating to recruitment and selection processes in respect of re-grading established civil servants to equivalent grades. The Public Service Management (Recruitment and Appointment) Act 2004 (Additional Function for Licence Holders) Order 2006 (S.I. No. 602 of 2006) provides for the following additional function to be conferred on the Commission for Public Service Appointments: making codes of practice relating to recruitment and selection processes in respect of re-grading established civil servants to equivalent grades. The order also enables an office-holder who holds a recruitment licence under Pt 4 of the Public Service Management (Recruitment and Appointment) Act 2004 to carry out assessments of established civil servants for the purposes of re-grading to equivalent grades.

STATE BODIES

Aer Lingus The Aer Lingus Act 2004 (Commencement of Section 3) Order 2006 (S.I. No. 348 of 2006) brought s.3 of the Aer Lingus Act 2004 (*Annual Review of Irish Law 2004*, pp.22–23) into force on June 30, 2006. The 2004 Act provided the legal framework to facilitate private sector investment in what had been the state-owned airline. The 2006 Commencement Order enabled the Minister of Finance to dispose of shares in the airline. This was followed by a part-flotation of the company's shares in 2006, with the State retaining a "golden share".

TRIBUNAL OF INQUIRY

Privacy in business affairs In *Caldwell v Mahon* [2006] I.E.H.C. 86, High Court, February 15, 2006, Hanna J. declined to grant an injunction to the applicant who had claimed that his business privacy interests were being put at risk, by the respondent, the members of the tribunal of inquiry into planning and payment to politicians, which had been established in 1997. As part of the investigation into allegations of corruption in the planning process, the tribunal of inquiry began an investigation into the ownership of certain lands. In the course of its enquiries, the tribunal examined the business affairs of the applicant who was the owner, through a limited liability company, of some of the lands under investigation, and his relationship with another businessman and a politician. The applicant sought to challenge the decision of the tribunal to move from the private phase into the public phase, alleging that the tribunal's enquiries would result in the disclosure of his confidential business affairs in breach of his constitutional right to privacy and Art.8 of the European Convention on Human Rights. In an earlier decision the High Court held that, at the time the tribunal made its decision to move into the public hearing phase, the Convention did not form part of domestic law.

It is worth noting that Hanna J. proceeded on the basis that the right to privacy did extend to business affairs, but he also took the view that such a right could only exist at the outer reaches of and the furthest remove from the core personal right to privacy. An individual's right to privacy in business affairs must, therefore, become subject to the limitations and exigencies of the common good, subject at all times to the requirements of constitutional justice and fair procedures, citing the views in the Canadian case *Bernstein v Bester* (1996) 4 B.C.L.R 449. Citing the Supreme Court decisions in *Haughey v Moriarty* [1999] 3 I.R. 1 and *Desmond v Moriarty* [2004] 1 I.R. 334, he held that the right to privacy in relation to private dealings with others was not absolute, even at its purely personal nucleus. When dealing with the applicant's business affairs in the context of the tribunal, Hanna J. concluded that such right to privacy as the applicant possessed had long since been overtaken by the exigencies of the common good. Even if the Convention had formed part of domestic law at the date of the tribunal's decision, and assuming the applicant had a protected right to privacy under the Convention in respect of his business affairs, the compromise or interference with that right was—in the words of Art.8—authorised by law and in accordance with it, necessary in a democratic society, related to a pressing social need, and proportionate. On that basis, he refused the injunctive relief sought.

Asylum and Immigration Law

PATRICIA BRAZIL B.L., Lecturer in Law, Trinity College, Dublin and
NUALA EGAN, B.L.

CASE LAW

**Application for discovery in judicial review proceedings alleging bias
against Refugee Appeals Tribunal** *Popovici v Nicholson and Refugee
Appeals Tribunal*, unreported, April 26, 2006 was an application for the
production of certain documents relating to the decisions and procedures of
the first- and second-named respondents in the course of conducting appeal
hearings concerning the applicants pursuant to the provisions of the Refugee Act
1996, as amended. The application was made subsequent to an order for leave
to proceed by way of judicial review which was made on February 9, 2005.

The applicants' case concerned a claim of general bias on behalf of the first-
and second-named respondents, evidenced by the alleged pattern of findings by
the first-named respondent and the procedures in assigning cases adopted by
the second-named respondent and a specific complaint concerning the manner
in which the first-named respondent conducted the appeal hearing in question.
The application for leave was not contested by the respondents.

De Valera J. commenced his judgment by noting that, in conceding the
application for leave to seek judicial review, the respondents must be taken
to have conceded that there were "substantial grounds" on which to base the
applicants' claim. This being so, the learned judge held that the dictum of Finlay
C.J. in *AIB Bank plc v Ernst and Whinney* [1993] 1 I.R. 375 was relevant:

> "The basis purpose and reason for the procedure of discovery ... is to
> ensure as far as possible that the full facts concerning any matter in
> dispute before the court are capable of being presented to the court by
> the parties concerned, so that justice on full information, rather than a
> partial or limited revelation of the facts arising in a particular action,
> may be done."

The learned High Court judge also adopted as a correct statement of law the
following passage from Delany and McGrath, *Civil Procedure in the Superior
Courts* (2nd ed., Thomson Round Hall, 2005), para.10–03:

> "... the discovery process is designed to narrow the issues which must
> be resolved between the parties and to facilitate the resolution of the
> case in as speedy and cost efficient manner as possible."

De Valera J. concluded:

> "I am satisfied, therefore, that there should be discovery of documents
> by the respondents to ensure that the full facts of this matter come before
> the court hearing the judicial review application but the scope of the
> documentation sought by the applicant is too extensive and it should be
> restricted to such documents as are necessary for the purpose of ensuring
> a proper and comprehensive hearing of the facts and arguments."

In so holding, reference was made to the decision of Finlay Geoghegan J. in
KA v Minister for Justice, Equality and Law Reform [2003] 2 I.R. 93 where
it was held:

> "The limitation on discovery ... is that it must not be considered to be a
> fishing exercise ... it is not sufficient for an applicant simply to make an
> assertion not based on any substantial fact and then seek discovery in the
> hope that there will exist documents which support the contention."

De Valera J. applied this principle to refuse discovery in respect of certain
categories of the discovery sought on the grounds that they constituted a
"fishing expedition" and furthermore were not relevant in the context of the
proceedings. However, de Valera J. granted discovery in respect of certain
categories relating to statistical information, pointing out that only statistics
already compiled and available were discoverable as "the discovery procedure
is not appropriate to seek to force the respondents to compile statistics from
information in their possession for the benefit of the applicant". In relation to
the applicants' request for documents relating to the assignment of cases to
tribunal members, both generally and specifically in relation to the applicants,
de Valera J. was satisfied that this was an appropriate heading pursuant to which
discovery should be allowed. Finally, it was noted that it was not clear that any
audio-visual recording or transcript in respect of the applicants' hearing with
the first-named respondent existed, but that this was an appropriate matter for
discovery if same was, in fact, available.

De Valera J. concluded that whilst it was appropriate for the respondents to
make discovery in terms of the order of the court, the extent of the obligation
on the respondents was as follows:

> "the respondents need only disclose documents already in existence for
> the purpose of this discovery and do not need to create, or extrapolate,
> statistics or tables not already in existence".

Thus, the learned judge clarified that this meant it was open to the respondents
to object to the production of certain documents as envisaged in the specimen

"Affidavit as to documents" set out at Appendix C, No.10 of the Rules of the Superior Courts.

Application of Art.31 of Convention Relating to the Status of Refugees in Irish law   In *Siritanu v DPP* [2006] I.E.H.C 26 the applicant sought an interlocutory injunction restraining the respondent, his servants or agents from taking any further step in the prosecution of the applicant in the proceedings entitled *People (DPP) v Siritanu*, bearing the charge sheet number 369913, pending the determination of the proceedings. The applicant also sought leave to apply for a declaration that the continued prosecution of the applicant was an abuse of the process of the court and an order of mandamus by way of application for judicial review directing the respondent to consider the request of the applicant that the said prosecution be withdrawn on the ground that the applicant was entitled to the benefit of Art.31 of the United Nations Convention Relating to the Status of Refugees 1951.

The applicant was a Moldovan national who arrived in the State on March 7, 2005. On arrival, the applicant was charged with certain offences under the Refugee Acts relating to the destruction of papers and his failure to establish his identity. Ultimately, these charges were withdrawn as his true passport was obtained by him. The applicant was subsequently rearrested and charged with an offence under s.26 of the Criminal Justice (Theft and Fraud) Act 2001 relating to the use of a false instrument. When the matter was before the District Court on foot of the said charge it was indicated to the District Court that an application was being made to the respondent seeking to have the proceedings withdrawn on the grounds that his prosecution would be in breach of Art.31 of the United Nations Convention Relating to the Status of Refugees 1951. The applicant relied on the decision of *R. v Uxbridge Magistrates Court, Ex p. Adimi* [2001] Q.B. 667 in support of his application. However, by letter dated September 8, 2005, the applicant's request for withdrawal of the proceedings was refused on the basis that the portion of the judgment of Simon Browne L.J. in *Adimi* which was favourable to the applicant had been reconsidered by the judge himself in *R. (European Roma Rights) v Prague Immigration Offices* [2004] 2 W.L.R. 147. The respondent further noted that the applicant's situation was governed by the decision of the High Court in this jurisdiction in *Sofinetti v Anderson*, unreported, High Court, March 18, 2004,[1] where O'Higgins J. rejected the suggestion that Art.31 of the Refugee Convention Act 1951 had been incorporated into Irish law and rejected the suggestion that the applicant in that case was immune from criminal prosecution by reason of the Convention.

The applicant sought to distinguish the decision of O'Higgins J. in *Sofinetti* on the basis that, in the present proceedings, the applicant was not making a claim for immunity from prosecution, but rather sought to request the DPP to

---

[1]   Referred to in *Annual Review of Irish Law 2005*, pp.34–38.

consider the provisions of Art.31. It was argued that the letter from the office of the respondent made clear that the respondent was refusing to consider the position under Art.31. Dunne J. referred to the detailed arguments of counsel for the applicant and the respondent, and the various submissions advanced on behalf of each party. The learned High Court judge accepted the submission of the respondent that the reliefs sought by the applicant in effect amounted to seeking prohibition (although that was not how the application was characterised), and accepted that in those circumstances the standard to be met by the applicant in order to succeed was to show that there was a real risk that he could not get a fair trial.

Dunne J. noted that this was a somewhat difficult conclusion to reach because, in the circumstances of this case, the applicant had not sought to demonstrate that there was a serious risk of an unfair trial if the relief sought was not granted, but rather the applicant simply sought to have the respondent make a decision, one way or another, having regard to the provisions of Art.31. In this regard it was noted that if, having made such decision, the decision was one to prosecute, then the only reliance that could be placed by the applicant on Art.31 in court would be in mitigation of any sentence on the basis that "[c]learly the provisions of Article 31 do not afford a defence to the prosecution". Dunne J. concluded that the applicant had failed to show a serious risk of an unfair trial and that his application must, therefore, fail.

Notwithstanding this conclusion, Dunne J. proceeded to consider the question as to whether or not the applicant had crossed the threshold necessary to apply for leave in this case. In doing so, the learned High Court judge noted that the decision of the respondent of September 8, 2005 had regard to the terms of Art.31 of the Convention, but proceeded on the basis of the decision of the High Court in *Sofinetti* to the effect that Art.31 could not be invoked by an applicant in relation to a prosecution undertaken by the DPP. Dunne J. referred to the conclusions of O'Higgins J. in this regard, where he held:

> "In the light of Article 29.6 of the Constitution taken in conjunction with the duties imposed on the DPP by the Constitution and the Prosecution of Offences Act, 1974 there can be no legitimate expectations in the applicant that Article 31 of the Convention could be successfully invoked by her so as to prevent the DPP prosecuting her and maintaining such prosecution."

Dunne J. concluded that there was no basis for disagreeing with the conclusion of O'Higgins J., nor was there any basis for distinguishing the conclusion on the issue of legitimate expectation in the circumstances of this case. On the basis that the respondent correctly had regard to the decision in *Sofinetti* and applied it appropriately, Dunne J. proceeded to consider whether there was any purpose in compelling the respondent to consider a request from an applicant in circumstances where there was no legitimate expectation that

Art.31 of the Convention could be successfully invoked so as to prevent the DPP from prosecuting and maintaining a prosecution such as that in the present circumstances, asking: "What right enforceable by mandamus could there be to compel a consideration by the respondent under Article 31 in circumstances where Article 31 cannot be invoked?"

Dunne J. held that no such right could exist, and that what the applicant sought to do was to delay his prosecution to have a request considered that would afford no benefit to the applicant in circumstances where the respondent had made his position abundantly clear. In the circumstances, the learned High Court judge was satisfied that the applicant had not satisfied the requirement to show that there were substantial grounds demonstrated which could give rise to leave to apply for judicial review.

Challenge to refusal of residency application by non-national parents of Irish citizen children pursuant to "IBC/05 scheme" As noted in the *Annual Review of Irish Law 2005*,[2] on January 14, 2005 the Minister for Justice announced revised arrangements for the processing of claims for permission to remain from the non-national parents of Irish children who were born before January 1, 2005, known as the "IBC/05 scheme". The Minister applied fixed criteria in deciding these applications, primarily: (a) continuous residency in the State since the birth of the Irish child; (b) evidence of good character since birth of the Irish child; and (c) evidence of involvement in upbringing of child. In practice, failure to satisfy the Minister of any one of these criteria resulted in the application for residency being refused. A total of 17,917 applications were received and processed under the IBC/05 scheme, and on the basis of the cases completed by January 31, 2006, 16,693 applicants were given leave to remain, with refusal decisions given in 1,119 cases. The manner in which the scheme was applied was challenged in a number of test cases, with the lead decision being that of *Bode v Minister for Justice, Equality and Law Reform*, unreported, High Court, November 14, 2006.[3] Each of the applicants sought orders of certiorari quashing the decision of the Minister to refuse their applications for residency pursuant to the scheme.

Finlay Geoghegan J. began by outlining the background to the promulgation of the IBC/05 scheme, including the decision of the Supreme Court in *Lobe and Osayande v Minister for Justice, Equality and Law Reform* [2003] 1 I.R. 1 and the Twenty-Seventh Amendment to the Constitution which was approved

---

[2] See *Annual Review of Irish Law 2005*, pp.11–12.
[3] The related cases were *Adio v Minister for Justice, Equality and Law Reform; Dimbo v Minister for Justice, Equality and Law Reform; Duman v Minister for Justice, Equality and Law Reform; Edet v Minister for Justice, Equality and Law Reform; Fares v Minister for Justice, Equality and Law Reform; Oguekwe v Minister for Justice, Equality and Law Reform; Oviawe v Minister for Justice, Equality and Law Reform.* Supplementary judgments in each of these proceedings were also delivered by Finlay Geoghegan J. on November 14, 2006.

by referendum on June 11, 2004 and signed into law on June 24, 2004. It was noted that the effect of the constitutional amendment was that since January 1, 2005 it is no longer possible for persons to bestow Irish citizenship on their children simply by arranging for their birth in Ireland.

Finlay Geoghegan J. then proceeded to consider the administrative arrangements of the respondent at issue in light of the factual dispute between the parties which was central to the challenges made by the applicants to the validity of the decisions of the respondent. It was contended by the applicants that the revised arrangements announced by the respondent were administrative arrangements according to which each of the applicants was invited or entitled as the parent of an Irish citizen child to apply for leave to remain in the State and which provided for the processing or consideration and determination of such applications. On behalf of the respondent it was submitted that the IBC/05 scheme was not addressed to all parents of Irish-born children born before January 1, 2005, but rather it was a scheme directed only towards those parents who fell within the class of person the respondent, as a matter of policy, had determined should be granted residency or leave to remain under the scheme. The distinction was crucial to the determination of the issue, in light of the primary complaints of the applicants that the Minister failed to have regard to the rights of the citizen child, including the child's right to have his or her best interests taken into account, when making a decision to refuse the parents' applications for residency. The learned High Court judge concluded in accordance with their plain meaning that the revised arrangements established by the respondent on January 15, 2005 were addressed to the non-national parents of Irish-born children born before January 1, 2005. It was held that such parents were invited or permitted to apply for permission to remain in the State based upon the parentage of their Irish-born child, and that the respondent by the announcement committed himself to consider and determine applications for permission to remain in the State from parents of Irish-born children born before January 1, 2005 made on form IBC/05.

The primary basis for the applicants' challenges to the negative decisions issued to them under the scheme was that the decisions were invalid or unlawful in that they were taken in breach of personal or fundamental rights of the citizen children guaranteed and protected by the Constitution and the European Convention on Human Rights. It was submitted that the taking of a decision to refuse a parent residency for failure to meet a requirement of continuous residency without considering the rights, including welfare, of the citizen child was in breach of the citizen child's rights under Arts 40.3 and 41 of the Constitution. It was further submitted that the taking of a decision to refuse a parent residency for failure to meet a requirement of continuous residency without considering the rights of the child to respect for his/her private and family life was in breach of the State's obligations under Art.8 of the European Convention on Human Rights and, consequently, in breach of the respondent's obligations under s.3 of the European Convention on Human Rights Act 2003.

The respondent opposed the applicants' contentions on the grounds that the IBC/05 scheme was introduced in the exercise of the inherent power of the Executive to formulate and execute immigration policy, and that the determination of the criteria according to which residency would be granted was a matter of immigration policy and, as such, was not subject to review by the courts. It was submitted that, if the refusal for failure to meet the requirement of continuous residency was subject to review by the court, then the respondent was not under any obligation to consider the rights of the Irish citizen child prior to refusing an application on IBC/05 as the refusal did not alter the status in the State of the refused parent; the refusal did not involve the deportation or breaking up of a family unit; the scheme operated to grant a privilege to which the parents had no entitlement to those who met the criteria under the Scheme; and prior to any deportation, the citizen child's rights and the rights of the family would be considered under the procedure set out in s.3 of the Immigration Act 1999. For similar reasons it was contended that there was no interference with the citizen child's right to respect for his/her private and family life in breach of Art.8 of the Convention.

The applicants asserted the existence of a number of rights which inhered in citizen children, which rights they submitted ought to have been considered by the Minister when refusing the applications for residency by the parents. The applicants asserted that the child enjoyed a right to reside in Ireland, as recognised by the Supreme Court in *Fajujonu v Minister for Justice* [1990] 2 I.R. 151. It was also submitted that each child enjoyed the right to be reared and educated with due regard to welfare, including a right to have his/her welfare considered in the sense of what is in his/her best interests in decisions affecting him/her. This right apparently derived from the personal rights guaranteed pursuant to Art.40.3.1° of the Constitution.[4] For those children whose parents were married to each other, the rights which the child enjoyed as an individual derived from being a member of a family within the meaning of Art.41. The existence of these rights, and in particular the personal rights arising under Art.40.3.1°, was not disputed by the Minister in these cases; rather, it was submitted that the Minister was not under an obligation to have regard to those rights in the context of a refusal under the IBC/05 scheme because such decision did not impact on the child. The Minister expressly declined to place any information before the court which might have justified the refusal, *e.g.* on

---

[4]   The applicants relied on a well-developed body of case law in the adoption context on the rights of children; the following dicta of O'Higgins C.J. in *G v An Bord Uchtála* [1980] I.R. 32 at 56 is a classic statement of those rights:

"Having been born, the child has the right to be fed and to live, to be reared and educated, to have the opportunity of working and of realising his or her full personality and dignity as a human being. These rights of the child (and others which I have not enumerated) must equally be protected and vindicated by the State."

the basis of the common good or proportionality grounds. Finlay Geoghegan J. concluded in relation to this aspect of the challenges:

> "that when the respondent established in January, 2005 the IBC/05 Scheme and when he received applications from the parents of the citizen children and proceeded to consider and determine those applications, at all times he was bound to act in a manner consistent with the State guarantee to defend and vindicate as far as practicable the personal rights of the citizen child including the right to live in the State and to be reared and educated with due regard for his welfare."

This decision was based on the apparently "anomalous" position of parents of citizen children whose applications for residency were refused—such parents had no right or entitlement to be in the State, and most particularly were not permitted to work. It was held by the learned judge that "this had obvious consequences for their ability to provide for their citizen child and also adverse consequences for the rights of the citizen child to be reared and educated with due regard for their welfare."

Having considered the constitutional rights at issue, Finlay Geoghegan J. went on to consider the applicability of the European Convention on Human Rights and the jurisprudence of the European Court of Human Rights. Although not satisfied that the applicants had demonstrated that rights of family life pursuant to Art.8 were engaged in the factual circumstances of each case, it was held that the right to respect for the private life of the citizen child *was* engaged by the refusal of an application under IBC/05, even if no deportation order had issued.[5] In so holding, reference was made to a number of decisions of the European Court of Human Rights, particularly *Sisojeva v Latvia*, unreported, European Court of Human Rights, June 16, 2005, where that court noted:

> "that no formal deportation order has been issued in respect of the applicants. It reiterates, however, that Article 8, like any other provision of the Convention or the Protocols thereto, must be interpreted in such a way that it guarantees not rights that are theoretical or illusory but rights that are practical and effective. Furthermore, while the chief object of Article 8, which deals with the right to respect for one's private and family life, is to protect the individual against arbitrary interference by public authorities, it does not merely compel the State to abstain

---

[5] In defining "private life", Finlay Geoghegan J. referred to the decision of the ECtHR in *Niemietz v Germany* (1992) 16 E.H.R.R. 97 where it was held (at para.29) that: "… it would be too restrictive to limit the notion [of private life] to an 'inner circle' in which the individual may live his own personal life as he chooses to exclude therefrom entirely the outside world not encompassed within that circle. Respect for private life must also comprise to a certain degree the right to establish and develop relationships with other human beings."

from such interference: in addition to this negative undertaking, there may be positive obligations inherent in effective respect for private or family life. In other words, it is not enough for the host State to refrain from deporting the person concerned; it must also, by means of positive measures if necessary, afford him or her the opportunity to exercise the rights in question without interference."[6]

On this basis, Finlay Geoghegan J. held:

"that each of the citizen children who has lived in the State since the date of their birth must be considered to have a private life in the State in the sense of personal and social relationships which result from living in the State. Further, as they are citizens with a constitutionally protected right to live in the State, it is a private life which demands respect from the respondent."

Finlay Geoghegan J. held that the Minister's explicit refusal to consider the best interests of the child when examining an application for residency under IBC/05 was a breach of the constitutional rights of the citizen child and failed to observe the key principles set out by the Supreme Court in *Lobe & Osayende*. Applying the relevant principles as derived from the Convention, Finlay Geoghegan J. concluded:

"Applying the above principles to the position of each citizen child in this and the related applications that the taking by the respondent of a decision to refuse the parent's application without considering the right to private life in the sense of the constitutionally protected personal rights of the citizen child was an interference with the citizen child's rights to respect for his/her private life within the meaning of article 8.1 of the Convention. A decision which constitutes an interference with the right to respect for private life is not necessarily in breach of article 8 of the Convention. It may be permissible if justified under article 8.2. However, counsel for the respondent expressly indicated to the court that no submission was being made on behalf of the respondent that the taking of decisions to refuse an application on IBC/05 by reason of a failure to establish continuous residency since the date of the birth of the citizen child was justified in accordance with the provisions of article 8.2 of the Convention.

Accordingly, it appears to me that in taking the decision to refuse the parent's application on IBC/05 the respondent must be considered to have acted in a manner which is not compatible with the State's obligations under article 8 of the Convention and hence contrary to s.

---

[6] European Court of Human Rights, June 16, 2005, para.104.

3(1) of the Act of 2003."

[**Note:** This decision was the subject of an appeal by the respondent to the Supreme Court, which was heard on May 22, 23 and 24, 2007.]

Constitutionality of statutory entitlement to deem application withdrawn on grounds of non-co-operation   The constitutionality of the statutory entitlement to deem an application for asylum withdrawn on grounds of non-co-operation was addressed in *Olufemi v Minister for Justice, Equality and Law Reform*, unreported, High Court, July 27, 2006.

The applicant was a Nigerian national who claimed to have arrived in Ireland in March 2004. The applicant further claimed that he remained illegally in the State until September 2004 when, while attempting to travel to the United Kingdom in possession of a false international student card, he was apprehended at Dublin Airport. The applicant alleged that he became ill, was taken to Beaumont Hospital, and was later taken back to the airport where he was interviewed by a member of the Garda National Immigration Bureau. It was at that stage that he made an application for refugee status.

The immigration officer who dealt with the applicant averred that, despite being asked, the applicant refused to provide his address or details of any addresses at which he had resided during the period in which he had been in the State. The applicant alleged that that refusal to furnish an address was due to his fear that the friends with whom he was staying would get into trouble. Further, the applicant originally swore that when making out his application for refugee status he was not given any notification of documentation advising him of his obligations. It did, however, later emerge that the applicant actually signed a receipt of notice of his obligations under s.9(4A), dated September 4, 2004.

It was not disputed that the applicant failed to supply the second-named respondent, the Office of the Refugee Applications Commissioner, with his address within the prescribed time. As a result thereof, an official on behalf of the Commissioner made a recommendation to the first-named respondent that the applicant not be declared a refugee and that his application for asylum was deemed withdrawn by virtue of the provisions of s.9(4A) of the Refugee Act 1996 (as amended by s.7 of the Immigration Act 2003), which provides:

> "(a) An applicant shall inform the Commissioner of his or her address and of any change of address as soon as possible.
> (b) Where 5 working days have elapsed since the making of an application for a declaration and the applicant has not informed the Commissioner of his or her address, the application shall be deemed to be withdrawn."

Section 13(2) of the Act provides that where an application for a declaration is withdrawn or deemed to be withdrawn pursuant to s.9 or s.11, then:

> "(a) Any investigation under section 11 shall be terminated.
> (b) The report referred to in subsection (1) shall state that the application is being withdrawn or deemed to be withdrawn, as the case may be, and shall include a recommendation that the applicant concerned should not be declared to be a refugee, and
> (c) No appeal under section 19 shall lie against a recommendation under paragraph (b)."

Section 17(1A) of the 1996 Act provides:

> "(1A) Where an application is withdrawn or (other than pursuant to section 22) deemed to be withdrawn, or an appeal under section 16 is withdrawn or deemed to be withdrawn, the Minister shall refuse to give the applicant a declaration."

Finally, s.17(7) provides that a person to whom the Minister has refused to give a declaration may not make a further application for a declaration without the consent of the Minister.

In these proceedings, the applicant sought a declaration that s.9(4A)(b) of the 1996 Act, as amended, and/or that provision in combination with s.13(2)(c) of the Refugee Act 1996, as amended, were repugnant to the provisions of the Constitution and Art.40.3 thereof. The applicant further sought an order of certiorari quashing the decision of the second-named respondent of September 21, 2004 and the recommendation of September 21, 2004 pursuant to s.13(1) refusing the applicant a declaration of refugee status. Finally, the applicant sought an order remitting the application of the applicant made pursuant to s.8 of the Refugee Act 1996, as amended, to the second named respondent in order that same may be considered in accordance with law and the State's obligations pursuant to the 1951 Convention on the Status of Refugees.

Butler J. noted that the legislation attacked was enacted after the adoption of Bunreacht na hÉireann and thus enjoyed a presumption of constitutionality, referring to the "double construction" rule established in *East Donegal Co-Op Ltd v Attorney General* [1970] I.R. 317. It was argued on behalf of the respondents that the impugned provisions could not be construed in isolation, but rather that they must be read in context and, in particular, the context of the surrounding legislative provisions and the statutory scheme of which they form part. In particular, it was argued that the ameliorating provisions of s.17(7) could not be ignored when looking at the operative effect of s.9(4A) and (B) and s.13(2)(c). Referring to the facility available under s.17(7), Butler J. commented that "this provision would give an applicant every opportunity of explaining why he or she did not act within the time limits referred to."

Butler J. concluded that the decision to refuse the applicant's application for refugee status had been made pursuant to s.17(1A) of the 1996 Act, and that the applicant was not precluded from seeking the consent of the Minister to make a further application for refugee status pursuant to s.17(7). The learned judge therefore refused the applicant's application.

Correct test to be applied by Minister to application for permission to make further application for declaration of refugee status under s.17(7) of Refugee Act 1996   The High Court in *Itaire v Minister for Justice, Equality and Law Reform*, unreported, High Court, May 5, 2006, considered the appropriate test to be applied to applications pursuant to s.17(7) of the 1996 Act in circumstances also dealing with the relevance of previous tribunal decisions in related cases.

On May 26, 2005, an application was made to the respondent pursuant to s.17(7) of the Refugee Act 1996 requesting his permission for a further application for a declaration of refugee status to be made by the applicant. The application was stated to be based on the availability of fresh information which was not previously available, and/or through no fault of the applicant had not been previously presented during the course of processing the applicant's application for refugee status by the office of the Refugee Applications Commissioner (RAC) and the Refugee Appeals Tribunal (RAT). The fresh information was stated to be matters concerning the successful outcome of an application for refugee status made by the applicant's sister-in-law, and in particular the content of a positive recommendation of the Refugee Appeals Tribunal in her appeal.

It was submitted by the applicant that the background circumstances, reasons and basis for fear of persecution of his sister-in-law were extremely similar to that of the applicant and that the applicant had resided as a family member with his sister-in-law since 1997. It was further submitted than an examination of the content of the respective applications for refugee status of the applicant and his sister-in-law disclosed a very close similarity in the background and basis for the applications. It was further submitted that an examination of the decisions of the Refugee Appeals Tribunal in the appeal of the applicant and that of his sister-in-law disclosed that the same objective material and basis were submitted before the tribunal members who adjudicated the appeals reached conflicting conclusions when presented with the same objective material.

By letter dated July 21, 2005, the applicant was informed by the respondent that his application pursuant to s.17(7) of the Refugee Act 1996 was refused. This letter stated that "each asylum application is assessed on its own individual merits and consequently, comparison cannot be accepted as having relevance." It was further stated that "the new evidence submitted does not significantly add to the likelihood of the applicant qualifying for asylum on the totality of the evidence already available and considered."

MacMenamin J. referred to the decision in *EMS v Minister for Justice Equality and Law Reform*, unreported, High Court, December 21, 2004[7] wherein Clarke J. addressed the appropriate standard to be applied by the Minister in assessing such applications, referring to the dicta of Bingham M.R. in the case of *R. v Secretary of State for the Home Department, Ex p. Onibiyo* [1996] 2 All E.R. 901 as follows:

> "The acid test must always be whether comparing the new claim with that earlier rejected, and excluding material on which the claimant could reasonably have been expected to rely in the earlier claim, the new claim is sufficiently different from the earlier claim to admit of a realistic prospect that a favourable view could be taken of the new claim despite the unfavourable conclusion on the earlier claim."

The applicant submitted that the respondent erred in the test applied to his application pursuant to s.17(7) on the basis that the respondent did not consider whether there was "a realistic prospect that a favourable view could be taken of a fresh claim despite the unfavourable conclusion reached in the earlier claim". Rather, the test applied was whether "the new evidence submitted significantly added to the likelihood of the applicant qualifying for asylum", which was submitted to be an incorrect test. The applicant relied on a series of United Kingdom determinations[8] to the effect that, having regard to the rule of law and consistency in decision-making process, particular regard must be had to the principle expressed by Lord Hoffman in *Arthur JS Hall v Simons* [2002] 1 A.C. 615 as: "The fundamental principle of justice which requires that people should be treated equally and like cases treated alike".

MacMenamin J. also referred to the decision of Sedley J. in the case of *Shirazi v Secretary of State for the Home Department* [2004] 2 All E.R. 602 wherein it was stated:

> "In a system which is as much inquisitorial as it is adversarial, inconsistency on such questions works against legal certainty. That does not mean that the situation cannot change, or that an individual's relationship does not have to be distinctly gauged in each case. It means that in any one period a judicial policy (with the flexibility that the word implies) needs to be adopted on the effect of the in country data in recurrent classes of case".

---

[7] Discussed in *Annual Review of Irish Law 2004*, p.61.

[8] *Tewedros Tadesse Haile v Immigration Appeals Tribunal* [2002] I.N.L.R. 283, *Immigration Appeal Tribunal, Ex p. Aziz v R.* [1999] E.W.H.C. 276 and *R. v Secretary of State for the Home Department, Ex p. Boybeyi*, unreported, Court of Appeal, May 14, 1997.

Reference was also made to the decision of *Dikulu v Minister for Justice, Equality and Law Reform* (*ex tempore* judgment of Finlay Geoghegan J., High Court, July 2, 2003). In that case three sisters with similarly situated circumstances regarding their fear of persecution had their appeals for refugee status heard contemporaneously. The appeal of one sister was successful and the other two were unsuccessful. In the decision in the substantive judicial review proceedings, Finlay Geoghegan J. examined the precise basis for the differing conclusions regarding the respective family members and the purported basis therefor. MacMenamin J. noted that the approach adopted by the court was to consider whether there was any relevant material to support the conclusion by reason of factual differences that the applicants who failed in their claims had not established a well-founded fear and that "to consider that, it is necessary to consider all three decisions and to consider the similarities and differences". Finlay Geoghegan J. engaged in a detailed examination of the three decisions, concluding that there was no evidence to support the differing decisions reached.

MacMenamin J. concluded that the applicant had established substantial grounds for the purposes of obtaining leave to challenge, by way of judicial review, the refusal of the applicant's application pursuant to s.17(7). In so finding, MacMenamin J. also held that an arguable case had been made out in relation to the intensity of review in asylum and human rights cases as considered by Fennelly and McGuinness JJ. in the case of *Osayande and Lobe v Minister for Justice* [2003] 1 I.R. 1. Reference was also made to the decision of Clarke J. in the case of *Gashi v Minister for Justice, Equality and Law Reform*, unreported, High Court, December 3, 2004[9] where he stated that he was satisfied that it was at least arguable that where constitutional or human rights are at stake, the standards of judicial scrutiny set out in *O'Keeffe* may fall short of what is likely to be required for their protection. On that basis it was also held to be arguable that the decision to refuse the application under s.17(7) was irrational.

Detention pursuant to s.5 of Immigration Act 1999 an abuse of power if deportation cannot be carried out within eight-week period   The decision of the High Court in *Obende v Minister for Justice, Equality and Law Reform* [2006] 3 I.R. 218 sets out important limitations on the powers of detention contained in s.5 of the Immigration Act 1999.

The applicant was a Nigerian national who arrived in the State as an unaccompanied minor and sought asylum. The applicant's application for refugee status was refused by the Refugee Applications Commissioner and, on appeal, by the Refugee Appeals Tribunal. A deportation order in respect of the applicant was made by the respondent on September 15, 2006. The applicant subsequently applied pursuant to s.3(11) of the Immigration Act

---

[9]   Discussed in *Annual Review of Irish Law 2004*, p.54.

1999 for leave to remain in the State on the basis of, *inter alia*, the fact that she had recently been reunited with her sister whose residence in the State was previously unknown to the applicant. It was contended by the respondent that no application for leave to remain on the basis of the applicant's relationship with her sister had been received prior to the institution of proceedings. It was further contended that the time for processing of any such application would be 18–24 months and that it was not necessary that the applicant be permitted to remain within the State while such application was pending.

By order made *ex parte* on April 4, 2006, the High Court (Dunne J.) ordered that the first-named respondent, his servants or agents be restrained until after April 24, 2006, or until further order in the meantime, from deporting the applicant. The court further ordered that the applicant's solicitor be at liberty to serve a notice of motion for an interlocutory injunction and for leave to apply for judicial review returnable on April 24, 2006. When the matter came on for hearing before Herbert J., the learned judge held that there were "special circumstances" why the application for interlocutory relief should be heard immediately,[10] namely, the fact that the applicant who was just over the legal age for detention under the provisions of s.5(4) of the Immigration Act 1999, had been in custody for five weeks, and because of the imminent expiration of the limitation period of eight weeks in aggregate imposed on such detention by s.5(6) of the 1999 Act.

Having regard to the affidavit evidence and the submissions of counsel, Herbert J. concluded that the applicant had established a serious question to be tried as to whether or not the applicant had placed "new" material, including her application for residency on family reunification grounds, before the first-named respondent in October or November 2005. It was further held that there was a serious question to be tried as to whether, having regard to the right to apply to the first-named respondent to revoke a deportation order pursuant to s.3(11) of the 1999 Act, it was in accordance with fair procedures for the first-named respondent to seek to enforce the deportation order regardless of the applicant's claim that allegedly important "new" material had been submitted for his consideration and in respect of which no decision had been made pursuant to s.3(11) of the 1999 Act.

In so holding, Herbert J. rejected the submission on behalf of the respondent based on the decision of the Supreme Court in *GAG v Minister for Justice, Equality and Law Reform* [2003] 3 I.R. 422 at 473, that the applicant had no entitlement to remain in this State and having regard to the duty of the first-

---

[10] Thus departing from the principle established by Finlay Geoghegan J. in *Margine v Minister for Justice, Equality and Law Reform*, unreported, High Court, February 14, 2004 that "[i]n all cases where interlocutory relief is sought and in the absence of various special circumstances, it appears to me undesirable in the interests of the efficient administration of justice and the saving of legal costs expenses and the saving of judicial time, that there be a separate hearing of the application for such interlocutory relief and the application for leave."

named respondent to maintain and enforce the national policy with regard to asylum-seekers and persons seeking residence in the State, the balance of convenience or, the "risk of doing an injustice" (*per* May L.J. in *Cayne v Global Natural Resources plc* [1984] 1 All E.R. 225 at 257), lay in refusing to stay the deportation of the applicant. It was held by the learned High Court judge that the applicant had established a serious question to be tried that if she were to be returned to Nigeria her circumstances might become such that she would be unable, for economic or other reasons, to continue to prosecute her application for residence in this State. Herbert J. concluded that, on the particular facts of this case, there was a greater risk of doing a serious injustice by refusing to grant the injunctive relief sought than by granting it, even though the first-named respondent might eventually refuse to grant the applicant permission to remain in the State, even for a limited period. The court therefore continued the order restraining the first-named respondent, his servants or agents, from deporting the applicant until the hearing of the application for leave to seek judicial review or until further order in the meantime.

Counsel on behalf of the applicant then submitted that the court had an inherent jurisdiction at common law or pursuant to Art.34 of the Constitution to admit the applicant to bail, notwithstanding the fact that the applicant had not challenged and was not challenging the validity of the deportation order of September 15, 2005 and had been an evader prior to her arrest and detention pursuant to the provisions of s.5 of the Immigration Act 1999. It was submitted that the exercise of this power could only be prevented or restricted by clear and express provisions to that effect in the Immigration Act 1999, and that no such provision was to be found. It was contended that the court should exercise this power in favour of the applicant because her continued detention in custody was unlawful, unnecessary, unjust and disproportionate. Counsel for the applicant invoked in support of this submission the decision of *R. v Secretary of State for the Home Department, Ex p. Turkoglu* [1998] 1 Q.B. 398 where it was held by the Court of Appeal that where the High Court is seised of an application for judicial review, that court has jurisdiction to grant or refuse bail, which decision is subject to a right of appeal unless expressly excluded by statute or judicial precedent.

Counsel for the applicant also relied upon the decision of the European Court of Human Rights in the case of *Dougoz v Greece* (2002) 34 E.H.R.R. 61 as supporting the proposition that if the High Court did not have an inherent jurisdiction to enquire into the applicant's detention and, if the circumstances merited it, to order her conditional or unconditional release, s.5 of the Immigration Act 1999 would be in breach of Art.5 of Sch.1 of the European Convention on Human Rights Act 2003. On behalf of the respondents it was submitted that the applicant was an evader and that her continued detention was necessary in order to enforce the deportation order made by the first-named respondent in respect of her.

Herbert J. referred to the decision of the Supreme Court in *Re Article 26 and ss.5 and 10 of the Illegal Immigrants (Trafficking) Bill 1999* [2000] 2 I.R. 360 where Keane C.J. considered the scope of the powers of detention contained in s.5 of the Bill, noting that a detainee:

> "is a person not entitled to be in the country at all. But this does not mean that he is without rights. The detention must be for the necessary statutory purposes … As already pointed out, the principles set out by this Court in *East Donegal Co-operative v Attorney General* [1970] I.R. 317, must be applied to the statutory powers of detention. It does not follow that because the section permits of detention for up to eight weeks in the aggregate, the proposed deportee may necessarily be detained for that period if circumstances change or new facts come to light which indicate that such detention is unnecessary."

Herbert J. concluded that the High Court "has a plenitude of powers which it may use and, which it must use if, it finds on the facts of any particular case that a person is being detained where it is quite clear that the deportation of that person cannot be effected within the aggregated period of eight weeks allowed for that purpose by the Statute." The learned judge was satisfied on the affidavit evidence that there was a concluded and present intention on the part of the first-named respondent to deport the applicant, and only thereafter to consider her application for leave to reside in the State pursuant to her application under s.3(11) of the 1999 Act. However, Herbert J. held that having regard to the stay now imposed by the court on her deportation, and the minimum period of time likely to elapse before her application for leave to seek judicial review could be heard and determined in its proper place in the court list, "the only lawful basis for her continued detention for the remaining three weeks of the permitted statutory period of eight week in aggregate, has effectively disappeared." In so holding, Herbert J. referred to the dicta of Keane C.J. at 411 in *Re Article 26 and ss.5 and 10 of the Illegal Immigrants (Trafficking) Bill 1999,* that "[i]t would be an abuse of the power to detain if it was quite clear that deportation could not be carried out within the eight weeks". Herbert J. thus made an order for the conditional release of the applicant upon a number of conditions.

Entitlement to be in the State of applicant who was family member of person recognised as a refugee   The High Court considered the entitlement to be within the State of a family member of a person recognised as a refugee under the Refugee Act 1996 in *Iatan v Commissioner of An Garda Síochána,* unreported, High Court, February 2, 2006 in a judgment which also addressed the precise relationship between visas, entitlements to remain, and the entitlement to family reunification pursuant to s.18 of the 1996 Act.

The first-named applicant was a Romanian national. He was the spouse of the second named applicant, who was granted refugee status on June 10,

2003. The minor applicants were the children of the first- and second-named applicants. Subsequent to the recognition of the second-named applicant as a refugee, her solicitors corresponded with the respondent indicating her desire to be reunited with her husband, the first-named applicant. It was indicated by officers of the respondent that an application for a visa should be made to the Irish Honorary Consul in Bucharest (being the appropriate Irish diplomatic location having regard to the first-named applicant's residency). On foot of that application, a visa was granted and the first-named applicant came to Ireland.

Upon being given permission to land at Dublin airport, the first-named applicant was advised to go to the Garda National Immigration Bureau ("GNIB"). On attending the GNIB, the first-named applicant was given a GNIB identity card and his passport was stamped with a permission to remain in Ireland for one year, until April 27, 2005. It was not intimated, either to the first- or second-named applicants or their legal representatives, that any further application was required in order to secure permission to remain indefinitely in the State in accordance with the family reunification scheme provided for in s.18 of the Refugee Act 1996. For that reason no further application was made. However, the first-named applicant subsequently lost his identity card and, on applying for a new card, was informed that his permission to be in the State had expired. In those circumstances the first-named applicant was informed that he no longer had any legal entitlement to remain in the State.

Correspondence from the applicants' solicitors ensued, culminating in a reply from the respondent dated September 21, 2005, setting out the distinction between different forms of visas and permissions and contending that no permission under s.18 of the 1996 Act had ever been granted. Finally it was indicated that it was open to the applicants "to make an application to remain/ family re-unification under Section 18 of the Refugee Act, 1996."

On behalf of the respondent, it was contended that there were significant legal and practical differences between a visa, a permission to be and remain in the State and a permission under s.18 of the Refugee Act 1996, conferring upon a person who is a member of the family of a refugee, rights analogous to those conferred by law on such refugee. The respondent submitted that the successful application of the first-named applicant to the Irish Honorary Consul in Bucharest resulted in him being given a visa and no more. Secondly, it was submitted that his application to the GNIB resulted in him being given a permission to remain in the State but no more than its terms provided for (that is to say, a permission for one year). Finally, it was said that no permission under s.18 had been given, although it was pointed out that if an application for such permission was made, it would be considered on its merits. Counsel for the applicants submitted that the manner in which the first-named applicant's application was made and responded to, gave rise to additional legal entitlements beyond those which might ordinarily be said to flow from the various visas and permissions given.

In those circumstances, Clarke J. considered the legal distinction between the visa, permission to stay and s.18 permission which arose in the context of this case. Clarke J. noted that the definition of a visa is to be found in s.1 of the Immigration Act 2003 as "an endorsement made on a passport or travel document other than an Irish passport or Irish travel document for the purposes of indicating that the holder thereof is authorised to land in the State subject to any other conditions of landing being fulfilled."

It was furthermore accepted that a visa does not give a right to remain in the State but merely confers a right to land. Clarke J. noted that s.4 of the Immigration Act 2004 confers on an immigration officer, acting on behalf of the Minister, an entitlement to give to a non-national appropriate documentation authorising such non-national to land or be in the State, which document is referred to in the Act as "a permission". Clarke J. accepted the submission on behalf of the respondent that, in the scheme of the legislation applicable, there is a clear distinction between a "visa" on the one hand and a "permission to be in the State" on the other hand, holding: "A 'visa' is a form of pre-clearance. A 'permission' confers an additional entitlement upon the holder of it to remain in the State in accordance with the terms of that permission."

In contrast, it was held that s.18 of the Refugee Act 1996 deals specifically with a different form of permission which can be given by the Minister (rather than an immigration officer) and is to be "in writing to the person to enter and reside in the State and on such permission being given the person shall be entitled to the rights and privileges specified in section 3 for such period as the refugee is entitled to remain in the State." Clarke J. noted that in order to obtain a s.18 permission, the person concerned must be a member of the family of someone who has been given a declaration of refugee status, in accordance with the 1996 Act. Reference was made to the procedure pursuant to s.18, namely, on the application of such refugee, s.18(2) requires that the application is referred to the Refugee Applications Commissioner who investigates the application and submits a report in writing to the Minister, setting out the relationship between the refugee concerned and the person who is the subject of the application and also the domestic circumstances of that person. If, following consideration of such a report, the Minister is satisfied that the person is a member of the family of the refugee, then the Minister is required to grant a permission under the section, subject to the entitlement of the Minister to refuse to grant such permission (or, indeed, to revoke it once granted) under s.18(5) in the interests of national security or public policy. Clarke J. thus concluded that "a person who is a member of the family of a refugee (as defined) and in respect of whom no national security or public policy reason exists for determining otherwise, is entitled to permission under the section from the Minister." It was noted that the Minister is also given a discretion to grant a similar permission to a dependent of the refugee who does not come within the formal definition of "member of the family".

Turning to the legal distinctions between the various schemes, Clarke J.

held:

> "[t]here can be little doubt ... that the three categories of document or
> permission to which reference has been made are separate and distinct.
> A visa is ... simply a permission to land and amounts to a form of pre-
> clearance to that end. A permission to remain in the State is given by
> an Immigration Officer under the Immigration Acts and, subject to its
> terms, allows the recipient to remain in the State for whatever period,
> and subject to whatever conditions, as may be properly attached to that
> permission. A permission under s.18 must be given by the Minister
> but can only be refused on the basis that the person who is the subject
> matter of the application for permission either is not a member of the
> family of the refugee concerned or that there are national security or
> public policy issues which lead to a proper refusal."

Considering the facts of the present case, Clarke J. held that a letter issued by
the Family Reunification Section of the respondent in December 2003 was
inaccurate in so far as it indicated that the Minister may "at his or her discretion"
grant permission to a dependent member of the family of a refugee to enter and
reside in the State, in the context of the implication that such persons include,
inter alia, spouses. Clarke J. held that "[t]he Ministerial discretion, as pointed
out above, does not arise (subject to security and public policy issues) in
relation to the immediate members of the family but only to dependents who
are somewhat more remote."

Clarke J. then proceeded to consider the applicants' contention that the
respondent's conduct had given rise to a legitimate expectation, referring
to the summary of the relevant principles in *Keogh v CAB and Revenue
Commissioner*, unreported, High Court, McKechnie J., December 20, 2002.
Clarke J. concluded that:

> "the letter of December 2003 from the respondent to the applicants'
> solicitor created a legitimate expectation that;
>   (a) an application for permission under s.18 would be dealt with
>   by means of same being originated by a visa application to the
>   Irish Honorary Consul in Bucharest and;
>   (b) that such an application would be treated as being an application
>   under the section so that the result of the visa application would
>   be taken to be the result of the application under the section."

Clarke J. concluded that the applicants were entitled to have the application
made to the Irish Honorary Council in Bucharest treated as an application
under s.18, and that in those circumstances, an application under s.18 had been
pending since that time and that the Minister was in default in not giving a

decision in respect of that application in a timely fashion. The learned judge noted that a consideration by the Minister of an application under s.18 involves, in reality, a consideration of two separate matters:

> "The first is a matter of substance concerning whether the person in respect of whom permission is sought is a 'member of the family' as defined. For the reasons analysed above that decision is not a matter in respect of which the Minister can be said to exercise any statutory discretion. Obviously the Minister may, on the facts of a particular case, not be satisfied that the person is a member of the family. However such a decision is not a matter of discretion. It is a matter of determination. The Minister can only come to a view as to whether a person is or is not a 'member of the family' in accordance with public law principles.
>
> [T]here is a second aspect of the Minister's consideration, being a determination as to whether there are public policy or national security issues that might lead to the refusal of permission under s.18. That aspect of the decision clearly does involve the exercise of a ministerial discretion."

Clarke J. thus granted an order of mandamus requiring the Minister to determine the entitlement of the first-named applicant under s.18 of the 1996 Act solely in respect of whether the relevant aspect of the Minister's decision involved the exercise of a statutory discretion, and the Minister was estopped from revisiting the question of whether the first-named applicant was a member of the family of the second-named applicant.

Impact of invalid age assessment of unaccompanied minor on substantive asylum application   In *Odunbaku v Refugee Applications Commissioner*, unreported, High Court, February 1, 2006, the applicant arrived in the State in June 2003 and gave her date of birth as September 8, 1988. On her arrival, she was unaccompanied and was the subject of age assessment interviews carried out by the Refugee Applications Commissioner on July 3 and 4, 2003. The overall conclusion reached was that the applicant was "estimated to be in the region of 16 going on 17", *i.e.* that although it was determined that the applicant was an unaccompanied minor, her true age was somewhat older than the age she had given. The applicant was thereafter placed in a hostel under the care of the East Coast Health Authority. In January 2004 a social worker at the hostel wrote to the Refugee Applications Commissioner indicating a suspicion that the applicant was, in fact, over 18 years of age. As a result of this communication a further interview was arranged with an official of the Refugee Applications Commissioner, which re-assessment was conducted by the same official who had carried out the initial age assessment of the applicant. The re-assessment led to a conclusion that the applicant was in fact over 18 years of age.

The applicant thereafter made an application for asylum which was processed in the ordinary way. She sought the services of the Refugee Legal Service on February 3, 2004 and was classified as a minor by that service. On her behalf the Refugee Legal Service wrote to the Commissioner on February 24, 2004 requesting reasons for the re-assessment of age. By faxed letter of February 27, 2004, the Refugee Legal Service wrote to the Commissioner expressing dissatisfaction with the age assessment and requesting an adjournment of the asylum assessment interview then scheduled for two days later. Notwithstanding this request, the applicant's interview was conducted by the Refugee Applications Commissioner two days later. By letter dated March 19, 2004, the Commissioner informed the applicant that her application was unsuccessful. Correspondence subsequently issued from the Refugee Legal Service contesting the age assessment. In those letters, judicial review of the age assessment was threatened, although the Refugee Legal Service was subsequently unable to institute such proceedings in the absence of a next friend owing to the applicant's status as a minor.

By virtue of the fact that the decision of the Commissioner contained one of the findings specified in s.13(6) of the Refugee Act 1996, no oral appeal was available to the applicant. Notwithstanding subsequent correspondence requesting further consideration of the issues raised in respect of the applicant's age, the tribunal proceeded to consider and refuse the applicant's appeal, notification of which was communicated by letter from the Minister dated September 22, 2004. On October 12, 2004, an application was submitted on behalf of the applicant for humanitarian leave to remain in the State. The solicitor acting on behalf of the applicant also attempted to gather the papers necessary to consider whether judicial review proceedings ought to be commenced. In that context a difficulty arose concerning the appointment of a next friend. On December 21, 2004, an application was made to the President of the High Court seeking an order from the court appointing a person for the purposes of acting as a next friend. The President indicated that it might be appropriate to approach an interested voluntary organisation for the purposes of seeking their consent to act as such next friend. On that basis, the solicitor concerned wrote to the Irish Refugee Council on December 24, 2004, requesting that it consider appointing a person to act as next friend. On January 26, 2005, it was confirmed that the Chief Executive of the Irish Refugee Council would so act and an application for leave was brought on February 7, 2005.

In light of the factual background, Clarke J. determined that although the application for leave was made significantly beyond the 14-day period specified in s.5 of the Illegal Immigrants (Trafficking) Act 2000, he was satisfied that there were "wholly exceptional circumstances" in this case. The learned judge concluded that if it were otherwise appropriate to grant leave to challenge a determination of the Commissioner that the applicant was not an unaccompanied minor, then it would be appropriate to approach the question of an extension of time on the basis of it being at least arguable that the applicant was, at all material times, a minor. Clarke J. so held also having regard to the significant technical difficulties which were encountered by those seeking to represent the applicant.

Clarke J. then proceeded to consider the core of the applicant's challenge, namely the age determination. Reference was made to the decision of the High Court in *Moke v Refugee Applications Commissioner* [2006] 1 I.R. 476[11] wherein the learned High Court judge outlined the procedures to be followed in age assessment in order to ensure that such procedure conforms with the principles of constitutional justice, namely:

> "(i) the applicant must be told the purpose of the interview in simple terms. It may be as straightforward as informing the applicant that the interviewers need to decide whether the applicant is or is not under the age of 18 years.
>
> (ii) where an applicant claims to be under 18 years of age and the interviewers form a view that this claim may be false, the applicant is entitled to be told in simple terms the reasons for or grounds upon which the interviewers consider the claim may be false and to be given an opportunity of dealing with those reasons or grounds.
>
> (iii) where, as in this instance, the applicant produces a document which purports to be an original official document which includes a record of his alleged date of birth and the interviewers are not prepared to rely upon such document, the applicant is entitled to be told of their reservations and given an opportunity to deal with same.
>
> (iv) if the decision is adverse to the applicant then he must be clearly informed of the decision and the reasons for same. The reasons need not be long or elaborate but should make clear why the applicant's claim to be under 18 is not considered credible. The initial information and communication may, of necessity, be given orally but should be promptly confirmed in writing.
>
> (v) where the decision is adverse to the applicant and, as stated, there exists the possibility of reassessment then such information should be communicated clearly to the applicant again initially orally and also in writing. Such communication should include how such reassessment may be assessed by the applicant".

On the basis that the procedures set out in *Moke* represented the current law in this jurisdiction on age assessments, Clarke J. was satisfied that there were substantial grounds for arguing that the appropriate procedures were not followed. Clarke J. noted that the applicant had not been informed of her

---

[11] Discussed in *Annual Review of Irish Law 2005*, p.44.

entitlement to a reassessment subsequent to the determination in January 2004 that she was not a minor. There were also substantial grounds for contending that the basis for the adverse finding as to age (including the assessment made by the social worker in the hostel in which she was then resident) was not put to the applicant. In those circumstances, Clarke J. held that there were substantial grounds, sufficient for the purpose of leave, to permit a full hearing of a challenge to the age assessment decision of the Commissioner.

Clarke J. then proceeded to consider the impact of such finding on the subsequent decisions made in respect of the applicant's application for refugee status, noting the finding in *Moke* that "the mere fact that there has been an invalid age assessment does not, of itself, necessarily lead to the conclusion that subsequent decisions made in the refugee process are themselves invalid". Clarke J. held that in order that an invalid age assessment might be said to have affected any subsequent decisions made by either the Commissioner or tribunal, it would be necessary for the court to be satisfied "that the impugned age assessment decision had some material and practical effect upon the process before those other bodies". In the present case it was submitted that in a number of material respects the consideration of both the Commissioner and tribunal had been materially affected by the earlier decision as to age, particularly in respect of the assessment of the applicant's credibility. Clarke J. held:

> "There can be little doubt that the assessment of an account given by a person (and in particular any alleged inaccuracies or inconsistencies in such an account) can be materially affected by the age of the person concerned. This is not, of course, a matter of technicality. While there may be formal consequences of a person being just over or just under 18 years of age it is unlikely that any significant difference as to the assessment of the credibility of such person would flow from the fact that a person was (say) 18 years and one month on the one hand or 17 years and 11 months on the other hand. However a more significant age disparity could well have a material effect on the assessment of an account given. On the facts of this case it would appear that the difference between the age contended for by [the applicant] and the age as found by the RAC was of the order of a minimum of three years. Material events, important to the assessment of the credibility of [the applicant's] account, therefore occurred at a time when, on her case, she may well have been barely a teenager but where, on the view taken by the RAC, she was significantly older."

Clarke J. concluded that it was at least arguable that the assessment of the applicant's credibility was potentially affected in a material way by the view of her age taken by the Commissioner. In those circumstances, the learned High Court judge distinguished the decision in *Moke* and held that it was arguable that there may have been a material effect on the process, both before the Commissioner and before the tribunal on appeal (not least because the appeal before the tribunal was a paper appeal), sufficient to provide substantial grounds for the proposition that both of those determinations would also fall if the original age assessment decision itself were to be set aside. In those circumstances, Clarke J. held that there were sufficient grounds for granting leave to challenge the decisions of both the Commissioner on the substantive refugee application and also the tribunal on appeal.

The decision of the High Court in *Odunbaku* reflects the ongoing difficulties which arise in respect of applications for asylum by unaccompanied minors in this jurisdiction and the absence of any guidance in the legislative scheme as to the appropriate procedures to be applied in respect of such applicants. The difficulties experienced by unaccompanied minors seeking asylum in Ireland, including access to legal representation, were highlighted by the Law Society in its *Report on Rights-based Child Law: The Case for Reform* (Law Society, March 2006) where it was noted that meeting the needs of this "particularly vulnerable group of children presents complex challenges for the State and for those who work and support children in the refugee and child law area." As the report makes clear, there remains much to be done to fully secure and vindicate the rights of unaccompanied minors seeking asylum in this jurisdiction.

No obligation to name country of deportation in deportation order The Supreme Court in *Sibiya v Minister for Justice, Equality and Law Reform*, unreported, Supreme Court, February 7, 2006 rejected the submission that there existed an obligation to name the country of deportation in a deportation order.

This was an appeal by the applicants from a decision of the High Court which refused the applicants' application for, *inter alia*, orders of certiorari in respect of deportation orders made by the Minister on August 7, 2003. Pursuant to s.5(3) of the Illegal Immigrants (Trafficking) Act 2000, the High Court granted leave to appeal to the applicant and certified that its decision involved a point of law of exceptional public importance and that it was desirable in the public interest that an appeal be taken to the Supreme Court on that point of law. The point of law so certified was:

> "The Deportation Order does not indicate to where the applicants are to be deported. Insofar as the former border is determined by the Immigration Act, 1999 (Deportation) Regulations, 2002 those regulations are ultra vires and void."

Giving the judgment of the Court, Murray C.J. noted that the country of origin of the first-named applicant was South Africa, and that the applicant had arrived in Ireland from that country and applied for refugee status. The Chief Justice noted that the process under which the applicant's application for refugee status was dealt with, included appeals from initial decisions and a review of her case on humanitarian grounds, and concluded that there was ample evidence before the court that the issue in that process was whether the applicant and her children should be allowed to remain in the State or be deported to her home country, South Africa.

On behalf of the applicants it was contended that the Immigration Act 1999 (Deportation) Regulations 2002 were void and *ultra vires* the provisions of s.7 of the Immigration Act 1999. The applicants complained that the deportation order, which was accepted to be in the form prescribed by the Regulations, did not state or mention the name of the country to which they were to be deported. It was contended that, in permitting this, the Regulations were *ultra vires* the provisions of the Act. In support of this submission the applicants relied on s.7(2) of the Act which provides that: "Regulations under this Act may contain such incidental, supplementary and consequential provisions as appear to the Minister to be necessary or expedient for the purposes of the regulations." It was submitted that the stating of the name of the country of deportation in the deportation order itself was necessary or expedient for the purposes of the Act as indicated by s.7(2).

However, Murray C.J. noted that s.7(1) provides that:

> "The Minister may –
> (a) by regulations provide, subject to the provisions of this Act, for any matter referred to in this Act as prescribed or to be prescribed…"

The Chief Justice further noted that s.3(7) of the Act makes express provision for the form of a deportation order to be prescribed by regulation. Although the Regulations, in setting out the form of the deportation order, did not specify that the name of the country to which the person is to be deported should be stated, the Regulations did achieve the purpose of s.3(7) of the Act, namely ,to prescribe a statutory form. It was noted that s.7(2) refers to "... incidental, supplementary and consequential provisions as appear to the Minister to be necessary or expedient, *for the purposes of the regulations*" (emphasis in original). It was held by Murray C.J.:

> "The Regulations themselves have served the purpose of the Act in prescribing the form and I cannot accept the argument on behalf of Dr. Forde that subsection 7(2), which grants a discretion to the Minister, but even if it was mandatory on the Minister to make provision for incidental, supplementary and consequential provisions, that it in any sense, requires that he have in the particular form of the deportation order, the name of the State in question. This is not necessary or expedient for the purpose of the regulations which prescribe the relevant

form, not for the purposes of the regulations but for the purposes of the Act."

The Chief Justice noted that it had been acknowledged in this case from the outset that the Minister accepted that a person was entitled to know the name of the country to which they were to be deported. It was also noted that applicants for refugee status are active and not passive participants in the process to which such an application is subjected, and that applicants are "very readily given access to the complete file, or a complete copy of it, after notification of an intention to make a Deportation Order." The Chief Justice was satisfied that the process was quite transparent in this respect, and concluded:

"it is undoubtedly the case, and there is no evidence to suggest otherwise, that an applicant for refugee status who has been refused and who has been notified of the intention of the Minister to make a Deportation Order or in respect of whom a Deportation Order has actually been made and who has any doubt, notwithstanding the process that they have been through, as to the country to which they are to be deported, can formally seek that information and obtain a reply."

Murray C.J. held that in the context of the actual legal issue raised by the applicant, there was nothing in the Act which required that the point in time and manner in which an applicant is notified of the country to which he or she is to be deported must be the time when the deportation order is made, on the basis that "[t]hat is not what the Act says nor what it requires the Minister to do." For those reasons, the Supreme Court dismissed the appeal.

Obligation of Minister to consider application for revocation of deportation order within reasonable period In *Awe v Minister for Justice, Equality and Law Reform*, unreported, High Court, June 24, 2006, the applicants were Nigerian nationals who had sought asylum in the State, which applications were ultimately rejected. On December 22, 2004, deportation orders were made in respect of each of the applicants, which were served in February 2005, with accompanying notices under s.3 of the Immigration Act 1999. The applicants were then required to present themselves on dates thereafter both in the Garda National Immigration Bureau, Burgh Quay, Dublin and subsequently in Cork.

In the interim, on March 2, 2005, correspondence issued from the applicants' solicitor to the Department of Justice indicating that they were awaiting updated medical reports in respect of the first-named applicant. The applicants' solicitor expressed the view that the Minister should not give effect to the deportation order without first having regard to the updated medical reports. It was also noted that the applicants were awaiting the departmental analysis which formed the basis of the decision to deport; an undertaking not to deport pending receipt of that analysis was also sought.

On March 7, 2005, the applicants' solicitor wrote a further letter to the Department, enclosing medical reports in respect of the first-named applicant and further representations in support of their application for leave to remain on a humanitarian basis. The letter then made representations as to why the Minister should not give effect to the deportation orders and in the last paragraph made a request that the deportation orders be revoked. An acknowledgment was received on March 9, 2005 indicating that the correspondence had been forwarded to the relevant unit, and no further communication thereafter issued.

The applicants instituted proceedings seeking an order of mandamus directing the respondent to consider and decide on the application made on behalf of the applicants in the letter of March 7, 2005. It appears that there existed some confusion as to the nature of the application made in the letter of March 7, 2005, having regard to the statutory scheme created by s.3 of the Immigration Act 1999. Although it was initially submitted on behalf of the applicants that the letter of March 7, 2005 contained "further representations under s.3(3)(b) of the Act of 1999 for leave to remain in the State on humanitarian grounds", Finlay Geoghegan J. agreed with the submission of counsel on behalf of the respondents that s.3(3)(b) of the Act of 1999 only relates to representations which may be made after a notice of a proposal to deport and prior to the making of a deportation order.

In response to this submission, counsel for the applicants then submitted that the letter of March 7, 2005 contained an application for revocation of the deportation orders. Having regard to the obligation of the Minister to consider an application for revocation of a deportation order pursuant to s.3 of the Immigration Act 1999, Finlay Geoghegan J. noted:

> "The Act of 1999 does not contain any time limit or procedure in relation to an application to the respondent to exercise his power to revoke a deportation order under section 3(11) of the Act of 1999. In accordance with the decision of the Supreme Court on the Article 26 reference in *In re the Illegal Immigrants (Trafficking) Bill, 1999* [2000] 2 I.R. 360, the applicants are entitled to have any statutory powers exercised in relation to them, exercised in accordance with the principles of constitutional justice and fair procedures."

The learned High Court judge concluded that, on the facts of this case, an arguable case in law had been made out that the principles of constitutional justice and fair procedures required the respondent to determine the application for revocation of the deportation orders contained in the letter of March 7, 2005. It was further held that such principles required the determination to be made within a reasonable period of time and that any such reasonable period of time had expired prior to the hearing of the leave application.

Obligation of Refugee Appeals Tribunal to disclose information pursuant to s.16 of Refugee Act 1996   The nature and extent of the obligations on the tribunal arising by virtue of s.16 of the Refugee Act 1996 were considered by the High Court in *Olatunji v Refugee Appeals Tribunal*, unreported, High Court, April 7, 2006. The applicant submitted that the decision of the tribunal member indicated that the tribunal member had relied upon three pieces of information which were not disclosed to the applicant and which the applicant and her advisers had no opportunity of commenting upon. It was submitted that this constituted a breach of s.16(8) of the Refugee Act 1996 (as amended by s.11(1)(k) of the Immigration Act 1999) which provides:

> "The Appeal Board shall furnish the applicant concerned and his or her solicitor (if known) with copies of any reports, observations, or representations in writing or any other document, furnished to the Appeal Board by the Commissioner copies of which have not been previously furnished to the applicant pursuant to section 11 (6) and an indication in writing of the nature and source of any other information relating to the appeal which has come to the notice of the Appeal Board in the course of an appeal under this section."

It was submitted on behalf of the applicant that the tribunal had failed to disclose a UNHCR position paper which was referred to in the decision, information in relation to African culture and family referred to by the tribunal member, and information from the Garda National Immigration Bureau in relation to the procedure at Dublin Airport.

Finlay Geoghegan J. concluded in respect of this element of the applicant's challenge:

> "The obligation in s.16 is a mandatory obligation. The obligation would appear to include all information relevant to the appeal. The Tribunal Member appears to have considered each of the above relevant to the appeal insofar as she has referred to them and relied on them in her reasoning. The third matter appears of particular importance insofar as it appears from the findings made in para.7 that the Tribunal Member relied upon this information to reject entirely 'from a credibility point of view' the applicant's account of her arrival and passage through Immigration at Dublin Airport and hence relevant to the assessment of the applicant's overall credibility."

The learned High Court judge thus granted an order of certiorari in respect of the decision of the tribunal on this ground.

Obligation of Refugee Appeals Tribunal to provide access to previous decisions of legal significance   In *Atanasov v Refugee Appeals Tribunal* [2007] 1 I.L.R.M. 288, the Supreme Court considered the existence and extent of any obligation on the Refugee Appeals Tribunal to provide access to appellants to previous decisions of legal significance.

Each of the applicants for judicial review sought, in advance of the holding of their refugee appeals before the Refugee Appeals Tribunal, access to previous relevant decisions of the tribunal. In making such application, the applicants relied on the provisions of s.19(4A) of the Refugee Act 1996, which provided that:

> "(a) The chairperson of the Tribunal may, at his or her discretion, decide not to publish (other than to the persons referred to in section 16(17)) a decision of the Tribunal which in his or her opinion is not of legal importance.
>
> (b) Any decision published shall exclude any matters which would tend to identify a person as an applicant under the Act or otherwise breach the requirement that the identity of applicants be kept confidential".

It was submitted by the applicants that the presenting officers, who act as advocates on the appeals on behalf of the State, were granted access to the tribunal's "master file" in respect of applicants and could therefore, in practice, share decisions with each other. It was submitted on behalf of the applicants that, in those circumstances, failure to afford the applicants access to those decisions was a breach of the applicants' rights to fair procedures and/or natural justice and, furthermore, infringed the requirement of equality of arms under Art.6(1) of the European Convention on Human Rights. The tribunal declined to make available the decisions as requested.

The applicants instituted judicial review proceedings seeking an order directing the tribunal to grant access to previous decisions and recommendations of the tribunal of relevance to the applicants' appeals. By order of the High Court (MacMenamin J.) on July 7, 2005,[12] the applicants were granted a declaration that the refusal of the tribunal to make available relevant tribunal decisions as requested or identified, and as sought by the applicants, was in breach of the applicants' rights to fair procedures and natural and constitutional justice pursuant to the provisions of Art.40.3 of the Constitution. The respondents appealed this decision to the Supreme Court.

Geoghegan J. delivered the decision of the court and, after reviewing the factual background of each case, considered the procedures which apply in the conduct of refugee appeals in this jurisdiction:

---

[12] *Annual Review of Irish Law 2005*, pp.24–29.

"It is of the nature of refugee cases that the problem for the appellant back in his or her country of origin which is leading him or her to seek refugee status is of a kind generic to that country or the conditions in that country. Thus, as in these appeals, it may be a problem of gross or official discrimination against homosexuals or it may be a problem of enforced female circumcision or it may be a problem of some concrete form of discrimination against a particular tribe. Where there are such problems it is blindingly obvious, in my view, that fair procedures require some reasonable mechanisms for achieving consistency in both the interpretation and the application of the law in cases like this of a similar category. Yet, if relevant previous decisions are not available to an appellant, he or she has no way of knowing whether there is such consistency."

Having determined that the tribunal was obliged to make available relevant previous decisions in certain cases, Geoghegan J. went on to consider the role which such disclosed decisions would play in the conduct of the appeal, saying that "[i]t is not that a member of a tribunal is actually bound by a previous decision but consistency of decisions based on the same objective facts may, in appropriate circumstances, be a significant element in ensuring that a decision is objectively fair rather than arbitrary."

Geoghegan J. cited, with approval, the decision of Lord Woolf M.R. in *Manzeke v Secretary of State for the Home Department* [1997] Imm. A.R. 524 on the usefulness of previous relevant decisions when he said the following:

"It will be beneficial to the general administration of asylum appeals for special adjudicators to have the benefit of the views of a tribunal in other cases of a general situation in a particular part of the world, as long as that situation has not changed in the meantime. Consistency in the treatment of asylum seekers is important in so far as objective considerations, not directly affected by the circumstances of the individual asylum seeker, are involved."

Geoghegan J. reiterated that:

"[p]revious decisions of the tribunal may be ones which if applied in the appellant's case would benefit the appellant but if there is no access he has no knowledge of them and indeed he has no guarantee that the member of the tribunal has any personal knowledge of the previous decisions made by different colleagues."

He concluded that "such a secret system is manifestly unfair".

Turning to the proper construction of s.19(4A) of the 1996 Act, Geoghegan J. held that the section authorised the chairperson not to publish decisions which, in his or her opinion, were not of legal importance. In this respect, Geoghegan J. cautioned that the term "legal importance" must not be given too narrow a definition, holding that it "does not have to be some narrow point of law in the technical sense". As against this, the learned judge accepted that there may be many cases that are based on particular facts that do not put the applicant into some particular category and would be of no legal relevance to any other applicant's case; it was held that s.19(4A) authorised the chairperson not to publish that type of decision. Ultimately, the jurisprudential basis for the obligation to provide access to previous relevant decisions was identified as the constitutional entitlement to fair procedures, and not simply the applicable statutory provisions.

Having thus determined the appeal in favour of the applicants, the Supreme Court clarified the impact of its decision in relation to the entitlement of access to previous decisions:

> "It would be wrong for this court, certainly in these proceedings, to hold that there was any statutory or constitutional obligation to provide some open library containing redacted previous decisions. That may well be the system adopted for the purposes of affording access if the chairman of the tribunal considers it appropriate. But I do not think that it would be the function of this court or of any other court to direct the establishment of systems of that kind. What this court is concerned with is the personal rights of the particular applicants before it. Provided each of those applicants is given reasonable access in whatever form the tribunal considers fit to previous decisions which are being reasonably required for legal relevance within the meaning which I have indicated, that aspect of the duty to provide fair procedures is complied with."

Finally, Geoghegan J. stated that the judgment related only to the rights of persons who in advance of a hearing by the tribunal had requested access to relevant precedents and had been refused. The Supreme Court held that its decision could have no application to cases where the tribunal hearings had been completed without such access having been sought; this limitation thus prevented the possibility of persons whose refugee appeals had been concluded seeking to have those decisions reopened by reference to the constitutional entitlement to seek access to previous relevant decisions.

The ramifications of this decision on practice and procedure in refugee appeals has yet to be fully explored. Whilst the tribunal subsequently put in place a procedure allowing for access to previous decisions, practical limitations in the operation of this procedure have been raised as a concern. Furthermore, it is anticipated that further litigation will be required to clarify the precise obligations of the tribunal when a previous relevant decision is cited, particularly in relation to the persuasive value of such previous decisions. Finally, although the Supreme Court made clear that its decision related only to the Refugee Appeals Tribunal and did not have any application to decisions of the Minister for Justice (in respect of applications for leave to remain on a humanitarian basis), no reference was made to the application of the entitlement to previous decisions in the context of the Refugee Applications Commissioner. This may also form the basis of future proceedings.

Obligations of Refugee Applications Commissioner when making determination under s.13(6) of the Refugee Act 1996 that there is a minimal basis for application The obligations of the Commissioner when making determination under s.13(6), that there is a minimal basis for an application for asylum, was considered in *Shirazi v Minister for Justice, Equality and Law Reform*, unreported, High Court, June 27, 2006. This was an application for leave to apply for judicial review, wherein the applicant sought to quash both the recommendation made under s.13 of the Refugee Act 1996 whereby the first-named respondent decided not to recommend that the applicant be granted a declaration of refugee status, and the decision made at the same time by the Commissioner to make a finding under s.13(6)(a) of the Refugee Act 1996. Both decisions were made on March 23, 2005.

Clarke J. began by noting the consequences of a finding under s.13(6)(a) of the Refugee Act 1996, namely the fact that an appeal from the decision of the Commissioner is made on the papers only and without the benefit of an oral hearing. Clarke J. accepted the submission of the respondents in this respect that there was no "absolute entitlement" to an oral appeal in any process. However, it was noted that the Oireachtas had determined that persons are entitled to an oral appeal unless there is a finding under one of the subsections of s.13(6), such that a finding under s.13(6)(a) is a significant finding, in that it affects what would otherwise be the statutory entitlement of the applicant to an oral appeal hearing.

In that context, two legal arguments were put forward concerning the manner in which the deciding officer of the Refugee Applications Commissioner approached the decision-making process. Section 13(6)(a) requires that, in order for the person charged with making the decision to come to the relevant conclusion, the officer concerned must be satisfied that either no basis, or a minimal basis, has been established. The decision in respect of the applicant specified that the officer concerned was satisfied that no basis or a minimal basis had been established. The applicant contended that the decision was therefore unclear, on the ground that the officer should have specified one or other of the bases, *i.e.* should have specified either that there was no basis or that there was a minimal basis. Clarke J. was not satisfied that this was a correct view of the law, holding:

"The substance of the requirement in Section 13(6)(a) is that in order to make the finding under that subsection the deciding officer is required to be satisfied that, at its height, the Applicant's claim has been shown

> to have a basis no more than minimal. Whether the decision to that
> effect, by the deciding officer, on the facts of this case is arguably open
> to challenge, is a matter to which I will return in due course. However,
> I am not satisfied that the mere fact that the deciding officer specified
> his decision in the terms which he did, provides as a standalone basis
> any grounds for mounting a challenge."

The second basis on which the applicant sought to impugn the decision of the
first-named respondent was the contention that the statutory regime involving
s.13(6)(a) requires two separate decisions, and that, in substance, the deciding
officer should first decide whether there is something more than a minimal
basis and then go on to decide whether, on balance, he or she proposes to
recommend refugee status. Clarke J. was also not satisfied this constituted a
correct view of the law, holding:

> "At the end of the day there is a decision involving an assessment
> of all of the relevant criteria for refugee status by reference to the
> legislation and the authorities. That decision must be made by reference
> to the two different standards. If the deciding officer is satisfied to
> recommend refugee status then that is the end of the matter. If such a
> recommendation is given then the statutory process leading to refugee
> status will flow from that.
>
> On the other hand, if the deciding officer is not satisfied, applying
> the appropriate criteria, to make a recommendation of refugee status
> then the deciding officer may also decide that the case made is such
> that it is does not provide even a minimal basis for the contentions of
> the Applicant. In those circumstances it is open to the deciding officer
> to record a decision under Section 13(6)(a), with the consequences
> which I have outlined.
>
> There are not, therefore, two entirely separate decisions, but a
> single determination by the deciding officer as to the strength, as it
> were, of the Applicant's case. At one extreme the deciding officer may
> determine that the case is so weak that it can properly be characterised
> as having no basis or only a minimal basis. At the other extreme the
> deciding officer may be persuaded by the case such as to recommend
> refugee status."

Clarke J. accepted that in certain cases there might arise an "intermediate
category" where the deciding officer may be satisfied that something more
than a minimal basis has been put forward, but that, nonetheless, it is not
sufficient to pass the threshold necessary to make a recommendation in favour
of refugee status. However, it was held that whichever of those three positions
the deciding officer determines upon, the same issues, materials, and criteria
are being applied to the question which requires to be addressed, and that

the view which the deciding officer takes of those matters will determine his decision on both his substantive recommendation and whether to reach a finding under s.13(6)(a).

Clarke J. then proceeded to consider whether the applicant had made out sufficient grounds to pass the substantial grounds test necessary for the purposes of an application for leave to challenge the decision of the Commissioner. It was noted that the applicant was an Iranian national who had spent much of the last 10 years in South Korea. The applicant claimed to have converted to Christianity (having been a Muslim) while in South Korea, and that he was subjected to physical mistreatment by other Muslims in South Korea. The applicant also claimed that he was informed that the Iranian Embassy in South Korea had been told of his conversion and he had heard that certain approaches had been made to his father who remained in Iran. In those circumstances, he claimed a fear of persecution on return to Iran.

In rejecting the applicant's application for refugee status, Clarke J. noted that the deciding officer appeared to place reliance on a finding that conditions applicable to Christians in Iran were more benign than contended for on behalf of the applicant. Clarke J. reviewed the country of origin information which was before the Commissioner, and which distinguished significantly between a number of different categories of person who may have a religion other than the Muslim religion in Iran. First, a distinction was made in relation to persons who were born into another religion, such as Christianity, in which circumstances a relatively benign regime applied. However, Clarke J. noted that a distinction was made in the country of origin information in relation to persons who may have converted from the Muslim religion to another religion such as Christianity, noting that "there can be little doubt that the position of such persons is less benign". Secondly, significant reliance was placed in the country of origin information on the manner in which a person, whether originally Christian or an apostate to Christianity, practises their religion and, in particular, whether they engage in an attempt to convert others. Clarke J. further noted that "there seems little doubt but that significant adverse consequences may continue to flow from an attempt to proselytise". Finally, it was held that the country of origin information did support the view that there had been a significant lessening in practical terms of the consequences for apostates in virtually all categories (with the exception of those engaged in aggressive proselytisation) in recent years. Clarke J. held that it was in that context that the fact that the relevant law in Iran still maintains a position that those who are apostates from Islam may suffer the death penalty must be seen, and concluded:

"There seems to be ample evidence for the view taken by the Refugee Applications Commissioner to the effect that, in practice, the mere fact that someone changes their religion from the Muslim to a religion such as Christianity does not of itself expose such a person to the death penalty at this stage."

Having considered all of the evidence that was before the Refugee Applications Commissioner and also having considered the determination of the Refugee Applications Commissioner, Clarke J. was not persuaded that there were substantial grounds for the suggestion that the s.13 recommendation was open to challenge. This finding was reached on the basis that the analysis conducted by the deciding officer provided a basis for the determination which was made by that officer to the effect that he was not prepared to recommend the applicant for refugee status.

However, Clarke J. came to a different view in respect of the finding under s.13(6)(a) of the 1996 Act, on the basis that the deciding officer did not set out in his determination precisely why he felt the claim was minimal. Clarke J. was critical of the failure on the part of the decision-maker to specify the basis for the view that the claim was minimal, rather than being a situation where on balance the applicant's contention for refugee status should be rejected. In those circumstances, Clarke J. granted leave to challenge by way of certiorari the decision of the first-named respondent pursuant to s.13(6)(a) of the 1996 Act, and also granted an order of mandamus compelling the Commissioner to refer the applicant's application for asylum for full consideration under the substantive procedures of the Refugee Act 1996.

The decision of Clarke J. is significant in that, whilst it rejects the applicant's contention for a "two-stage" decision-making process when the Commissioner makes a finding pursuant to s.13(6) of the 1996 Act, it does require the decision-maker to state the basis for making such a finding, which basis is reviewable by the High Court by way of judicial review.

Trial of preliminary issue in judicial review proceedings alleging bias against tribunal member In *Nyembo v Refugee Appeals Tribunal*, unreported, High Court, October 6, 2006, the applicant had been granted leave by the High Court (Butler J.) on March 8, 2006 to seek an order prohibiting the second named respondent from hearing his refugee appeal and an order of mandamus requiring that the applicant's appeal be assigned to another tribunal member. The grounds on which leave was granted related to the applicant's belief that the second-named respondent was biased and predisposed against appellants who appeared before him by way of oral hearing. The respondents, thereafter, made an application to have a preliminary issue of law determined prior to the full hearing relating to the admissibility of statistical evidence on the outcome of decisions of the second-named respondent as a member of the tribunal, and whether as a matter of law such statistics could constitute a basis for a finding of actual and/or apparent bias.

Feeney J. noted that the purpose behind a court order permitting the trial of a preliminary issue of law was primarily to save time and costs, with the authorities governing such procedure referring to the utility of such order where it has the capacity to result in the dismissal and/or significant truncating of the applicant's claim. It was held by Feeney J. that in considering an application for the trial of a preliminary issue of law, particular regard must be had to the likelihood of achieving savings in costs and time, and whether there would be "a saving or a duplication". It was held that, in the present case, there were a number of factors which were of importance in that weighing exercise. The first was that the proceedings were by way of judicial review where the legal issues and grounds had been clearly defined and limited by the order granting leave. Secondly, the learned High Court judge held that this did not appear to be a case where the proposed preliminary issue would cause any duplication of evidence. Thirdly, it was held that the legal issue sought was one that would require to be fully argued involving the same time either at a preliminary stage or at the full hearing. Fourthly, and most importantly, Feeney J. held that the determination of the preliminary issue in favour of the respondent would be likely to result in the applicant's claim being either concluded or very significantly curtailed. Fifthly, it was held that the hearing of the preliminary issue would be likely to bring order and direction to any full hearing and reduce its duration and define the scope and extent of discovery.

Reference was made to the decision of the Supreme Court in *Tara Exploration and Development Ltd v Minister for Industry and Commerce* [1975] I.R. 242, where the court identified the circumstances in which it is appropriate to permit the trial of a preliminary issue. Feeney J. noted that the decision of the Supreme Court established that an order pursuant to Ord.34 of the Rules of the Superior Courts for the preliminary determination of certain questions of law should not be granted if the proposed question or questions could not be answered without reference to the relevant facts where such facts have not been determined. In the words of O'Higgins C.J. at 257: "Order 34, Rule 2 can only apply to questions of pure law where no evidence is needed and no further information is required." Feeney J. thus accepted that where the question or questions are dependent on facts that have not been ascertained, that the procedure or rule should not be utilised, referring to the dicta of O'Flaherty J. in *Duffy v News Group Newspapers Ltd (No.2)* [1994] 3 I.R. 63 at 76, where he stated that the trial of a preliminary issue "... is only appropriate where words can be placed before the Judge without the necessity of calling evidence."

It was held that the lack of the requirement for evidence is central to the determination of the court in deciding whether to order the trial on a preliminary issue, noting that it was clear from the authorities that this could be achieved where the facts were agreed, where there were no facts in dispute, and where the defendant agreed facts for the purposes of a preliminary issue of law only without prejudice to the entitlement to contest the facts if the actual determination of the preliminary issue would not result in the disposal of the case.[13]

Feeney J. thus concluded that the use of the procedure is of limited application and it is also a discretionary one, noting that the court must be careful to avoid creating an unfair situation of duplication or delay when the very purpose of the rule is the opposite. It was held that, in the present case, the facts agreed or, more accurately, accepted, by the moving party were set out in the respondent solicitor's letter of June 28, 2006, and that such facts were facts contended for by the claimant in the grounding affidavits. The learned High Court judge noted that there were other matters claimed which remained in dispute as to the belief of certain practitioners as to bias on the part of the second-named respondent in respect of refugee appeals, but Feeney J. held that the accepted facts gave rise to a real and substantial issue as to what are the legal consequences and conclusions to be drawn from such accepted facts and as to the status and admissibility of evidence. It was noted that such legal consequences and the status in evidence would be required to be addressed at an early stage in the proceedings to allow for the efficient disposal of the claim, and that this consideration would be vital to the conduct of the case.

Feeney J. was satisfied that no additional facts were necessary for these matters to be addressed and that this was not a case where extra evidence would be required on this issue or where it could be said that the legal issues were being tried *in vacuo*. The learned judge thus concluded that it was appropriate to exercise his discretion to order the trial of two preliminary issues of law as follows:

> "1. Whether as a matter of law statistical evidence on the outcome of decisions of the second respondent as a member of the Refugee Appeals Tribunal is admissible in evidence.
> 2. Whether as a matter of law statistics and/or evidence relating to the outcomes or results of decisions made by the Refugee Appeals Tribunal can without more constitute a basis for a finding of actual and/or apparent bias."

In so holding, Feeney J. noted that the trial of the proposed preliminary issues would have a real likelihood of reducing the costs and time of the proceedings, and that if the respondent was to be successful on the preliminary issues as argued for by the respondent, the applicant's case would be potentially determined or at least significantly reduced in scope. It was also held that the trial of these issues on a preliminary basis and in advance of any potential discovery would have the effect of reducing or eliminating the requirement for discovery.

---

[13] Feeney J. noted that the capacity of the defendant/respondent to accept facts alleged by the moving party for the purposes of the trial of a preliminary issue of law was confirmed by the Supreme Court in *McCabe v Ireland* [1999] 4 I.R. 151.

[**Note**: The applicants' appeal against the decision of Feeney J. was allowed by the Supreme Court on June 19, 2007 on the basis that there were contested facts which were relevant to the issues of law, and that there was no agreement as to those facts. The Supreme Court held that, in those circumstances, it was not appropriate, practical or convenient to have preliminary issues of law determined, and remitted the matter to the High Court.]

Whether decision to deport applicant ought to be rescinded having regard to the applicant's threat to commit suicide in the event of deportation In *Cosma v Minister for Justice, Equality and Law Reform*, unreported, High Court, February 15, 2006, the High Court considered whether the Minister was required to revoke a deportation order in the light of a threat by the applicant to commit suicide in the event of deportation.

The applicant was a Romanian national whose application for asylum on grounds of religious oppression was refused. The applicant was subsequently invited to make representations pursuant to s.3 of the Immigration Act 1999, which were not successful and a deportation order was made in respect of her on July 4, 2003. On September 23, 2003, the applicant's solicitors submitted a psychiatric report on her behalf and sought reconsideration of the applicant's deportation on the basis of an alleged threat of suicide by the applicant in the event of her deportation. Two further psychiatric reports were submitted on October 8, 2003, along with further representations. By letter dated October 31, 2003, the respondent refused the applicant's application.

The applicant instituted proceedings seeking an order of certiorari quashing the decision of the respondent to deport the applicant under s.3 of the Immigration Act 1999, an injunction restraining such deportation and an order of mandamus directing the Minister to consider and decide the applicant's case in the light of the suicide threat.

Counsel for both parties accepted that the applicant was entitled to the unspecified personal rights guaranteed by Art.40.3.2° of the Constitution. It was submitted on behalf of the applicant that this was a case in which there was a real and substantial risk of suicide and, as a consequence, there was a clear risk that the applicant's right to life would be jeopardised if she were deported. In light of the applicant's rights both under the Constitution and under the European Convention on Human Rights, it was submitted that in reviewing the respondent's decision, the court had to apply anxious scrutiny to the Minister's decision and to the materials and evidence relied upon by him in coming to his conclusion to proceed with the deportation. On behalf of the respondent it was submitted that there was, in reality, no evidence of any real and substantial risk of suicide upon which the Minister could or should act. It was submitted that the threat of self-harm and the circumstances giving rise to it were not raised by the applicant until 2003, that the applicant's application for asylum had made no reference to the circumstances which allegedly gave rise to her suicide threat, and that the documents submitted by the applicant's solicitors did not amount to psychiatric reports to which any great weight should be attached. It was submitted that these documents were inadequate and offered no sufficient diagnosis or prognosis, but instead comprised no more than a handwritten record of a narrative account given by the applicant to the doctor as a result of one meeting with her and subsequent observations of an unsatisfactory and inconclusive nature.

In relation to the arguments on the appropriate standard of review, Hanna J. considered the nature of the "anxious scrutiny" test and concluded:

> "I would view such phrases as enjoining the court to apply a special and particular rigour to its analysis of the questioned decision where the court is satisfied that a prima facie issue has arisen concerning a possible significant interference with a person's right to life or bodily integrity. An applicant should face only a modest hurdle in impressing the court to embark upon this course. However, the court should be wary of such rights being invoked in circumstances which are manifestly frivolous, vexatious, clearly ill founded or which amount to an abuse of process."

Turning to the core of the applicant's challenge, Hanna J. reviewed numerous authorities on the right to life both under Irish law[14] and the European Convention on Human Rights,[15] and held that in order for the applicant to succeed it would be necessary to establish three factors on the balance of probabilities:

1. When the Minister decided to refuse to rescind the deportation order, there then existed, to the Minister's knowledge, a real and substantial threat to the applicant's life by suicide as a direct consequence of his decision.

2. The applicant's threatened act of suicide could only be forestalled by him acceding to the applicant's request and stopping the process of deportation and not by any other means such as medical intervention.

3. The Minister either missed or disregarded, to the point of irrationality, compelling medical and other material evidence of the foregoing.

Hanna J. reviewed the document submitted on behalf of the applicant in support of the application for revocation, and noted that whilst the applicant's solicitors clearly intended it to be treated as a psychiatric report, it comprised

---

[14] *Ryan v Attorney General* [1965] I.R. 294; *State (C) v Frawley* [1976] I.R. 365; *Attorney General v X* [1992] 1 I.R. 1.
[15] *D v United Kingdom* (1997) 24 E.H.R.R. 423; *Ahmed v Austria* (1996) 24 E.H.R.R. 278; *Soering v United Kingdom* [1989] E.C.H.R. 14; *R. (Razgar) v Secretary of State for the Home Department* [2003] E.W.C.A. Civ. 840.

almost entirely a narrative by the applicant offering reasons as to why she was threatening to commit suicide and there was no diagnosis made of any actual mental illness nor any suggested modality of treatment for same. Hanna J. concluded that whilst a prima facie issue concerning potential compromise of the applicant's right to life and bodily integrity was raised in the circumstances, the applicant had failed to establish that there was a real and substantial risk that she would kill herself. In relation to the psychiatric reports submitted, it was noted that these "fall well short of what one would expect in terms of actual analysis of the applicant's condition, an objective diagnosis and, most significantly, no attempt to address the issue of treatment even in the event of the deportation going ahead." Further, it was held that the applicant had not established that revocation of the deportation order would avert her threatened suicide; it was noted in this regard that no consideration had been given to removing the alleged danger by treatment either in this State or in Romania. Finally, Hanna J. was not satisfied that any material evidence, documentary or otherwise, was either missed or disregarded by the Minister or his officials.

Finally, Hanna J. referred to the policy aspect of the respondent's decision not to revoke the deportation order and the memorandum accompanying the affirmation of the deportation order including a comment from a principal officer in the respondent's department, noting:

"This is a situation becoming more common—where a case is being made that a deportation order should be revoked on the basis that the person will harm herself if sent back to her country.

No-one can say whether such a threat will be effected or not. Suicides happen among nationals and non-nationals. However, public policy cannot be such that the law will not be applied in the face of such a threat."

Addressing the applicant's challenge to such determination, Hanna J. held as follows:

"The letter from Mr. Dowling dated 31st October, 2003, correctly points out that the applicant has no right to be in the State, evidences careful consideration of the medical evidence, makes what is an unobjectionable statement of public policy with regard to the threat of suicide and focuses on dealing with any such threat medically. It is, in my view, a proper response to a threat of suicide."

This finding would appear to be at variance with the decision of Finlay Geoghegan J. in *Makumbi v Minister for Justice, Equality and Law Reform*, unreported, High Court, November 15, 2005,[16] which decision is under appeal.

---

[16] See *Annual Review of Irish Law 2005*, p.57.

It is to be hoped that the decision of the Supreme Court in *Makumbi* will clarify the extent of the obligations of the State in cases involving threats of suicide in the event of removal from the State.

Whether deportation of child diagnosed with attention deficit hyperactivity disorder and intellectual disability in breach of Constitution and/or Arts 3 and 8 of European Convention on Human Rights   The High Court was called upon to address the threshold for successfully invoking Arts 3 and 8 of the European Convention on Human Rights in challenging a deportation order in the leave application in *Agbonlahor v Minister for Justice, Equality and Law Reform* [2007] 1 I.L.R.M. 58.

On March 5, 2003, the first-named applicant and her two children arrived in the State and sought asylum. On December 30, 2003, the first-named applicant was notified by the Refugee Applications Commissioner that her application for refugee status was unsuccessful. On April 20, 2004, she was notified by the Refugee Appeals Tribunal that her appeal from the decision of the Refugee Applications Commissioner was unsuccessful. The applicants' application for leave to remain in the State on humanitarian grounds was refused by the Minister and on October 4, 2005, the first-named applicant was notified to present herself to the Garda National Immigration Bureau.

On October 4, 2005, the second-named applicant was scheduled for assessment at a Regional Autistic Spectrum Disorder Clinic. On October 11, 2005, the second- and third-named applicants were taken into the care of the appropriate health and welfare authorities after the first-named applicant had harmed herself. On November 4, 2005, the applicants' solicitors sought revocation of the deportation orders made by him on September 15, 2005 on grounds of the changed circumstances of the second-named applicant. On November 8, 2005, the second-named applicant was assessed by a speech and language therapist and a senior clinical psychologist. They concluded that the second-named applicant did not have sufficient features to meet the criteria required for autistic spectrum disorder, but held he did meet the criteria for a diagnosis of attention deficit hyperactivity disorder in addition to intellectual disability. On January 20, 2006, the Minister for Justice affirmed the deportation orders on the basis that the second-named applicant was not autistic, and that the making of the deportation orders was consistent with domestic and international legal obligations.

The applicants subsequently sought leave by way of judicial review to quash the decision of the Minister for Justice to implement the deportation orders which had been made in respect of each of them. The applicants also sought declarations that the decision of the Minister to enforce the deportation orders was *ultra vires*, arbitrary and unreasonable, disproportionate, contrary to natural and constitutional justice and contrary to the Minister's obligations under the European Convention on Human Rights.

It was submitted that the Minister had acted *ultra vires* and in violation of Art.40.3.2° of the Constitution and Arts 3 and 8 of the European Convention on Human Rights Act. Considering this submission, Herbert J. noted:

"It has been decided that despite the reference to 'citizen' in Article 40.3.2° of the Constitution, the State is obliged to defend and to vindicate the life and possessions of those persons who are not citizens of the State but who are present in the State. Whether or not this obligation on the State extends to what are generally termed, 'socio-economic rights', such as the right to medical treatment, is a matter of doubt even in the case of citizens of the State. However, there can be no doubt but that Article 42.4 of the Constitution obliges the State to make available free primary education, which has been held to include, primary education suitable for children with special educational needs. However, the existence of such rights is not absolute and unqualified. In the instant case they are subject to the right of the State in the interests of the common good to deport persons who have been refused refugee status, (subject to the provisions of s.5 of the Refugee Act, 1996, (prohibition on refoulement) and s.4 of the Criminal Justice, (United Nations Convention Against Torture) Act, 2000) and now, in my judgment, Article 3 of the First Schedule of the European Convention on Human Rights Act, 2003."

Herbert J. rejected the applicants' claims in so far as they related to Arts 40 and 42 of the Constitution, applying the dicta of Keane C.J. in the *Baby O* case,[17] where it was held that "[i]f the State's right to deport persons who have been refused refugee status were thus circumscribed, it would be, in a great range of cases, virtually negated".

Herbert J. then proceeded to consider the potential application of Arts.3 and 8 of the European Convention on Human Rights. Referring to the decision of the House of Lords in *N v Secretary of State for the Home Department* [2005] 2 A.C. 296 on the threshold for Art.3-complaints in medical treatment cases, the learned High Court judge concluded that the applicants did not have an arguable case that the decision of the Minister was an infringement of their rights under Art.3 of the European Convention on Human Rights Act, on the basis that "the facts of the instant case are nowhere approaching the level of a certainty of immediate appalling suffering or loss of life that would be required to establish an arguable case for judicial review based on 'exceptional circumstances' as that term has been defined by the Strasbourg Court."

However, Herbert J. noted that Baroness Hale in *N* adverted to the fact that the case law of the European Court of Human Rights "did not exclude that treatment which does not reach the severity of article 3 treatment may

---

[17] *O v Minister for Justice, Equality and Law Reform* [2002] 2 I.R. 169.

nonetheless breach article 8 in its private life aspect where there are sufficiently adverse effects on physical and moral integrity", referring to the decisions of *R. (Razgar) v Secretary of State for the Home Department* [2004] 2 A.C. 368, *Bensaid v United Kingdom* [2001] 33 E.H.R.R. 205 and *Henao v The Netherlands* (Application No.13669/03), unreported, European Court of Human Rights, June 24, 2003. Herbert J. adopted the following statement of Lord Bingham in *Razgar* in relation to Art.8:

> "the rights protected by article 8 can be engaged by the foreseeable consequences for health of removal from the United Kingdom pursuant to an immigration decision, even where such removal does not violate article 3, if the facts relied on by the Applicant are sufficiently strong. In so answering I make no reference to 'welfare', a matter to which no argument was directed. It would seem plain that, as with medical treatment so with welfare, an Applicant could never hope to resist an expulsion decision without showing something very much more extreme than relative disadvantage as compared with the expelling State."

Herbert J. concluded that, applying the "arguable test" case set out by the Supreme Court in *G v DPP* [1994] 1 I.R. 374, the applicants had established arguable grounds that the refusal of the Minister to revoke the deportation orders was a violation of their rights under Art.8(1) of the First Schedule of the European Convention on Human Rights. The applicants were, accordingly, granted leave on this sole ground.

Whether entitlement to tape-record interview conducted by Refugee Applications Commissioner   In *Hakizimana v Minister for Justice, Equality and Law Reform*, unreported, High Court, November 14, 2006, the applicant was a national of Burundi who arrived in Ireland in January 2004 and immediately upon arrival sought asylum as a refugee. The applicant was interviewed pursuant to s.11 of the 1996 Act on August 15 and 30, 2005. That resulted in a recommendation from the Commissioner that refugee status be refused. The Commissioner's recommendation was the subject of a judicial review application, which proceedings resulted in an agreement whereby on consent the Commissioner's recommendation was set aside. The settlement also provided that the report which had been prepared pursuant to s.13(1) of the 1996 Act would be withdrawn and removed from the applicant's file and it was agreed that a fresh consideration of an application for refugee status would be considered.

Thereafter, the applicant was notified that, in relation to his application for a declaration as a refugee, an interview would take place on March 23, 2006. The applicant's solicitors wrote to the Commissioner in advance of the interview seeking that the interview be electronically recorded in full rather than being merely reduced to writing by way of "notes of interview" or otherwise, and that a copy be provided to him as soon as possible after the interview. Alternatively, the applicant sought permission to record the interview with his own equipment. This request was based upon the fact that the previous High Court proceedings had disputed the accuracy of the records of previous interviews. By letter dated March 22, 2006, the Commissioner refused the applicant's request on the basis that it was not the policy of the Commissioner to electronically record interviews.

The applicant instituted judicial review proceedings seeking a declaration that he was entitled to make his own tape-recording of the proposed interview or alternatively that the applicant was entitled to require the Commissioner to tape-record the said interview. A further declaration was sought that the failure or refusal of the Commissioner to tape-record the interview or permit the applicant to do so and/or to furnish the record to the applicant prior to a decision being made, was contrary to the applicant's rights under Art.40.3 of the Constitution and/or was an unlawful exercise of the Commissioner's statutory powers.

Feeney J. began by setting out a comprehensive account of the procedures which apply to interviews pursuant to s.11 of the Refugee Act 1996. It was accepted by the learned High Court judge that "[t]here is no issue but that procedural fairness in compliance with the rules of natural and constitutional justice should and must attend the process to determine an application for refugee status". It was further accepted that the process being carried out by the interviewer was an inquisitorial process and not an adversarial process, in accordance with para.196 of the UNHCR Handbook which indicates that, whilst the burden of proof in principle rests on the applicant, the duty to ascertain and evaluate all the relevant factors is shared between the applicant and the examiner.

It was submitted by the applicant that the absence of an entitlement on the part of the applicant to keep an electronic record of his interview, either by having it recorded by the Commissioner or recorded on the applicant's behalf, amounted to an absence of fair procedures and a breach of the rules of natural and constitutional justice. It was submitted that this claim was to be viewed against a statutory framework which can result in any appeal which the applicant would have being determined without an oral hearing, where a finding is made pursuant to s.13(6) of the 1996 Act.

It was held by Feeney J. that:

> "There is no doubt but that the second named Respondent must apply fair procedures. However fair procedures vary depending upon the nature of the process being conducted. The process being conducted by the second named Respondent is an important and significant quasi judicial process with the result impacting upon the potential safety, welfare and life of an Applicant."

Feeney J. held that, in considering the requirements of fair procedures, assistance
can be gleaned from the approach adopted by the Irish courts in relation to
criminal investigations leading to a criminal trial, on the basis that:

> "it could not be reasonably contended that the obligations for fair
> procedures as viewed by the courts in respect of criminal investigations
> or trials could be in any way lower than the requirements for fair
> procedures to be followed in an administrative body albeit one
> carrying out an important quasi judicial function. In other words this
> Court is satisfied that the requirements identified as being necessary in
> criminal investigations and trials represent the imposition of the highest
> requirements for fair procedures. The asylum process is of such moment
> that only high standards of fairness will suffice."

It was noted that the issue of recording interviews during a criminal investigation
was considered by the Supreme Court in *People (DPP) v Quilligan (No.3)*
[1993] 2 I.R. 305, where O'Flaherty J. expressed a clear view that the issue
of the introduction of audio/visual recordings, even where there was a statute
providing for same which had yet to be implemented, was a matter of policy
for the Oireachtas.

In the context of the asylum process, and in particular the conduct of
interviews by the Commissioner, Feeney J. was satisfied that:

> "The procedures followed by the second named Respondent, set forth in
> detail above, clearly go well beyond what is strictly required by statute
> and provide *inter alia* that the interview notes must be signed and agreed
> by an Applicant on a page by page basis. The notes are a summary of
> what has been said rather than a verbatim account. The Respondents
> submitted that such procedures are sufficient to ensure compliance
> with natural justice in the conduct of refugee interviews and pointed
> out that there is no legal authority to support the proposition that where
> interpretative facilities are provided and interview notes are read back
> and signed by the interviewee, that there is a residual obligation either
> to permit an interviewee to make a separate recording or to furnish the
> interviewee with a recording."

Feeney J. relied on the decision of the Supreme Court in *Lavery v Member
in Charge* [1999] 2 I.R. 390 as demonstrating the reluctance of the courts to
prescribe the manner in which interviews must be conducted or recorded,
holding that such approach does not remove the overall requirement of the
court to ascertain if the overall process offends objective considerations of
fairness.

It was noted that the courts in England have, on two recent occasions,
considered the question of the tape-recording of interviews as part of the asylum

process. The first consideration was by Pitchford J. in *Mapah v Secretary of State for the Home Department* [2003] E.W.H.C. 306 (Admin.) and the later decision is that of the Court of Appeal in *R. (Dirshe) v Secretary of State* [2005] 1 W.L.R. 2685. In *Mapah*, Pitchford J. determined that the policy of the Secretary of State to refuse permission to tape interviews during an immigration interview was lawful and did so on the basis that his consideration of the overall procedure in place did not, in his judgment, offend objective considerations of fairness. Subsequently, in *Dirshe*, the Court of Appeal arrived at a different view but expressly did not overrule the decision in *Mapah*. Feeney J. regarded the difference in view as being based upon the different administrative procedures in place at the time of the Court of Appeal's consideration of the matter.

Feeney J. concluded that "[t]his Court is satisfied that an analysis of the entire process demonstrates that the procedure cannot be said to offend objective considerations of fairness." It was held that the approach adopted by the Court of Appeal in *Dirshe* to declare that it was unlawful to decline to permit an applicant who is not accompanied at his asylum or human rights interview by a legal representative and/or an interpreter to tape-record that interview was based upon the precise procedures in England. Feeney J. referred to the significant differences which applied to procedures in this jurisdiction, including the fact that the procedure in this jurisdiction does not seek to have a verbatim account and therefore a central finding of the Court of Appeal to the effect that a tape-recording provides the only sensible method did not apply in this jurisdiction. Reference was also made to the fact that the process followed in this jurisdiction is that each and every page is signed by the applicant and agreed by the applicant, which did not appear to be the procedure in England as of the date of the Court of Appeal hearing in 2005. Further, it was noted that there is also no time gap between the applicant hearing what is recorded and signing and agreeing same as the procedures provide for it to be done on the day of the interview and at the time of the interview. Feeney J. referred to the availability of free legal advice in advance of the interview and the possibility of being accompanied at an interview by a representative of the Refugee Legal Service if there is advice to that effect. Finally, Feeney J. noted that s.11(2) did not require a verbatim account of the interview but rather a report in writing in relation to the interview. On this basis, Feeney J. held:

> "I am satisfied that the answer to the central question is that having regard to the entirety of the procedure adopted by the second named Respondent that that procedure meets the appropriate standard of fairness and the procedure in place does not offend objective considerations of fairness. That is not to say that there is not always scope for refinement and improvement of procedures but in the light of the above determination it is not for this court to make such judgment."

It is submitted that the decision of the judge, particularly in respect of the finding that s.11(2) of the 1996 Act does not require a verbatim account of the interview, fails to engage with the central complaint of the applicant, namely, that the constitutional entitlement to fair procedures may require such an account. Furthermore, it is submitted that the learned judge's reliance on the principle of judicial deference was misplaced given the matters in issue; whilst judicial deference might be exercised in respect of the matters which fall within the expertise of a designated administrative body, the nature and extent of any procedural obligations in the context of constitutional guarantees are surely a matter for the High Court and not the administrative body.

Whether failure to seek state protection sufficient to render irrelevant any country of origin evidence of failure on part of applicant's country of origin to provide protection   The extent and application of the principle of "internal protection alternative" was considered by the High Court in *Kvaratskhelia v Refugee Appeals Tribunal* [2006] 3 I.R. 368.

The applicant was a Georgian national who sought asylum in this State arising from a fear of persecution on the ground of his sexual orientation. The applicant sought an order of certiorari quashing the respondent's refusal of his refugee appeal. It was contended on behalf of the applicant that the first-named respondent, the member of the Refugee Appeals Tribunal, erred in law in finding that there was a presumption in favour of state-of-origin protection in refugee applications or, alternatively, that the matters referred to by the first-named respondent were sufficient to give rise to such a presumption in the instant case. It was further contended that the tribunal member erred in finding that the fact that the applicant did not seek state protection in Georgia from homophobic abuse and assaults was sufficient to render irrelevant any country of origin evidence of a failure on the part of the Georgian state authorities to provide protection to homosexual men. Finally, it was submitted that the member of the Refugee Appeals Tribunal failed to have any proper regard to the country-of-origin information, to the evidence of complaints made by the applicant, and to the instances of persecution suffered by the applicant as establishing the non-availability of a system for the protection of the citizen or a reasonable willingness by the state authorities to operate such a system.

Counsel for the respondents submitted that the first-named respondent had properly relied upon the dicta of La Forest J. in the decision in *Canada (Attorney General) v Ward* (1993) 2 R.C.S. 689 at 725 and 726 where that learned judge, in giving the decision of the Canadian Supreme Court, stated as follows:

> "Absent some evidence, the claim should fail, as nations should be presumed capable of protecting their citizens. Security of nationals is, after all, the essence of sovereignty. Absent a situation of complete breakdown of state apparatus, such as that recognised in Lebanon in *Zalzali*, it should be assumed that the state is capable of protecting a

claimant. (...)

I find that state complicity is not a necessary component of persecution either under the 'unwilling' or under the 'unable' branch of the definition. A subjective fear of persecution combined with state inability to protect the claimant creates a presumption that the fear is well-founded. The danger that this presumption will operate too broadly is tempered by a requirement that clear and convincing proof of a state's inability to protect must be advanced. I recognise that these conclusions broaden the range of potentially successful refugee claims beyond those involving feared persecution at the hands of the claimant's nominal government. As long as this persecution is directed at the claimant on the basis of one of the enumerated grounds, I do not think the identity of the feared perpetrator of the persecution removes these cases from the scope of Canada's international obligations in this area."

Herbert J. found the reasoning and conclusions of La Forest J. "both persuasive and compatible with the jurisprudence of this State in considering applications for refugee status." Referring to the principle that the onus is on the applicant for refugee status to establish both a subjective fear of persecution for one, at least, of the reasons specified in s.2 of the Refugee Act 1996 and an objective basis for that fear, Herbert J. held:

"Apart from those calamitous cases where the total failure or repressive subversion of all state institutions has become so notorious that the fact that a particular state is no longer capable or willing to vindicate the human rights of all of its nationals must be accepted without the need for actual evidence, it would in my judgment be contrary to reason to require a requested state to approach every application for refugee status from the premise that the state of origin is or may be unable or unwilling to provide protection from persecution to the claimant."

Thus, the judge agreed that subject to such exceptional cases:

"the fact that the power of the state to provide protection to its nationals is a fundamental feature of sovereignty and, the fact that the protection afforded by refugee status is 'a surrogate coming into play where no alternative remains to the claimant', renders it both rational and just for a requested state to presume, unless the contrary is demonstrated by 'clear and convincing proof', on the part of the Applicant for refugee status, that the state of origin is able and willing to provide protection to the Applicant from persecution, even if at a lesser level than the requested state."

Herbert J., therefore, held that the tribunal member did not err in law in applying the presumption that state-of-origin protection was available in Georgia to someone in the position of the applicant.

It was submitted by counsel for the applicant that even if the first-named respondent acted *intra vires* in concluding that the applicant had not sought protection from any state authority, she failed to consider whether, if such an application had been made by him, state protection might reasonably be forthcoming. Counsel for the applicant relied upon the judgment of La Forest J. in *Canada (Attorney General) v Ward* at 724 where the learned judge said that "like Hathaway, I prefer to formulate this aspect of the test for fear of persecution as follows: only in situations in which state protection 'might reasonably have been forthcoming' will the claimant's failure to approach the state for protection defeat his claim."

Counsel for the applicant also relied upon the case of *Skenderaj v Secretary of State for the Home Department* [2002] E.W.C.A. Civ. 567, where Auld L.J. held: "if the State cannot or will not provide a sufficiency of protection, if sought, the failure to seek it is irrelevant, and that is so whether the failure results from a fear of persecution or simply an acceptance that to do so would be futile."

Counsel for the respondents submitted that the first-named respondent had expressly concluded that the applicant had not shown by "clear and convincing proof" that he suffered or would suffer from a failure of state protection as it related to his claim. Counsel pointed to the further finding by the first-named respondent that the applicant's evidence did not displace the presumption that his state of origin was capable of protecting him in circumstances where state assistance had not been sought by him.

Having regard to the decision of the first named-respondent, Herbert J. held that the only inference reasonably capable of being drawn was that the conclusion that the applicant had not shown by 'clear and convincing' evidence that he suffered or would suffer from a failure of state protection as it relates to his claim, was based on her finding that the applicant had not sought the assistance of the state authorities in Georgia. He could not, therefore, rebut the presumption that those state authorities were capable of protecting him from persecution by reason of his membership of a particular social group. Herbert J. held that no other construction could in the particular context be placed upon the conclusion of the first-named respondent that "[t]he appellant's evidence does not displace this presumption in circumstances where assistance was not sought. Where, in Professor Hathaway's words, the refugee claimant ought reasonably to vindicate his or her basic human rights against the home state, refugee status is inappropriate."

Thus, Herbert J. stated:

> "Unfortunately, it appears to me that the first named Respondent has not addressed at all the question of whether, having regard to the Applicant's own evidence and to the country of origin information submitted with

> his appeal to the Refugee Appeals Tribunal, state protection 'might reasonably have been forthcoming' from the state authorities of Georgia had the Applicant sought it. In my judgment, the first named Respondent misdirected herself in law in concluding wrongly that the failure of the Applicant to seek protection from the state authorities of Georgia was sufficient in itself to defeat his claim for refugee status."

Herbert J. concluded that the first-named respondent had not once considered whether the evidence of the applicant and the country of origin information furnished by him was sufficient to rebut the presumption of state-of-origin protection in this case. In so holding, the learned High Court judge held that the legal position as stated by La Forest J. in *Canada (Attorney General) v Ward* and Auld L.J. in *Skenderaj v Secretary of State for the Home Department* was entirely compatible with the jurisprudence of this State, and that the decision of the first-named respondent was in breach of the principles articulated in those decisions. Accordingly, Herbert J. granted an order of certiorari quashing the decision of the first-named respondent dated February 11, 2005, upholding the decision of the Refugee Appeals Commissioner that the applicant's claim for asylum in this State be refused.

Whether obligation on Minister to provide reasoned decision in relation to non-refoulement altered by incorporation of European Convention on Human Rights In *Dada v Minister for Justice, Equality and Law Reform*, unreported, High Court, May 3, 2006, the applicants sought leave to challenge by way of judicial review, the decision of the respondent communicated by letter dated April 4, 2006, whereby he refused to revoke a deportation order already made in respect of the applicants. The applicants sought to challenge the refusal to revoke on the basis that the decision relied upon country of origin information which had not been brought to the attention of the applicants so that they could comment on same, and that this was a breach of the applicants' rights to constitutional justice and fair procedures. It was, furthermore, submitted that there was a failure by the respondent to consider whether the applicants were at risk of unlawful detention upon return to Nigeria, which risk was a breach of s.4 of the Criminal Justice (United Nations Convention Against Torture) Act 2000 and also was contrary to Art.3 of the European Convention on Human Rights. The applicants also complained that the respondent failed to consider the position and status of the applicants as integrated aliens in this State and failed to consider and balance the rights of the applicants pursuant to Art.8 of the European Convention on Human Rights to private and family life.

O'Neill J. began by considering the scope of the review or inquiry to which the applicants were entitled. Noting that "the decision sought to be challenged comes at the end or at the last potential stage of an elaborate and lengthy process of inquiry into the status in this State of the applicants", O'Neill J. held that "[i]t is clear that the nature and extent of the inquiry which is appropriate in this later phase of the process, thus described, is significantly more restricted than for example in the asylum phase. Likewise the extent of review of the later phase is undoubtedly more restrictive than in the earlier phase."

It was noted that in *O v Minister for Justice, Equality and Law Reform* [2002] 2 I.R. 129, the Supreme Court held that an applicant seeking to oppose a deportation order relying upon the prohibition on refoulement under either s.5 of the Refugee Act 1996, or s.4 of the Criminal Justice (United Nations Convention on Torture) Act 2000, was merely entitled to have his representations considered and was not entitled to a discursive reserved judgment. Applying this principle, O'Neill J. held that it was not open to the High Court to review the decision to refuse to revoke the deportation orders.

As to the nature of the challenge, O'Neill J. noted that "[w]hilst in the *Baby O* case, what was in issue was a consideration of a refoulement issue, in my view, issues of lesser weight such as arise, in a reliance on Article 8 would a fortiori have to be dealt with in the same restrictive fashion." O'Neill J. rejected the submission on behalf of the applicants that the effect of the incorporation of the European Convention on Human Rights into Irish law by the European Convention on Human Rights Act 2003 was such that the approach adopted by Keane C.J. in the *Baby O* case to alleged breaches of Convention rights could no longer be considered to be good law:

> "In my view that submission must fail as the applicants have not demonstrated to my satisfaction that the rule in the Baby O case, is contrary to any aspect of the ECHR or that in interpreting or applying that rule, pursuant to s.2(1) of the European Convention on Human Rights Act 2003, that any departure from the application of the rule is required."

There is no reference in the judgment of the learned High Court judge to the scope of review which the court ought to apply in cases concerning alleged breaches of Convention rights, and in particular whether a higher standard of "anxious scrutiny" might be required in reviewing decisions pertaining to *non-refoulement*.[18] The impact of the Convention on judicial review was highly anticipated in the light of the 2003 Act, but a Supreme Court decision on this key issue is still awaited. Whether the nature or scope of review might require to be altered in accordance with the Convention, as occurred in the

---

[18] See, *e.g. WM (DRC) v Secretary of State for the Home Department* [2006] E.W.C.A. Civ. 1495 where Lord Buxton held "importantly, since asylum is in issue the consideration of all the decision-makers, the Secretary of State, the adjudicator and the court, must be informed by the anxious scrutiny of the material that is axiomatic in decisions that if made incorrectly may lead to the applicant's exposure to persecution. If authority is needed for that proposition, see per Lord Bridge of Harwich in *Bugdaycay v SSHD* [1987] A.C. 514 at 531F" [para.7].

United Kingdom in light of the Human Rights Act 1998, is an issue in urgent need of clarification.

Whether Refugee Appeals Tribunal entitled and/or obliged on appeal pursuant to s.13(6) of 1996 Act to permit oral hearing The powers of the Refugee Appeals Tribunal in respect of an appeal which is governed by the provisions of s.13(6) of the Refugee Act 1996 were considered by the High Court in *Darjania v O'Brien (sitting as the Refugee Appeals Tribunal)*, unreported, High Court, July 7, 2006.

The applicant was born in Abkhazia, a region within the state of Georgia, in 1971. The applicant arrived in Ireland on May 21, 2004, having left Georgia on April 30, 2004. On June 22, 2004 she applied for asylum on the basis of persecution suffered as a result of her ethnicity. The Refugee Applications Commissioner found that the applicant had not established that she had a well-founded fear of prosecution as defined under s.2 of the Refugee Act 1996, as amended, and further made a finding pursuant to s.13(6)(c) by reason of the applicant's failure, without reasonable cause, to make an application as soon as reasonably practicable after arrival in the State. As a result of that finding the applicant's subsequent appeal to the Refugee Appeal Tribunal was held without an oral hearing.

The finding in respect of the failure to make an application as soon as reasonably practicable was appealed to the Refugee Appeals Tribunal on the basis that the applicant was ill and due to medical difficulties was unable to make her application upon arrival. Medical evidence was produced which indicated that she was suffering significant symptoms of post-traumatic stress disorder including flashbacks, nightmares, depression and insomnia.

It was submitted by the respondents that the Refugee Appeals Tribunal's jurisdiction to make decisions was confined by s.16(2) to either: (a) affirming the recommendation of the Commissioner, or (b) setting aside the recommendation of the Commissioner and recommending that the applicant should be declared a refugee. It was submitted that there was no "intermediate option" available, whereby a tribunal member could set aside part of the recommendation of the Commissioner, such as the part denying the applicant an oral hearing under s.13(6) of the Act, and permit an oral hearing.

It was noted by McGovern J. that this issue was discussed to some extent in the case of *Moyosola v Refugee Appeals Commissioner*, unreported, High Court, Clarke J., June 23, 2005,[19] wherein Clarke J. stated:

"It would appear that where the RAT hears an appeal in a case to which s.13(6) applies the only options open to the Tribunal are to allow the appeal or affirm the decision of the RAC. It does not appear that the case can be referred back to the RAC. This raises difficult questions as

---

[19] Discussed in *Annual Review of Irish Law 2005*, pp.38–41.

to the jurisdiction of the RAT in a case where there is a s.13(6) finding which is based in material part on a view as to credibility. If the RAT feels, for example, that such a finding (i.e. a s.13(6) finding) was not justified but nonetheless has doubts as to the credibility of the applicant the RAT cannot, apparently, conduct an oral hearing to satisfy itself on credibility. How should it then act? I would leave a consideration of this question to a case where it directly arises."

Clarke J. further noted:

"I therefore express no view on the question as to whether the procedures now mandated by s.13 (as amended) would be inconsistent with the principles of constitutional justice in a case where the report of the RAC made no finding in respect of any of the matters specified in s.13(6) so that the applicant concerned would have the opportunity to have a full oral hearing before the RAT at a time subsequent to the receipt by them of all of the relevant materials which were likely to be relied on at such a hearing. Nor does it necessarily follow from the view which I have expressed above that the relevant procedures would be inconsistent with the principles of constitutional justice in cases where the view taken by the RAC so as to bring the application within the ambit of s.13(6) was not one based upon the credibility of the applicant but rather was based on, for example, a finding under s.13(6)(d) that the applicant had lodged a prior application in a Geneva Convention country or that the factual grounds put forward by the applicant concerned were not such that even if accepted same would give rise to a finding consistent with the granting of refugee status."

McGovern J. held that the tribunal member did not consider the issue of delay and whether the application was made "..as soon as reasonably practicable" after the applicant arrived in the State, although it was clear that the member had regard to the medical evidence, gave the applicant the benefit of the doubt in relation to the allegations of rape and assault, and also accepted that the applicant had been traumatised as a result.

McGovern J. accepted the contention made on behalf of the respondent that "under the Refugee Act 1996 as amended the jurisdiction of the Refugee Appeals Tribunal to make decisions is confined by s.16(2) to either (a) affirming a recommendation of the Commissioner or (b) setting aside a recommendation of the Commissioner and recommending that the Applicant should be declared a refugee." The learned judge continued:

"The wording of s.13(5) and s.13(6) is unambiguous and once the commissioner made one of the findings specified in s.13(6), as he did, it followed that the appeal would be determined without oral hearing and the first named Respondent did not in my view have power to permit an oral hearing."

McGovern J. noted that the issue could have been determined if the decision of the Refugee Applications Commissioner had been challenged in addition to or independently of the challenge to the tribunal, and concluded that "the first named Respondent was not acting *ultra vires* in dealing with this case without an oral hearing".

The decision in *Darjania* thus emphasises the importance of challenging decisions of the Commissioner pursuant to s.13(6) of the 1996 Act prior to the conducting of the appeal, in light of the finding of the High Court that the tribunal has no jurisdiction to convert an appeal on the papers to an appeal by way of oral hearing.

Whether Refugee Appeals Tribunal erred in assessment of internal protection alternative   The obligations of the Refugee Appeals Tribunal in the assessment of international protection alternatives was addressed in *Okeke v Minister for Justice, Equality and Law Reform*, unreported, High Court, February 17, 2006.

The applicant was a Nigerian national who sought asylum in the State. The applicant's application was refused by the Refugee Appeals Tribunal and the applicant thereafter sought leave, by way of judicial review, to challenge the refusal of her appeal. The applicant's challenge related largely to the tribunal member's treatment of the issue of an internal protection alternative. It was submitted that the applicant was not given an adequate opportunity to address the issue of relocation and that no evidence was produced to the tribunal to support the contention that she could access state protection by moving to places such as Benin, Port Harcourt and Lagos, as suggested by the tribunal member. It was thus submitted that the tribunal member had engaged in speculation in this aspect of her decision. The applicant also submitted that the tribunal made no inquiry as to whether in the proposed relocation sites there would be a risk of further persecution of the same kind or whether there were other risks which would amount to persecution, and that the tribunal had, therefore, failed to take into account relevant considerations. The decision was also criticised in so far as the tribunal member stated that it would not be "unduly harsh to expect the appellant to relocate to the locations identified within the country of origin". It was submitted on behalf of the applicant that there was no explanation for this finding and no consideration of the effect of displacement on the applicant, or the extent of the applicant's connection to any area she was expected to relocate to, or to the fact that the applicant was physically disabled.

In relation to the question of whether the tribunal failed to take into account relevant considerations when finding that the applicant could have relocated, Peart J. held that the applicant had failed to establish substantial grounds for so establishing, having regard to the principle of "curial deference". Peart J. held that "the Tribunal is entitled to the assumption that it is generally aware of the size and population of Nigeria, as well as the general political situation, and the nature and extent of the state protection authorities which exist in that State."

In respect of the submission that the tribunal member erred in law by not considering the applicant's claim in the context of the wider human rights situation in Nigeria, reference was made to the decision of Gilligan J. in *BP v Minister for Justice, Equality and Law Reform* [2003] 4 I.R. 201 in which substantial grounds were found to exist for quashing the decision of the tribunal arising out of the manner in which it was concluded that the applicant could relocate in his country of origin. Peart J. noted that the frailty identified in that case was that the tribunal member had failed to undertake any detailed consideration of whether the risk of the applicant facing persecution extended to any other areas of Georgia to which it was proposed that the applicant ought to have internally relocated. However, Peart J. distinguished the decision in *BP* from the present case by reference to the nature of the persecution feared, which in *BP* concerned persecution at the hands of state agents. Having regard to this essential difference, Peart J. concluded that there could be no substantial grounds for arguing that the tribunal member could not reasonably conclude, without specific evidence and inquiry, that in a country of the size and population of Nigeria, the applicant could access meaningful state protection from any further threats from her husband.

Finally, Peart J. considered the applicant's complaint that the tribunal member acted in breach of fair procedures by failing to give the applicant prior warning that the issue of internal relocation alternative might be raised. The learned High Court judge rejected this challenge on the basis that the applicant shared the responsibility to bring forward material and facts to support her claim, continuing:

> "The concept of relocation as an antidote to a well-founded fear of persecution is well-known, and it is relevant that the applicant was legally represented by experienced lawyers in this area. It must have been clear to all concerned even before the appeal itself that even in a situation where the Tribunal might arrive at a view that the applicant has a well-founded fear of persecution, she would not be granted a declaration of refugee status unless there was no reasonable prospect of safety being assured through relocation. This is not something novel. This Court cannot accept that there are substantial grounds for contending for a lack of fair procedures in a situation where the applicant simply did not anticipate that this question might arise."

Peart J. thus refused leave to seek relief by way of judicial review on the basis that no substantial grounds had been disclosed in the application, characterising the grounds put forward as falling "more within the concept of 'tenuous' rather than 'weighty'."

Whether Refugee Appeals Tribunal failed to have regard to applicant's HIV status as potential discrimination-based claim for asylum

In *Msengi v Minister for Justice, Equality and Law Reform*, unreported, High Court, May 26, 2006, the applicant was a South African national who sought asylum in the State. She sought leave to apply for judicial review quashing the decision of the first-named respondent dated November 26, 2004 refusing her application for refugee status. The applicant stated that she had been raped in February 2003, and had thereafter been threatened by her rapist that she would be killed if she reported the rape. The applicant stated that as a result of the rape she became pregnant. Her second child was born in this country. Both herself and the child were HIV-positive. It was submitted on behalf of the applicant that if she were to return to South Africa she would be concerned for her own safety and was also concerned about the health and well-being of herself and her child.

At the hearing of the applicant's refugee appeal on August 23, 2004, counsel on her behalf made submissions to the first-named respondent that to contract HIV in South Africa was like "a death sentence". A number of documents were also submitted, including submissions to the Parliamentary Portfolio Committee, a South Africa Country Report on Human Rights Practices 2003, and the Human Rights Review South Africa 2004. The tribunal member found that he was not satisfied that the applicant was a refugee within the meaning of s.2 of the Refugee Act 1996. The finding was based on a number of considerations, including a finding that state protection was available to the applicant concerning the rape. The tribunal member further held that the applicant did not constitute a member of a particular social group, but that she had been targeted as an individual and was the subject of a number of specific criminal acts of violence.

The applicant challenged the decision of the tribunal on a number of grounds, including the tribunal's treatment of the applicant's evidence that she was HIV-positive, and that the tribunal erred in law in the manner in which it defined "particular social group". The applicant also alleged that the tribunal member erred in law in the manner in which he satisfied himself that state protection was available to the applicant. The essential case made by the applicant was that the tribunal member did not deal with her claim that she was entitled to refugee status on the basis that she was HIV-positive.

Counsel for the applicant relied on the decision of *EMS v Minister for Justice, Equality and Law Reform*, unreported, High Court, Clarke J., December 21, 2004, where Clarke J. held that where there is an inappropriately low level of healthcare given within South Africa to a group who form a social group for the purposes of refugee law, and where, having regard to the level of healthcare provided within that country, the treatment of that group from a health perspective may be regarded as discriminatory to a significant degree, it was, therefore, arguable that this would amount to a sufficient level of discrimination to give rise to a claim for persecution. On behalf of the applicant it was submitted that, in the light of the applicant's statement that to contract HIV in South Africa was tantamount to a death sentence, and the country of origin information before the tribunal objectively grounding this claim, the tribunal was obliged to consider the applicant's claim *vis-à-vis* a particular social group and women in South Africa who are HIV-positive. Although it was accepted that the issue was not put explicitly to the tribunal in Convention terms, it was submitted that it was an obvious point of Convention law favourable to the applicant that did not appear in the tribunal's decision and had a strong prospect of success.

The applicant relied on two English authorities; the first of these was *R. v Home Secretary, Ex p. Robinson* [1997] Imm. A.R. 568 where Brooke L.J. held that the Immigration Appeals Tribunal had a purpose or obligation to consider Convention law whether or not the specific Convention point was advanced by the applicant. The applicant further relied on the authority of *Ravichandaran v Secretary of State for the Home Department* [1996] Imm. A.R. 97 to the effect that a decision-making body has a general obligation to determine an appeal on the basis of the facts placed before it. Further reliance was placed on a decision of Peart J. in *AO v Refugee Appeals Tribunal*, unreported, High Court, Peart J., May 26, 2004,[20] where one of the applicants sought asylum explicitly on the grounds of religion and also stated in her questionnaire that she was HIV-positive and that HIV patients "are seen as something else in Nigeria and are deserted". Peart J. held that as it was beyond doubt that the applicant had been diagnosed as HIV-positive it therefore became a possibility, once she articulated this in a limited way, that there might be discrimination against the group of HIV-sufferers and that the burden of proof was then initiated whereby it was necessary to pass to a further degree of investigation of the application "perhaps by obtaining any available country of origin information about the condition or plight of HIV sufferers in Nigeria". Relying on these authorities it was submitted that in the instant case, the applicant's evidence, coupled with the corroborating country of origin information, together with the submissions made and the case law opened, obliged the tribunal to consider whether the applicant had a well-founded fear of persecution by reason of her membership of a particular social group of women with HIV in South Africa, and as distinct from the category of a particular social group who are victims of rape in South Africa.

On behalf of the respondents it was contended that, on the face of the documentation before the court, the applicant never made a case that she was at risk of persecution by reason of the facts that she was a person in South Africa who was HIV-positive, nor was such a claim made in the notice of

---

[20] Discussed in *Annual Review of Irish Law 2005*, p.62.

appeal to the tribunal. It was submitted that the applicant did not appear to have given any evidence to the effect that she feared persecution from the State or non-state agents by reason of her status as a person who was HIV-positive. It was submitted that the onus was on the applicant to show she was a refugee pursuant to s.11(a)(3) of the Refugee Act, and further that this onus existed even when the applicant was before the Commissioner, as she was a national of a country standing designated by order under s.12(4) as a safe country of origin (pursuant to the Refugee Act 1996 (Safe Countries of Origin) Order 2004 (S.I. No. 714 of 2004)).

MacMenamin J. held that there were arguable and substantial grounds for the applicant's contention that "there were materials before the Tribunal that placed the Tribunal itself on inquiry as to whether the applicant would be the victim of discrimination as a HIV positive woman in South Africa which the South African authorities would not only be unwilling to counteract but [would] be instrumental in perpetuating." It was held that there were arguable grounds for the proposition that in those circumstances an onus devolved on the tribunal itself to investigate and consider these issues as a consequence. Accordingly, leave was granted to the applicant to challenge the decision of the tribunal on that basis.

MacMenamin J. then proceeded to consider the question of discrimination and persecution of a particular social group. The applicant relied on the case of *Rostas v Refugee Appeals Tribunal*, unreported, High Court, July 31, 2003, wherein Gilligan J. identified and adopted the principles put forward by Lord Hoffman in *R. v Immigration Appeals Tribunal, Ex p. Shah and Islam v Secretary of State for the Home Department* [1999] 2 A.C. 629:

> "Persecution consists in serious and sustained or systematic violation of fundamental human rights, civil, political, social or economic, together with an absence or failure of state protection. This includes circumstances where there may be specific hostile acts, or such a situation may result from the cumulative effects of various measures of discrimination where they may have serious prejudicial consequences, thus giving rise to a fear of persecution".

It was noted that with regard to persecution by non-state actors, Lord Hoffman in *Shah and Islam* approved the succinct formula: "Persecution equals Serious Harm plus Failure of State Protection". Gilligan J. continued:

> "Apart from the risk of persecution from non-state actors, there may be a separate issue of whether there is a risk of persecution from other sources, including agents of the State, having regard [to] evidence of discrimination, human rights violations and abuses by the police and other state organs against members of the Roma community. If this is so it may give rise to a risk of persecution on the Convention ground

of membership of the Roma race from either or both state and non-state actors".

It was submitted that the applicant belonged, arguably, to a potential social group of relevance. This social group was:

(a) women in general and/or vulnerable women in respect of rape;

(b) women who have been the subject of sexual violence in the past (in respect of a subsequent gun attack); and

(c) women with HIV.

It was submitted that HIV-positive women in South Africa constituted a particular social group and that the tribunal neither considered this nor whether this was a particular social group. The applicant relied on a number of authorities including *Shah and Islam* regarding the proper approach to a particular social group wherein discrimination is isolated as the key factor.

MacMenamin J. referred to the decision of *Skenderaj v Home Secretary* [2002] 4 All E.R. 555, where Auld L.J. summarised the authorities as concluding that membership of a particular social group included:

"1. some common characteristic either innate or which by reason of conviction or relief cannot readily be changed

2. shared or internal defining characteristics giving particularity though not necessarily cohesion to the group

3. (subject to possible qualification) a characteristic other than a shared fear of persecution, and

4. (subject to possible qualification) in non-state persecution cases, a perception by society of the particularity of the social group."

On behalf of the respondent it was submitted that the proposition advanced by the applicant was misconceived and contrary to the accepted view as expressed in *Shah* that it was a general principle that there can only be a "particular social group" if the group existed independently of the persecution. In this case because the group was defined by reference to rape it was submitted that the applicant was engaged in circular reasoning which was rejected by the House of Lords in *Shah*. It was further submitted on behalf of the respondent that this issue had been litigated previously in the case of *Lelimo v Minister for Justice, Equality and Law Reform*, unreported, O'Sullivan J., November 12, 2003, where the High Court rejected a claim by a South African national who had been a victim of rape that there was insufficient de facto state protection and that without more she was thereby a member of a social group for the purposes of the Convention. MacMenamin J. held that the court could not, and must not, grant leave on grounds which have been previously litigated and determined, as by definition therefore there were no "substantial grounds" for challenging the decision on this point.

On the issue of state protection, MacMenamin J. noted that it was established that protection afforded by a state "needs neither to be perfect or absolute", relying on *Horvath v Home Secretary* [2001] 1 A.C. 489 where it was stated by Lord Hope:

> "The standard to be applied is therefore not that which would eliminate all risk and would thus amount to a guarantee of protection on the home state. Rather it is a practical standard, which takes proper account of the duty which the state owes to all its own nationals … it is axiomatic that we live in an imperfect world. Certain levels of ill-treatment may still occur even if steps to prevent this are taken by the state to which we look for our protection."

MacMenamin J. concluded that there were substantial grounds for arguing that HIV-positive women in South Africa constituted a particular social group and received state protection, and granted leave to challenge the decision of the tribunal on the ground:

> "The first named respondent failed to take into account adequately or at all the fact or significance of the applicant's status as an HIV positive person in the consideration of persecution in the future and as to her membership of a particular social group in the consideration of whether State protection was available to her."

It was held that the applicant had not established substantial or sufficient grounds to permit leave to be granted in respect of her status as a woman in South Africa in respect of the rape alleged or in respect of women who have been victims of sexual violence in the past as these were matters previously determined by the High Court.

Whether rights of citizen child properly weighed in decision to deport non-national father In *Elukanlo v Minister for Justice, Equality and Law Reform*, unreported, High Court, July 4, 2006, the applicants, a Nigerian national and his Irish citizen son, sought judicial review of the refusal of the respondent to revoke a deportation order in respect of the first-named applicant. The applicants sought declarations that the deportation of the first-named applicant would infringe their rights to a private and family life as guaranteed by Art.8 of the European Convention on Human Rights, and their constitutional rights.

It was submitted on behalf of the first-named applicant that he enjoyed family life with his son in accordance with Art.8 of the Convention, as recognised in

Keegan v Ireland (1994) 18 E.H.R.R. 342 and *Lebbink v Netherlands* [2004] 2 F.L.R. 463. It was further submitted that the respondent's refusal to revoke the deportation order failed to comply with the principle of proportionality in the context of Art.8 rights, in accordance with the decision in *Kozhukarov v Minister for Justice, Equality and Law Reform*, unreported, High Court, December 14, 2005. On behalf of the second-named applicant it was submitted that he also enjoyed a right to family life pursuant to Art.8 in addition to the personal rights enjoyed by a child pursuant to Art.40.3 of the Constitution. The second-named applicant relied upon the decision of the European Court of Human Rights in *Berrehab v Netherlands* (1988) 11 E.H.R.R. 322, to the effect that deportation of a non-national parent may constitute an infringement of the right to family life of a citizen child. The respondent complained that the first-named applicant had not made full disclosure of his circumstances to the Minister at the appropriate time. It was submitted, by way of analogy with the circumstances in *L & O v Minister for Justice* [2003] 1 I.R. 1, that "this was a similar situation in which purely by virtue of the fortuitous circumstances of the birth of a child, the first named applicant seeks to stop the execution of a deportation order." The respondent relied upon the dicta of Keane C.J. in *L & O* that "[t]he inherent power of Ireland as a sovereign State to expel or deport non-nationals (formerly described in our statute law as 'aliens') is beyond argument" and submitted that whilst the second-named applicant enjoyed rights guaranteed by the Constitution, those rights were not absolute.

Dealing first with the submissions of the first-named applicant, Dunne J. held that "[i]t is clear from the authorities before me that the father of a non-marital child has certain rights under Article 8 of the European Convention", although it was accepted that the extent of those rights will vary from case to case, depending upon the circumstances in each case. Having regard to the facts in the instant case, it was held that:

> "insofar as the first named applicant has rights under Article 8 those rights would appear to be at the lower end of the scale of such rights. Nonetheless, I have no doubt that the first named applicant has rights under Article 8 of the Convention which, having regard to the jurisprudence of the European Court of Justice as exemplified in cases such as Berrehab referred to above, have to be considered in the context of a decision under s.3(11)."

It was also held by Dunne J. that the rights of a father under Art.8 when being considered by the respondent must be weighed against the rights of the State to regulate its immigration and asylum system, requiring a "balancing exercise" to be carried out. Turning to the decision of the respondent not to revoke the deportation order, Dunne J. held that it was:

> "manifestly clear from that decision that in coming to the view that he

would not rescind his decision or vary it that the respondent clearly weighed the rights of the first named applicant as a father against the rights of the State. In other words he carried out a balancing exercise. Nothing has been put before me to suggest that this is not so. He clearly considered the first named applicant's rights as a father which had just been made known to him and decided that was not sufficient to tip the balance in favour of the first named applicant."

Dunne J. concluded that the respondent had, at every stage, given an opportunity to the first-named applicant to make submissions and had considered those submissions in full. It was held that so far as the first-named applicant had rights by virtue of Art.8 of the Convention, those rights were not absolute rights and were properly weighed in the decision by the respondent not to rescind or vary the deportation order. Accordingly, the learned High Court judge could see no basis upon which leave could be granted to the first-named applicant.

Turning then to consider the submissions of the second-named applicant, Dunne J. held:

"that there is at least an arguable issue to be tried as to whether or not a child who is not born at the time of the making of the decision is entitled to have its rights considered under s.3(11). Such a child by virtue of Article 8 and indeed under the provisions of the Constitution, has rights which have to be safeguarded and considered."

Dunne J. held that the second-named applicant was entitled to argue that the respondent did not consider at all the rights of the second-named applicant in reaching his decision under s.3(1). It was further held to be open to the second named applicant to raise the issue that the rights of the second-named applicant were not given due regard by the respondent in reaching the decision under s.3(11). The learned High Court judge thus granted leave to the second-named applicant to challenge the decision of the respondent made on March 15, 2006 not to revoke the deportation order in respect of the first-named applicant.

Whether Supreme Court should grant injunction restraining deportation of appellant pending determination of appeal In *Cosma v Minister for Justice, Equality and Law Reform*, unreported, Supreme Court, July 10, 2006, the Supreme Court was required to consider whether injunctive relief should be granted restraining the deportation of the appellant pending the determination of her appeal from the decision of the High Court (considered above).

The applicant, having been refused leave by the High Court to challenge the refusal of the Minister to revoke a deportation order made in respect of her, subsequently issued a motion to the Supreme Court seeking, *inter alia*, an injunction restraining the respondent from executing the deportation order pending the determination of the appeal a declaration that s.3(11) of the Immigration Act 1999 was not governed by s.5 of the Illegal Immigrants (Trafficking) Act 2000 and, therefore, that the applicant did not require a certificate from a High Court judge in order to institute an appeal before the Supreme Court.

In argument before the court it was conceded by counsel for the respondent that the provisions of s.5(3) of the Illegal Immigrants (Trafficking) Act 2000, which provided that no appeal should lie from a decision of the High Court in certain immigration and refugee matters without a certificate that the decision involves a point of law of exceptional public importance, did not apply to a challenge by way of judicial review to the refusal by the respondent to amend or revoke the deportation order under s.3(11) of the Immigration Act 1999. Furthermore, it was conceded by counsel for the appellant that the appeal was limited to the consideration of the refusal of the Minister under s.3(11) of the 1999 Act, as a certificate had been refused in relation to other matters being challenged in the proceedings.

Thus, the only issue remaining before the court was whether an injunction ought to be granted restraining the respondent from deporting the appellant pending the determination of this appeal. McCracken J. noted that there was, unquestionably, a valid deportation order in being, and the issue in this appeal was whether the Minister ought to have revoked that order, but the validity of the order itself was not being, and could not be, challenged in the appeal. McCracken J. accepted that as a matter of general principle, "the Supreme Court has an inherent power to grant interlocutory orders pending the hearing of an appeal where such order is necessary to protect the rights of the parties." However, he held that any such order must be made sparingly and only in circumstances where it will not conflict with the undisputed rights of any of the parties. Reference was made in this regard to Ord.58, r.18 of the Rules of the Superior Courts 1986, which provides:

> "An appeal to the Supreme Court shall not operate as a stay of execution or of proceedings under the decision appealed from, except so far as the High Court or the Supreme Court may order; and no intermediate act or proceeding shall be thereby invalidated, except so far as the High Court or the Supreme Court may direct."

McCracken J. noted that in this case the "decision being appealed from" was a decision of the respondent made under s.3(11) not to revoke a deportation order against the appellant, which challenge in no way impugned the validity of the deportation order itself, and concluded that "[i]f the court were to grant an injunction such as is being sought by the appellant, the effect would be to thwart the operation of the perfectly valid deportation order and would, at least to some degree, prevent the operation of a perfectly valid and unappealable High Court order."

It was accepted that there might be circumstances where the Supreme Court might exercise its inherent jurisdiction to grant an injunction which could have this effect, *e.g.* when a previously unknown fact comes to light, being a fact which was unknown at the time of making of the deportation order, and which is one of such gravity as might stay implementation of the deportation order. However, this was not the case which had been made out before the Supreme Court and, in the circumstances, the court declined the injunctive relief sought.

LEGISLATION

European Communities (Eligibility for Protection) Regulations 2006 (S.I. No. 518 of 2006) The European Communities (Eligibility for Protection) Regulations 2006 (S.I. No. 518 of 2006) which came into force on October 10, 2006, purport to give effect to Council Directive 2004/83/EC of April 29, 2004 on minimum standards for the qualification and status of third-country nationals or stateless persons as refugees or as persons who otherwise need international protection and the content of the protection granted. The Directive, in turn, stemmed from the Tampere Agreement of the European Council in October 1999 to work towards the establishment of a common European asylum system.

The Regulations provide guidance to decision-makers in the asylum process regarding the content of many of the core aspects of the refugee definition. In that regard, for example, reg.10 provides a number of examples of the content of the concepts of race, religion, nationality and, perhaps most instructively, provides guidance as to how membership of a particular social group shall be identified. Regulation 9, in setting out those acts which shall constitute persecution for the purposes of s.2 of the Refugee Act 1996, refers to acts of persecution or an accumulation of measures, which are "sufficiently serious by their nature or repetition as to constitute a severe violation of basic human rights, in particular the rights from which derogation cannot be made under Article 15(2) of the European Convention on Human Rights". It must therefore be queried whether the prospect of entitlement to recognition of refugee status on the basis of one singular particularly grievous incident constituting persecution has been removed by this provision. An illustrative list of acts of persecution is thereafter set out.[21]

Paragraph 45 of the UNHCR Handbook,[22] which recognises a presumption

---

[21] The Regulations also provide guidance in relation to refugees *sur place* (reg.6), issues pertaining to internal protection (reg.7) and the control of a state or a substantial part of the territory of a state by international organisations (reg.8).

[22] The courts have recognised that the handbook provides guidance regarding the standards to be applied in this jurisdiction in the context of applications for asylum; see, for example, Finnegan P. in *Z'gnatev v Minister for Justice, Equality and Law Reform*, unreported,

of well-founded fear of persecution on the part of a person who has suffered past persecution, finds reflection in reg.5(2).[23] The handbook also recognises that an applicant for asylum may not be able to support his or her statement by documentary or other proof and adds that "cases in which an applicant can provide evidence of all his statements will be the exception rather than the rule. In most cases, a person fleeing from persecution will have arrived with the barest necessities and very frequently even without personal documents."[24] Bearing that in mind, reg.5(3) appears to place an onerous obligation upon applicants for asylum. It provides that if aspects of an applicant's statements are not supported by documentary or other evidence, those aspects shall not need confirmation if the applicant has made a genuine effort to substantiate his or her application, all materials at the applicant's disposal have been submitted and a satisfactory explanation proffered regarding the absence of the other documents, the application has been made at the earliest possible opportunity,[25] the applicant's statements are found to be coherent and plausible and his or her general credibility affirmed.

It should be noted that many of the provisions of the Regulations apply not only to persons seeking to apply for asylum but those who allege a real risk of suffering serious harm and thus seek to avail of a protective regime introduced via the Regulations, the subsidiary protection regime. This regime of subsidiary protection should, it is hoped, meet the needs of some persons who fall outside the narrow definition of refugee employed in the Geneva Convention and mirrored in s.2 of the Refugee Act of 1996. The definition of the Geneva Convention reflects the Cold War concerns of its drafters who sought, by and large, to offer protection to political dissidents facing individualised threat in their home country, but fails to reflect today's needs. Many applicants for asylum at this point in time are at risk of serious harm from violence and instability in their home countries, yet fall outside the parameters of the refugee definition as they cannot establish a Convention basis for their fears. It is to be hoped that the concept of subsidiary protection will offer protection for such persons. Regulation 2(1) provides that a person shall be eligible for subsidiary protection if he or she is: (a) not a national of a member State; (b) does not qualify as a refugee; (c) is a person in respect of whom substantial grounds have been shown for believing that he or she would, if returned to his or her country of origin, face a real risk of suffering serious harm; (d) is a

---

High Court, March 29, 2001.

[23] This presumption shall not apply where "there are good reasons to consider that persecution or serious harm will not be repeated." It does provide, however, that compelling reasons arising out of a previous persecution or serious harm alone may, nevertheless, warrant a determination that the applicant is eligible for protection, where such good reasons exist to consider that such persecution or serious harm will not be repeated.

[24] Para.196.

[25] Unless the applicant demonstrates good reason for not doing so; reg.5(3)(d).

person to whom the exclusion clause on Art.13[26] does not apply; and, finally
(e) is unable, or owing to such risk, unwilling to avail himself or herself of the
protection of that country. Serious harm shall consist of the "death penalty or
execution, torture or inhuman or degrading treatment or punishment or serious
and individual threat to civilians or persons by reason of indiscriminate violence
in situations of international or internal armed conflict".[27]

Although the Directive does not appear to limit the point in time at which
an application for subsidiary protection must be made, reg.4(1)(a) provides that
notification[28] of the Minister's proposal to deport a given person shall include
a statement to the effect that a person whose application for refugee status has
been refused shall be entitled to make an application for such protection to
the Minister within a 15-day period. Thus, it would appear that the regulation
envisages that applications for refugee status and for subsidiary protection shall
be made and considered sequentially.[29] It would also therefore appear that the
regulation envisages that a person who has made an application for asylum
in another Member State of the EU shall not be permitted to an application
for subsidiary protection within this State. The Directive, however, does
not appear to impose any such limitation. It is also noted that the Dublin II
Regulation does not apply to applications for subsidiary protection and therefore
a person should, it appears, be entitled to apply for subsidiary protection in
this jurisdiction following the refusal of his or her asylum application in other
Member State.

If, however, an applicant for subsidiary protection is unsuccessful, reg.4(5)
provides that the Minister shall thereafter proceed to consider whether a
deportation order should be made. It would, furthermore, appear that it has
already become the practice of the Minister for Justice to refuse to consider
applications for subsidiary protection on behalf of persons already the subject
of deportation orders. Leave to apply by way of judicial review was granted
by the High Court on an *ex parte* basis in a number of cases in which that
practice was challenged and the issue of the failure to properly transpose
the Directive raised. In *Hila and Djolo v Minister for Justice, Equality and
Law Reform,* unreported, High Court, July 27, 2007, Feeney J. held that the
Minister's practice in this respect was unlawful on the basis that there was

---

[26] Article 13 provides that a person shall be excluded from eligibility for subsidiary
protection where there are serious reasons for considering that he or she has committed
a crime against peace, war crime or crime against humanity as defined, has been guilty
of acts contrary to the purposes and principles of the UN, has committed a serious crime,
or more worryingly by reason of its vagueness and breadth, "constitutes a danger to the
community or to the security of the State".

[27] The reference to an "individual threat" may give causes for concern, although it is arguable
that, in this context, the expressions should be understood to mean that the person with
the applicant in question faces a risk because of the indiscriminate violence and merely
that violence must pose a particular threat to his or her life or person.

[28] Pursuant to s.3(3) of the Immigration Act 1999.

[29] See Brazil, "Subsidiary Protection under Irish Law" (2006) 4 *The Researcher* 1.

a failure to recognise the discretion vested in the minister under reg.4(2) to consider an application for subsidiary protection from a person the subject of a deportation order, if such person could identify facts or circumstances which demonstrated a change or alternation from their position at the time the deportation order was made.

The Regulations set out the entitlements of persons to whom subsidiary protection is granted. Regulation 17 provides that subject to the exclusion and cessation clauses, a person deemed eligible for subsidiary protection shall be granted permission to remain in the State for three years. The permission shall be renewable, unless compelling reasons of national security or public order otherwise require. Again, the Regulation has provided a more generous reading than that set out in the Directive which specifies that such person to whom refugee status is granted shall be entitled to residence for three years whilst those to whom subsidiary protection is afforded shall merely be entitled to a residence permit valid for at least one year.

Regulation 16(1) envisages that a person who has been deemed eligible for subsidiary protection may apply to the Minister for Justice for permission to be granted to a member of his or her family to enter and to reside in the State. The Minister *shall* then grant permission in writing to a person to reside in the State, if satisfied that the person is a member of the family of the applicant as defined to include a spouse pursuant to a subsisting marriage, the parents of an unmarried minor and a minor and unmarried child of a successful applicant. The Minister *may*, in addition, grant permission to "dependent members" of the successful applicant's family to enter and to reside in the State. Such persons shall include a grandparent, parent, brother, sister, child, grandchild, ward or guardian of the applicant who is wholly or mainly dependent upon the applicant or is suffering from a mental or physical incapacity to such extent that it is not reasonable to expect him or her to maintain himself or herself fully. It is to be noted that this provision extends beyond that specifically provided for in the Directive and thus the Minister has in this regard exercised the discretion referred to in Art.3 of the said Directive to introduce or retain more favourable standards in respect of those eligible for subsidiary protection.

European Communities (Free Movement of Persons) Regulations 2006 (S.I. No. 206 of 2006) The European Communities (Free Movement of Persons) Regulations 2006 (S.I. No. 226 of 2006)[30] were signed into law on April 30, 2006. These Regulations purport to implement Directive 2004/38/EC on the right of citizens of the Union and their family members to move and reside freely within the territory of the Member States. That Directive sought to replace and supplement the existing legislative framework which consisted of nine Directives and two Regulations on the freedom of movement within

---

[30] The 2006 Regulations were replaced by the European Communities (Free Movement of Persons)(No.2) Regulations 2006 which came into force on January 1, 2007.

the European Union of citizens and their family members. It addresses, in essence, the conditions in which Union citizens and their families should exercise their right to move and reside freely within the Member States, the issues pertaining to a right of permanent residence, and outlines the relevant restrictions on the aforementioned rights and grounds of public policy and public security or health.

The Regulations provide that a European Union citizen may reside in the State for a period of up to three months provided he or she holds a national identity card or passport. It also provides that family members shall enjoy comparable rights of residence in the State if, however, the family member satisfies a pre-condition which is not imposed in the Directive itself. Thus, reg.3(2) provides that the entitlements conferred therein shall not apply to a family member unless the family member is lawfully resident in another Member State and is seeking to enter the State with the Union citizen spouse or seeking to join that Union citizen spouse who is lawfully present in the State. This imposition of a previous lawful residence requirement in another Member State does not mirror any provision in the Directive and concerns may, therefore, arise regarding the *vires* of this provision.[31]

If that precondition is met, the Regulations confer benefits upon "qualifying family members" of Union citizens who shall include that citizen's spouse, a child who is under 21 years of age or who is otherwise dependent, and a grandparent or parent of the Union citizen or his or her spouse. The Regulations also apply to other "permitted family members" who are not qualifying family members of the Union citizen but who are dependent members of the household strictly requiring the personal care of the Union citizen on the basis of serious health grounds or, finally, is the partner of a Union citizen in a duly-attested durable relationship. Family members may reside in the State for up to three months if they are in possession of a valid passport and do not become an unreasonable burden on the social welfare system of the State. Residency for a period in excess of three months may be obtained by the Union citizen and the family member if the Union citizen is in employment or is self-employed in the State, or otherwise has sufficient resources to support himself or herself and the accompanying family members. Comprehensive sickness insurance for the said family members shall also be required in order to enjoy this lengthier right of residence. Alternatively, if the Union citizen is enrolled in an educational

---

[31] In *Secretary of State for the Home Department v Akrich (C109/01)* [2003] E.C.R. I–9607, the European Court of Justice upheld the decision of the United Kingdom authorities made under the previous regime based upon Regulation 1612/68 refusing to readmit to the United Kingdom a third-country national spouse of an EU citizen. The court endorsed the view that the non-national spouse must be lawfully resident in a Member State when he moves to another Member State to which the Union citizen's spouse is migrating or has migrated. This decision does not appear to be fully consistent with other decisions, both previous and subsequent, of the European Court of Justice; in that regard see *MRAX v Belgium* [2002] E.C.R. I–6591 and *Commission v Spain* [2005] E.C.R. I–2911. See also *Jia v Migrationsverket*, unreported, European Court of Justice, January 9, 2007.

establishment in the State for the principle purpose of following a course of study there, to include a vocational training course, and has comprehensive sickness insurance, such an extended period of residence may be obtained. Once resident here for a period of at least three months, the family member may apply to the Minister for Justice, Equality and Law Reform for a residence card and, once the Minister is satisfied that the above conditions are met, reg.7(2) provides that he or she shall, within six months of the application, have a residence card issued to them. Such a card shall be valid for the duration of the envisaged period of residence or for five years, whichever is the lesser period.[32] Once the right of residence is conferred upon a family member of a Union citizen, that right will survive the death or departure from the State of the Union citizen and, furthermore, will persist in the event of a divorce or annulment of the marriage in question. A Union citizen or family member who falls within the terms of the Regulation and who has resided in the State for a continuous period of five years may reside herein on a permanent basis.[33]

---

[32] Once the right of residence is conferred, the person in question shall continue to enjoy that right as long as he or she satisfies the conditions in question.

[33] *Per* Art. 12. Article 13 recognises that a Union citizen or family member who has been in employment in the State or has pursued an activity of a self-employed person herein shall enjoy a right of permanent residence which shall persist even when he or she ceases working in the State.

Commercial Law

COMPETITION

Competition (Amendment) Act 2006   The Competition (Amendment) Act 2006 amended the Competition Act 2002 (*Annual Review of Irish Law 2002*, pp.24–30) in order to revoke the ban on below-cost selling in the Restrictive Practices (Groceries) Order 1987 (*Annual Review of Irish Law 1987*, pp.34–35) in its entirety and to deal with practices such as unfair discrimination, advertising allowances and what is termed "hello money". The changes were based on a report on the 1987 Order by the Competition Authority and another report by the Consumer Strategy Group. The Government accepted that the statutory restrictions in the 1987 Order should be replaced by more general provisions now contained in the 2002 Act, as amended by the 2006 Act. The 2006 Act (with the exception of s.5(2)) came into force on March 20, 2006 (Competition (Amendment) Act 2006 (Commencement) Order 2006 (S.I. No. 127 of 2006)).

It was pointed out during the Oireachtas debate on the 2006 Act that s.4 of the 2002 Act (based on Art.81 of the EC Treaty) prohibits agreements and concerted practices that have the effect of distorting competition. The undertakings participating in such activity do not have to be dominant for their activity or conduct to be captured by s.4. Section 5 of the 2002 Act (based on Art.81 of the EC Treaty) prohibits similar unilateral conduct, where no agreement or concerted practice is necessary, on the part of dominant undertakings. The 2006 Act prohibits certain unilateral conduct on the part of non-dominant undertakings in the grocery trade, which it was feared might emerge following revocation of the Groceries Order 1987 and which might not be captured by either s.4 or s.5 of the 2002 Act because they are not conduct of a dominant undertaking.

Section 1 of the 2006 Act inserted three new sections into the 2002 Act, ss.15A, 15B and 15C. Section 15A of the 2002 Act (as inserted by the 2006 Act) includes new definitions. Thus, "grocery goods" are defined as food and drink for human consumption, including alcohol but excluding anything sold in a restaurant or bar. This includes the vast bulk of products sold in conventional grocery stores. A "grocery goods undertaking" is defined as any undertaking engaged in the production, supply or distribution of grocery goods. A "retailer" is defined as anyone who sells grocery goods to the public.

Section 15B(1) of the 2002 Act (as inserted by the 2006 Act) prohibits resale price maintenance in connection with the supply of grocery goods. Resale price maintenance arises where manufacturers or suppliers specify the minimum prices at which their goods may be resold. This practice was prohibited by Art.3 of the Groceries Order 1987. Notwithstanding this, the provisions of the 1987 Order preventing sale below invoice price legitimised the practice, which appeared to contradict provisions in the Prices Act 1958. The amendment effected by the 2006 Act was thus intended to restate the position in the 1958 Act. Section 15B(2) prohibits unfair discrimination in connection with the supply of grocery goods, so that a supplier cannot offer preferential terms to one buyer over another when the transactions involved are equivalent in nature. Section 15B(3) prevents an undertaking from forcing another to pay for the advertising or display of grocery goods. By contrast with Art.18 of the Groceries Order 1987, which prevented the payment of such advertising allowances in all cases, the provision inserted by the 2006 Act prevents any undertaking from being forced into making such payments. This does not prevent collaborative advertising arrangements which are mutually beneficial to the participants and which promote competition by bringing the availability of grocery goods to the attention of consumers. Section 15B(4) prohibits a retailer from forcing a supplier to pay "hello money", by which a retailer demands a payment from a supplier before agreeing to stock that supplier's products. As in Art.18 of the Groceries Order 1987, the circumstances in which the practice is prohibited by the provision in the 2006 Act include on the opening of a new store, an extension to an existing store or a change of ownership of a store. However, the 2006 Act also deals with what was regarded as a flaw in the 1987 Order by specifying a period of time, 60 days, during which the prohibition applies. Section 15B(5) replicates language already used in s.4 of the 2002 Act by providing that the conduct described is only prohibited when it has the object or effect of preventing, restricting or distorting competition in the grocery trade, either in the State or in any part of the State.

Section 15C of the 2002 Act (as inserted by the 2006 Act) provides a right of action for any party aggrieved by prohibited conduct. A party may apply to the Circuit Court or the High Court for injunctive relief and damages, including exemplary damages. The Competition Authority also has a similar right of action under this section.

Section 2 of the 2006 Act applies s.30 of the Competition Act 2002 to the right of action in s.15C of the 2002 Act (as inserted by the 2006 Act). In particular, it applies s.30(4)(b) of the 2002 Act, which does not allow the Competition Authority to delegate the power to initiate legal proceedings to a member of the Authority or a member of staff of the Authority. Section 3 of the 2006 Act applies s.45 of the Competition Act 2002, which contains provisions in respect of authorised officers of the Competition Authority and their warrants of appointment.

Section 4(1) of the 2006 Act revokes the Restrictive Practices (Groceries) Order 1987, while s.5 contains further repeals of the Acts listed in the Schedule. These were confirming Acts in respect of orders made under the Restrictive

Practices Acts (replaced by the Competition Act 1991, the predecessor of the 2002 Act), which had become redundant.

During the debate on the 2006 Act, the Opposition had suggested that a specific provision be included in the 2006 Act to prohibit predatory pricing. This was resisted on the ground that such conduct is already prohibited by s.5 of the Competition Act 2002, which prohibits abuse of a dominant position. It was noted that s.5 of the 2002 Act is based on Art.82 of the EC Treaty and that there is a strong body of case law to the effect that these provisions can be and are used to prohibit and punish predatory pricing. Furthermore, dominance does not have to be assessed on a national basis. An individual supermarket outlet in a rural town, whether part of a multiple or not, could be considered dominant within the meaning of the 2002 Act, and thus prosecuted if it engaged in predatory pricing.

Regulatory body: Medical Council *Guide to Ethical Conduct and Behaviour* In *Hemat v Medical Council* [2006] I.E.H.C. 187, High Court, April 11, 2006, McKechnie J. held that the public interest should be a factor in determining whether ethical guidelines issued by a regulatory body such as the Medical Council, and which restrict the ability of a doctor to engage in practice, were in breach of competition law. The issue arose against the following background.

The plaintiff is a qualified medical doctor and the defendant is the statutory body with the powers, duties and responsibilities specified in the Medical Practitioners Act 1978 (since replaced by the Medical Practitioners Act 2007, to which we will return in the *Annual Review of Irish Law 2007*). The plaintiff claimed that the defendant was an undertaking or an association of undertakings and that certain provisions of the *Guide to Ethical Conduct and Behaviour*, drawn up by the Council and binding on its members, was in breach of ss.4 and 5 of the Competition Act 2002 or, alternatively, Arts 81, 82 and 86 of the EC Treaty. McKechnie J.'s judgment dealt with the single issue of whether the Medical Council is an undertaking or an association of undertakings for the purposes of the 2002 Act and the EC Treaty. The plaintiff had been registered as a medical practitioner with the Council since 1985 and over the years had worked with a number of Irish hospitals in the fields of urology and oncology. The plaintiff also had a "practice in integrated medicine", and had publicly advertised his skills as a self-employed practitioner of integrated medicine, which involved a combination of conventional medicine and clinical orthomolecularisation. Following complaints about this advertisement and correspondence with the plaintiff, the defendant, pursuant to its *Guide on Ethical Conduct and Behaviour*, considered that there was a prima facie case for the holding of an enquiry into his conduct in publishing the advertisement. The inquiry found the plaintiff guilty of professional misconduct and he was removed from the register of medical practitioners for one month with certain conditions attached to his ongoing registration.

Evidence was given for the plaintiff concerning the restriction on advertising imposed by the Council. While accepting that a level of restrictions is necessary in the medical field, the witness called for the plaintiff, who dealt with the economic aspect of competition law, considered that the restrictions imposed by the Council were significant and substantial and therefore did have economic consequences. The plaintiff also submitted that the vast majority of the Medical Council members were individual undertakings in that they were providing medical services for a fee and that, therefore, the Medical Council as a whole must be considered an association of undertakings and, furthermore, that its decision to restrict advertising is one which correctly should be considered as an economic activity. It followed, the plaintiff submitted, that the decision of the Council came within the ambit of competition law. It was accepted on behalf of the Medical Council that its decision was one capable of having economic consequences. However, in looking at the composition of the Medical Council it was submitted that more than 30 per cent of the full membership of the Council were not undertakings and, therefore, it could not be said that the body as a whole constituted an association of undertakings. It was accepted that a public authority could be an undertaking but that, equally, it should not be so categorised where the activity in question is of a public nature and carried out in the public interest. The Council also submitted that it could not seriously be claimed by the plaintiff that the issuing of the Council's *Guide to Ethical Conduct and Behaviour* was an economic activity. The true test should be the nature of the activity carried on rather than the precise composition of the body in question. The Council argued that the court should not isolate one function entrusted to the Council in deciding this issue but rather should look at the nature and effect of the activities entrusted to the Council under the Medical Practitioners Act 1978. In this respect it was argued that the Council should be considered as purely regulatory in nature and therefore the decision taken by it in respect of the plaintiff was not one taken by an association of undertakings for the purposes of competition law.

As already indicated, the arguments of the Council were, in effect, accepted by McKechnie J. and he concluded that, in issuing the *Guide to Ethical Conduct and Behaviour*, the Medical Council was not an undertaking or association of undertakings for the purposes of competition law. He considered that the term "undertaking" must be construed in a broad and functional way. He accepted that public authorities and bodies subject to public law have been held to be undertakings but he also noted that no general set of rules has been set down to date by the European Court of Justice as to what constitutes an undertaking; rather, the court had tended to determine the issue on a case-by-case basis. McKechnie J. pointed out that that Arts 81 and 82 of the EC Treaty are designed to capture conduct by bodies which is unfavourable to healthy competition and, save in the most limited of circumstances, have no application to sovereign acts of individual states, including in the operation of their laws and regulations. He accepted that it is more difficult to apply this in practice, as in this situation where a regulatory body, heavily influenced by public law, is said by its actions to have engaged in economic activity which distorts competition. Crucially, he considered that the Medical Council does not act for or represent the interests of individual doctors, noting that it is not composed exclusively of members of the medical profession, nor are all of its members undertakings in their own rights (in this respect, he distinguished the present case from the circumstances in *Pavlov and Wouters* (Case C–180/98) [2000] ECR 1–6451). Finally, he accepted the Medical Council's submission that the principles by which it must perform its functions are driven by public interest criteria and, accordingly, the performance of such functions is carried out in the public interest and for the general good. In that respect, the relevant provisions of the 2002 Act and EC Treaty did not apply.

Takeover bids   The European Communities (Takeover Bids) (Directive 2004/25/EC) Regulations 2006 (S.I. No. 255 of 2006) implemented Directive 2004/25 on takeover bids. They came into force on May 18, 2006.

CONSUMER PROTECTION

Cross-border co-operation   The European Communities (Cooperation Between National Authorities Responsible for the Enforcement of Consumer Protection Laws) Regulations 2006 (S.I. No. 290 of 2006) implemented Regulation No. 2006/2004 on co-operation between national authorities responsible for the enforcement of consumer protection laws. The 2004 Regulation requires Member States to link up national enforcement authorities and enables them to take coordinated action against rogue traders who target consumers across EU borders. The Regulation removes barriers to information exchange and co-operation and also empowers enforcement authorities to seek and obtain action from their counterparts in other Member States.

FINANCIAL SERVICES

Building societies   The Building Societies (Amendment) Act 2006 amended the Building Societies Act 1989 and gave belated effect to the report of an Expert Review Group on Building Societies. The Building Societies (Amendment) Act 2006 (Commencement) Order 2006 (S.I. No. 394 of 2006) brought the 2006 Act into force on July 26, 2006. The expert group recommended that any building society wishing to demutualise and develop as a public company should not be unduly restricted as regards the conditions under which it could pursue that option. However, the group also recommended that any society wishing to continue to develop as a mutual society should be adequately protected in retaining its mutual status. Sections 19 to 27 provide for amendments of the legislative provisions relating to demutualisation. The criterion in the 2006 Act for opting out of the protective provisions was intended to ensure sufficient protection for a society that wishes to remain a mutual society, by making it a condition for opting out of the protective provisions that a building society has, for at least five years prior to demutualisation, restricted access to membership by requiring a minimum deposit of €10,000 to open a share account. There is also a five-year period of protection either before or after demutualisation, depending on whether a society wants to have the option of being sold following conversion to a public company or not. The 2006 Act results in building societies having four possible options with regard to their status: to remain mutual; to demutualise under the existing protective provisions in the 1989 Act; to opt out of those provisions and be taken over immediately; or to opt out and be sold at any later date.

Demutualisation   The main change involves allowing a building society discretion to decide to opt out of the five-year post-conversion protective provisions in the 1989 Act, which preclude any individual or institution holding 15 per cent or more of the shares of a demutualised society for five years. There are two elements involved in this matter in the 2006 Act. First, s.21 amends s.101 of the Building Societies Act 1989 to allow a building society, in specified circumstances, to propose a conversion scheme that will, effectively, disapply the provisions of s.102. This opt-out provision is designed to operate in a way that will not adversely affect any society wishing to retain mutual status. A society will only be able to disapply the protective provisions if it has, for the preceding five years, required a minimum of €10,000 to open a share account. Section 19 contains a further provision intended to protect against pressure for demutualisation being brought to bear through members of a mutual building society. It extends s.74 of the 1989 Act, precluding members from proposing conversion resolutions at AGMs, though the wording of the change was amended during its legislative passage to ensure that there is no question of restricting the right of members to raise any issue for discussion.

     The second element of the provisions relating to conversion and sale of a building society involves the insertion of a new section into the 1989 Act providing for an integrated process of conversion and immediate acquisition. Section 22 of the 2006 Act provides that a society opting to convert without the protection of the five-year post-conversion protective provisions will be empowered to do so through a combined "conversion-acquisition scheme" which will form part of the conversion scheme and, as such, will be approved by the members of the society. This will enable the society to agree a trade sale of the company to be implemented immediately on demutualisation. If, for any reason, that acquisition did not proceed, for example, due to some condition of the agreement not being fulfilled, the conversion would be terminated and the society would continue as a mutual building society.

Other changes to powers of building societies   In addition to dealing with demutualisation, the 2006 Act also implemented recommendations of the expert group to widen the powers and flexibility of building societies, subject to an appropriate level of approval by the Central Bank. These include amendments to increase the powers and discretion of societies, subject to approval by the Central Bank, as appropriate, in regard to matters such as the range of services they provide; how they source funding; bodies in which they can invest; categories of customers that can be given membership; and the extent to which specific approval of society members and the Central Bank is needed in order to undertake certain functions.

Section 7 allows building societies to extend membership to additional categories of customers and to establish loyalty schemes for members. Section 8 broadens the scope of building societies to raise funds from different sources in line with other financial institutions and also extends the power of building societies to provide security for borrowings by various bodies in which they are empowered to invest. Section 9 brings the powers of building societies in regard to mortgages into line with those of other financial institutions, including clarification of powers relating to refinancing and top-up loans and allows mortgages to be provided without the society having a first charge against the property.

Section 10 permits a building society to make unsecured or partly secured loans without first having to adopt the power specifically to do so. The Central Bank will have a general supervisory role with regard to the making of these loans rather than prescribing a specific loan limit as is currently the case. Section 12 extends the existing powers of building societies to invest in or support other bodies, including investment in unincorporated bodies such as partnerships, as well as corporate bodies.

Section 13 extends the range of financial services that can be offered by a building society, including any activities under the EC Codified Banking Directive that were not otherwise permitted by the 1989 Act. Examples of new services that could be provided arising from this include trading for the accounts of customers in money market instruments and other financial instruments and portfolio management and advice. Section 15 provides that powers that are ancillary or incidental and related to powers that have already been adopted by members of a building society and approved by the Central Bank, will not have to be separately adopted and approved.

GUARANTEE

Surety not discharging debt: summary summons   In *McGrath v O'Driscoll*, High Court, June 14, 2006 the plaintiff acted as guarantor for the defendants in an agreement in which a bank loaned the defendants substantial sums of money for the purchase of a vessel. The bank subsequently brought proceedings against the plaintiff, as surety, in respect of the money it was owed by the defendants. The plaintiff now claimed to be entitled to recover the sum of money awarded against him together with his own costs of defending the proceedings brought by the bank against the defendants on the basis that they were the primary debtors and were obliged to indemnify him as a surety against whom judgment had been obtained by the bank, the principal creditor. The plaintiff commenced proceedings against the defendants by way of summary summons. The defendants argued that the plaintiff was not entitled to do so on the basis that the plaintiff had not yet discharged the amount he was claiming from them to the bank and therefore the debt was not due to him. The defendants argued that were the principal debtor obliged to pay the sum due to the guarantor in circumstances where the guarantor had not yet discharged the debt due to the principal creditor, there would be no certainty that the guarantor would use that money to discharge the liability to the creditor. Clarke J. agreed and dismissed the plaintiff's claim. He considered that a guarantor can only obtain an unconditional order for the payment of a debt or liquidated sum against a principal debtor in circumstances where the guarantor has, in fact, paid the debt or otherwise given value. The position of a guarantor in respect of whom the principal creditor has obtained a judgment, but where no money has in fact been paid on foot of that judgment, gave rise to potential difficulties. He considered that an absolute requirement that such a person must pay the debt before having the opportunity to recover any sums paid from the principal debtor, could lead to a situation where an impecunious guarantor might be faced with an impossible situation in that he would be unable to recover from the principal debtor simply because he would be unable to pay the principal creditor. On the other hand, if a guarantor had, simply because judgment had been entered against him, an entitlement to recover the amount of that judgment against the principal debtor, a serious injustice could arise. Were the principal debtor to be obliged to pay the sum due to the guarantor, there would be no certainty that the guarantor would use that money to discharge the liability to the principal creditor. If the guarantor, having obtained the sum from the principal creditor on foot of a court order, were not to pay that sum to the principal creditor, then the principal debtor would, notwithstanding the fact that he had discharged the debt once, by paying it to the guarantor, still be liable to discharge it a second time if he was pursued by the principal creditor. To meet those competing difficulties, Clarke J. noted that the courts had developed appropriate practices to ensure that no injustice would arise. However, cases such as this were not suited to summary disposal and so he concluded that the use of the summary summons procedure was not appropriate in this case.

INTELLECTUAL PROPERTY

Artist's resale right   The European Communities (Artist's Resale Right)

Regulations 2006 (S.I. No. 312 of 2006) implemented Directive 2001/84 on the resale right for the benefit of the author of an original work of art. They allow creators of original works of visual and plastic art, through a system of royalty payments, to benefit from resales of those works when they are sold through the professional art market. They came into force on June 13, 2006.

Cross-border enforcement of intellectual property rights The European Communities (Enforcement of Intellectual Property Rights) Regulations 2006 (S.I. No. 360 of 2006) implemented the elements of Directive 2004/48 on the enforcement of intellectual property rights. The 2004 Directive harmonises civil remedies and measures available for the enforcement of intellectual property rights across the European Community. The Regulations came into force on July 5, 2006. The European Communities (Enforcement of Community Judgments on Trade Marks and Designs) Regulations 2006 (S.I. No. 646 of 2006) ensure that decisions, accompanied by an order for costs, made by the Office of Harmonisation for the Internal Market (OHIM), can be executed in Ireland. OHIM is a community body whose main function is to register trade marks and designs which have unitary effect throughout the Community. The Regulations nominate the High Court as the competent authority before which such orders should be brought for execution. See also the changes effected by the Patents (Amendment) Act 2006, below.

Patents (Amendment) Act 2006 The principal purpose of the Patents (Amendment) Act 2006, which began its legislative life as the Patents (Amendment) Bill 1999, was to implement the 1993 Agreement on Trade-Related Aspects of Intellectual Property Rights, the TRIPS Agreement, which was an Annex to the Agreement establishing the World Trade Organisation, WTO. In the time lapse between 1999 and its enactment in 2006, a number of additional provisions were added to take account of other international developments and to make a number of amendments to domestic intellectual property legislation. In spite of its short title, therefore, the 2006 Act amended not only the Patents Act 1992 (which, admittedly, is its main focus) but also the Trade Marks Act 1996, the Copyright and Related Rights Act 2000 and the Industrial Designs Act 2001.

During the Oireachtas debate in 2006, the developments in the second half of the 20th century and early years of the 21st century to support the protection of inventive processes were outlined. These included the creation of a common patent system in Europe under the 1973 European Patent Convention (EPC). The 1973 Convention established a European Patent Office in Munich, the function of which is to grant, on the basis of one central application to that office, patents which would be valid in each Contracting State designated by the applicant. In effect, a bundle of national patents emerge from a European patent application and in each designated country the European patent has the same legal effect as one granted by the local national patent office. European patents are granted only after an in-depth examination following a comprehensive novelty search in a collection of several million documents and, therefore, offer a high level of legal certainty. The 1993 TRIPS Agreement, referred to above, added a significant global trade element to patent rules. Since 1993 there have been a number of other international developments concerning patents, including amendments arising from revisions to the EPC; provisions to give effect to the Patent Law Treaty which was concluded under the auspices of the World Intellectual Property Organisation (WIPO), the UN agency which administers international treaties in the field of intellectual property; and miscellaneous necessary amendments to domestic intellectual property legislation.

TRIPS Agreement on patents   It was noted that Art.3 of the 1993 TRIPS Agreement obliges each member country to accord the same treatment to non-nationals as it does to its own nationals. Article 4 includes a most favoured nation provision according to which any advantage, favour, privilege or immunity granted by a member country to the nationals of any other country in regard to intellectual property rights must be accorded immediately and unconditionally to nationals of all other WTO member countries. The standard for patentable subject-matter is set in Art.27 of the TRIPS Agreement. Patents shall be available for any inventions, whether products or processes, in all fields of technology provided that they are new, inventive and capable of industrial application. Patents shall be available and patent rights enjoyable without discrimination as to the place of the invention, the field of technology and whether products are imported or locally produced. There are three permissible exemptions to the basic rule on patentability. First, inventions, the commercial exploitation of which would be contrary to public order or morality, may be exempted. Secondly, inventions concerning diagnostic, therapeutic and surgical methods for the treatment of humans or animals may be exempted. Thirdly, member countries may exclude from patentability "plants and animals other than micro-organisms and essentially biological processes for the production of plants and animals other than non-biological and micro-biological processes". It was noted that the Patents Act 1992 generally complied with the provisions of the TRIPS Agreement relating to both the standard for patentable subject-matter and the subject-matter which may be excluded from patentability.

The main area where the 1992 Act required amendment to comply with the TRIPS Agreement concerned the provisions concerning compulsory licences. Sections 70 to 75 of the 1992 Act concern the compulsory licensing of patents without the authorisation of the patentee. It was noted that Art.27.1 of the TRIPS Agreement requires that "patents shall be available and patent rights enjoyable without discrimination as to place of invention, the field of technology and whether products are imported or locally produced". Essentially, this means that where a patented product is exploited in any member country of the WTO and is then imported into another country in sufficient quantities to satisfy domestic demand there, a compulsory licence cannot be granted in that other country.

Additionally, pursuant to Art.31 of the TRIPS Agreement, numerous conditions must be adhered to by member countries of the WTO should such countries provide for the possibility of granting compulsory licences under a patent. Prior to the granting of a compulsory licence, the applicant for the licence must show that reasonable efforts to obtain a contractual licence from the patentee have failed. The licence shall be limited as to its scope and duration and it shall be of a non-exclusive nature. The compulsory licence shall be non-assignable and shall be granted predominantly for the supply of the domestic market. The compulsory licence shall be terminated if and when the circumstances which led to it cease to exist and are unlikely to recur. The patentee shall be compensated adequately depending on the circumstances of each case. The legal validity of the compulsory licences as well as any decision relating to the compensation shall be subject to judicial review. Where compulsory licences are granted to permit exploitation of a second patent which cannot be exploited without infringing a first patent, three additional conditions apply: the invention claimed in the second patent shall involve an important technical advance of considerable economic significance; the patentee of the first patent shall be entitled to a cross-licence, that is, a licence to use the invention claimed in the second patent; and the licence in respect of the first patent shall be non-assignable except with the assignment of the second patent. Sections 19 to 23 of the 2006 Act amended the existing provisions concerning compulsory licensing of patents in ss.70 to 75 of the 1992 Act to bring them into line with the TRIPS Agreement.

Amendments to EPC The 2006 Act also amended the 1992 Act arising from the revision of the European Patent Convention (EPC) in 2000. The revised text of the EPC will enter into force, at the latest, two years after the 15th Contracting State has deposited its instrument of ratification or accession. The 15th State deposited its instrument of accession in December 2005, so that other EPC Member States were required to do so by December 2007 to avoid being excluded from the European Patent Organisation. The main changes made by the 2006 Act concerned patentability criteria and, in particular, explicit recognition that a patent may be obtained for a second medical use of a known substance; limitation of the effect of European patents following the central limitation procedure before the European Patent Office (EPO), introduced in the EPC revision; and provision for the protection of third parties where a patent is restored by the enlarged board of appeal of the EPO following its review of a decision of a board of appeal of the EPO.

WIPO Patent Law Treaty The 2006 Act also brought the 1992 Act into compliance with the Patent Law Treaty. The purpose of the treaty, which was concluded under the auspices of WIPO, is to harmonise the formal requirements for patent applications set by national and regional patent offices such as elements of an application, filing date, priority, time limits and other procedural matters, and to streamline the procedures for obtaining and maintaining a patent. The Patent Law Treaty does not relate in any way to substantive patent law, for example, the criteria to be satisfied for an invention to be eligible for patentability. Its focus is on procedural requirements involved with filing and prosecuting a patent application, such as filing date requirements and procedures to prevent loss of the filing date; formal requirements regarding patent applications; and mechanisms to avoid unintentional loss of rights. While there is no obligation to accede to the treaty, the adoption of its provisions will make it easier for applicants to prosecute and to maintain a patent application.

Human and animal body treatment   Sections 3 and 4 of the 2006 Act amend ss.9 and 10 of the 1992 Act to bring them into line with Art.27.1 of TRIPS and Arts 52 and 53 of the EPC, as amended. The changes provide that methods of treatment of the human or animal body and diagnostic methods practised on the human body which had previously been excluded from patentability under s.9 by the fiction of their lack of industrial applicability are now included as exceptions to patentability on public policy grounds under s.10. The amended s.9 makes it clear that patents are to be available for inventions in all fields of technology. Section 5 amends s.11 of the 1992 Act to bring it into line with the new Art.54(5) of the EPC and will now explicitly allow patent protection to be obtained for second and further medical uses of known substances or compositions.

Filing   Section 6 of the 2006 Act inserts a completely substituted s.23 of the 1992 Act to reflect the requirements of Art.5 of the Patent Law Treaty and sets out the requirements that must be fulfilled to get a filing date for a patent application. The changes include a right to be accorded a date of filing even when the description does not comply with the language requirements of the legislation or other requirements. They also allow a reference, in lieu of filing a description, to a previously filed application to be used to obtain a date of filing. Another change is that if a missing drawing or part of the description is filed subsequent to the date of filing of the application, the application will not be re-dated to that later date, if priority from a previous application is claimed and the requirements to be prescribed are met. One of those will be that the missing part of the description or drawing is present in the earlier application. Section 7 amends s.25 of the 1992 Act and extends the existing right to claim priority from an earlier application filed in a state party to the Paris Convention for the Protection of Industrial Property to a right to claim priority based on an earlier application in any Member State of the WTO. Section 8 amends s.33 of the 1992 Act and provides for the possibility of correcting an error in the withdrawal of an application. Section 9 amends the 1992 Act by the insertion of new ss.35A and 35B to allow for the re-establishment of rights as provided for in Art.12 of the Patent Law Treaty in the case of applications which had been refused or deemed withdrawn for failure to comply with a time limit.

Section 35A sets out the conditions and procedures under which the Controller of Patents, Designs and Trade Marks shall reinstate an application, and s.35B sets out the effects of reinstatement of a patent application, including the protection for third parties. Section 10 amends s.37 of the 1992 Act to clarify the protection afforded to third parties where a patent has been restored and to set out the effects of restoration. The pre-2006 protection for the intervening rights of third parties had been set out in r.38 of the Patent Rules 1992, but the Attorney General's Office had advised that it should be set out in the Act itself. Section 11 amends s.38 of the 1992 Act to ensure consistency in approach to post-grant amendment in national proceedings and before the EPO. Section 12 amends s.42 of the 1992 Act regarding the use of patents on board vessels, aircraft and land vehicles. That arises from Ireland's ratification of the WTO Agreement. Section 13 amends s.45 of the 1992 Act and is a drafting revision to reflect minor amendments to Art.69 of the EPC. Section 14 amends s.50 of the 1992 Act to provide that relief for the infringement of a partially valid patent may be granted also on condition that the proprietor of a European patent designating the state limits the patent at the EPO.

Section 15 amends s.53 of the 1992 Act to introduce a further restriction on the bringing of proceedings for groundless threats of infringement. The effect of the 2006 Act is that proceedings may not now be brought by an aggrieved party where a person, for example, a patent proprietor, has threatened that party with proceedings in respect of acts of secondary infringement—such as selling or stocking the patented product or offering the patented process for use—provided the person being threatened has made or imported that product for disposal or used that process. Section 16 amends s.58 of the 1992 Act to bring it into conformity with Art.138(1)(*d*) of the European Patent Convention. It clarifies that s.58(*d*) relates only to amendment of the patent that occurred after it had been granted. Section 17 amends s.59 of the 1992 Act to provide that, in the case of a European patent designating the state, where the controller or the court has found that the grounds of revocation affect the patent only in part, the specification of the patent can be amended under s.38 of the Act, or the claims of the patent can be limited by the proprietor under the new central limitation procedure provided for in the revision of the European Patent Convention.

Section 18 amends s.68 of the 1992 Act to remove any discriminatory restriction on the importation of a patented product from another member country of the WTO. Sections 19 to 23, inclusive, substantially amend ss.70, 71, and 73 to 75, inclusive, of the 1992 Act to bring the provisions concerning compulsory licences into line with the requirements of Art.27.1 and Art.31 of TRIPS: see the discussion above.

Evidence taken by the Controller of Patents, Designs and Trade Marks Section 24 of the 2006 Act amends s.92 of the 1992 Act to clarify that the provisions applicable to the taking of evidence by the Controller of Patents, Designs and Trade Marks applies equally to later enactments under which the controller has functions. Section 25 amends s.96 of the 1992 Act to ensure that the three-month period for filing an appeal against a decision or order of the controller, in the instance where written grounds of the controller's decision have been sought, is computed from the date that the written grounds are furnished rather than from the date of the decision. Section 26 amends s.110 of the 1992 Act and is consequential on the revision of s.33. It sets out the procedure to be followed where the controller receives a request to restore an application that has been withdrawn in error. Section 27 introduces a new s.110A to set out the effect of restoration of a withdrawn application, particularly the protection of the intervening rights of third parties. Section 28 inserts a new s.118A into the 1992 Act to reflect Art.11 of the Patent Law Treaty and to provide that where the applicant or proprietor of a patent has failed to observe a time limit specified by the controller the person may be granted one extension as of right.

European patents   Section 29 amends s.119 of the 1992 Act to reflect that European patents may be limited or revoked by the European Patent Office at the request of the proprietor under the new central limitation procedure contained in the revision of the EPC. That section also provides for the consequences of the restoration of a European patent which has been revoked by a board of appeal and is subsequently restored by an enlarged board of appeal. Section 30 inserts a new s.119A into the 1992 Act to provide for the possibility of relief where a translation of a European patent designating the state published in French or German has not been filed within the prescribed period. Again, that is to provide for re-establishment of rights under Art.12 of the Patent Law Treaty. Section 31 amends s.120 of the 1992 Act to reflect the omission of the current Art.54(4) from the revised EPC. The effect is that a European application designating the state will have prior effect under s.11(3) on publication, even if the designation of the state has been withdrawn prior to publication. Also, consequent on the proposed amendment to s.37, the intervening rights of third parties, following the re-establishment of the applicant's rights under the EPC, are now set out in the section. Section 32 amends s.121 of the 1992 Act to set out the protection afforded to a third party who may have begun to do an act which would not have constituted infringement based on the original translation of a patent or application, but which would constitute infringement based on a corrected translation. Section 33 makes a minor drafting amendment to s.122 of the 1992 Act to bring it in line with the terminology in Art.77 of the EPC. Section 34 repeals the transitional provision set out in para.4 of the First Schedule to the 1992 Act as that provision is inconsistent with Art.28 of the TRIPS Agreement. Section 35 amends the Second Schedule to the 1992 Act to introduce a new provision with regard to "equivalents", consequent on the revision of the Protocol on the interpretation of Art.69 of the EPC.

Section 36 repeals two orders made under s.25(5) of the 1992 Act, relating to agreements concerning priority with countries not party to the Paris Convention, which will become superfluous when s.7 of the 2006 Act comes into operation.

Section 37 amends s.2 of the Trade Marks Act 1996 to include a reference to the "Agreement establishing the World Trade Organisation".

Amendments to Trade Marks Act 1996   Section 38 of the 2006 Act amends s.10 of the Trade Marks Act 1996 to bring it into line with decisions of the European Court of Justice which established that a trade mark can be refused on the basis of earlier rights if the earlier mark enjoys a reputation in the State and the later mark would take unfair advantage of that reputation, regardless of the issue as to whether the goods in both cases are similar or not. Section 39 is linked in that it relies also on decisions of the European Court of Justice, and it amends s.14 of the 1996 Act to make it an infringing act for the proprietor of a mark to use a similar or identical mark to an earlier mark where the earlier mark enjoys a reputation in the State and the later mark would take unfair advantage of that reputation.

Section 40 amends s.25 of the 1996 Act to align the search and seizure provisions with those prevailing under more recent legislation in the intellectual property area such as the Copyright and Related Rights Act 2000. It extends the list of activities which can be carried out during a search and seizure operation, for example, making an inventory of the infringing articles; allowing the seizure of anything found which may be required in evidence; and the power to require any person found on the premises to give his or her name or address for use in any subsequent legal proceedings.

Section 41 amends s.29 of the 1996 Act to include changes affecting the proprietorship of a mark to be regarded as transactions to be recorded in the Register of Trade Marks. Section 42 amends s.41 of the 1996 Act and extends the priority right, based on an earlier application in a country or territory with which Ireland has entered into an agreement for the reciprocal protection of trade marks, to successors in title of a person. Section 43 amends s.60 of the 1996 Act to include a reference to the WTO. Section 44 amends s.79 of the 1996 Act to ensure that the three-month period for filing an appeal against a decision of the Controller of Patents, Designs and Trade Marks, in the instance where written grounds of the Controller's decision has been sought, is computed from the date written grounds are furnished rather than from the date of the decision. Section 45 is aimed at ensuring full TRIPS compliance in that anywhere in the Trade Marks Act where the Paris Convention is referenced, such references are expanded to include also the WTO agreement. Section 46 augments the transitional provisions of the 1996 Act arising from ratification of the WTO agreement. It safeguards the continuation of any bona fide use by any person who was, prior to the entry into effect of the WTO agreement, using a mark.

Copyright   Section 47 of the 2006 Act amends s.364 of the Copyright and Related Rights Act 2000 by ensuring that in any court proceedings in which the Controller is involved under the 2000 Act, the Controller can neither be the recipient of an award for costs nor be ordered to pay costs. Section 48 repeals s.367(2) of the Copyright and Related Rights Act 2000, the effect of which is that the Controller of Patents will no longer be required, within a period of three months, to refer to arbitration a dispute referred to him under the terms of the Act as this has, in practice, proved impossible.

Industrial designs   Section 49 amends s.57 of the Industrial Designs Act 2001 and clarifies that infringement proceedings cannot be instigated before the date of publication of registration of a design and, equally, that no criminal offence can be committed before that date. Section 50 amends s.84 of the Industrial Designs Act 2001 to ensure that the three-month period for filing an appeal against a decision or order of the Controller, in the instance where written grounds of the Controller's decision have been sought, is computed from the date that the written grounds are furnished rather than from the date of the decision. Section 51 provides for citation and commencement.

Trade mark: confusion   In *Zockoll Group Ltd v Controller of Patents, Designs and Trade Marks*, High Court, October 17, 2006, the plaintiff appealed under the Trade Marks Act 1996 against the decision of the controller to refuse its application to register the terms "800 FLOWERS" and "800 FLORISTS" as trade marks. The Controller had ruled that there was no connection in trade between the plaintiff and the intended trade mark, and also ruled as a matter of discretion that the registration would frustrate the legitimate expansion by the second defendant of its business in an unjustifiable manner. The plaintiff argued that there was a sufficient connection through their exercise of quality control over the goods in question. The plaintiff also argued that the second defendant company was incorporated in the United States and that there was no significant evidence of a spillover of reputation into this jurisdiction. O'Sullivan J. upheld the appeal. He held that there was no basis for opposing the registration by the plaintiff of the terms as trade marks. Applying the decision of Costello J. in the "PASS" case, *Bank of Ireland v Controller of Patents, Designs and Trade Marks*, High Court, March 31, 1987 (*Annual Review of Irish Law 1987*, p.46), he held that the evidence established, on the part of the plaintiff, an intention to use the trade mark in connection with the relevant product in the course of trade. Applying *Smith Hayden & Co. Ltd's Application* [1945] 63 R.P.C. 97, he also concluded that there was no evidence of a potential for deception or confusion if the plaintiff were to use the marks sought to be registered.

PUBLIC WORKS CONTRACTS

The European Communities (Award of Public Authorities' Contracts) Regulations 2006 (S.I. No. 329 of 2006) implemented Directive 2004/18 on the co-ordination of procedures for the award of public works contracts, public supply contracts and public service contracts. To that extent, they are also linked to the revised Government Contracts Committee (GCC) Standard Contracts, which constitute the "Framework Agreements" for the purposes of the 2004 Directive: see the discussion in the Law Reform Commission's *Consultation Paper on Privity of Contract: Third Party Rights* (LRC CP–40–2006), para.1.76. The 2006 Regulations came into force on June 22, 2006.

Company and Insolvency Law

GRÁINNE CALLANAN, Lecturer in Company Law,
Waterford Institute of Technology

DISQUALIFICATION/INVESTIGATIONS

Access to and discovery of documents held by inspectors In *Re National Irish Bank Ltd (under investigation) and Re National Irish Bank Financial Services Ltd (under investigation)* [2006] 2 I.L.R.M. 263, the Director of Corporate Enforcement (the Director) sought access to or discovery of documents held by inspectors appointed to investigate the affairs of National Irish Bank Limited and National Irish Bank Financial Services Limited (the companies). The Director grounded his application for access pursuant to s.12 of the Companies Act 1990 (the 1990 Act) or alternatively, the Director sought non-party discovery against the inspectors pursuant to Ord.31, r.29 of the Rules of the Superior Courts (RSC).

Following the publication of the inspectors' report in July 2004 the Director sought disqualification orders against a number of persons named in the report. Eight of these respondents were contesting the Director's application. When the Director commenced the disqualification proceedings against the respondents, he made it clear in the originating notices of motion that he would be relying on the report of the inspectors on foot of s.22 of the 1990 Act. A number of the respondents had sought and were granted access to documents held by the companies to adduce evidence to rebut the findings of the inspectors. The Director contended that as the respondents intended challenging the findings of the inspectors he would be disadvantaged in his s.160 applications if he did not have access to the documents upon which the inspectors based their findings.

The Director sought numerous documents from the inspectors who submitted that these documents were already available from either the respondents or the companies themselves. The Director had also requested that the inspectors identify background or supporting documents which were material to their findings. The inspectors submitted that this would involve them in a mammoth task of reviewing the entire of a substantial amount of material and information which was available to them in the course of their investigation. The inspectors also submitted that this task would incur further costs over and above any legal costs and that the 1990 Act did not make provision for the payment of further costs once the inspectors had delivered their final report. The inspectors' statutory function was to investigate and deliver a report and any further obligations following the delivery of the report required clarification and any decision in this regard would have implications for future investigations.

The Director contended that s.12(1) of the 1990 Act gives the court a wide discretion to direct the inspectors to provide access to the documents sought. Section 12(1) provides:

> "Having considered a report made under s.11, the court may make such order as it deems fit in relation to matters arising from that report including –
>
> (a) an order of its own motion for the winding up of the body corporate, or
> (b) an order for the purpose of remedying any disability suffered by any person whose interests were adversely affected by the conduct of the affairs of the company, provided that, in making any such order, the court shall have regard to the interests of any other person who may be adversely affected by the order."

The Director relied upon the general provision of s.12 whereby the court is given a discretion to make such order as it deems fit in relation to matters arising from an inspector's report. On this basis, the Director contended that the court had power to order the inspectors to provide access to the documents which the Director was seeking.

Kelly J. referred to the judgment of Finnegan P. in *Re Ansbacher (Cayman) Ltd* [2004] 3 I.R. 193 (see *Annual Review of Irish Law 2004*) where the Revenue Commissioners sought access to documents obtained by the inspectors in the course of their investigation, but which were not included in the appendices to their report. Finnegan P. stated:

> "The first legal issue to arise is the construction of s.12(1) of the Act of 1990. The section gives the court a wide discretion — it may make such order as it deems fit. Accordingly in determining whether to make an order the court must take into account all relevant circumstances. What is relevant in the circumstances of any particular application may vary and I propose only to deal with those circumstances which I consider relevant on the present application. However on every application in exercising the discretion, the court must have regard to the interests of any person who may be adversely affected by its order. While this is expressly mentioned where reliance is placed on s.12(1)(b) of the Act of 1990, it equally applies to every other application under the section. It is to be noted that the discretion conferred upon the court is not limited to the circumstances mentioned in ss.12(1)(a) and (b) of the Act of 1990, in that these provisions are regulated by the word 'including' so that the discretion of the court may be exercised in cases falling outside these provisions."

Kelly J. was satisfied that the court had an absolute discretion as to what order it could make under s.12. Despite such a wide discretion, it was observed that any order on foot of this discretion must be consistent with other provisions of the 1990 Act. In this regard the court did not consider that the legislation envisaged "some form of rolling process where, notwithstanding the delivery of the final report by them inspectors might be asked to revisit all of the documents in their possession in order to identify which documents support particular findings made by them. Such an exercise would be inconsistent both with the notion of a final report and indeed the task which the statute requires inspectors to undertake." Kelly J. further observed that s.13 of the 1990 Act, which provides for the payment of the expenses of investigations, does not include provisions in respect of expenses incurred after the investigation is completed. Accordingly, it was clear that the legislature did not intend an order of the type sought by the Director to be granted. The court considered the implications if the application was acceded to:

> "[I]t is possible, perhaps likely, that the respondents might seek similar access to other documents which they perceived might be helpful to their contentions. Indeed, applications for further and better access might also manifest themselves thereby giving rise to an almost endless obligation being placed upon the inspectors to revisit their report and to identify documents which are supportive of conclusions reached or opinions expressed. In my opinion this was never envisaged or contemplated by the legislation. It is also to be noted that in affording the inspectors' report the special status which it has under s.22 of the Act, value was placed on the inspectors' conclusions and opinions rather than on the information gathered."

On this basis, Kelly J. agreed with the inspectors' view that "just as there is a need for finality in litigation so there is also a need for finality in investigations." The application for access under s.12 was, accordingly, refused.

The Director also sought to rely on Ord.31 r.29 of the Rules of the Superior Court which provides as follows:

> "Any person not a party to the cause or matter before the Court who appears to the Court to be likely to have or to have had in his possession custody or power any documents which are relevant to an issue arising or likely to arise out of the cause or matter or is or is likely to be in a position to give evidence relevant to any such issue may by leave of the Court upon the application of any party to the said cause or matter be directed by order of the Court to answer such interrogatories or to make discovery of such documents or to permit inspection of such documents. The provisions of this Order shall apply mutatis mutandis as if the said order of the Court had been directed to a party to the said

cause or matter provided always that the party seeking such order shall indemnify such person in respect of all costs thereby reasonably incurred by such person and such costs borne by the said party shall be deemed to be costs of that party for the purposes of Order 99."

The Director submitted that the court's discretion should be exercised in his favour as the inspectors were no different to any other non-party to litigation who may have documents in their possession. The court was not inclined to agree. Kelly J. observed:

> "The inspectors came into possession of such documents as they hold on foot of their appointment as inspectors to conduct an investigation pursuant to an order of this court. They did so. Their investigation is over. Their final report has been delivered. They should not in my view be asked to do more since their task is complete. If the director cannot obtain the documents under s. 12 of the Act because to do so would be inconsistent with the final nature of the report and the scope and scheme of the legislation, then he cannot do so by transforming the application into one for non-party discovery. In other words he cannot circumvent the refusal of his s. 12 application and seek to obtain the documents by the side wind of non-party discovery. The inspectors' task is done: their statutory function is complete. They cannot in my view be asked to revisit their report and the documents generated by their investigations so as to make discovery as sought."

The court observed that case law in relation to Ord.31, r.29 demonstrates the tendency of the courts to interpret it in a restrictive manner (*Fusco v O'Dea* [1994] 2 I.R. 93; *Chambers v Times Newspapers Ltd* [1999] 2 I.R. 424 and *Allied Irish Banks Plc v Ernst and Whinney* [1993] 1 I.R. 375). Accordingly, such an order should only be made where there was a real and pressing need or where a substantial benefit would be gained. The court was not satisfied that the Director had demonstrated a real and pressing need so as to justify an order being made under s.12 or under Ord.31, r.29. Many of the documents required by the Director could be obtained from the respondents to the s.160 motions or from the companies themselves. With regard to the request by the Director that the inspectors identify the relevant documents and submissions that lead to their conclusions Kelly J. stated:

> "As I already pointed out s.22 of the Act gives a special status to the facts found and the opinions expressed by the inspectors in their report. It is not concerned with the information gathered by them. They were not appointed as evidence gatherers and they should not now be asked to identify the documentary evidence which they relied upon in finding the facts and forming the opinions which they did."

On this basis the court refused the order sought.

Delay in proceedings   *Re Kentford Securities Ltd (Under Investigation); McCann v Director of Corporate Enforcement*, unreported, High Court, Peart J., March 7, 2006, concerned an application to have disqualification proceedings dismissed on the grounds of pre-commencement delay and/or for want of prosecution on the basis that the delay had been inordinate and inexcusable. An authorised officer was appointed to exercise the powers conferred by s.19 of the Companies Act 1990 and, having done so, produced a report in 2002 into the affairs of the company. The report found that the company was used by Mr Des Traynor during the period 1989–1994 to facilitate the evasion of taxes. As part of the substantive proceedings a number of allegations had been made against the applicant in relation to his activities as auditor of the company.

The applicant claimed that the application for his disqualification was "grossly prejudicial" as it was being sought over 15 years after the alleged first complaint relating to his actions in 1990, and he maintained that the delay was both inordinate and inexcusable, and that it would be unjust to allow the application to proceed. The respondent asserted that the first complaint made against the applicant was after November 2002 when the report of the authorised officer was provided to the Office of the Director of Corporate Enforcement. The respondent also contended that some of the allegations made in the disqualification proceedings related to events occurring in the context of the investigation.

Central to the applicant's claim that he had been prejudiced by the delay was that Mr Des Traynor died in 1994, and accordingly the applicant had been deprived of the opportunity to call evidence from him in respect of some of the allegations. The respondent submitted that even if Mr Traynor were to give evidence substantiating the applicant's claims, this would still not be sufficient to avoid an order for his disqualification, given the entirety of the complaints and allegations made about how he conducted himself as the auditor to the company.

The court was satisfied that even though the respondent did not commence his application to have the applicant disqualified under s.160 of the Act until March 2005, the report did not come to his attention until November 2002. Accordingly, it was only from that date that the court should consider whether there has been any excessive or unreasonable delay. The respondent submitted that after the report was received it was necessary to obtain legal advice and a report from an auditing expert before considering how the matter should proceed. The report of the auditing expert was dated February 2005. The respondent commenced the substantive application in March 2005.

The court was satisfied that as the matters relevant to the application for disqualification occurred many years prior to the application, the interests of justice required that any application should proceed with all reasonable and possible haste once a decision was made (*Toal v Duignan* [1991] I.L.R.M.

135 and *Ó'Domhnaill v Merrick* [1984] I.R. 151 referred). The court observed that there was no suggestion in the present case that the application, once commenced, did not proceed other than with reasonable expedition. Furthermore, the court was satisfied that the applicant was in a position to resist the substantive application without injustice or unfairness. The application was accordingly dismissed.

Disqualification of person following a report of inspectors   Section 22 of the Companies Act 1990 (the 1990 Act) provides that a report of inspectors appointed to investigate a company shall be admissible in any civil proceedings as evidence of the facts set out therein without further proof unless the contrary is shown, and of the opinion of the inspector in relation to any matter contained in the report. Under s.160(2)(e) of the 1990 Act the court may, in consequence of a report of inspectors, disqualify a person if it is satisfied that the conduct of such person makes him unfit to be concerned in the management of a company. The Director of Corporate Enforcement (the Director) is given *locus standi* under s.160(6A) to make such an application.

In *Re Ansbacher (Cayman) Ltd; Director of Corporate Enforcement v Collery,* High Court, Finlay Geoghegan J., March 9, 2006, the Director made such an application. Following the publication of the report of inspectors appointed to enquire into the affairs of Ansbacher (Cayman) Limited (Ansbacher), the Director applied to have the respondent disqualified under s.160(2)(e). The Director relied exclusively on the content of the inspectors' report, and submitted that its findings and conclusions established as a matter of probability that Mr Collery was guilty of a serious lack of commercial probity in relation to the affairs of Ansbacher such that it made him unfit to be concerned in the management of a company within the meaning of s.160(2)(e). The respondent did not oppose the application and furthermore he did not contest any of the findings in the inspectors' report. Nonetheless, the court accepted that the onus was on the Director to satisfy the court that the conduct of Mr Collery, as referred to in the inspectors' report, made him unfit to be concerned in the management of the company. The report found that the respondent had knowingly assisted Ansbacher and a related company in unlawful activities including, *inter alia*, unlicensed banking activities, breaches of the Companies Acts and tax evasion. Referring to the principles set out by Kelly J. in *Director of Corporate Enforcement v D'Arcy*, High Court, October 26, 2005 (see *Annual Review of Irish Law 2005*) the court was satisfied that Mr Collery's conduct was such to make him unfit to be concerned in the management of a company.

A number of decisions in 2005 considered the principles relevant when fixing the period of disqualification (see *Annual Review of Irish Law 2005*). Finlay Geogheghan J. accepted the principles set out by Kelly J. in *D'Arcy* (see above) and stated as follows:

"the principles applicable to determining the appropriate period in this
case appear to be the following:

(1) The primary purpose of an order of disqualification is not to
punish the individual but to protect the public against future
conduct of companies by persons whose past record has shown
them to be a danger to creditors and others.

(2) The period of disqualification should reflect (in relation to an
order under s.160(2)(e)) the gravity of the conduct as found by
the Inspectors which makes the respondent unfit to be concerned
in the management of a company.

(3) The period of disqualification should contain deterrent
elements.

(4) A period of disqualification in excess of ten years should be
reserved for particularly serious cases.

(5) The court should firstly assess the correct period in accordance
with the foregoing and then take into account mitigating factors
prior to fixing the actual period of disqualification."

Applying these principles she concluded that given the serious nature of
the conduct of the respondent as outlined in the report of the inspectors, the
appropriate period of disqualification before taking into account any mitigating
factors should be one of 12 years. The relevant mitigating factors were that
the conduct complained of in the inspectors' report took place between 1991
and 1997 and that no complaint has been made in respect of the conduct of
the respondent in any subsequent period. The respondent had also assisted
the inspectors with "promptness and courtesy in difficult circumstances". The
respondent also recognised and took responsibility for his conduct. On this
basis Finlay Geoghegan J. concluded that the disqualification period should
be reduced by three years.

Having outlined the principles applicable, Finlay Geoghegan J. took the
opportunity to clarify her approach in fixing the period for disqualification. The
Director had, in correspondence with the respondent's solicitors, indicated that
the period of disqualification was a matter for the court. However, in the same
correspondence, the Director had analysed and compared the findings of the
inspectors in relation to Mr D'Arcy in the National Irish Bank investigation
with the findings of the inspectors in relation to the respondent in the Ansbacher
investigation. The court observed that such a comparison appeared to have
been carried out in the context of the 10-year disqualification period ordered
by Kelly J. in the *D'Arcy* case. In this regard, Finlay Geoghegan J. referred
with approval to the approach of Lord Woolfe M.R. in *Re Westmid Packing
Services Ltd* [1998] 2 All E.R. 124 where he stated:

"(8) This court was referred to the decision of Nourse J in *Re Civica
Investments Ltd.* [1983] BCLC 456 at 457–458, in which he said:

'It might be thought that [the appropriate period of disqualification] is something which, like the passing of sentence in a criminal case, ought to be dealt with comparatively briefly and without elaborate reasoning. In general I think that that must be the correct approach. More important, as more of these cases come before the court, it is obviously undesirable for the judge to be taken through the facts of previous cases in order to guide him as to the course he should take in the particular case before him. No doubt in this, as in other areas, it is possible that there will emerge a broad and undefined system of tariffs for defaults of varying degrees of blame, but there must come a point when it is no longer either necessary or desirable to go through the facts of previous cases. For my part I think that the point has now been reached.'"

Finlay Geoghegan J., having observed that Nourse J.'s approach should be adopted in all cases involving disqualification, considered that the principles applicable to the court's jurisdiction under s.160(2) were now clear. On this basis she concluded:

"The application of those principles to the facts of the particular case is a matter for the trial judge. The citation of cases as to the period of disqualification will, in the great majority of cases, be unnecessary and inappropriate. I would respectfully agree that the approach of this Court to the appropriate period of disqualification should be the application of the principles now established to the facts of the particular case and that the citation of the facts of other cases and periods of disqualification is unnecessary and inappropriate."

Cross-examination of affidavit evidence In *Re National Irish Bank Ltd, Director of Corporate Enforcement v Seymour*, unreported, High Court, O'Donovan J., May 16, 2006, the applicant applied to the court under Ord.75B, r.7 and/or Ord.40, r.1 of the Rules of the Superior Courts and/or under the court's inherent jurisdiction for an order that the respondent attend the trial of this action and be cross-examined on his affidavit evidence. The applicant also applied for an order that, in the event that the respondent failed to attend for cross-examination, the affidavits should not be used at the trial of this action. The respondent maintained that cross-examination on his affidavits was inappropriate and he disputed the applicant's entitlement to the relief sought.

Order 75B, r.7 of the Rules of the Superior Courts provides:

"Every application under the Act shall be grounded upon the affidavit of the party making such application and shall be heard and determined on affidavit unless the court otherwise orders."

Order 40, r.1 of the Rules of the Superior Courts provides:

> "Upon any petition, motion or other application, evidence may be given
> by affidavit, but the court may, on the application of either party, order
> the attendance for cross examination of the person making any such
> affidavit."

Order 75B, r.9 of the Rules of the Superior Courts also enables a court to direct
a plenary hearing "in any case in which the court considers that it is either
necessary or desirable in the interests of justice to do so."

Following a report of inspectors appointed to investigate the affairs of
National Irish Bank and National Irish Bank Financial Services Ltd, the
applicant sought an order of disqualification against the respondent under
s.160(2) of the Companies Act 1990. As part of the substantive proceedings,
a number of affidavits were filed by the applicant and the respondent. The
respondent contended that as he disputed the criticisms of his conduct and the
inferences and opinions which the inspectors drew from the evidence, but not
the factual findings, it was not an appropriate case in which to direct a cross-
examination of the respondent on those affidavits.

O'Donovan J. considered that the discretion of the court should only be
exercised in favour of a cross-examination if the court considers that it is
necessary for the purpose of disposing of the issues which the court has to
determine (*per* Keane C.J. in *Holland v Information Commissioner*, unreported,
High Court, December 15, 2003). The court accepted the respondent's
submissions that he did not dispute the facts relied on by the inspectors in
support of their findings in any material way, but rather the constructions of
and inferences from those facts. Nonetheless, as the respondent had challenged
virtually every conclusion that the inspectors drew from those facts, and given
that the court was entitled to know the mindset of the respondent, the court
was satisfied that in order for a trial judge to come to a reasonable conclusion
with regard to the commercial probity of the respondent, the interests of justice
required that the cross-examination be conducted. The court directed that the
respondent attend the trial of this action for the purpose of being cross-examined
on his affidavit evidence and in the event that he failed to attend for such cross-
examination the said affidavits should not be used at the hearing.

RESTRICTION OF DIRECTORS

Partial relief from restriction declaration   In *Re Xnet Information Systems
Ltd (in Voluntary Liquidation)*, unreported, High Court, O'Neill J., October 10,
2006, the applicant sought an order pursuant to s.152 of the Companies Act
1990 (the 1990 Act), for relief from a declaration of restriction made pursuant to
s.150 of the 1990 Act. As the liquidator did not make submissions, the Director

of Corporate Enforcement was joined as a notice party to the proceedings. Section 152 of the 1990 Act provides, *inter alia*, that a person to whom s.150 applies may, within not more than one year after a declaration has been made, apply to the court for relief, either in whole or in part, from the declaration, and the court may, if it deems it just and equitable to do so, grant such relief on whatever terms and conditions it sees fit.

The applicant submitted that s.152 gives the court the broadest of discretion to relieve against the restriction where it is just and equitable to do so (*per* Laffoy J. in *Re Ferngara Associates Ltd: F & R Robinson v Forrest* [1999] 1 I.R. 426 *per* Finlay Geoghegan J. in *Carolan and Cosgrave v Fennell*, unreported, High Court, October 24, 2005). It was further submitted that where it was just and equitable to so do, the court had an unfettered discretion to give grant relief against the entirety of the restriction order.

In assessing whether there were just and equitable grounds for relief, the court was asked to have regard to a number of matters. One of the key matters related to the applicant's constitutional right to earn his livelihood. The applicant submitted that while the right is not absolute, any statutory provision which sought to curtail such a right should be closely scrutinised by the courts to ensure that the restriction was not, having regard to the legitimate objective of the statutory restriction, either arbitrary or excessive (relying on *Murphy v Stewart* [1973] I.R. 97; *Attorney General v Paperlink Ltd* [1984] I.L.R.M. 373 and *Cox v Ireland* [1992] 2 I.R. 503).

The applicant also relied on the matter of the hardship he had incurred as a result of the restriction order. In this regard, the applicant had been unable to engage in commercial activity and had been forced to rely upon his wife's earnings for the support of his family. Furthermore, the collapse of the company had resulted in personal losses to the applicant in the region of €150,000. As the applicant was an entrepreneur with an expertise in the computer industry, he was restricted from developing ideas with commercial potential without forming and being a director of a company. Given his financial situation, he could not raise the €63,000 in order to gain the benefit of the exemption from restriction under s.150(3) of the 1990 Act. Accordingly, he would be placed at a gross disadvantage *vis-à-vis* potential investors who could extract from him an unfair and disproportionate share of the enterprise because of his restricted status.

In regard to the deterrent value of the s.150 restriction, it was submitted that where there was no dishonesty or bad motive found, that the element of deterrence involved in these restrictions in order to protect the public, *i.e.* the creditors and others who would have dealings with the director in question, was much less engaged. The applicant endured the stigma which attaches to a restriction declaration in the commercial world and beyond. Having regard to the length of time (in excess of two years) for which the restriction had applied, it was submitted that, having regard to the nature of the applicant's conduct, the deterrent value of a s.150 restriction in this case would not be undermined if the restriction were lifted at this point in time.

The Director's submissions were broadly as follows:

(a) The applicant had not demonstrated a "need" or "legitimate interest" in having the restriction lifted; he had failed to provide any particulars of the companies which he proposed to engage in. The applicant had not demonstrated that he could not earn his living using his entrepreneurial skills otherwise than through a limited company.

(b) While a restriction order necessarily involves hardship of some sort, it must be assumed that, in enacting these provisions, Parliament intended that the objective of protection of the public outweighed the punitive effect on the person to whom the restriction applied.

(c) The court must be satisfied that the public is adequately protected in respect of the concerns giving rise to the original restriction and that the deterrent value of restriction in general is not thereby undermined. Accordingly, given that the reasons which led to the imposition of the restriction were extremely serious in that there was a serious disregard of the applicant's obligations under the Companies Acts, and an entirely inadequate appreciation of the duties and responsibilities of directors, relief was not warranted.

(d) The capitalisation requirement, requiring as it did an "equity cushion", was a valuable protection of creditors and the court should very carefully evaluate the reasons put forward by an applicant as to why the requirement to put up this capital is unduly onerous.

(e) The court should consider whether the public interest can be adequately protected in the context of a partial or total relief from restriction and in doing so the court should consider the imposition of appropriate conditions to protect the public interest. In this regard, the Director submitted that if the court was disposed to grant relief, it should do so subject to a range of specific conditions which included that manner in which decisions of any board, on which the applicant was a director, should be made.

O'Neill J. considered that the fundamental purpose of s.150 is to protect the public from persons who, in the discharge of their duties as directors of companies, have acted dishonestly or irresponsibly. He suggested that the implication of the statutory requirement that an applicant for relief must apply within "not more than one year after a declaration has been made" is that the Oireachtas envisaged applications for relief would be made within a short time of the restriction order being made. Accordingly, he inferred that the term of a restriction was not to be viewed in a manner similar to a sentence, in that the restricted person must be required to endure the full term of five years. Taking into account the relatively low capitalisation threshold required by s.150(3) together with the one-year requirement, O'Neill J. was satisfied that the Oireachtas was intent on the relatively speedy rehabilitation of directors in respect of whom declarations of restriction were made. O'Neill J. noted that the practical effect of the low capitalisation threshold in s.150(3) meant that the public may be relatively unprotected from restricted directors who happen to have access to modest levels of wealth. Accordingly, as a matter of fairness and to ensure equality of treatment of persons in similar circumstances as required by Art.40.1 of the Constitution, this statutory provision cannot be applied in such a way as to work an invidious discrimination against impecunious persons.

O'Neill J. further observed that a court must, when asked to lift the restriction either wholly or partially, be satisfied that the risk to third parties from either the dishonesty or irresponsibility of the applicant in the future is of such a low order as to leave the court satisfied that the restriction can be safely, either wholly or partially, lifted.

The court accepted that an applicant must, in seeking relief, demonstrate a "need" or "interest" to engage in trade through the medium of a limited company rather than a need to restore his reputation. Furthermore, the applicant must satisfy the court that the capitalisation threshold is, having regard to his impecuniosity, an insurmountable obstacle to him. If the court is satisfied, having considered the reasons for the restriction, that a risk to the public remains, however low, the appropriate course to follow is to reduce the capitalisation threshold to a level which is attainable to the applicant in question. O'Neill J. observed that the other relevant factors were:

(a) the deterrent effect of the restriction order, *i.e.* the deterring of directors from dishonest or irresponsible conduct and thereby the promotion of high standards of corporate governance;

(b) the conduct of the applicant since the winding-up;

(c) the hardship suffered by an applicant which should not outweigh the protection of the public.

Assessing the evidence, in particular, the applicant's repayment of monies despite his dire financial situation and the expensive lesson he learned from the collapse of the company, the court was satisfied that the risk to the public of a repeat of irresponsible behaviour by the applicant in the discharge of his duties as a director of a company was very low. With regard to whether the deterrent effect of a s.150 restriction would be undermined, the court observed that the applicant had been unable to engage in trade through the medium of a limited liability company and had had to live with the stigma associated with the declaration under s.150. Having regard to the "need" or "interest" of the applicant, the court accepted that the applicant is entitled, if he has ideas which have commercial potential, to exploit these ideas using his own entrepreneurial skills. As this would normally involve the medium of a limited liability company, the court was satisfied that the applicant would be significantly disadvantaged by the restriction order because he would be susceptible to exploitation in dealing with other investors. According to O'Neill J., such a consequence would be an unjust and inequitable result of the restriction. Finally, O'Neill J. was satisfied that while the factors which led to the restriction were very serious in themselves, given the applicant's prior responsible behaviour in relation to the company and his conduct since the winding-up, there was very little risk to the public of being exposed to any damage or injury if the applicant was permitted to act as a director of a company again.

Given the applicant's real impecuniosity and his inability to acquire the capital necessary to comply with the capitalisation threshold, the court considered it appropriate to reduce the amount required by s.150(3) to €7,500. The court further held that all other aspects of the restriction order should remain in place until their statutory expiration. The court also imposed the condition that the applicant notify the Director of the name of any company of which he became a director or secretary or in which he took up any position which is the subject-matter of the declaration of restriction. Furthermore, the court gave liberty to the Director to apply to the court to vary any of the conditions attached to the granting of relief, including the revoking of the relief, should the circumstances warrant it.

Costs of successful restriction applications   Section 56(2) of the Company Law Enforcement Act 2001 imposes a mandatory obligation on liquidators to apply to the court for the restriction of directors of insolvent companies unless the Director of Corporate Enforcement has relieved him of this obligation. This statutory mandate has proved onerous for liquidators, particularly where the company in question is without funds. A number of judicial decisions relating to the costs of such applications have exacerbated the position of liquidators to such an extent that many are reluctant to take on the liquidation of some insolvent companies. The decisions in *Re Mitek Holdings Ltd (in liquidation); Grace v Kachkar*, unreported, High Court, Finlay Geoghegan J., May 5, 2005 and *Re Tipperary Fresh Foods (in liquidation); O'Riordan v O'Connor*, unreported, High Court, Finlay Geoghegan J., May 5, 2005 (see *Annual Review of Irish Law 2005*) demonstrated the potential cost to creditors of the restriction scheme provided for in s.150 of the 1990 Act. Section 150(4B) provides:

> "The court, in hearing an application for a declaration under subsection (1) from the Director, a liquidator or a receiver, may order that the directors against whom the declaration is made shall bear the costs of the application and any costs incurred by the applicant in investigating the matter."

In these cases the court held that s.150(4B) of the 1990 Act did not include the remuneration of the liquidator for the time spent investigating the matter and reporting thereon to the Director of Corporate Enforcement. On the basis of these decisions, if the liquidator cannot recoup his remuneration from the directors for the extra time spent investigating the restriction matters, the creditors of the company or indeed the liquidator himself will incur this extra cost. The cost provision has now been amended to include the remuneration of the applicant. Section 11(1) of the Investment Funds, Companies and Miscellaneous Provisions Act 2006 amends s.150(4B) of the 1990 Act to enable the court to order that the directors against whom a restriction declaration is made, shall bear not just the costs of the application but also the costs and expenses (including remuneration) of the applicant in investigating the matter and collecting evidence in relation to the application.

Costs of unsuccessful restriction application   In *Re Doherty Advertising Ltd (in Official Liquidation),* unreported, High Court, O'Leary J., July 14, 2006, the applicants sought an order for their costs in successfully defending an application for restriction. The court was satisfied that Ord.99, r.1 of the Rules of the Superior Courts applied (approving the decision of Finlay Geoghegan J. in *Visual Impact and Displays Ltd (in liquidation) v Murphy* [2003] 4 I.R. 451). Order 99, r.1 RSC provides as follows:

> "Subject to the provisions of the Acts and any other statutes relating to costs and except as otherwise provided by these Rules:
> (1) The costs of and incidental to every proceeding in the Superior Courts shall be at the discretion of those Courts respectively.
> (2) No party shall be entitled to recover any costs of or incidental to any proceeding from any other party to such proceeding except under an order or as provided by these Rules.
> (3) ...
> (4) The costs of every issue of fact or law raised upon a claim or counterclaim shall, unless otherwise ordered, follow the event."

O'Leary J. then considered these rules in the context of the s.150 application. He observed that the primary provision of the Order is that costs are at the "discretion of the court". Where the Order provides that the costs should "follow the event", this generally means that the "successful" party is awarded his/her costs against the "unsuccessful" party. Where, as is the situation in the majority of cases, there is a "losing" and a "winning" side, the rule is applied in a manner whereby the unsuccessful party bears the cost of the action. In the context of the present application, the question arose as to whether this general rule applied. In this regard O'Leary J. stated:

> "It is clear that the directors feel that they have succeeded as they have

proved to the satisfaction of the court that they had acted in an honest and responsible fashion. Therefore they submit they are justified in claiming that as they have won (i.e. were successful) they should as a matter of normal practice, get costs. But has anybody 'lost' (i.e. been unsuccessful)? Is there any reason why the applicant cannot also maintain that he was equally successful in the sense that he put before the court an application for the court's determination and the decision of the court (irrespective of the outcome) is the fulfilment by him of his legal duty. When the necessity to make the application, on the instructions of the Director of Corporate Enforcement, is backed by a criminal sanction is the application itself not the 'event' in question rather than the adjudication of the court?"

He went on to say:

"This possible interpretation is in the view of the Court supported by (but not dependant on) the description (amounting possibly to a qualification) of the issues falling with the rule within O.99, r.1 (4) as relating to a 'claim or counterclaim'. Can an application (pursuant to a legal duty) by a liquidator for adjudication by a court on the pre-liquidation (or post liquidation) behaviour of a director be properly called a claim or a counterclaim? The liquidator is merely the presenter of the application not a claimant or party with any interest in the outcome either for himself or on behalf of the creditors."

O'Leary J. compared the situation to that which arises in a criminal prosecution where an accused is under an obligation to use his/her funds to defend his case. O'Leary J. noted that in such circumstances the awarding of costs is very unusual and limited to cases where the prosecution has misbehaved in some way.

On the basis of the foregoing, O'Leary J. concluded that on the proper application of Ord.99, r.1. of the RSC, costs should not be normally awarded to a director who satisfies the court that he/she should not be the subject of a restriction order under s.150. Having observed that in exceptional circumstances the normal rule may not apply, O'Leary J. considered whether there was a reason to depart from the normal rule. While the court was critical of some of matters raised by the liquidators, it was also satisfied that the applicants' behaviour while directors, while not amounting to irresponsibility, represented a real failure on their behalf. Accordingly, the court refused to make an order as to costs.

LIQUIDATIONS

Winding up on the ground of substratum failure   Section 213(f) of the
Principal Act provides that a company may be wound up by the court if it is
of the opinion that it is *just and equitable* to do so. One such circumstance
where this ground has been invoked successfully is where the substratum of the
company has failed (*Re German Date Coffee Co* [1882] 20 Ch D 169). Given the
propensity for companies to include multiple business activities in their objects
clause, and the ability of a company to alter its objects clause, it is unusual to
see an application on the ground of substratum failure. Nonetheless, such was
the reason for an application to wind up the company in the recent case of *Re
Metafile Ltd*, unreported, High Court, Laffoy J., December 12, 2006.

Metafile Limited (the company) was incorporated to carry on, *inter alia*,
a manufacturing business. The memorandum further authorised the company
to carry on such a broad and diverse range of other businesses that Laffoy J.
suggested:

> "In order to illustrate how comprehensive that range was, it is only
> necessary to record that, while it did not include the business of
> candlestick maker, it did include the businesses of butchers and bakers
> in addition to hairdressers and glaziers."

A shareholders' agreement provided that the business of the company was to
be the manufacturing and production and sale of various steel products and
such other activities as would be agreed upon by the parties to the shareholders'
agreement and all other business the company is empowered to carry out by
virtue of its memorandum of association. The company never carried on the
type of manufacturing business envisaged in the primary objects set out in a
memorandum of association and in the shareholders' agreement. However, a
related company, Carrig, carried on the business of mechanical engineering
contractors. The shareholders and the proportion of shares held by them in
the company and in Carrig were identical. The company was the owner of
the factory premises and other assets. Carrig conducted its business from the
company's premises using these assets.

Tensions developed between the petitioner and other members which
ultimately resulted in the petitioner successfully petitioning the court to wind
up Carrig. The petitioner then sought to wind up the company by invoking
s.213(f) and (g). The court was satisfied on the basis of the petition and on the
hearing of the petition that the sole basis on which the petitioner was grounding
his entitlement to relief was that there had been a failure of substratum. The
petition was resisted by the company primarily on the basis that there had been
no failure of substratum.

Laffoy J., noting that she had not been referred to Irish authorities dealing
with the issue, referred to a number of English decisions on substratum failure.

In *Re Kitson & Co. Ltd* [1946] 1 All E.R. 435, Lord Greene M.R. rationalised the substratum ground as follows:

> "It must be remembered in these substratum cases that there is every difference between a company which on the true construction of its memorandum is formed for the paramount purpose of dealing with some specific subject-matter and a company which is formed with wider and more comprehensive objects. I would explain what I mean. With regard to a company which is formed to acquire and exploit a mine, and, accordingly, if the mine cannot be acquired or if the mine turns out to be no mine at all, the object of the company is frustrated, because the subject matter which the company was formed to exploit has ceased to exist. It is exactly the same way with a patent, as, in the well known *German Date Coffee* case. A patent is a defined subject matter, and, if the main object of a company is to acquire and work a patent and if it fails to acquire that patent, to compel the shareholders to remain bound together in order to work some other patent or make some unpatented article is to force them into a different adventure to that which they contracted to engage in together; but, when you come to subject matter of a totally different kind like the carrying on of a type of business, then so long as the company can carry on that type of business, it seems to me that *prima facie* at any rate, it is impossible to say that the substratum has gone."

The court also referred to the decision in *Re Perfectair Holdings Ltd* [1990] B.C.L.C. 423. Here, the company, which was the subject-matter of the petition, was a holding company which held property. A wholly-owned subsidiary of the company carried on business from that property. Following a dispute between the shareholders, it was agreed that one group of shareholders would purchase the shares of the subsidiary, the holding company would sell the property and the holding company would be put into liquidation. The share purchase was completed and the holding company sold its property and its only asset was the proceeds of this sale. Subsequently, one group of shareholders sought to have the holding company wound up. The petition was resisted on the basis that the company had a pending action for damages against the subsidiary and that the prosecution of this claim constituted a justification for keeping the holding company in existence. In this regard Scott J. observed that, on construction of the memorandum, if there are commercial activities that the company is capable of carrying out and some of the shareholders wish to pursue such activity, then prima facie the just and equitable ground will not have been made out. However, as it was clear to the court that the intention of the shareholders was that the company would never again engage in any commercial activity and that the sale of the principal asset and the prosecution of the claim were not for the purpose of any trading object but for the purpose of liquidation, Scott

J. allowed the petition and ordered that the company be wound up.

Laffoy J. distinguished *Perfectair* on the ground that, in the context of the present application, it was not envisaged by the members that the company would be wound up. Construing the objects clause, whether standing alone or read in conjunction with the shareholders' agreement, Laffoy J. observed:

> "[T]he paramount purpose for which the Company was incorporated was to carry on a manufacturing business of a general kind. The fact that the members carried on a mechanical engineering contractor's business through the medium of Carrig does not take from the fact that the Company can carry on the type of manufacturing business envisaged in its memorandum. That being the case, in my view, it cannot be said that the substratum has gone. Indeed the Shareholders' Agreement expressly provided for the Company carrying on such other activities as should be agreed between them from time to time and all other business which the Company was empowered to carry out under its memorandum of association."

On this basis Laffoy J. concluded that the petition should be dismissed.

Pre-liquidation legal advices   In *Re Compustore Ltd (in voluntary liquidation)*, unreported, High Court, Laffoy J., February 22, 2006, the company's solicitors made an application under s.280 of the Companies Act 1963 (the Principal Act) asking the court to determine whether fees and expenses due to the applicants in respect of advices given in relation to the procedures to be followed to place the company into creditors' voluntary liquidation were "expenses properly incurred in the winding up of the company" within the meaning of s.281 of the Act of 1963. Section 281 provides:

> "All costs, charges and expenses properly incurred in the winding up, including the remuneration of the liquidator, shall be payable out of the assets of the company in priority to all other claims."

The liquidator submitted that the words of s.281 were clear and unambiguous. The reference in s.281 to costs "incurred in the winding up" presupposed that the winding-up was in being when the costs were incurred. Accordingly, the fees and expenses in issue were not expenses properly incurred in the winding-up within the meaning of s.281.

Laffoy J. held that a proper construction of the words "costs, charges and expenses properly incurred in the winding up" referred to those costs incurred after the resolution to wind up the company had been passed (*Re AV Sorge & Company Ltd* [1986] B.C.L.C. 490 distinguished). In this regard, Laffoy J. was satisfied that "in enacting s.281, the legislature intended that there would be a rigid temporal cut-off at the time of the passing of the resolution to wind up voluntarily". Accordingly, she held that the fees and expenses due to the applicants for pre-resolution advice and services were not "expenses properly incurred in the winding up of the company" within the meaning of s.281 and the application was dismissed.

Removal of liquidator   *Re Doherty Advertising Ltd (in liquidation)*, unreported, High Court, McGovern J., June 16, 2006. In 2004 the court had approved a proposed settlement on terms whereby the applicant would enter into a binding agreement that he would pay, to the credit of the winding-up, a certain sum of money. This money represented an amount paid to him by the company from an account which contained funds that did not belong to the company and had since been repaid to its rightful owners. In the present application the applicant sought, *inter alia*, an order for the removal of the liquidator. Section 228(c) of the Companies Act 1963 (the Principal Act) provides that a liquidator appointed by the court "may resign or, on cause shown, be removed by the court". The liquidator contended that the applicant had no *locus standi* to apply to have the liquidator removed. The court was referred to the decision of the Privy Council in *Deloitte & Touche AG v Johnson* [2000] 1 B.C.L.C. 485 where it was held that the proper person to make an application would be a person interested in the outcome of the liquidation. The Privy Council further observed that a contributory who was not a creditor could not apply to have a liquidator removed. Furthermore, an applicant would have to show that he was a person qualified to make the application and that he was a proper person to make the application.

In the present application the court was satisfied that the applicant was not a person qualified to make the application for the removal of the liquidator. The court accepted that the applicant may become a creditor at some stage in the future, when he had repaid the monies alleged to have been improperly obtained by him. However, for present purposes the applicant was challenging the liquidator in a manner which put his interests adverse to those of the creditors in the liquidation. On this basis, the court held that the applicant was not a person entitled to bring this application. Irrespective of the *locus standi* issue, the court observed that the applicant had not shown sufficient cause for the removal of the liquidator as required by s.228(c) of the Principal Act. The burden of proof on the applicant had not been discharged as he had failed to show unfitness of the liquidator to act.

DIRECTORS' POWERS

Directors' discretion to refuse to register a transfer of shares   By virtue of model reg.3 of Table A, Pt II, the directors of a company may, without assigning any reason therefore, refuse to register a transfer of shares. Where a company adopts this model regulation, the directors' power in this regard is very broad but is subject to an important proviso, *viz.* such power must be exercised bona fide in the interests of the company (*Re Smith and Fawcett Ltd* [1942] 1 Ch. 304). Section 122 of the Companies Act 1963 (the Principal Act) provides, *inter alia*, that if the name of any person is, without sufficient cause, omitted from the register of members, the aggrieved person may apply to the court for rectification of the register.

In *Banfi Ltd v Moran*, unreported, High Court, Laffoy J., July 20, 2006, the plaintiff applied for an order under s.122 to have shares registered in its name. The company's articles of association provided, *inter alia*, that the directors could, in their absolute discretion and without assigning any reason therefore, decline to register any transfer of any share. A number of shares in the company—the issue of these proceedings—were held by a nominee company, ICT Nominees Limited (ICT). ICT controlled and managed by two of the defendants, but ICT acknowledged in a declaration of trust that it held the shares in trust for the plaintiff who was beneficial owner. By virtue of a stock transfer of May 2003, ICT transferred the shares to the plaintiff. Following the execution of the transfer, the plaintiff sought to be registered as a member of the company. Before deciding the matter, the board of the company requested various information and answers from the plaintiff. The plaintiff did not respond. This lack of response related to proceedings under s.205 of the Principal Act which were pending before the High Court. These proceedings were brought by the plaintiff against a number of persons, including the defendants. The s.205 proceedings were successfully struck out on the basis that, in the absence of registration, the plaintiff did not have *locus standi*.

Before the conclusion of the s.205 proceedings, the board of the company unanimously agreed to refuse to register the transfer from ICT to the plaintiff. The minutes of the meeting indicated that the decision was made after the board had considered various matters including the impact of the registration on all "interested parties". The first-named defendant submitted that the decision to refuse the registration was taken bona fide in the interest of the company. He also specifically claimed by affidavit that given the lack of response for the information sought by the board, it did not appear to be in the interests of the company to approve the transfer. Laffoy J. observed that this lack of response was not recorded or reflected in the minutes of the board meeting where the decision was made.

In the present application, the plaintiff made a number of serious allegations against the defendants, that their refusal was actuated by fraud and mala fides and was motivated by the desire to enable the defendants to continue diverting business to their other company. The defendants disputed the claims. The general principles considered by Laffoy J. to be relevant can be summarised as follows:

(a) The exercise of the directors' power to refuse to register must be gauged by reference to the company's articles of association subject to the proviso that the decision must be exercised bona fide and for the benefit of the company as a whole.

(b) Where the material part of the relevant regulation replicates verbatim model reg.3 of Table A, Pt II, as in this case, the directors have the most unfettered of powers (*Re Smith and Fawcett Ltd* [1942] 1 Ch. 304).

(c) While the Table A model permits directors to refuse registration without giving any reasons for their decision, there are exceptions to that rule (*Re Hafner* [1947] I.R. 426). The respondents had given reasons both in the minutes of the meeting and in the proceedings themselves.

(d) The court, in exercising its jurisdiction under s.122, may review the result of the exercise of their power by the directors where it is established that they have acted otherwise than bona fide and for the benefit of the company.

On the basis of these principles Laffoy J. concluded that the crucial matter was whether in exercising its discretion, the board acted bona fide in what it considered to be the interests of the company as a whole and the burden was on the plaintiff to prove that the board had not so acted. As the defendant directors had not stood on their right to remain silent and had given reasons for refusing to register the plaintiff, the court considered that their evidence could be assessed and inferences drawn from it. On this basis, Laffoy J. concluded that the reason for the refusal to register the plaintiff as a member was to ensure that the pending s.205 proceedings would be struck out and that the plaintiff would not be in a position to initiate any further proceedings under s.205. While the board minutes had recorded that regardless of the decision "the directors would act to protect the interests of all the beneficial owners including [the plaintiff]", Laffoy J. considered this, against the background of the s.205 proceedings, to be a "meaningless platitude". She suggested that the defendants:

> "could, if they wished, ensure that the interests of the plaintiff are protected by enabling it to pursue the remedies which are open to all shareholders since 1963, the remedies available under s.205, either through the trustee which is the registered owner of the shares, or by allowing it to become registered. They have effectively closed off one avenue by the decision to refuse to register the transfer to the plaintiff and they are in control of the other avenue. Having regard to the position they have adopted in relation to registering the transfer, and given their position as directors of ICT, the registered owner of the plaintiff's shares, it is reasonable to assume that ICT as a transferor member will not be pursuing the statutory remedies available under s.205 on behalf of the plaintiff. Through ICT, and in the face of their fiduciary duties, [the defendants] have maintained a stranglehold on the plaintiff's shareholding in the Company and have wholly stymied the plaintiff in pursuing the statutory redress which is available to all

> shareholders. I have no doubt, on the evidence, that in participating and, in effect, carrying the resolution to refuse to register the plaintiff as a member they were pursuing their own self interests, not the interests of the Company as a whole."

On this basis Laffoy J. directed the rectification of the register of the members of the company to provide for the registration thereon of the plaintiff as the owner of the shares.

RECEIVERS

Re Red Sail Frozen Foods Ltd and Related Companies, unreported, High Court, Laffoy J., October 20, 2006. The applicant was appointed receiver and manager of a number of related companies. The receiver sought the directions of the court pursuant to s.316 of the Companies Act 1963 (the Principal Act) on the following matters:

(1) whether the receiver should pay preferential claims in relation to contracts of employment where there existed a pre-receivership practice of making "under-the-counter" payments to employees;

(2) whether the receiver's commission within the meaning of the Conveyancing Act 1881 included his remuneration and the costs, charges and expenses incurred and whether the court should exercise its discretion in allowing the receiver a commission exceeding the statutory 5 per cent of the gross amount of the money received by him in realizing the security; and

(3) whether the bank could recover certain costs, charges and expenses incurred in connection with the receivership from the secured assets.

Under-the-counter payments The first matter concerned the question of whether it is lawful for the receiver to pay preferential claims made by the Minister for Enterprise, Trade and Employment to employees of some of the companies under s.285 of the Act of 1963, in circumstances where there was a pre-receivership practice of making "under-the-counter" payments to employees without deduction of PAYE and PRSI. Both the subrogated claims of the Minister/Department and the residual employees' claims are made in respect of payments where PAYE and PRSI deductions were properly operated. The receiver had notified the Department of the practice and it was agreed that the claims would exclude payments in respect of which the appropriate PAYE/PRSI deductions had not been made. When the claims were being made to the Department, the receiver made it clear that he was not making any determination as to whether the relevant employees had enforceable contracts of employment notwithstanding the cash payments and that he was not admitting any future subrogated claim by the Department in respect of any payment which it would make to the employees. Subsequently, the Department made payments to employees of certain companies in respect of arrears of wages, holiday pay, minimum notice and unfair dismissal. The Department claimed that it had a preferential claim in respect of the amounts which were so paid against certain companies. The receiver's concern was whether, having regard to the manner in which the employment contracts of employees were operated in practice, as a matter of law, the employees' contracts were enforceable and whether the Department's claim to be subrogated was valid.

The court was satisfied that it was lawful for the receiver to pay the unfair dismissals' and minimum notice components of the Department's claim and any residual claims of employees on the basis of existing statutory provisions. The matter of the arrears of wages and holiday pay were not subject to statutory intervention in the same manner and, accordingly, it was accepted that common law principles would apply. In this regard the court considered helpful the decision of the Court of Appeal in *Hall v Woolston Hall Leisure Ltd* [2001] 1 W.L.R. 225, where Peter Gibson L.J. identified two types of case where illegality renders a contract unenforceable from the outset: contracts entered into with the intention of committing an illegal act, and contracts expressly or implicitly prohibited by statute. Peter Gibson L.J. also identified a third category of case wherein a person may be prevented from enforcing the contract, *viz.* where a contract, lawful when made, is illegally performed and the party participated in that illegal performance. Laffoy J. considered that in relation to such cases, the requirement of "active participation" in addition to knowledge was necessary to render a contract of employment unenforceable. On the facts, the court observed that it was impossible to come to a conclusion as to the extent, if any, to which any employees actively participated in the illegal performance of their contracts in the context of determining whether the debt was enforceable. Accordingly, Laffoy J. considered that the Department's subrogated claim for holiday pay and arrears of wages should receive similar treatment as the other claims and directed payment by the receiver.

The remuneration of the receiver   With regard to the second matter, the receiver essentially sought directions on the following:

(a) his entitlement to remuneration and future remuneration under the security documents; and

(b) the restriction, if any, on his entitlement to remuneration on the basis of s.24(6) of the Conveyancing Act 1881 (the 1881 Act).

The relevant statutory provisions applicable to this matter were s.24(6) and s.24(8) of the 1881 Act. Section 24(6) covers the receiver's commission and provides that:

"The Receiver shall be entitled to retain out of any monies received by him, for his remuneration, and in satisfaction of all costs, charges, and expenses, incurred by him as receiver, a commission at such rate, not exceeding five per centum on the gross amount of all money received, as is specified in his appointment, and if no rate is so specified, then at the rate of five per centum on that gross amount, or at such higher rate as the court thinks fit to allow, on application made by him for that purpose."

Section 24(8) which is concerned with the order of priority of the application of the monies received by a receiver provides:

"The receiver shall apply all money received by him as follows (namely):
- (i) In discharge of all rents, taxes, rates, and outgoings whatever affecting the mortgaged property; and
- (ii) In keeping down all annual sums or other payments, and the interest on all principal sums, having priority to the mortgage in right whereof he is receiver; and
- (iii) In payment of his commission, and of the premiums on fire, life, or other insurances, if any, properly payable under the mortgage deed or under this Act, and the cost of executing necessary or proper repairs directed in writing by the mortgagee; and
- (iv) In payment of the interest accruing due in respect of any principal money due under the mortgage; and shall pay the residue of the money received by him to the person who, but for the possession of the Receiver, would have been entitled to receive the income of the mortgaged property, or who was otherwise entitled to that property."

The court then considered the provisions of the relevant debentures relating to the remuneration, costs, charges and expenses incurred by the receiver in so far as they may have varied the application of the relevant provisions of s.24. The debentures broadly provided that the provisions of s.24(6) and s.24(8) of the 1881 Act would apply as if they were contained in the debenture, save that all monies received by the receiver after providing for the matters specified in clauses (i) to (iii) of s.24(8) and for all statutorily preferred payments, and for all costs, charges and expenses of or incidental to the exercise of any of the powers of such receiver, shall be applied in or towards the satisfaction of the debentures. The court observed that the significant aspect of the debentures' provisions was that the costs, charges and expenses of the receivership were treated separately from the receiver's "commission", as provided for in s.24(8)(iii). Construing the incorporation of the provisions of s.24(6) and s.24(8) into the debentures to give consistency *inter se* to the incorporated provisions, the court was satisfied that the commission referred to in s.24(6) and s.24(8)(iii) excluded the receiver's costs, charges and expenses which were expressly provided for in the incorporation of subs.(8) subject to variation (*Marshall v Cottingham* [1982] Ch. 82 approved).

As to the matter of the *quantum*, the court was satisfied that s.24(6), as incorporated in the debenture, was not varied by the provisions of the debenture. As the receiver had incurred substantial trading expenses in addition to the normal expenses of the receivership, a strict application of the 5 per cent rule would have resulted in a substantial shortfall for the receiver. Accordingly, the receiver requested that the court exercise its discretion under s.24(6) and agree to a higher amount, which was circa 8.5 per cent of the amounts received by him under the debentures. The court referred to the decision of Geoghegan J. in *In the Matter of City Car Sales Ltd*, unreported, High Court, October 5, 1994, where he exercised his discretion under s.24(6) of the 1881 Act and approved an amount over the 5 per cent where the receiver had conducted the receivership at all times bona fide. Laffoy J. also considered the statements of principle in the judgment of Ferris J. in the English High Court in *Mirror Group Newspapers plc v Maxwell* [1998] B.C.L.C. 638, where he observed that receivers, as with all office-holders, are fiduciaries whose fundamental obligation is a duty to account, both for the way in which they exercise their powers and for the property with which they deal. With regard to the remuneration of office-holders, Ferris J. observed:

> "Certain more particular consequences follow from what I have said so far. First, office holders must expect to give full particulars in order to justify the amount of any claim for remuneration. If they seek to be remunerated upon, or partly upon, the basis of time spent in the performance of their duties they must do significantly more than list the total number of hours spent by them or other fee-earning members of their staff and multiply this total by a sum claimed to be the charging rate of the individual whose time was spent. They must explain the nature of each main task undertaken, the considerations which led them to embark upon that task and, if the task proved more difficult or expensive to perform than at first expected, to persevere in it. The time spent needs to be linked to this explanation, so that it can be seen what time was devoted to each task. The amount of detail which needs to be provided will, however, be proportionate to the case."

Ferris J. further observed:

> "In my judgment it is vital to recognise three things in this field. First, time spent represents a measure not of the value of the service rendered but of the cost of rendering it. Remuneration should be fixed, so as to reward value, not so as to indemnify against cost. Second, time spent

is only one of a number of relevant factors, the others being, as I have said, those which find expression in r.2.47 and similar rules. The giving of proper weight to these factors is an essential part of the process of assessing the value, as distinct from the cost, of what has been done. Third, it follows from the first two points that, as the task is to assess value rather than cost, the tribunal which fixes remuneration needs to be supplied with full information on all the factors which I have mentioned."

In the present application, the companies had contended that the information provided by the receiver fell short of allowing any analysis of either the remuneration claimed or the legal costs in respect of which he seeks reimbursement. The receiver submitted that his report outlined the history of the receivership; the steps he took to get in the assets; his trading at three locations for approximately four months; his dealing with the employees of the companies, including matters covered by the first issue; dealing with title and planning issues in relation to the fixed assets; disposing of the fixed assets; dealing with stock in trade, which was disposed of over an eight-month period; dealing with trade debts and trade creditors; and miscellaneous other matters, including litigation. The companies argued that the receiver ought to have, but did not, explain the nature of each of the main tasks undertaken, the considerations which led him to embark on those tasks, and whether and how the tasks proved more expensive or difficult. The court did not accept such criticisms but did accept that the receiver had failed to link the time spent to the tasks he was required to perform in the receivership. The receiver submitted that in furnishing his report he had followed the practice in court liquidations, by giving an overview of the operational activity of the receiver. Furthermore, no objection had been advanced as to the manner in which the receiver had conducted the receivership. The receiver also submitted that as there was no controversy in this case as to the manner in which the receivership was conducted, the court should follow the decision of Geoghegan J., which, it was submitted, was to sanction remuneration that was reasonable and calculated in the normal way.

The court observed that there was no mechanism in Ireland whereby the court could refer the measurement of remuneration and costs, charges and expenses (other than legal costs) in respect of which the receiver is entitled to a venue or forum more equipped to deal with the issue than the court. As the receiver had conducted the receivership in a proper and bona fide manner and the basis on which the remuneration was claimed conformed with normal accountancy practice, the court was satisfied that it would allow a rate higher than 5 per cent which would allow him the remuneration claimed.

Cost recovery by debenture-holder The third matter on which the receiver sought directions related to whether the debenture-holding bank was entitled to recover from the receiver, out of the assets of the company, the legal costs and expenses incurred by the bank in connection with the appointment of the receiver, litigation taken against the bank and receiver by the companies and the receivership in general.

The court re-affirmed the principle whereby a mortgagee is entitled to add to the secured debt his costs, charges and expenses properly incurred, but observed that there are exceptions to this principle. First, costs and expenses incurred where there is no express contractual justification, such as defending a third party challenge to the rights of the mortgagee, are not payable (citing with approval *Gomba Holdings Ltd v Minories Finance* [1993] Ch. 171; *Parker-Tweedale v Dunbar Bank plc (No.2)* [1991] Ch. 26 and *Re Baldwin's Estate* [1900] 1 I.R. 15). However, the court was satisfied that the litigation in question could not be characterised as a third-party challenge, so as to come within the exception. Secondly, costs, charges and expenses which have not been "properly incurred" will not be added to the liabilities unless express contractual provisions provide otherwise. Thirdly, the entitlement of a mortgagee to receive its costs "properly incurred" requires the costs to be taxed on a party and party basis unless the express terms of the debenture could justify a departure from that rule. As the debentures did not contain an express provision in relation to legal costs or expenses incurred by the bank as distinct from the receiver, the court examined each category of costs and expenses sought by the bank in order to decide upon the bank's entitlement to reimbursement.

In the matter of the litigation, the bank had agreed to a settlement of €100,000 as a contribution to the plaintiffs' costs. The court drew a distinction between the costs in relation to the proceedings, both the €100,000 contribution to the plaintiffs' costs and the bank's own costs, on the one hand, and the other costs claimed by the bank, on the other hand. In relation to the costs of the proceedings, the court was satisfied that the clear intent of the settlement was to remove all challenges to the bank's security and the validity of the appointment of the receiver and to bring the proceedings to a final conclusion. Furthermore, the court stated that it was implicit in the settlement that the intention of the parties was to terminate all liability of each party to the other party arising out of the proceedings, including liability for costs. In particular, it was an implied term that the plaintiffs would have no liability to the defendants for costs and that the defendants would have no further liability to the plaintiffs for costs, beyond the contribution of €100,000. Accordingly, as the effect of this contractual compromise was to render inapplicable any entitlement the bank would have had to costs, the court concluded that the bank had no entitlement to recoup from the assets of the companies, the sum of €100,000 it paid under the settlement or to its own costs of the proceedings.

In relation to the bank's claim to be entitled to be paid the legal costs and expenses incurred in connection with the appointment of the receiver, the court was satisfied that those costs and expenses were reasonably and properly incurred by the bank in relation to the enforcement and preservation of its security and were payable out of the secured assets.

With respect to the costs relating to any legal advice or assistance required in connection with the conduct of the receivership and the exercise of the receiver's powers, the court held that these costs must be to the account of the receiver, under the provisions of the debentures. The court observed that to decide otherwise would be to charge the assets of the companies twice for the cost of legal services which could only properly be incurred once.

INSOLVENCY REGULATION 1346/2000

On May 2, 2006 the European Court of Justice (ECJ) delivered its decision on *Eurofood IFSC Ltd* (see *Annual Review of Irish Law 2004*). The ECJ upheld the decision of the High Court that Eurofood's centre of main interest was Ireland. The ECJ confirmed that the appointment of the provisional liquidator on January 27, 2004 opened main insolvency proceedings under Art.16 of the Insolvency Regulation.

TAKEOVERS

The European Communities (Takeover Bids (Directive 2004/25/EC) Regulations came into effect on May 20, 2006, the due date for transposition of Directive 2004/25/EC on Takeover Bids. The Directive is one of the measures adopted under the EU Financial Services Action Plan (the FSAP) and provides for harmonised rules for the conduct of takeovers in the EU and equal protection for minority shareholders. The implementation of the Directive took almost 14 years to complete—the last attempt collapsed after a deadlock vote in the European Parliament in 2001. The Directive in its final form is a somewhat diluted version of the Commission's original proposals, considered necessary to garner sufficient support for its implementation. The Directive does not, therefore, result in a uniform set of takeover rules, rather it sets minimum standards and Member States may impose their own additional rules which may be more stringent than those set by the Directive. The rules for the supervision of takeovers in Ireland are provided for in the Takeover Panel Act 1997 and the Takeover Rules made pursuant to this Act. The 2006 Regulations, together with the necessary amendments to the Takeover Rules, apply those provisions of the Directive which are not already part of Ireland's existing regime. The key provisions of the Directive relate to the following:

1. Application By virtue of Art.1, the Directive applies to takeover bids for securities admitted to trading on a regulated market other than securities issued by collective investment undertakings, apart from the closed-end type or securities issued by a Central Bank of a Member State (Reg.3(1)).

2. The competent authority   Member States are obliged to designate the authority or authorities competent to supervise bids. Regulation 5 designates the Irish Takeover Panel (the panel) as the competent authority. In terms of supervision, the authority competent to supervise a bid is that of the Member State in which the offeree company has its registered office if that company's securities are admitted to trading on a regulated market in that Member State. In all other cases (*e.g.* where securities are not admitted or are admitted to trading on more than one regulated market), the Directive lays down rules for deciding the competent supervisory authority for a particular takeover which must, in certain cases, share responsibility with the competent authority of the Member State where the company has its registered office. In such a situation, the issue will arise as to which set of takeover rules will apply. The Directive sets out, in very general terms, which matters will be determined by the takeover rules of the Member State where the company has its registered office (matters relating to employees, company law matters, defence mechanisms permitted) and matters to be determined by the Member States where the company is listed (consideration and procedural rules). However, there is no method for resolving disputes as to any jurisdictional conflicts should they arise.

Regulation 6 sets out the jurisdiction of the Panel in accordance with the provisions of the Directive. Regulation 9 requires the Panel to co-operate with the relevant authorities in other Member States wherever necessary for the application of measures adapted in those states to implement the Directive. Regulation 10 confers on the Panel the additional powers to ensure it can carry out its functions under the Regulations.

3. Defensive measures   In relation to defensive mechanisms adopted by companies in respect of a hostile takeover bid, the Directive establishes two rules—the board neutrality rule (Art.9) and the breakthrough rule (Art.11).

The board neutrality rule (Art.9) provides that any defensive measures taken by the board of the target company, after a bid has commenced, must be authorised in advance by the general meeting of shareholders. Member States must adopt rules requiring the general meeting to be convened at short notice. Where decisions are made prior to a bid but have not been fully implemented, the general meeting must also approve or confirm any such decisions where they are not part of the normal course of the company's business and where the implementation of the decision might result in the frustration of the bid. Regulation 15 gives effect to this rule.

The breakthrough rule applies at two different stages. The first stage is where a bid is made public. Once this occurs, any restrictions on transfer of shares (whether imposed by the articles of association or shareholders' agreements) are unenforceable against the offeror during the period allowed for acceptance of the bid. Furthermore, restrictions on voting rights (such as multiple voting shares) will not have effect in the general meeting of the shareholders which is voting on any defensive mechanisms. The second stage involves the offeror obtaining the 75 per cent threshold of voting capital. Once this occurs, the offeror has the right to call a general meeting and vote in accordance with the normal provisions of company law in order to facilitate changes in the target company (*e.g.* alteration of the articles). The offeror cannot be hindered by any voting restrictions in place, any special rights attaching to shares in relation to appointment and removal of directors or multiple voting rights. Regulations 18 and 19 give effect to the break-through rules, where they are applicable.

One of the controversial aspects of the Directive is Art.12, which permits Member States to opt out from the application of Arts 9 and 11, provided that companies registered in that Member State are permitted to opt in. Where Member States opt out, this will allow their companies to take defensive actions to frustrate bids and/or the break-through provisions which essentially protect the offeror will not apply. This provision is likely to give rise to increased protectionism across the Member States, particularly where certain companies are regarded as central to a Member State's national interests. The optional nature of Arts 9 and 11 was considered a necessary compromise to achieve the European Parliament's approval, but the Commission remains vehemently opposed to this compromise position and is determined that when the Directive is reviewed after 2011, the optional elements will be removed.

As expected, Ireland has opted out of the "breakthrough provisions" of Art.11. However, as required by the Directive, Pt 3 of the Regulations provides that companies with voting shares may, by special resolution, resolve to opt in, provided certain conditions are satisfied. Those conditions are broadly that the company has securities admitted to trading on a regulated market; the articles of association of the company do not contain restrictions incompatible with Art.11; no securities conferring special rights in the company are held by a Minister of the Government; and no special rights in the company are exercisable by a Minister of the Government by or under any enactment. Once a company opts in they are prohibited from those actions which infringe Art.11, as described above (Regs 18 and 19).

A company may revoke an opting-in resolution by a further special resolution (an "opting-out resolution"). If a company passes an opting-in resolution or an opting-out resolution, notification of that fact shall be given to the Irish Takeover Panel and any other competent authority where the company has been, or has requested to be, admitted to trading on a regulated market (Reg.20).

In order to ensure a level playing field, the Directive provides for a reciprocity arrangement. Accordingly, where a company is subject to the rules on defensive measures and that company becomes the target of an offer, the Member State where the company has its registered office may exempt the offeree company from the application of those rules if the offeror company does not apply Arts 9 and/or 11. Regulation 10 provides that the Panel is empowered, by virtue of this Regulation, to specify, in rules, the circumstances in which the Panel is enabled to grant derogations from, or waive, the rules.

4. Transparency   Article 10 of the Directive requires all companies which have securities admitted to trading on a regulated market to disclose in the annual report their capital and control structures. Regulation 21 gives effect to the above requirements. Accordingly, the report of the directors under s.158 of the Principal Act must include, in addition to the existing statutory requirements, details of:

(a) the different classes of securities including those not listed for trade;

(b) significant direct and indirect shareholdings;

(c) existing restrictions on the transfer of securities;

(d) special control rights;

(e) any restrictions on voting rights;

(f) any rules which the company has in force concerning the appointment and replacement of directors of the company, or the amendment of the company's articles of association;

(g) the powers of the company's directors, including in particular any powers in relation to the issuing or buying back by the company of its shares;

(h) any significant agreements to which the company is a party that take effect, alter or terminate upon a change of control of the company following a bid, and the effects of any such agreements;

(i) any agreements between the company and its directors or employees providing for compensation for loss of office or employment (whether through resignation, purported redundancy or otherwise) that occurs because of a bid;

(j) any rules which the company has in force concerning the appointment and replacement of directors of the company.

5. Equivalent treatment of shareholders   The Directive provides that all target shareholders of the same class must be afforded equivalent treatment (Art.3). The use of the word "equivalent" rather than "equal" treatment would appear to leave some flexibility to the offeror to differentiate between shareholders. However, given the purposive approach of the Directive, provisions contained there relating to mandatory bids, pricing and the Irish Takeover Rules, it is unlikely that offerors will have much flexibility to discriminate.

6. Mandatory bid rule   The mandatory bid rule (Art.5) ensures that the acquirer shall make an offer at an equitable price to all holders of securities for all their holdings, once a certain percentage of the voting rights in the target company is obtained which gives him control of the company. A further criticism of the Directive is that the percentage threshold is left to be determined by the Member States and the percentage of voting rights which confer control is to be determined by the takeover rules of that Member State. Such a lack of uniformity will detract from the idea of a level playing field throughout Europe. In Ireland, the Takeover Rules prescribed by the Panel make detailed provision in this regard and, in general terms, a mandatory bid will be required where the offeror has acquired 30 per cent of the controlling securities of the target company.

7. Partial offers in voluntary bids   The Directive does not prohibit partial offers in voluntary bids. A bidder can make an offer for less than 100 per cent of the voting rights of the target company provided that it does not exceed the threshold determined by each Member State which would trigger the application of the mandatory bid rule. That does not mean, however, that Member States are not free to prohibit partial offers even in cases of voluntary bids. This is the case in Ireland where the Takeover Rules prohibit any partial offers except with the consent of the Takeover Panel and subject to certain conditions.

8. Equitable price   In cases where a mandatory bid is required, the Directive requires that the bid must be made at an equitable price. This is the highest price paid for the same securities by the offeror, over a period determined by the Member States. Such a period, however, cannot be less than six months or more than 12 months prior to the launch of the bid. Regulation 13 empowers the Panel to specify rules to enable the Panel to adjust the equitable price by reference to specified criteria which must be substantiated and published. Under the existing Takeover Rules the longer period of 12 months is specified as the relevant period.

   Furthermore, the bidder must also match the highest price paid for any securities acquired after the launch of the bid and before it lapses, if it is higher than the initial offer. Member States are free to allow deviations from the highest price rule as long as the price is adjusted by the competent regulatory authorities, for special reasons, and provided that the price adjustment does not defeat the purpose of the mandatory bid rule. The Takeover Rules make provision in this regard (r.9.4).

9. Squeeze out–sell out rights   Once a bidder has acquired a certain portion of the target companies' securities as a result of a takeover bid, it can "squeeze out" the remaining by compelling them to sell their securities at a *fair* price. Member States can set the threshold for triggering the squeeze-out right by reference to capital (between 90 and 95 per cent) or, alternatively, by reference to the number of acceptances in the offer (90 per cent). The offeror must exercise the "squeeze out" right within a period of three months after the end of the bid and is required to offer a fair price and the same form of consideration offered in the bid, or cash. Following a mandatory bid, the consideration offered in the bid is presumed to be fair, while in voluntary bids the consideration offered in the bid is presumed to be fair where the offeror has acquired, through acceptance of the bid, securities representing not less than 90 per cent of the capital carrying voting rights comprised in the bid. By virtue of Reg.23, Ireland has adopted the 90 per-cent threshold for a squeeze-out. Accordingly, s.204 of the Principal Act (which sets the takeover threshold at 80 per cent) is amended in so far as a takeover bid is made for a company which is subject to these Regulations. Conversely, minority shareholders will have the right to compel an offeror who has obtained 90 per cent or more of the capital to purchase their securities at a fair price (Reg.24).

10. Consideration of offer   The Directive protects shareholders of the target company from being forced to accept an offer that is not considered to be optimal with regard to severe time pressure and/or inadequate or misleading information by the following:

(a) Holders of securities of an offeree company must be afforded sufficient time to enable them to reach a properly informed decision on the bid. Article 7 of the Directive provides that the minimum period for which an offer must remain open to acceptances can be no less than two weeks and no more than 10 weeks from the date of publication of the offer document. In Ireland the minimum period is 21 days, and after 60 days an offer that remains conditional as to acceptances will lapse unless the Panel decides otherwise.

(b) Increased transparency and disclosure in relation to the announced bid, including prior communication of the offer document to the Member State's supervisory authority before the offer document is made public; notification to the employees' representatives once the bid is made public; prompt dissemination of information in all Member States that the securities of the target company are listed so as to ensure market transparency and integrity for all securities of the offeree company; and a minimum content of the offer document, to enable the holders of securities to reach a properly informed decision on the bid. The Takeover Rules provide extensive requirements relating to these matters.

11. Sanctions   Article 17 requires that the Member States will determine the appropriate sanctions to be applied in the event of infringement. While the Directive requires that these sanctions are "effective, proportionate and dissuasive", there will obviously be a lack of uniformity in application across the EU.

12. Review   As there are a number of controversial aspects of the Directive, particularly in relation to the optional provisions, the lack of uniformity in relation to mandatory bid requirements and the perceived difficulties in relation to shared supervisory rules, the Directive provides that the Commission must review the Directive after 2011 and, where necessary, propose amendments.

COMPANIES LEGISLATION

Investment Funds, Companies and Miscellaneous Provisions Act 2006 (No. 41 of 2005) The Investment Funds, Companies and Miscellaneous Provisions Act 2006 ('the 2006 Act') was signed into law on December 24, 2006. Section 1(2) of the 2006 Act provides that Pts 2 and 3, and the Companies Acts 1963–2005, may be cited together as the Companies Acts 1963 to 2006 and shall be construed together as one.

PART 1

Sections 1–5 provide for preliminary matters including, *inter alia*, commencement, interpretation, the making of orders and regulations.

PART 2

Sections 6–18 provide for a number of amendments to the Companies Acts. The key provisions are as follows:

Statutory declarations Section 6 provides for the amendment of existing procedures regarding statutory declaration made in pursuance of or for the purposes of the Companies Acts. Statutory declarations which are made outside the State before a person entitled to practice as a solicitor in Ireland or by a person authorised to administer oaths in that state will be valid. Provisions regarding the authentication of such persons under international Conventions to which Ireland is a signatory must be complied with.

Private companies By virtue of s.7 the meaning of a private company under s.33(1) of the Companies Act 1963 has been amended. The amendment broadly provides for an increase in the maximum membership from 50 to 99 members (excluding employees and ex-employees), and that certain offers of debentures and/or shares including, *inter alia*, offers to qualified investors or to fewer than 100 persons, will not constitute an invitation or offer to the public which is prohibited by s.33(1)(c) of the Companies Act 1963. These changes will enhance Ireland's competitive position as a location for structuring asset securitisation transactions through Special Purpose Vehicles (SPVs). Heretofore, issuers used public limited companies to form SPVs as a means of offering debt or other asset-backed securities to investors. SPVs can now be formed using private companies and, provided the offer of securities complies with the conditions imposed by s.33, it will not constitute an offer to the public. This will result in time- and cost-efficiencies and eliminate the capital requirements associated with forming public companies.

Audit threshold exemptions   Sections 9–10 provide for amendments to the existing audit threshold exemptions. The audit exemption thresholds for private companies, as provided for in the Companies (Amendment) (No.2) Act 1999, have been increased to allow for the maximum limit permitted by the EU, which is €7.3 million for turnover (previously €1,500,000) and €3.65 million for balance sheet (previously £1,500,000).

Restriction and disqualification   The costs provisions of the Companies Act 1990 in relation to restriction and disqualification applications have been amended by s.11 to enable applicants for declarations of restriction and disqualification to recover not only the costs of the applications, but also the costs and expenses (including remuneration) in investigating the matters which form are the subject of the application and collecting evidence in respect of those matters (see RESTRICTION OF DIRECTORS, above).

Dematerialisation   Section 12 amends s.239 of the Companies Act 1990 to allow the Minister to provide by regulation for the mandatory dematerialisation of securities of public companies trading on a regulated market, a market other than a regulated market (*e.g.* the IEX) and other specified public companies. The process of dematerialisation is considered necessary to provide a more efficient and harmonised processing of securities transactions and to ensure the Irish market remains internationally competitive.

Liability of guarantors in relation to prospectuses   Section 13 amends s.43 of the Investment Funds, Companies and Miscellaneous Provisions Act 2005 (the 2005 Act) to restrict the liability of guarantors where a prospectus is being issued in respect of non-equity securities. The liability of guarantors will now only apply in respect of statements included in, or information omitted from, the prospectus, that relates to the guarantor or the guarantee given by the guarantor. This amendment addresses the potential liability of credit insurers for untrue statements in or omissions from a prospectus under the 2005 Prospectus Rules (see *Annual Review of Irish Law 2005*). The consequences of this potential liability had an impact on the asset securitisation industry, because SPVs which use a credit insurer to enhance the attraction of a particular issue were locating in other jurisdictions.

Consent of experts in relation to prospectuses   Section 14 amends s.45 of the 2005 Act by clarifying matters relating to the requirement to obtain the consent of experts to the inclusion in a prospectus of reports prepared by such experts. Under the new regime, the expert's consent is only required in relation to the inclusion of a statement or information attributed to that expert, which is required to be included in a prospectus under EU prospectus law. Therefore, where historical financial information is being used in the prospectus, and such information has been audited, the consent of the auditor will not be required.

PART 3

Transparency requirement   Sections 19–24 of Pt 3 of the Investment Funds, Companies and Miscellaneous Provisions Act contain provisions designed to facilitate the transposition of the Transparency (Regulated Markets) Directive (Directive 2004/109/EC). The Directive was introduced to enhance transparency in EU capital markets by establishing rules relating to periodic financial reports, other reporting obligations and the disclosure of major shareholdings in respect of issuers whose securities are admitted to trading on a regulated market in the EU. Section 20 gives the Minister power to make regulations to give effect to the Transparency Directive and any other supplemental measures. It is expected that these Regulations will be introduced early in 2008.

PART 4

Part 4 contains, *inter alia*, a number of miscellaneous amendments to the Takeover Panel Act 1997. These amendments are necessary to enable the Irish Takeover Panel to make provision in their rules to give effect to EU law in this area (see TAKEOVERS, above). The Schedule to the Irish Takeover Panel Act 1997 is also replaced in order to align the General Principles with those of the Takeover Bids Directive as transposed into Irish law by the Takeover Regulations discussed above. However, the Substantial Acquisition of Securities General Principles will be retained. The General Principles applicable to the conduct of takeovers are now as follows:

1.   All holders of the securities of an offeree of the same class must be afforded equivalent treatment; moreover, if a person acquires control of a company, the other holders of securities must be protected.

2.   The holders of the securities of an offeree must have sufficient time and information to enable them to reach a properly informed decision on the bid; where it advises the holders of securities, the board of the offeree must give its views on the effects of implementation of the offer on employment, conditions of employment and the locations of the company's places of business.

3. The board of an offeree must act in the interests of the company as a whole and must not deny the holders of securities the opportunity to decide on the merits of the offer.

4. False markets must not be created in the securities of the offeree, of the offeror or of any other company concerned by the offer in such a way that the rise or fall of the prices of the securities becomes artificial and the normal functioning of the markets is distorted.

5. An offeror must announce an offer only after ensuring that he or she can fulfil, in full, any cash consideration, if such is offered, and after taking all reasonable measures to secure the implementation of any other type of consideration.

6. An offeree must not be hindered in the conduct of its affairs for longer than is reasonable by an offer for its securities.

7. A substantial acquisition of securities (whether such acquisition is to be effected by one transaction or a series of transactions) shall take place only at an acceptable speed and shall be subject to adequate and timely disclosure.

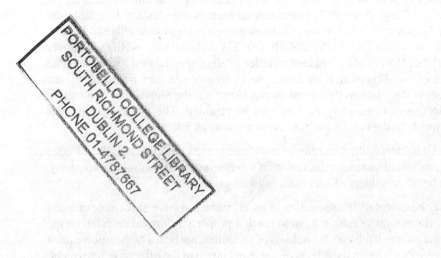

Conflicts of Law

ADOPTION

In *Attorney General v Dowse* [2007] 1 I.L.R.M. 81, a case which involved much public controversy, MacMenamin J., exercising powers under s.7(1)(A) and (B) of the Adoption Act 1991, as inserted by the Adoption Act 1998, made wide-ranging orders in relation to the guardianship, maintenance and succession rights of an Indonesian child adopted by an Irish citizen and his Azeri wife who were both ordinarily resident in Indonesia at the time of the adoption in 2001. The adoption had been entered in the Register of Foreign Adoptions. Later, the adoptive parents, claiming that bonding had not occurred, had placed the child in a private orphanage in Indonesia. When this fact became known to the Adoption Board, very strenuous efforts were made by the Irish authorities to deal effectively with the situation in the child's interest. The child finished up back with his natural mother. The Attorney General initiated proceedings in Ireland on behalf of the child. The adoptive parents sought an order under s.7(1)(B), seeking the cancellation of the entry of the adoption of the child in the Register of Foreign Adoptions.

MacMenamin J. held that the provisions of Arts 41 and 42 of the Constitution applied. The adoptive parents had failed in their duty to the child. Cancellation came at a price—a lump sum maintenance payment of €20,000 and periodical payments of maintenance throughout the child's minority followed by a further substantial lump sum payment; the child's succession rights were also preserved.

The case raises very significant issues of principle and policy. We will postpone detailed consideration of these until the *Annual Review 2007*, when we will analyse the Law Reform Commission's *Consultation Paper on Aspects of Intercountry Adoption Law* (LR CP 43–2007). Here we need merely observe that the dearth of private international law rules in Ireland and many other common law jurisdictions on the revocation of adoption orders is largely attributable to the previous relative unfamiliarity of these systems with the phenomenon of *adoptio minus plena*, which contains the possibility of revocation. The rapid globalisation of child adoption has transformed the position. This also requires further reflection on the international remit of protection of children under the Irish Constitution. What formerly may have seemed to many to be a naive universalism in the judicial interpretation of the range of protection afforded by the Constitution is beginning to look prophetic, anticipating the interrelationship of international human rights norms and private international law.

CHILD ABDUCTION

1. Hague Convention

Rights of custody   Under Art.3 of the Convention, for a removal or retention of a child to be wrongful it is necessary to show that, at the time of the removal or retention, the custody rights breached "were actually exercised … or would have been so exercised but for the removal or retention".

In *Re K McD, E McD and J McD (minors); VG v P McD* [2006] I.E.H.C. 69, the parties were unmarried parents of three children. Their relationship had been in serious difficulties for some time. The father was Irish; the mother "had lived most of her life in England". At one point the father was living in Ireland and the mother was living in England with the children. She was having difficulty coping with them and she brought them to Ireland without any prior agreement with the father as to the period they were to be left in his care. She did not stay with the children then but returned to the father's house about a week later and sought to take the children back to England. The father refused.

Finlay Geoghegan J. held that, immediately prior to the father's retention of the children, the mother had been exercising her rights of custody:

> "The fact that she may have had difficulty in coping with the children and partly, at least, for that reason brought them to Ireland and placed them in the care of their father for approximately one week does not mean that she should be considered for the purposes of Article 3 of the Hague Convention not to be in fact exercising her rights of custody. Also, the alleged wrongful retention only occurred when the mother turned up at the father's house in Ireland, sought to take the children back to England and was refused. In so turning up and requesting the children she was exercising her rights of custody."

The holding in this case is surely correct. One should, however, hesitate about ascribing to every demand for return of a child the quality of the exercise of rights of custody. Clearly there can be cases where there is no such necessary connection.

In *Re LD and CAD (Children); TD v A-MP and JR* [2006] I.E.H.C. 68, the applicant, the father of two children who had been taken by the respondent, their mother, from Michigan to Ireland, sought to establish that he had rights of custody for the purposes of Art.3. He was not married to the mother. The children had lived with him for almost a year before they were taken to Ireland, though they spent some time with his maternal grandmother. There was no question that the children had been removed without his consent; the only issue, therefore, concerned his legal standing under Art.3.

It will be recalled that the Supreme Court had to deal with a somewhat similar question in *HI v MG (Child Abduction: Wrongful Removal)* [2000] I.R. 110, analysed in the *Annual Review of Irish Law 1999*, pp. 57–60. The court held that "rights of custody" did not extend to "inchoate" rights which a court in the state of habitual residence was likely to uphold but which had not yet formally been recognised or granted by law. This approach has the effect of excluding many unmarried fathers from the entitlement to take proceedings under the Hague Convention. In *HI*, the father had actually married the mother, with whom he lived, in a religious ceremony but the marriage was not recognised under New York law. In the instant case there was disputed expert evidence as to the father's legal rights under Michigan law. Finlay Geoghegan J. did not blame the experts for this as they had been "attempting to answer different questions put to them and which in part were based upon the differing facts put forward by the parties". She adjourned the proceedings to obtain further clarification, based on a draft of issues regarding Michigan law.

Finlay Geoghegan J. declined the request from counsel for the father that he be permitted to obtain through the Central Authority a further affidavit of laws pursuant to Art.8 of the Convention. Article 8(f) provides that an application for the return of a child may be accompanied or supplemented by:

"(f) a certificate or an affidavit emanating from a Central Authority, or other competent authority of the State of the child's habitual residence, or from a qualified person, concerning the relevant law of that State."

In Finlay Geoghegan J.'s view, fair procedures might require that the court permit the mother to obtain an affidavit of laws on the same issues. This might well result in a further dispute between US deponents as to the relevant law of Michigan which would not easily be resolved.

Nor did Art.15 offer a solution. It provides that:

"The judicial or administrative authorities of a Contracting State may, prior to the making of an order for the return of the child, request that the applicant obtain from the authorities of the State of the habitual residence of the child a decision or other determination that the removal or retention was wrongful within the meaning of Article 3 of the Convention, where such a decision or determination may be obtained in that State. The Central Authorities of the Contracting States shall so far as practicable assist applicants to obtain such a decision or determination."

A decision by the Michigan courts that the removal had been wrongful would not be determinative of the proceedings in Ireland:

"This Court must decide in accordance with the law of this jurisdiction whether the removal was wrongful. Accordingly, whilst such a decision may well be of assistance to this Court, it would only potentially help this Court resolve all the issues in this application if, in the course of the decision, the Court was able to address and determine the relevant issues of law of the State of Michigan which would permit this Court then to determine whether either the father or the courts of Michigan had a right of custody within the meaning of the Convention in relation to the children…".

The scope of "rights of custody" under Art.3 of the Convention is analysed incisively by Emer Long in "The Hague Convention and Irish Law: Rights of Custody or Rights of Access" [2007] Ir. J. of Fam. L. 12.

Consent   In *SR v MMR,* Supreme Court, February 16, 2006, affirming, with variations, High Court, January 25, 2006, the parameters of the defence of consent under Art.3 were probed. The case concerned the removal to Ireland by the mother of two children from Massachusetts. The father was a US citizen; the mother, originally from Ireland, had spent the previous 12 years in America. The parties had married in 1997. In December 2004 the mother told the father that her parents had given her a present of air tickets for herself and her children. In January 2005 she and the children flew to Ireland, having been driven by the father to the airport. She remained in Ireland thereafter with the children. The father, in seeking their return, contended that the mother had represented to him that she was going to Ireland on a short vacation; the mother denied this and claimed that he had consented to a stay of indefinite duration.

Finlay Geoghegan J. relied on Hale J.'s elaboration of the relevant principles in *Re K (Abduction: Consent)* [1997] 2 F.L.R. 212:

> "(i) the onus of proving the consent rests on the person asserting it; and
> (ii) the consent must be proved on the balance of probabilities; and
> (iii) the evidence in support of the consent needs to be clear and cogent;
> (iv) the consent must be real; it must be positive and it must be unequivocal;
> (v) there is no need that the consent be in writing;
> (vi) it is not necessary that there be proof of an express statement such as 'I consent'. In appropriate cases consent may be inferred from conduct but where such is alleged it will depend upon the words and actions of the allegedly consenting parent viewed as a whole and his or her state of knowledge of what is planned by the other parent."

Applying this test, Finlay Geoghegan J. held that the respondent had not discharged the burden resting on her to establish that the applicant had given his consent. The evidence indicated that the information communicated by the mother to the father in relation to the proposed trip to Ireland had been that it was a vacation visit of short duration in the order of three to three-and-a-half weeks and that it was on the basis of such information that the father had consented to the children travelling to Ireland. In making this finding Finlay Geoghegan J. accepted that the mother had not specified a precise return date but that did not appear to Finlay Geoghegan J. to be of significance:

> "In real terms there is a substantial difference between a vacation and a change of residence or move for an indefinite period. A vacation necessarily implies a return to the normal residence at the end of the vacation period. The latter two do not necessarily imply a return. I find that prior to leaving the US this trip was at all material times characterised by the mother to the father as being a vacation."

Even if the mother had intended the trip to be of a long or indefinite duration she had not communicated that fact to the father by words or deeds. The mother and the children left with one suitcase each. The father had not been aware that the mother had sent six boxes of belongings prior to leaving for Ireland.

The Supreme Court on appeal upheld Finlay Geoghegan J.'s holding as correct, and as being based on credible evidence. Denham J. (McGuinness, Hardiman, Fennelly and McCracken JJ. concurring) quoted the passage from Hale J.'s judgment in *Re K (Abduction: Consent)* without demur.

In *Re O, M, N and GL; FL v CL* [2006] I.E.H.C. 66, Finlay Geoghegan J. held that a father had not consented to the taking of his four children from Northern Ireland to the Republic where their mother, his wife, had represented to him that the journey involved a weekend trip to visit her parents. The mother had secretly put in place arrangements to secure rental accommodation in the Republic and had apparently made enquiries at the local school about enrolling the older children there.

Acquiescence   Under Art.13(a) of the Hague Convention, the court of the requested state is not bound to return a child who has been wrongfully removed or retained where the person seeking the order for return had subsequently acquiesced in the removal or retention. A body of jurisprudence has now built up on what constitutes acquiescence. In *RK v JK (Child Abduction: Acquiescence)* [2000] 2 I.R. 416 (analysed in the *Annual Review of Irish Law 1998*, pp. 76–78), both Denham J. and Barron J. cited with approval Waite J.'s comments in *W v W (Abduction: Acquiescence)* [1993] 2 F.L.R. 211:

> "The gist of the definition can perhaps be summarised in this way. Acquiescence means acceptance. It may be active, arising from express words or conduct, or passive, arising by inference from silence or inactivity. It must be real in the sense that the parent must be informed of his or her general right of objection, but precise knowledge of legal rights and remedies and specifically the remedy under the Hague

Convention is not necessary. It must be ascertained on a survey of all relevant circumstances, viewed objectively in the round. It is in every case a question of degree to be answered by considering whether the parent has conducted himself in a way that would be inconsistent with his later seeking a summary order for the child's return."

All the judges in *RK v JK* referred approvingly to the speech of Lord Browne Wilkinson in *Re H (Abduction: Acquiescence)* [1998] A.C. 72, where he expressed the view that:

"the applicable principles are as follows. (1) For the purpose of article 13 of the Convention, the question whether the wronged parent has 'acquiesced' in the removal or retention of the child depends upon his actual state of mind. As Neill L.J. said in *In re S. (Minors) (Abduction: Acquiscence)* [1994] 1 F.L.R. 819 at p. 838: ... 'the court is primarily concerned, not with the question of the other parent's perception of the applicant's conduct, but with the question whether the applicant acquiesced in fact.' (2) the subjective intention of the wronged parent is a question of fact for the trial judge to determine in all the circumstances of the case, the burden of proof being on the abducting parent. (3) The trial judge, in reaching his decision on the question of fact, will no doubt be inclined to attach more weight to the contemporaneous words and actions of the wronged parent than to his bare assertions in evidence of his intention. But that is a question of the weight to be attached to evidence and is not a question of law. (4) There is only one exception. Where the words or actions of the wronged parent clearly and unequivocally show and have led the other parent to believe that the wronged parent is not asserting or going to assert his right to the summary return of the child and are inconsistent with such return, justice requires that the wronged parent be held to have acquiesced."

Lynch and Barron JJ. expressed agreement with the statement of the views expressed by Balcombe L.J. in *Re A (minors) (Abduction: Custody Rights)* [1992] 2 W.L.R. 536, in relation to the weight that should be given to a single letter written by a father to the mother. The majority in the English Court of Appeal held that the letter established acquiescence on the father's part. Balcombe L.J. did not agree. He considered that this would:

"give 'acquiesced' far too technical a meaning for the context in which it is used. As I have already said, the main object of the Hague Convention is to require the immediate and automatic return to the state of their habitual residence of children who have been wrongfully removed. To this there are a limited number of exceptions, but it is apparent that the purpose of the exceptions is to preclude the automatic return of the children to the country whence they were removed, only if it can be shown or inferred that this could result in unnecessary harm or distress to the children. In other words, it is to the interests of the children that the exceptions are directed, not (except insofar as these directly affect the interests of the children) the interests of the parents or either of them. In my judgment, this requires the court to look at all the circumstances which may be relevant and not, as is here submitted, to the terms of a single letter.

Added force is given to this view by the English and French dictionary definitions of 'acquiesce' which I have quoted above. 'Accept' and 'adhesion' to my mind connote a state of affairs which persists over a period. 'Acquiesce' is not, in my judgment, apt to refer to a single expression of agreement taken in isolation from all surrounding circumstances."

Barron J., having referred to Balcombe L.J.'s remarks, said:

"I agree. In my view, acquiescence in the context of the Convention means an acceptance of the changed circumstances arising from the wrongful removal and/or the wrongful retention, as the case may be, by a parent in such circumstances that it is reasonable that he or she should be bound by it. It must be such that it would be inconsistent for the parent who has acquiesced to seek later to rely upon the rights given to such parent under the Convention to have the child or children returned summarily. The acceptance may be by words or conduct."

In *SR v MMR,* Supreme Court, February 16, 2006, affirming, with variations, High Court, January 25, 2006, the question of acquiescence arose where a wife took two children from Massachusetts to Ireland in January 2005, ostensibly on a vacation, and refused to return them in February 2005. She unsuccessfully sought to argue that her husband had given his consent: see above p.134. She also contended, again unsuccessfully, that the husband had acquiesced.

The father had not made contact with the US Central Authority to seek the return of the children until May 2005. Proceedings were commenced in September 2005. The husband explained his reluctance to contact the Central Authority on the basis that his wife had been maintaining that she was simply extending the vacation; moreover, he had been anxious to encourage a voluntary return as he recognised that, if he took proceedings under the Hague Convention, this would inevitably mean an end to the marriage. In the High Court, Finlay Geoghegan J. accepted this explanation and the Supreme Court affirmed her holding that the husband had not acquiesced.

In *Re O, M, N and GL; FL v CL* [2006] I.E.H.C. 66, Finlay Geoghegan J. held that the father of four children habitually resident in Northern Ireland had acquiesced in their wrongful retention by their mother in the Republic.

The mother had taken them to the Republic in November 2004, ostensibly for a weekend visit to her parents. Over the next three months the father was motivated by the desire to achieve a reconciliation with the mother and her voluntary return with the children to the family home. During this period he did not expressly seek the return of the children to the jurisdiction of Northern Ireland nor expressly object to their remaining in the Republic. By agreement between him and the mother, the mother went on holidays without the children to mainland Europe for around three weeks at the end of December. During this time, the children stayed with their father in Northern Ireland and then in their rented accommodation in the Republic. On her return, the mother told the father that she intended to seek a divorce. The father quickly realised that reconciliation was unlikely. He suspected that a third party was involved.

The father did not commence proceedings until September 2005. In the meantime relations with his wife were acrimonious. She obtained an initial barring order against him in the District Court in late February which was discharged in early March. The father had no direct access to his children from February to September.

Finlay Geoghegan J. held that the father had acquiesced; although he was a successful businessman with full legal advice, throughout the period of separation from his children there had been "a total lack of either direct demand or demand through his solicitors for the return of the children to Northern Ireland".

In *Re K McD, E McD, and J McD (minors); VG v P McD* [2006] I.E.H.C. 69, Finlay Geoghegan J. held that a mother resident in England whose three children had been unlawfully retained by their father in Ireland in late October 2004 had not acquiesced in their retention where she had not taken proceedings under the Hague Convention until July 2005. She was psychologically frail and unable to cope well with adversity; the legal position did not become clear to her until July 2005 when, with the assistance of a politician, she obtained an appointment with a legal aid centre in Ireland and, she said, was first advised of her rights under the Hague Convention. A letter written in January 2005 on her instructions to the father in which he was described as the children's primary carer and able to obtain guardianship in order to claim childrens' allowance, was not indicative of acquiescence as its purpose was to ensure that the immediate physical needs of the children would be met.

In view of the several reasons why acquiescence was not established in this case, it was unnecessary for Finlay Geoghegan J. to elaborate on the extent to which a person's psychological frailty should be regarded as preventing conduct that would otherwise constitute acquiescence from having that character. The subjective test laid down by Lord Browne Wilkinson and approved by the Supreme Court speaks in terms of "intention". This concept works well where the person has full rational control over his or her choices and conduct. Where there is some degree of inhibition of that independence on account of psychological factors, it is less helpful to approach the question of acquiescence from an intention perspective. It can be a hallmark of particular psychological conditions that the person may not be able to act effectively on his or her intentions. If a parent can show that he or she intended to seek the return of a child but was prevented from implementing that intention by reason of psychological frailty, should a court be deprived of the entitlement to make a finding of acquiescence, save in cases falling within the fifth consideration mentioned by Lord Browne Wilkinson?

In *Re TK and RK (Children); AK v AK* [2006] I.E.H.C. 277, Gilligan J. rejected the defence of acquiescence. The mother had taken the children from England to Ireland in April 2005. The father, from whom she had been divorced in 2001, invoked the assistance of the English courts and made efforts to find her. Searches were activated in the United States of America by the central authorities for the Hague Convention and the husband went to Sierra Leone on a fruitless visit. Although the mother and children were living openly in Ireland, they were not found for many months. The husband's proceedings under the Hague Convention were instituted one year and 19 days after the wrongful removal.

In the light of these facts, Gilligan J. considered that a finding of acquiescence "would be at odds with the applicant's persistent efforts in the family courts in England".

Grave Risk   In *SR v MMR,* Supreme Court, February 16, 2006, affirming, with variations, High Court, January 25, 2006, the defence of grave risk was not sustained. A mother who had taken her children from Massachusetts to Ireland made allegations of wrongdoing against the father, unspecified in Finlay Geoghegan J.'s judgment or on appeal. Finlay Geoghegan J. observed that at no stage had the mother considered it necessary to seek help from any authority in the United States of America during the time that she and the children had resided with the father in the matrimonial home. Even if the allegations were well founded, the protection that the mother might need was available from the Massachusetts courts. The Supreme Court did not disturb this holding on appeal.

Wishes of the Child   Article 11(2) of Council Regulation 2201/2003 requires the court to ensure that a child is given the opportunity to be heard in proceedings when applying Arts 12 and 13 of the Hague Convention "unless this appears inappropriate having regard to his or her age or degree of maturity".

In *Re O, M, N and GL; FL v CL* [2006] I.E.H.C. 66, the four children were aged respectively nine, seven, five and three. Finlay Geoghegan J. was satisfied that, having regard to their ages, it was appropriate that the eldest child be interviewed by the court-appointed child psychiatrist rather than giving evidence either formally or informally. While acknowledging that the court "should in accordance with the rights of the eldest child take into account the objections expressed by [her] to the return to Northern Ireland",

Finlay Geoghegan J. went on to conclude, in the light of the child psychiatrist's
evidence "as to the reasons for the objections and source of anxiety of the child",
without wishing in any way to appear to be disrespectful to those objections,
that it did "not appear appropriate to give any significant weight to th[em] in
determining whether or not to make an order for return in the exercise of the
discretion now given to the court by Article 13 of the Convention". This laconic
statement makes it hard to know why precisely the child's wishes were not
being taken into account. She was admittedly young and the objective basis
for her objections may have been insubstantial. What is not clear from this
passage is the extent, if at all, to which the wishes of a child were being given
any stand-alone status, rather than being considered but one, non-distinctive
element in the broad judicial discretion whether to return a child which was
articulated by the Supreme Court in *B v B* [1998] 1 I.R. 299 and applied by
Finlay Geoghegan J. in the instant case.

In *Re K McD, E McD and J McD (minors); VG v P McD* [2006] I.E.H.C.
63, where the children were aged, respectively, six, three and two, Finlay
Geoghegan J. considered it inappropriate that the court should hear them.

In *Re TK and RK (Children); AK v AK* [2006] I.E.H.C. 277, the exact basis
on which Gilligan J. departed from the wishes of a child is not entirely clear
from the text of the judgment. The mother had wrongfully removed her two
children, T, aged 9, and R, aged 5, from England to Ireland in breach of their
father's rights of custody. It appears that a child psychiatrist had earlier been
appointed by Finlay Geoghegan J. to assess the children and "report to the court
for the purposes of the court exercising its discretion pursuant to Article 13 of
the Hague Convention" on the degree of maturity of T, whether she objected to
being returned to England and "if so, the grounds of this objection and whether
any objections expressed had been independently formed or resulted from the
influence of any other person including a parent". Gilligan J. considered that
three issues remained to be decided: whether the children were settled in their
new environment; if so, whether the court had a discretion to order a return;
and "if appropriate the position relating to the older child, T and her indication
that she does not wish to be returned to England".

Gilligan J. concluded that the children were settled in their new environment,
having referred in detail to the psychiatrist's report, which clearly indicated
that the elder child, who "was of age appropriate maturity", preferred to stay
in Ireland, even if this would mean not seeing her father for a long time.
Notwithstanding this conclusion, Gilligan J. stated:

> "I take the view that I have a discretion to order a return pursuant to
> Article 18 of the Convention. I am satisfied that this discretion must
> be exercised in the context of the approach of the Convention bearing
> in mind the best interests of the children. I also have to bear in mind
> the view that has been expressed by the older child T. that she does not
> wish to be returned to the place of her habitual residence."

Gilligan J. noted that, while the children had a very strong and loving attachment to their mother, who appeared to have brought them up particularly well, the children had also enjoyed and benefited from their father's company and his contact with them "was a necessary and essential ingredient of their childhood". Gilligan J. referred to Lowe, Everall and Nicholls, *International Movement of Children: Law, Practice and Procedure* (Jordans, Bristol, 2004) 3 which "succinctly" dealt with the question of the relevant age at which the views of a child can be taken into account:

> "So far as age and maturity of the child is concerned, as the Perez-Vera report says, 'all efforts to agree on a minimum age at which the views of the child could be taken into account failed since all the ages suggested seemed artificial even arbitrary.' Consequently the Convention itself is silent on the matter although it seems fair to say that those involved in the drafting process generally had in mind older children and probably would have agreed that a child under the age of 12 would not normally be considered as possessing sufficient maturity."

Gilligan J. also noted that Balcombe L.J.'s statement in *Re R (Child Abductions: Acquiescence)* [1995] 1 F.L.R. 716 at 729 had stated that English courts had refused to lay down any chronological threshold below which a child's objections would not be taken into account but he added that the younger the child was the less likely it was that the child would have the maturity which makes it appropriate for the court to take its other objections into account.

Gilligan J. went on to observe:

> "The general impression that I deduce from the information available to me is that T. as a nine year old girl has attained age appropriate maturity. It also appears that she is a bright, bubbly child who does well at school and has the capacity to adjust to given situations. While quite clearly she is of a very tender age, I take the view that I must have regard for the view as expressed by her, but primarily I look to the reasons as advanced by her for not wishing to be returned to England."

The basis of T's objection to being returned was that she was happy in her new environment, had friends there, was settled at school and that overall she had a nicer life than she had in London in terms of the quality of her house which she described as bigger, the quality of her play area which she described as larger, and the social network of which she was part and which appeared to offer more opportunity for fun and friendship from her perspective. Gilligan J. attached significant importance to the fact that T had made no objection to being returned to England on any ground associated with her father and the evidence available suggested that all her previous dealings with her father had been harmonious and that she was sad at the lack of ongoing contact with him.

Gilligan J. stated:

> "In coming to a conclusion on this aspect, I am acutely conscious of the best interests of T. and her sister R. I am conscious that both children, against the background circumstances of this unfortunate case, have had a contact relationship with their father and that the severance of that relationship has caused sadness to both children and that the view of … the social worker who prepared his report … was to the effect that an ongoing lack of contact between the children and their father is potentially emotionally harmful to the children and that the risk of harm will increase with age. I take the view that I have to bear in mind the approach and purpose of the Convention itself, and the fact that the children are settled in their new environment. I accept without reservation that an order for the return of the children will undoubtedly at this point in time cause them considerable upset. Against this background, I have to weigh the nature and basis of the objections as advanced by T. for not wishing to be returned to her place of habitual residence and, in doing so, I come to the conclusion in the exercise of my discretion that the long term best interest of T. far outweighs the nature and extent of the basis of the objections as raised by her in coming to a decision that she should be returned to England. It follows that R. should also be returned."

This analysis appears to be based on the court's general discretion to return a child under Art.18 (or, just possibly, under Art.13: see below p.144) rather than on the basis that the court should not have regard to T's wishes. Curiously, there is no express holding on this latter issue, though Gilligan J.'s quotations from English academic and judicial authorities suggest that he regarded T as being too young to have her wishes taken into account under that Article. In seeking to assess the merits of the objective grounds for the child's wishes, Gilligan J. was adopting a welfare-based approach rather than seeking to defer to these wishes in their own right. At the heart of this deference is a deeper philosophical debate between paternalism and autonomy. The thrust of the global movement towards greater emphasis of the views of children is driven by concern for the latter value.

Undertakings   An interesting question of policy arose in *SR v MMR*, Supreme Court, February 16, 2006, affirming, with variations, High Court, January 25, 2006. To what extent should the court of the receiving state be permitted to seek an undertaking by the party seeking the return of a child not to initiate prosecution proceedings in the home state? In favour of giving the court such a power, it may be considered to contribute to the welfare of the child by protecting the child's relationship with the abducting (or wrongfully retaining) parent. As against this, the idea that restraints should be placed on the operation of a state's criminal justice system, albeit for a good motive, is troubling.

In *SR v MMR,* a mother had taken her two children from Massachusetts to Ireland on the pretext of a vacation and had refused to return them. The father, who was married to the mother, took successful proceedings under the Hague Convention. One of the undertakings to which Finlay Geoghegan J.'s order for return was subject was that the father would "not pursue or facilitate a prosecution" against the mother in the US or elsewhere arising out of the subject-matter of the proceedings. On appeal, the Supreme Court, bearing in mind that the courts of Massachusetts would have seisin and jurisdiction, and in recognition of the comity of nations, amended this undertaking to read as follows:

> "Without prejudice to the powers of prosecution of the authorities and courts of the State of M., U.S.A., the father will not make a formal complaint or initiate a prosecution against the mother in the U.S. or elsewhere arising out of the subject matter of these proceedings."

Settlement in new environment   Article 12(2) of the Hague Convention provides as follows:

> "The judicial or administrative authority even where proceedings have been commenced after the expiration of the period of one year … shall also order the return of the child unless it is demonstrated that the child is now settled in its new environment."

In *Re N (minors) (Abduction)* [1991] 1 F.L.R. 413, Bracewell J. saw some force in the argument that:

> "the presumption under the Convention is that children should be returned unless the mother can establish the degree of settlement which is more than mere adjustment to surroundings. I find that word should be given its ordinary natural meaning, and that the word 'settled' in this context has two constituents. First, it involves a physical element of relating to, being established in, a community and an environment. Secondly, I find that it has an emotional constituent denoting security and stability. Purchas L.J. in *Re S* [(*A Minor*) (*Abduction*) [1991] 2 F.L.R. 1] did advert to article 12 at p. 35 of the judgment and he said:
> > 'If in those circumstances it is demonstrated that the child has settled, there is no longer an obligation to return the child forthwith, but subject to the overall discretion of art. 18 the court may or may not order such a return'.
> He then referred to a 'long-term settled position' required under the article, and that is wholly consistent with the approach of the President in *M. v M.* [Fam Div, October 8, 1990] and at first instance in *Re S.* The

phrase 'long-term' was not defined, but I find that it is the opposite of 'transient'; it requires a demonstration, by a projection into the future, that the present position imports stability when looking at the future, and is permanent insofar as anything in life can be said to be permanent. What factors does the new environment encompass? The word 'new' is significant, and in my judgment it must encompass place, home, school, people, friends, activities and opportunities, but not, per se, the relationship with the mother, which has always existed in a close, loving attachment. That can only be relevant insofar as it impinges on the new surroundings."

In the Supreme Court decision of *Re R (A minor); P v B (No. 2)*, [1999] 4 I.R. 18, Denham J. (Hamilton C.J. and Barrington J. concurring) said she found this to be "a very helpful analysis".

In *Re TK and RK (Children); AK v AK* [2006] I.E.H.C. 277, Gilligan J. dealt with the issue where a mother and two children, aged nine and five, had been living in Ireland for over a year. The parties agreed that the children should not be separated, and Gilligan J. would have in any event taken the same view.

Gilligan J. noted that Bracewell J.'s analysis had been followed in England but not in Australia, in *Director General Departure of Community Services v M and C* [1998] 24 Fam. L.R. 178. Without referring to *Re R (A minor); P v B (No. 2)*, Gilligan J. followed Bracewell J.'s approach. After a review of the evidence relating to the children, which showed that the elder daughter was well integrated at school, and their mother, who was happily employed, Gilligan J. concluded that the children were settled into their new environment.

Gilligan J. went on, however, to exercise his discretion to order the return of the children under Art.18, as he considered that this would be in their long-term welfare. We consider this aspect of the decision below p.146.

Judicial discretion to return   In *B v B* [1998] 1 I.R. 299 the Supreme Court determined that, where a defence under Art.13 of the Convention is made out, the court has a discretion as to whether an order for the return of the children should be made. In that case Denham J. stated that, in the exercise of this discretion:

"[f]actors to be considered include:
　(1) the habitual residence of the child at the time of the removal
　(2) the law relevant to her custody and access.
　　　These two first factors raise the issue of the comparative suitability of the competing jurisdictions: whether the decisions as to the best interest of the child should be taken in an English or Irish court: in light of the Hague Convention.
　(3) The overall policy of the Convention and its objective to secure protection for rights of access.

      In this latter regard the fact that the mother of a two year old girl has not had access other than on the day of the court hearing of the child is a relevant consideration, though not decisive on its own.

(4) The object of the Convention to ensure that the rights of custody and of access under the law of one contracting state are effectively respected in the other contracting states.

(5) The circumstances of the child, information relating to the social background of the child, as stated in the final paragraph of art. 13 of the Hague Convention.

(6) The nature of consent of the appellant. Was it consent to the removal of the child from England for some time or in effect a waiver of custody of the child until she was 16? In this regard the circumstances of the making of the consent are relevant.

(7) The litigation in England and the decision of the 5th August, 1996, by the English High Court, Family Division, that V.B. be a ward of court, that the respondent return the child to that jurisdiction, and that V.B. reside with the appellant.

(8) The matter of undertakings, which are settled law in this jurisdiction, especially in relation to very young children."

Clearly, some of these factors related to the particular facts of the case before the court but others were of more general application.

In *Re O, M, N and GL; FL v CL* [2006] I.E.H.C. 66, four children of habitual residence in Northern Ireland had been wrongfully retained by their mother in the Republic. Their father, who took proceedings under the Hague Convention, was found to have acquiesced in their retention: see above p.137. As regards the discretion to be exercised by the court under the principles set out in *B v B*, Finlay Geoghegan J. thought it important to stress that:

"whilst the court in exercising a discretion under Article 13 to determine whether or not to make an order for return may take into account the interests of the child, it does not appear that it is intended to engage in the type of wider welfare inquiry in relation to the future needs of the child which it would do if the application were a dispute in relation to custody or residence between the parents. The court in determining whether or not to make an order for return under Article 13 is not determining such a custody or residence dispute. Article 11 of Regulation 2201/2003 retains to the courts of the State of habitual residence of the child prior to the wrongful removal or retention the right to decide on a question of custody notwithstanding an order for non-return."

Finlay Geoghegan J. took into account the similarity of laws and approaches of the courts in both jurisdictions to issues of custody and access; the ability of the parties to access lawyers in both jurisdictions; the facts that the children had been in the Republic for 14 months and the elder ones were in their second academic school year and the fact that this period had resulted at least in part from the acquiescence of the father.

There was no geographical obstacle to the father's exercising access if the children remained in the Republic and the protection of the father's right to access could be secured equally by the courts of either jurisdiction. These factors led Finlay Geoghegan J. to exercise her discretion by refusing an order for the return of the children to Northern Ireland. It was in her view in the children's interests that their place of residence and schooling should not be changed without a full and wide-ranging welfare enquiry by a court.

We have noted above, pp.139–140 and p.144 that, in *Re TK and RK (Children); AK v AK* [2006] I.E.H.C. 277, Gilligan J. held that two children who had been living in Ireland for over a year were settled into their new environment but nonetheless he ordered their return to England in the exercise of his discretion under Art.18. He was "satisfied that this discretion must be exercised in the context of the approach of the Convention bearing in mind the best interests of the children". He came to his conclusion even though the elder child had expressed the wish not to go back to England. At no point did Gilligan J. refer to the court's discretion under Art.13 to order the return of the children.

It would be most desirable for our courts in the future to address the whole question of judicial discretion to return in a comprehensive way. Among the questions on which we need clarification are the following. Is the entitlement under Art.18 intended to refer to situations, *outside the context of the Hague Convention*, where a court is entitled to order a return or is this entitlement to be fashioned from a reading of the Convention itself? (The English and New Zealand authorities on this question are discussed by Lowe, Everall and Nicholls, *op. cit.*, paras 17.2–17.4.) If Arts 13 and 18 are to be interpreted as mutually reinforcing, what are the practical implications? Should the judicial discretion prescribed in Art.13 differ having regard to the particular bar— consent, serious risk of harm or the child's wishes—that is raised?

In this general context it is worth referring to the constitutional dimension. It will be recalled that, in *Re GM and CM and DM (minors); London Borough of Sutton v RM, JM and MJ* [2002] 4 I.R. 488, analysed in the *Annual Review of Irish Law 2002*, pp. 68–71, Finlay Geoghegan J. exercised her discretion under Art.13 not to return children "present and living in Ireland" to England, where they were likely to be adopted without their parents' consent in circumstances wider than permissible under Arts 41 and 42 of the Constitution. In *Re SCC (a child); Foyle Health and Social Services Trust v EC and NC* [2006] I.E.H.C. 448, Dunne J. took the same approach where the facts were a good deal starker. The parents had both engaged in criminality, alcohol abuse was a factor in their lives and their six other children had been taken into care on account of neglect and physical abuse. The child in question had been born in Northern

Ireland and had been placed in care there before being wrongfully removed to the Republic. Even though the facts in the instant case were quite different from those in the *Sutton* case, Dunne J. thought that the constitutional implications were sufficiently strong to warrant a refusal to return the child. Her judgment suggests that she may have been relying on Art.20 rather than Art.13, since she interpreted Finlay Geoghegan J.'s judgment as relying on the provisions of Art.13(b). It is, perhaps, not easy to find a clear basis for that interpretation.

Habitual residence   In the *Annual Review of Irish Law 2004*, pp. 134–9, we analysed the important decision of *Re CAS (a minor); PAS v AFS*, Supreme Court, November 24, 2004, where Fennelly J. emphasised the need to keep to a minimum the resort to technical legal rules when determining a child's habitual residence under the Hague Convention. This wise counsel was not always fully heeded in 2006.

In *SR v MMR,* Supreme Court, February 1, 2007, affirming, with variations, High Court, January 25, 2006, a mother long resident in the United States of America took her two children from Massachusetts to Ireland in January 2005 on the pretext of a short vacation. She refused to return them a few weeks later to Massachusetts when requested to do so by their father to whom she was married, and whose consent to their removal from Massachusetts had not been validly obtained: see above p.134. When the father sought their return under the Hague Convention, the question arose as to their habitual residence at the time of the failure to return them to Massachusetts.

Finlay Geoghegan J. quoted the following passage from McGuinness J.'s judgment in *Re CM (a minor); CM and OM v Delegacion Provincial de Málaga Consejería de Trabajo y Asuntos Sociales Junta de Andalucia* [1999] 2 I.R. 363 at 381:

> "Having considered the various authorities opened to me by counsel, it seems to me to be settled law in both England and Ireland that 'habitual residence' is not a term of art, but a matter of fact, to be decided on the evidence in this particular case. It is generally accepted that where a child is residing in the lawful custody of its parent (in the instant case the mother), its habitual residence will be that of the parent. However, the habitual residence of the child is not governed by the same rigid rules of dependency as apply under the law of domicile and the actual facts of the case must always be taken into account. Finally, a person, whether a child or an adult, must, for at least some reasonable period of time, be actually present in a country before he or she can be held to be habitually resident there."

Finlay Geoghegan J. held that the state of habitual residence of the children at the time of failure to return was Massachusetts rather than Ireland. She stated:

"On the facts of this application the two children were, in January, 2005, in the joint custody of both parents. Immediately prior to February, 2005, they had been in Ireland for approximately four weeks. Having regard to my conclusion that the father consented to their travelling to Ireland only for a vacation, even if their mother had in January, 2005 a settled intention to return permanently to Ireland it does not appear to me that the two children can be considered, by the fourth week of February, 2005 to have lost their habitual residence in Massachusetts and acquired a new habitual residence in Ireland. Whilst I accept that a new habitual residence may be acquired in a short time, in the case of young children such as these where there is no agreement by their parents and joint custodians that they change their residence, I do not consider that they acquired a new habitual residence in approximately four weeks."

The Supreme Court affirmed this holding on appeal. Denham J. (McGuinness, Hardiman, Fennelly and McCracken JJ. concurring) dismissed the submission that the children had acquired an Irish habitual residence in a single sentence: "[A]bsent the father's consent, or a court order, the mother may not unilaterally alter the minor's habitual residence."

Although there can be no doubt that the rejection of an Irish habitual residence was correct, one can note a certain difference of approach between Finlay Geoghegan J. and Denham J. Finlay Geoghegan J. emphasised the factual dimension of the enquiry as to habitual residence; Denham J. set out a legal rule.

In *Re K McD, E McD and J McD (minors)*; *VG v P McD* [2006] I.E.H.C. 69, the parties were unmarried. The father was Irish; the wife had lived most of her life in England. When in England, they had lived together with their three children. The parties and their children came to live in Ireland in March 2004. The father had sold land which he owned there and had purchased a house for the family to live in. The move to Ireland had been under discussion for six to 12 months previously. The father had a strong desire to return to Ireland; the mother agreed that the family should move but believed that, if she did not like it, she could return to England with the children. Within a short period, she became unhappy with the move. The relationship between the parties broke down and the mother and children returned to England in July 2004 where they stayed until the following October.

At that time, the mother took the children to Ireland, unannounced, and placed them in the care of their father. She was having difficulty coping with them on her own. A week later she sought their return, but the father refused.

Finlay Geoghegan J. held that at all stages the children had an English habitual residence. Again invoking the holding in *CM v Delegacion de Malaga* [1999] 2 I.R. 363 that a child's habitual residence for the purposes of the Hague

Convention is a matter of fact, Finlay Geoghegan J. observed:

> "Whilst the habitual residence of a child is not governed by any rigid
> rule of dependency it appears to me on the facts of this case the court in
> determining the habitual residence of the children must have regard to
> the fact that the mother is in Irish terms the sole guardian of the children
> or in English terms the person with parental responsibility. The father is
> not a guardian and it was not contended on his behalf that he has parental
> responsibility in accordance with the laws of England and Wales. I
> have concluded that the children did not acquire a habitual residence in
> Ireland between the period of March and July, 2004. Whilst the father
> undoubtedly moved to Ireland with the settled intention to remain here I
> have concluded the mother did not have such a settled intention. Further,
> within a short space of time difficulties had arisen and the future of the
> family unit consisting of the mother, father and the three children had
> become precarious. The mother was the only person with a legal right
> to custody of the children. I have concluded that the children did not
> change their habitual residence to Ireland in the spring and summer of
> 2004 prior to returning to England with the mother in early July, 2004.
> They were therefore habitually resident in England in the approximate
> one week period prior to their wrongful retention in Ireland. Even if the
> mother brought them to Ireland to their father partly at least by reason of
> an inability to cope and without agreement on a definite date for return,
> I do not consider she then had any settled intention of permitting them
> to reside long term or permanently in Ireland."

In *Re SCC (a child); Foyle Health and Social Services Trust v EC and NC*
[2006] I.E.H.C. 448, Dunne J. held that a child born and very shortly there after
taken into care in Northern Ireland had acquired a habitual residence there,
in spite of the fact that his parents' habitual residence was in the Republic.
She stressed the factual character of the enquiry into habitual residence. She
acknowledged that it might be difficult to imagine circumstances in which a
child born to married parents living together could acquire a habitual residence
in a particular state as a result of the unilateral actions of one of the parents. In
the instant case, however, the father had acquiesced in his wife's move from
the Republic to Northern Ireland even though, being in prison, he had no prior
knowledge of it. Moreover, neither he nor his wife had taken any steps to have
the child (lawfully) returned to the Republic.

Costs   In *FL v CL* [2006] I.E.H.C. 70, Finlay Geoghegan J. addressed the
question of costs in proceedings under the Hague Convention in which the
applicant had been unsuccessful in his application for the return of his children
to Northern Ireland: see above p.137. Normally, under Ord.99, r.1 of the Rules
of the Superior Court, costs follow the event. Here the applicant argued that, in

respect of the period where the respondent had retained solicitors at her own expense prior to being represented by solicitors nominated by the Legal Aid Board, he should not have to pay the respondent's costs. He had effectively been prevented from having access to his children and had been obliged to take the proceedings under the Hague Convention in pursuit of his entitlement to access. He had been successful in a number of interim applications relating to access. There had been no element of *mala fides* on his part in taking the instant proceedings.

Finlay Geoghegan J. acceded to the applicant's argument, taking into account the following five factors when exercising her discretion:

> "Firstly, the nature and the purpose of these proceedings; that is, that they are proceedings under the Hague Convention and in particular the obligation imposed on the central authorities under article 7 of the Hague Convention in subparagraphs f and g to initiate and facilitate the institution of proceedings and where circumstances so require to provide or facilitate the provision of legal aid for such proceedings.
>
> Secondly, the importance to the children who are the subject matter of these proceedings of the court not now making orders which would exacerbate unnecessarily the relationship between their parents. It remains of paramount importance that the parents of the children, to whom these proceedings relate, should attempt to work in cooperation to secure an orderly arrangement for the upbringing of the children.
>
> Thirdly, the fact that the applicant undoubtedly instituted these proceedings and failed in the relief sought in the proceedings.
>
> Fourthly, the nature of the interlocutory applications necessitated to secure the applicant access to the children whilst these proceedings were before the court, the outcome of these applications, and the manner in which the respondent handled some aspects of these proceedings.
>
> Next, the probable expenses incurred by the respondent in connection with the proceedings."

2. Luxembourg Convention

In the *Annual Review of Irish Law 1993*, pp. 131–5, we examined the Supreme Court decision in *RJ v MR* [1994] 1 I.R. 271, where Finlay C.J. interpreted the word "manifestly" in Art.10(b) ("...the effects of the original decision are manifestly no longer in accordance with the welfare of the child") as placing on the party objecting to the making of an order "an onus to prove the incompatibility as a matter of high probability". In the *Annual Review of Irish Law 2004*, pp. 140–147, we discussed *RW v CC* [2004] 2 I.R. 108, where Finlay Geoghegan J. applied this test. In *Re PJ HR and JM JHR.; RGHR v LMG* [2006] I.E.H.C. 262, Finlay Geoghegan J. again invoked this test when rejecting the claim that Art.10(b) applied. Two years had elapsed since an access order had been made by the Oxford County Court in favour of the father. The children had been resident in Ireland during that time. Whilst Finlay Geoghegan J. acknowledged it might be desirable that future applications be made in Ireland, this fell far short of complying with the test set out in Art.10(b).

SPOUSAL MAINTENANCE

In *DT v FL* [2006] I.E.H.C. 98 the parties had been divorced in the Netherlands in 1994 on the application of the husband. The Dutch court awarded maintenance to the wife. It did not, however, address the questions of custody or child maintenance as it "decided that it had no authority to deal with such matters". The husband later sought a declaration in the Irish High Court that the divorce should be recognised, pursuant to s.29(1)(d) and (e) of the Family Law Act 1995. Morris P., on November 23, 2001, refused to make this declaration, on the basis that the husband's domicile at the time of the divorce had been Irish. The Supreme Court affirmed, on November 26, 2003: see our analysis in the *Annual Review of Irish Law 2003*, pp. 95, 99. The wife later took judicial separation proceedings in Ireland. The husband challenged her entitlement to do so.

The focus of the husband's attention was on the ancillary reliefs that might be awarded by the court in the context of judicial separation. These could include an order for maintenance. The husband, in effect, argued that there was already in place a maintenance order, under the Dutch divorce, and that European law prevented a second order, irreconcilable with it, from being made in another state.

Two principal issues confronted McKechnie J. Was the Dutch maintenance order still in force and, if so, did its currency constitute a barrier to the granting of ancillary relief in the Irish proceedings? Should it be treated as a judgment entitled to recognition in spite of the Supreme Court's refusal to recognise the divorce? McKechnie J. did not think that the case raised a *lis pendens* problem; rather it was concerned with the question of recognition of a foreign judgment originally entitled to recognition (if at all) under the Brussels Convention. This proved more intractable than might have been anticipated since the manner in which the process of maintaining the enforceability of prior judgments as European law moved from Convention to Regulation had been somewhat inelegant. At all events, McKechnie J. concluded that, while it appeared that no express provision had been made to cover earlier judgments in the transition between the Convention and the Regulation, the Dutch order simply had to remain enforceable if it was so originally. The academic commentators were divided as to whether this continuity should be attributable to the terms of the Convention or the Regulation; McKechnie J. favoured the former interpretation.

This brought McKechnie J. to the question whether the fact that the Supreme Court had declined to recognise the Dutch divorce decree meant that the maintenance element of the decree also should be denied recognition. He

held that the Dutch judgment was not entitled to recognition on the basis of
Art.27(3) of the Brussels Convention, which provided that a judgment should
not be recognised if irreconcilable with a judgment given in a dispute between
the same parties in the state in which recognition is sought, and Art.27(4),
which denied recognition to a judgment if the court in the state of origin, in
order to arrive at its judgment, had decided a preliminary question concerning
the status or legal capacity of natural persons or rights in property arising out
of a matrimonial relationship in a way that conflicted with a rule of the private
international law of the state in which the recognition was sought, unless the
same result would have been reached by the application of the rules of private
international law of that state.

McKechnie J. observed:

> "The maintenance order in question is predicated on the divorced status
> of the parties, as declared by the court of the Netherlands, in its judgment
> of September, 1994. That decision was arrived at in circumstances
> covered by Article 27(4) of the Convention. The recognition and
> enforcement of that judgment, in this State, could only take place on the
> basis that both parties are divorced in this country. Quite evidently, that
> proposition is diametrically opposed to the conclusion reached by the
> Supreme Court, namely that the parties remain validly married in this
> jurisdiction. Thus to enforce the maintenance order would be directly in
> conflict with the decision of the Supreme Court. That being so, I don't
> believe that it could ever have been recognised in this jurisdiction under
> the Brussels Convention. Accordingly, the maintenance order is not a
> provision for the purposes of applying Article 21 of the Convention.
> Therefore if this court should proceed with the present case, and make
> ancillary orders, when granting a decree of judicial separation, that
> judgment in respect of such orders will not be in conflict with any other
> judgment for the purposes of Article 21 of the Convention."

McKechnie J. also rejected the argument that the maintenance order had
been entitled to recognition during the period from 1994 under the Supreme
Court decision in 2003 and that it would be curious if thereafter it lost that
entitlement:

> "In 2003, the Supreme Court ruled that the 1994 divorce had no effect
> in Ireland. It did not say that it was effective up to 2003, but then
> ceased to be effective. Rather it declared as a matter of Irish law that the
> divorce never had the effect of dissolving the marriage of the parties. It
> therefore said, by necessary implication, that the maintenance decree
> was inconsistent with what, as a matter of Irish law, had always been
> the status of the parties. A delay in clarification does not change that
> fact."

In his judgment, McKechnie J. addressed the troublesome question of how to distinguish "matters relating to maintenance" from "rights in property arising out of a matrimonial relationship". Orders relating to the former are enforceable under the Brussels Regulation; orders relating to the latter are not.

In *Van den Boogaard v Laumen*, C–220/95; [1997] ECR 1–1147, the Court of Justice threw some light on the matter:

> "Owing precisely to the fact that on divorce an English court may, by the same decision, regulate both the matrimonial relationships of the parties and matters of maintenance, the court from which leave to enforce is sought must distinguish between those aspects of the decision which relate to rights in property arising out of a matrimonial relationship and those which relate to maintenance, having regard in each particular case to the specific aim of the decision rendered.
>
> It should be possible to deduce that aim from the reasoning of the decision in question. If this shows that a provision awarded is designed to enable one spouse to provide for himself or herself or if the needs and resources of each of the spouses are taken into consideration in the determination of its amount, the decision will be concerned with maintenance. On the other hand where the provision awarded is solely concerned with dividing property between the spouses, the decision will be concerned with rights and property arising out of a matrimonial relationship and will not therefore be enforceable under the Brussels Convention.
>
> It makes no difference in this regard that payment of maintenance is provided for in the form of a lump sum. This form of payment may also be in the nature of maintenance where the capital sum set is designed to ensure a pre-determined level of income."

McKechnie J., having quoted this passage, commented:

> "It seems therefore that once the purpose, focus or intention of the decision is to make provision for the needs of one party, having regard to the resources of the other, then the resulting order will be within Article 5(2) of the Brussels I Regulation. Provided that the intention of the decision is as I have specified, the actual form of the award is immaterial. It matters not whether the order is for the payment of a periodic sum, a lump sum, or the transfer of ownership of moveable or immoveable property. Provided that the court is not simply dividing property in a matrimonial context, but rather is looking after the needs of one party by reference (at least in part), to the assets of the other party, then that is sufficient to constitute 'maintenance' for the purposes of the Regulation."

While this distinction will be clear in many cases, in others it will not. When making orders for financial provision or divorce or judicial separation, the court is engaging in a process of financial planning which considers a range of options, long term and short term. The maintenance option is but one of these; it does not reflect any clear assumption about gender roles and obligations. In some cases unquestionably the purpose of the maintenance order will be to meet the alimentary needs of a dependent spouse; in other cases the making of orders of financial provision involving the sale or transfer of assets may be designed to take account of alimentary needs but in a less overt or conscious way.

FOREIGN JUDGMENT

In *Re Flightlease (Ireland) Ltd (in voluntary liquidation)* [2006] I.E.H.C. 193, Clarke J. had to resolve two important issues under the rules of Irish private international law: whether to characterise certain proceedings arising in the context of foreign insolvency proceedings as *in personam* or *in rem* and whether to extend the recognition of foreign judgments by adding a "real and substantial connection" ground.

The joint liquidators of *Flightlease (Ireland) Ltd* sought permission from the court to distribute the assets without reference to a claim by Swissair, which was in a form of debt-restructuring liquidation in Switzerland. An application was currently before the Swiss courts seeking the return of certain monies paid by Swissair to Flightlease. The question was whether recognition would be afforded by the Irish courts to any judgment obtained by Swissair against Flightlease in the Swiss courts. If it were to be clear that the courts in Ireland would not recognise the judgment of the Swiss court as being binding upon the joint liquidators of Flightlease, then it might well be appropriate for the joint liquidators to decide not to participate in the Swiss proceedings, since their very participation had the potential (on one view of the law) to render any judgment of the Swiss courts enforceable in Ireland.

Under the Swiss federal statute on debt enforcement and bankruptcy, a claim of the nature brought by Swissair against Flightlease in the Swiss proceedings could arise only where the transaction in question, occurring during the period of five years prior to the granting of the debt-restructuring moratorium, had been carried out with the intention of either putting certain creditors at a disadvantage or favouring certain creditors to the disadvantage of others and that this was apparent to the other party to the transaction.

As to the first issue, the joint liquidators of Flightlease argued that, while some orders made in insolvency proceedings might be enforced as judgments *in personam*, the nature of the claim in the instant case was so closely connected to the Swiss insolvency proceedings as to render it a judgment *in rem*, in contrast to a judgment for a debt, for example, which would clearly be *in personam*.

For Swissair to succeed, the Swiss court would have to be satisfied that the transaction in favour of Flightlease had been carried out for the purposes of effecting what, in the analogous jurisdiction of the courts in Ireland in respect of liquidations, might be seen as similar to a fraudulent preference. The transaction must have occurred during the period of five years prior to the commencement of the insolvency proceedings. Thus, the joint liquidators argued, proceedings of the type contemplated could arise only where there was an insolvency and an insolvency process before the courts.

Clarke J. did not consider that this should lead to an *in personam* characterisation. He observed:

> "While that much is true it does not, it seems to me, at the end of the day, take away from the substance of the order which will be made which is to the effect that on foot of the application of the relevant Swiss law, Flightlease will, if it is unsuccessful, be ordered to pay a liquidated sum of money back to Swissair. While some weight must be attached to the fact that the relevant proceedings could only have arisen in the event of an insolvency it seems to me that greater weight must be attached to the nature of the order to be made.
>
> Similar orders could be made in this jurisdiction even in circumstances where there was no insolvency. For example moneys can be paid out by a solvent company which are paid *ultra vires* to a third party. Where that third party was aware that the company did not have the power to pay the moneys, same can be ordered to be repaid. Such an order would, in my view, be clearly an *in personam* order against the recipient. Therefore orders requiring persons to repay monies to a company can be *in personam*. It is the character of such an order that seems to me to be the principal factor in determining whether it can properly be described as *in personam*. Notwithstanding, therefore, the fact that the particular circumstances giving rise to the making of the order in the Swiss proceedings could only occur in the event of the company concerned being the subject of insolvency proceedings, I am nonetheless satisfied that any order which might be made should properly be characterised as an *in personam* order and its enforceability should, therefore, depend on the application of the appropriate rules for the recognition of *in personam* orders at common law."

Clarke J. turned to consider the second issue, as to whether the traditional common law rules for recognition of foreign *in personam* judgments should be supplemented by a "real and substantial" ground. If such a ground were to receive judicial benediction, a compelling case could be made out on the facts that a real and substantial connection existed. A "significant part" of Flightlease's commercial decisions had been made in Switzerland by Swiss members of the board. Both Flightlease and Swissair were ultimately subsidiaries of SAirGroup. The transaction in question involved a payment by another company within the same group, also based in Switzerland. If, however, the traditional common law rules for recognition of foreign judgments were applied, a judgment in the Swiss courts would not be recognised if Flightlease had not participated in the Swiss proceedings as it was not present in Switzerland when the proceedings were commenced and had not submitted to the jurisdiction.

Swissair sought to encourage Clarke J. to follow the lead of the Supreme Court of Canada in adding a "real and substantial connection" ground for recognition. This ground had received the support of the House of Lords, in the context of foreign divorces, in the controversial decision of *Indyka v Indyka* [1969] 1 A.C. 33. In *De Savoye v Morguard Investments Ltd* [1990] 3 S.C.R. 1077, the Supreme Court of Canada held that it should apply in respect of the recognition of *in personam* judgments in sister provinces. La Forest J. observed:

> "In a word, the rules of private international law are grounded in the need in modern times to facilitate the flow of wealth, skills and people across state lines in a fair and orderly manner. Von Mehren and Trautman have observed in 'Recognition of Foreign Adjudications: A Survey and A Suggested Approach' (1968), 81 Harvard Law Review 1601, at p. 1603: 'The ultimate justification for according some degree of recognition is that, if in our highly complex and interrelated world each community exhausted every possibility of insisting on its parochial interests, injustice would result and the normal patterns of life would be disrupted.'
>
> Yntema (though speaking more specifically there about choice of law) caught the spirit in which private international law, or conflict of laws, should be approached when he stated ["The objectives of Private International Law", (1957) 35 Can. Bar Rev. 721]: 'In a highly integrated world economy, politically organized in a diversity of more or less autonomous legal systems, the function of conflict rules is to select, interpret and apply in each case the particular local law that will best promote suitable conditions of interstate and international commerce, or, in other words, to mediate in the questions arising from such commerce in the application of the local laws'. As is evident from throughout his article, what must underlie a modern system of private international law are principles of order and fairness, principles that ensure security of transactions with justice. This formulation suggests that the content of comity must be adjusted in the light of a changing world order. The approach adopted by the English courts in the 19th century may well have seemed suitable to Great Britain's situation at the time. One can understand the difficulty in which a defendant in England would find himself in defending an action initiated in a far corner of the world in the then state of travel and communications... The approach, of course, demands that one forget the difficulties of the plaintiff in bringing an

action against a defendant who has moved to a distant land. However, this may not have been perceived as too serious a difficulty by English courts at a time when it was predominantly Englishmen who carried on enterprises in far away lands. As well, there was an exaggerated concern about the quality of justice that might be meted out to British residents abroad ...

The world has changed since the above rules were developed in 19th century England. Modern means of travel and communication have made many of these 19th century concerns appear parochial. The business community operates in a world economy and we correctly speak of a world community even in the face of decentralized political and legal power. Accommodating the flow of wealth, skills and people across state lines has now become imperative. Under these circumstances, our approach to the recognition and enforcement of foreign judgments would appear ripe for reappraisal. Certainly, other countries, notably the United States and members of the European Economic Community, have adopted more generous rules for the recognition and enforcement of foreign judgments to the general advantage of litigants.

However, that may be, there is really no comparison between the interprovincial relationships of today and those obtaining between foreign countries in the 19th century. Indeed, in my view, there never was and the courts made a serious error in transposing the rules developed for the enforcement of foreign judgments to the enforcement of judgments from sister-provinces. The considerations underlying the rules of comity apply with much greater force between the units of a federal state, and I do not think it much matters whether one calls these rules of comity or simply relies directly on the reasons of justice, necessity and convenience to which I have already adverted. Whatever nomenclature is used, our courts have not hesitated to cooperate with courts of other provinces where necessary to meet the ends of justice."

In *Beals v Saldanha* [2003] 3 S.C.R. 416, the Supreme Court of Canada went further and held that the "real and substantial connection" test should apply also to the reconition of foreign judgments.

In *Flightlease*, Clarke J. considered that, in substance, the judgment in *Salndahna* "simply made what was implicit in the judgment of *De Savoye* explicit", as the logic of the views expressed in *De Savoye* necessarily required the extension of the principle to the recognition of foreign judgments.

Clarke J. decided not to go the same way. No such trend had been detected in any other common law jurisdiction; some academic commentary had leaned against adopting that course. In *KD v MC* [1985] I.R. 697, where the Supreme Court had not adopted the "real and substantial" ground for recognising foreign divorces for a number of reasons, not least that the issue had not been raised in the High Court, McCarthy J. had stressed the disruption that recognition would cause for those who had ordered their family arrangements on the assumption that the law did not extend so far. Clarke J. commented:

> "It seems to me that McCarthy J was emphasising that a radical change in the common law had the potential, in some cases, to create significant effects (including retrospective effects) on many parties (and not just the parties before the court) and should not, therefore, be lightly engaged in. I fully agree with that view.
>
> It is inherent in the common law that it will necessarily evolve to meet new circumstances and that, in the course of any such evolution, new principles may, in time, be developed to reflect the changing world in which the law has to operate. To that extent a gradually evolving common law system can, in certain circumstances, have advantages over a more rigid statutory regime where change can only occur after a full statutory process and may be too late to meet the needs of individual cases. The other side of the same coin is, however, that decisions as to the common law declare the law as it was at the time of the events giving rise to the proceedings in which the issue arises. A radical change in the common law has, therefore, the potential to have a retrospective effect which would not, in the ordinary way, arise in the event of a statutory amendment. It was the potential injustice of such an effect that McCarthy J was referring to in the passage which I have quoted.
>
> Subject to the overall limitation that the courts in this jurisdiction could not, in any event, engage in an alternation in the common law which amounted to legislation (an issue not raised by the parties in this case), the courts remain free to allow for the orderly evolution of common law principles. However the passage from McCarthy J which I have quoted seems to me to be a reason for exercising significant caution where an over radical alteration in common law principles is suggested."

Having regard to that caution and to the fact that there did not, as yet, appear to be any real consensus in the common law world as to a need for a change in the direction identified by the Supreme Court of Canada, Clarke J. concluded that adding the new ground, as suggested by Swissair, "would have the potential to do more harm than good".

JURISDICTION

1. Contract
Article 5 of the Brussels Regulation 44/2001 provides as follows:

> "A person domiciled in a Member State may, in another Member State

be sued:
   (a) In matters relating to a contract, in the courts for the place of performance of the obligation in question;
   (b) For the purpose of this provision and unless otherwise agreed, the place of performance of the obligation in question shall be:
      — in the case of the sale of goods the place in a Member State where, under the contract, the goods were delivered or should have been delivered,
      — in the case of the provision of services, the place in a Member State where, under the contract the services were provided or should have been provided,
   (c) if subparagraph (b) does not apply then subparagraph (a) applies."

Following *De Bloos v Bouyer* (Case 14/76) [1976] 3 E.C.R. 1497 at para.13, the Supreme Court in *Bio-Medical Research Ltd t/a Slendertone v Delatex SA* [2004] I.R. 307 noted that, for the purposes of determining the place of performance within the meaning of Art.5, the obligation to be taken into account is the obligation which corresponds to the contractual right on which the plaintiff's action is based.

In *General Monitors Ireland Ltd v SES ASA Protection SpA* [2005] I.E.H.C. 223, Finlay Geoghegan J. noted that Art.5(1)(b) of the Regulation sought to address some of the previous difficulties that had arisen under the former Brussels Convention regarding the determination of the place of performance of multiple obligations. Article 5(1)(b), she said, gave "an autonomous definition for the place of performance in the case of contracts for the sale of goods and in the case of contracts for the provision of services".

In *Nestorway Ltd t/a Electrographic International v Ambaflex BV* [2006] I.E.H.C. 235, the plaintiff invoked Art.5(1) when claiming that the defendant had wrongfully terminated an exclusive distribution agreement. In Clarke J.'s view, such type of agreement encompassed at least two separate and equal principal obligations: an obligation to supply the distributor, within the terms of the agreement, with the goods concerned and a further obligation not to supply any other person within the parameters defined by the agreement.

While performance of the terms of the contract would, necessarily, involve separate individual contracts for the sale of goods, it did not seem to Clarke J. that the obligations in question in the instant case could be said to be a "sale of goods". Accordingly the deeming provisions of Art.5(1)(b) did not apply. When assuming the place of performance of the obligation in question, under Art.5(1)(a), the court should apply the rules of Irish private international law, under which Dutch law was that chosen by the parties. The plaintiffs had failed to adduce evidence of the Dutch law on this question. Clarke J. was "inclined to take the view" that, under Irish law, Ireland would be considered to be "at least a place" where the obligations in question were to be performed, given

that these obligations involved the supply of goods to the territory covered by
the agreement and the requirement to refrain from supplying goods to others
within that territory. The French courts had taken a similar view in *SARL Noge
v Gotz GmbH* [1998] I.L. P.r 189. It was not possible, however, to tell whether
Dutch law would be the same. Since the onus rested on the plaintiffs to establish
jurisdiction under Art.5(1)(a) and they had failed to show that Ireland was the
place of performance of the relevant obligation under Dutch law, Clarke J. set
aside the service on the defendant for want of jurisdiction.

2. Companies and other organs

Montani v First Directors Ltd [2006] I.E.H.C. 92 involved a dispute regarding
the ownership of assets, consisting almost entirely of "real property and related
assets", physically located in Italy. They were vested in an Italian company.
Shares in the company were held in an Irish company, Liberty Security Systems
Ltd. The plaintiff claimed he had a beneficial interest in the Irish company and
that, as a result of a series of unlawful transactions, including conspiracy, there
had been an unlawful attempt to put the assets beyond his reach. He sought,
inter alia, a declaration that he was the beneficiary owner of 50 per cent of
the shares of the Irish company and damages for conspiracy, breach of trust
and breach of duty. He invited the court to assume jurisdiction under Art.5(3),
6(1) and 22(2) of Brussels Regulation 44/2001.

The plenary summons stated that there were no proceedings between
the parties pending in another contracting Member State arising "from the
said cause of action". Hanna J., on a motion seeking that the court decline
jurisdiction or stay the proceedings, thought that "a question mark" had to
be raised over the validity of the endorsement. There were three sets of civil
proceedings already in progress in Italy relating to the wider saga of the history
of the company and an Italian subsidiary. Nonetheless, he held that the motion
should not succeed. The plaintiff's "terse" pleading had, in his view, made
out a prima facie ground under Art.6(1) based on the allegation of conspiracy,
which was a tort in circumstances where one of the defendants was an Irish
domiciliary. Under Art.6(1) a person domiciled in a Member State may also
be sued where he or she is one of a number of defendants in the courts for the
place where any one of these is domiciled, provided the claims are so closely
connected that it is expedient to determine them together to avoid the risk of
irreconcilable judgments resulting from separate proceedings.

Under Art.22(2), courts of the Member State where a company has its seat
have exclusive jurisdiction, regardless of domicile, where the proceedings
have, as their object:

> "the validity of [its] constitution, ... nullity or ... dissolution ... or the
> validity of decisions of its organs ...".

Hanna J. considered that Art.22 applied to the facts of the instant case:

"It is beyond question but that Liberty is an Irish limited-liability company and subject to Irish law. The fundamental issue in the case, it seems to me, is the validity of the decisions of the organs of that company causing the shares, the shareholding in that company, to move to a number of parties ... Article 22, in my view, therefore, renders mandatory the determination of that issue by the courts of Ireland and Article 28 must defer to Article 22 in those circumstances."

Article 28 deals with cases where related actions are pending in the courts of different Member States. Hanna J. did not believe that Art.28 required consideration (for reasons that are not exactly clear); had it been relevant it would not have assisted the defendants:

"I think the Court has to adopt a common-sense approach, and this applies as much to Article 22 as it would were we to go on to consider Article 28. It has to be pragmatic. It is further worthy of note that the Italian proceedings have the appearance of conditionality in that they expressly look forward to and await decisions of the Irish courts, and this is not surprising because ... the assets are here and no decision of the Italian courts, however much respected and honoured in this jurisdiction, can have a binding effect with regard to the assets in this jurisdiction which are regulated by Irish law. Therefore, as I say, were I to have gone on to consider Article 28, I would have been satisfied that the plaintiff has satisfied the onus to derogate from the general principle enunciated in Article 2 of Brussels 2, and it follows, from what I have said and the general tenor of my judgement, that I would have found in favour of the plaintiff."

In *Hassett (a minor) v South Eastern Health Board* [2006] I.E.H.C. 105, a surgeon sued for negligence sought an indemnity from the Medical Defence Union. This was refused. The surgeon claimed that the decision to withdraw cover from him was based on a broader decision not to grant an indemnity to Irish obstetrician members or former members and that this constituted a breach of contract and interference with his legitimate expectation that cover would be provided. He also pleaded estoppel. The Medical Defence Union contested jurisdiction, invoking Art.22. It stressed that it was not an insurance company and that the benefits of membership were all discretionary, subject to individual decision in each case as to whether cover should be given. It invoked Megarry V.C.'s decision in *Medical Defence Union Ltd v Department of Trade* [1980] 1 Ch. 82, as authoritative support of this interpretation of its functions. The surgeon in reply invoked a passage from Geoghegan J.'s judgment in *Barry v Medical Defence Union Ltd,* Supreme Court, June 16, 2005:

"Twenty five years have passed since that decision [*Medical Defence*

Union Ltd v Department of Trade] and it is common knowledge in
this jurisdiction that very large claims for damages have been made
and recovered against members of the respondent especially arising
out of obstetric mishaps and they in turn have been indemnified by the
respondent. As a consequence huge 'premiums' are paid. As suggested
by Sir Robert Megarry it must be assumed that in the ordinary way
despite the discretionary nature of the liability the respondent considers
such a claim in much the same way as an insurance company would do
and for the most part provides indemnity in all appropriate cases. It is
not disputed that there are some contractual obligations on the part of
the respondent under the statutory contract. I do not find it necessary
to explore the extent of these obligations but I do not rule out that
they might not more correctly be expressed in rather stronger terms
than is suggested in the judgment of Sir Robert Megarry delivered in
a different context. Presumably if a person is entitled to discretionary
assistance there cannot be an improper exercise of the discretion and
arguably the improper exercise of the discretion would itself be a breach
of contract."

Finnegan P. adopted a purposive approach to the interpretation of Art.22. Since
it was an exception to the basic jurisdiction rules contained in Arts 2, 5 and 6, it
"must not be given a wider interpretation than... required by its objective and
accordingly construed narrowly...". The Article, in its original manifestation as
Art.16(2) of the Brussels Convention, had as its objective the internal regulation
and management of a company in accordance with its public documents; this
was Professor Jenner's view, expressed in his report. There was "no suggestion"
that Art.22 was intended to affect simple contract litigation.

Finnegan P. interpreted the surgeon's claim for an indemnity as not being
based on a contract contained in the memorandum and articles of association
of the Medical Defence Union but rather on a collateral contract. It was thus
"not a claim based on the validity in terms of company law of any decision of
an organ" of the Medical Defence Union. He parsed the details of the surgeon's
claim. Some clearly fell outside the scope of Art.22(2); others needed closer
scrutiny but, having given that scrutiny, Finnegan P. concluded that they
also were not caught by Art.22(2) since they related, not to the *validity* of a
decision of an organ of the Medical Defence Union, but rather to the *propriety
or correctness* of the decision.

3. Prorogation
Article 23 of the Brussels Regulation confers jurisdiction on courts agreed
by the parties to a contract. Article 23 provides that an agreement conferring
jurisdiction must be either:

"(a) In writing or evidenced in writing; or

(b) In a form which accords with practices which the parties have established between themselves; or

(c) In international trade or commerce, in a form which accords with the usage of which the parties are or ought to have been aware and which, in such trade or commerce, is widely known to me and regularly observed by, parties to contracts of the type involved in the particular trade or commerce concerned."

In *Nestorway Ltd t/a Electrographic International v Ambaflex BV* [2006] I.E.H.C. 235, the plaintiffs entered into an exclusive distributorship argument with the defendant which it claimed had been wrongfully terminated. They sought to ground jurisdiction under Art.5(1) of the Regulation. The defendant contested jurisdiction, arguing that the parties had agreed to confer jurisdiction on the courts of the Netherlands. It argued that a set of conditions which had been incorporated in the contract so provided. Clarke J. rejected the defendant's argument. Applying Irish legal rules of construction, he inclined to the interpretation that these conditions had been incorporated only to the extent that they covered conditions regarding warranties and guarantees (and possibly, individual sales), with which the current litigation was not concerned. Article 23 would thus have no application. The contract was, however, governed in Dutch law but the defendant had not produced evidence of the construction of the contract under Dutch law. Accordingly, Clarke J. held that the defendant's argument in relation to Art.23 should not succeed.

PROCEEDS OF CRIME

In *F McK v BM and KM* [2006] I.E.H.C. 395, the applicant sought a disposal order pursuant to s.4 of the Proceeds of Crime Act 1996 in respect of sums of money standing to the credit of the respondents in an Austrian Bank. In 1997 the Superior Court for Criminal Cases in Vienna had made a preliminary injunction in the nature of a restraint order over the accounts the subject-matter of the proceedings. That injunction remained valid until the final disposition of the proceedings before that court. The Austrian prosecutor had applied for a permanent confiscation order in respect of the monies.

On behalf of the respondents it was submitted that as a matter of private international law the Irish High Court should cede jurisdiction to the Austrian court on the basis of comity of courts. It was also argued that without the concurrence of the Austrian court the respondents could not themselves ensure compliance with an order pursuant to s.4 and that accordingly such an order should not be made.

Finnegan P. rejected these arguments. He stated:

"It is wrong to think that the court can only act in one of two ways *in personam* or *in rem*. If the party to be subject to the order is within the jurisdiction of the court it may act *in personam* and require him to take steps within his power to give effect to the court's order in respect of assets situate in another jurisdiction. I see no difficulty in the court making an order pursuant to section 4 thereby depriving the respondents of such title or interest as they may have in the sums on deposit in Austria. In this case the section 4 order would transfer the estate right and title of the respondents in the funds to the Minister or to such other person as the court may determine. The ultimate release of the funds is a matter which would require to be dealt with before the court of Austria. In making the order the court is not determining any question of Austrian law but merely substituting the Minister (or the other person so determined) for the respondents and giving them no better right or title to the funds than the respondents themselves may have. By way of analogy the order has the like effect of a transfer of immovable property subject to a mortgage."

Finnegan P. also considered that the argument as to extraterritoriality was misconceived. Extraterritorial legislation simply meant legislation which attached significance for courts within the jurisdiction to facts and events occurring outside the jurisdiction. It did not imply that one state could pass laws for another state or that several systems of law would be in operation regulating a particular sphere within any given state. It did "not *per se* offend against the comity of courts".

Constitutional Law

ORAN DOYLE, Lecturer in Law, Trinity College, Dublin
and
ESTELLE FELDMAN, Research Associate, Trinity College, Dublin

ACCESS TO COURTS

Frivolous and vexatious litigant   *Riordan v An Taoiseach* [2006] I.E.H.C.
312 is, it has to be said, not the easiest of judgments to follow. This is not at all
because of the effective decision of Smyth J., far from it. Rather it is because
it is one of a long line of cases taken by Denis Riordan, a litigant who has:

> "not merely repeatedly sought to re-open decisions of this Court, he has
> also persistently abused the locus standi he has been afforded by the
> High Court and this Court in cases in which he has no direct personal
> interest, in order to make scandalous allegations, not merely against
> members of the judiciary, but other persons whom he chose to join as
> defendants in his proceedings" (*Riordan v An Taoiseach (No. 4)* [2001]
> 3 I.R. 365 *per* Keane C.J. at 370).

The hearing followed a Supreme Court order dated November 21, 2003
granting the plaintiff leave to institute limited proceedings in the High Court.
Smyth J. recorded some difficulty in understanding parts of the order as no
written judgment of the Supreme Court was available to him. An example
of the confused state of affairs was demonstrated by a lack of reasons given
by the court for its departure from its judgment of October 19, 2001 on an
application first made within two years against parties intended to be protected
from unnecessary harassment. The judgment of the Supreme Court in October
2001 concluded:

> "This Court is extremely reluctant, as the High Court has been, to
> restrain the access of any citizen to the courts. The stage has clearly been
> reached, however, where the proper administration of justice requires
> the making of such an order as against the Applicant. Accordingly, in
> addition to dismissing the present motion the Court will, in exercise
> of its inherent jurisdiction, order that the Applicant be restrained from
> instituting any proceedings, whether by way of appeal or otherwise,
> against any of the parties to these proceedings or the holders of any of the
> offices named as Defendants or against the Oireachtas, the Government,

or any member thereof or Ireland (other than in relation to the taxation of costs), whether in the High Court or the Supreme Court, except with the prior leave of this Court, such leave to be sought by application in writing addressed to the Registrar of the Supreme Court" (quoting *Riordan v An Taoiseach (No. 4)* [2001] 3 I.R. 365 at 370).

Smyth J. went on to note that the plaintiff had previously sought to institute proceedings making a similar constitutional challenge which had been substantially refused in the High Court by Ó Caoimh J. in May 2001 (*Riordan v An Taoiseach (No. 5)* [2001] 4 I.R. 463):

"I have no evidence or advices or confirmation at the hearing that the decision of Ó Caoimh J refusing leave to institute proceedings on the same points was brought to the attention of the Supreme Court. The Defendants were unaware if such decision had been brought to the attention of the Supreme Court."

Ó Caoimh J. held that the (then intended) now actual plaintiff had not shown the necessary locus standi to impugn the constitutionality of ss.1(3), 2(3), (4) and (5) of the Courts (Establishment and Constitution) Act 1961, applying *Cahill v Sutton* [1980] I.R. 269, and that the proposed constitutional claim against the division of the Supreme Court, which had heard earlier proceedings, was vexatious as it sought to determine an issue previously determined by a court of competent jurisdiction, and was one which obviously could not succeed and was an action from which no reasonable person could reasonably expect to obtain relief. In concluding his judgment, Ó Caoimh J. stated: "I am further of the view that the purpose for which this proposed action is sought to be brought is an improper purpose, namely the harassment and oppression of the various parties referred to in the proceedings already determined by the Supreme Court and that the proposed action is other than the assertion of a legitimate right."

In the instant case Smyth J. comprehensively dealt with all issues for which the plaintiff had leave to bring proceedings. His determination is presented *in extenso*:

"1. The Plaintiff lacks locus standi to challenge the various claims referable to the Court of Criminal Appeal.
2. I reject as without foundation the contention that the Supreme Court as the court of final appeal established under the Constitution has not convened since December 1995 and has never heard an appeal or issued a determination since that time. This finding is referable as to whether the judges sat on a court of appeal comprising three or more judges at any time since that date.
3. The allegations made against the Court of Criminal Appeal

referable to *DPP v Gilligan* are scandalous and unwarranted.

4. The Plaintiff has abused the locus standi which he has been afforded by the Supreme Court in seeking to litigate before this court cases and decisions already made by the courts of which there is no evidence that he brought to the attention of the Supreme Court in late 2003.

5. In my judgment none of the statutory provisions in suit are repugnant to the provisions of the Constitution.

6. It is not the function of the courts to make decisions on academic issues of law where there is no dispute to resolve. It is undesirable that important constitutional provisions requiring decision should be imported into litigation in a dispute which no longer exists for the purpose of determining who pays the cost for litigation which has otherwise come to an end.

7. A court system that becomes preoccupied with how it is perceived, and is intent to permit, in an anxiety to ensure the right of access to the courts, any person who may benefit from a declaration of the unconstitutionality of a statute indirectly or consequently, is in danger of fostering or encouraging needless litigation at the whim of every and any citizen.

The right of access to the courts is to be protected, but it is not an absolute automatic right in all and every case and circumstance. In the context of this case the words of Henchy J in *Cahill v Sutton* [1980] IR 269 at p286 have a particular relevance:

> 'It would be contrary to precedent, constitutional propriety and the common good for the High Court or this Court to proclaim itself an open house for the reception of such claims'.

In vindicating the constitutional rights of any person it is of importance that the rights of the community as a whole or identifiable persons or officers or offices in it are not disregarded (e.g. by being open to harassment, oppression or scandalous or vexatious litigation). The common good and the respect of society and of the community for a justice system is not served or ensured by a disproportionate concern for the rights of the individual at the almost inevitable expense of a disregard for the rights of society by an over indulgence of every or any complaint of an individual. The courts in respecting the rights of all those who seek access to the court must also have some self-respect. Otherwise there is the real possibility nay probability, that the justice system will be abused and/ or manipulated for unworthy purposes.

Accordingly, in addition to dismissing this action I will (as did the Supreme Court in *Riordan v Ireland (No.4)*) in exercise of inherent jurisdiction, order the Plaintiff be restrained from instituting any proceedings whatsoever whether by summons or notice of motion or otherwise against any of the parties to these proceedings or the holders of any of the offices named as Defendants or against the Oireachtas, the Government or any member thereof or Ireland (other than in relation to any issue as to the amount of costs and an appeal on this instant decision) except with prior leave of this court, or only if appropriate (as determined in the first instance by this court) by the Supreme Court: Such leave to be sought by application in writing on notice to the intended defendant(s)/respondent(s) supported by affidavit referring in full and complete detail to all earlier applications, motions, actions or proceedings of any nature whatsoever and the status, result or determination thereof and vouching the payment in full of all costs and expenses referable to such directions as the Plaintiff may have been liable by order or orders of the court or the Supreme Court in all and every earlier application, motion, action or proceedings of any nature whatsoever. Notwithstanding that this foregoing element of this judgment may in isolation and devoid of context appear as imposing an impermissible price on the rights of access to the courts under the Constitution or in common law going back to Magna Carta, it is not such. It is an affront to the principle that not only must justice be done, but seen to be done if the public purse is to be regarded as a full indemnity fund to permit the Plaintiff to continue what, in this instance is, under the guise of constitutional concern, vexatious litigation."

Leave to take legal proceedings   It may be seen from the foregoing that the courts deal most fairly with a vexatious litigant. While, at the same time, condemning the nature of frivolous and, indeed at times, scandalous litigation the superior courts are willing and bound to analyse the approaches of such a plaintiff in order to allow any proceedings which might have merit. Readers are referred to the section headed ELECTORAL ISSUES in this chapter for analysis of a case in which the plaintiff, Denis Riordan, had been given leave to litigate (*Cooney, King and Riordan v Minister for the Environment* [2006] I.E.S.C. 61).

ADMINISTRATION OF JUSTICE IN PUBLIC

In *Independent Newspapers of Ireland Ltd v Anderson* [2006] I.E.H.C. 62, the newspaper challenged an order made by a district judge restraining media outlets from reporting the name of an accused person charged with offences in relation to the possession of child pornography. Clarke J. held that the only basis on which such an order could be made was if it was necessary to ensure a fair trial. In this case, the district judge had erred by making an order on the basis of the likely effect to the good name of the accused person. Clarke J. approved a procedure whereby the district judge could make an order without hearing argument from the media outlets concerned. However, having made such an order, a district judge had to have the power to reconsider the order having heard argument from the media outlets concerned. In assessing what circumstances would justify the grant of such an order, Clarke J. relied on the principle of proportionality:

> "If any restrictive order is justified under *Irish Times Ltd* principles then, in order to amount to a justified interference with Article 34.1, such an order must, in my view, comply with principles analogous to those which have been developed under the doctrine of proportionality. Such an order should, therefore:
>
> (i) be designed only to restrict the publication of material which, it is adjudged, would cause serious prejudice leading to a real risk to a fair trial; and
>
> (ii) should do so in a manner which interferes as little as possible with the entitlement to report fully on all aspects of the administration of justice; and
>
> (ii) should do so in a way which is proportionate.
>
> Against such a test it seems to me that the restrictive orders in this case fail. The orders seem more designed to protect the anonymity of the first-named notice party rather than preventing the publication of any material that would not be admissible at a trial and where publication might, therefore, be prejudicial to such trial. The orders of themselves do not prevent the publication of material which makes any accusations against the first-named notice party but which do not specify that he stands charged with offences now before the courts. The jury at the trial will, of course, know the identity of the accused."

CONSTITUTIONAL CHALLENGE TO INFRASTRUCTURAL PROJECTS

Dunne v Minister for Environment, Heritage and Local Government [2006] I.E.S.C. 49 was an appeal against the decision of Laffoy J. dismissing the applicant's challenge that s.8 of the National Monuments (Amendment) Act 2004 offends Arts 5, 10, 15 and 40 of the Constitution and specified European Council Directives. The High Court judgment was dealt with in great detail in the *Annual Review of Irish Law 2004*. Since the Supreme Court declared itself "entirely satisfied" to adopt Laffoy J.'s comprehensive analysis of the statutory provisions and dismissed the appeal, it is unnecessary to consider these matters in this *Annual Review*. The court concluded the portion of its judgment on the constitutional issues as follows:

"The various contentions of the plaintiff under these invoked Articles relate entirely to the plaintiff's alternative view of the appropriate policy for the protection of the natural heritage of Carrickmines. As noted by the learned trial judge, it is not inconceivable that in a hypothetical case, a person in the position of the plaintiff might successfully challenge a statutory measure on the basis that it purported to permit a clear-cut breach of the State's duty to protect the national heritage. As noted by the learned trial judge, this is not such a case. In inviting the Court to review s.8 in the light of the State's duty to safeguard the national heritage and on the basis of the other requirements of the common good, the plaintiff is inviting the courts to undertake a policy role which is conferred on the Oireachtas by the Constitution."

Accepting the importance of preserving the separation of powers, concern nonetheless needs to be expressed that neither court presented any real hope to a potential litigant that a Minister's discretionary decision under s.8 could be successfully challenged.

CRIMINAL LAW RIGHTS

Criminal procedures have been heavily influenced by the Constitution. However, the effect on substantive criminal law has been far less marked. In *King v Attorney General* [1981] I.R. 233 at 257, the Supreme Court struck down parts of s.4 of the Vagrancy Act 1824 which created the offence of "loitering with intent" which applied to "every suspected person or reputed thief" who was proved to have been frequenting or loitering in various public places "with intent to commit a felony". To prove the intent it was not necessary to prove any overt act; the intent could be inferred from the circumstances and from the accused's previous convictions. In a memorable passage, Henchy J. identified the following constitutional defects with the provision:

"In my opinion, the ingredients of the offence and the mode by which its commission may be proved are so arbitrary, so vague, so difficult to rebut, so related to rumour or ill-repute or past conduct, so ambiguous in failing to distinguish between apparent and real behaviour of a criminal nature, so prone to make a man's lawful occasions become unlawful and criminal by the breadth and arbitrariness of the discretion that is vested in both the prosecutor and the judge, so indiscriminately contrived to mark as criminal conduct committed by one person in certain circumstances when the same conduct, when engaged in by another person in similar circumstances, would be free of the taint of criminality, so out of keeping with the basic concept inherent in our legal system that a man may walk abroad in the secure knowledge that he will not be singled out from his fellow-citizens and branded and punished as a criminal unless it has been established beyond reasonable doubt that he has deviated from a clearly prescribed standard of conduct, and generally so singularly at variance with both the explicit and implicit characteristics and limitations of the criminal law as to the onus of proof and mode of proof, that it is not so much a question of ruling unconstitutional the type of offence we are now considering as identifying the particular constitutional provisions with which such an offence is at variance."

It is apparent from this reasoning that substantive provisions of the criminal law must be certain. For many years this stood as the only identified, constitutional requirement pertaining to the substantive content of the criminal law, as distinct from the many requirements as to how accused persons could be treated and the commission of offences proven.

In *Re the Employment Equality Bill 1996* [1997] 2 I.R. 321, the Supreme Court identified a further constitutional requirement in relation to the substantive content of the criminal law. Section 15 of the Bill imposed vicarious criminal liability on an employer for any discriminatory acts of an employee that infringed s.14, subject to the defence that the employer took such steps as were reasonably practicable to prevent the employee from infringing s.14. The court held (at pp. 374–375) that this breached both Art.38.1 and Art.40.1 of the Constitution:

"[T]he Court is of the opinion that the condition by which [the offences] may be held to pass muster under our present constitutional system is that ... they should essentially be regulatory in character; apply where a person has a particular privilege (such as a licence) or a duty to make sure that public standards as regards health or safety or the environment or the protection of the consumer, and such like, are upheld, and where it might be difficult, invidious or redundant to seek to make the employee liable.

However, what is sought to be done by this provision is that an employer, devoid of any guilty intent, is liable to be found guilty on indictment of an offence carrying a fine of £15,000 or a prison sentence of two years, or both such fine and imprisonment, and to be tainted with guilt for offences which are far from being regulatory in character but are likely to attract a substantial measure of opprobrium. The social policy of making the Act more effective does not, in the opinion of this Court, justify the introduction of so radical a change to our criminal law. The change appears to the Court to be quite disproportionate to the mischief with which the section seeks to deal.

The Court concludes that to render an employer liable to potentially severe criminal sanctions in circumstances which are so unjust, irrational and inappropriate would make any purported trial of such a person not

one held in due course of law and, therefore, contrary to Article 38, s.1
of the Constitution and also repugnant to the provisions of Article 40,
s.1 of the Constitution."

In *C v Ireland (No. 2)* [2006] I.E.S.C. 33, the Supreme Court in effect stated a
more general principle that underlay the specific decision in *Re Employment
Equality Bill*. This judgment followed on from that in *C v Ireland (No. 1)*
[2005] I.E.S.C. 48, in which the first applicant (C) was awaiting trial on
offences contrary to s.1(1) of the Criminal Law (Amendment) Act 1935, which
provides: "Any person who unlawfully and carnally knows any girl under the
age of fifteen years shall be guilty of a felony, and shall be liable on conviction
thereof to penal servitude for life or for any term not less than three years or
to imprisonment for any term not exceeding two years.

    C was charged with having on several occasions had unlawful carnal
knowledge of a female under the age of 15. He submitted that he had reasonable
grounds for believing that the complainant was over the age of 15 and that he
would plead that by way of defence, were it not for the apparent exclusion of
that defence by the statute. By way of judicial review, C sought a declaration
that a reasonable mistake as to the age of the complainant was a defence or, in
the alternative, a declaration that the exclusion of such a defence was repugnant
to the Constitution. The second applicant (G) was charged with the sexual
assault of a complainant, who was under the age of 13 at the time. Section 14
of the 1935 Act provided that consent would not be a defence to a charge of
sexual assault (then called indecent assault) upon a person under the age of 15.
G argued, however, that the defence of reasonable mistake as to age should be
open to him. Both applicants were unsuccessful before the High Court.

    A majority of the Supreme Court (Geoghegan and Fennelly JJ., Hardiman
and McCracken JJ. concurring) refused C's application for a declaration that
s.1(1) of the 1935 Act allowed for a defence of reasonable belief as to age. They
held that the offence was non-regulatory in character and that the presumption
of *mens rea* could therefore be rebutted only by express language or necessary
implication. Silence as to the *mens rea* requirement would not rebut the
presumption. However, they reasoned that the *mens rea* presumption was in
this case rebutted by necessary implication. This necessary implication arose
from a comparison of the 1935 Act with certain provisions of the Criminal Law
Amendment Act 1885, which it replaced. The 1885 Act, which itself replaced
certain provisions of the Offences Against the Person Act 1861, created as
a felony an offence involving a younger girl (unlawful carnal knowledge of
a girl under 13) and as a misdemeanour an offence involving an older girl
(unlawful carnal knowledge of a girl aged between 13 and 16). With regard to
the misdemeanour offence involving the older girl, s.5 of the 1885 Act provided
a defence where the accused had reasonable cause to believe that the girl was
of or over the age of 16. The 1935 Act replaced these provisions but moved
the age limits so that the felony offence applied with respect to girls under

the age of 15, and the misdemeanour offence applied with respect to girls between the ages of 15 and 17. However, it provided no reasonable mistake as to age defence in respect of either offence. The majority judges held that it was a *necessary implication* of this legislative history that the presumption of *mens rea* was rebutted. Denham J. dissented, reasoning that while that would be a *reasonable implication* of the legislative history, it was not a *necessary implication* (the test under *Murray*). On that basis, she was prepared to grant C a declaration that there was a *mens rea* requirement implicit in s.1(1).

With regard to G, however, the court unanimously granted a declaration that the offence of sexual assault implicitly provided a defence of reasonable mistake as to the age of the complainant. As this was a common law offence, there was no legislative history to rebut the presumption of *mens rea*.

The Supreme Court then invited further argument as to whether the legislative exclusion of *mens rea* in relation to s.1(1) was unconstitutional. This was the point at issue in *C v Ireland (No. 2)* [2006] I.E.S.C. 33, the Supreme Court unanimously holding that s.1(1) of the 1935 Act was unconstitutional. Hardiman J., with whom all other members of the court agreed, noted the absolute character of the offence: once the *actus reus* was established, no defence was open to the accused person. He reasoned that it was proper to assess the seriousness of the offence by reference to the maximum punishment that could be ordered. The maximum sentence of penal servitude for life, the social stigma attached to the offence and the consequences of enrolment on the Sexual Offenders Register combined to render the offence created by s.1(1) very serious. Hardiman J. reasoned:

> "It appears to us that to criminalise in a serious way a person who is mentally innocent is indeed 'to inflict a grave injury on that person's dignity and sense of worth' and to treat him as 'little more than a means to an end', in the words of Wilson J. quoted earlier in this judgment. It appears to us that this, in turn, constitutes a failure by the State in its laws to respect, defend and vindicate the rights to liberty and to good name of the person so treated, contrary to the State's obligations under Article 40 of the Constitution. These rights seem fundamental in the sense of that word as used in *Jedowski*; cited above...
>
> The English decisions, of course, were addressing matters of construction and not of compatibility with a Constitution. But they, like this Court in the Employment Equality Bill case, and like the Canadian Supreme Court in the cases cited, speak powerfully to the central importance of a requirement for mental guilt before conviction of a serious criminal offence, and the central position of that value in a civilised system of justice.
>
> Speaking of such a system in a constitutional context, O'Higgins CJ in *The State (Healy) v Donoghue* [1976] IR 325 said:
>> In the first place the concept of justice, which is specifically referred

to in the preamble in relation to the freedom and dignity of the individual appears again in the provisions of Article 34 which deals with the Courts. It is justice which is to be administered in the Courts and this concept of justice must import not only fairness and fair procedures, but also regard to the dignity of the individual. No court under the Constitution has jurisdiction to act contrary to justice.

I cannot regard a provision which criminalises and exposes to a maximum sentence of life imprisonment a person without mental guilt as respecting the liberty or the dignity of the individual or as meeting the obligation imposed on the State by Article 40.3.1 of the Constitution ..."

Hardiman J. rejected any utilitarian justification (*e.g.* the protection of young girls) for the abrogation of the right of an accused person not to be convicted of a true criminal offence in the absence of *mens rea*. It is this heavy emphasis on dignity that appears to provide the philosophical underpinning for this development in constitutional law. On this argument, the State must respect each individual as an independent, autonomous agent. Individuals must not be treated as a means to an end. Accordingly, as a matter of constitutional law (as well as criminal law theory), it is impermissible for the State to punish people for crimes of which they are mentally innocent. Although s.1(1) of the Criminal Law Act 1935 was unquestionably a serious offence (or a "true crime", if one prefers that terminology), it is possible that Hardiman J.'s comments may have some application to less serious (or "regulatory") offences. This is an issue to which the courts will surely return.

DECLARATIONS OF UNCONSTITUTIONALITY

While the decision in *C* was controversial, it quickly produced a far more controversial case, that of *A v Governor of Arbour Hill Prison* [2006] I.E.S.C. 45. On June 15, 2004, A had pleaded guilty to the offence of unlawful carnal knowledge of a girl under the age of 15 years, contrary to s.1(1) of the Criminal Law (Amendment) Act 1935. The girl in question was the 12-year-old friend of A's daughter. When sleeping over at A's house, she was plied with alcohol by A who then raped her. For this crime, A was sentenced to a term of imprisonment of three years. This was the offence declared unconstitutional in the *C* case, above.

On May 26, 2006 A instituted habeas corpus proceedings. Article 40.4.1° of the Constitution provides that no citizen shall be deprived of his personal liberty save in accordance with law. Article 40.4.2° prescribes a procedure whereby detained persons can seek an order from the High Court declaring their detention illegal and ordering their release. On May 29, 2006 the High

Court ordered the release of A, Laffoy J. principally reasoning that A's continued detention in custody had been rendered unlawful by the declaration that s.1(1) of the 1935 Act was unconstitutional. The State appealed and on June 2, 2006 the Supreme Court allowed the appeal, ordering the re-arrest of A. The court provided its reasons on July 10, 2006. The issues in this case can best be addressed by comparing how the court characterised the effects of the declaration of unconstitutionality in *C* with its previous dicta on the effects of such declarations. This can be subdivided into a number of issues.

When do declarations of unconstitutionality date to? The *A* case concerned a pre-1937 statute; a majority did not question that pre-1937 statutes are void from the enactment of the Constitution. Hardiman J. noted arguments advanced by the State for the over-ruling of *Murphy v Attorney General* [1982] I.R. 241 on this point, but was reluctant to consider such arguments in the context of Art.40 proceedings (designed for speed), particularly given that the case could (in his view) be decided against A on the basis of existing jurisprudence.

The effects of a declaration of unconstitutionality The Supreme Court endorsed the distinction, drawn in *Murphy*, between the principle that a statute declared unconstitutional is void either *ab initio* or from 1937 and the retroactive effect that such a declaration might have. In *Murphy v Attorney General, McDonnell v Ireland* [1998] 1 I.R. 134 and arguably *State (Byrne) v Frawley* [1978] I.R. 328, the courts had drawn exceptions to retroactivity based effectively on delay and acquiescence on the part of the litigant seeking relief. However, it is clear from *Muckley v Attorney General* [1985] I.R. 472 that these were exceptions to a general principle. Following the decision in *Murphy*, the Oireachtas had enacted s.21 of the Finance Act 1980, which provided for a system under which the tax collected from married persons, in respect of the tax years prior to 1979/1980, would not be any less than would have been collected under the provisions impugned in *Murphy*. This gave rise to the situation in *Muckley v Ireland*. The plaintiffs had overpaid their tax in 1979/1980. However, they had underpaid their taxes in the years 1975/1976 to 1978/1979, under the legislation subsequently struck down as unconstitutional. The inspector of taxes sought to offset the previous underpayments against the more recent overpayment, with the result that the Revenue Commissioners would not have to repay the amount of the overpayment. This would have been the correct position if s.21 of the 1980 Act were constitutionally valid; however, both the High Court and the Supreme Court held that s.21 was unconstitutional on the grounds that it penalised the married state. On that basis, Barrington J. summarised the situation as follows, casting considerable light on the extent to which the declaration of voidness in *Murphy* had retrospective effects:

"It appears to me that the logic of the Supreme Court judgment in the *Murphy Case* [1982] IR 241 indicates that there was no power to

compute and to levy taxes under the impugned provisions of the Act of
1967. If these taxes have not been paid there is no power to collect them.
Taxes which have been paid under the impugned provisions cannot,
generally, be recovered but this is not because the impugned provisions
ever had any validity but because of the unfortunate fact that it is not
possible to rectify all the injustices of life.

This line of reasoning has however the unpalatable result that
conscientious citizens who paid their taxes on time cannot recover them
but people who delayed or defaulted may escape liability altogether.
Mr. O'Neill, on behalf of the Attorney General, referred to this as a
'monstrous' result.

It is however only fair to point out that there is no question of Mr
and Mrs Muckley being defaulters. They met all their tax liabilities in
accordance with the PAYE system and, in retrospect, we now know
that they in fact paid more tax than they were constitutionally obliged
to pay. The logic of this would appear to be that, on the basis of the
Murphy decision, they are not obliged to pay any further taxes in respect
of the financial years 1975/76 to 1978/79 (inclusive), and that they
are entitled to a refund of the full amount of tax over-paid in the year
1979/1980 free of any set off in respect of the earlier years" ([1985]
I.R. 472 at 477).

This clarifies a number of points. First, the decision in *Murphy* was characterised
as an exception justified by the practical difficulties of paying back taxes that
had already flowed into the central fund. It was an exception to the general
principle that voidness means having no legal effect. Secondly, the Muckleys
were in effect able to avail themselves of the declaration of unconstitutionality
granted in *Murphy* to affect transactions entered into prior to *Murphy*.
Although these points were not argued before the court, they certainly reflect
the understanding of *Murphy* at the time. If *Muckley* correctly stated the law,
the presumptive principle to apply to A was that he should be released unless
there was some reason why it was not practicable to do so.

However, the Supreme Court in *A* preferred O'Flaherty J.'s statement in
McDonnell v Ireland [1998] 1 I.R. 134 as being the correct statement of the law.
In that case, the Supreme Court unanimously refused a claim for damages from
a postman who had forfeited his employment on foot of s.34 of the Offences
Against the State Act, a section subsequently declared unconstitutional in *Cox
v Ireland* [1992] 2 I.R. 53. Most members of the court relied on the fact that
Mr McDonnell had delayed for many years in seeking damages, long after
any limitation period would have elapsed. However, O'Flaherty J. made some
more general observations:

"[S]ince the provision was in place when the plaintiff was prosecuted
on the 30th May, 1974, he cannot now avail of its extirpation as giving

him a cause of action. This is established in both the majority judgments, as well as in the minority judgment, of the Court in [*Murphy*]...

The approach of the majority in [*Murphy*], while holding that declarations of invalidity of legislation worked to make the impugned legislation void *ab initio*, produced more or less the same results [as the minority judgment of O'Higgins CJ that such legislation was void only from the date of the declaration]. It was held that the plaintiffs were not entitled to recover tax paid by them for any period prior to the tax year 1978/79, which was the tax year in respect of which the constitutionality of those sections was first effectively impugned...

The correct rule must be that laws should be observed until they are struck down as unconstitutional. Article 25.4.1 of the Constitution provides that:

'Every Bill shall become and be law as on and from the day on which it is signed by the President...'

and that, unless the contrary is expressed, that law is effective from that day forth ...

From that date, all citizens are required to tailor their conduct in such a way as to conform with the obligations of the particular statute. Members of society are given no discretion to disobey such law on the ground that it might later transpire that the law is invalid having regard to the provisions of the Constitution. Every judge on taking office promises to uphold 'the Constitution and the laws'; the judge cannot have a mental reservation that he or she will uphold only those laws that will not someday be struck down as unconstitutional. We speak of something as having 'the *force* of law'. As such, the law forms a cornerstone of rights and obligations which define how we live in an ordered society under the rule of law. A rule of constitutional interpretation, which preserves the distinct status of statute law which, as such, is necessitated by the requirements of an ordered society and by 'the reality of the situation' ... should have the effect that laws must be observed until struck down as unconstitutional. The consequence of striking down legislation can only crystallise in respect of the immediate litigation which gave rise to the declaration of invalidity. This is what occurred in *Murphy v The Attorney General* ... as well as in *Cox v Ireland* ... [1998] 1 IR 134, at 143–144."

Although this approach of Flaherty J. was consistent with the result in *Murphy*, it was not consistent with the reasoning of the majority. The majority clearly viewed the limitation in *Murphy* as an exception to a general principle of retroactive effect for declarations of voidness. For O'Flaherty J., however, there is a general principle against retroactive effect for declarations of voidness, with perhaps a limited exception for those engaged in the litigation in which the declaration of constitutionality is granted. Moreover, the approach suggested by O'Flaherty J. is inconsistent with the result in *Muckley*. For if laws must be observed until struck down and the consequences of striking down legislation only crystallise in respect of the immediate litigation, the Muckleys should not have been able to avoid the effects of their underpayment of taxes prior to the declaration that such legislation was unconstitutional, as they themselves had not challenged the constitutionality of that legislation.

In *A v Governor of Arbour Hill Prison*, the Supreme Court adopted and approved O'Flaherty J.'s approach, although it is perhaps worth noting that *Muckley* does not appear to have been cited to the court in either *McDonnell* or in *A*. Murray C.J. put the matter as follows:

> "[O'Flaherty J's] statement of the law I am quite satisfied is correct. It is the logical and ineluctable application of the principles and considerations set out in the judgment of this Court in *Murphy* and indeed other judicial dicta which I have cited … Save in exceptional circumstances, any other approach would render the Constitution dysfunctional and ignore that it contains a complete set of rules and principles designed to ensure 'an ordered society under the rule of law' in the words of O'Flaherty J."

Although Murray C.J. was correct to note that the courts have not enforced a rigidly retroactive effect for declarations of unconstitutionality, it is arguable that he reversed the principle and the exception. O'Flaherty J.'s statement of the law does not logically and ineluctably follow from the principles and considerations laid down in *Murphy*. Indeed, as O'Flaherty J. himself had implicitly conceded, his proposition was consistent with the result of *Murphy* but not with the reasoning employed. Moreover, it was inconsistent with the result of *Muckley*.

The judgment of Denham J. neatly captured the way in which the implications of *Muckley* were overlooked by the Supreme Court:

> "The plaintiffs [in *Murphy*] were the only tax payers entitled to maintain a claim for restitution of tax in pursuance of the Court's decision, unless proceedings had already been instituted by any other taxpayer challenging the validity of the sections impugned in the proceedings. Thus, this decision on unconstitutionality did not render the State liable to repay all excess monies gathered, *bona fide*, by the State, since 1967, to the plaintiffs, or to the many affected married couples. There was no retrospective application of unconstitutionality."

This is incorrect, however. There was retrospective application of the declaration in *Murphy*; otherwise, the plaintiffs in *Muckley* could not have maintained their claim that they had overpaid their taxes. What *Murphy* precluded was certain forms of action for the repayment of taxes already paid. An exception was made to the principle of retroactive effect.

In addressing *Murphy* itself, Hardiman J. focused on Henchy J.'s assertion that a condemned provision would *normally* provide no legal justification for any acts done or left undone or for transactions undertaken in pursuance of it. He relied on the word "normally" to support Murray C.J.'s restatement of the principle:

> "In a criminal prosecution where the State relies in good faith on a statute in force at the time and the accused does not seek to impugn the bringing or conduct of the prosecution, on any grounds that may in law be open to him or her, including the constitutionality of the statute, before the case reaches finality, on appeal or otherwise, then the final decision in the case must be deemed to be and to remain lawful notwithstanding any subsequent ruling that the statute, or a provision of it, is unconstitutional. That is the general principle.
>
> I do not exclude, by way of exception to the foregoing general principle, that the grounds upon which a court declares a statute to be unconstitutional, or some extreme feature of an individual case, might require, for wholly exceptional reasons related to some fundamental unfairness amounting to a denial of justice, that verdicts in particular cases or a particular class of cases be not allowed to stand."

Although Henchy J.'s use of the word "normally" clearly envisaged exceptions to retroactive application of declarations of unconstitutionality—a point supported by the decision in both *Murphy* itself and *McDonnell*—it is questionable whether it is consistent with a general principle that criminal convictions will stand notwithstanding a subsequent declaration of unconstitutionality. Such a general principle substitutes the rule for the exception.

The relevance of collateral challenges and *ius tertii* Both Murray C.J. and Hardiman J. emphasised the fact that A's claim for release was in the nature of a collateral challenge, Hardiman J. also relying on the concept of *ius tertii*. Murray C.J. defined collateral challenges in the following way:

> "A collateral attack arises where a party, outside the ambit of the original proceedings seeks to set aside the decision in a case which has already been finally decided, all legal avenues, including appeal, having been exhausted, for reasons that were not raised in the original proceedings but for reasons arising from a later court decision on the constitutionality of a statute."

The last phrase of this definition is crucial, as the courts have clearly allowed collateral challenges in the past where the basis for the challenge did not turn on a declaration of unconstitutionality. For instance, in *Shelly v Mahon* [1990]

1 I.R. 36, an applicant for judicial review succeeded in having his conviction quashed when it transpired that the district judge who convicted him had been invalidly in office at the time, on account of a misunderstanding as to his age. The applicant had applied for judicial review 22 months after his conviction, well outside the normal time for such an application. This point is even more starkly illustrated by *Glavin v Governor of Mountjoy Prison* [1991] 2 I.R. 421. One month after the Supreme Court decision in *Shelly*, Mr Glavin sought an order of habeas corpus pursuant to Art.40.4. He had been sent forward for trial by the same district judge and subsequently pleaded guilty to larceny in the Circuit Criminal Court. The High Court ordered that the relief be sought by way of an application for judicial review and, three-and-a-half years after Mr Glavin had been sent forward for trial, quashed his conviction. This decision was upheld on appeal by the Supreme Court. Indeed, it is almost in the nature of a habeas corpus application that it is a collateral challenge. Rather than utilise the normal appeal procedures, an applicant challenges her detention under a special provision on the basis that the legal wrong done (which could be appealed on its own terms) brings into play a further wrong: unconstitutional deprivation of liberty.

For these reasons, it cannot be said that collateral challenges have never been successful. Murray C.J.'s limitation of his point to collateral challenges based on declarations of unconstitutionality renders correct the statement that collateral challenges have never been permitted. However, if the point is limited to collateral challenges based on declarations of unconstitutionality, one wonders whether it adds anything (either by way of support or rationale) to the general principles identified by the court in relation to declarations of unconstitutionality.

Hardiman J. placed considerable emphasis on the concept of *ius tertii*, repeatedly noting that Mr A could not have advanced the argument advanced by Mr CC in the earlier case—Mr A clearly knew the age of his victim. Hardiman J. considered that this accentuated the collateral character of Mr A's challenge:

> "[Henchy J referred] to the entitlement of such a person 'normally' to relief, and to the limitations of that entitlement in certain circumstances. But a person such as the present applicant who is mounting an oblique or collateral attack on a prison sentence, on the basis of another person's successful attack on the statute under which it was imposed, is clearly in a weaker position. His position is weaker again if he himself could never have lodged the initial attack, since the statute offended no right of his. He is not a person 'damnified by the operation of the invalid provision' and thus not a person 'normally' entitled to relief, within Henchy J's categories."

However, this seems to offer little more than rhetorical support to the contention that Mr A was not entitled to release. His argument was not based on any constitutional infirmity in the section under which he was first convicted but was rather based on the constitutional infirmity of his continued detention on the basis of a legislative provision which the court accepted no longer existed. Murray C.J. accepted this point:

> "I accept that this application is not based on the assertion of a *jus tertii*. It is not a general assertion of unconstitutionality without regard to the applicant's circumstances or a claim based on the infringement of rights of another person or persons. The applicant claims to be directly affected by the decision in *CC* because he was convicted pursuant to the section of the 1935 Act which in *CC* was subsequently found unconstitutional."

This is surely the correct position. Although one's attitude to Mr A's claim is coloured by his attempt to derive a benefit from arguments on which he could never himself have relied, Mr A's claim was not a *ius tertii*.

The continuing effect of official acts done before the declaration of unconstitutionality In the High Court, Laffoy J. ordered the release of Mr A largely on the basis that his *continuing* detention could not be justified on the basis of the statute declared to be void *ab initio*. She put the matter as follows:

> "As I have said, the only consequence of the declaration of the inconsistency of s. 1(1) with the Constitution with which I am concerned on this application is whether it has rendered the detention of the applicant unlawful as of now. If it is undoubtedly the case that the consequences of a declaration under Article 50.1 may be determined by a variety of factors, for example, the conduct of the person relying on the declaration or the fact that an irreversible course of events has taken place, so that what was done on foot of the condemned statutory provision may not necessarily be relied on as a ground for a claim for mollification or other legal redress, as Henchy J noted in *Murphy v The Attorney General*, citing the decision of the Supreme Court in *The State (Byrne) v Frawley*. However, on this application I am not concerned with whether the applicant may be in a position to maintain a civil action for wrongful imprisonment in the future... In the light of the declaration by the Supreme Court of the inconsistency of s.1(1), the only offence of which the applicant was convicted, the conviction is a nullity, and the warrant is bad on its face... [H]is detention was rendered unlawful by the declaration and cannot continue."

This is the most cogent ground for the release of Mr A. Notwithstanding any limitations there may be to the effects of declarations of unconstitutionality,

Art.40.4 requires that a person not be deprived of her liberty save in accordance with law. Once s.1(1) of the 1935 Act was declared unconstitutional, even prospectively, what continuing basis could there be for A's imprisonment? This issue was not squarely addressed by the Supreme Court. Hardiman J. provided the only detailed consideration of the habeas corpus issues:

> "The particular difficulties affecting an applicant for Article 40.4.2 relief who is a convicted prisoner have been well epitomised in this Court in the judgment in *The State (Aherne) v Cotter* [1982] IR 1 88 as follows:
>
>> Before a convicted person who is serving his sentence may be released under our constitutional provisions relating to *habeas corpus*, it has to be shown not that that detention resulted from an illegality or a mere lapse from jurisdictional propriety, but that it derives from a departure from the fundamental rules of natural justice, according as those rules require to be recognised under the Constitution in the fullness of their evolution at a given time and in relation to the particular circumstances of the case. Deviations from legality short of that are outside the range of *habeas corpus*.
>
> That passage puts part of the applicant's difficulties squarely. He has not been able to allege any departure from natural justice in the way he has been treated. He acknowledges his guilt and that his claimed release would be a 'windfall'. On the other hand, it must be manifest that his release would be a great injustice to others. But it is not necessary to decide the case on that basis. A is here attempting to do what no-one has done before: to set up a declaration based on the right of a third party in order to invalidate a past and closed transaction, his criminal trial. This cannot be done because, on the long established and unchallenged jurisprudence the trial and sentence are things which require to be given continued force and effect. A's release would require a departure from that line of authority which I am satisfied there is no warrant for doing. I am satisfied, in other words, that A is now and always has been detained in accordance with law."

This reasoning is not wholly convincing. As is clear from *Shelly* and *Glavin*, the courts have not generally exercised any bar on people re-opening their criminal convictions several years later. In relation to the habeas corpus issue, while it is difficult for convicted prisoners to obtain habeas corpus, it is not impossible. If a person, having been convicted of an offence for which the only penalty was a fine, were sentenced to a term of imprisonment, it scarcely seems plausible that a court would refuse habeas corpus on the basis that the prisoner had been properly convicted. This is surely *a fortiori* the case if a person is *now* in prison on foot of a law which *now* does not exist.

Ultimately, the Supreme Court's conclusions on this point must rest on the proposition that any official action taken on foot of a statute before that statute is declared unconstitutional shall continue to have full force and effect even after the declaration of unconstitutionality. There is oblique support for this proposition in the judgment of Griffin J. in *Murphy*. Griffin J. agreed with Henchy J. that post-1937 statutes declared unconstitutional were void *ab initio*. He sought to support this point with reference to previous cases decided by the courts and the orders made therein:

> "The construction at which I have arrived is also reinforced by decisions of this Court when declaring enactments of the Oireachtas invalid under Article 15, s.4, subs.2. In *In re Evelyn Doyle* the Court held that certain provisions of s.10, subs.1(*d*) and (*e*), of the Children Act, 1941, were repugnant to the Constitution. The child in question had been sent by the District Court to an industrial school under subs.1(*e*)(iii) of s.10 of the Act of 1941 on the consent of one parent, the other parent having deserted the home. The Court held the detention of the child to be invalid and the High Court, in consequence, directed her release. There is nothing in the judgment of Maguire C.J. to suggest that the section was valid until it was declared to be repugnant—indeed, the contrary is to be implied from the order of the Court. [1982] IR 241, at 330–331."

Griffin J. inferred from the facts (a) that the statute was declared unconstitutional; and (b) that the detention was declared invalid, that the statute must have been void *ab initio*. However, this inference only holds if one assumes that a prospective-only declaration of unconstitutionality would not undo the continuing effect of an official action taken before such a declaration. That assumption, however, would also entail that, where statutes are void *ab initio* yet provide authority to official actions taken on foot of them, there is no reason to stop such official actions having effect after the declaration of unconstitutionality. This was not a particularly important issue for Griffin J.—or the other majority judges in *Murphy*—because they only accorded legal effects to void statutes in exceptional circumstances. However, where legal effects are routinely accorded to void statutes, it becomes a far more significant issue, as evidenced by the *A* case itself. This difference in context means that the comments of Griffin J. cannot be taken as anything more than the most oblique support for the proposition that official actions taken before a declaration of unconstitutionality can continue to have effects after the declaration of unconstitutionality.

As noted above, the Supreme Court has effectively reversed the general principle and the exception. Murray C.J. stated the new position as follows:

> "In a criminal prosecution where the State relies in good faith on a statute in force at the time and the accused does not seek to impugn

the bringing or conduct of the prosecution, on any grounds that may in law be open to him or her, including the constitutionality of the statute, before the case reaches finality, on appeal or otherwise, then the final decision in the case must be deemed to be and to remain lawful notwithstanding any subsequent ruling that the statute, or a provision of it, is unconstitutional. That is the general principle.

I do not exclude, by way of exception to the foregoing general principle, that the grounds upon which a court declares a statute to be unconstitutional, or some extreme feature of an individual case, might require, for wholly exceptional reasons related to some fundamental unfairness amounting to a denial of justice, that verdicts in particular cases or a particular class of cases be not allowed to stand."

The exact contours of the exception are unclear. Some of the concerns over the possible release of Mr A stemmed from the fact that it would be an unjustified windfall, in the sense that he himself would never have been able to challenge the statute on the basis relied on by Mr C. If this is the concern that prompted Murray C.J. to suggest this exception, it is possible that the courts might order habeas corpus in future cases where it would not be an unjust windfall. The relevance of such a value-laden determination to the primarily procedural question of whether a deprivation of liberty is in accordance with law is questionable.

Summary of position   After the *A* case, the position with regards to declarations of unconstitutionality appears to be as follows. Statutes declared unconstitutional are void either from 1937 or *ab initio*. The term "void" suggests that such statutes are deprived of all legal effects, save the legal effect of normally providing sufficient authority for each and every official action taken on foot of them prior to the declaration of unconstitutionality. Such official actions that have a continuing effect will continue to have that effect indefinitely, even after the statute has been struck down. There are limited exceptions (a) for those who instituted the litigation leading to the declaration of unconstitutionality; and (b) in situations where it would amount to a fundamental unfairness to keep someone in prison.

The *A* case demonstrates a legitimate concern for the proper ordering of society. However, all the dicta (perhaps not surprisingly, given the context of the case) focus on situations where public officials have acted. But the law also plays a role in guiding the activities of private individuals. It seems likely that cases will emerge in the next few years in which a person is accused of committing acts that breached s.1(1) prior to it being struck down as unconstitutional. The rights of victims and the proper ordering of society would seem to be prejudiced just as much by not prosecuting such persons as they would have been by releasing Mr A. Yet nothing in the judgments of the Supreme Court would allow any action to be taken on foot of the statute in those cases.

The Supreme Court's decision in *A* thus creates and/or entrenches three contentious distinctions. First, there is the distinction between a legal measure being void on the one hand and providing near absolute legal authority for official action on the other. Secondly, there is the distinction between those for whom release would be an unjustified windfall and those for whom release would not be an unjustified windfall. Finally, there is the distinction between giving continuing effect to official actions taken in reliance on the law but not giving any recognition to the extent to which private citizens have ordered their lives in reliance on the law. All these distinctions could be avoided if the Supreme Court were to reverse *Murphy* and simply hold that statutes declared unconstitutional are void only from the date of the declaration forwards, perhaps with a limited exception for those who had instituted the litigation. Although such a re-interpretation might not be the best interpretation of Art.15.4 and Art.50.1, it would produce a more consistent and defensible set of propositions than exists in the current case law.

ELECTORAL ISSUES

A series of cases challenging the constitutionality of certain statutory provisions governing the nomination of candidates for election to Dáil Éireann culminated in 2006 in the Supreme Court appeal *Cooney, King, Riordan v Minister for the Environment* [2006] I.E.S.C. 61. The appellants claimed that ss.46(4A) and (4B) of the Electoral Act 1992 as inserted by s.1(a) of the Electoral (Amendment) Act 2002, for the nomination of eligible persons as candidates in Dáil elections, are incompatible with the provisions of the Constitution, in particular Art.16 and Art.40, because, in general terms, those conditions and procedures are not permitted by Art.16 of the Constitution, are unduly onerous so as to be an impermissible impediment to their constitutional rights to be nominated as candidates and also constitute an invidious discrimination against non-party candidates as compared with candidates who are affiliated to a registered political party and are nominated by that party. The Supreme Court held that portions of s.46(4B) were unconstitutional and declared that section severable in its entirety.

The judgment in this case is likely to assume considerably greater significance than might be first thought. In 2007 a constitutional challenge to the element of the Electoral Acts, s.41 of the 1992 Act, which disqualifies undischarged bankrupts from membership of Dáil Éireann and, thus, standing for election, was withdrawn prior to hearing (see contemporaneous media reports from June 2007, Ms Beverly Cooper Flynn TD, litigant). Thus, it is possible that in the future similar challenges may be taken which will go to judgment. In this Supreme Court appeal the first two named appellants had taken separate actions, heard together and dismissed by Kearns J. in the High

Court; the third appellant's claim had been dismissed by Carney J. who had
relied upon and applied the judgment and decision of Kearns J. in the earlier
determined proceedings. Further, he dismissed the third appellant's claim
that s.46(5) of the 1992 Act is unconstitutional because it requires that he be
described as "non-party" on the ballot paper rather than as "independent"
(*Riordan v Ireland* [2005] I.E.H.C. 44 *Annual Review of Irish Law 2005*). By
agreement the appeals were heard together.

The most relevant provisions of Art.16 of the Constitution provide:

> "1.1° Every citizen without distinction of sex who has reached the age
> of twenty-one years, and who is not placed under disability or incapacity
> by this Constitution or by law, shall be eligible for membership of Dáil
> Éireann.
>
> > 2°(i) All citizens, and
> >   (ii) such other persons in the State as may be determined by
> >   law,
>
> without distinction of sex who have reached the age of eighteen years
> who are not disqualified by law and comply with the provisions of the
> law relating to the election of members of Dáil Éireann, shall have the
> right to vote at an election for members of Dáil Éireann.
>
> 3° No law shall be enacted placing any citizen under disability or
> incapacity for membership of Dáil Éireann on the ground of sex or
> disqualifying any citizen or other person from voting at an election for
> members of Dáil Éireann on that ground.
>
> 4° No voter may exercise more than one vote at an election for Dáil
> Éireann, and the voting shall be by secret ballot."

Article 16.7 states: "Subject to the foregoing provisions of this Article, elections
for membership of Dáil Éireann, including the filling of casual vacancies, shall
be regulated in accordance with law."

The impugned provisions of the Electoral Act 1992 as amended by the
Electoral (Amendment) Act 2002 are, in particular, ss.46(4A) and 46(4B),
Pt X of the 1992 Act. The relevant portions of s.46, as amended, provide as
follows:

> "46(1) At a Dáil election a person may nominate himself as a candidate
> or may, with his consent, be nominated by another person (being a
> person registered as a Dáil elector in the constituency for which he
> proposes to nominate the candidate) as proposer. ....
>
> (4) A candidate may include in his nomination paper the name of the
> political party registered in the Register of Political Parties as a party
> organised to contest a Dáil election of which he is a candidate, provided
> that, at the time the nomination paper is delivered to the returning officer,
> a certificate in the form directed by the Minister (in this Act referred to

as a 'certificate of political affiliation') authenticating the candidature is produced to the returning officer, being a certificate signed by the officer or officers of such party whose name or names appear in the said Register pursuant to section 25(4)(c) ...

(4A) In the case of a candidate whose candidature is not authenticated by a certificate of political affiliation under subsection (4), the candidate's nomination shall, before delivery of his nomination paper to the returning officer in accordance with section 50, be assented to by 30 persons (excluding the candidate and any proposer) who are registered as Dáil electors in the constituency.

(4B) The following provisions apply in respect of the assents required by subsection (4A) to the nomination of a candidate referred to in that subsection:

   (a) the candidate or the candidate's proposer, if any, shall complete part of a nomination paper as directed on that paper and lodge the paper in the prescribed local authority offices for the constituency;

   (b) the local authority shall number any nomination papers lodged under paragraph (a) in the order in which they are lodged;

   (c) where more than one nomination paper for the same candidate is lodged with the local authority, the first such nomination paper shall be deemed to be the nomination paper for that candidate for that election unless the candidature is withdrawn under section 54 or is deemed under section 62(1) to have been withdrawn;

   (d) to assent to the nomination, a person registered as a Dáil elector in the constituency shall sign the candidate's nomination paper and produce a prescribed photographic identification to the local authority official;

   (e) the local authority official shall note the following details on the nomination paper and then sign the note:

      (i) the assentor's number on the register of electors;

      (ii) the form of identification produced by the assentor, including any number on it;

      (iii) the time and date of the assentor's signature on the paper;

   (f) where the nomination paper bears the signatures of more than the required number of qualified assentors, the signatures (up to the required number of those assentors) appearing first on the nomination paper shall be taken into account to the exclusion of any others;

   (g) where a person registered as a Dáil elector in the constituency signs as assentor the nomination papers of 2 or more different candidates in the same election, that person's signature on the first such nomination paper lodged with the local authority shall

alone be regarded and that person's signature on every other
nomination paper shall be disregarded."

Section 52(1) of the Electoral Act 1992, as amended, confers on a returning
officer the function of ruling on the validity of each nomination paper lodged
by any candidate and he is authorised to treat a nomination paper as invalid if
he, as returning officer, considers that: "(a) in the case of the nomination paper
of a candidate referred to in s. 46(4A), [a non-party candidate] the nomination
is not assented in the manner required by s. 46…".

The Electoral Regulations 2002 (S.I. No. 144 of 2002) made by the Minister
pursuant to powers conferred on him by, *inter alia,* s.46 of the Act of 1992
provide for the photographic identification which an assentor must produce
for the purpose of authenticating his assent to the relevant local authority
officials. Article 5 of the Regulations, in conjunction with the Second Schedule,
prescribes the local authority offices for each constituency at which a non-
party candidate must lodge the nomination paper, incorporating the 30 assents,
as required by s.46(4B). The Regulations also set out, in the First Schedule,
the prescribed form of nomination paper at Dáil Éireann with accompanying
explanatory notes.

It is obvious from the foregoing that some of the statutory procedures
required for non-party candidates are cumbersome and, indeed, the Supreme
Court recognised this: "The marshalling of thirty persons either individually or
collectively or in separate groups to commit up to a day travelling to and from
the designated office is, in the view of the Court, a heavy burden to impose on
a person seeking to validate his nomination papers."

This aspect of the judgment will be dealt with first.

Disproportionate administrative procedures The court found that the
statutory provisions, imposed by virtue of s.46(4B), were disproportionate to
the particular objective to be achieved, namely the due authentication of the
nomination papers of a prospective election candidate. A number of risks in the
procedures were identified. There was a real risk of impeding a candidate from
lodging validated nomination papers within a reasonable time after the first
date for the lodgment of such papers was announced. In addition, a potential
candidate would have to devote a disproportionate amount of time over a
disproportionate period of the election campaign to making such arrangements.
The court held that the administrative procedures imposed an undue impediment
on the otherwise lawful right of the candidate to be nominated and was not
satisfied by the State's evidence that no other administrative arrangements
could be introduced which would be significantly less onerous regarding the
verification of a signature on a nomination paper.

The court dismissed the additional claim, upholding Carney J. that the
Oireachtas is entitled to regulate by law pursuant to Art.16.7.

Regulate by law The substantive portion of the judgment dealt with a consideration of the right of the Oireachtas to regulate elections by law. The court considered it self-evident that the State has a legitimate interest in regulating the conduct of elections by law, subject to the Constitution, in the interests of, *inter alia*, protecting and maintaining the integrity and efficacy of the electoral process for Dáil Éireann as well as ensuring that those elections are conducted free from abuse and in an orderly fashion consistent with democratic values acknowledged by the Constitution including Art.5 which declares Ireland to be "a sovereign, independent, democratic State". Further, it is a matter of judgment for the Oireachtas and not for the courts as to what regulatory or preventative measures are desirable. This is provided, of course, that they are otherwise consistent with the Constitution and serve a legitimate purpose, are proportionate to that purpose and avoid invidious discrimination.

Referring to the High Court action the court found that Kearns J. had incorrectly interpreted the Constitution when he concluded that the power to regulate the manner in which eligible candidates may be nominated derived from Art.16.1.1°. The Supreme Court found instead that Art.16.7 applied:

> "Certainly, Article 16.1.1. confers on the Oireachtas the power to determine which categories of persons may, by law, be placed under a disability or incapacity for the purposes of membership of Dáil Éireann so as to render them ineligible from membership of Dáil Éireann and thus in becoming candidates at all. Article 16.1.3. expressly excludes the sex of the person as being a ground for placing a citizen under disability or incapacity for membership of Dáil Éireann. That is not to say that the Oireachtas is otherwise unfettered as to which category or kind of person should be placed under a disability or incapacity for membership of the Dáil. The exercise of any such power may be subject to other constitutional considerations such as the pursuit of a legitimate State interest and the principle of proportionality.
>
> Article 16.1.1 is concerned with persons who by reason of their condition or status belong to a category of persons whose membership of Dáil Éireann could legitimately be considered as undermining or conflicting with, *inter alia*, such matters as the legitimacy and integrity of Dáil Éireann exercising the traditional and constitutional functions of a democratic legislature.
>
> In this respect the Oireachtas must be considered to have a reasonable degree of discretion to determine the categories of persons who may be excluded from eligibility from membership of Dáil Éireann on the basis of Article 16.1.1 provided that the categories of persons concerned are so determined in a manner which is rational and not arbitrary and which serves a legitimate interest of the proper functioning of the Dáil as the legislative organ of government, independent of other organs of government, State institutions and similar bodies ..."

[The court quoted s.41 of the Electoral Act 1992.]

In short Article 16.1.is concerned with persons who by reason of their status or capacity belong to a defined category who are disqualified by law from *membership* of Dáil Éireann. Thus it is persons who are so disqualified from membership of Dáil Éireann by reason of their disability or incapacity as defined by the Constitution or by law who are governed by that provision. The question of the eligibility of such persons to stand as Dáil candidates does not arise since they are disqualified from membership.

On the other hand it is common case that the appellants are not disqualified from *membership* of Dáil Éireann by reason of any disability or incapacity. They are eligible not only for membership of Dáil Éireann but they are eligible to be candidates in a Dáil election. What the impugned measures purport to do is to require them to fulfil certain conditions so as to demonstrate, as claimed by the State, a real or *bona fide* commitment to the electoral process. Article 16.7. provides:

'*Subject to the foregoing provisions of this article, elections for membership of Dáil Éireann, including the very filling of casual vacancies, shall be regulated in accordance with law.*'

Accordingly, when the State, by means of legislation adopted by the Oireachtas, exercises a power to regulate the manner and conditions according to which persons may seek to be nominated as candidates for Dáil Éireann it is exercising a power pursuant to 16.7.of the Constitution and not 16.1.1."

The court observed that Kearns J. in the High Court judge may have felt himself constrained to follow the decision of the High Court in *Redmond v Minister for the Environment* [2001] 4 I.R. 61, which had not been appealed, and in particular the manner in which Herbert J. interpreted and applied the decision of the Supreme Court in *Re Article 26 of the Constitution and The Electoral Amendment Bill 1983* [1984] I.R. 268. In that case the issue with which the court was concerned was whether the Constitution permitted the right to vote to be extended to persons other than citizens. In concluding that the Bill was incompatible with the Constitution, the court was concerned primarily with an interpretation of Art.16.1.2° which specifically concerned the right to vote in Dáil elections albeit, *inter alia*, in the context of Art.16 as a whole and in conjunction with Art.12.4.1°: "In that context the general observations of the court with regard to Article 16 generally must be seen as that, namely, general observations since no issue arose or was argued concerning, for example, the powers which might generally be exercised in regulating elections pursuant to 16.7." The court concluded that:

"Article 16.7 of the Constitution, in providing that elections for membership of Dáil Éireann may be regulated in accordance with law, conferred on the Oireachtas the power to regulate, *inter alia*, matters with which citizens must comply in order to be nominated.

For the reasons outlined above, the conclusions expressed in *Redmond v Minister for the Environment & Ors* [2001] 4 IR 61 to the effect that the Oireachtas does not have powers pursuant to Article 16.7. to regulate by law the conduct of elections by establishing conditions, monetary or otherwise, for the nomination of candidates is not a correct statement of the law."

FAMILY RIGHTS

Article 41 protects the family based on marriage in its constitution and authority. This had led to a strong protection for decisions made by married parents in respect of their children. In *Re JH* [1985] I.R. 375, the Supreme Court considered the situation of a child who had been placed for adoption. Prior to the adoption order being made final, the natural parents married and the mother withdrew her consent. Notwithstanding that the child had spent nearly two years with the proposed adoptive parents prior to the Supreme Court hearing, the court ruled that she should be returned to her natural (and now married) parents. In this regard, Finlay C.J. reasoned that s.3 of the Guardianship of Infants Act 1964, which requires the court to have regard to the best interests of the child in any guardianship or custody disputes, must be interpreted as involving a constitutional presumption that the best interests of the child lie with the married parents, unless the court is satisfied that there are compelling reasons why this cannot be achieved. A more extreme result had been reached in *M v An Bord Uchtála* [1977] I.R. 287, in which the child had been placed for adoption after six weeks and the adoption order had been made final. However, the court held that a defect in the process rendered the adoption order invalid and the child should be returned to its natural (now married) parents, notwithstanding that it had lived for six years with its adoptive parents. In 2006, the courts were presented with an opportunity to reconsider these principles.

In *N v HSE* [2006] I.E.H.C. 278, the applicants sought the return to them of their daughter. Their daughter had been born to them in July 2004 while they were unmarried. She was placed for adoption and since November 2004 was in the care of the proposed adoptive parents. The applicants got married in January 2006 and six weeks later instituted habeas corpus proceedings to secure the return of their daughter. The High Court gave its judgment in June 2006. As with the earlier cases, no final adoption order had been made at this stage so their daughter had not yet become the child of the constitutional family of the proposed adoptive parents. The dealings between the birth parents, the proposed adoptive parents and the HSE were complicated in the extreme. Moreover, there was little agreement over the events and the correct characterisation of those events. In particular, there were issues over how well the HSE had advised both sets of parents as to their rights in the process, the precise reasons for the marriage of the birth parents and the actions taken by the proposed adoptive parents in an attempt to find out information about the birth parents. These details perhaps best illustrate the corrupting effect of applying the law and legal procedures to the most intimate and delicate of interpersonal relations. Ultimately the conclusions of both the High Court and the Supreme Court turn largely on the statement of general legal principles and psychological evidence as to how the child would be affected by a return to her natural parents, not on contested issues of fact as to how the adult parties interacted with one another. Accordingly, I will not set out that detailed factual background here.

There was considerable expert evidence as to the likely effect on the child of being transferred back to her birth parents. McMenamin J. summarised the effect of this evidence as follows:

> "Taken together I consider that the effect of this evidence is that, in the event of an abrupt transfer, or one effected without cooperation, or in circumstances where cooperation is likely to breakdown, there is a *probability* that Ann will sustain psychological or emotional damage. This must be seen in the light of many factors which regrettably demonstrate the breakdown in trust that has occurred between the parties and which is through much of the evidence...
>
> This is not to ignore the risk, which must not be ignored, that for bona fide reasons the Doyles may be unable to cooperate in a transfer process. But in no circumstances could a court countenance a 'veto', based either on bona fide reasons or otherwise, when issues of this type are at stake.
>
> All these factors must be seen in the light of the evidence relating to the degree of trust between the Byrnes, the HSE and the Doyles. When one takes the expert evidence together with the absence of trust and cooperation, the question must arise as to whether a very short term phased transfer of the type (which is the only way in which Ann's emotional development might be protected) can now take place.
>
> In these circumstances, and having regard to the fact, I consider that the evidence goes significantly further than that adduced in two cases; *Re J* [1966] IR 295 and in *Re JH (An Infant)* [1983] IR 375. Developments have taken place in psychology which have considerably advanced the knowledge now available as to attachment, bonding, style of parenting and with regard to the effect of the transfer of care and custody of children, particularly in circumstances where such transfer may be abrupt or which break down because of distrust."

McMenamin J. accepted that the appropriate test was that laid down in *Re JH*, but considered (a) that the current case could be distinguished on its facts; and (b) that the test in *Re JH* had to be read in light of more recent constitutional pronouncements on the rights of the child. In relation to the factual issue, McMenamin J. commented: "The evidence in the earlier authorities did not establish the probability of a risk of harm or psychological damage such as gave rise to the consideration of the rights of the child. Here the evidence establishes such probability having regard to the circumstances.

In relation to the rights of children, McMenamin J. particularly relied on various dicta of the Supreme Court in *HW v NWHB* [2001] 3 I.R. 622, in which the personal rights of the child were recognised. However, he concluded that the test remained that of "compelling reasons" as stated in *Re JH*. He also considered the alternative test, relying directly on the wording of Art.42.5 of the Constitution itself. This provides: "In exceptional cases, where the parents for physical or moral reasons fail in their duty towards their children, the State as guardian of the common good, by appropriate means shall endeavour to supply the place of the parents, but always with due regard for the natural and imprescriptible rights of the child."

McMenamin J. applied both the "compelling reasons" test and the "failure of duty" test. In relation to the failure of duty, McMenamin J. considered that a number of incidents, taken together, constituted a failure in duty on the part of the birth parents to their daughter. These included the initial placement of the child for adoption, the re-affirmation by signature of the form in April 2005 and the signature of the final adoption form. Addressing the "compelling reasons" test, McMenamin J. held that there was a probability of psychological harm to the child if she were to be transferred back to her birth parents. This was largely because the relationship between all the parties had become so mistrustful that there was, in his view, no realistic prospect of a phased transfer. For these reasons, McMenamin J. concluded that the child should remain with her adoptive parents.

This decision was quickly appealed to the Supreme Court, which unanimously ruled that the child should be returned to her natural parents (*N v HSE* [2006] I.E.S.C. 60). However, it is clear that some members reached this conclusion with far greater happiness than did other members. The different judgments therefore cast interesting light on the issues raised by the Constitution in relation to children's rights, parents' rights and the position of the marital family.

Hardiman J. provided a cogent justification for the primacy given to parental rights by the Constitution. He endorsed the test in *Re JH*, emphasising that there was a constitutional presumption that the welfare of the child is to be found within the family; accordingly, state intervention can only be justified if it is established that there are compelling reasons why the welfare of the child *cannot* be secured in the custody of the parents. Responding to the general public debate on the issue of parental authority, he offered the following defence of this constitutional position:

"I do not regard the constitutional provisions summarised above, or the jurisprudence to which they have given rise, as in any sense constituting an adult centred dispensation or as preferring the interests of marital parents to those of the child. In the case of a child of very tender years, as here, the decisions to be taken and the work to be done, daily and hourly, for the securing of her welfare through nurturing and education, must of necessity be taken and performed by a person or persons other than the child herself. Both according to the natural order, and according to the constitutional order, the rights and duties necessary for those purposes are vested in the child's parents. Though selflessness and devotion towards children may easily be found in other persons, it is the experience of mankind over millennia that they are very generally found in natural parents, in a form so disinterested that in the event of conflict the interest of the child will usually be preferred...

There are certain misapprehensions on which repeated and unchallenged public airings have conferred undeserved currency. One of these relates to the position of children in the Constitution. It would be quite untrue to say that the Constitution puts the rights of parents first and those of children second. It fully acknowledges the 'natural and imprescriptible rights' and the human dignity, of children, but equally recognises the inescapable fact that a young child cannot exercise his or her own rights. The Constitution does not prefer parents to children. The preference the Constitution gives is this: it prefers parents to third parties, official or private, priest or social worker, as the enablers and guardians of the child's rights. This preference has its limitations: parents cannot, for example, ignore the responsibility of educating their child. More fundamentally, the Constitution provides for the wholly exceptional situation where, for physical or moral reasons, parents fail in their duty towards their child. Then, indeed, the State must intervene and endeavour to supply the place of the parents, always with due regard to the rights of the child.

If the prerogatives of the parents in enabling and protecting the rights of the child were to be diluted, the question would immediately arise: to whom and on what conditions are the powers removed from the parents to be transferred? And why?"

Hardiman J. repeated his comments in *HW v NWHB* to the effect that although the primacy of parents, as a constitutional idea, had its source in natural law theory, it was also consistent with quite different strands of thought, even a Benthamite one.

Addressing the "compelling reasons" test in more detail, Hardiman J. emphasised that the test was whether there were compelling reasons why the welfare of the child *could not* be achieved within the natural family. The test was not whether there were compelling reasons why the child *should* remain within the adoptive family. The presumption was therefore strongly in favour of the natural family.

In addressing the High Court's findings in relation to the "compelling reasons" test, Hardiman J. was not prepared to accept that the court could legitimately consider the possibility of the adoptive parents failing to cooperate with a phased return as a ground for refusing to allow that return. Agreeing with Geoghegan J.'s detailed review of the evidence, Hardiman J. was satisfied that a phased and gradual return of the child to her natural parents would substantially reduce the risk of any long-term damage to the child. On that basis, he was not satisfied that there was any compelling reason which could displace the constitutional presumption that the welfare of the child would be best served in the natural family. In relation to the "failure of duty" test, Hardiman J., relying on previous authority as well as first principles, held that participation in the adoption process (*i.e.* the taking of steps that could lead to adoption) could not constitute a failure of duty.

Hardiman J.'s judgment is consistent with *Re JH* and effectively restores the constitutional *status quo* that was unsettled by McMenamin J.'s judgment in the High Court. However, his rationalisation and statement of the constitutional position raises three broader issues that perhaps suggest some shift in constitutional thinking. First, his judgment referred repeatedly to the constitutional presumption that the welfare of the child is to be found in her natural family. However, this is not what was held in *Re JH*. In that case, Finlay C.J.'s comments were explicitly referenced to a context where there was "a contest between the parents of a legitimate child—who with the child constitute a family within the meaning of Articles 41 and 42 of the Constitution—and persons other than the parents as to the custody of the child". Thus Hardiman J.'s judgment effectively replaces a presumption in favour of the marital family with a presumption in favour of the natural family. This raised few issues in *Re JH* itself as the natural family had got married, but it is not difficult to see how it could pose difficulties. At an ideological level, it is clearly inconsistent with the whole ethos of Arts 41 and 42. From *State (Nicolaou)* onwards, the courts have been consistent in their view that Arts 41 and 42 protect the marital family, not natural families. While natural mothers have many rights in respect of their children, natural fathers do not. This points up the second difficulty with Hardiman J.'s presumption in favour of natural families: what happens where the natural parents do not agree on the custody of the child? Thirdly, consider the situation where the adoption had been completed and the child had become part of the adoptive parents' marital and constitutionally-protected family before her natural parents got married. On the basis of Hardiman J.'s presumption in favour of the natural family, the child would have to be returned to her natural parents. On the basis of the *Re JH* presumption, however, the child would have to remain with her married adoptive parents. The courts will have to resolve this conflict in a future case.

In this regard, Geoghegan J.'s judgment took a slightly different approach. He commented that the marriage was obviously of the utmost importance "because it would be perceived as having a dramatic effect on the legal position". He also commented that it was fundamental to any consideration of the issues in the case that the applicants were now married. However, he subsequently tempered this somewhat by referring to the "importance of family and marriage and quite frankly also the biological link". He also commented: "Many people, I suspect, would consider that there is an appreciable advantage for a child to be reared within a natural family and having real parents and real aunts and uncles."

Finally, he recasts the constitutional presumption as being a "presumption that the child's welfare is better served with the natural parents in a marriage". This is not wholly consistent with *Re JH* and raises obvious difficulties where it is the adoptive parents who are married and the natural parents remain unmarried.

Setting aside these difficulties, which may simply be issues of terminology, Hardiman J.'s account of the constitutional primacy of parents is surely the most compelling defence of that position. That is, he is right to reject the contention that a preference for parents over third parties renders the Constitution adult-centred rather than child-centred. For children (at least young children) cannot make important decisions for themselves. Someone must decide where a child should live, what a child's best interests require and whether a child wishes to assert her right to bodily integrity, for example. A view that these choices are better made by parents than by third parties (whether the courts, priests or social workers) does not elevate the rights of parents over the rights of children. Parents do not have rights over their children in the same way as they may have a right over the family car or the family pet. Rather, parents have an autonomous decision-making role in relation to their children, a role which can only be displaced in exceptional circumstances by the State. All that said, one wonders whether the Constitution, as interpreted by the courts, has rendered it too difficult for the State to intervene where parents make seriously misguided decisions for their children. In my view, the facts of *N v HSE* did not provide a compelling case for state intervention. The balance of the evidence seemed to be that, provided a gradual transfer of custody was achieved, the interests of the child could be protected by a transfer back to her natural, now married, parents. However, the earlier case of *HW v NWHB* remains troubling, even if one agrees with Hardiman J.'s views in *N v HSE*. Provided that one accords primacy to parental decision-making on the basis that one believes it is most likely to serve the best interests of children (and not because one views the family as a pre-civil entity emerging from the mists of time and therefore impervious to regulation), there must surely come a point where the decisions of the parents affect a child so badly that the State should intervene. If the reason for deference to parents in the first place is a belief that parents are the best at making decisions that respect the best interests of the child, the threshold for state intervention must turn on some concept of the best interests of the child. That is, the threshold should depend not on the bona fides of the parents but rather on the effect of the decisions on the child. However, in *HW v NWHB* there was no basis on which anyone could conclude that the refusal of the PKU test was in the child's best interests. The parents had made a fetish out of bodily integrity at considerable risk to the long-term health of their child. If the Constitution precludes the State from intervening where parents make a decision that no reasonable parent could conceivably make, we should have concerns about the Constitution.

The final point of general interest that arises from Hardiman J.'s judgment is his view, first stated in *HW v NWHB*, that the position of parental primacy is as consistent with Benthamite philosophy as it is with natural law philosophy. This is half correct, and is correct in so far as it applies to the sort of fact situations raised in *HW* and in *N*. However, it misses important aspects of natural law thinking. For the natural law speaks not so much of the primacy of parents as the subsidiarity of the State. The State has a subsidiary role in the sense that it must provide *subsidium* (help) to parents. It is for that reason that the State should not interfere with parental decision-making: its role is to give help, not to override parents. However, the State must give that *subsidium*. When one considers cases such as *Sinnott v Minister for Education*, one can readily see the differences between a laissez-faire non-interventionist approach and a support-giving approach. Writing in the different context of property rights, Gerard Hogan has adverted to the way in which the courts have given a liberal interpretation to the property guarantee, possibly out of step with the natural law origins of the provision. It is arguable that a similar process is occurring with respect to the family provisions. Articles 41 and 42 are being deracinated and re-imagined as protections of families on the basis that the family is a private institution with which the State should not be involved. This removes the support which the State would be obliged to give to the family under a natural law understanding of the State's subsidiary role.

Fennelly J. agreed with the judgments of both Hardiman and Geoghegan JJ., but placed particular emphasis on an additional factor that had featured less prominently in those judgments—the anomalous position of the child if she were not returned to her natural parents:

> "In present circumstances, Ann cannot be adopted. She is registered as a child of the Byrnes. She bears their name. If she stays with the Doyles, the relationship must be that of long-term fosterers. In addition, the Byrnes, remaining her lawful parents and guardians retain rights and obligations in respect of her health, education and general welfare. This situation can, at best be described as anomalous. It is a long way from a completed adoption. I cannot regard it as being in the long-term interests of Ann. This is an aspect of the case which, in my view, weighs heavily in the balance in favour of a return to the Byrnes."

Murray C.J. agreed with Hardiman, Fennelly and Geoghegan JJ. but devoted his own judgment to the issue of how the transfer of the child back to her natural parents should be effected.

McGuinness J. came to the same conclusion as the other members of the court on the application of the tests of "failure of duty" and "compelling reasons". However, she did so with considerable doubt as to whether the constitutionally-mandated tests adequately represented a child-centred approach. Her comments stand in stark contrast to those of Hardiman J. Addressing the difficulties with the constitutional approach, she commented as follows:

> "It is this constitutional context which leaves me to consider the dramatic and remarkable part played in the life and future of Ann by the marriage of her parents. Prior to the Byrnes marriage Ann was placed with entirely suitable prospective adopters in the hope of shortly becoming part of a constitutional family. No criticism has been made of her care and development. Following the natural mother's decision to withdraw her consent to adoption (a decision which, of course, she had a perfect right to make) it was open to the Doyles to initiate proceedings under section 3 of the Act of 1974, a course which it appears they planned to take. Given the evidence before the High Court and the conclusions drawn from that evidence by the learned trial judge, the probability is that there was a full agreement to place the child for adoption. In such a case, the central issue before the court to which all evidence would be directed would be the best interests of Ann.
>
> On 9th January, 2006 the Byrnes intermarried. I have no doubt that their marriage reflected their commitment to each other and their determination to recover custody of their child; it admittedly also reflected their legal advice. Once the marriage took place the Byrnes became a constitutional family with all the concomitant rights and presumptions. The present Article 40 proceedings were then initiated. The central issue to be considered by the court underwent a metamorphosis; it was no longer the best interests of the child but the lawfulness or otherwise of the Doyles' custody of her. When deciding whether the Doyles' custody of Ann is in accordance with law it is no longer possible for the court to follow the original approach of Lynch J. in *In Re J.H.*—*"to look at it through the eyes, or from the point of view of the child"*. It is clear that the court is bound by the decision in *In Re J.H.*; the full rigour of the test established in that case must be applied.
>
> Ann, on unchallenged evidence, is now a happy and secure little two-year-old girl. She is in the loving care of David and Eileen Doyle whom she knows as her father and mother. She has the love and companionship of Eileen Doyle's mother, whom she sees as her grandmother, and of other extended family and friends. She faces an uncertain future. The expert evidence as to whether she will suffer long term harm by being

transferred to the care of her natural parents is predictive rather than certain. But so too is the assessment evidence of S. C. concerning the parenting ability of the Byrnes. Indeed the very concept of a presumption is in itself predictive rather than certain.

In common with Lynch J. in *In Re J.H.*, I remain uncertain and apprehensive about the effects of a transfer of Ann's custody, and about her future in general.

Nevertheless, I do not consider that the medical and other evidence before the High Court judge met the heavy burden of establishing that there were compelling reasons that her welfare could not be achieved in the custody and care of her natural parents. An additional and crucial factor in my reaching this conclusion is that, given her parents' marriage and the re-registration of her birth, there is now no realistic possibility that Ann can be adopted by the Doyles. The Byrnes cannot be held to have failed in their duty towards her or to have abandoned their rights as parents. If Ann remains with the Doyles in what amounts to continuing fosterage this would give rise to practical problems for her in the future. Her position would be insecure and anomalous and there would be no way of guarding against further litigation in the future concerning either her continuing care and custody or the extent of access to her by her natural parents.

In his judgment, Geoghegan J. refers to the fact that in 'some quarters' the decision taken by the Supreme Court in *In Re J.* has been subjected to criticism. The learned judge rightly expresses the view that unless and until the Constitution itself is amended there is no justification for that criticism. I am in agreement with this view. The judgment of this court, as expressed by Finlay C.J., reflects the unequivocal wording of Articles 41 and 42 of the Constitution, as does the judgment of the court in *In re The Adoption Bill 1987* (already cited).

It would be disingenuous not to admit that I am one of the 'quarters' who have voiced criticism of the position of the child in the Constitution. I did so publicly in the report of the Kilkenny Incest Inquiry in 1993. The present case must, however, be decided under the Constitution and the law as it now stands. With reluctance and some regret I would allow this appeal."

The rights of the child were also to the fore in *Bode v Minister for Justice* [2006] I.E.H.C. 341 and related cases. In *Lobe v Minster for Justice* [2003] 1 I.R. 1, the Supreme Court had held that the non-Irish parents of Irish children could not assert, on their child's behalf, a right to have its family members provide it with care and companionship within Ireland. In effect, the non-Irish parents of Irish children did not have any derivative right to remain in the State, although there was an obligation on the Minister for Justice, before issuing any deportation order, to consider the right of the child to have its parents provide it with care and companionship within the State. Following this decision, the citizenship referendum in 2004 and alterations to the patterns of births to non-Irish parents within Ireland, the Minister decided that "rather than engaging in a case by case analysis, as a gesture of generosity and solidarity to the persons concerned, a general policy would be adopted of granting those persons (the non-Irish parents of Irish born children) permission to remain in the State provided that they fulfilled certain criteria". For this reason, the Minister established IBC/05. There was some dispute over the terms of the scheme and, in particular, whether a non-Irish parent had to be continuously resident in the State in order to avail herself of the scheme. Finlay Geoghegan J. summarised the scheme as follows:

> "Considering each of the above documents I have concluded in accordance with their plain meaning the revised arrangements (which became known as the IBC/05 Scheme) established by the respondent on 15th January, 2005 were, as the title of the notice of that date states, "Revised arrangements for the consideration of application(s) for permission to remain (in the State)". Further, the persons to whom they were addressed were non-national parents of Irish born children born before 1st January, 2005. Such parents were invited or permitted to apply for permission to remain in the State based upon the parentage of their Irish born child. The respondent by the announcement committed himself to consider and determine applications for permission to remain in the State from parents of Irish born children born before the 1st January, 2005 made on form IBC/05.
>
> There is nothing in any of the documents which expressly, or by implication states that the revised arrangements do not apply to a person who was not continuously resident in the State with his or her Irish born child since the date of birth in the sense of precluding such persons from making an application on IBC/05 (at 15–16 of the unreported judgment)."

The Minister accepted that, in administering the scheme and deciding on particular applications, no consideration was given by him or on his behalf to the position or rights of the Irish-born child.

The right asserted in *Lobe* had been the right of the child to have the care and companionship of its parents within the State. The right most strongly asserted in *Bode*, however, was the right to be reared and educated with due regard to welfare including a right to have her welfare considered in the sense of what was in her best interests in decisions affecting her. The Minister did not contend that there were common good reasons that justified him in not taking into account the rights of the child, nor that there were common good reasons that required him to refuse an application where continuous residency had not been established. This was in many ways a high stakes argument. It is generally not difficult, within an administrative decision-making process, to establish that something has been "considered" (see *McEvoy v Meath County Council* [2003] 1 I.L.R.M. 431). In effect, the Minister was seeking a strong statement from the courts ensuring a near absolute discretion for the Minister in relation to immigration matters. The high stakes argument failed in the High Court.

Finlay Geoghegan J. reasoned that a positive decision on an IBC/05 application is one which has a considerable impact on a child's life. It prima facie defends and vindicates the personal rights of the citizen child to live in the State and to be reared and educated with due regard to her welfare. It was therefore a breach of the rights of the citizen child for a decision to be taken in relation to IBC/05 without any consideration of the rights of that child. She put the position as follows:

> "Applying the above to the rights identified herein and the IBC/05 application the position appears to be as follows. The citizen child of the non-national parent has, *prima facie*, a right to remain in the State. While in the State (at least) the citizen child has a right to be educated and reared with due regard to his/her welfare and in a decision affecting this, to have considered what is in his/her best interests. These are qualified rights in the sense that the respondent having had due regard to these rights and taking account of all relevant factual circumstances may decide for good and sufficient reason, in the interests of the common good, that the parent be refused permission to remain in the State even if this is a decision which is not in the best interests of the child. In deciding whether there is such good and sufficient reason in the interests of the common good to refuse the application of the parent on IBC/05 for permission to remain in the State the respondent should ensure that his decision, in the particular circumstances of the citizen child and parent is not disproportionate to the ends sought to be achieved" (at 34 of the unreported judgment).

At the time of writing, this decision has been appealed to the Supreme Court by the Minister.

The start of 2006 saw the publication of the Tenth Progress Report of the All-Party Oireachtas Committee on the Constitution, focusing on the family. The report proposed to examine the changes that were occurring in Irish society and sought to evaluate what, if any, changes were needed in the Constitution to enable the State to deal adequately with those changes. The work of the committee provoked considerable interest. It received 7,989 submissions and 16,143 petitions. It also heard 52 oral presentations. The committee's report first provides a helpful exegesis on changes in the demographic and social context of the family. It then addressed the following issues in a thematic way: the definition of the family, cohabiting heterosexual couples, same-sex couples, children, the natural or birth father, lone parents, and women in the home. The changes recommended by the committee were fairly minimal. Moreover, many of the proposed changes have been overtaken by more recent suggestions on the part of the Government. Nevertheless, the committee provided a useful analysis of the issues and it remains appropriate to outline its suggestions and the reasoning behind them.

In relation to the recognition of non-traditional family units, the committee stated that a constitutional amendment would be necessary to effect a change in the definition of family to allow for gay marriage. However, it considered that legislation could extend a wide range of marriage-like privileges both to unmarried opposite-sex and unmarried same-sex couples. This view is not shared by everyone, however. In coming to this conclusion, the committee appears to have adopted the views of the Law Reform Commission in its *Consultation Paper on the Rights and Duties of Cohabitees* in 2004. This view interprets the line of authority commencing with *Murphy v Attorney General* [1982] I.R. 241 as prohibiting merely the penalisation of marriage. However, as has been argued by John Mee, it may be that the obligation to protect marriage prohibits *both* the penalisation of marriage *and* any inducement not to marry. If this is the case, it could be argued that the existence of a civil partnership scheme for opposite-sex couples might induce such people not to marry; such a problem does not arise in relation to same-sex couples (assuming that sexuality is not radically fluid). There may therefore, notwithstanding the committee's views, be constitutional problems in providing a civil partnership scheme for opposite-sex couples. If the Oireachtas moves with more political circumspection, however, providing a civil partnership scheme only for same-sex couples, it is unlikely that there would be constitutional difficulties.

The committee recommended against any change in the definition of the family. It noted that there was not a consensus that the definition of the family in the Constitution should be extended. It noted the views on one side of the debate to the effect that any constitutional recognition for non-traditional family types would undermine the uniqueness of the traditional family. In concluding that the constitutional definition of family should not be changed, the committee effectively sided with this rather extreme viewpoint:

> "In the case of the family, the committee takes the view that an amendment to extend the definition of the family would cause deep and long-lasting division in our society and would not necessarily be passed by a majority. Instead of inviting such anguish and uncertainty, the committee proposes to seek through a number of other constitutional changes and legislative proposals to deal in an optimal way with the problems presented to it in the submissions" (at 122).

In this way, the committee sought to side-step the recognition question by dealing with practical benefits. But the recognition question cannot be so easily avoided. For in refusing constitutional recognition for non-traditional families, the committee was affirming the uniqueness of the traditional family. While one can recognise the realpolitik that lies behind this position, it misses the point of the recognition arguments put forward by non-traditional families. People in such families seek equal recognition because they believe that they are equal to traditional families. Dealing with practical problems while maintaining differential recognition maintains the inequality.

A minority of the committee dissented on this issue. They proposed that an additional provision be inserted at the end of Art.41: "The state also recognises and respects family life not based on marriage. All persons, irrespective of their marital status, have a right to family life. The Oireachtas is entitled to legislate for the benefit of such families and of their individual members."

In relation to children, the committee did recommend a constitutional amendment in the following terms: "All children, irrespective of birth, gender, race or religion, are equal before the law. In all cases where the welfare of the child so requires, regard shall be had to the best interests of that child."

This proposed amendment has a number of drafting flaws. First, "irrespective of birth" is presumably intended to mean "irrespective of civil status at birth" and not irrespective of whether the child is born or not. Secondly, there is some concern over enumerating certain proscribed grounds of discrimination without including a "such as" phrase. Is the implication that grounds of discrimination such as disability or religious belief are to be permitted? That said, the prohibition of discrimination on the grounds of race might have provided a welcome uplift to the rights of Irish children with non-Irish parents. The second sentence of the proposed amendment marked a considerable watering down of what had been proposed by the Constitution Review Group in 1996. That report had suggested: "In all actions concerning children, whether by legislative, judicial or administrative authorities, the best interests of the child shall be the paramount consideration."

In keeping with its recommendation against changing the definition of "family", the committee recommended against granting any explicit rights to unmarried fathers. However, it suggested that the position of unmarried fathers could be improved by the new protection for the rights of the child:

> "The committee ... believes that its proposed amendment in respect of the rights of children will indirectly improve the status of the natural or birth father. Thus, for example, if no child could henceforth be discriminated against on grounds of birth, this would surely oblige the courts to re-fashion a line of (highly controversial) jurisprudence since the Supreme Court's decision in *The State (Nicolaou) v An Bord Uchtála* [1966] IR 567 in which it was held that the natural mother (and not the natural father) had a constitutional right to the custody of the child. If the Constitution were to contain an express guarantee of non-discrimination on the grounds of birth and to have regard to the best interests of the child, this would mean that some of the *Nicolaou*

rationale would disappear. The child under those circumstances would have the same right to the company and care of his or her father as would a child born within marriage. In any event, the welfare and best interests of the child (which considerations would, if the committee's proposals were to be accepted, now be elevated to constitutional status) would generally mean that the child had a constitutional right to have the company and care of his or her father and to ensure that the father played a part in decision-making concerning his or her welfare (at 124)."

This reasoning is not particularly convincing. Much of the concern that unmarried fathers have in relation to the courts is based on a belief (right or wrong) that gendered attitudes to child-rearing count against them when decisions are being made. It is difficult to see why the elevation of a best interests test from legislative status to constitutional status would alter the gendered way in which that term is interpreted, if that is indeed the case. At a more general level, it is noteworthy for those interested in judicial activism that our elected politicians have practically invited the courts to achieve by way of judicial reinterpretation what the politicians themselves refuse to do through popular politics on the basis that it would be divisive and unlikely to have the support of a majority of the population.

The committee recommended that Art.41.2 of the Constitution (the role of woman in the home) should be replaced with a gender neutral version:

"1. The State recognises that by reason of family life within the home, a parent gives to the State a support without which the common good cannot be achieved.

2. The State shall, therefore, endeavour to ensure that both parents shall not be obliged by economic necessity to work outside the home to the neglect of their parental duties."

The conjunction of the phrases "both parents" and "shall not be obliged" is awkward as it could suggest, on one reading, that both parents should be assisted to work within the home.

In conclusion, the committee's report provided useful analysis of the legal and social issues. However, as a programme for change, it has avoided many issues and relied on some questionable views as to the likelihood (not to mention permissibility) of judicial activism.

JUDICIAL IMPEACHMENT

As reported in the *Annual Review of Irish Law 2005*, Judge Brian Curtin unsuccessfully challenged the constitutionality of a number of aspects of the manner in which the Oireachtas proposed to consider his impeachment. In

2006 the Supreme Court rejected his appeal (*Curtin v Clerk of Dáil Éireann* [2006] I.E.S.C. 14). Judge Curtin had been acquitted, by way of direction, of a charge of possessing child pornography. Notwithstanding his acquittal, there remained considerable public concern. Both houses of the Oireachtas by resolution adopted a new procedure to allow for investigations into judicial conduct. Following those new procedures, a motion was moved noting the concerns about the applicant's conduct and calling for his removal from office. Again following the new procedures, both houses by resolution established a joint select committee to take evidence in relation to the applicant's conduct. The Oireachtas also amended s.3 of the Committees of the Houses of the Oireachtas (Compellability, Privileges and Immunity of Witnesses) Act 1997 to allow judges to be compelled to give evidence and to produce documents to Oireachtas committees, subject to the consent of the compellability committee of the Houses. Pursuant to this power, the committee ordered the applicant to produce his computer, including its hard drive, for the examination of the committee. The applicant sought judicial review of the committee's decision, challenging both the inquiry process established by the resolutions and the constitutionality of s.3 of the 1997 Act, as amended.

On appeal, Judge Curtin adapted his arguments somewhat, narrowing them down to three principal contentions. First, Judge Curtin claimed that the impeachment process was inconsistent with Art.35.4.1 because it did not require the charges against him to be proved before the Houses of the Oireachtas debated the impeachment resolution. Secondly, Judge Curtin claimed that s.3 of the 1997 Act (as amended), which allowed judges to be compelled to give evidence and provide documents to the Oireachtas committee, was unconstitutional as it infringed judicial independence. Thirdly, Judge Curtin claimed that the particular direction issued by the Oireachtas committee requiring him to produce his computer was invalid, having regard to the exclusionary rule.

The constitutionality of the impeachment process   Article 35.4.1° of the Constitution, the provision on which Judge Curtin relied, provides simply: "A judge of the Supreme court or the High Court shall not be removed from office except for stated misbehaviour or incapacity, and then only upon resolutions passed by Dáil Éireann and by Seanad Éireann calling for his removal.

As s.39 of the Courts of Justice Act 1924 extended to Circuit Court judges the same tenure as that afforded to judges of the High Court and Supreme Court, it was common case that the procedural protections of Art.35.4.1° applied to Judge Curtin. That said, Art.35.4.1° itself is quite vague as to the procedures to be followed. Murray C.J., who delivered the judgment of the court, commenced with a consideration of the appropriate interpretative principles to be applied to such a provision:

"Where words are found to be plain and unambiguous, the courts must apply them in their literal sense. Where the text is silent or the meaning of words is not totally plain, resort may be had to principles, such as the obligation to respect personal rights, derived from other parts of the Constitution. The historical context of particular language may, in certain cases, be helpful… This is not to say that taking into account the historical context of certain provisions of the Constitution excludes its interpretation in the context of contemporary circumstances."

Although all of these methods of interpretation may indeed help one to add content to under-specified constitutional provisions (and, by that light, count as useful interpretative aids), difficulties would arise if the different extrinsic sources would lead one to add different content. The problem is that, apart from the interpretative aid itself, one has no guidance as to what the "correct" meaning is. The fact that the meaning seems correct by reference to the interpretative aid amounts only to self-justification. Applying the various methods to the terms of Art.35.4.1°, Murray C.J. first observed:

"Some of the words in Article 35.4.1 are clear and unambiguous. A judge cannot be removed other than in accordance with Article 35.4.1: both Houses must pass the required resolution; the resolution must call for the judge's removal. This apparently refers to the resolution as proposed. A resolution of one House alone will not suffice. It is also clear, by necessary implication, that the resolution itself must specify the '*misbehaviour or incapacity,*' as the case may be, (or indeed, though not relevant in this case, the '*incapacity*') which purports to justify the judge's removal.

Apart from these matters, Article 35.4.1 is silent. It does not define misbehaviour or state whether misbehaviour relates to the performance of judicial duties or may be misbehaviour of a general kind. Article 35.4.1 prescribes no procedures to be followed by the Houses of the Oireachtas. Article 15.11.1, however provides that: '*All questions in each House shall, save as otherwise provided by this Constitution, be determined by a majority of the votes of the members present and voting other than the Chairman or presiding member.*' In particular, Article 35.4.1 contains no guidance on the power of the Houses to appoint investigating committees or the powers it may delegate to any such committees.

In these circumstances, it is reasonable to consider whether there is any history or background to the enactment of the Constitution capable of elucidating what was in the contemplation of the framers. More particularly, however, it will be necessary to consider the constitutional context of Article 35.4.1."

In this regard, he considered that three elements were particularly relevant: the function and standing of the judiciary in the constitutional scheme, the express power conferred on the Oireachtas and the obligation to respect principles of fairness and justice in the exercise of that power. Murray C.J., citing a number of provisions of the Constitution, identified the role of the courts (and, by implication, judges) as follows: "The courts are required to act as custodians of the Constitution and as such, to act as a check on the actions of the other two arms of government and to ensure that they act in accordance with the rule of law, respect individual constitutionally protected rights and observe the provisions of the Constitution."

An essential prerequisite to the performance of this function was, he reasoned, that the independence and integrity of the courts be guaranteed and respected. This independence was effected by a number of provisions, including Art.35.4.1°. Importantly, this independence did not exist for the benefit of the judges themselves, as individuals, even though it might have that effect. Rather, it existed for the benefit of the people as it was only an independent judiciary that could ensure that the organs of the State conducted themselves in accordance with the rule of law.

Referring to many of the seminal cases on the separation of powers, Murray C.J. emphasised that each organ of the State must be allowed to exercise its own powers and that the presumption of constitutionality applies to resolutions of the Houses of the Oireachtas, including those adopted in relation to Judge Curtin. Moreover, the Oireachtas had an exclusive power—under Art.15.10—to pass the resolutions contemplated by Art.35.4.1°.

The nub of Judge Curtin's complaint was that fair procedures could not be followed within the method adopted by the Houses of the Oireachtas. It would have been superior, he argued, for the committee to make decisions in relation to the evidence and present a non-binding report to both Houses. Moreover, he argued that he would not be able to present evidence to the Houses even if he thought it necessary. The court was not convinced by this latter point, noting that there was nothing in the standing orders to prevent the Houses hearing evidence, however unprecedented that might be. That said, the court accepted that Judge Curtin's suggested approach "might well have been more satisfactory". It clarified that the judgment in *Maguire v Ardagh* would not preclude such a committee in the context of the specific power and duty accorded exclusively to the Houses of the Oireachtas under Art.35.4.1°. However, based on the earlier separation of powers case law, the court reasoned that the appropriate constitutional test was whether the approach adopted by the Houses of the Oireachtas was "in clear disregard" of the Constitution. The court concluded that it was not *clearly in disregard* of the Constitution for the Oireachtas to decline to adopt a procedure that was not, on the face of Art.35.4.1°, constitutionally required. In any event, the court considered that Judge Curtin had taken an unduly narrow view of the powers of the committee. Although the committee was precluded from making findings of fact, recommendations concerning the facts or expressing any opinions about the facts, it was not precluded from organising the material and evidence into manageable form.

A separate but related argument was made by Judge Curtin during the Supreme Court appeal. It was argued that there was a risk that the Houses of the Oireachtas might conflate two issues into one, by deciding on the issue of misbehaviour and the possible consequence of removal from office in one resolution. The court considered that this issue was premature as the procedures had not yet reached that stage and as neither the standing orders nor the resolution prescribed any method for debating the resolution. However, given the exceptional character of the case, the court felt it appropriate to provide some guidance to the Oireachtas:

> "It is the opinion of the Court that, as a matter of basic fairness, the Appellant should be entitled to a distinct hearing and decision on the issues of fact before he must confront the ultimate and drastic decision to remove him from office. Some support is to be found in the words of Article 35.4.1. The first part of the sentence declares that a judge may not be removed *'except for stated misbehaviour or incapacity.'* The second part goes on to provide that this may happen: *'and then only upon resolutions passed...'* These remarks are not intended to impose onerous legal requirements on the Houses. They retain a large area of discretion as to how the resolutions are put. They are not necessarily obliged to break the allegations against the Appellant into several components. They may decide that the factual issues may fairly be expressed in the form of a single proposition."

The constitutionality of the power to compel judges   The court held that s.3A of the Houses of the Oireachtas (Compellability, Privileges and Immunity of Witnesses) Act 1997 was constitutional, for much the same reasons as underlay its decision in relation to the impeachment process under Art.35.4.1°. Judicial independence existed for the benefit of the people, not the benefit of the individual judge. A particular responsibility had been conferred on the Oireachtas by Art.35.4.1°. In order to consider whether to remove a judge from office, it was necessary for the Oireachtas to have a power of the type granted by s.3A of the Act.

The direction to produce the computer   Judge Curtin sought to rely on the exclusionary rule to maintain that the committee could not direct him to produce his computer. The Supreme Court rejected this argument. Section 3A was a lawful basis for ordering production of the computer. This lawful basis was not undermined by the fact that the computer had been unlawfully seized in the past. Moreover, the Oireachtas had also amended the Child Trafficking and Pornography Act 1998 in order to exempt any proceedings of the Oireachtas from criminality by reason of the possession or distribution of child pornography. There was therefore no reason why it would be unlawful to provide the computer to the committee. Note: As Judge Curtin subsequently resigned, the proposed impeachment process did not proceed.

NON-SPECIFIC CONSTITUTIONAL RIGHTS

McStay v Minister for Health and Children Ireland and the Attorney General [2006] I.E.H.C. 238 dealt with a preliminary issue of law as to whether the substantive proceedings between the parties gave rise to a justiciable issue, whereby the plaintiff might impugn the legality and/or seek damages in respect of the manner of establishment and/or operation of the Post Mortem Inquiry into infant organ retention as established by the respondents. The applicant, a member of the organisation of Parents for Justice and the mother of a deceased infant whose organs had been retained by Our Lady's Hospital for Sick Children, Crumlin, claimed, *inter alia*, that both her and her deceased infant's constitutional rights had been breached. Smyth J. held that there was no justiciable issue.

PENAL SANCTIONS

In *Osmanovic v DPP* [2006] I.E.S.C. 50 (and related cases), the Supreme Court considered the constitutionality of s.89(b) of the Finance Act 1997, which amended s.186 of the Customs Consolidation Act 1876. Section 89(b) provides:

> "In s.186 of the Customs Consolidation Act, 1876, there shall be substituted, in lieu of the penalty for each such offence specified therein (being forfeiture of either treble the value of goods including the duty payable thereon, or one hundred pounds, whichever is the greater)–
>
> (a) on summary conviction, a fine of £1,000, or at the discretion of the court, to imprisonment for a term not exceeding 12 months or to both the fine and the imprisonment,
>
> (b) on conviction on indictment, a fine of treble the value of the goods, including the duty payable thereon, or £10,000, whichever is the greater, or at the discretion of the court, to imprisonment for a term not exceeding 5 years or to both the fine and the imprisonment."

The Supreme Court rejected various arguments that these provisions were unconstitutional. First, it was argued that the provision breached the separation of powers as it left the sentencing court with no discretion as to the level of fine to impose. Delivering the judgment of the Court, Murray C.J. reasoned that s.89(b) did not stipulate a particular penalty. A sentencing judge had a choice between imposing the fixed fine or any term of imprisonment up to the maximum specified. The Oireachtas was entitled to lay down parameters for sentencing and the fact that the fine (if selected by the judge) was fixed did not breach any limits on the powers of the Oireachtas.

It was next argued that the provision amounted to a discrimination based on wealth. Murray C.J. described the crude version of this argument as being that "the rich are fined and the poor are sent to prison". He did not accept that an argument of this type could demonstrate unconstitutional discrimination:

> "In the case of an ordinary offence a judge might well be dealing with somebody who had no money and would, therefore, form the view that some kind of custodial or suspended sentence would be more appropriate as otherwise there would be no punishment. If, on the other hand, the person he is sentencing has money the fine becomes a real option. Normally, there is no element of unconstitutional discrimination in this process."

As a statement of general principle, this is somewhat disturbing. If personal liberty ranks higher on the scale of constitutional values than does personal property, it would be disturbing if the poor were more likely to be deprived of their liberty than the rich. Perhaps the difficulty flows from the false premise of a defendant "who had no money". In a welfare state such as ours, while there may unfortunately be great inequality, everybody has some money. It is thus possible for a sentencing court to impose fines on the rich and the poor. In order for the punitive effect on a particular rich person and a particular poor person to be equivalent, the fine on the particular rich person should presumably be greater. The difficulty with s.89(b) would seem to be that, as the fine was fixed at a certain amount, it might not be a feasible fine for the particular poor person at all, thereby requiring the term of imprisonment instead. Such a wealth discrimination is of concern. At several points in his judgment, Murray C.J. alluded to the fact that the offences in question were revenue offences. In those circumstances, the accused person clearly had had sufficient money at some point; otherwise, the fiscal obligation would not have arisen. Also, the punishment of the accused person involved the restitution of money to a person (the State) who had been fraudulently deprived of that money. Both of these facets of revenue offences would seem to provide a justification for any sort of wealth discrimination that s.89(b) might effect. However, as a statement of general principle, the court's conclusion remains troubling.

In one of the related cases, it was argued that an effect of s.89(b) was that a person might be forced, against her will, to plead guilty in the District Court so as to avoid the higher fine that might be imposed in the Circuit Court. Unsurprisingly, the court rejected this argument. Finally, the court rejected an argument that the provision was disproportionate (in the sense of allowing for disproportionate sentences), again relying on the range of options open to a sentencing judge.

In *PH v Ireland* [2006] I.E.H.C. 40, the applicant challenged the constitutionality of certain provisions of the Sex Offenders Act 2001. He had been convicted of various sexual offences prior to the coming into force of that Act. On the coming into force of the 2001 Act the applicant became subject to the various obligations on sex offenders under that Act, principally an obligation to notify the Garda Síochána of any change in address. The State argued that the applicant did not have any standing to challenge the constitutionality of the Act as he had indicated to the court that he was in full compliance with its provisions and did not intend to breach any of its requirements. In short, the State argued that the applicant would not be threatened with prosecution if he complied with the notification provisions. Unsurprisingly, Clarke J. rejected this argument:

> "4.3 If there were to be a constitutional infirmity about those provisions then an application of the standing rule in the manner which the respondents contend for, would place persons such as Mr. H. in what, in my view, would be an invidious position. They would either have to comply with what would, on that view, be a constitutionally impermissible restriction on their activities, and thus lack standing to challenge the validity of those restrictions or, alternatively, would be forced, in order that they might have standing, to commit what would, *prima facie,* be a criminal offence under a statute enjoying the presumption of constitutionality. Such an interpretation of the standing rule would not, in my view, be consistent with a harmonious interpretation of the Constitution as a whole.
>
> 4.4 I am, therefore, satisfied that where, as here, a regulatory provision imposes a burden on a small and defined group of persons on pain of a criminal sanction, any person subject to the burden concerned has, in general terms, standing to challenge the imposition of that burden notwithstanding the fact that they have chosen to obey the regime imposed upon them."

However, there was one respect in which Clarke J. held the applicant not to have standing. One of the arguments advanced by the applicant was that the retrospective character of the 2001 Act meant that persons sentenced before it came into force were deprived of the opportunity to make submissions to the sentencing court about the notification provisions and how the existence of such provisions should affect what would be an appropriate sentence. However, the applicant's own sentence had been varied by the Court of Criminal Appeal after the 2001 Act came into force. He therefore had had an opportunity to make such submissions and accordingly did not have standing to impugn the constitutionality of the legislation on those grounds.

The applicant's substantive argument was that the provisions of the 2001 Act amounted to the retrospective imposition of a penal sanction, contrary to Art.15.5 of the Constitution. This argument had been rejected by Finlay Geoghegan J. in *Enright v Ireland* [2003] 2 I.R. 321. Clarke J. held that it would be inappropriate, given the comity between courts of equal jurisdiction, for him to revisit this matter unless the applicant could point to some defect in the earlier judgment or some significant change in circumstances. In this regard, the applicant sought to rely on the judgment of the Court of Criminal Appeal in *DPP v NY* [2002] 4 I.R. 308, decided the day after Finlay Geoghegan J.'s judgment in *Enright*. In this case, Fennelly J. had accepted that, in determining a sentence, the court could have regard to the effect on the convict of the provisions of the 2001 Act. Similarly, in *DPP v GD*, Court of Criminal Appeal, July 13, 2004, McCracken J. had referred to the provisions of the 2001 Act as a "punishment". On this basis, the applicant sought to argue that the notification provisions of the 2001 Act constituted a stipulated punishment for the offence and accordingly amounted to an unconstitutional retroactive imposition of penal sanction. Clarke J. rejected this argument:

> "I do not agree with that proposition. As was pointed out by Fennelly J. in *N.Y.* a court imposing a criminal sanction is entitled to take into account all relevant circumstances. The description of the imposition of the burden contained in the 2001 Act as a 'punishment' in those cases, it seems to me, simply records the fact that, for the purposes of sentencing, it is an additional burden placed upon a convicted person which must be weighed in the balance in all the circumstances of the case in order to determine an appropriate sentence. The range of matters which can properly be taken into account in sentencing is, of course, extremely wide. For many years courts imposing sentence have properly taken into account the fact that conviction of the offence concerned may well have led to serious adverse consequences for the accused wholly independent of the criminal process."

For this reason, Clarke J. concluded, the decision in *Enright* should not be reconsidered.

PRIVACY RIGHTS

Constitutional privacy rights arose for consideration in two cases in 2005; *Atherton v DPP* [2005] I.E.H.C. 429 was considered in *Annual Review of Irish Law 2005*, pp.236-237.

The second case was *Aherne v RTE* [2005] I.E.H.C. 180. The applicants sought to restrain RTE in advance from broadcasting a report in relation to the Leas Cross Nursing Home, run by the applicants. Assessing the privacy interest involved, Clarke J. held that while the applicants had raised an arguable case that their privacy had been infringed, the filming related to the applicants in their capacity as the managers of a nursing home and not in relation to their own private life. As such, it did not infringe to a great extent on their privacy. In addition, there were real issues of public interest and concern raised by the programme. Bearing in mind the general principle against prior restraint orders, Clarke J. held that it would be inappropriate to make the order sought.

In 2006 privacy rights werre considered at some length in *Caldwell v Judge Mahon* [2006] I.E.H.C. 301. This case concerned a challenge to a decision of the tribunal of Inquiry into Certain Planning Matters and Payments, colloquially known as the Mahon Tribunal, formerly known as the Flood Tribunal. Hanna J. observed that the applicant was fundamentally endeavouring to address the Tribunal on whether or not it should move from its private investigations into public hearing. In so doing the applicant contended that the respondents had acted *ultra vires*, in breach of the requirements of natural and constitutional justice and in breach of the applicant's constitutional right to privacy and the right to respect for his privacy under Art.8 of the European Convention on Human Rights.

Wide measure of discretion to tribunal The applicant contended, *inter alia*, that the holding of public hearings into phases 2–8 of the Carrickmines II Module of the tribunal's proceedings constituted an unjustified, unnecessary and disproportionate invasion of his right to privacy under Art.40.3 of the Constitution. In response it was contended that the applicant was possessed of such rights under the Constitution and the Convention and any interference with same was both justified and proportionate. Much of the hearing dealt with this "centrally important issue". A number of authorities had been cited, including *Haughey v Moriarty* [1999] 3 I.R. 1 and the Law Reform Commission's *Consultation Paper on Public Inquiries including Tribunals of Inquiry* (LRC CP 22–2003) (Dublin, 2003). This paper, in dealing with the shift of a tribunal of inquiry from private to public hearings concluded at paras 8.24 and 8.25:

> "There is an implicit rejection here of any contention that, because the right to privacy is established on the authority of the Constitution, it follows that there must be an especially stringent review (or in U.S. jargon, 'hard look'), where there is any disturbance of it. The net result seems to be that, on the two major constitutional points (constitutional justice and privacy), which often arise together, a wide measure of discretion is allowed to a tribunal."

However, in a contemporaneous case, *Dublin City Council v Fennell*, unreported, Supreme Court, May 12, 2005, Kearns J. had held, *inter alia*, that the provisions of the European Convention on Human Rights Act 2003 were not retrospective in the circumstances of that case. In *Caldwell*, Hanna J. considered that since the constitutional and convention rights of the applicant, although distinct, were debated in tandem, it would be preferable to postpone giving judgment on this aspect of the case until he had heard further from counsel on the impact, if any, of the decision in *Fennell. Caldwell v Judge Mahon (No.2)* [2006] I.E.H.C. 301 is a supplemental judgment dealing with the issue of the Convention and with the right to privacy. It was found that the Convention had no retrospective effect and, therefore, did not apply.

Privacy in business dealings   Hanna J. noted that the applicant's complaint was to the effect that the tribunal's enquiries would engender disclosure of his confidential business affairs. It was acknowledged that the right to privacy is well established (*Kennedy v Ireland* [1987] I.R. 587), but the question arising was whether this right extends to a person's business dealings. In particular, where the respondents are inquiring into, *inter alia*, myriad private companies through which the applicant had sought to conduct his affairs (Hanna J. stressed that this statement carried no implication of wrongdoing), "does this transport the applicant's business affairs beyond the protective shade of the Constitution and into the sunlight of public scrutiny?"

Hanna J. observed that the private citizen conducting his business privately is not subject to the legislative requirements imposed upon private companies. Moreover, the privileges of incorporation and limited liability could only be viewed in tandem with the obligations that attend them such as the publication of annual accounts, etc. *Kennedy v Ireland* deals with personal rights and it is unclear to what extent, if any, *Haughey v Moriarty* [1999] 3 I.R. 1 comes any nearer to identifying a right to privacy in the context of business transactions conducted through limited liability companies.

Two points of importance were distinguished in considering *Hanahoe v Hussey* [1998] 3 I.R. 69, about a raid under warrant on a solicitor's premises, the circumstances of which differed greatly from the instant application. First, although the plaintiffs were awarded damages for interference with the solicitor's right to privacy, this arose from a leak to the media, probably from a garda source, about the impending raid on the premises for files. Secondly, the solicitor involved sued both as a firm, and also personally:

> "There is no doubt as to the existence of a personal right. Therefore, insofar as the focus of the Court was turned upon the 'invasion' of the applicant's privacy, it was done so in the context of the solicitors carrying on their practice as solicitors in premises belonging to them. This they did with all the panoply of confidentiality and security attendant upon such practice, long recognised and protected by the courts. And yet in lawfully authorised circumstances, their premises could be 'raided' and documents and materials removed.
>
> Indeed, we live in an age where the veil of confidentiality and secrecy which used to protect dealings between lawyers and other professional

persons and their clients from the exposure to the gaze of others has been pierced, albeit in circumstances mandated by the common good and in pursuit of wrong doing."

Core of privacy Thus, Hanna J. held that the common good can and does permit interference in appropriate circumstances with the relationship between a client and his professional adviser. However, he noted that an individual's business affairs, conducted through what the respondents described as a 'maze of offshore companies', must fall well beyond the level of constitutional protection afforded to, *e.g.* a solicitor–client relationship. He was reluctant to hold that no right to privacy existed with regard to the applicant's business affairs, seeing no logical reason why it should not. He did observe that the question merited far more debate than the context of the case permitted. Notwithstanding this, he was satisfied to proceed on the basis that the right to privacy does extend to business affairs: "It seems to me, however, that such right can only exist at the outer reaches of and the furthest remove from the core personal right to privacy."

The following quote from the judgment of Ackerman J. in *Bernstein v Bester* [1996] (4) *Butterworth's Constitutional Law Reports (South Africa)* 449 was adopted by Hanna J.:

"A very high level of protection is given to the individual's intimate personal sphere of life and the maintenance of its basic preconditions and there is a final untouchable sphere of human freedom that is beyond interference from any public authority. So much so that, in regard to this most intimate core of privacy, no justifiable limitation thereof can take place. But this most intimate core is narrowly construed. This inviolable core is left behind once an individual enters into relationships with persons outside this closest intimate sphere; the individual's activities then acquire a social dimension and the right to privacy in this context becomes subject to limitation."

Hanna J. continued: "Given the distance at which the applicant's right to privacy in his business affairs stands from the 'inviolable core', such right must become subject to the limitation and the exigencies of the common good and they weigh all the more heavily against it, subject at all times to the requirements of constitutional justice and fair procedures."

Public conduct of tribunals Reliance was placed on the judgment of Hamilton C.J. in *Haughey v Moriarty* [1999] 3 I.R. 1 and Denham J.'s judgment dealing with privacy and tribunals in *Desmond v Moriarty* [2004] 1 I.R. 334 at 367. This line of authority requires the public conduct of the Tribunal's business save as where otherwise mandated or in the most exceptional circumstances. Hanna J. held that the right to privacy in relation to private dealings with others is not absolute, even at its purely personal nucleus. When it comes to dealing with business affairs in the context of the tribunal, such right to privacy as any applicant may possess has long since been overtaken by the exigencies of the common good. He continued:

> "There is one further matter of importance. Details of the applicant's business affairs entered into the public domain through the opening statement of counsel for the Tribunal on the 20th January, 2004. That being the case, I cannot see how, to borrow a well-known colloquialism, 'the genie can be put back in the bottle'. Even if the nature and extent of the applicant's right to privacy could confront with greater force the rights and obligations of the Tribunal, it would seem pointless to contemplate prohibiting the Tribunal from being about its business."

Turning to a consideration of Art.8 of the European Convention of Human Rights with a view to its persuasive authority, it seemed to Hanna J. that in Irish law and under the Convention, a court is faced with broadly the same questions. Thus, he concluded that assuming the applicant had a protected right which had been compromised, the compromise or interference was authorised by law, such compromise was necessary in a democratic society, it related to a pressing social need and it was proportionate. So, both under the Constitution and the Convention, had it been considered part of domestic law at the time of the case, the court found that the applicant's right to privacy had not been breached.

PROPERTY RIGHTS

In the *Annual Review of Irish Law 2004* the major case considered under the heading of property rights was *Re Health (Amendment) (No. 2) Bill 2004* [2005] I.E.S.C. 5. This dealt with the property rights of the most vulnerable, and in many cases, most impoverished members of society. By contrast, *Shirley v Gorman* [2006] I.E.H.C. 27 deals with litigants at the far extreme of both scales, wealthy and established corporate bodies rather than elderly private persons. In this case, arising from Peart J.'s earlier judgment in an appeal from the Circuit Court, the plaintiffs challenged the constitutionality of provisions of s.7 of the Landlord & Tenant (Amendment) Act 1984 by which the first-named defendant had been found entitled to acquire the fee simple interest in a business premises owned by the plaintiff. The statutory scheme contained in the impugned section included a price-fixing mechanism which, it was contended, was an unjust attack on the plaintiffs' property interests and was disproportionate, arbitrary, unjust and unconstitutional in that it went far beyond what is necessary or required to satisfy the principles of social justice and the exigencies of the common good as contained in Art.43 (property rights).

Article 43.2 provides:

> "2.1. The State recognises, however, that the exercise of the rights
> mentioned in the foregoing provisions of this Article ought, in civil
> society, to be regulated by the principles of social justice.
>   2.2. The State, accordingly, may as occasion requires delimit by law
> the exercise of the said rights with a view to reconciling their exercise
> with the exigencies of the common good."

The impugned s.7(4) of the Landlord & Tenant (Amendment) Act 1984 provides
as follows:

> "7(4)(a) Where at the relevant date, the land is held under a lease that has
>   expired or is held at a rent which, whether under the terms of the
>   lease or by operation of a statute, is subject to a review which
>   is due but has not been made, the purchase of the fee simple
>   shall, subject to the other provisions of this section, be a sum
>   equal to one-eighth of the amount which, at that date, a willing
>   purchaser would give and a willing vendor would accept for the
>   land in fee simple free of all estates, interests and incumbrances,
>   but having regard to any covenant which continues in force by
>   virtue of section 28 of Act (No.2) of 1978, and assuming that
>   the lessee has complied with any other covenants or conditions
>   in his lease that could affect the price.
>   (b) Deduction shall be made from that amount equal to the value
>   of the goodwill, if any, in the premises of the person acquiring
>   the fee simple.
>   (c) A deduction shall also be made from that amount equal to any
>   addition to the value of the premises resulting from such works
>   as would qualify for the special allowance mentioned in section
>   35 of the Act of 1980.
>   (d) In determining the amount referred to in paragraph (a) any
>   addition to value deriving from contemplation of substantial
>   rebuilding, or a scheme of development (such as are mentioned
>   in section 33(1)(b)(i) and (ii) of the Act of 1980 shall be
>   disregarded."

Peart J. had no hesitation in granting *locus standi* citing the judgment of Keane
J. in *Iarnrod Eireann v Ireland* [1996] 3 I.R. 321 who had held that some of
the enumerated rights under Art.40.3.2° are not of relevance to corporate
bodies:

> "Property rights are, however, in a different category. Not only are
> corporate bodies themselves capable in law of owning property, whether

movable or immovable, tangible or intangible... There would be a
spectacular deficiency in the guarantee to every citizen that his or her
property rights will be protected from 'unjust attack', if such bodies
were incapable in law of being regarded as 'citizens, at least for the
purpose of this Article, and if it was essential for the shareholders to
abandon the protection of limited liability to which they are entitled by
law in order to protect, not merely their own rights as shareholders but
also the property rights of the corporate entity itself, which are in law
distinct from the rights of its members" (at 345 as quoted in *Shirley*).

Social justice principles   Peart J. held that the impugned legislation could be
seen as aimed at principles of social justice in the sense of distributive justice.
He observed that social justice in the context of property rights means that there
ought to be at least a fair, as opposed to equal, distribution of property amongst
all members of the society, so that justice is achieved. Where an open market
operates in a democratic society there will always be those who have more than
others. He noted that the plaintiffs submitted that they are obliged under the
impugned scheme to transfer their property to an already prosperous entity, the
first-named defendant, and that there can be no social justice principle which
requires that this be done. He adopted the reasoning in *James v United Kingdom*
8 E.H.R.R. 123 that it was not unreasonable for a legislature to determine that
landlords should be deprived of the enrichment which would otherwise ensue
on reversion of the property, even if in a number of cases "undeserving" tenants
thereby benefited and that the scale of the anomalies under it did not render
it unacceptable. No evidence had been produced that other landlords besides
the plaintiffs were similarly adversely affected by anomalies such as those
complained of by the plaintiffs. While there would be some others similarly
affected, during the great many years of the scheme's existence Peart J. had
no knowledge of any other challenge as to its constitutionality:

> "The lack of any evidence as to the extent to which so-called wealthy
> or prosperous tenants are availing or have availed already of the scheme
> is of relevance, because even though undoubtedly some such anomalies
> or unintended consequences of the legislation may have occurred, it
> does not follow that the scheme should be seen as no longer pursuing
> its intended objective in respect of which the legislation enjoys the
> presumption of constitutionality. In my view, these features of the
> operation of the legislation cannot in themselves disturb the integrity
> of the social justice principles pursued by the legislation, and the
> presumption of constitutionality in that regard."

The court had heard comprehensive evidence on the relevant landlord and
tenant legislation and the social and historical background to its development.
Peart J. stated that the impugned legislative provisions must not be viewed as

an isolated piece of legislation, but rather as part of a continuum of legislation all of which was designed in different ways to improve, as the legislature saw it, the position of tenants. It is permissible in legislation designed to regulate rights by principles of social justice to permit all tenants regardless of whether they are residential or business lessees to be entitled to purchase the freehold interest of their premises: "It is still a regulation by principles of social justice so to permit, even if it could be said both at the time and in later years that the class of business tenants in the country, or at least some of them, may not be generally regarded as deserving or needy." He was satisfied that the landlord does receive fair compensation under the scheme.

The exigencies of the common good   Peart J. held that the word "accordingly" appearing in Art.43.2.2° has significance: "It is only where the State is pursuing a social justice principle that it may as occasion requires delimit the exercise of property rights with a view to reconciling their exercise with the exigencies of the common good." In addition, he accorded significance to the phrase 'as occasion requires', also in Art.43.2.2°. This phrase introduced a consideration of proportionality:

> "Such delimitation of property rights by the State when pursuing a principle of social justice, must therefore at the relevant time (i.e. the hearing of these proceedings) be 'required' for the purpose of reconciling their exercise with the exigencies of the common good. Not only does the phrase suggest that the legislative measures may have a certain in-built obsolescence, since the 'requirement' for same could disappear after a passage of time, but it would seem also to feed into the concept of proportionality in the sense that while a particular measure may well assist or have assisted in reconciling the exercise of certain property rights with the exigencies of the common good while in pursuit of a social justice principle, it may not be 'required' in order to do so. That is consistent with the proportionality argument that constitutional rights should be interfered with, restricted or delimited as little as is necessary for the attainment of the desired social justice objective."

Much turns on the meaning of the word "exigencies". It appeared that the plaintiffs predicated their arguments on a meaning equating to something like absolute necessity. Peart J. observed that if that were the case "the legislature would be under such a strict requirement of proof of absolute necessity in every instance where they wish to amend the law in relation to delimiting property rights that the situation would become impossible." In his view a meaning far short of absolute necessity would be adequate. Further, he held that the courts should be slow in any way to substitute its own view of what may or may not be required in order to reconcile the exercise of property rights with the exigencies of the common good: "Until some point of absolute extremity is reached where legislation is patently and manifestly not in pursuit of any possible common good exigency, the Court should abstain from interfering with the role of the legislature in deciding what measures are needed." He found that the fact that some anomaly is thrown up by the scheme, such as where the first-named defendant is a wealthy entity, does not mean that the legislation does not meet the exigencies of the common good in a broad sense.

Proportionality Peart J. dealt separately with the issue of proportionality relying on the reasoning of Costello J. in *Heaney v Ireland* [1994] 3 I.R. 593. He noted that the first-named defendant's eligibility to acquire the fee simple was derived simply because, by virtue of the very precise way in which the conditions and definitions for eligibility are crafted in this very detailed legislation, he was able by chance to come within them. The plaintiffs contended that the first-named defendant was in effect getting a benefit which the legislation did not intend him to get, and that it was by some unfair and arbitrary chance that this was so and that it is unconstitutional. Peart J. agreed with those submissions as far as the element of chance or good fortune of the tenant is concerned. However, it was another matter to conclude therefore that the scheme is an unjust attack on the plaintiffs' property rights on proportionality grounds, having regard, *inter alia*, to the fact that fair compensation is to be paid.

Peart J. continued:

> "Where there is a statutory scheme of general application under which a great number of premises are intended to be included, and certain criteria are decided upon by the Oireachtas for eligibility into the scheme, it is reasonable that a certain margin of appreciation be permitted to the Oireachtas in the manner in which the scheme is devised. In any such scheme there will inevitably be premises which happen for one reason or another to come within the scheme even though the particular category of premises was not the intended target of the legislation. It would be virtually impossible to avoid such a situation arising no matter how carefully and painstakingly the criteria for eligibility into the scheme are crafted."

In the present case compliance with the compensation requirement of the Supreme Court as stated in *Re Planning and Development Bill 1999* [2000] 2 I.R. 321 meant the market value of the landlord's residual interest in the property.

Peart J. declared himself satisfied that the very detailed provisions contained in the statutory scheme as to what factors are to be taken into account and what factors are to be excluded from consideration:

> "represents a balanced approach to valuation of the residual interest of the landlord, and that the figure arrived at ensures that fair, reasonable

and appropriate compensation is paid to the landlord for that interest. The fact that some already prosperous tenant thereafter may achieve a windfall by the onward sale of the freehold premises is not something which can affect the constitutionality of the scheme, even in the case of the first-named defendant who one may safely say, for the reasons already stated, was not a category of lessee whom it was intended to benefit under the scheme."

Peart J. found that the plaintiffs had failed to rebut the presumption of constitutionality of the impugned statutory provisions.

RIGHT TO LIBERTY

Detention for Mental Treatment The Mental Treatment Act 1945 was referred to in the *Annual Review 2004* when considering *Blehein v Minister for Health* [2004] I.E.H.C. 374, a case challenging the constitutionality of s.260 of the Mental Treatment Act 1945. In 2005 the High Court considered the interaction between Art.40 of the Constitution and persons who may be detained under the provisions of the Mental Treatment Act. In *Re Article 40.4.2 and Kelly v Clinical Director of Lakeview Unit Naas General Hospital* [2006] I.E.H.C. 196, Clarke J. relied on *Croke v Smith* [1998] 1 I.R. 101 in which the Supreme Court noted that there were a number of safeguards available to persons who may be detained under the Act including the entitlement of such a person to invoke the provisions of Art.40.4.2° of the Constitution. Having ordered an inquiry under Art.40.4.2°, the question at issue for the court was how in practice a hearing of the type contemplated in the *Croke* decision should be approached.

In the instant case in which there was no procedural dispute as to compliance with the statutory requirements of the Act, Clarke J. held the following: "Where a person seeks an inquiry under article 40.4.2 and alleges that they ought not be detained the onus is on the custodian of the person, and that onus is to show that the detainee remains as of the date of the inquiry, in need of care by virtue of being of unsound mind such that deprivation of liberty is necessitated."

Clarke J. then cited three non-procedural tests set out in *Croke* with which the High Court must be satisfied when hearing the habeas corpus inquiry, namely that:

"(1) the person detained is a person of unsound mind and in need of care and treatment;.

(2) that the procedures outlined in the Act have been complied with;.

(3) the person detained has not recovered;" (*Croke v Smith* [1998] 1 I.R. 101 at 124).

He also found that as a consequence of that entitlement, a detainee must be entitled to a reasonable opportunity to deal at the hearing of the inquiry with each of the components of the test.

Inevitable procedural difficulties The procedural difficulty confronting the court when proceeding with a potential inquiry under Art.40.4.2 in the case of a person detained under the Mental Treatment Act related to a number of potential circularities with which all participants, including the court, are faced.

The first, noted by counsel for the applicant, is the difficulty that may be encountered by a person in the position of the applicant who wishes to contest the validity of her continued detention and needs, for the purposes of putting forward a cogent case to that effect, access to medical records, but may be refused access to those medical records by virtue of a view taken by those in whose custody he or she may be, of a lack of capacity.

Clarke J. continued that:

> "certainly there is a circularity from the perspective of the custodians in that if a bona fide view has been taken that a person remains in need of care in detention that may well also in many cases lead to a conclusion that the person does not have the capacity to authorise any release of records. It may well be that in many cases it will therefore be inconsistent for the custodian to take the view that the person concerned has capacity while at the same time maintaining the view that the person requires to be kept in continued detention at least for the time being."

However, two points had to be noted in this regard. First, there is not necessarily an identity between a person having capacity to give instructions in legal proceedings and them requiring to be detained under the provisions of the Mental Health Act. Yet, "there is likely to be a significant overlap in practice in most cases between the two questions". Secondly, there may be cases such as the instant case where it is asserted on behalf of the custodians that the disclosure of the relevant notes would be inappropriate for clinical reasons independent of the legal process.

Creative approach by court required Thus, there is a requirement for the court to be creative as to the procedures that need to be followed. Procedures must be designed such as to ensure a fair hearing; but, without at the outset making any assumptions either way, the procedures "must be crafted in a manner which avoid, insofar as it may be possible, the risk of doing any harm to the person who may be in the position of an applicant in such proceedings". Equally, the procedures have to operate on the basis of not prejudging any of those issues.

Clarke J. then outlined a number of principles necessarily emerging from his comments:

"Firstly, it seems to me that it necessarily follows from *Croke* that the minimum entitlement of an applicant in a position such as [the applicant] is to a reasonable facility to enable her to put before the Court an expert view on the material factual matters to the issues which arise. On the facts of this case the expert view would appear to be potentially relevant to three matters: firstly, [the applicant's] capacity; secondly, the appropriateness or otherwise of the disclosure of information; thirdly, and ultimately, whether this court should be satisfied that the *Croke* test for continued detention has been met."

The court then directed that the following process, "which will hopefully lead to consideration of the issues that arise in the case", should be followed. Clarke J. in the course of formulating the process endeavoured to meet the various competing requirements already identified:

"Firstly, I propose directing that a consultant psychiatrist on the nomination of Mr. Finucane should have such reasonable accesses as that consultant may require to [the applicant] and to all relevant medical records regarding [the applicant]. I did not understand there to be any contest about the appropriateness of that action to be taken. Secondly, for the avoidance of doubt I direct that such consultant may report to Mr. Finucane on his views arising out of his inquiries on any of the issues relevant to this case as I have identified them. Thirdly, and again for the avoidance of doubt, given that such report may well require to contain materials taken from or references to clinical notes and other medical records, I will direct that for the time being Mr. Finucane should not disclose the contents of any report received by him from such medical consultant save: (1) to counsel instructed in the case, and (2) save to the disclosure for the purposes of discussion of the general conclusions of the report with [the applicant]."

The court further directed that there should be a hearing of the following issues in the following order:

"firstly, whether a wider access than I have already directed to the records is, as a matter of law, required to render [the applicant's] detention lawful, either: (a) as an absolute legal entitlement; (b) as a qualified legal entitlement, arising generally but not excluded on the facts of this case; or (c) in order to render on the facts of this case the process of inquiry with which the court is charged by the *Croke* decision to be fair."

In addition the court noted that clearly some of those issues are matters of pure legal argument, but some of them have the potential to depend on facts.

Finally, the court emphasised the need for urgency in dealing with that process in accordance with the constitutional imperatives for an Art.40 procedure, but Clarke J. also accepted the importance of the issues arising:

> "both the legal issues and potentially the factual issues and at least, to some extent, the novelty of some of those issues. While emphasising the need that the matter be dealt with urgently, I suppose I am also putting a caveat to that to the effect that they should be dealt with properly as well, not only from the point of view of the interest of the parties but also because the process may have a potential to affect other cases."

Similarly, for those reasons stated in the judgment it seemed desirable to deal with this case in some detail.

Access to Medical Records It certainly appears that the procedures outlined in this case would be applicable in a far wider context than liberty or detention. It is common place that access to patient records is refused on the basis of the diminished mental capacity of the patient. The judgment in this case may open the way for an aggrieved patient to mount a more effective challenge in such situations.

RIGHT TO LIFE OF THE UNBORN

In *R v R* [2006] I.E.H.C. 359, the High Court considered the application of Art.40.3.3° of the Constitution to embryos created *in vitro*. The plaintiff was married to the first defendant. In 2002 the plaintiff underwent IVF treatment. In preparation for this, the plaintiff agreed to the removal of eggs from her ovaries and a mixing of the eggs with the sperm of her husband. Both signed a document in which they consented to the cryo-preservation (freezing) of their embryos and undertook full responsibility on an ongoing basis for those embryos. The first defendant also signed documents in which he consented to the fertilisation of his wife's eggs and the implantation of three embryos. He acknowledged that he would become the father of any resulting child. As a result of the IVF treatment, six viable embryos were created and three were implanted in the plaintiff's womb, the other three being frozen. As a result of this process, the plaintiff gave birth to a daughter. Towards the end of the pregnancy, marital difficulties arose and the plaintiff and her husband separated. The issue came before the court because the plaintiff wished to have the three frozen embryos implanted in her uterus. Her husband did not want this to happen and did not wish to become the father of any child that might be born as a result of the implantation of the frozen embryos.

McGovern J. directed a trial of a preliminary issue. This established that there was no agreement between the husband and wife as to what should happen to the frozen embryos and that the husband had given neither express nor implied consent to the implantation of the frozen embryos. If there had been agreement or consent to implantation on the part of the husband, there would have been no possible conflict between the wishes of the parties and constitutional requirements. However, as there was no consent to implantation on the part of the husband, the court was required to assess whether there was any constitutional reason why the embryos should be implanted. This turned largely on an interpretation of Art.40.3.3° of the Constitution: "The State acknowledges the right to life of the unborn and, with due regard to the equal right to life of the mother, guarantees in its laws to respect, and, as far as practicable, by its laws to defend and vindicate that right."

Animating McGovern J.'s judgment is a purportedly rigid distinction between law, on the one hand, and moral beliefs on the other. At the outset, he put the matter as follows:

> "It is possible for scientists and embryologists to describe in detail the process of development from the ovum to the embryo and on to the stage when it becomes a foetus after implantation of the embryo in the wall of the uterus, but in my opinion, it is not possible for this Court to state when human life begins. The point at which people use the term 'human being' or ascribe human characteristics to such genetic material depends on issues other than science and medicine. For example, it is a matter which may be determined by one's religious or moral beliefs and, even within different religions, there can be disagreements as to when genetic material becomes a 'human being'. But it is not the function of the courts to choose between competing religious and moral beliefs... [W]hat I have to decide is whether the three frozen embryos at issue in this constitute the 'unborn' for the purposes of Article 40.3.3° of the Constitution."

It is of course unarguable that the case required to be determined by reference to the Constitution rather than by reference to moral or religious beliefs. This did not mean, however, that the court was not choosing between competing moral and religious beliefs. Such a choice was unavoidable: the court had to choose the moral (and/or religious) belief that was constitutionally endorsed in Art.40.3.3°.

In approaching this issue, McGovern J. relied largely on the historical approach. He noted Murray C.J.'s comments in *Curtin v Dáil Éireann* that it was reasonable, where there was no textual guidance, to consider the history or background to the enactment of the Constitution in order to elucidate what was in the contemplation of the framers. On this basis and given the lack of any definition of "unborn" in Art.40.3.3°, McGovern J. had regard to the history and background to the amendment of the Constitution. In this regard, McGovern J. referred to a number of cases decided after the enactment of Art.40.3.3° which suggested that that constitutional amendment was intended to prevent the legalisation of abortion. The cases referred to were *Attorney General (SPUC) v Open Door Counselling Ltd* [1988] I.R. 593, *Attorney General v X* [1992] 1 I.R. 1 and *Baby O v Minister for Justice* [1992] 1 I.R. 1. McGovern J. drew the following conclusion:

> "These remarks seem to further confirm the linking of Article 40.3.3 with the abortion issue. If this is correct then it equates 'unborn' with an embryo which has implanted in the womb, or a foetus... What clearly emerges from the authorities that I have referred to is that the Courts have declared that the Eighth Amendment to the Constitution giving rise to the wording in Article 40.3.3 was for the purpose of making secure the prohibition on abortion expressed in s.57 and 58 of the Offences Against the Person Act, 1861 and not to permit abortion or termination of pregnancy except where it is established as a matter of probability that there is a real and substantial risk to the life of the mother if such termination were not effected. The Courts have never, thus far, considered whether the word 'unborn' in Article 40.3.3 includes embryos in vitro... If Article 40.3.3 and the 1861 Act are concerned with the termination of pregnancy this does not mean that they are concerned with embryos *in vitro*. There has been no evidence adduced to establish that it was ever in the mind of the people voting on the Eighth Amendment to the Constitution that 'unborn' meant anything other than a foetus or child within the womb. To infer that it was in the mind of the people that 'unborn' included embryos outside the womb or embryos in vitro would be to completely ignore the circumstances in which the amendment giving rise to Article 40.3.3 arose. While I accept that Article 40.3.3 is not to be taken in isolation from its historical background and should be considered as but one provision of the whole Constitution, this does not mean that the word 'unborn' can be given a meaning which was not contemplated by people at the time of the passing of the Eighth Amendment and which takes it outside the scope and purpose of the amendment."

It is questionable whether McGovern J.'s unequivocal conclusion on the scope and purpose of the Eighth Amendment is consistent with his recognition of the fact that no court had ever considered whether the word "unborn" in Art.40.3.3 includes embryos *in vitro*. In this regard, it is noteworthy that McGovern J. did not cite any pre-1983 source to support his view on the meaning of Art.40.3.3. Cases post-1983 that concerned abortion and explained the purpose of Art.40.3.3 in relation to its impact on abortion law scarcely count as reliable support for the proposition that the purpose and scope of Art.40.3.3 concerned abortion and only abortion. In considering the purpose of Art.40.3.3°, it is perhaps significant that the framers of that amendment did not simply enact a ban on abortion (similar to the constitutional offences of treason and blasphemy) but rather sought to articulate a statement of rights, a philosophical basis as to why abortion was prohibited. That philosophical basis—explicitly stated in the Constitution—was the right to life of the unborn. McGovern J. avoided the need to explore what was meant by the right to life of the unborn essentially by concluding that the Constitution did not so much protect the right to life of the unborn as prohibit abortion. This is an insecure basis for such a far-reaching judgment.

Towards the end of his judgment, McGovern J. returned to the distinction between law and morality:

> "The fact that something is not prohibited by the law does not of itself mean that it is morally acceptable to carry out that act. There may be many people who, because of their moral or religious outlook regard the process of IVF as unacceptable even though it is permitted by the law. There are others who see this as a great advance in medical science giving the opportunity to infertile couples to have children. In issues such as this there may well be a divide between Church and State, and between one religion and another. It is not for the Courts to weigh the views of one religion against another, or to choose between one moral view point and another. All are entitled to equal respect provided they are not subversive of the law, and provided there are no public policy reasons requiring the Courts to intervene. Moral responsibility exists even in the absence of law and arises out of the freedom of choice of the individual. People have many different ideas of morality. Society is made up of people of various religious traditions and none. If the law is to enforce morality then whose morality is it to enforce? The function of the Courts is to apply the law, which are the rules and regulations that govern society. Where these rules and regulations are to be found in articles of the Constitution they are approved of by the people, and where they are to be found in legislation they are passed by the Houses of the Oireachtas. Laws should, and generally do, reflect society's values and will be influenced by them. But at the end of the day it is the duty of the Courts to implement and apply the law, not morality."

In so far as this extract suggests that the law can avoid making moral decisions, it is questionable. McGovern J. paints a picture of the law allowing people to make their own moral choices in certain respects. This limited role for law would be supported both by those of a liberal persuasion (who value the autonomy of the individual very highly) and by those of a natural law persuasion (who view the moral role of the State as subsidiary to the moral responsibility of the individual). On either account, the law—in leaving certain moral choices to individuals—is itself making a moral decision. A belief in individual autonomy and/or the subsidiary role of the State are both moral beliefs. Where the State allows individuals to make their own moral decisions, it does so on the basis of a moral belief that those sorts of decisions are best made by individuals. This idea is well captured by the first part of the extract quoted above: just because the State—assume for the sake of argument—allows the destruction of non-implanted embryos, this does not mean that it is morally correct to destroy such embryos. This is an area in which the law has chosen (for moral reasons) to allow people to make their own moral choices. However, has Irish law really made that choice? Is it really the case that in guaranteeing the right to life of the unborn, the Irish Constitution takes the view that it is legally (if not necessarily morally) permissible to destroy unborn life that was conceived *in vitro*? For this was the effect of McGovern J.'s decision, as he himself recognised. In holding that the word "unborn" was unclear, he ultimately came to the conclusion that the unborn outside the womb had no constitutional right to life. As such, it was a matter for the Oireachtas to determine the legal status of embryos *in vitro*. Pending such determination, however, those embryos had no legal status and could be destroyed. This was a result consistent only with a view that unborn life does not include embryos *in vitro*, a point the judge purported not to be deciding.

RIGHT TO MARRY

The right to marry was considered in two cases in 2006. In *O'Shea v Ireland,* October 17, 2006, the High Court declared unconstitutional s.3(2) of the Deceased Wife's Sisters Marriage Act 1907 as amended by s.1(2)(b) of the Deceased Brother's Widow's Marriage Act 1921. The first plaintiff had married her former husband in 1980. They separated in 1985 and were granted a divorce in 2000. The former husband subsequently remarried. After the separation, the former husband's younger brother (the second plaintiff in the proceedings) assisted the first plaintiff financially in a number of ways and helped in looking after the children. A relationship developed between the two plaintiffs and he moved into the home in 1985 or 1986. They had cohabited there since and had looked after the children of the marriage together. The plaintiffs sought to marry each other, but this was prohibited by the statutory provisions cited above. The relevant bar in s.3(2) was a prohibition on a man marrying the divorced wife of his brother during the lifetime of such brother. This bar was part of a wide scheme of restrictions based on consanguinity and affinity.

Laffoy J. reasoned that the principal issue was whether this marriage bar was consistent with the Constitution as amended, in particular as amended in 1996 to allow for the dissolution of marriage. Laffoy J. held that there was a right to marry protected by Art.40.3 of the Constitution, approving the dicta of Kenny J. in *Ryan v Attorney General* [1965] I.R. 294. The location of the right in Art.40.3, characterising it as a personal right, is of some importance as it ensures that it can be invoked by unmarried persons. Arguably, if the right were implied into Art.41, the constitutional provision dealing with marriage, it could not be relied on by unmarried people who were seeking to marry, a "Catch 22" situation. Laffoy J. held that the prohibition contained in s.3(2) was a prima facie restriction of the constitutional right of each of the plaintiffs to marry, commenting: "It is an impairment of the essence of the right of each because it prevents each marrying her and his chosen partner." The question was whether the plaintiffs had established that the restriction was not justified.

The plaintiffs did not rely on the European Convention on Human Rights. Although their case had commenced before the European Convention on Human Rights Act 2003 came into force, Laffoy J. considered that if the Convention had been invoked it would apply to the facts of the case as the prohibition of the plaintiffs' marriage to each other was a continuing and ongoing state of affairs. The plaintiffs did not seek to rely directly on the 2003 Act, but did rely on a judgment of the European Court of Human Rights as supportive of their constitutional argument. In *B and L v United Kingdom* (Application No. 36536/02, European Court of Human Rights, December 13, 2005) the court declared in breach of the Convention a provision of the UK Marriage Act 1949 which precluded a daughter-in-law from marrying her former father-in-law following her divorce from her husband. The court held that this ban was in breach of Art.12 of the Convention which guarantees the right of men and women to marry and found a family, according to the national laws governing the exercise of the right.

Laffoy J. described the defendants' arguments in defence of the marriage bar in the following terms:

> "The defendants' defence of the consistency of s.3(2) with the Constitution is founded on two constitutional imperatives: the State's obligation to promote the common good, a concept referred to in the Preamble; and the State's guarantee to protect the family and to guard with special care the institution of marriage as provided for in Article 41. As I have stated, the defendants did not adduce any evidence and, accordingly, their defence is based entirely on legal argument.
>
> The argument... addressed the perceived danger to the institution of marriage by permitting marriage within close degrees of affinity. The argument was based on a premise with which nobody could disagree, that marriage ought to be a secure, stable unit. It was developed on the basis of an assertion with which, I suspect, many would disagree, that a person who marries into a family adopts as his or her own the siblings of the other spouse. A barrier should exist to the possibility of marriage with those siblings. Permitting marriage between a divorced spouse and a sibling of the other spouse would undermine the stability of the marital unit, it was urged" (at 26–27).

Laffoy J. rejected these arguments on two related grounds. First, she did not perceive a factual basis for the defendants' arguments. They simply had not adduced evidence to support the proposition that the statutory prohibition would provide a strong emotional barrier by encouraging the feeling that siblings-in-law are in the same relationship as natural brothers and sisters. Moreover, the defendants had not established that the children of a family would be adversely affected by such relationships forming. Indeed, the plaintiffs' circumstances provided evidence from which it could be inferred that the plaintiffs had successfully reared the first plaintiff's children without subjecting them to confusion and hurt.

Secondly, Laffoy J. reasoned that even if these two adverse effects were to arise, the bar would not stop the relationships occurring. As the plaintiffs' circumstances demonstrated, the prohibition on marriage had not stopped them forming their relationship in the first place. This second ground for rejecting the defendants' arguments does not seem to be a stand-alone ground. Where a possible marital relationship is prohibited because it would purportedly lead to adverse consequences, it is of some relevance that the law does not prohibit the same relationship in non-marital form even though it would still give rise to the same adverse consequences. However, the mere fact that non-marital relationships of the same type would form irrespective of a legislative prohibition is not generally taken to be a good reason for the removal of such a prohibition, a point well illustrated by the next case in which the right to marry was invoked.

Zappone v Revenue Commissioners [2006] I.E.H.C. 404 was argued before Laffoy J. gave her decision in *O'Shea* but was decided after that judgment. The plaintiffs were two women who were Irish citizens, although Dr Zappone was originally Canadian. They had lived together as a cohabiting couple since their relationship began in 1981. On March 13, 2003 the plaintiffs married each other in Vancouver, British Columbia in Canada. In April 2004 the plaintiffs wrote to the Revenue Commissioners requesting that they should be allowed to claim their allowances as a married couple under the Taxes Consolidation Acts. The Revenue Commissioners refused to do so on the basis that the relevant Acts referred to 'husband' and 'wife' and the Oxford English Dictionary defined those terms in gender-specific ways. Accordingly, the Revenue Commissioners' view was that the plaintiffs could not be treated as a married couple for the purpose of the tax laws.

In November 2004 the plaintiffs were granted leave to apply for judicial review but were ordered to serve a plenary summons and statement of claim. Ireland was a defendant to the proceedings, as well as the Revenue Commissioners. Although the case initiated as a claim to have the plaintiffs' Canadian marriage recognised for the purposes of Irish tax law, its parameters were changed somewhat by s.2(2)(e) of the Civil Registration Act 2004, which precludes marriage by same-sex couples. This provision only came into force in December 2005 and was not directly challenged in the proceedings. However, counsel on behalf of the plaintiffs accepted that this provision had the effect of depriving the plaintiffs of capacity to marry in Irish law; as a result, Irish law could not recognise the foreign marriage of the plaintiffs. The case therefore turned on whether the plaintiffs had an entitlement to marry as a matter of Irish law. Nevertheless, there was no direct challenge to the constitutionality of s.2(2). The defendants placed considerable emphasis on the absence of such a challenge in their submissions. Dunne J. referred to this in her conclusions, noting that she found it "extremely difficult to comprehend how an assertion of a constitutional right to marry could incidentally have the effect of rendering unconstitutional an Act passed by the Oireachtas as recently as 2004". Nevertheless, there is nothing in her reasoning to suggest that the outcome of the case would have been different had s.2(2)(e) been directly challenged.

The argument advanced by the plaintiffs essentially turned on three propositions: (a) there is a constitutionally protected right to marry; (b) discriminations on the ground of sexuality (and gender) must meet a higher standard of justification; (c) to the extent that previous judicial dicta suggested a constitutional conception of marriage as limited to opposite-sex couples, the Constitution should be re-interpreted in the light of changing values and attitudes to gay people. The defendants did not contest that there was a right to marry. However, they argued that discrimination against same-sex couples in the context of access to marriage was constitutionally authorised. Moreover, either it was inappropriate to change the constitutional conception of marriage or there was no general shift in the understanding of marriage that would warrant such a change.

Reviewing the evidence, Dunne J. held that the two plaintiffs were not treated differently from unmarried opposite-sex couples but that they were treated differently from married couples. She accepted the evidence of a Professor Kennedy who had commented that homosexuality was a feature of the human condition, an aspect of normality. More contentious was the evidence as to the suitability of same-sex partners as parents. In this regard, Dunne J. held that the various research studies presented in evidence did not allow the court to conclude either that children raised by same-sex couples fared as well as those raised by opposite-sex couples or that such children fared less well than those raised by opposite-sex couples: "[T]here is simply not enough evidence from the research done to date that could allow firm conclusions to be drawn as to the consequences of same sex marriage particularly in the area of welfare of children."

Dunne J. did not analyse the plaintiffs' arguments that discrimination on the grounds of sexuality required a higher level of scrutiny. Instead she accepted two justifications for the discrimination. She first referred to Art.41 of the Constitution:

> "I accept the arguments made by the defendants in relation to the issue
> of discrimination on the basis that the right to opposite sex marriage
> is derived from the Constitution and thus that this is a justification

for any distinction between the position of the plaintiffs and married
couples...

> The final point I would make on this topic is that if there is in fact
> any form of discriminatory distinction between same sex couples and
> opposite sex couples by reason of the exclusion of same sex couples
> from the right to marry, then Article 41 in its clear terms as to guarding
> [with special care the institution of marriage] provides the necessary
> justification" (at 129).

Although the courts have consistently held that the special position of marriage
provides a justification for legislative discrimination against unmarried couples,
this cannot resolve the question of access to the institution of marriage itself.
That must rest on an anterior view that marriage is constitutionally defined to
exclude same-sex couples. Dunne J.'s final conclusion that Art.41 in its clear
terms provides the necessary justification for such a view seems to stretch the
language of Art.41 too far. That Article does not define marriage. While it may
well be reasonably (and perhaps necessarily) implicit in Art.41 (by reason of its
background, ethos and the views of the framers) that it refers to opposite-sex
marriage, Art.41 does not so state in clear terms. Accordingly, the support for
Dunne J.'s final point must be found elsewhere.

In this regard, Dunne J. referred to many cases such as *T v T* [2003] 1
I.L.R.M. 321 and *Foy v An tArd Claraitheóir*, High Court, July 9, 2002 in
which the courts had suggested that the constitutionally-guaranteed concept
of marriage involved a man and a woman. Interestingly, she did not refer to
Murphy v Attorney General [1982] I.R. 241 at 286 where Kenny J., giving
the judgment of the Supreme Court, described marriage as a "permanent,
indissoluble union of man and woman". As a statement carrying the full
weight of the Supreme Court, this arguably has more authority than the other
cases relied on. The plaintiffs had attempted to circumvent such dicta on the
grounds (a) that they were only obiter dicta; and (b) that the interpretation of
the Constitution should be allowed to change over time. Although the plaintiffs
were correct that the statements were obiter dicta, as the issue of same-sex
marriage did not arise in any of the cases, the dicta nonetheless represent a
long-settled understanding of what the constitutional terms mean.

The issue of whether the meaning of the Constitution should change
over time raises more difficult points. In this regard, Dunne J. seems to have
suggested three different bases on which the definition of marriage should
not be deemed to be different from that in the mind of the framers in 1937.
First, she referred to the guidelines suggested by Professor Kelly in 1988,
whereby the values-based provisions of the Constitution should be interpreted
in a present-tense manner, while the more law-based provisions should be
interpreted in a manner that has regard to the historical background. In this
regard, Dunne J. relied on the judgment of Murray J. in *Sinnott v Minister for
Education* [2001] 2 I.R. 545 at 681 in which those guidelines were approved.

She then commented:

> "It is interesting to note that in the *Sinnott* case which was also relied
> on by the plaintiffs in this context, the Supreme Court held that the
> concept of primary education must be interpreted in the light of practice
> in 1937 but a majority of the court held that the word 'child' in Article
> 42 must be understood as extending up to eighteen years, that is the
> present age of majority. If one was to transpose that reasoning to the
> facts of the present case one would say that one looks at the concept of
> marriage as it was defined in the light of practice or understanding in
> 1937 and that issues such as capacity must be understood in the light
> of prevailing law" (at 127).

The difficulty with this line of reasoning is that it does not reflect the approach
taken by Murray J. in *Sinnott*, on whose judgment Dunne J. first relied. Although
Murray J. held that the duration of primary education should be determined
by reference to the understanding in 1937, he strongly suggested that the
concept of primary education was a values issue that required a contemporary
understanding:

> "The late Professor John Kelly, writing in *The Constitution of Ireland
> 1937–1987* (Institute of Public Administration, 1988) suggested
> guidelines to achieve a balance as between possible competing
> claims of the historical approach to constitutional interpretation and
> the contemporary or 'present-tense' approach. The 'present-tense' or
> contemporary approach, he suggested is appropriate to standards and
> values. 'Thus elements like "personal rights", "common good", "social
> justice", "equality", and so on, can (indeed can only be) interpreted
> according to the lights of today as judges perceive and share them.' He
> felt that on the other hand the historical approach was appropriate 'where
> some law-based system is in issue, like jury trial, county councils, the
> census.' This he said was not to suggest that the 'shape of such systems
> is in every respect fixed in the permafrost of 1937. The courts ought to
> have some leeway for considering which dimensions of the system are
> secondary, and, which are so material to traditional constitutional values
> that a willingness to see them diluted or substantially abolished without
> a referendum could not be imputed to the enacting electorate'.
> There is undoubted value in such an approach which Professor
> Kelly clearly had in mind as a *guide* to, rather than formal canons of,
> interpretation.
> As correctly emphasised by counsel for the first plaintiff, the
> obligation to provide for free primary education in Article 42.4 is
> unique in the extent to which it circumscribes the discretion which the
> organs of State, government and Oireachtas, normally enjoy under the

Constitution as to the allocation of national resources. That particular
obligation is limited to primary education. It excludes other forms of
education. If Article 42.4 was intended to extend that constitutional
obligation to the provision of free primary education to all adults,
irrespective of their age, according to their need, I think it can fairly
be said that one would have expected such a far reaching limitation
on the powers of the Oireachtas to have been expressly stated in the
provision.

That is not to say that the content or nature of the education to
be provided for cannot be interpreted in the light of present day
circumstances. The nature and quality of the primary education to be
provided is a more abstract concept with connotations of standards and
values. Historically there is no doubt that many persons who suffered
from mental or physical handicap were not capable of benefiting from
the kind of education that was traditionally available. However, with
greater insight into the nature of people's handicaps, the evolution of
teaching methods, new *curricula* as well as new tools of education there
is no doubt that the nature and content of primary education must be
defined in contemporary circumstances. That means where children are
capable of benefiting from primary education (however its content is
defined) the State have an obligation to ensure that it is provided free
to children who can benefit from it including those who suffer from
severe mental or physical handicap.

In my view, primary education taken in its ordinary and natural
meaning is at once both inclusive and exclusive. It relates to the teaching
of children only. It includes children but excludes adults. I do not find
in the Constitution authority for interpreting it otherwise."

It is thus questionable whether Dunne J. was correct to conclude—on the
basis of *Sinnott*—that the meaning of marriage (and the capacity to enter into
marriage) had to be interpreted in a manner consistent with the intention in
1937. Dunne J.'s second basis for adopting a 1937 understanding of the term
marriage turned on a distinction between unenumerated rights and implied
rights. In this regard, she accepted the defendants' submission that the living
Constitution approach was more appropriate to the context of ascertaining
unenumerated rights than to the task of redefining a right that was implicit in the
Constitution. This proposition reduced the relevance of Walsh J.'s judgment in
McGee v Attorney General [1974] I.R. 284, on which the plaintiffs had placed
considerable reliance. In that case, Walsh J. had stated that "no interpretation
of the Constitution is intended to be final for all time. It is given in the light
of prevailing ideas and concepts." This had led him to enumerate the right
to marital privacy. However, the division of constitutional rights into two
types, unenumerated and implicit, is difficult to draw. If a different method of
interpretation is to apply to each type of right, where one draws that dividing

line becomes a matter of some significance. These difficulties could be avoided if the courts were simply to adopt the approach suggested by Professor Kelly without superimposing additional distinctions between the appropriate methods of interpretation for explicit, implicit and unenumerated rights.

Dunne J.'s third basis for determining that the 1937 understanding of marriage should be adopted appears more obliquely but is probably the most convincing. She noted that the *T v T* case, in which Murray J. referred to marriage as being between a man and a woman, was decided in 2003 and that, therefore, the opposite-sex understanding of marriage could not be described as fossilised. She commented that the court was being asked to redefine marriage to mean something which it has never done to date, and that the definition of marriage had always been understood as being opposite-sex marriage. She concluded:

> "Having regard to the clear understanding of the meaning of marriage as set out in the numerous authorities opened to the Court from this jurisdiction and elsewhere, I do not see how marriage can be redefined by the Court to encompass same sex marriage. The Plaintiffs referred frequently in the course of this case to the 'changing consensus' but I have to say that there is little evidence of that. The consensus around the world does not support a widespread move towards same sex marriage. There has been some limited support for the concept of same sex marriage as in Canada, Massachusetts and South Africa together with [Spain, Belgium and the Netherlands] but, in truth, it is difficult to see that as a consensus, changing or otherwise" (at 127).

Although the meaning of marriage is contested now in a way that would have been inconceivable in 1937, it is not the case that the meaning of marriage has unequivocally shifted. Accordingly, even if one accepts that the Constitution's protection of marriage is a values issue and requires a present tense interpretation, it does not necessarily follow that the constitutional meaning of marriage should be expanded to include same-sex marriage. This does raise questions of the role that the courts should play in social change: should they lead change by lending their weight to the questioning of traditional concepts (such as marriage) or should they reflect change by only adapting constitutional interpretations where there has been an unequivocal shift in how the term is understood? A constitution with a strong egalitarian guarantee could require a court to lend its weight to the questioning of traditional concepts. However, given the limited force that has been accorded to Art.40.1 and the explicit approval of legislative discriminations against non-marital families, it is (at least) fully consistent with existing case law for the courts to rely on a traditional, albeit now contested, understanding of marriage in order to exclude same-sex couples from that institution.

As noted above, Dunne J. provided one further, rather terse, justification for the limitation of marriage to opposite-sex couples:

> "The other ground of justification must surely lie in the issue as to the welfare of children. Much of the evidence in this case dealt with this issue. Until such time as the state of knowledge as to the welfare of children is more advanced, it seems to me that the State is entitled to adopt a cautious approach to changing the capacity to marry albeit that there is no evidence of any adverse impact on welfare" (at 130).

Dunne J. had concluded that the sociological research was not rigorous enough to establish whether children raised by same-sex couples either fared less well or as well as those raised by opposite-sex couples. In this light, her conclusion on this point suggests a cautious scientific view that the State wait for conclusive (or at least stronger) social scientific evidence before allowing same-sex marriage. However, there is an important assumption underlying this conclusion, namely that opposite-sex parents raise children adequately. It could—*ex hypothesi*—be possible that same-sex parents would raise children better. Insisting that the State wait until there is evidence that same-sex parents are no worse at raising the children runs the risk of opposite-sex parents raising children who could have been better raised by same-sex parents. Moreover, it posits as a test not a requirement that same-sex parents be shown to be good parents, but rather that same-sex parents produce similar results as opposite-sex parents, according to various measure. The purpose of these observations is neither to argue that opposite-sex parenting is inadequate nor to maintain that same-sex parents would be better. Rather it is simply to demonstrate that Dunne J.'s conclusion on this point is based as much on an unproven view of opposite-sex parenting as the ideal as it is on a cautious scientific approach.

RIGHTS OF FAMILY

In *McK v Information Commissioner* [2004] I.E.H.C. 49, [2004] 2 I.R. 12 the Supreme Court held that it should be presumed that parents are entitled to access to their child's medical records. This, however, is a rebuttable presumption. See elsewhere the chapter on Information Law and the Ombudsman.

TRESPASS INTO SEPARATION OF POWERS

Executive by law subject to civil servant control Section 20 of the Freedom of Information (Amendment) Act 2003 gives discretionary power to Secretaries General of Government Departments to certify that a record of whatever nature relates to a deliberative process of government and is thus exempt from release. Such a certificate is not amenable to internal review and cannot be appealed to the Information Commissioner. Section 20(1)(c) states, *inter alia*, that such a certificate shall be final. Effectively this means that the decision is entirely in the hands of the senior civil servant and that *all* Ministers, not just the departmental Minister, are bound by this unreviewable decision. In 2006 the first such certificate was issued by the Secretary General of the Department of Justice, Equality and Law Reform.

This event is such a serious attack on the proper role and function of Ministers and Secretaries General that the comment of the Information Commissioner on this amendment to the Freedom of Information Act 1997 bears repeating:

> "[I]t would seem inappropriate that a certificate issued by a Secretary General under the proposed section 20(1A)(a) be final when, amongst other considerations, in contrast, a certificate issued by a Minister under section 25 of the 1997 FOI Act is appellable under section 42 to the High Court on a point of law. Moreover, it would seem inappropriate, in circumstances where such a Minister may declare a record to be exempt in such a Certificate by virtue of section 23 [Law Enforcement and Public Safety] or 24 [Security, Defence and International Relations] only if he/she is satisfied that the record concerned is of sufficient sensitivity or seriousness to justify his/her doing so, that a Secretary General of a Department of State may certify a record of *whatever nature* to relate to the deliberative processes of any Department of State, *whatever their nature*" [emphasis included in original]. (*The Application and Operation of Certain Provisions of the Freedom of Information Act, 1997* (Office of the Information Commissioner 2003), previously quoted in discussion on this issue in *Annual Review of Irish Law 2003,* 135 *et seq.*)

See chapter on Information Law and the Ombudsman.

Executive abdicates functional responsibilities   It is ironic that in *Minister for Enterprise, Trade and Employment v Information Commissioner* [2006] I.E.H.C. 39 (see chapter on Information Law and the Ombudsman), counsel for the Minister suggested that the Information Commissioner "had usurped or purported to lawfully interfere with the powers granted to the Minister for Finance under the Acts to proscribe a body as a 'public body' for the purposes of the Act". This, according to counsel, if upheld by the court, would constitute "usurpation by the judicial power of an executive function". The circumstances of this case do, indeed, suggest a trespass of the separation of powers but it is of quite a different nature than that suggested in the case. The question to ask is whether the executive, in setting up these independent agencies which are obviously public bodies but are excluded from monitoring such as that provided by the Information Commissioner or the Ombudsman, is in effect engaging in undue delegation of executive power. Where is the accountability and where is the safeguard of openness and transparency in the public interest?

There is yet another irony in the suggestion that the Information Commissioner is trespassing in the realm of the separation of powers. In relation to access to the records of minors the Supreme Court, by reason of its limited judgment in *McK*, has left the Commissioner no option but to interpret her mandate to uphold the Freedom of Information Act by encouraging a view that minor children should be consulted in decisions relating to requests from their parents for access to their personal medical and other records. It is by no means certain that this was the intention of the Supreme Court. It is probable that were a parent to take an action objecting to this interpretation by the Commissioner that the court would find against the Commissioner. Yet, given the abdication of their responsibilities by both the executive in its failure to legislate for oversight of executive functions and of the judiciary to interpret legalisation with guidance for future action, there is no other course of action open to the Commissioner.

TRIBUNALS OF INQUIRY

In *Murphy and Reynolds v Mahon* [2006] I.E.H.C. 75, the applicants were refused *locus standi* to challenge the constitutionality of s.6(1) of the Tribunals of Inquiry (Evidence)(Amendment) Act, 1979 as substituted by s.3(1) of the Amendment Act of 1997. This might be deemed sufficient service to the case, much of which lies in the sphere of procedure and of administrative rather than constitutional law. But at the risk of emulating the apparently interminable nature of the tribunal process itself, this would be to do a disservice to the judgment of Smyth J.

The case was a judicial review hearing following leave of Kelly J. that certain matters be determined in relation to a challenge to decisions of the Tribunal of Inquiry into Certain Planning Matters and Payments initially known popularly as the Flood Tribunal and subsequently as the Mahon Tribunal.

The proceedings had been commenced following publication of the second and third interim reports of the Flood then Mahon Tribunal in both of which reports the applicants had been found to have "obstructed" and to have "hindered" the progress of the tribunal.

Obstruction and hindrance   In his determination Smyth J. dealt with the issue of delay, finding against the applicants in this regard:

> "Given the alleged sense of grievance of the Applicants concerning the 2nd Report, making findings of obstruction and hindrance, which they did not challenge for 19 months, there was in my opinion an added sense of obligation to challenge the 3rd Report promptly. This they did

not do. They left it to one day within the period set as the latest under the rules to challenge the 3rd Report."

Nevertheless, Smyth J. did not wish to rest his judgment on that basis and he has presented a comprehensive analysis of a tribunal of inquiry's findings of obstruction and hindrance.

Equality of treatment   Smyth J. rejected the applicants' challenge to the tribunal in this regard based on the evidence, the inexcusable, indeed the inexplicable delay in bringing the proceedings, and in allowing the work of the tribunal to proceed until such time as the outcome was not to the liking of the applicants, at which stage they issued proceedings. He observed that equality of treatment of witnesses does not mean that identical treatment must be accorded to each witness, "for such does not allow for differences of capacity, age, the role and relative importance of each witness or the variants that context provides before courts or tribunals".

Tribunal findings do not carry punitive sanction   Holding that the tribunal was entitled to make its finding and rulings based on the evidence before it, Smyth J. queried whether the tribunal had the power in law so to do. He noted that it was agreed that under s.6 of the 1979 Act as amended by s.3 of the 1997 Act it was envisaged that a tribunal had power to make findings of, *inter alia*, failure to cooperate:

> "It seems reasonable and in my opinion necessary to infer that the legislature in so providing would not emasculate such power as to inhibit a Tribunal from making findings as to degrees of culpability in this regard. To so limit the tribunal would be to fail to distinguish between formal non-cooperation, perhaps through oversight or genuine misunderstanding, and active or deliberate or sustained conduct of omission or commission such as hindered a Tribunal. To so limit or circumscribe the power of the Tribunal in the context of the legislation could work a manifest injustice. In my judgement, in making such distinctions as it did in the instant case, the Tribunal went no further than was necessary and properly required to do to carry into effect the task entrusted to it and that in its making findings of obstruction and hindrance, such may be fairly regarded as incidental and consequential upon those things which the Oireachtas authorised. The fact that in a different forum and evidence tendered to it tested by a different standard of proof, conduct set out in Section 3(2) of the Act of 1979 is a criminal offence did not make the decision of the Tribunal ultra vires. Further, only the Courts have the punitive power in the event of a successful prosecution."

Right to good name   Smyth J. found it evident that the tribunal's findings that the applicants were guilty of a corrupt payment seemed of less concern to them then the consequences flowing from the finding of obstruction and hindrance:

> "Against the undisputed fact that a payment to Mr. Burke was not for a legitimate purpose and that payment to Mr. Redmond was corrupt, I fail to see any validity or reality in the argument that respect for constitutional right to a good name requires as a matter of construction that the Court find that there is no power to make a finding of obstruction and/or hindrance, which in my judgement is of far less serious significance than making illegitimate or corrupt payments."

WAR

In *Dubsky v Government of Ireland* [2005] I.E.H.C. 442 Mr Dubsky challenged the Government's decision to allow US aircraft involved in the military action in Afghanistan to overfly the State and/or refuel in Shannon. Mr Dubsky argued that the assent of the Dáil was required, pursuant to Art.28.3.1° of the Constitution, which provides: "War shall not be declared and the State shall not participate in any war save with the assent of Dáil Éireann." Macken J. addressed the meaning of this provision:

> "On the question of the scope of the Article, I find that this is both wide and narrow. It is required to be met, in conformity with the constitutional process therein envisaged, on each and every occasion on which there is an intended declaration of war on the part of the State or when there is an intended participation by the State in a war, whether declared by it or not. In that sense it is very wide. It is narrow in the sense that it requires such an assent only in those two circumstances, and not otherwise, as is clear from its wording. In the event there is no declaration of war, or no participation in a war, there is no requirement for any assent. The Article does not require that the Dáil determine that the State has not declared war. Equally it does not require that the Dáil determine that the State is not participating in a war."

Mr Dubsky relied on the statement in Art.28.3.3° that—in that subsection—"time of war" includes a time when there is taking place an armed conflict in which the State is not a participant but in respect of which each of the Houses of the Oireachtas shall have resolved that, arising out of such armed conflict, a national emergency exists affecting the vital interests of the State. He contended that this demonstrated that "an armed conflict" was "a war". Macken J. rejected this argument, on the basis that the purpose of the definition in Art.28.3.3° was to allow the Oireachtas to declare a state of emergency. Accordingly, the definition could not be carried across to the quite different context of Art.28.3.1°, nor used to determine the general meaning of "war".

Macken J. held that neither Mr Dubsky nor the Government had established that there was or was not a war in Afghanistan. As Mr Dubsky bore the onus of proof, however, he could not be successful in his claim. Nevertheless, she considered the issue of "participation" for the sake of completeness. She adopted Kearns J.'s statement in *Horgan v Ireland* to the effect that there would have to be an "egregious disregard of constitutional duties" before the courts should intervene on the grounds of Art.28. Applying this exacting test, she was not satisfied that Mr Dubsky had demonstrated that Ireland was participating in the conflict in Afghanistan, even if that conflict were to be constitutionally characterised as a war.

Contract Law

FERGUS RYAN, Head, Department of Law,
Dublin Institute of Technology

APPEALS ON FINDINGS OF FACT

See also *Advanced Totes Ltd v Bord na gCon*, Supreme Court, McGuinness J.; Hardiman, McCracken, Kearns and Macken JJ. concurring, March 23, 2006, [2006] I.E.S.C. 17 (below under PUBLIC PROCUREMENT).

Guilfoyle v Farm Development Co-operative Limited, Supreme Court, March 23, 2006, [2006] I.E.S.C. 18   The decision in *Guilfoyle* underlines the traditional and long-held reluctance of the Supreme Court to overrule courts of original jurisdiction on findings of fact.

In this case, the Supreme Court dismissed an appeal by the plaintiff against a High Court finding that a contract which he claimed had been entered into had not in fact been agreed. The plaintiff, Barry Guilfoyle, was a former employee of the defendant company, Farm Development Co-operative (hereinafter FDC). In a meeting in 1999 he informed Mr Murphy, the Managing Director of FDC, of his intention to leave the company to set up his own business elsewhere. During the course of this meeting Mr Guilfoyle alleged that Mr Murphy, on behalf of FDC, had agreed to buy the plaintiff's shareholding in FDC for IR£120,000. Murphy disputed this claim, alleging that no such agreement had been reached.

At the time, the plaintiff held 150 "B" ordinary shares in the company. Another employee, Jack Barlow, who had 75 "B" ordinary shares, had previously been paid IR£60,000 for his shareholding. At the 1999 meeting, Mr Guilfoyle alleged that he had cited Mr Barlow's payment as precedent, and was given to understand that he would receive payment on roughly the same valuation of shares.

The net question in the case was whether the alleged oral agreement had in fact been concluded. While Mr Guilfoyle asserted that he had been promised £120,000, Mr Murphy claimed that he (Murphy) had merely indicated in broad terms that FDC would "deal honourably and fairly with [Guilfoyle's] share encashment, as we always have done with all parties with FDC". Given the disputed recollection of the meeting, Smyth J. in the High Court effectively sided with Murphy, concluding that "although Mr. Guilfoyle genuinely believed he was going to get the same treatment as Mr. Barlow, I am equally satisfied that Mr. Murphy did not agree to give Mr. Guilfoyle £119,555 or £120,000 in respect of his shares in the company".

The judge thus concluded that no agreement had been made to buy the shares at £120,000 and, as such, he refused to grant specific performance as requested by the plaintiff. The plaintiff appealed to the Supreme Court, alleging that Smyth J. had erred in law and in fact in holding that no agreement had been entered into arising from the 1999 meeting.

The Supreme Court nonetheless upheld the High Court verdict. Noting the limitations of its appellate role, Denham J. (Fennelly and Macken JJ. concurring) refused to overrule the High Court. She found that Smyth J. was entitled to rule in the manner he did. He had been entitled, moreover, based on the contested evidence, to make conclusions on the credibility of each of the witnesses.

In her judgment, Denham J. referred to the reluctance of the Supreme Court to overrule a lower court on points of fact. She referred, in particular, to *Hay v O'Grady* [1992] 1 I.R. 210. In that case the Supreme Court highlighted that an appellate court does not enjoy the opportunity of seeing and hearing witnesses, or have the benefit of observing the manner in which the evidence is given or the demeanour of those giving it. As such, the Supreme Court should be wary of overruling judges on questions of fact and credibility:

> "This is the type of case where an appellate court treads very carefully, because at issue are questions of fact and credibility. These are quintessentially matters for the trial court. In this case the findings of the learned trial judge as to which witness he believed were findings of primary fact... If the findings of fact made by the trial judge are supported by credible evidence, this Court is bound by them, however voluminous and weighty the testimony against them."

In the Supreme Court's view, the determination of fact was "...supported by credible evidence" and thus the higher court was bound by the findings.

ARBITRATION

See also *Malcolm Marshall v Capital Holdings Limited t/a Sunworld*, High Court, Roderick Murphy J., July 21, 2006; [2006] I.E.H.C. 271 (discussed below under CONSUMER PROTECTION).

O'Sullivan and O'Sullivan v Eagle Star Insurance Ltd, High Court, Laffoy J., July 10, 2006   The claimants in this case sought an extension under s.45 of the Arbitration Act 1954 to the time permitted for referral of a dispute to arbitration. The claimants had taken out insurance on their home, the insurer being the defendant company. During the currency of the policy, a contractor working on the home (Mr O'Neill) was injured and, as a result, sought to sue the plaintiffs for personal injury, loss and damage. On inquiry, the respondent insurer (in a letter dated March 2003) refused to indemnify the claimants on the basis that the insurer had (it claimed) been misled as to the condition of the home. The insurer had, Eagle Star asserted, offered the policy on the basis that the home was in good repair, whereas in fact there was no stairway fitted at the time:

> "If we had been aware of this position we would not have accepted the risk. Due to the breach of policy conditions by failure to disclose this material fact we are not in a position to consider indemnity under the policy."

The insurer added that, given the circumstances, the "matter may be more appropriate for Mr. O'Sullivan's business liability insurers for their consideration".

In March 2003 the claimants sought an indemnity from their business liability insurers, Quinn Direct. Quinn Direct subsequently nominated solicitors to represent the plaintiffs in the proceedings taken by Mr O'Neill. Nonetheless, in October 2003 the contractor was granted liberty to enter judgment in default of an appearance by the O'Sullivans, the assessment of damages being due shortly after the decision in this case. In March 2005 Quinn Direct notified the plaintiffs that it was unwilling to provide an indemnity and the lawyers nominated to act for the plaintiffs were withdrawn.

This withdrawal by Quinn Direct explains in part what happened next. In December 2005 the claimants sought to invoke the arbitration clause in the Eagle Star policy. The respondent, however, objected on the grounds that, under the policy, either party had to invoke the clause within one year from the date on which the indemnity had been denied (being March 2003). As the deadline for invoking the clause was thus March 2004, the claim was, the insurer asserted, deemed to have been abandoned.

Section 45 of the Act of 1954 allows a court to extend the contractually agreed time limit for referral of a dispute to arbitration if it is of opinion that in the circumstances of the case undue hardship would otherwise be caused. If this is the case it may, subject to normal statutory periods of limitation, extend the time for such period as it thinks proper.

Laffoy J. considered the ruling of Hamilton J. in *Walsh v Shield Insurance Company Ltd* [1976–1977] I.L.R.M. 218. In that case, Hamilton J. held that there had been an inexcusable delay in commencing arbitration proceedings and in seeking relief under s.45. Nonetheless, he proceeded to extend the time for invoking arbitration on the basis that undue hardship would otherwise be caused to the applicant. He further concluded that such an extension would not prejudice the respondent company. A condition was added, however, rendering the applicant liable for its own costs, even if it succeeded in arbitration.

In considering the instant case, Laffoy J. rejected the proposition that Eagle

Star's letter of March 2003 had encouraged or advised them to pursue Quinn Direct. She accepted furthermore that both the delay in seeking arbitration and in seeking a s.45 extension of time were inexcusable. The respondent claimed that it would be prejudiced by the fact that judgment had already been entered in default of appearance, and the respondent would thus have very little prospect of success against Mr O'Neill. It further asserted that any hardship caused to the claimants should be addressed by pursuing Quinn Direct or the solicitors appointed by the latter.

The judge nonetheless concluded that the delay did not prejudice Eagle Star, in that the insurer would still be able to make its case in arbitration regarding the indemnity. In so far as the claimants were concerned, however, the prospect of damages being awarded against them was inevitable and, as such, undue hardship would ensue "if the respondent has wrongfully declined an indemnity and [the claimants] are deprived of the opportunity of establishing that at arbitration". The respondent furthermore would be entitled, if it lost in arbitration, to seek a remedy from any third party whose participation led to any alleged mismanagement of the claimants' defence in the O'Neill case, there being a subrogation clause in the Eagle Star policy.

Laffoy J. thus concluded that the time for referring the dispute to arbitration should be extended for one week from the date of her judgment, subject to the caveat that the applicant would be responsible for the costs of this motion and arbitration, even if successful.

Templeville Developments v Leopardstown Club, High Court, O'Sullivan J., May 4, 2006; [2006] I.E.H.C. 129   This case essentially concerns the extent to which an arbitrator was entitled to determine certain disputed matters that were submitted to arbitration. The Leopardstown club owns and manages a well-known racecourse situate on lands in Co. Dublin. Under the terms of a 1998 lease, part of these lands had been leased to the plaintiff, which owns and operates a large leisure and sports facility. The parties shared the right to a number of car parking facilities.

As a result of a compulsory purchase order made by the Dún Laoghaire–Rathdown County Council, a portion of the lands used by the plaintiff was compulsorily acquired. On foot of this acquisition, the first defendant entered into a licence agreement with the plaintiff, under which the defendant agreed that the plaintiff would be entitled to a new site sufficient for its needs, to include car parking spaces. A provision in the agreement provided that:

> "...any dispute relating to the location of the new site or the suitability of same shall be resolved between the parties by a single arbitrator in accordance with the provisions for arbitration hereinafter contained."

A further arbitration clause stipulated that in case of a dispute on any of the terms, provisions or conditions of the agreement, such dispute shall be referred to the decision of an agreed arbitrator.

A disagreement arose regarding the location of the new site (particularly concerning the siting of a parking ramp). The dispute was referred to arbitration. In earlier proceedings (High Court, O'Sullivan J., December 10, 2003) an interlocutory order was granted to prevent the construction of a parking ramp by the plaintiff pending the conclusion of arbitration. This injunction was later lifted (High Court, Murphy J., July 30, 2004).

The crux of these new proceedings concerned the powers of the arbitrator regarding the location of a new site. The plaintiff asserted that, under the licence agreement, the arbitrator was entitled, in his own right and on his own initiative, to select a new site to which the plaintiff would be relocated. The defendant disputed this, alleging that under the terms of the agreement the arbitrator's role was limited to assessing the suitability of any site offered by the defendant as licensor. The defendant argued that, given the complex uses of its lands by diverse users, no reasonable businessperson would have agreed to allow a third party to select and determine the new site without reference to an existing proposal by the defendant. In particular, the defendant noted the terms of clause 5 of the agreement, reserving the latter's right to nominate a new site.

Nonetheless, the court concluded, on an interpretation of the licence agreement, that the arbitrator was entitled *on his own initiative* to determine the location of the new site. He was entitled to do so, moreover, without reference to any site proposed by either of the parties and without the need for either party to nominate a location for his consideration. As a matter of general policy, the judge suggested that the courts generally tended to favour an expansive interpretation of the role of the arbitrator, that all disputes should be referred to him or her for final resolution. On the particular wording of the licence agreement, the court concluded that the references to "any dispute" being "resolved" conferred on the arbitrator in this case an unfettered right to determine for himself and on his own initiative the location of a new site for the plaintiff's business.

Greyridge Developments Ltd v Laurence McGuigan t/a McGuigan Construction and Reddy, High Court, Gilligan J., June 28, 2006; [2006] I.E.H.C. 441   This case concerns an attempt to revoke the instigation of an arbitration arising from a dispute between the parties. The plaintiff company, which had commenced building on its lands in Carrick-on-Shannon, Co. Leitrim, had hired the defendant as building contractor. There were in fact two contracts between the parties, both of which contained an arbitration clause requiring that any dispute or difference arising between the parties be referred to an arbitrator, whose decision in the matter was deemed to be final and binding.

Subsequently a dispute arose, the defendant claiming that the plaintiff owed him €525,623, with the plaintiff counterclaiming for non-completion of the project. Works ceased and the matter was referred to arbitration before the second defendant. Though the arbitration process commenced in 2001, there had yet to be a formal hearing.

The plaintiff subsequently sought an order declaring that by reason of what it claimed was fraud on the part of the defendant, the arbitration should cease with the matter proceeding instead before the High Court. Section 39(2) of the Arbitration Act 1954 allows a court to revoke the appointment of an agreed arbitrator where a dispute has arisen as to fraud. In this case the plaintiff alleged that the defendant had furnished a purported invoice for STG£8,547.50 for deliveries of concrete, which invoice, it claimed, was a forgery. The defendant admitted that this was so, but denied any fraud, asserting that the concrete had in fact been delivered, further asserting that it was possible to verify this by observation of the building site.

The judge agreed that the concrete invoice was indeed a forgery, and moreover that "...very serious issues as to credibility have been raised" in respect of other invoices which had been presented. Nonetheless, the judge refused to exercise his discretion to terminate the arbitration and allow the matter to proceed to a plenary hearing. Noting the traditional reluctance of the courts to interfere in an arbitration process to which both parties had agreed, the judge had regard to the decision in *Cunningham-Reid v Buchanan-Jardine* [1988] 2 All E.R. 438. In that case, the Court of Appeal ruled that where the party accused of fraud wished to have the matter heard in court, the court would invariably allow the case to proceed to plenary trial, the rationale being that the accused should have an "opportunity to clear his name in open court". On the other hand, if the person accused of fraud wanted the arbitration to proceed, "the allegation of fraud was not by itself sufficient reason for the court to refuse a stay [to the arbitration]. Instead the court has discretion dependent on all the circumstances of the case."

Gilligan J., noting the strong judicial preference for non-interference in matters of arbitration, observed that where parties had agreed under contract to refer a dispute to arbitration, the courts generally would not step in unless there was good reason to do so. The parties in this case had entered into a valid and binding agreement. Although the plaintiff had a bona fide concern regarding forgery and fraud, there was nothing to suggest that the experienced arbitrator would be unable to deal with these issues. While the charge of fraud was serious, the points of law arising were not complex, and the experienced and distinguished arbitrator was, the judge concluded, well able to deal with all issues raised and to draw all necessary inferences from the facts as determined.

The judge was further persuaded by the fact that the arbitration process had been ongoing for five years, with considerable costs having arisen in respect thereof. He observed, in particular, that the amounts in respect of which fraud was alleged were relatively insignificant in the context of the defendant's total claim for €525,623. Nor could the court justify causing further delay to proceedings by requiring that the whole case be set back to "square one". He concluded, moreover, that despite the defendant's allegedly "unorthodox" *modus operandi*, no issue of public interest arose in the matter such as would require a plenary hearing. As such, a decision to revoke the power of the arbitration was not justified. The court thus refused to stay the arbitration.

BREACH OF CONTRACT

Taylor Flynn v Sulaiman and Advanced Cosmetic Surgery Ltd, High Court, O'Neill J., May 23, 2006; [2006] I.E.H.C. 160   The plaintiff in this case, a 54-year-old woman, underwent liposuction at the second defendant's clinic, with the first defendant operating. Unhappy with the results, she sought damages for breach of contract, alleging in particular that she had not been properly informed in advance about certain possible consequences of the procedure and any suitable alternatives thereto.

Having made an appointment, the plaintiff attended the clinic on July 12, 2000, the plan being that she would meet a Dr Kingdon, the clinic's lipo-sculpture specialist. On the day, Dr Kingdon did not turn up as arranged, but Ms Taylor Flynn nonetheless met with Ms Shiels, manager of the clinic. At that meeting Ms Shiels, who had personally undergone the liposuction procedure, displayed her own abdomen to the plaintiff as evidence of what the former claimed were the great advantages of the procedure. Although the plaintiff did, at that meeting, speak to another doctor, the latter pointed out her lack of familiarity with liposuction. It was accepted, in particular, that there was at that meeting no discussion of the alternative options or of the possible complications arising from liposuction.

An operation was arranged for July 19, at which Dr Kingdon was due to preside. Prior to the operation, Ms Taylor Flynn signed what she believed to be a consent form (though this was not discussed with her at that point), and paid the balance of the IR£2,500 fee for the treatment. Dr Kingdon not having appeared, the first defendant, Dr Sulaiman, took over the operation. Although he claimed that he had fully discussed with the plaintiff the options available and the possible consequences of the operation, the judge concluded, on the evidence, that it was improbable that there had been a sufficiently detailed discussion:

> "...The first-named defendant's involvement occurred at very short notice because of the failure of Dr. Kingdon to turn up. I am satisfied that the first-named defendant assumed that a normal pre-procedure consultation had taken place in which all of the various relevant matters had been discussed, as he was entitled to do."

The result, the judge concluded, was that the plaintiff underwent the procedure:

"...wholly bereft of the knowledge derived from qualified medical practitioners that would have enabled her to have given an informed consent to the procedure involved."

The plaintiff had not been made aware, in particular:

- of the choice of procedures available and which would be most suitable for her;

- that abdominal plasty may have been more appropriate in her particular circumstances;

- that she was required to lose weight before the operation;

- that bumps and irregularities might arise as a result of the operation;

- that the operation would leave a flap of loose skin that would need to be "tucked"; and

- that the operation would not address muscle laxity.

The inadequacy of consent was, he added, compounded by the conduct of Ms Shiels in representing herself as typical of what the plaintiff might expect after liposuction.

As such, the court concluded that the clinic had breached its contractual obligation to ensure that the plaintiff was fully informed prior to undergoing the procedure. Dr Sulaiman, however, was not at fault. Having replaced Dr Kingdon at short notice, the judge ruled that Dr Sulaiman was entitled to assume that the plaintiff had been properly advised and thus that Dr Sulaiman had not been deficient in his standard of care.

On the question of damages the court ruled that the plaintiff was entitled to compensation "...for undergoing a procedure which in the circumstances should not have happened". She was entitled, in particular, to recompense in respect of the pain, discomfort and inconvenience caused to her, along with the cost of the procedure.

The plaintiff further alleged that her condition had been rendered worse as a result of the operation. Though she herself clearly perceived a deterioration, the court observed that an objective test should be employed, the question being whether a reasonable observer would conclude that she had been cosmetically damaged or degraded. The judge did not think that she had, though he did accept that loose skin on the abdomen had caused a red rash. A procedure of abdominal plasty would rectify this, though the plaintiff was (the judge added) "understandably unwilling" to undergo further treatment. In the final analysis, the judge awarded general damages of €15,000 plus the cost of the procedure, making a total of €18,300.

>50span> *Annual Review of Irish Law 2006*

COLLATERAL CONTRACTS

Slaney Foods International Ltd v Bradshaw Foods Ltd, High Court, Kelly J., March 22, 2006; [2006] I.E.H.C. 97 This case concerned a written agreement affording the plaintiff an option to purchase a 90 per cent interest in a Co. Kilkenny-based abattoir. The defendant had purchased the property in September 2003 for €1.4 million. It subsequently entered into negotiations with the plaintiff which resulted in a written agreement, signed by both parties. Under the agreement, the plaintiff would take a one-year lease on the premises subject to certain conditions. The agreement also contained an option under which the plaintiff was granted a right to purchase a 90 per cent interest in the property after the conclusion of the lease.

On the conclusion of the lease, the plaintiff sought to exercise its option. Having encountered opposition from Mr Bradshaw, the main shareholder in the defendant company, the plaintiff sought specific performance of the agreement. In its defence, the defendant, while conceding the existence of an agreement in those terms, claimed that the plaintiff was not entitled to relief as the latter was in breach of a collateral agreement entered into between the parties.

In all, the defendant claimed that the collateral contract comprised nine separate matters, orally agreed between the parties at various stages. On examination of the facts, Kelly J. concluded that agreement on five of the matters had, on the balance of probabilities, not been established (the onus being on the defendant). On the remaining four matters, the court held that while there was agreement, there had been no breach in respect of these matters. The defendant thus had not discharged the onus of proving that a collateral agreement, to the extent that it existed, had been breached in any way. Given the absence of such a breach, the plaintiff was entitled to specific performance.

The judge also rejected the defendant's counterclaim to the effect that, given the expiry of the lease, the plaintiff was in unlawful possession. The court concluded that the plaintiff was lawfully in possession as "purchaser in possession". The plaintiff was ready and willing to complete the purchase; the only factor preventing it from doing so was the defendant's opposition. The court thus ordered specific performance of the sale to the plaintiff, as per the option agreement.

COMPLETE, NOTICE TO

Ochre Ridge v Cork Bonded Warehouses, High Court, Smyth J., February 28, 2006 (below under CONDITIONS PRECEDENT) and *Hegarty and Hogan v Fusano Properties*, High Court, Laffoy J., February 24, 2006; [2006] I.E.H.C. 54 (below, MISREPRESENTATION).

Courtney v McCarthy, High Court, Laffoy J., December 21, 2006; [2006] I.E.H.C. 417 On March 4, 2005 an auction took place for the sale of a portion of lands belonging to the plaintiff, though the plaintiff retained some adjacent land for herself. The defendant having made the highest bid, the parties entered into a contract of sale, under which the defendant agreed to pay €1.8 million for the auctioned property. A deposit of 10 per cent was to be paid on execution of the contract. Furthermore, the closing date for completion of the sale was set as April 8, 2005.

The contract of sale contained a number of pertinent conditions. In particular, the plaintiff, having retained adjacent land for herself, agreed in special condition 11 that she would allow the defendant a right of way over the retained lands if the defendant was given planning permission for a development on the sold portion of the land. Condition 12 further stipulated that to facilitate any planned development on the land which had been sold, the defendant would build roads and services thereon, maintaining these facilities until such time as they were taken over by the local county council.

The conditions also stated that, in default of a timely closing, the defendant would be required to pay interest at 12 per cent in respect of the balance of purchase monies owed. Under conditions 40 and 41, moreover, the contract entitled the plaintiff, if the sale did not proceed by April 8, to issue a notice requiring completion within 28 days, in default of which the plaintiff would be entitled to retain the deposit paid and regard the contract as rescinded and the land as free for resale.

On April 22, 2005, the defendant having failed to complete on time, the plaintiff issued a notice to complete. The defendant having failed to complete in the interim, on May 30, 2005 the plaintiff wrote to the defendant informing her that the contract had been rescinded on foot of the failure to comply (within 28 days) with the notice to complete.

Nonetheless, in the period that followed, the parties and their legal teams continued to discuss the sale. The defendant, while in principle willing to close, contested a number of points. In particular, the defendant claimed that condition 12 of the contract was void for uncertainty. She further contested any liability on her part to pay interest, which the plaintiff maintained was due under the contract. While the plaintiff, during this period, was also willing in principle to conclude the sale, she continued to maintain her entitlement to rely on the contract, and her right to rescind. In particular she maintained throughout that she was entitled to claim interest in respect of the delay in closing.

Efforts to break the deadlock eventually faltered, whereupon the plaintiff again claimed that the contract was rescinded and the deposit forfeit. The defendant having intimated that she would seek specific performance of the agreement, the plaintiff sought declarations to the effect that this was not possible as the contract had been validly rescinded and the deposit was validly deemed forfeit.

The court granted these declarations. It first concluded that as of May 30,

2005 (the date on which the defendant had been notified of the rescission), the contract had been validly rescinded. The defendant having failed to close in compliance with the notice to complete, the contract was properly terminated on May 30, 2005. The contract, moreover, entitled the plaintiff to retain the deposit if there was a failure to comply with the notice to complete.

While the plaintiff had indicated her willingness thereafter to engage in negotiations aimed at reinstating the contract, her conduct in doing so was expressed as being strictly without prejudice to her legal right to regard the contract as having ended. Her participation in negotiations did not undermine her continuing right to rescind.

On July 4, 2005 the plaintiff had indicated that, provided certain conditions were met, she would be willing to close the contract in a face-to-face meeting on July 11, 2005. There having been some miscommunication in the interim between the various parties and their solicitors, the parties never met up on that date. On July 11, 2005 the defendant, nonetheless, transferred to the plaintiff's solicitors the €1.62 million balance owed in respect of the sale. The plaintiff, however, claimed that the conditions for reinstatement of the contract had not been met. Her solicitors thus repaid the €1.62 million and again notified the defendant that the contract was at an end.

On the specifics of what transpired in the week ending July 11, 2005, the court ruled that although the plaintiff had being willing to reengage during that period, she had done so strictly on the basis of conditions that the defendant had not met. First, the plaintiff had agreed to negotiate on the basis that the defendant would agree to pay the interest, on which point the defendant had not conceded. As a matter of probability, the court found, the defendant had not acknowledged her liability to interest and would not have paid such interest. Secondly, although the plaintiff had conceded a willingness to grant an immediate right of way over retained lands (thus varying condition 11), she had done so on the basis that there would be agreement on the precise location of that right of way. In fact, despite some discussions between the parties, the exact location remained undetermined, due primarily to the failure of the defendant to specify the precise right of way.

Having failed to meet these conditions, the court concluded that the plaintiff was entitled as of July 11, 2005 to revert to her original stance that the contract had been rescinded. On the facts, moreover, no new contract had arisen as a result of the dealings in the week preceding July 11.

The defendant had also claimed that, as a result of the plaintiff's actions, she was now estopped from relying on her right to regard the contract as having been rescinded. The defendant claimed that on July 4, 2005 the plaintiff had represented that if the defendant met certain conditions, she would be prepared to close at a face-to-face meeting the following July 11. The defendant alleged, moreover, that she had relied to her detriment upon this representation, specifically in releasing €1.62 million to the plaintiff's solicitor.

Although the court ruled that the plaintiff's representation (of July 4) had resulted in a temporary suspension of her right to rescind, any resulting estoppel was subject to conditions, namely that the defendant would agree to pay interest and agree on the precise location of the right of way. The defendant had not in fact met these conditions, and was asserting instead her right to close on her own conditions. Although the plaintiff had suffered detriment in releasing the €1.62 million (and incurring a week's interest thereon), this detriment had not occurred on foot of the representation, which required compliance with the terms of the contract. This included a commitment to pay interest, which the defendant had continued to resist.

The defendant, in sum, had failed to indicate, by July 11, 2005, a willingness to complete in accordance with the terms of the original contract. The representation of the plaintiff only suspended, and had not extinguished, her right to rescind. The court thus concluded that as the defendant had not, by July 11, met the conditions for reinstatement of the contract, the plaintiff was entitled to regard her right to rescind as having been restored. Given that the defendant had not proved willing to meet her end of the bargain, it was not unconscionable, the judge ruled, to allow the plaintiff to go back on her representation. As such, Laffoy J. declared that the contract had been validly rescinded, and the deposit legally forfeited.

CONDITIONS PRECEDENT

See also *Lombard and Ulster Banking Ltd v Mercedes Benz Finance Ltd and Vincent Hughes*, MacMenamin J., January 11, 2006; [2006] I.E.H.C. 168 (below under CONSIDERATION).

Ochre Ridge Ltd v Cork Bonded Warehouses and Port of Cork Company Ltd, High Court, Smyth J., February 28, 2006; [2006] I.E.H.C. 107   The plaintiff in this case had entered into a contract to purchase from the first defendant a leasehold interest in an old bonded warehouse in Cork. The completion date—in respect of which time was expressly deemed to be "of the essence" —was April 10, 2000.

The warehouse was subject to a 99-year lease held by the first defendant, which in turn had been created from a 999-year lease held by the second defendant (the Port of Cork Company Ltd). The plaintiff's contract of sale with the first defendant was expressly stated to be conditional on obtaining permission from the second defendant to assign the lease, as well as the latter's consent to the development of the property and to the plaintiff's proposed change of use thereof.

The second defendant, however, refused to consent to the proposal unless and until identified dilapidations on the property were rectified by the first defendant. The plaintiff and first defendant sought to persuade the Port of Cork to defer the requirement to fix dilapidations until after the new lease was granted, the parties asserting that there was little point in making the required adjustments if the plaintiff was going to re-develop. The plaintiff had agreed, in particular, to meet the Port of Cork's requirements as to dilapidations if the latter's consent was granted. The consent was not, however, forthcoming. The consent of the Port of Cork was, of course, a condition precedent to the enforcement of the contract. The date for completion having passed before this condition was met, the first defendant claimed that the contract had lapsed.

The plaintiff sought specific performance of the contract, damages for breach of contract and conspiracy. It alleged, in particular, that the consent of the second defendant had been wrongfully withheld, and that both defendants had conspired to frustrate the completion of the contract.

Smyth J. dismissed the claim, refusing to grant the relief sought by the plaintiff. Essentially, he concluded that the contract was subject to a condition precedent. Given that the condition—approval from the second defendant—had not been satisfied, the contract was no longer binding after the completion date. Smyth J. thus concluded that the first defendant was not in breach of contract. Citing *Aberfoyle Plantations Ltd v Cheng* [1960] A.C. 115, the judge observed that:

> "...where a conditional contract of sale fixes a date for the completion of the sale then the condition must be fulfilled by that date;...[in particular] where a conditional contract of sale fixed (whether specifically or by reference to the date fixed for completion) the date by which the condition is to be fulfilled, then the date so fixed must be strictly adhered to, and the time allowed is not to be extended by reference to equitable principles."

He further held that the defendant parties had not conspired to bring about the particular result. There was no requirement, he held, for the first defendant to sue the second, challenging the refusal through litigation; indeed the contract expressly relieved the first defendant of any obligation to do so. The first defendant had at all times, the judge concluded, complied with its contractual obligations, and had acted at all times in good faith (though on the latter point the court found that there was no obligation to act in good faith, as the relationship was contractual rather than fiduciary in nature).

Nor could the plaintiff pursue the second defendant, there being no contract in place between the plaintiff and second defendant. Some evidence was presented to the effect that the plaintiff had sought (unbeknownst to the first defendant) to persuade the Port of Cork to present a schedule of dilapidations, apparently with a view to strengthening the plaintiff's hand in negotiating a price with the first defendant. Nonetheless, no agreement had been entered into between them, and the Port of Cork had, moreover, no legal obligations toward Ochre Ridge. The doctrine of privity of contract thus applied, excluding the plaintiff from suing the second defendant. Thus, even if the consents had been unreasonably withheld, only the first defendant would have been entitled to pursue an action. Neither did any estoppel or legitimate expectation arise regarding the granting of consents.

CONSIDERATION

Lombard and Ulster Banking Ltd v Mercedes Benz Finance Ltd and Hughes, High Court, MacMenamin J., January 11, 2006; [2006] I.E.H.C. 168 This case concerns a number of areas of contract law, including consideration, misrepresentation and conditions precedent. The case arose from a proposal made by the second defendant, Mr Hughes, seeking finance from the plaintiff for the purchase of three Mercedes trucks which he proposed to buy from the first defendant. The first defendant, Mercedes, was seeking STG£62,667 for the three trucks. Mr Hughes proposed that he would pay a deposit of STG£22,667 while the plaintiff would provide finance to the tune of STG£40,000. Effectively, the proposal was that Lombard and Ulster and Mr Hughes would enter into three separate hire-purchase agreements in respect of each of the trucks respectively.

Unbeknownst to the plaintiff, the trucks in question had previously been the subject-matter of hire-purchase agreements between Mr Hughes and Mercedes. In fact it transpired that Mr Hughes had defaulted on some of the payments and that one of the trucks (the "1991 truck") had been repossessed. To complicate the matter, Mr Hughes had subsequently paid off the debt in respect of the 1991 truck, which meant technically that he now owned it (even though Mercedes still had possession). By contrast, the other two trucks were in the possession of Mr Hughes, though under the retention of title clause these technically belonged to Mercedes. The plaintiff was not aware of these facts and had not been informed, in the course of its discussions with Mercedes, of the true situation. It had understood that Mercedes owned and had possession of the three trucks. It had not realised that it was essentially refinancing an existing deal in respect of which there had been significant problems; had it known the truth, it would have refused to engage.

Still labouring under this misunderstanding, the plaintiff paid the £40,000. Mr Hughes, however, failed to pay the deposit. The defendant claimed that the plaintiff owed it the value of the deposit and that, until such time as this was paid, title could not pass (as under the invoice, all goods would remain the property of the vendor until the full price was paid). The defendant argued that, essentially, the plaintiff had accepted the risk of Mr Hughes not paying the £22,667 deposit.

In the circumstances, MacMenamin J. ordered rescission of the contract. He observed first that where a contracting party did not receive any part of what had been contracted for, this amounted to a total failure of consideration. Relying on *Chartered Trust v Healy*, unreported, High Court, Barron J., December 10,

1995 and *United Dominions Trust (Ireland) Ltd v Shannon Caravans* [1976] I.R. 225, the judge noted that Lombard and Ulster had contracted for title to the property; this was not in fact received, as the title would not pass until the full price was paid. Moreover, in the case of 1991 truck it appeared that title vested in Mr Hughes. The plaintiff was thus entitled, on this basis alone, to rescind the contract.

The court also concluded that there had been a misrepresentation of the true facts in the case, a rare example of non-disclosure (indeed, silence) amounting to an actionable misrepresentation. Mercedes, having failed to disclose the true situation, argued that it was up to the plaintiff to conduct a credit search on Mr Hughes. It had, it was alleged, no obligation to disclose its prior dealings with Mr Hughes. The judge rejected this proposition, noting that the plaintiff had (unknown to itself) effectively been placed in the position of surety in respect of the sale. As there was an unusual risk arising which was materially different in nature to that which one might normally expect in such a transaction, the first defendant had a duty to disclose the real situation. Having failed to do so, the plaintiff was entitled to rescind.

The court further concluded that the payment of the deposit by Mr Hughes was a condition precedent to the formation of the contract. As this had never been paid, the condition precedent had failed, with the result that the contract failed.

CONSUMER PROTECTION

Marshall v Capital Holdings Limited t/a Sunworld, High Court, Roderick Murphy J., July 21, 2006; [2006] I.E.H.C. 271 This case centres on a challenge to the jurisdiction of an arbitrator in a dispute between a travel agent and a consumer. The proceedings, in particular, address the circumstances in which an arbitration clause might infringe consumer law. The case also underlines the traditional reluctance of the courts to interfere in arbitration awards otherwise than in exceptional circumstances.

The plaintiff in this case was injured as a result of a fall sustained on a sun holiday in Gran Canaria. The plaintiff's travelling companion, Mr McElroy, had booked the holiday with the defendant tour organiser, on his own behalf and on behalf of the plaintiff, the vacation spanning the Christmas break of 1999/2000. In accordance with the standard conditions of the tour organiser, an arbitrator was appointed to hear and determine the dispute. Having heard submissions from both parties, the arbitrator dismissed the claim and awarded costs against the plaintiff.

Some two-and-a-half years after the arbitrator made his decision, the taxing master assessed and awarded costs against the plaintiff, on foot of which the latter sought a declaration setting aside the arbitrator's decision. The plaintiff claimed that the arbitration lacked jurisdiction, as he had not validly agreed to submit himself to arbitration in lieu of legal proceedings. He further sought a declaration that any consumer to such a contract should be informed of the presence of the arbitration clause and its potential consequences prior to signing such a contract. The plaintiff added that even if such steps were taken, the consumer should still be entitled to proceed to court in lieu of arbitration. He claimed, moreover, that the arbitration clause infringed the terms of the European Communities (Unfair Terms in Consumer Contracts) Regulations 1995 (S.I. No. 27 of 1995). The plaintiff finally asserted that the arbitrator had erred in failing to give reasons for his decisions, and had generally misconducted himself in the administration of the arbitration.

In a thorough and carefully reasoned decision, Roderick Murphy J. found against the plaintiff, and refused to set aside the arbitration award. The court concluded that although Mr McElroy claimed he had could not remember signing a booking form, the plaintiff had in fact consented to have the matter referred to arbitration and had participated in the reference without objection at that time. Given this action and the failure, at the time of the reference, to object to arbitration, the plaintiff was deemed to have acquiesced in the reference. Having so acquiesced, he could not now raise the point that the conditions contained in the booking form did not apply. The plaintiff had only complained about the clause after the ruling in the defendant's favour. He had been fully advised by both a solicitor and a barrister, and there was no evidence of his unwillingness, at the time, to proceed to arbitration. Nor was there any evidence, at the time the arbitration was proceeding, of the plaintiff's intention to litigate.

The plaintiff had alleged generally, as a matter of public interest, that every consumer dealing with a supplier of goods or services had a right not only to be informed of any arbitration clause in an agreement involving the consumer, but also to have the consequences of such a clause fully explained to him or her. This claim was made, it seems, in the public interest generally, *i.e.* on behalf of all consumers, a stance which, the court concluded, the plaintiff had no standing to make. Again the court noted that the plaintiff had acquiesced in invoking the arbitration procedure and, having been fully advised, submitted himself without complaint to the process.

On the allegation that the clause contravened the European Communities (Unfair Terms in Consumer Contracts) Regulations 1995, the judge again ruled against the plaintiff, finding that the clause in question was not unfair. The 1995 Regulations stipulate that a term will be unfair if (the contract not having been individually negotiated) it causes (contrary to the requirement of good faith) a significant imbalance in the parties' rights and obligations, to the detriment of the consumer. Examples of such terms are suggested in the Schedule to the Regulations and include:

> (b) terms that inappropriately exclude or limit the legal rights of the consumer in cases of non-performance or inadequate performance

of the contract; and ...

(q) terms that seek to exclude or hinder the right to take legal action or pursue a legal remedy, in particular, by requiring exclusive arbitration not covered by legal provisions.

The judge concluded, however, that the arbitration process in this case did not exclude the application of legal provisions. Although the arbitrator enjoyed a general discretion on matters of fact, he was bound nonetheless to follow and apply the law and had no power to disregard legal provisions. The arbitrator was required to make his decision according to legal principles; there was no evidence that the arbitrator in this case had ignored this requirement. Nor had the agreement in question excluded the right to pursue a legal claim in the courts. Clause 12 of the impugned conditions left open the possibility of litigation, while clause 16 expressly referred to the possibility of a claim being made through the Small Claims Court. It thus did not in fact exclude the right of the consumer to take legal proceedings.

The plaintiff had moreover, the court found, delayed in taking proceedings. Order 56, r.4 of the Rules of the Superior Courts requires that a party seeking to set aside an arbitration award must commence proceedings within six weeks. Having delayed two-and-a-half years, the plaintiff was now out of time, and the delay was inordinate. On the facts, the plaintiff had only initiated his action when costs were confirmed by the taxing master. While this may have spurred him into action, it did not excuse or justify such a lengthy delay.

The judge also upheld the arbitrator's right to award costs. Under s.29 of the Arbitration Act 1954, an arbitrator enjoys the same discretion as a judge in relation to costs. Indeed s.30 of the Act invalidates any clause in an agreement purporting to require each of the parties to pay their own costs of any future arbitration, regardless of the result thereof. The judge thus concluded that the arbitrator was wholly entitled to award costs against the plaintiff.

The plaintiff had further challenged the failure of the arbitrator to give a reasoned award. The judge concluded, however, that in general there was no legal requirement on arbitrators to give reasons for their decisions. The parties in this case had in fact agreed to forego the option of a reasoned award and, as such, the plaintiff could not now complain after the fact that reasons had not been given. The court further concluded that there had been no evidence of misconduct or improper procurement on the part of the arbitrator, contrary to s.38 of the 1954 Act.

In the course of his judgment, Murphy J. reiterated the courts traditional reluctance to interfere with arbitrations awards. Citing *Doyle v Kildare County Council* [1996] I.L.R.M. 252 and *Keenan v Shield Assurance Ltd* [1998] I.R. 89, the judge invoked the desirability for finality and the courts' unwillingness to intervene. He relied on s.27 of the 1954 Act, which provides that:

"Unless a contrary intention is expressed therein, every arbitration agreement shall, where such a provision is applicable to the reference, be deemed to contain a provision that the award to be made by the arbitrator or umpire shall be final and binding on the parties and the person claiming under them respectively."

Murphy J. concluded, noting that while a court "has a common law jurisdiction to set aside an award of an arbitrator where an error of law appears on the face of the award", nonetheless:

"…such an error must be so fundamental that the court cannot stand aside and allow it to remain unchallenged. An award will not be set aside merely because the decision on the question of law is an erroneous one as the parties are deemed to have agreed to abide by the decision of the arbitrator."

EQUITABLE RELIEF

On promissory estoppel see *Courtney v McCarthy*, High Court, Laffoy J., December 21, 2006; [2006] I.E.H.C. 417 (above under COMPLETE, NOTICE TO). See also cases under SPECIFIC PERFORMANCE, below.

Shiel v McKeon, High Court, Clarke J., May 31, 2006; [2006] I.E.H.C. 194   This case centres on the application of an equitable principle arising out of *Pallant v Morgan* [1953] 1 Ch. 43. The plaintiff in this case sought to prevent the defendant from reneging on the terms of an alleged informal agreement between the parties regarding the purchase of a property in Enniscrone, Co. Sligo.

The property comprised a house and garden (in which the plaintiff, Mr Shiel, was primarily interested) with a plot of land at the rear, adjacent to the sea (the portion of most concern to the defendant, Mr McKeon). When the property came on the market, both parties expressed an interest in purchasing it. The defendant (McKeon) in particular wished to incorporate a portion of the property into a significant development on adjacent land which he owned and in respect of which he had received planning permission. On August 11, 2005, the defendant thus offered to purchase the property for €435,000. Although no formal contract was exchanged or deposit submitted, it was McKeon's understanding that the vendor had agreed in principle—and subject to contract—to sell to him.

Prior to the formalisation of the agreement with McKeon, the plaintiff, Mr Shiel contacted the vendor indicating that he too wished to purchase the property. He made an offer of €415,000. Subsequently, an agent acting on Mr Shiel's behalf was told by the vendor that unless Shiel entered an offer of €500,000 by August 12, the property would be sold to the defendant (McKeon was unaware of this discussion). That deadline passed without any further offer being made.

The parties subsequently met on August 14 to discuss the matter. It was alleged by the plaintiff, Mr Shiel, that at this meeting the parties orally agreed that the defendant (McKeon) would purchase the property, as planned, in part trust for the plaintiff, the latter (Shiel) agreeing to pay €275,000 for the house and garden. The defendant would keep the portion at the rear. On the facts, Clarke J. concluded that, although unenforceable by means of specific performance (for lack of certainty and lack of formalities), the parties had entered into an informal arrangement to this effect.

The defendant, having purchased the property, sought to renege on the bargain. It was accepted that the arrangement between the parties was not legally enforceable. Nonetheless, the plaintiff argued that an equity arose such that Mr McKeon should be deemed to hold the property in part trust for Mr Shiel. Citing *Pallant v Morgan*, the plaintiff argued that he had refrained from bidding on the basis of an understanding that the land would be divided between the parties as per the arrangement. The defendant should not, thus, be permitted to retain the benefit of the plaintiff not making a further bid "without conceding the substance of the arrangement".

Clarke J. examined the principle in *Pallant v Morgan*. He accepted that an equity might arise where an arrangement between parties regarding the division of property precedes the acquisition of the property by one of the parties. Either on the basis of the maxim "equity regards as done that which ought to be done" or on the basis of proprietary estoppel, the arrangement is deemed "to colour the subsequent acquisition" such that the acquiring party may be deemed a trustee if he seeks to act inconsistently with the arrangement. The arrangement need not be legally enforceable, nor will uncertainty act as a bar to relief. It was, however, necessary that either the acquiring party gained an advantage or the non-acquiring party suffered a detriment as a result of the arrangement. In such circumstances, it would be inequitable to permit the acquiring party to retain a benefit absent compliance with the arrangement.

Though the nature of the arrangement was disputed, the court accepted that the defendant had indicated a sufficient level of agreement to lead Shiel to believe that he could safely refrain from further bidding. The defendant's motive in so doing, the court suggested, was to prevent Shiel from "gazumping" him. As such, prima facie, an equity arose such that—all else being equal— McKeon may have been restrained from dealing with the property in a manner inconsistent with the agreement.

However, the court refused to enforce the equity. At the time of their meeting, Mr McKeon had been unaware of the fact that Shiel had been issued with and had missed the August 12 deadline for making a €500,000 bid. Although in law, Shiel had no duty to reveal this fact, in equity, "he who seeks equity must do equity". As such, the judge concluded:

"…it does not seem to me that [Shiel] can invoke equitable principles when he procured the arrangement upon which he relies in circumstances where he was aware that Mr. McKeon was unaware of the fact that his position was far weaker than might otherwise be believed".

Shiel knew that McKeon was unaware of "a significant weakness" in Shiel's position. This being the case, the court ruled that:

"…Mr. Shiel has lost his entitlement to resort to equity to pursue the matter by reason of his failure to disclose his weakened position at the meeting on Sunday 14th. While the parties were not, on any view, on equal terms prior to the meeting of the 14th, the extent of that inequality was concealed by Mr. Shiel."

EXCLUSION CLAUSES

See *Hegarty and Hogan v Fusano Properties*, High Court, Laffoy J., February 24, 2006; [2006] I.E.H.C. 54 (below under MISREPRESENTATION).

"GOOD FAITH"

Triatic Limited v Cork County Council, High Court, Laffoy J., March 31, 2006; [2006] I.E.H.C. 111   This case concerned some protracted negotiations for the proposed purchase and development of Fort Camden (also known as Fort Meagher), a coastal artillery fort dating back to the late 1700s and based in Crosshaven, County Cork. It was acquired by the State in 1938. In 1988, the Department of Defence ceded physical possession of the fort to the defendant, on the understanding that it would be developed for tourist/amenity purposes, though it remained in the possession of the State.

In 1989 the defendant publicly advertised the availability of several unspecified sites for the purpose of industrial, commercial and touristic development. The plaintiff was initially associated with a development proposal for Fort Camden, made by a company called Valcoast, but in December 1994 Valcoast decided not to proceed with its plans. On foot of this withdrawal the plaintiff, Triatic Ltd, wrote to the council seeking an option to purchase Fort Camden, the option giving the plaintiff up to two years to formulate a development plan and arrange for finance and planning permission. In response the defendant wrote to the plaintiff in 1995 indicating that the council was willing to deal exclusively with the plaintiff "in regard to the submission of a comprehensive development proposal for Fort Camden". The duration of the period of exclusive dealing was to be six months from March 10, 1995. The letter also stated that in the absence of satisfactory progress by September 8,

1995, the defendant would be free to deal with other parties. Subsequently, the period of exclusive dealing was extended on various separate occasions, ultimately to November 6, 1996. In particular, in a further letter of May 7, 1996, the defendant indicated that it would deal exclusively with Triatic in relation to the submission of a development proposal, for a period of six months, though the letter was stipulated to be "without prejudice/subject to contract".

In the meantime the plaintiff had actively commenced planning and had, in particular, inquired as to the purchase price for the property which, the defendant indicated by letter, would be IR£500,000. On November 4, 1996 a formal proposal document was submitted, but did not meet the expectations of the council. In particular, the council queried the appropriateness of a proposal for a 100-bedroom hotel. The council believed that this constituted a fundamental change in the proposal, and that the request for expressions of interest would need to be re-advertised. The council intimated, in particular, that it may be required, under public procurement rules, to re-advertise.

These proceedings were taken seeking to prevent the re-advertisement. In particular the plaintiff submitted that it had, *inter alia*, a contract with the defendant council to the effect that the council would continue to deal exclusively with the plaintiff and to negotiate in good faith with the plaintiff. The plaintiff claimed that the council was obliged under that contract to continue to negotiate in good faith with the plaintiff, and that it was not entitled arbitrarily to resile from such negotiations. The plaintiff sought damages claiming that, in expressing its intention to re-advertise, there had been an anticipatory breach of contract on the part of the defendant council. The defendant for its part denied the existence of such a contract.

While the judge accepted that the council had agreed to deal exclusively with the plaintiff from March 1995 to November 1996, she refuted the suggestion that there was an open-ended obligation to negotiate beyond that point. Between those dates the court ruled that the plaintiff had enjoyed an exclusive opportunity to prepare and submit a proposal for development of the property. She did not accept, however, that this meant that the parties had to keep negotiating indefinitely until agreement was reached. Nor did she accept that the defendant could only withdraw from negotiations if adjudged to have a "good reason" for so doing.

Relying on *Walford v Miles* [1992] 2 A.C. 128, Laffoy J. effectively rejected the proposition that a court could enforce an agreement to negotiate "in good faith". Such an agreement would, she observed, be unworkable, and more than likely void for lack of certainty. The courts could not enforce an obligation to continue negotiating until such time as there was a good reason to withdraw from discussions. How could a court, she argued, objectively determine that a proper reason existed to terminate negotiations? How would a court police such an agreement? In the instant case, for instance, Laffoy J. noted that there had yet to be agreement on the price of the property. On what grounds could a court determine objectively whether a withdrawal from negotiations, on foot of a particular asking price, would be reasonable or not?

Laffoy J. did accept that a "lock-out agreement"—where the parties agree to negotiate to the exclusion of other interested parties—could be enforceable provided that the duration for negotiations was time-defined. She further accepted that the Irish courts had previously recognised a duty to use best endeavours to bring about certain results, though she distinguished these precedents on the basis that in those earlier cases the duty arose on foot of concluded contracts (which was not the case here).

In this case the parties had, in March 1995, entered into a lock-out agreement under which the plaintiff had enjoyed the exclusive opportunity to prepare and submit a proposal. The council had adhered to that agreement, accepting and considering the proposal. It acted (the court concluded) at all times in a bona fide manner and had not dealt with any other party. However, the agreement came to an end in November 1996. In so far as the period subsequent to that date was concerned, the parties were merely in open-ended negotiations, with no obligation of exclusivity arising. There was no requirement, moreover, to deal in good faith, still less to continue negotiating until there was agreement or a valid reason to withdraw.

Given the particular complexity of the issues in this case, and the range of matters yet to be resolved, Laffoy J. did not accept that the parties had agreed indefinitely to continue negotiations until they blossomed into a full contract. Such an agreement had not been entered into, and even if it had it would have been void for lack of certainty. (The judge also refuted, on much the same grounds, the claim that the plaintiff had a legitimate expectation.)

GUARANTEE/SURETY AGREEMENTS

McGrath v O'Driscoll, High Court, Clarke J., June 14, 2006; [2006] I.E.H.C. 195 The net question in this case concerns the circumstances in which a guarantor of a loan may seek summary judgment against the principal debtor in respect of an unpaid debt. The defendants in this case had formed a partnership which had purchased a ship. In order to fund the purchase, the individual defendants had sought and obtained a loan from Anglo Irish Bank, in respect of which the plaintiff had made a personal guarantee. It also entered into a management agreement with a company, MSV Solstice II Ltd, in respect of the management and operation of the ship, which agreement the plaintiff again contracted personally to guarantee. Having encountered difficult trading conditions, the partnership defaulted on the loan. On foot of the guarantee, Anglo Irish successfully sued the plaintiff for €6.375 million plus interest and costs.

Although Mr McGrath had not yet paid any monies in respect of the judgment against him, he commenced proceedings requiring the defendants to indemnify him in respect of the amount of the judgment plus interest and costs. He claimed that as they were the primary debtors, he was entitled to recover the amount from them. He claimed moreover that he was entitled to summary judgment on the matter.

The defendants opposed summary judgment on the basis, first, that the matters in contention could not properly be the subject of a summary summons. They claimed further that the proceedings were premature in that the plaintiff had not yet paid any monies to Anglo Irish. Finally, they asserted that as a result of several alleged breaches of the management agreement, the defendants were entitled to pursue a counterclaim which, if successful, would result in an amount similar to the quantum of the debt being advanced to them. On the basis of the counterclaim they thus asserted that they should be given leave to defend.

The judge concluded that, in the circumstances of the case, summary proceedings were not appropriate. Order 2, r.1 of the Rules of the Superior Courts allows summary judgment in cases where, *inter alia*:

> "...the plaintiff seeks only to recover a debt or liquidated demand in money payable by the defendant, with or without interest arising."

The defendants claimed, however, that as the plaintiff had not yet paid anything to Anglo Irish, he could not claim entitlement to pursue the debt by means of summary judgment.

The judge outlined the difficulties that arose where a guarantor was successfully sued on foot of his guarantee. On the one hand, if forced to pay the debt as a condition of pursuing the primary debtors, the guarantor may suffer an injustice. If required to pay the debt before pursuing the primary debtor, he might be rendered unable to pursue the latter if he (the guarantor) had insufficient funds to pay the amount owed. On the other hand, if the guarantor were allowed to sue the primary debtor before he had paid the creditor, the risk would arise that the guarantor might collect the money but, nonetheless, not pay the creditor. In such a case, the primary debtor would be required to discharge the debt twice over.

The judge noted that a solution to this dilemma was put forward in *Wolmerhausen v Gullick* [1893] Ch. 514. In reliance on the decision, Clarke J. concluded that:

> "...the court can make an order in favour of a guarantor declaring the entitlement of the guarantor in respect of the principal debtor and putting in place appropriate arrangements to ensure that the guarantor will be protected from any inappropriate failure on the part of the principal debtor to meet his liability."

Such an order would, however, not be deemed merely to be an order "only to recover a debt or liquidated amount of money" as required by Ord.2, r.1. As such, the order could not be sought by means of a summary summons.

The guarantor, Clarke J. concluded, could only obtain an *unconditional* order for payment of the debt *after the guarantor had in fact already paid the sum owed.* It would, he continued, be inappropriate to make an unconditional order where the guarantor had yet to pay the debt. While the guarantor may be entitled to a conditional order along the lines suggested in *Wolmerhausen,* such an order did not fall within the ambit of Ord.2, r.1. As such, summary judgment would be inappropriate in such a case.

Despite this ruling, the judge turned to consider whether, independently of the aforementioned conclusion, the defendants should be afforded leave to defend. He rejected the proposition that the proceedings were premature, noting that the court was entitled to make an order in the terms outlined in *Wolmerhausen.* The judge did, nonetheless, accept that the defendants had an arguable case arising from their counterclaim against the plaintiff. The test to be applied here was whether the defendants had a "fair and reasonable probability of ... having a real and *bona fide* defence". While it was not, he added, enough simply to assert a defence, without more:

> "...any evidence of fact which would, if true, arguably give rise to a Defence will, in the ordinary way, be sufficient to require that leave to defend be given so that that issue of fact can be resolved."

Questions of law or construction might, he continued, be resolved in summary proceedings, though this should only be done where the issues are relatively straightforward and where there is no real risk of doing injustice.

On the facts, the court concluded that the defendants had indeed established an arguable case that they were entitled to counterclaim on foot of an alleged breach of the management agreement. As such, there was at least an arguable case that they did not in fact owe the plaintiff anything. The judge further concluded that the counterclaim could constitute a defence in these proceedings. The test to be applied was whether the counterclaim "arises out of circumstances which are sufficiently connected to" the plaintiff's claim. If so:

> "a set off in equity arises because it would be inequitable to allow the plaintiff's claim without taking the defendant's cross-claim into account."

On the facts, the court concluded that there was indeed sufficient connection between the claim and counterclaim, the loan and management agreement both being "part of a package". In so ruling, the judge dismissed the plaintiff's argument that whereas the counterclaim arose from the agreement with the partnership as a group, the loan had been advanced to the defendants as individuals. This did not, he ruled, break the connection between the claim and counterclaim. If made out, the counterclaim was such, he concluded, as to provide the defendants with a set off in equity against the claim sufficient to extinguish the latter. On that basis, the defendants were granted liberty to defend.

ADM Londis plc v Arman Retail Ltd, Arman and Arman, High Court, Clarke J., July 12, 2006; [2006] I.E.H.C. 309   The first defendant in this case, Arman Retail Ltd, was a shop trading under the Londis brand, the second and third defendants being its proprietors. Arman Retail having gone insolvent, the plaintiff obtained judgment against the first defendant for €162,110 owed to it in respect of goods supplied by Londis. In these subsequent proceedings, Londis sought summary judgment against the second and third defendants on foot of guarantees given by them securing the liability of the first defendant.

The defendants sought to oppose summary judgment, claiming that they had substantial grounds for being granted leave to defend the case. Admitting that the requirements for establishing leave to defend such a case were not very high (see *Aer Rianta v Ryanair* [2001] 4 I.R. 607), the judge cited his own decision in *McGrath v O'Driscoll* [2006] I.E.H.C. 195 (discussed above), noting that, while it was not enough simply to assert a defence without more:

> "...any evidence of fact which would, if true, arguably give rise to a
> Defence will, in the ordinary way, be sufficient to require that leave to
> defend be given so that that issue of fact can be resolved."

While questions of law or construction might, he added, be resolved in summary proceedings, this should only be done where the issues are relatively straightforward and where there is no real risk of doing injustice. The fundamental question was whether the defendant had alleged facts which if true might arguably give rise to a defence. Five separate possible defences were raised.

The defendants first alleged a defence of *non est factum*. They claimed that, owing to the fact that a large volume of documents had been presented to them during franchise negotiations, they had been unaware of the content of the guarantee. The judge noted that for a claim of this nature to be made out, the defendants would have to establish that the document was radically and fundamentally different from that which they believed they were signing. Their mistake, moreover, had to relate to the general character rather than the legal consequences of the documents. The defendants would further need to establish that they were blameless in the matter, having taken all necessary steps to determine the nature and general content of the agreement.

On the facts, however, the defendants had clearly signed documents that on their face made it manifestly clear that a contract of guarantee was being entered into. This fact, the judge argued, could easily have been verified even on a cursory reading of the documents. As there was no likelihood that this defence would be made out, liberty to defend on the point was denied.

The defendants raised a further plea based on a change in the legal nature of the plaintiff, although the court concluded that this change in legal status was not such as to disbar the plaintiff from pursuing the guarantees. The court further refuted the proposition that the plaintiff, having had the option of pursuing an independent guarantee provided by a financial institution in the same matter, could not recover from the defendants. Subject to the principle against double discovery, the existence of an alternative guarantor or other basis for recovery did not, the judge ruled, preclude recovery from the defendants, jointly and severally.

The court did accept, however, that the defendants had an arguable case regarding the correct amount of the principal liability in respect of certain specific items claimed by the plaintiff, the disputed sums amounting to €12,000 in total. Thus, liberty to defend was granted on this basis, but only to the extent of the disputed sum of €12,000.

The court further ruled that the defendants should be granted liberty to defend on foot of a possible counterclaim that the principal debtor may have had against a company associated with the plaintiff. While noting the potential legal difficulties facing sureties seeking to rely on a counterclaim available to the principal debtor, and accepting that the counterclaim related to the conduct of a company other than the plaintiff, the court nonetheless concluded that the matter could not be resolved at a summary stage without a real risk of injustice arising. While hinting that many of the first defendant's problems were likely not attributable to the plaintiff or related companies, there was, the judge ruled, at least an arguable case that the counterclaim against the associated company was sufficiently connected to the contractual relationship with the plaintiff to allow for a defence claiming set off in equity against the amount of the guarantee.

The judge ruled that the likely amount of the counterclaim, having first subtracted from the total debt the €12,000 in respect of which the defendants had already been granted liberty to defend, was unlikely to exceed 50 per cent of the value of the remaining €150,000. He thus awarded the plaintiff €75,000, granting the defendants liberty to defend on the basis of the possible counterclaim in respect of the remaining €75,000.

IMPLIED TERMS

See *MR v TR*, High Court, McGovern J., July 18, 2006; [2006] I.E.H.C 221 (discussed below under INTERPRETATION OF CONTRACTS).

INTERLOCUTORY INJUNCTIONS

Damien Sheridan v Louis Fitzgerald Group Ltd and Burston Ltd, High Court, Clarke J., April 4, 2006; [2006] I.E.H.C. 125 The first defendant is the owner of a number of Dublin city centre pubs, including the Temple Bar-based Quays Bar. The plaintiff, together with a business partner, had run a catering business called Damal Catering Ltd, which had run a restaurant in another of the defendant's pubs. Damal had entered into an agreement (the specific terms of which were in dispute) to run a restaurant based at the Quays Bar. Sheridan claimed that Damal had an oral agreement with the defendant for a five-year lease of the restaurant, at a rent of €100,000 per annum for the first 18 months, reviewable thereafter. A deposit of €30,000 was to be paid. Fitzgerald Group denied any such agreement on the alleged terms.

Having experienced some financial difficulties, Damal Ltd went into liquidation. Sheridan alleged that the defendant subsequently agreed to grant the lease to Sheridan personally on the same terms as he claimed were agreed with Damal. On foot of this agreement, Sheridan sought specific performance. While Sheridan ran the restaurant for some time, on January 30, 2006 the defendant asked the plaintiff to vacate the premises. At the end of February, the plaintiff was effectively locked out of the restaurant.

Pending the plenary trial of these issues, the plaintiff sought an interlocutory injunction restraining his exclusion from the premises. A three-fold test was set out:

- Was there a fair issue to be tried between the parties?

- In the case of an injunction being refused, would damages be inadequate to compensate the plaintiff for any resultant losses?

- On whose side did the balance of convenience lie?

On the first point, although the court noted that a variety of issues were in dispute between the parties, Clarke J. concluded that there was a fair issue to be tried, there being a dispute on the facts as to whether the parties had entered into an agreement for a lease. In so ruling the court rejected the defendant's claim that as there was no mechanism in the alleged contract to determine the amount of rent payable after the first 18 months, the contract was void for uncertainty. Although the court acknowledged that the plaintiff might have some difficulty proving the mechanism for review, the possibility arose that such a mechanism might be implied by the court. Alternatively, a contract in respect of the first 18 months might be severed from the remaining 42-month period, the contract being deemed void for uncertainty only in respect of the latter 42-month period.

The defendant further alleged that the contract being an oral agreement, the terms of s.4 of Deasy's Act (requiring that a contract for a lease be in writing or evidenced in writing) had not been fulfilled. The court noted, however, the possibility that the plaintiff might be able to argue part performance, having personally entered into possession of the premises. Though there would be a significant number of "major hurdles" in establishing part performance (not least the fact that an associated company, Damal, had already been in possession, staying in possession not being indicative of part performance) there was at least a triable issue to be resolved. Likewise, the court concluded that there was a fair issue to be tried on whether the agreement entered into granted a lease or a licence, the effect of such agreements to be characterised not by reference to the words employed, but by the substance of the relevant agreement.

However, on the second criterion the plaintiff fared less well, the court concluding that he had failed to establish the inadequacy of damages as a remedy in circumstances where an injunction was not granted. Relying on *Curust Financial Services Ltd v Loewe-Lack-Werk Otto Loewe Gmbh and Company* [1994] I.R. 450 the court concluded that while damages might be difficult to assess, such assessment was not impossible. Although exclusion from the premises would likely have a "retardant" effect on the business, which would be felt even after the plaintiff was restored to the premises, the court would be able to account for such future loss as well as losses sustained during the exclusion. There was no suggestion, moreover, that the defendant would be unable to pay damages. The request for an injunction was thus refused.

In further support of this conclusion (and underlining the discretionary nature of equitable remedies) the judge observed that the plaintiff had delayed almost a month in taking proceedings, allowing the notice period for departure to expire before seeking an injunction. The court also noted, citing *Ó Murchú v Eircell Ltd*, unreported, Supreme Court, Geoghegan J., February 21, 2001, the traditional reluctance of the courts to grant an injunction requiring the court's ongoing supervision to ensure compliance. In this case, given that the parties would have been working in close quarters, it would have been difficult to enforce an injunction, if granted. The parties effectively would have been required to continue working together in circumstances where they were in significant dispute. This would have been impractical to enforce and difficult to supervise given the extent of the dispute *inter partes*.

Whelan Frozen Foods v Dunnes Stores, High Court, MacMenamin J., February 17, 2006; [2006] I.E.H.C. 171   In this case, the plaintiff sought an interlocutory injunction restraining the defendant from unilaterally varying agreed prices for goods supplied to the latter.

The plaintiff in this case, Whelan Foods, ran a wholesale business which bought stock and then sold it on to the defendant. Though the plaintiff had a large operation with 477 employees, for most of its existence its sole customer and source of income had been Dunnes Stores. The plaintiff claimed that the defendant had purported, in breach of two contracts, unilaterally to vary downwards agreed prices for stock—namely frozen and chilled foods and textiles products—which it acquired and stored with a view to supplying the defendant. The defendant proposed to deduct the difference from the account it had set up in respect of the plaintiff's business, and that it would, furthermore, backdate these changes.

Whelan Foods submitted that this could only be done by agreement, which had not been forthcoming on the part of the plaintiff. The plaintiff further claimed that it had suffered losses due to a failure, on the part of the defendant, to source promised volumes from the plaintiff. It alleged, moreover, unlawful withholding of sums due to the plaintiff, as well as undue interference (amounting it claimed, to economic duress) in Whelan's internal business affairs (including attempts to require it to take cost-cutting measures).

The plaintiff asserted that the changes proposed evidenced an intention unilaterally to vary the relevant contracts, a step which constituted an anticipatory repudiatory breach thereof. If implemented, it would amount to a repudiation of the contracts. The defendant on the other hand claimed that there was nothing in the contracts entered into in respect of the goods to require them indefinitely to adhere to the agreed rates, or to prevent periodic review thereof. Both parties nonetheless appeared to accept that a termination of relations, given the heavily dependent nature of the plaintiff's relationship with Dunnes Stores, would require between nine and 12 months' notice.

Pending full resolution of the matters at plenary trial, Whelan Foods sought an interlocutory injunction restraining the imposition of the proposed price changes. While it was accepted that there was a fair issue to be tried, the parties clashed on the matter of the adequacy of damages. The plaintiff claimed that the proposed changes would render its business unviable and thus created a serious risk of insolvency. Though disputed by the defendant, the court accepted that there was a real risk of financial collapse if an injunction was not granted. Any changes, the judge accepted, would, if implemented, impact seriously on its ability to continue trading. Although there was no doubt that the defendant would be able to pay damages, there was at least, the judge concluded, some doubt as to the adequacy of damages if the plaintiff were to have to cease trading. On this count, the judge noted that there was more than a mere assertion but real evidence of a real risk of insolvency.

The judge then turned to consider the balance of convenience which, he ruled, lay in preserving the *status quo ante* pending full trial. The potentially detrimental effects of not granting an injunction outweighed the potential inconvenience that might arise if an interlocutory injunction was granted pending trial. The judge granted the interlocutory injunction pending trial, requiring in effect the preservation of prices at the agreed rates and on agreed credit terms.

INTERPRETATION OF CONTRACTS

MR v TR, High Court, McGovern J., July 18, 2006; [2006] I.E.H.C. 221   This case concerned the status and interpretation of an agreement regarding the use of three frozen embryos created for the purpose of IVF treatment. The parties in this case were an estranged husband and wife (the wife being the plaintiff and the husband, the defendant). Prior to their separation the parties had undergone IVF treatment, for the purpose of which six embryos were created outside the womb using the eggs and sperm of the respective parties. Prior to implantation the husband had signed a consent form agreeing to the implantation of three of the embryos, and accepting that he would be legal father of any child born as a result of the treatment. Three of the embryos were implanted, resulting in the birth of a child. The remaining three embryos were kept in frozen storage, with the intention that they would be used if the first implantation did not succeed. Subsequently, the parties separated.

After the separation, the wife (who wanted to have another baby) sought to have the remaining three (frozen) embryos implanted. She claimed that her husband had consented, either expressly or implicitly, to such a course of action. The husband objected, claiming that he had never agreed to the implantation of the embryos in such circumstances as these, where the parties were now separated and where the first implantation had been successful.

This gave rise to two distinct questions:

- By signing the original consent form, had the husband agreed to the implantation of the remaining embryos for the purpose of allowing his estranged wife to have a second child?

- If not, and having regard to the terms of the Constitution guaranteeing the right to life of the unborn child, could the embryos be implanted notwithstanding the absence of the husband's consent? The plaintiff wife claimed, in particular, that the embryos had a right to life and a right to a family life and, thus, that the destruction of the embryos would be unlawful.

The first stage of proceedings turned on the extent and nature of the husband's consent. The husband's consent acknowledged that he (TR) was the husband of the plaintiff, and would be the legal father of any child born as a result of the treatment. He had also signed a further declaration that the sperm sample used in the treatment was his. Both parties, furthermore, had agreed in writing to the freezing of the embryos and that they both would, in particular, "…take full responsibility on an on-going basis for these cryopreserved embryos". The documents in question did not, however, address a number of contingencies, including what would happen if the parties separated, or what would happen to the second set of embryos if the initial treatment was successful.

On the facts, the court concluded that the husband had consented only to the implantation of the first three embryos. There was, the court concluded, nothing in the husband's consent to indicate express agreement to the subsequent implantation of the three frozen embryos in the uterus of the plaintiff. The court then considered whether such agreement could be implied either from the presumed intent of the parties, or (having regard to the nature of the contract) as a matter of law. On the matter of presumed intent, McGovern J. noted the well-worn maxim that a court could not imply a term simply because the judge considered it to be reasonable to do so. He cited, with approval, the judgment of MacKinnon L.J. in *Shirlaw v Southern Foundries (1926) Ltd* [1939] 2 K.B. 206 at 227 in which the latter noted that:

> "*Prima facie* that which in any contract is left to be implied and need not be expressed is something so obvious that it goes without saying; so that, if while the parties were making their bargain an officious bystander were to suggest some express provision for it in their agreement, they would testily suppress him with a common, 'oh of course'."

On the facts, the court concluded that it was impossible to presume that the parties implicitly intended that it would be "so obvious as to go without saying" that in circumstances where the first implantation had been successful and the parties had separated, the frozen embryos could be implanted. Nor could such a term be implied as a matter of law by reference to the nature of the contract. It was clear in these circumstances that the purpose of freezing the embryos was to ensure that further embryos would be available, if the first treatment was unsuccessful:

> "Looking at all the consent forms signed by the plaintiff and the first defendant and having regard to the evidence I am not satisfied that a term requiring that the frozen embryos should be implanted in the uterus of the plaintiff, derives from the nature of the agreement itself. I accept the submission of the Attorney General that to imply a term, the contractual provisions alleged must be necessary, they must be capable of being formulated with precision and they must be terms both parties would have agreed if suggested at the time of the conclusion of the contract."

Although this latter passage appears to conflate somewhat terms implied in fact and those implied by law, the net points are as follows:

(a) The parties could not be taken implicitly to have agreed that the frozen embryos could be used in circumstances where a child had already resulted from the treatment and the parties had subsequently separated.

(b) There was nothing in the nature of the contracts agreed to suggest that such a conclusion was legally necessitated.

In subsequent proceedings, the court ruled that the embryos did not fall under the protection of Art.40.3.3 of the Constitution as, pending implantation in the womb, they were (the court maintained) not "unborn" (High Court, McGovern J., November 15, 2006).

JURISDICTION

Stryker Corporation t/a Stryker Howmedica v Sulzer Metco AG, High Court, O'Neill J., March 7, 2006; [2006] I.E.H.C. 60   Although a number of questions arise from this case, the decision essentially turns on whether or not the parties had agreed to an exclusive jurisdiction clause which required that any dispute between the parties be heard in the Swiss courts, and under Swiss law. The case is also illustrative of the "battle of the forms" scenario under which different parties in a negotiation make competing offers and counter-offers with a view to having the contract governed by the conditions most favourable to each of the respective parties.

The plaintiff in this case was a company based in Cork specialising in the manufacture of orthopaedic implants made from titanium. The plaintiff secured the defendant, a company based in Switzerland, to design, manufacture and install a machine which the plaintiff would use in its plant in Cork. Less than six months after delivery the machine exploded and caught fire while being cleaned, as a result of which the plaintiff suffered, it said, serious loss and damage. The plaintiff sued for breach of contract and negligence, breach of duty and breach of statutory duty, as well as negligent misrepresentation.

As a preliminary matter, the defendant claimed that the Irish courts had no jurisdiction in the matter, as the contract agreed between the parties reserved the sole and exclusive jurisdiction in cases of dispute to the Swiss courts. During negotiations, the defendant had sent three separate quotations to the plaintiff, all of which stipulated that they were subject to the defendant's general conditions of contract. The defendant had, indeed, enclosed a copy of these conditions with each of the second and third quotations conveyed to the plaintiff. These conditions stipulated, *inter alia*, that "the contract shall be governed by Swiss substantive law" and that "the place of jurisdiction for both the customer and the supplier shall be at the registered office of the supplier" (though it reserved the right of the defendant supplier to sue at the customer's registered address).

The plaintiff, in response to the third quotation, faxed a purchase order to Sulzer, requesting the defendant "to design, supply, commission and validate an automatic inert gas wire coating system" in accordance with the defendant's third quotation. The plaintiff followed up this fax with a letter in identical terms in which it also enclosed the plaintiff's standard conditions (these conditions had *not* been included in the plaintiff's previous fax). The latter-mentioned conditions stipulated that the "seller's acknowledgement of this order or commencement of work pursuant to this order, whichever occurs first, shall be deemed an acceptance of this order",. The plaintiff's conditions went on to reject any alternative terms and conditions proposed by the seller that were different or additional to those in the plaintiff's standard conditions. On receipt by the defendant, the letter, together with the plaintiff's standard conditions, were simply filed and apparently not read.

An initial point arose regarding the appropriate standard of proof in jurisdictional disputes, the defendant asserting that it needed only to establish "a good arguable case" that its jurisdictional clause applied. Rejecting this claim, O'Neill J. ruled that if the clause were to be upheld, the defendant would have to satisfy the court on the balance of probabilities that the clause applied in this case. O'Neill J. pointed out that as a matter of fairness to the plaintiff (who may also have an arguable case) the onus was on the defendant to demonstrate the correctness of any submissions made by it.

The case turned largely on the terms of the Lugano Convention on Jurisdiction and the Enforcement of Judgments in Civil and Commercial Matters, a 1988 treaty incorporated into Irish law by the Jurisdiction of Courts and Enforcement of Judgments Act 1998. Article 2 of the Convention requires generally (and notably "subject to the provisions of this Convention") that persons domiciled in a Contracting State be sued in the courts of their home state. Ordinarily this would suggest that the Swiss courts would have jurisdiction in this instant case.

Article 17 of the Convention allows parties to agree a place of jurisdiction. On the facts, however, the judge concluded that the parties were not *ad idem* regarding the conditions governing the contractual relationship. In coming to this decision, O'Neill J. had regard to the objective intention of the parties as manifested by the documentation exchanged by them. In particular, he concluded that the plaintiff's inclusion of its standard conditions in its letter confirming the order could not be regarded as consistent with the acceptance of the defendant's general conditions. As such, the parties were not, objectively speaking, in agreement on the matter of jurisdiction as no consensus was evident on this point. The defendant's jurisdictional clause, thus, was not binding on the parties.

The judge then turned to the terms of Art.5(1) of the Convention, which allows a person domiciled in a Contracting State to be sued (notwithstanding Art.2) "in matters relating to contract, in the courts for the place of performance of the obligation". Although much of the work carried out by the defendants was completed in Switzerland, O'Neill J. concluded, on the facts, that the entirety of the obligation could only be fulfilled once the machine was assembled and installed in Cork. In other words, although the design and manufacture of the machine took place in Switzerland, the overall obligation arising from the contract was to supply, assemble and install a machine for use in the plaintiff's factory, an obligation that could only be carried out in Cork. This being the case, the court concluded that it had jurisdiction in the matter. Although the plaintiff had initiated a debt collection procedure in Switzerland, the court ruled that this essentially ancillary move did not detract from the plaintiff's overall case that the proceedings should be heard in Ireland.

Nestorway Ltd t/a Electrographic International v Ambaflex BV, High Court, Clarke J., July 19, 2006; [2006] I.E.H.C. 235   In 2001 the parties in this case entered into an exclusive distribution agreement under which the plaintiff secured the right to sell the defendant's product in four specified territories— Ireland, the UK, the USA and Spain—for a period of five years. In January 2006 Ambaflex (the defendant in this case) sought to terminate the agreement, claiming that the plaintiff had failed to discharge certain invoices. The plaintiff claimed that this stance amounted to a breach of contract and sought damages, as well as injunctions restraining the premature termination of the agreement. It also sought to prevent the defendant from selling within the specified territories for the remainder of the agreement. The parties were in dispute regarding the correct date of expiry of the contract.

While the contract was expressly stated as being governed by Dutch law, the plaintiff initiated proceedings in the Irish courts. The defendant disputed this, claiming that the appropriate forum under the contract, or in the alternative under Council Regulation 44/2001 (the "Brussels Regulation"), was a court of the Netherlands.

The first question that arose was whether the parties had agreed to confer jurisdiction on the Dutch courts under the terms of their agreement, Art.23 of the Brussels Regulation permitting the parties to agree a mutual choice of forum. The court concluded that although there had been agreement on the jurisdiction of the Dutch courts in respect of individual warranties and guarantees as well as individual sales involving the parties, this agreement applied only to those individual transactions and not to the exclusive distribution agreement as a whole. Although Clarke J. observed that under Dutch law a different view might be taken, he concluded that the onus lay on Ambaflex to establish that the conclusion under Dutch law would be different, an onus that it had failed to discharge.

Under Art.2 of the Brussels Regulation, the default court of jurisdiction (in the absence of agreement) is the court of the jurisdiction in which the defendant is domiciled. Article 5, however, creates an exception which confers jurisdiction on the courts of the place in which the obligation is to be performed. The obligation for this purpose, Clarke J. concluded, was the obligation which corresponded to the contractual right on which the obligation was based. This being an exclusive distribution agreement, that obligation was twofold—the obligation to supply Nestorway with the goods and not to supply others with goods in respect of the territories covered by the agreement.

Clarke J. noted that under the principles of private international law as they applied in Ireland, the proper law of the contract was Dutch. The onus of proving jurisdiction under Art.5 was, furthermore, on the person who sought to assert such jurisdiction, namely the plaintiff. Clarke J. observed that under Irish law the place of performance of the obligation more than likely included Ireland—one of the places in respect of which the agreement gave the plaintiff an exclusive right to supply. Ireland was, after all, one of the places where the obligations were due to be performed. Crucially, however, Irish law did not apply in this case. It was not possible to tell if Dutch law would take a similar view as no evidence on the possible stance of Dutch law had been adduced before the court. The onus of proving the Irish court's jurisdiction was on the person seeking to establish such jurisdiction, namely the plaintiff. As that onus had not been discharged, the court concluded that the jurisdiction of the Irish courts had not been established. The service of proceedings on Ambaflex was thus lifted for want of jurisdiction.

O'Connor v Masterwood UK Ltd, High Court, DeValera J., June 20, 2006; [2006] I.E.H.C. 217   In this case the High Court enforced a clause in an agreement granting sole jurisdiction in cases of dispute to the courts of Rimini, Italy. The judge observed that the original agreement between the parties was subject to the terms and conditions of sale of Masterwood SPA Rimini, though these terms and conditions were not specified. Nonetheless, the plaintiff subsequently signed an agreement containing a clause stipulating that "…[i]n any controversy … the Court of Rimini shall have sole jurisdiction".

The clause having been set out clearly in the body of the agreement, just above the plaintiff's signature, the court considered (though this did not seem necessary given the fact that the plaintiff had signed) that "[n]o one signing this agreement could fail to observe it;—it could not go 'unnoticed'". The judge observed, moreover, that neither Art.27 nor Art.28 of Council Regulation EC 44/2001 applied, "as only one set of proceedings is in being and in one jurisdiction only".

On the evidence, the judge thus concluded that the plaintiff had agreed to the jurisdiction clause "freely and without any deceit or subterfuge". This being the case, the court had no jurisdiction in the matter.

MISREPRESENTATION

See also *Lombard and Ulster Banking Ltd v Mercedes Benz Finance Ltd and Hughes*, High Court, MacMenamin J., January 11, 2006; [2006] I.E.H.C. 168 (above under CONSIDERATION). On alleged fraudulent misrepresentation, see *Greyridge Developments Ltd v McGuigan t/a McGuigan Construction and Reddy*, High Court, Gilligan J., June 28, 2006; [2006] I.E.H.C. 441 (above under ARBITRATION). On informed consent, see *Taylor Flynn v Sulaiman and Advanced Cosmetic Surgery Ltd*, High Court, O'Neill J., May 23, 2006; [2006] I.E.H.C. 160 (above under BREACH OF CONTRACT).

Hegarty and Hogan v Fusano Properties, High Court, Laffoy J., February 24, 2006; [2006] I.E.H.C. 54   This case concerned a contract entered into between the plaintiffs and the defendant in November 2002, in which the latter agreed to build and sell and the former to buy (off plans) an apartment in Smithfield Market, near Dublin city centre. The price agreed was stated as IR£625,000, though the judge accepted that this was a patent error and was meant to read

€625,000. The dispute centred on two points:

- whether the defendant was entitled to serve a notice of completion on the date it purported to do so;

- whether the concierge service (involving the employment of a caretaker for the premises) promised as a part of the contract was in fact delivered as described.

On May 3, 2005 the defendant issued a purported notice to complete. The plaintiffs claimed that this notice was invalid and of no effect. At that time the necessary building work was not, they claimed, complete.

The plaintiffs further claimed that the defendant had misrepresented "the quality of the appurtenances and services available", effectively arguing that the property and services that were in fact supplied were not worth the consideration agreed in the contract. In particular, they asserted that the concierge service promised as part of the contract differed significantly from the service in fact delivered.

In September or October 2002 the plaintiffs paid a deposit of €5,000 on the flat. At the time, they had been supplied with a brochure making a number of claims in respect of the property. In particular, the brochure stated that the property would be served by a concierge and that each apartment would have a video entry facility to allow residents to monitor visitors. The plaintiffs claimed that it was understood that the exterior entrance to the block in which their apartment was located would be served by a dedicated concierge. In other words, they claimed that the brochure had represented that their apartment could be accessed through the "conciergerie" (where the concierge service would be located). In fact, although the property as a whole contained three conciergeries, the plaintiffs' apartment could not be accessed through any of these. The relevant concierge service serving the plaintiffs was located elsewhere on the property, and could only be accessed by leaving their apartment block and walking outside. The plaintiffs thus sought a reduction in the agreed price to reflect the misrepresentation alleged.

The parties disagreed as regards whether the property had been completed at the time notice to complete was served. While the defendant claimed that the property was fit for habitation at the relevant time, the plaintiffs argued that the access approaches to the site remained a "hard hat site" and that construction was still ongoing at the time in question. They further alleged that the interior of the residence was not completed. The judge concluded that it was not possible to determine the point without further evidence. She noted that although the notice to complete purported to be based on conditions 40 and 41 of the Law Society of Ireland's General Conditions of Sale (2001), neither party had submitted any evidence as to the content of these conditions. As such, "it is not possible to express any view on whether the notice to complete was properly served in accordance with the conditions invoked by the defendant".

Furthermore, the parties had chosen to submit evidence as to the facts by means of affidavits which differed substantially as to whether the property was suitable for habitation or had been completed. In the absence of oral evidence and cross-examination, it was impossible to tell who was correct. Thus "it is not possible to find that the plaintiffs have established that the notice to complete was ineffective." While "that does not mean that it was effective", the judge effectively declined to rule on the point until further evidence was adduced.

In relation to the concierge service, the judge ruled in favour of the defendant builder. The representations made to the plaintiffs, she concluded, could not be interpreted as having promised the purchasers that they would be able to access their apartment through the conciergerie. The defendant had promised that the whole development would have a concierge, a promise that was in fact fulfilled as the development as a whole had no less than three concierges. The brochure was not, on the facts, open to the interpretation claimed by the plaintiffs that there would be a concierge at the entrance to each block.

Interestingly, neither party sought to rely on an exclusion clause, common to property sales brochures, stating that:

> "These particulars and accompanying price list are issued strictly on the understanding that they do not form part of any contract. Measurements are approximate and maps are not drawn to scale. The builder reserves the right to make any alterations to the design and specifications in the interest of the overall quality of the development."

In commenting on the failure to invoke this clause, Laffoy J. appeared to cast some doubt (albeit *obiter*) on the efficacy of such clauses:

> "Neither side brought that provision to the court's attention, understandably, perhaps, because it is an example of 'small print' in the physical sense."

She noted, however, that as the clause had not been invoked she would place no reliance on it.

OFFER AND ACCEPTANCE

On the "battle of the forms" see *Stryker Corporation t/a Stryker Howmedica v Sulzer Metco AG*, High Court, O'Neill J., March 7, 2006; [2006] I.E.H.C. 60 (above under JURISDICTION).

Smart Telecom plc v Radio Teilifís Éireann, High Court, Kelly J., May 26, 2006 This case concerns the status of referential bids in a tendering process. A referential bid is a response to an invitation to tender proposing that the bidder will pay a stipulated amount (or percentage) more than the next highest fixed sum bid received.

The first defendant in this case, RTÉ, indicated that it was seeking a sponsor for its broadcasted weather forecasts, available for €1.25 million per year for a minimum of two years. Four parties expressed an interest, including the plaintiff. In order to determine which party would get the contract, RTÉ held a competition inviting tenders from the four parties which had initially expressed an interest. The highest bidder, RTÉ indicated, would win the sponsorship contract.

The terms of the invitation to tender requested that each party submit its "best offer in the form of a sealed bid" clearly stating "what price you will commit to for this contract—per annum and in total for the two year period under negotiation". The offer was to be stated as a gross figure, including agency commission.

In response, Smart Telecom purported to make two distinct bids, one through a subsidiary, Smart Telecom Holdings Ltd, (which subsidiary had not in fact been one of the original four companies expressing an interest) and a second via the parent company's Chief Executive. The Holdings' bid expressed "our agreement to bid the sum of €1,5100,000 [sic] on behalf of our company". Smart subsequently clarified that this bid was in fact for €1.51 million per year over the two years of the contract.

The Chief Executive, on behalf of Smart Telecom itself, subsequently sent an e-mail stating "our agreement to bid a sum equal to 5% above the highest priced bid received by you by [sic] any other business for the minimum two year deal".

RTÉ ultimately awarded the contract to Glanbia Consumer Foods, the latter having bid €1.595 million per annum. On the basis that it had offered to pay 5 per cent over the highest bid received, Smart contested this award and brought proceedings seeking specific performance of what it alleged was a contract with RTÉ, or damages in lieu of specific performance. Additionally, Smart sought an injunction restraining RTÉ from awarding the sponsorship deal to Glanbia.

Generally, an invitation seeking tenders does not constitute an offer. The invitation is usually interpreted as an invitation to prospective customers to make the invitor an offer, which the latter may accept or reject at its discretion. Where, however, the terms of the invitation indicate that the highest bid will be accepted, different principles apply. In such a case, the invitation to tender in fact is deemed an offer to contract with whoever turns out to be the highest bidder, which is, in turn, accepted by the highest bidder.

The net question in this case was whether Smart's offer to pay 5 per cent over the next highest bid was a valid response to RTÉ's offer, and thus constituted the highest bid. In this regard, the court ultimately ruled against Smart, concluding that its bid was not a valid response to RTÉ's offer. The Smart bid—generally termed a "referential bid", in that the precise amount offered can only be determined by reference to the highest bid expressed as a fixed sum—did not, the court determined, meet the terms of the offer. Each interested party was asked to submit their best offer, clearly outlining the price it would pay per annum and for the two-year period. The RTÉ offer stated that the price was to be expressed as a *gross figure* including agency commission. This suggested, the judge concluded, that the RTÉ offer sought "actual figures" and thus excluded the making of a referential bid.

In coming to this conclusion, the judge relied on the House of Lords' decision in *Harvela Ltd v Royal Trust Company* [1986] A.C. 207. In particular, Kelly J. concluded that "where referential bids are sought there ought to be an express provision in the invitation permitting such bids to be made". In other words, a referential bid will only be valid where it is *expressly* permitted by the terms of the request for tenders.

PRACTICE AND PROCEDURE

On the criteria for summary judgments, see also *McGrath v O'Driscoll*, High Court, Clarke J., June 14, 2006; [2006] I.E.H.C. 195 and *ADM Londis plc v Arman Retail Ltd, Arman and Arman*, High Court, Clarke J., July 12, 2006; [2006] I.E.H.C. 309 (both discussed above under GUARANTEE/SURETY AGREEMENTS) and *Powderly v McDonagh and McDonagh*, High Court, Kelly J., January 31, 2006; [2006] I.E.H.C. 20 (below under SET-OFF, RIGHT OF).

On time limits, and the extension thereof, see *Veolia Water UK plc v Fingal County Council*, High Court, Clarke J., May 2, 2006; [2006] I.E.H.C. 157 (below, under PUBLIC PROCUREMENT).

Smart Mobile Ltd v Commission for Communication Regulation, High Court, Kelly J., March 13, 2006; [2006] I.E.H.C. 82 The decision in this case essentially concerned a procedural matter: whether a case alleging the breach of a contract by a statutory body should be progressed by means of a plenary summons or whether judicial review was more appropriate. The plaintiff in this case, alleging a breach of contract by the defendant, a statutory body, sought relief in the Commercial Court by means of a plenary summons. In preliminary argument the defendant contended that, on account of the fact that it was a public body performing a public function, the appropriate avenue for relief was by means of judicial review. The defendant alleged, in particular, that the use of a plenary summons was unreasonable and constituted an abuse of process.

The Commission for Communication Regulation (also known as "ComReg"), was established under the Communications Regulation Act 2002 as the statutory body responsible for the regulation of communications via electronic transmission networks (including communication by telephone, television, radio and wireless communication, mobile telephone and satellite) and of the postal sector. One of its objectives is to facilitate competition through the authorisation of access to networks and the regulation of such access, with a view ultimately to enhancing consumer choice.

In mid-2005 ComReg invited tenders for new 3G mobile telecommunications licences. The tender document specifically requested applicants to furnish, as part of the tender, a performance bond to support performance targets made in applications for the licence. Three companies—Eircom, Meteor and Smart Telecom—tendered for the licences. In its application, Smart gave a voluntary binding commitment to supply a performance bond of €100 million in support of performance targets to which it had committed itself in its tender application.

Following evaluation of the bids, Smart was informed that its bid had scored highest on the criteria for consideration and, as such, that a licence would be issued subject to the fulfilment of certain requirements. One of those conditions was that the plaintiff would produce the €100 million performance bond that it had promised to supply by December 16, 2005. A second condition stipulated that Smart would furnish, initially by December 1, 2005, a guarantee to the tune of €7.6 million to cover "spectrum access fees" for the first five years of the licence. By agreement, the latter deadline was extended to December 15.

Nonetheless, Smart sought, on December 15, a further extension to both deadlines. In response, ComReg wrote to Smart indicating that the bond and guarantee should be delivered by January 30, 2006 at the latest. In their letter, ComReg noted that no further extensions would, it said, be granted and that if Smart did not meet the January deadline, it would not get the licence. Throughout the following month, the defendant on several occasions stressed that, in relation to the deadline, time was of the essence.

On January 27, 2006 the plaintiff delivered draft performance bonds to the defendant. The defendant asserted, however, that these bonds did not meet the defendant's stipulated requirements and were thus, in its view, not acceptable. As such, it refused to grant the licence, alleging that the conditions for issuance thereof had not been met.

The plaintiff sought, by means of plenary summons, a declaration to the effect that the parties had a concluded contract for the award of the licence to Smart. The plaintiff contended, in particular, that the documents it had proffered met the conditions laid out by the defendant. In the alternative, Smart sought declarations (in para.2 of its claim) that the defendant was obliged to afford the plaintiff a reasonable period of time to comply with the conditions and that the January 30, 2006 deadline was unreasonable. It further sought declarations to the effect that the conditions set out by ComReg were unreasonable, or that the defendant should not regard the negotiations as ended until such time as Smart was given a reasonable period to satisfy those conditions.

The defendant argued, on a procedural point, that the declarations sought in para.2 of the claim raised points of public law more suited to judicial review.

The plaintiff was effectively alleging, in seeking these declarations, breaches of the defendant's statutory duties, in particular the duty to set reasonable deadlines for compliance. This second leg of the proceedings, ComReg argued, should in fact have been initiated by means of judicial review seeking an order of certiorari quashing ComReg's decision. Smart had, the defendant argued, abused the process of the court by using a private law summons to obtain a public law remedy.

The judge rejected this contention. First, he noted that, unlike certain other statutory agencies, there was no legislative requirement on those challenging the decisions of ComReg to proceed by way of judicial review and by no other means. For instance, under statute, decisions of An Bord Pleanála may only be challenged by judicial review. No such statutory restriction applied in the case of ComReg decisions. Kelly J. could find, moreover, no Irish case in which a litigant was found to have abused the court processes by making a plenary summons in lieu of seeking judicial review. Relying on *Landers v Garda Síochána Complaints Board* [1997] 3 I.R. 347 and *O'Donnell v Dún Laoghaire Corporation* [1991] I.L.R.M. 301, Kelly J. further considered the effect of Ord.84 of the Rules of the Superior Courts in cases where litigants were not confined by statute to challenging decisions solely by judicial review. Did Ord.84 mandate judicial review as the exclusive remedy for aggrieved persons seeking to sue in such circumstances? The judge concluded that it did not. Kelly J. cited with approval the judgment of Costello J. in *O'Donnell* to the effect that the courts were not at liberty to apply policy considerations to restrict the avenues for those seeking relief against a body with statutory powers.

The defendant had further argued that, by issuing a plenary summons, the plaintiff had circumvented certain procedural safeguards available on judicial review. In particular, the defendant asserted that the conditions precedent to the initiation of judicial review were more onerous than in the case of a trial founded on a plenary summons (leave for judicial review, for instance, requires sworn testimony before a judge). Kelly J. noted, however, that an interim injunction had previously been granted in this case, the standard of proof for obtaining such an injunction being higher than in the case of judicial review. Additionally, the defendant had conceded that the plaintiff, if it had sought leave for judicial review, would in fact have met the threshold for being granted such leave.

The judge further rejected the contention that, as judicial review normally proceeds by way of affidavit, the defendant would have been prejudiced by the plenary trial. Kelly J. noted that there was nothing to stop the Commercial Court from requiring a trial on affidavit in respect of the public law elements of the case. Nor would the defendant be prejudiced by the fact that more restrictive rules of discovery apply to judicial review proceedings. In practice, the court noted, the management of Commercial Court cases was such that discovery could and would quite precisely be confined and that "insofar as public law issues are concerned, the discovery pertinent to them will only be that which would be available in Judicial Review proceedings". In so far as public law issues arose in the case, they would be dealt with in accordance with public law principles.

Nor did the court believe that there would be any prejudice to third parties, namely the two unsuccessful licence applicants, in plenary proceedings. While the judge accepted that in judicial review he would have a jurisdiction to join notice parties, he proposed that if there was any likelihood of prejudice in this case, third parties would have an opportunity to state their case.

Finally, the judge noted that a private law issue also arose, which could not have been considered by means of judicial review. The judge felt that it would be inappropriate to "bifurcate" proceedings, progressing half of the case in judicial review and the other in a plenary trial. Nothing would be gained by requiring that the proceedings be dropped and recommenced by means of judicial review. In fact, such a step would likely result in unnecessary costs and delay.

PRIVITY OF CONTRACT

See also *Ochre Ridge v Cork Bonded Warehouses*, **High Court, Smyth J., February 28, 2006** (above under CONDITIONS PRECEDENT).

Law Reform Commission, *Consultation Paper on Privity of Contract and Third Party Rights* **LRC CP–40–2006**   The doctrine of privity of contract generally precludes a person from suing or being sued under a contract to which that person was not a party. Although there are certain exceptions to the doctrine, the concept of privity has been known to result in considerable injustice in cases where contracts entered into for the benefit of a third party are not honoured. In such cases, the third party typically cannot seek enforcement, while the promisee may be restricted in seeking damages if she has not personally suffered a loss.

The Law Reform Commission has invited public comment on a proposal to allow third parties to enforce rights under contracts made for their benefit. In its paper the Commission outlines the current law in Ireland, noting the exceptions to the general principle that only the parties to a contract may rely on its terms. It notes some of the difficulties that the rule has produced, particularly in complex transactions where there are multiple parties. It gives examples of dealings in the construction trade, in shipping and in insurance contracts, as well as in the consumer law context where intricate chains of supply may considerably distance the consumer from the contractual reach of the original supplier. Given the increasing complexity of modern transactions, where a myriad of contracts and contractors come into play, the privity rule potentially poses a serious barrier to obtaining relief.

The Commission sets out a number of options for reform. These include the possibility of judicial development of existing exceptions, reform of remedies for promisees (which, currently are limited in cases where the promisee herself has not borne any loss) and statutory reform. On the last point, the Commission separately discusses three options:

- a general legislative provision allowing third parties to rely on contracts entered into for their benefit;
- more detailed legislation providing for third party remedies; and
- piecemeal additions to the currently existing exceptions.

Provisionally, the Commission recommends that the doctrine of privity of contract requires reform to permit third parties to enforce contracts made for their benefit. While not ruling out the possibility of judicial development of the exceptions, the Commission provisionally opts for legislative reform. In this regard, the Commission considers whether to recommend a general provision giving a broad right to third parties to sue, or, in the alternative, to seek more detailed legislation. Although, again, its recommendation is stated to be subject to public consultation, the Commission favours the option of comprehensive detailed legislation. While it does not recommend the option of extending currently available exceptions in a piecemeal fashion, it suggests that existing exceptions should be safeguarded and preserved. The paper invites submissions on the appropriateness or otherwise of the codification of such existing remedies. It also provisionally opts against extending promisees' right to sue, favouring granting remedial rights to the third parties instead.

On the type of legislation needed in this context, the Commission opts for detailed provision over a general catch-all clause. In particular, the Commission appears to caution against the approach adopted in England and Wales, in the Contracts (Rights of Third Parties) Act 1999, creating a broad general clause entitling third parties to rely on contracts expressed to be for their benefit. A more detailed scheme is, they conclude, required:

> "2.44… while a general clause might be easier to enact initially, it does not properly address the complex issues that arise in relation to privity. For this reason, it is not likely that the tools of the common law can match the precision that legislation can provide."

In particular, the Commission observes:

> "2.45… while a general clause removing the bar to third party enforcement has the advantage of simplicity, it does not adequately deal with the difficulties that arise in practice. If anything, legislation such as the England and Wales *Contracts (Rights of Third Parties) Act 1999* has been criticised for not being detailed enough."

Given the complexity of the issues, a general enabling clause would not be sufficient.

In its recommendations, the Commission proposes a test for the determination of eligible third parties. It first suggests that entitlement to claim as a third party should be predicated on the identification of the party by name or description in the relevant contract, though the party need not be in existence at the time of contracting. Members of a class of persons should also be entitled to benefit, if that class of persons is sufficiently identified. For a third party to make a successful claim, the Commission suggests that the following conditions be observed:

"1. The parties intend that the third party is to receive the benefit of the contract or a term of the contract; and

2. The parties intend that the term benefiting the third party should be enforceable by the third party in their own name."

It would be open to the contracting parties to rebut any presumption in favour of the third parties.

The Commission further suggests that either reliance or acceptance or both should mark the "crystallization" of third party rights. Thus, where a third party relies on, or alternatively accepts, a benefit set out in a contract to which she is not a party, the contracting parties should be precluded from contractual variation absent the consent of the third party. Although the rights of the promisee should be preserved even in the face of a claim by a third party, the Commission recommends that measures be introduced to prevent double recovery. In particular, where a promisor fulfils his contractual duty to the third party, in whole or in part, the Commission suggests that the person making the promise should proportionately be relieved of any obligation to the promisee.

PUBLIC PROCUREMENT

Advanced Totes Limited v Bord na gCon, Supreme Court, McGuinness J.; Hardiman, McCracken, Kearns and Macken JJ. concurring, March 23, 2006; [2006] I.E.S.C. 17 This case turned on the requirements set out in EU law for the proper conduct by public bodies of tendering processes for public contracts. The applicant in this case sought to challenge the award of a contract by the respondent, alleging that the tender process failed in certain respects to comply with EU requirements.

The respondent Board, a statutory body responsible, *inter alia*, for the running of several greyhound racecourses, sought tenders for the supply of totalisator ("tote") services for some of those stadiums. The applicant, a company providing hardware, software and consultancy for the purpose of operating totalisator services, tendered, along with three other companies, for the contract but was ultimately unsuccessful.

For the purpose of considering bids, an Award Committee was established. On the merits, the Award Committee initially favoured the bid from a company called Amtote, though a concern was raised that the latter's asking price was too high. The Committee obtained advice to the effect that it would not have been possible to negotiate on price with one party alone. Thus, the Committee decided to seek re-tenders. (The High Court ruled, and the Supreme Court accepted, that the respondent was entitled to do so.) On foot of the re-tender, a company called Autotote was deemed to have won the contract.

It was accepted that Autotote's bid was successful primarily because it had offered, as part of its bid, to operate the IT infrastructure necessary to run the totalisator services from an "external hub". This approach had the benefit of relieving the respondent, Bord na gCon, of any responsibility to manage the system internally. Advanced Totes, on the other hand, had not proposed any external hosting service, thus casting the burden of management (Bord na gCon argued) on the respondent.

The applicant objected to this decision, seeking an order of certiorari and a declaration that the contract entered into with Autotote was void. It claimed in particular that, in applying the criterion regarding the presence or otherwise of an external hub, the respondent had failed to comply with EU law regarding the conduct of processes of public procurement.

Overturning the High Court on this matter, the Supreme Court ruled that the process adopted did indeed fail to comply with EU law. Speaking for a unanimous court, McGuinness J. noted that the terms of Council Directive 92/50/EEC relating to the co-ordination of procedures for the award of public service contracts ("the Services Directive") require compliance with certain criteria in the awarding of such contracts. In particular, Art.36 of the Directive (as well as the Irish regulations on which it is based) stipulates that the criteria for awarding the contract must be mentioned in the document setting out the terms of the request for tender in such a manner as to indicate the relative importance of each criterion. There was, moreover, a clear requirement that the criteria be set out and ranked in such a way as to ensure that "normally diligent tenderers" would be able clearly and unambiguously to interpret the criteria and their relative importance.

In particular the court cited, with approval, the comments of the European Court of Justice in *SIAC Construction Ltd v Mayo County Council* [2002] 2 I.L.R.M. 401 to the effect that a procurement process would only be upheld:

> "…on condition that the transparency and objectivity of the procedure are respected, which presupposes that *the criterion is mentioned in the contract document or contract notice*, that it is there *formulated in such a way as to allow all reasonably well informed and normally diligent tenderers to interpret it in the same way*, and that the adjudicating

> authority must keep to that interpretation throughout the procedure and
> apply the criterion in question objectively and uniformly to all tenders
> (emphasis added)."

While the High Court judge had concluded that it was unclear whether all of the strict requirements of EU law had been met, he did not believe that there had been any breach of the principles of equal treatment or transparency set out in EU law. As such, he refused to set aside the award.

Although the Supreme Court refused to overrule the High Court judge on certain findings of fact, it nonetheless concluded that on the central issue as to whether EU law had been breached, the award should indeed be quashed. It was clear, McGuinness J. argued, that the offer of external or internal hosting was central to the decision made by the Award Committee. Nonetheless, this very significant criterion was not formulated in the request for tender documents in such a way as to indicate clearly that the matter of internal or external management of the system would be a criterion, still less that it would be so crucial a criterion. Furthermore, the documents failed to suggest any ranking of the relevant criteria, such that the issue of hub location had not been signalled as so significant a concern. Thus, the request for tender documents clearly lacked the transparency and objectivity sufficient to meet the standards set out in the Services Directive. On this basis, the decision of the High Court was reversed, and the appeal allowed, thus quashing the award of Bord na gCon.

The court did, however, refuse to overrule the judge on certain findings of fact, namely that the members of the Award Committee had not improperly communicated with the applicant regarding matters of pricing, nor had the committee made any decision in favour of the applicant. The Supreme Court further accepted that the decision of the award committee was in the nature of a recommendation to Bord na gCon that was not binding (in other words the final decision was to be made by An Bord itself). Citing *Hay v O'Grady* [1992] 1 I.R. 210, the Supreme Court concluded that there was amply sufficient evidence on which to justify the decisions made on facts. Nonetheless, in so far as the judge's conclusion on the application of EU law was concerned, he had erred in law, and the decision was thus reversed.

Veolia Water UK plc v Fingal County Council, High Court, Clarke J., May 2, 2006; [2006] I.E.H.C. 157   This case turned on a procedural point regarding time limits for a challenge to the decision of a local authority awarding a public contract. EU law requires Member States to charge businesses and other non-domestic users for the use of water and water waste facilities, based on actual usage. On behalf of the four Dublin local authorities, Fingal County Council sought tenders for the supply of water-metering systems for non-domestic users in order to give effect to these requirements.

The particular tendering process was complex and requires some explanation. It distinguished, first, between proposals for a "drive-by" monitoring system and a "fully fixed" system. The "drive-by" system, which was cheaper to install, but may have been more expensive to run, presupposed that a vehicle could monitor usage simply by "driving by" the location of the user. On the other hand, the fully fixed system, while more expensive to install, would have facilitated more frequent monitoring of usage.

The candidates were invited to submit tenders based on what they considered to be the optimal mix of the two different monitoring methods. However, the tender documents also stipulated that each party should submit a further tender detailing the price for upgrade to a wholly "fully-fixed" system. To further complicate the matter, tenderers were permitted to submit, alongside tenders that complied with the requirements of the tender process, alternative tenders that were not compliant therewith.

Two competitors, including Veolia, submitted bids, with each supplying a compliant bid and a number of non-compliant bids each. In September 2005, Veolia was informed that its bids were unsuccessful. In January 2006, Veolia instituted judicial review proceedings challenging this decision on the basis that:

- the Council had failed to have regard to the price in each bid of the upgrade to a fully fixed system. While it had assessed the bids containing an upgrade, consideration of these "upgrade" bids did not contribute in any way to the Council's final decision.

- the successful tender did not comply with the tendering requirements as it contained no provision for the upgrade to a fully-fixed system or a quoted price for such an upgrade.

- the successful tender was not in fact upgradeable to a fully-fixed system.

Fingal objected to the review on the basis that Veolia was out of time for raising this challenge. Order 84A, r.4 of the Rules of the Superior Courts stipulates that a judicial review of a decision to award a public contract had to be initiated at the earliest opportunity. At the furthest extreme, a challenge should be mounted within three months of the date on which the grounds first arose. The rule provides, nonetheless, for an extension of time if the court believes there is good reason for so doing.

An initial question arose as to when time begins to run under the relevant rule. Veolia argued that time only began to run when the applicant became aware of facts giving it grounds for challenge. Refuting this claim, Clarke J. concluded that on the ordinary meaning of the words of the rule, time begins to run from the date on which the event occurs, regardless of the knowledge of the parties. (The state of knowledge of the parties would, however, be relevant in considering whether it was appropriate to *extend* the time for mounting such a challenge). The relevant date in determining when time begins to run under this rule was the date on which:

"...any formal adverse consequence has crystallised to the extent that a formal step in the process [had been] taken adverse to the interests of the applicant concerned."

In this case, he ruled, time began to run from at least the date on which the decision to award the contract to its competitor was notified to Veolia. In support of his conclusion he cited dicta from Fennelly J. in *Dekra Éireann v Minister for the Environment and Local Government* [2003] 2 I.R. 270, justifying the strict approach to time limits in challenging public procurement decisions on the basis that "[t]hey relate to decisions in the commercial field, where there should be little excuse for delay". There was, moreover, nothing in EU law to displace this conclusion. Provided that the application of EU law on public procurement is not rendered ineffective thereby, and that the rules do not discriminate between procedures invoking domestic and EU law respectively, EU law leaves it to the Member States to set the applicable procedural requirements.

This strict approach was offset, however, and justified by the discretion of the court to extend time for consideration of the challenge. On this point, Clarke J. observed that in determining whether to extend time, the knowledge and actions of the parties were relevant. Having considered the facts, Clarke J. concluded that an extension of time would be permitted in relation to some but not all of the grounds.

- From at least October 2005, Veolia had been aware that the provisional bids setting out a price for upgrade had not been properly considered by the Council, or at least had not been considered relevant by the Council in making its decision. Given this state of knowledge, and the failure to act promptly, it was not, the judge concluded, appropriate to extend time in relation to this ground.

- Different considerations applied, however, to the second ground, that the successful tender did not contain a price for the upgrade. Despite repeated enquiries, Veolia had not become aware of this fact until December 19, 2005. On this basis, Veolia would be allowed an extension of time to pursue this matter.

- On the matter regarding the upgradeability of the successful bid, the judge did not reach a firm conclusion, but allowed the parties leave to make further argument. If there were arguable grounds for so doing, he indicated that he would be willing to extend the time.

REPUDIATION

O'Dwyer and Jones-O'Dwyer v Boyd and Dillon, High Court, Finnegan P., May 17, 2006; [2006] I.E.H.C. 157   In 1998, by means of a written agreement, the plaintiffs agreed to buy, and the first defendant to sell, a 27-acre property (including a house) in Mallow, Co. Cork, the purchase price being IR£300,500. In error, the agreement included in the lands conveyed a large slurry tank and a small portion of ground associated therewith. The plaintiffs subsequently sought specific performance of this agreement subject to an abatement of the purchase price in respect of the error and some other matters. Pending the conclusion of arbitration, the proceedings were stayed.

As a result of the arbitration, a total award of €53,010 was made in respect of the aforementioned error as well as certain other defects in the property. No award was made in respect of other defects while claims for stress and loss of rent were held not to be within the scope of the arbitrator's jurisdiction. While the arbitrator's fees plus VAT were to be divided equally between the parties, no other costs were awarded.

On resumption of the case before the High Court, the plaintiffs raised a number of complaints against the second defendant, who had acted as solicitor for the defendant. In particular, the solicitor had acted under a power of attorney issued by the first defendant. The court, however, refused to entertain the plaintiffs' attempt to make the solicitor personally liable for the defaults of the vendor. Finnegan P. ruled that, as with any contract entered into by an agent, the actions of the agent bound the principal, the agent not being liable on the agreement. The court further refuted the proposition that the solicitor had defamed the plaintiffs. Following a robbery, the plaintiffs had removed a number of marble fireplaces from the Mallow property, claiming they were doing so in order to protect the property. The second defendant (the first defendant's solicitor) reported this removal to the Gardaí. The court concluded that, given that the fireplaces remained the property of the vendor until completion of the sale, the report was factually correct and thus not defamatory. The fact that the plaintiffs had a contract for purchase of the property, and thus an interest in equity:

> "...does not carry with it a right to possession of the premises or fixtures nor does it carry a right to a lien. While the Plaintiffs may have been well motivated in securing the [fireplaces] once demand for the return was made and refused the Plaintiffs were in wrongful possession of the same."

On August 11, 2004 the proceedings between the plaintiff and first defendant were compromised, with a settlement being concluded. Subsequently, however, a disagreement arose regarding costs. The defendant claimed that, under the settlement, such orders for costs as existed would be honoured and all other costs would be borne by each side "back to back". The plaintiffs disputed any such agreement, asserting that the August 11 settlement did not include any resolution on costs—it covered only the balance of the purchase price and the wording of the deed of conveyance.

The plaintiff subsequently made a proposal that the parties would simply allow these costs awarded against each other to balance each other out. On the evidence, the judge concluded that this proposal had not been accepted. He ruled furthermore that the August 11 settlement required the parties to honour existing orders for costs, and had prevented the parties, moreover, from seeking further orders as to costs.

Despite this, the plaintiffs subsequently applied for and received an order in their favour in respect of reserved costs. This, the first defendant claimed, constituted a repudiation of the August 11 settlement, thus negating the agreement for sale of the premises.

In considering whether there had been a breach sufficient to discharge the defendant from performance, Finnegan P. noted that if a party refuses to perform a contract

> "giving therefor a wrong or inadequate reason or no reason at all he may yet justify his refusal if there are at the time facts in existence which would have provided a good reason even if he did not know of them at the time of his refusal."

Despite the fact that the terms of the settlement had been disputed, the defendant had nonetheless written to the plaintiffs in October 2004 to indicate his willingness to complete. In December 2004, however, the defendant wrote to the plaintiffs asking whether they intended to rely on the new order for reserved costs and thus "resile" from the August 11 settlement. The defendant disputed the entitlement to reserved costs and noted that if the plaintiffs persisted in demanding payment thereof "we shall regard that persistence and demand as a repudiation of the 11th August agreement." The plaintiff's response, while maintaining the right to pursue reserved costs, offered to consider any proposal the defendant might have as to the costs.

On January 11, 2005 the first defendant offered to close the sale if the plaintiffs withdrew their demand for reserved costs, but the plaintiffs insisted on same. The court concluded that there had nonetheless been no repudiation of the August 11 agreement. While the plaintiffs had taxed the costs in question, they had not demanded payment thereof up to the date of the hearing before Finnegan P. They were unlikely, moreover, to do so in the future given that the judge had ruled that they were not entitled to seek such costs:

> "I am satisfied that in not making a demand on foot of the Certificate of Taxation and in not seeking to execute on foot of the same the Plaintiffs prevented their stance in relation to these costs from amounting to a repudiation of the [August 11] settlement."

As such, the court concluded that the parties were obliged to complete the purchase in line with the August 11 settlement. In particular, he ruled that the parties were bound by that agreement in relation to costs.

A further issue arose out of the aftermath of a robbery on the premises in which some damage had been caused to fixtures and fittings, including three fireplaces. The judge concluded that as a result of the August 11 settlement, the parties would complete the sale in accordance with the Agreement for Sale, the provisions of which cast the risk pending completion of the sale on the defendant/vendor. The plaintiffs having claimed compensation, the judge assessed that they were owed €39,355 in respect of the damaged fixtures.

The plaintiffs made further claims regarding the alleged deterioration of the premises since the arbitration award. The judge concluded that the condition of the premises remained largely unchanged since the arbitration, though he did award some compensation in respect of fallen ridge tiles. He refused furthermore to compensate the plaintiffs for costs arising from their involvement in investigating and engaging with the Gardaí regarding the break-in, the judge noting that (as they did not bear the risk in respect of the theft) they had no reason to involve themselves in such matters.

The judge also refuted the plaintiffs' claim for damages arising from the delay in completion. While accepting that a purchaser may recover damages where there has been delay on the part of the vendor (*Raineri v Miles* [1979] 3 All E.R. 763), the plaintiffs' actions in insisting on a conveyance of the lands on which the slurry tank was located (for which they had already received compensation) and costs to which they were not entitled had contributed to the delay such that they were equally at fault.

The plaintiffs also claimed €171,412 as damages for loss of rent from the date on which completion was due. The judge noted, however, that this claim for special damages had not been raised in their Statement of Claim. The original completion date, moreover, had been superseded by the August 11 settlement which presupposed foregoing any entitlement in respect of matters preceding that date. The damage was, moreover, too remote, given that the defendant had not been on notice of the plaintiffs' intention to rent the premises.

The original Agreement for Sale had allowed the purchaser to let a cottage on the premises from the date of execution to the completion of the sale at IR£50 rent a month. Following the robbery, the defendant had removed the ornamental gates to this property for safekeeping and replaced them with locked farm gates preventing the plaintiffs from driving to the cottage. While the judge noted that they could still gain access by foot, he concluded that they were entitled to damages under s.41 of the Landlord and Tenant Law (Amendment) Act (Ireland) 1860 in the amount of €500 for lack of vehicular access. The total award in the plaintiff's favour thus came to €41,670.

The judge expressed the hope that the sale would be completed as quickly as possible.

SET-OFF, RIGHT OF

See also *McGrath v O'Driscoll*, High Court, Clarke J., June 14, 2006; [2006] I.E.H.C. 195 and *ADM Londis plc v Arman Retail Ltd, Arman and Arman*, High Court, Clarke J., July 12, 2006; [2006] I.E.H.C. 309 (both discussed above under GUARANTEE/SURETY AGREEMENTS).

Powderly v McDonagh and McDonagh, High Court, Kelly J., January 31, 2006; [2006] I.E.H.C. 20   In 2001 the defendants secured the services of the plaintiff as main contractor in the renovation of Corbalton House, a 200-year-old period house belonging to the defendants. Although it was initially envisaged that a formal contract would be agreed in respect of the work, no written contract was ever made. In May 2004 the defendants dismissed Mr Powderly, alleging that the renovation work in question fell below acceptable standards.

The plaintiff claimed that, at the time of dismissal, sums of approximately €2.8 million were owing to him in respect of the work carried out on Corbalton House. The defendants disputed this, alleging that Mr Powderly had in fact been overpaid. They counterclaimed for the return of monies that they stated were owing to them, alleging that the work of the contractor was substantially defective and that he had overcharged for work done. They claimed, in particular, that the cost of remedying the defects allegedly attributable to the plaintiff builder was in the region of €1.5 million. An application by the defendants for the submission of the dispute to arbitration was rejected on the grounds that the parties had not in fact agreed to arbitrate their differences.

The plaintiff subsequently sought summary judgment on two points, on the basis that the defendants had not demonstrated that their defence revealed a triable issue. The plaintiff asserted that he was owed monies in respect of his work and that these monies should be paid outright, without the need to proceed to plenary trial. The test to be employed to determine whether summary judgment should be issued or whether leave to defend should be granted was, Kelly J. concluded, that set out by the Supreme Court in *Aer Rianta v Ryanair Ltd* [2002] 1 I.L.R.M. 381:

> "...whether, looking at the whole situation, the defendant has satisfied the court that there is a fair and reasonable probability that he has a real and *bona fide* defence".

The first point on which the plaintiff sought summary judgment related to monies allegedly owed on foot of an architect's certificate issued on May 10, 2004. An architect's certificate may be issued, pending the completion of the contract, to confirm that certain aspects of the work have been completed and that the contractor should be paid therefor. The purpose of doing so is to ensure that contractors have a regular cashflow to enable them to complete the work while the contract is ongoing. The plaintiff claimed that the architect's certificate had approved the payment of €645,886 to the plaintiff on account of work completed over a six-week period. The defendants claimed, for their part, that they were entitled to set off monies allegedly owed to them.

The judge concluded that summary judgment should not be granted on this issue, the defendants being entitled to argue in plenary trial that they had a right to set off the monies owed to them. Rejecting the contrary view expressed by Lord Denning M.R. in *Dawnays Ltd v FG Minter Ltd* [1971] 1 W.L.R. 1205, Kelly J. concluded that there was nothing in law excluding the defendants from claiming set-off in respect of monies owing under an architect's certificate. This was not, he noted, a debt of a particular character, and there was, as such, no special immunity from a counterclaim. If the right of set-off was to be excluded, this could only be achieved by written agreement, of which there was in this case none. On the facts, the judge concluded, the terms of the contract between the parties were not inconsistent with a right of set-off. As the defendants' claim was at least arguable, summary judgment would be inappropriate.

The second point related to an additional sum of €564,180 allegedly owed to the plaintiff. The judge reviewed, for this purpose, the evidence of a quantity surveyor acting for the defendants. The surveyor observed that, although certain work had been performed by the plaintiff, for which the latter was entitled to be paid, the plaintiff was not entitled to the full cost that he had claimed in respect of that work. The surveyor noted that it was not sufficient simply to make an arithmetic calculation based on the number of hours worked and the quantity of materials used. One also had to have regard to the quality of the work performed and the extent to which substantive progress had been made on the project. On this latter score, the surveyor concluded, the plaintiff fell short. The overall hours claimed were, he asserted, unjustified when viewed in the light of what he felt was the lack of progress made on the project. The surveyor thus indicated that, in his opinion, the full sum claimed should not have been allowed and, in particular, that deductions should have been made for lack of productivity and lack of progress on the project.

The judge concluded that the surveyor's evidence did not constitute an admission of liability in respect of the claimed sum. As such, he rejected the motion for summary judgment. On both counts the judge concluded that he was satisfied, looking at the whole situation, that there was a fair and reasonable probability that the defendants had a real and bona fide defence. The case should, the judge ruled, proceed to plenary trial.

SOLICITOR'S LIEN

***Mulheir and Arnold v Gannon and Claffey Gannon Solicitors*, High Court, Laffoy J., July 17, 2006**   In November 1998 the plaintiffs' home was subject to a search by the State. On foot of this search, and at the request of the plaintiffs, the defendant solicitor initiated proceedings on their behalf against the State.

Prior to the plenary hearing, however, the relationship between the plaintiffs and the defendant had deteriorated to the point that, in May 2003, the defendant advised his clients to seek alternative legal representation.

Having retained a new solicitor, the plaintiffs sought an order requiring the defendant to release all files relating to the plaintiffs' case. The defendant, however, refused to release the relevant papers until such time as he was paid what he claimed were outstanding costs relating to his work on their behalf. The precise amount of costs was disputed—in particular the defendant refused to cash a draft for €1005.44 submitted to him by the plaintiffs. A complete bill of costs had not been given to the plaintiffs, nor had costs been taxed.

The defendant, in sum, maintained that until such time as his costs were paid, he held a common law lien over the papers, effective as a security for those costs. He claimed that if an order for the release of the files was granted, it would effectively negate that lien, thus undermining his prospects of seeking full costs.

Laffoy J. first rejected the proposition that the lien was contingent on a taxed bill of costs, accepting that the plaintiffs did owe costs and that the defendant enjoyed a lien in respect of the case files until these costs were paid. She noted that where a solicitor's retainer is discharged in the course of litigation, "the determining factor is whether the solicitor is discharged by the client or, alternatively, the solicitor discharges himself from the case". Where the client withdraws, the solicitor is entitled to exercise a possessory lien over the client's files pending payment of outstanding costs. If, on the other hand, the solicitor determines the retainer, with reasonable cause, the solicitor's lien arises subject to the caveat that the court may (in order to permit the client to continue exercising his right to litigate) order the solicitor to submit the files to the client's new legal team. To rule otherwise would, she suggested, potentially compromise the client's constitutional right to litigate:

> "...where litigation is in progress, that litigation should not be stymied by the refusal of a solicitor, who has discharged himself, to hand over the papers in relation to the litigation, provided that his lien is secured..."

If such an order were made, however, the new solicitor would be required to undertake "to preserve the original solicitor's lien" and to return the files on completion of the litigation. This would safeguard the benefit of the lien in pursuing costs (see *Heslop v Metcalfe* (1837) 3 My. & C. 183). Such an order could be made on terms, for instance, that the costs would be paid in whole or in part.

Although the point was in dispute, and no oral evidence had been adduced thereon, the judge assumed for the purpose of the case that Gannon had discharged himself for reasonable cause. Following relevant case law, Laffoy J. concluded that:

"...subject to such conditions as the court considers necessary to be imposed in the interests of justice, the client is entitled to a mandatory order directed to his former solicitor to hand over the file to his new solicitor on an undertaking by the new solicitor to preserve the former solicitor's lien."

In other words, while the defendant would be obliged to hand over the disputed files to the plaintiffs' new solicitor, the latter would be required to protect the files so as to preserve the integrity of the defendant's lien.

On the evidence, the court concluded that costs of at least €1013.05 were outstanding. Though the defendant claimed that further sums were also outstanding, the court noted that, despite having ample time to do so, he had yet to submit a detailed bill or to have the costs taxed. The court also rejected the defendant's argument that the risk of recovering costs increased due to the fact that the plaintiffs now lived outside Ireland, Laffoy J. noting the relative ease with which Irish judgments could be enforced in other EU Member States. She further dismissed the proposition that the release of files would destroy Gannon's lien, noting that the lien would be "...protected by the undertaking from the new solicitor retained by the client".

Although the first plaintiff was pursuing some aspects of his litigation as a lay litigant, Laffoy J. nonetheless refused to contemplate direct delivery of the files to the plaintiffs themselves, favouring instead submission to their new solicitors:

"...the plaintiffs are not entitled to an order directing the delivery of the files maintained by the defendant in a manner that would destroy the defendant's lien, for example, by ordering delivery directly to them."

Laffoy J. thus ordered the delivery of files within two weeks to the new solicitors, on the condition that (i) the plaintiffs reimburse Gannon €1013.05 in costs; and (ii) that the new solicitor undertake to keep the files subject to the defendant's lien, and to return them to the defendant when proceedings ended. The delivery was, moreover, stated to be without prejudice to the defendant's claim for costs.

SPECIFIC PERFORMANCE

See also *Slaney Foods International Ltd v Bradshaw Foods Ltd*, High Court, Kelly J., March 22, 2006; [2006] I.E.H.C. 97 (above under COLLATERAL CONTRACTS); *Guilfoyle v Farm Development Co-operative Limited*, Supreme Court, March 23, 2006; [2006] I.E.S.C. 18 (above under APPEAL ON FINDINGS OF FACT); *Ochre Ridge v Cork Bonded Warehouses*, High Court, Smyth J., February 28, 2006 (above under CONDITIONS PRECEDENT); and

Smart Telecom plc v Radio Teilifís Éireann, High Court, Kelly J., May 26, 2006 (above under OFFER AND ACCEPTANCE).

Cosmoline Trading v DH Burke and Son Ltd and DHB Holdings, High Court, Finnegan J., February 8, 2006; [2006] I.E.H.C. 38   This case centred on a lease of a supermarket premises in Tuam, County Galway. The defendants owned a series of commercial properties throughout Galway and surrounding counties. In particular, it owned a premises called "Abbey Trinity", situate in Tuam. In 1997 the defendants and plaintiff entered into a lease granting the plaintiff, for a period of 35 years, a leasehold interest in a portion of the premises at Abbey Trinity, as well as in nine other premises throughout the Connacht/North Midlands region. These premises were to be operated by the plaintiff as supermarkets. A consolidated rent was agreed in respect of all 10 premises, with an agreement to review the rent in the sixth year and every five years thereafter.

The plaintiff's fortunes in the meantime proved to be mixed. While the Abbey Trinity premises appeared to be successful, its other supermarket locations faltered, with the result that the plaintiff had, one by one, surrendered several of the premises back to DHB.

In 2003 the parties agreed that, with a view to facilitating the redevelopment of the Abbey Trinity premises, the plaintiff would temporarily move the supermarket to the rear of the premises. The plaintiff subsequently did so, but experienced a drop in trading due to the disruption caused by construction and the lack of parking spaces. As a result, the parties agreed that the plaintiff could move to another premises owned by the defendants.

The question that arose was whether the parties had agreed that, on completion of the renovations, the plaintiff could move back into the Abbey Trinity premises. On this point the parties were fundamentally in dispute. The defendants claimed that it was their understanding that the plaintiff intended to seek alternative premises in a proposed shopping centre known as the "Tiernan development" and would thus be surrendering its interest in the Abbey Trinity premises. The plaintiff disputed this, and sought specific performance of what it alleged was an agreement that the plaintiff would be allowed to move back to Abbey Trinity once re-developed.

Much of the confusion arose from the fact that the plaintiff's directors were involved in a miscellany of projects involving different associated companies. It transpired that while the plaintiff company had been unsuccessful in securing premises in the Tiernan development, an associated company run by some of the directors of Cosmoline had been successful. The defendants believed that in fact Cosmoline had secured the Tiernan supermarket deal and would not be returning to Abbey Trinity. On foot of this understanding, they made arrangements to secure an alternative client. In fact, the plaintiff still intended to move back to its original premises.

On the facts, the judge ruled that, in his opinion, all parties had honestly represented their perspective. As such, he concluded that the parties had fundamentally misunderstood each other's intentions and were genuinely not *ad idem* regarding the return to the Abbey Trinity premises.

Two questions thus arose:

- Had there been an agreement for a new lease of premises at the renovated Abbey Trinity?

- If not, had the plaintiff surrendered its interest in the lease of the original premises?

A new lease On the first point, the plaintiff sought to rely on a letter sent by the defendant in August 2003, detailing the arrangements for the renovation. In the letter, the defendant confirmed its understanding that the plaintiff would temporarily move to the rear of the premises. The letter also proposed that the plaintiff would move back to the front of the premises on completion of renovations. The judge observed that while an agreement for a lease was, in equity, enforceable as a lease, specific performance would only be granted if there was certainty as to a number of factors including: (1) the parties; (2) the premises; (3) the terms of the lease; (4) the commencement date of the lease; and (5) the rent payable under the lease. Other material terms would also have to be agreed. For instance, given the fact that the supermarket was to be located in a larger premises containing various establishments, agreement was required on mutual covenants of support and protection (though this could be implied, the judge observed). The management structure and service charge would, moreover, have to be discussed.

On the facts, the judge concluded that some essential preconditions to the enforcement of a contract for a new lease had not been met. In particular there had been no agreement as to the date of commencement or the term of years. Nor were the parties *ad idem* on the precise boundaries of the premises to which the plaintiff was entitled, a dispute having arisen as to whether the plaintiff was entitled to a portion of the property which the defendants intended to run as a coffee shop. The location of storage facilities and the management structure had, furthermore, yet to be settled. The letter of August 2003 thus amounted to no more than a general proposal on the part of the defendant. Negotiations did not result in a completed contract and, as such, there was no concluded agreement upon which specific performance could be based. Fundamentally, there was a lack of consensus on material and essential terms and thus no contract.

The old lease The judge concluded, however, that despite the mixed signals sent out by the plaintiff's directors, the plaintiff had not surrendered its original interest in the Abbey Trinity premises. Under s.7 of Deasy's Act, a surrender of a lease may only be carried out by deed, or a signed note in writing, or by act and operation of law. Clearly there had been no deed, and no written surrender. It was suggested, however, that certain acts might be considered, in law, to permit the court to consider that there had been a surrender by act and operation of the law. A court may regard a surrender by act and operation of the law as having occurred if, having regard to the acts of the parties, the court could construe such actions as having been consistent only with an intention to surrender. Examples might include the vacation of a premises coupled with the handing back of keys to the landlord, or an abandonment of premises followed by a resumption of the landlord's possession thereof.

Thus, the question arose as to whether the plaintiff's conduct could be construed as indicating an intention to surrender the lease. Although the plaintiff had indicated that it might be willing to take cash in exchange for an agreement to vacate, no agreement was reached on this proposal. On the facts, the judge concluded that there was no intention to vacate Abbey Trinity and that the plaintiff retained an interest in the premises.

This left the parties in a curious conundrum. Whereas the plaintiff was not entitled to a new lease for the renovated property, neither could the defendant deny that the plaintiff's original interest subsisted. In the circumstances, the judge suggested (though he left it to the parties to conclude) that compensation might be offered to the plaintiff to buy out this interest.

Quinn and Quinn v Greally and Liddy, High Court, Roderick Murphy J., May 12, 2006; [2006] I.E.H.C. 148   In December 2001 the first plaintiff, Mary Quinn, entered into an agreement with Mr Greally, a property developer, under which Mrs Quinn had agreed to exchange property in her sole name for a new home to be built by Mr Greally. This agreement was in consideration for Mrs Quinn's agreement to withdraw an objection she had made to the defendant's application for planning permission. The plaintiffs sought specific performance of this agreement, or damages for breach thereof, along with costs.

The first defendant, Mr Greally, had sought planning permission for a Co. Longford development called Clonbalt Woods. Initially Mrs Quinn had objected to the development, but withdrew her objection on foot of an agreement with Mr Greally. Under this agreement, Mr Greally promised to pay Mrs Quinn €47,139 so that she could purchase a site for a new home in the Clonbalt Woods development. The defendant further agreed to build a house for Mrs Quinn on the Clonbalt Woods site once purchased, and to pay her further monies in respect of the transaction, including €25,395 in respect of any inconvenience caused to her.

The defendant initially provided a deposit of €4,190 towards the price of the site for Mrs Quinn's new home, the balance to be paid by March 1, 2002. Nonetheless, having subsequently fallen into financial difficulties, Mr Greally never paid the balance. Mrs Quinn alleged that she was entitled to an order for specific performance of the contract, or damages in lieu thereof. Mr Greally, while admitting the existence of the agreement, alleged that Mrs Quinn was not willing to complete her side of the bargain. Effectively, he sought to renegotiate the contract, which Mrs Quinn proved unwilling to do.

The court granted the order for specific performance. While noting that such an order would not have been granted had the agreement not been "certain, fair and just", the court concluded that the plaintiff had acted at all times in good faith. She was in particular, ready, willing and able to complete her side of the bargain under the contract. Subject to a variation in the agreed completion date, the court ordered specific performance of the contract.

A related issue initially arose involving the second defendant, Mr Brendan Liddy, the solicitor for the first defendant, Mr Greally. Mr Liddy had, in December 2001, entered into a personal indemnity under which he had promised to pay Mrs Quinn the balance owed by Mr Greally in the event that Mrs Quinn was called upon to pay the developer of the new site in circumstances where Mr Greally had not delivered on his contractual promise. This indemnity would not operate until after March 1, 2002, the date by which Mr Greally had agreed to pay the balance. Although an action on the indemnity was originally contemplated, this was dropped when Mr Liddy paid the amount owed, though the interpretation of the indemnity was considered in this case. The court concluded, in particular, that the solicitor's obligation to indemnify arose not on the failure of the defendant to pay the balance by the set date, but *"only where the plaintiff had a liability to pay the balance to the developer"* of the site on which her new house was to be developed (emphasis added). In any event, this did not, the court ruled, prevent specific performance being granted in respect of the first defendant.

Fitzsimons v Value Homes, High Court, Clarke J., May 12, 2006; [2006] I.E.H.C. 144   The plaintiff, Ms Fitzsimons, entered into a contract with the defendant, Value Homes, under which the defendant agreed to build, and the plaintiff to buy, a new apartment to be constructed in north Co. Dublin. The original price agreed under the contract (accounting for a minor variation) was €142,655 with a February 2003 closing date being set for completion. The plaintiff laid down a deposit in respect of the property.

Having encountered difficulties in completion at the contemplated price, the defendant sought to renegotiate the contract price and deadline. On foot of these negotiations, the parties agreed to a new price of €162,655 and an extended deadline of November 2003. As it transpired, however, the defendant failed even to meet this new deadline and at the time of judgment—almost two-and-a-half years late—the apartment had yet to be completed. The defendant again sought to renegotiate the contract price upwards by another €20,000, but this time Ms Fitzsimons resisted. In the circumstances, the plaintiff sought specific performance of the original contract. In an earlier judgment, Butler J. made an order for damages, to be assessed by the taxing master.

The first question that arose was whether or not the variation agreement (under which the price was increased to €162,655) was valid and binding. The court agreed that it was. At face value the agreement to increase the price may not have appeared to be supported by valuable consideration. Nonetheless, the court concluded that there were practical benefits to be derived by the plaintiff in agreeing to this variation. In reasoning reminiscent of that found in *Williams v Roffey* [1990] 1 All E.R. 512, the court observed that there was a real risk that without the increase the building project would not have been completed. This being the case, Ms Fitzsimons avoided potentially serious consequences by agreeing to the increase, in particular in evading the risk that (practically speaking) she might not have been able to recover her deposit if the builder went bankrupt. As such, the builder had provided valuable consideration for the agreed increase in price.

The plaintiff had further argued that the person who witnessed the plaintiff's signature of the variation agreement had not in fact seen her sign. The purpose of the witness, the court reasoned, was to prevent a dispute arising regarding whether the signature was that of the plaintiff. Given that the plaintiff was not disputing that the signature was hers, nothing turned on the failure properly to witness her signature. Similarly, the court rejected the proposition that the defendant's failure to execute the variation agreement was fatal. Given that it was seeking to rely on the latter agreement, the defendant was estopped from denying its validity.

In the final analysis the court concluded that specific performance should be granted but on the basis of the contract as varied and *not* the original contract. Ms Fitzsimons, the court decided, was entitled to specific performance only on the basis of the varied contract (with the increased price). To allow her to rely on the original contract would have been inequitable. The fact that she had not issued a completion notice was irrelevant, as specific performance depended not on a breach of contract but on the equitable duty to perform the contract. There was, the court reasoned, ample evidence of her willingness and ability to close the sale.

On the other hand, the court accepted that it would be unfair to allow the defendant to have the benefit of a contract part of which it had failed to complete on time. The resulting 30-month delay had caused the plaintiff significant losses. The judge thus concluded that specific performance of the upwardly varied agreement would be granted subject to the abatement of the contract price by the value of the loss (which would be assessed separately). The court further indicated that the defendant should make good on its promise to deliver the apartment complete with white goods.

Criminal Law

CRIMINAL JUSTICE ACT 2006

Because of the range and complexity of the subject-matter of the Criminal Justice Act 2006, we discuss its provisions separately at the beginning of this chapter.

Background   The Criminal Justice Act 2006 began its legislative life as the Criminal Justice Bill 2004, which in turn had been published by the Department of Justice, Equality and Law Reform in draft form in 2003 as the Scheme of a Criminal Justice Bill 2003. As introduced, the 2004 Bill contained 38 sections, which implemented the principal recommendations of the 1999 *Report of the Expert Group on Changes to the Criminal Law* (chaired by the late Eamonn Leahy, S.C.), appointed to consider changes in the criminal law as recommended in the 1997 *Report of the Steering Group on the Efficiency and Effectiveness of the Garda Síochána*. As initiated, the 2004 Bill contained a range of significant reforms. These included amendments to the powers of the Garda Síochána in relation to the investigation of offences, including the designation of crime scenes and the taking of forensic evidence. It also included provision for the admissibility in evidence of certain witness statements which had been later recanted at trial. The 2004 Bill also provided for an extension of the circumstances in which the DPP may bring a "without prejudice" appeal to the Supreme Court. The 2004 Bill also proposed the imposition of fixed charge penalties (sometimes mistakenly referred to as "on-the-spot-fines") in respect of certain offences under the Criminal Justice (Public Order) Act 1994, changes to the requirements for the issue of a firearms certificate and an amendment of the Petty Sessions (Ireland) Act 1851 relating to the issue and execution of certain warrants. As we discuss below, all of these provisions were enacted when the 2004 Bill became the Criminal Justice Act 2006.

The 2004 Bill received considerable public attention when it was published. Thus, the Irish Human Rights Commission (IHRC), to which the Scheme of the 2003 Bill and the 2004 Bill were referred by the Minister pursuant to the Human Rights Commission Act 2000, expressed serious reservations as to the compatibility of the Bill with national and international human rights standards, notably in connection with the provisions on taking forensic samples and the admissibility of witness statements (the IHRC's observations on the 2003 Scheme and 2004 Bill are available at www.ihrc.ie).

The 2004 Bill came under more intense scrutiny when, in late 2005, as the 2004 Bill completed the Second Stage in Dáil Éireann, the Minister for Justice, Equality and Law Reform stated his intention to introduce significant additional elements to the 2004 Bill at committee stage. This would not have attracted particular comment but for the range and extent of the proposed amendments announced, which were published in March 2006. The effect of the amendments was that a 2004 Bill containing 38 sections would be transformed into a 2006 Act containing 196 sections. The additional elements introduced at Committee Stage included the following: amendments to the Firearms Acts 1925 to 2000, including increasing fines and penalties generally for firearm offences, creating mandatory minimum sentences for certain offences, introduction of a "gun amnesty" and amendments governing the grant of firearm certificates; amendments to the Explosives Act 1875 to provide for new offences relating to fireworks and increased penalties; new offences relating to organised crime, including an offence of participating in or contributing to any activity of a criminal organisation for the purpose of enhancing the ability of such an organisation to commit or facilitate a serious offence whether inside or outside the State, an offence of committing an offence for the benefit of a criminal organisation and an offence of conspiracy to commit a serious offence; amendments to the Misuse of Drugs Act 1977 in order to strengthen the pre-2006 sentencing provisions for drug trafficking offences, to create a new offence of importation of drugs with a value of €13,000 or more, and a new offence of supplying drugs to prisons; a requirement obliging persons convicted on indictment of certain drug trafficking offences to notify certain information to the Garda Síochána; provisions on sentencing, including creating a statutory basis for suspended or partially suspended sentences, imposition of a fine and deferral of sentence, restriction on movement orders and electronic monitoring of offenders; civil proceedings in relation to Anti-Social Behaviour Orders (ASBOs) for adults and, separately, for children, resulting in amendments to the Children Act 2001; and the establishment of the Criminal Law Codification Advisory Committee to advise on the drawing up of a criminal code and monitor its implementation. As indicated, these additional amendments attracted considerable comment and were so extensive that they required a detailed Motion to Recommit to Committee—not in itself unprecedented, but which was itself debated over two days in Dáil Éireann.

We now turn to outline the main elements of the 2006 Act. It should be noted here that an explanatory memorandum was published with the 2006 Act as enacted (available at www.oireachtas.ie), in line with stated Government policy (not yet universally applied). The overview that follows has drawn on some elements of that explanatory memorandum. In view of the nature and extent of the many elements in the 2006 Act, we provide a general overview of these provisions only.

Investigation of offences   Part 2 of the 2006 Act (ss.5 to 14) contains several provisions concerning the investigation of offences.

Crime scene   Section 5 provides for a statutory basis for the designation of a place as a crime scene. Section 5(1) provides that a member of the Garda Síochána when in a public place, or any other place under a power of entry authorised by law or to which or in which he or she was expressly or impliedly invited or permitted to be may, pending the giving of a direction under subs.(3), take such steps as considered reasonably necessary to preserve any evidence of, or relating to the commission of an arrestable offence. The steps which may be taken are specified in subs.(4) of the section. The member must have reasonable grounds for believing that an arrestable offence (within the meaning of s.2 of the Criminal Law Act 1997) was, is being, or may have been committed in the place or that there is, or may be, evidence relating to, the commission of an arrestable offence that was, or may have been committed elsewhere. Section 5(2) provides that a member who exercises such powers shall, as soon as reasonably practicable, seek the making of a direction under subs.(3) by a member of the Garda Síochána not below the rank of superintendent in relation to the place. Section 5(3) provides that a direction may be given by a member of the Garda Síochána not below the rank of superintendent designating a place as a crime scene. The member who makes the direction must have reasonable grounds for believing that either an arrestable offence was, is being, or may have been committed in the place, or there is, or may be, evidence in the place of the commission of an arrestable offence that was, or may have been, committed elsewhere, and it is necessary to designate the place as a crime scene to preserve, search for and collect evidence of, or relating to, the commission of the offence. Subsection (4) provides that a direction shall authorise such members of the Garda Síochána as considered appropriate to take such steps as considered reasonably necessary, including all or any of those listed in the subsection, to preserve, search for and collect evidence at the crime scene. Section 5(5) provides that a member of the Garda Síochána not below the rank of superintendent can authorise such persons as he or she considers appropriate to enter a crime scene for a specified purpose and for such period as he or she may determine. Section 5(6) provides that a direction shall be in force no longer than is reasonably necessary to preserve, search for and collect evidence. Section 5(7) provides that a direction in relation to a place other than a public place shall cease to be in force 24 hours after it is given. Section 5(8) sets out the requirements in relation to the recording of the giving of the direction. Section 5(9) provides that a judge of the District Court may, in specified circumstances, including that the investigation is being conducted diligently and expeditiously, continue the direction in force for a period not exceeding 48 hours. Section 5(10) provides that an order continuing the direction in force may be made not more than three times. Section 5(11) provides that the High Court may, in particular where exceptional circumstances exist which warrant the continuance of the direction, make an order continuing a direction in force for such period as it considers appropriate. Subsection (12) provides that a member of the Garda Síochána who intends to make an application to a judge of the District Court or of the High Court for an order continuing a direction in force shall, if it is reasonably practicable to do so before the application is made, give notice of it to the occupier of the place or if it is not reasonably practicable to ascertain the identity or whereabouts of the occupier or the place is unoccupied, the owner, unless it is not reasonably practicable to ascertain the identity or whereabouts of the owner. Section 5(13) provides that if the occupier or owner of the place applies to be heard by the court, an order shall not be made under subs.(9) or (11) unless an opportunity has been given to the person to be heard. Section 5(14) provides that the High Court or a judge of the District Court may attach such conditions as the court or the judge considers appropriate to an order for the purpose of protecting the interests of the occupier or owner. Section 5(15) provides that a person who obstructs a member of the Garda Síochána in the exercise of his or her powers under the section or who fails to comply with a direction under the section shall be guilty of an offence and shall be liable on summary conviction to a fine not exceeding €3,000 or imprisonment for a term not exceeding six months or both. Section 5(16) provides that a member of the Garda Síochána may arrest without warrant any person whom the member suspects of committing an offence under subs.(15). Section 5(17) provides that nothing in this section prevents the designation of a place as a crime scene, or a member of the Garda Síochána from taking any of the steps referred to in subs.(4), if the owner or occupier of the place consents.

Search warrants   Section 6 provides a revised general provision on the issuing of search warrants where an arrestable offence has been committed or suspected by the substitution of a new s.10 into the Criminal Justice (Miscellaneous Provisions) Act 1997. The new s.10 of the 1997 Act provides as follows. Section 10(1) of the 1997 Act, as amended, provides that where a judge of the District Court is satisfied by information on oath of a member not below the rank of sergeant that there are reasonable grounds for suspecting that evidence of, or relating to, the commission of an arrestable offence is to be found in any place, the judge may issue a warrant for the search of that place and any persons found at that place. Section 10(2) of the 1997 Act, as amended, provides that a member not below the rank of superintendent may, in certain circumstances, if he or she is satisfied that there are reasonable grounds for suspecting that evidence of, or relating to, the commission of an arrestable offence is to be found in any place, issue a warrant for the search of that place and any persons found at that place. Section 10(3) of the 1997 Act, as amended, provides that a member not below the rank of superintendent shall not issue a search warrant under subs.(2) unless he or she is satisfied that the warrant is necessary for the proper investigation of the offence concerned and that circumstances of urgency giving rise to the need for the immediate issue of the warrant would render it impracticable to apply to a judge of the District Court for the issue of a search warrant. Section 10(4) of the 1997 Act, as amended, provides that subject to subs.(5), a search warrant under the section shall be expressed, and shall operate, to authorise a named member, accompanied by such other members or persons or both as the member thinks necessary, to enter, at any time or times within one week of the date of issue of the warrant, on production if so requested of the warrant, and if necessary by the use of reasonable force, the place named in the warrant, to search it and any persons found at that place, and to seize anything found at that place, or anything found in the possession of a person present at that place at the time of the search, that that member reasonably believes to be evidence of, or relating to, the commission of an arrestable offence. Section 10(5) of the 1997 Act, as amended, provides that a search warrant issued under the section by a superintendent shall cease to have effect after a period of 24 hours has elapsed from the time of the issue of the warrant. Section 10(6) of the 1997 Act, as amended, provides that a member acting under the authority of a search warrant under the section may require any person present at the place where the search is being carried out to give to the member his or her name and address, and may arrest without warrant any person who obstructs or attempts to obstruct the member in the carrying out of his or her duties, fails to give the member his or her name and address or gives a name or address which the member has reasonable cause for believing is false or misleading. Section 10(7) of the 1997 Act, as amended, provides that a person who obstructs or attempts to obstruct a member acting under the authority of a search warrant under this section, who fails to comply with a requirement under subs.(6)(a) or who gives a false or misleading name or address to a member shall be guilty of an offence and shall be liable on summary conviction to a fine not exceeding €3,000 or imprisonment for a term not exceeding six months or both. Section 10(8) of the 1997 Act, as amended, provides that the power to issue a warrant under s.10 is without prejudice to any other power conferred by statute to issue a warrant for the search of any place or person.

Power to seize and retain evidence   Section 7(1) provides that where a garda, who is in a public place or any other place under a power of entry authorised by law or to which or in which he or she was expressly or impliedly invited or permitted to be, finds or comes into possession of anything and he or she has reasonable grounds for believing that it is evidence of, or relating to, the commission of an arrestable offence, he or she may seize and retain it for use as evidence in any criminal proceedings for such period from the date of seizure as is reasonable or, if proceedings are commenced in which it is required for use in evidence, until the conclusion of the proceedings. The provisions of the Police (Property) Act 1897 apply to the item so seized. Section 7(2) provides that the member shall not seize or retain a document where it is represented or appears that the document was, or may have been, made for the purpose of obtaining, giving or communicating legal advice, unless he or she suspects with reasonable cause that the document was not made for that purpose. Section 7(3) provides that the power under the section to seize and retain evidence is without prejudice to any other power conferred by statute or otherwise to seize or retain evidence of, or relating to, the commission or attempted commission of an offence.

Arrestable offences includes common law offences Section 8 amends s.2(1) of the Criminal Law Act 1997. As enacted, the 1997 Act had provided that an "arrestable" offence is one for which a person of full capacity and not previously convicted may, under or by virtue of "any enactment", be punished by imprisonment for a term of five years or by a more severe penalty and includes an attempt to commit any such offence. Section 8 of the 2006 Act amended s.2(1) of the 1997 Act by the substitution of "under or by virtue of any enactment or the common law" for "under or by virtue of any enactment". The effect of the amendment is, of course, to bring common law offences carrying a term of imprisonment of five years or more for which there is no statutory penalty within the definition of "arrestable offences".

Increased period of detention under Criminal Justice Act 1984 The main purpose of s.9 of the 2006 Act was to amend s.4 of the Criminal Justice Act 1984 to provide for an increased power of detention under the 1984 Act. As enacted, s.4 of the 1984 Act had provided for a total of up to 12 hours' detention (made up of an initial period of six hours with provision for a further period of up to six hours) where the offence involved carries a penalty of five years' imprisonment or more. Section 9 amended s.4(c) of the 1984 Act to provide for the possibility of a further period of 12 hours' detention on the approval of an officer of at least the level of chief superintendent, who must have reasonable grounds for believing that the increased detention is necessary for the proper investigation of the offence concerned. Mirroring the change made in s.8 of the 2006 Act, above, s.9 also amended s.4(a) of the 1984 Act to apply the 1984 Act to offences punishable under common law with a term of imprisonment of five years or more where there is no statutory penalty provided for. Section 9 also made a number of amendments to s.4(b) of the 1984 Act to the effect that the detention provisions of the section apply to a person arrested within a Garda station as well as to a person taken to a Garda station.

Detention under Criminal Justice (Drug Trafficking) Act 1996 Section 10 amended ss.2 and 4 of the Criminal Justice (Drug Trafficking) Act 1996 to the effect that the detention provisions in the 1996 Act apply to a person arrested within a Garda station as well as to a person taken to a station (mirroring the changes made in s.9 of the 2006 Act, above).

Detention for more than one offence As enacted, s.42 of the Criminal Justice

Act 1999 provided that a prisoner may be arrested by a member of the Garda Síochána on the authority of a judge of the District Court in connection with an offence other than the offence for which he or she was imprisoned and brought to a Garda Station and detained there for the period authorised by s.4 of the Criminal Justice Act 1984. Section 11 of the 2006 Act amended s.42 of the 1999 Act to apply it in circumstances where there may be more than one offence or suspected offence involved.

Power of Garda Síochána to photograph arrested persons   Section 12 of the 2006 Act provides that, on the authority of a member of the Garda Síochána not below the rank of sergeant, a person arrested by a member of the Garda Síochána may be photographed in a Garda Síochána station as soon as may be after his or her arrest. A photograph taken in these circumstances may only be used to assist in the identification of the arrested person in connection with any proceedings which may be instituted against him or her in respect of the offence for which he or she was arrested. Section 12(3) provides that s.8 of the Criminal Justice Act 1984, which deals with the destruction of records, shall apply to photographs (including the negatives) taken under s.12. Section 12(4) provides that a person who refuses to allow a photograph to be taken pursuant to this section shall be guilty of an offence and shall be liable on summary conviction to a fine not exceeding €3,000 or imprisonment for a term not exceeding six months or both.

Further amendments to Criminal Justice Act 1984   Section 13 of the 2006 Act amended ss.6, 8 and 28 of the Criminal Justice Act 1984. Subsection 13(*a*) increases the fine contained in s.6(4) of the 1984 Act to €3,000 in respect of a detained person who obstructs or attempts to obstruct or otherwise fails to cooperate with a garda exercising powers under that section. The powers which a member of the Garda Síochána may use under s.6 of the 1984 Act include the power to demand the name and address of the person, the power to search or cause the person to be searched and the power to take or cause to be taken fingerprints and palm-prints. Subsection 12(b) of the 2006 Act increased the period for which photographs, palm-prints and fingerprints can be retained by the Gardaí in the absence of proceedings before they must be destroyed. Where proceedings for an offence to which s.4 of the 1984 Act applies are not instituted against the person, the period within which the destruction of the record must be carried out is increased from six months to twelve months. The period for which a judge of the District Court may, on the application of the DPP, authorise the preservation of a record as provided for in s.4(7), is increased from six months to twelve months. Section 13(*c*) increases to €3,000 the fine in respect of a person dealt with under the Probation of Offenders Act 1907 or who is convicted and who refuses to comply with a requirement under s.28 of the 1984 Act or to allow his or her fingerprints, palm-prints or photograph to be taken pursuant to that section.

Taking forensic evidence Section 14 of the 2006 Act makes a number of amendments to the Criminal Justice (Forensic Evidence) Act 1990. Section 14(*a*)(i), (ii) and (iii) provide that mouth swabs and saliva become samples which may be taken without the consent required by s.2(4)(b) of the Criminal Justice (Forensic Evidence) Act 1990. Section 14(a)(v) inserted a new s.2(8)(A) into the 1990 Act to the effect that where a sample of hair, other than pubic hair, is taken in accordance with its terms, the sample may be taken either by cutting hairs or by plucking hairs singly with their roots and where hairs are plucked, no more can be plucked than the person taking the sample reasonably considers to be necessary to constitute a sufficient sample for the purpose of forensic testing. Section 14(a)(iv) applies these provisions to a drug trafficking offence within the meaning of s.3(1) of the Criminal Justice Act 1994. Section 14(a)(vi) increases from £1,000 to €3,000 the maximum fine where a person obstructs or attempts to obstruct any member of the Garda Síochána or any other person acting under the powers conferred by the 1990 Act. Section 14(b) extends from six to 12 months the time period for which samples obtained from persons can be retained before being destroyed in circumstances where proceedings are not instituted. Section 14(c) amended s.5(2) of the 1990 Act to provide that the Minister for Justice, Equality and Law Reform may make regulations concerning the manner in which samples may be taken, the location and physical conditions in which samples may be taken, and the persons (including members of the Garda Síochána), and the number of such persons, who may be present when samples are taken. It may be noted that, in response to critical comments by the Irish Human Rights Commission, the Criminal Justice Act 2007 (to which we will return in the *Annual Review of Irish Law 2007*) expressly provides that only reasonable force may be used in connection with sample-taking under the 1990 Act. It was also noted during the Oireachtas debate on s.14 that, following the publication of the Law Reform Commission's *Report on the Establishment of a DNA Database* (LRC 78–2005) (*Annual Review of Irish Law 2005*, pp.266–8, 501–504) the Government had agreed to the drafting of legislation on the establishment of a DNA database.

Admissibility of certain witness statements Part 3 of the 2006 Act (ss.15 to 20) deals with the admissibility of certain witness statements. In particular, it deals with circumstances where a witness recants and refuses to stand over a previous statement. These provisions were in response to some highly-publicised criminal trials in recent years in which this had occurred. It was pointed out during the Oireachtas debate that the position prior to 2006 (referred to as the position at common law, though this should more properly have referred to the Criminal Procedure Act 1865: see the *Annual Review of Irish Law 2003*, p.234) was that a previous statement made to Gardaí cannot be admitted in evidence as proof of any fact contained in it; the fact that a witness may have previously said something different can be used to attack the credibility of the witness but the assertions in the earlier statement cannot constitute proof of those assertions.

The changes effected by Pt 3 added significantly to some pre-2006 statutory changes to the general rule, and it was also acknowledged that they were based on principles applied by the Canadian Supreme Court to the admission of prior inconsistent statements by witnesses in *Queen v TGB* (1993) 1 S.C.R. 740, which was discussed in *People (DPP) v McArdle* [2003] 4 I.R. 186 (*Annual Review of Irish Law 2003*, pp.234–36). Section 16 of the 2006 Act sets out the circumstances in which such statements can be admitted. Section 16(1) provides that where a person is sent forward for trial in relation to an arrestable offence, a relevant statement made by the witness may be admitted as evidence of any fact contained in it if the witness is available for cross-examination but refuses to give evidence, denies making the statement or gives evidence which is inconsistent with it. Section 16(2) lists the conditions which a court may take into account in deciding on its admissibility. These are, confirmation by the witness or proof that he or she made the statement, satisfaction by the court that direct oral evidence of the facts in the statement would have been admissible in court as evidence, that it is voluntary, reliable, and that it was given on oath or affirmation or contains a statutory declaration by the witness as to its truth or the court is satisfied the person understood the requirement to tell the truth. Section 16(3) provides that in deciding on the reliability of the statement the court should have regard to whether it was video-recorded or given on oath or solemn affirmation or whether there is, in the absence of the foregoing, other sufficient evidence of reliability. The court must also have regard to any explanation given by the witness for refusing to give the statement, for giving evidence inconsistent with it, or for any evidence given in relation to denial of making the statement. Section 16(4) provides that the statement will not be admitted if the court is of the opinion that in all the circumstances, including whether its admission or exclusion would be unfair to the accused, it is not in the interests of justice to do so or if its admission is unnecessary having regard to other evidence. Section 16(5) provides that in estimating the weight to be given to the statement regard must be had to all the circumstances from which any inference could be drawn as to its accuracy or otherwise. Section 16(6) clarifies that the section is without prejudice to certain existing statutory procedural requirements regarding matters such as proof of statements. Section 17 provides that in relation to an arrestable offence where a witness makes a statement to a garda, the witness may make a statutory declaration that the statement is true and a garda may take and receive it. Alternatively the garda may administer an oath or affirmation. Section 18(2) provides that a witness may make a statutory declaration that his or her statement is true to a competent person. Section 18(1) defines competent person as a person employed by a public authority. Section 19 provides that the Minister may make regulations for the video-recording or audio-recording of witness statements made to the Garda Síochána. Section 20 amended s.4E of the Criminal Procedure Act 1967, which deals with an application by the accused for dismissal of a charge, to allow for the admissibility of any video-recording or audio-recording, which may be admitted by the trial court as evidence of any fact stated in it.

Prosecution appeals Part 4 of the 2006 Act (ss.21 to 24) expands in a limited respect the circumstances in which the prosecution may bring a "without prejudice" appeal under s.34 of the Criminal Procedure Act 1967, and also deals with other aspects of prosecution appeals.

As noted during the Oireachtas debate, the limited prosecution right of appeal has its basis in the common law principle against double jeopardy, that no person should be tried twice for the same offence. The pre-2006 position under s.34 of the 1967 Act restricted the "without prejudice" prosecution right of appeal to a point of law arising from a directed acquittal arising from a "terminating ruling". The change effected by s.21 of the 2006 Act is that such appeals are available in respect of "non-terminating" rulings, where a decision by the trial judge may not have led directly to an acquittal. Section 21 of the 2006 Act amends s.34 of the Criminal Procedure Act 1967 to provide that the DPP (or the Attorney General if he or she is the prosecuting authority) may, on a *without prejudice* basis, refer a question of law arising during the trial to the Supreme Court for determination. Section 34(3), as amended, provides that the Supreme Court can hear argument by the Attorney General or the DPP as appropriate or by counsel on their behalf, by counsel on behalf of the acquitted person or by that person if the court agrees. The court can also hear argument by counsel appointed by the court, if in accordance with the provisions of s.34(4), as amended, the acquitted person waives his or her rights in this respect or if the court considers it desirable in the public interest to appoint such counsel. The identity of the acquitted person should not be disclosed unless that person agrees otherwise. The section also provides for free legal aid for the acquitted person if he or she opts to be represented and if the person's means are insufficient to obtain legal aid.

Section 22 of the 2006 Act inserts an amended s.29 of the Courts of Justice Act 1924, to provide for an appeal to the Supreme Court from the Court of Criminal Appeal where the court or the Attorney General certifies that the decision involves a point of law of exceptional public importance and that it is desirable in the public interest that the appeal be taken. The Supreme Court had found in *People (Attorney General) v Kennedy* [1946] I.R. 517 that a prosecution appeal did not lie under s.29 of the 1924 Act. The amendment is similar to s.21 in that it provides the prosecution with a "without prejudice" right of appeal to the Supreme Court in relation to a point of law involved in a decision by the Court of Criminal Appeal. In accordance with subs.(3) the court or the Attorney General or the DPP, as appropriate, must certify that the decision involves a point of law of exceptional public importance and that it is desirable in the public interest that the Attorney General or the Director should take the appeal. The arrangements in relation to appeals under subs.(3) for representation, anonymity and for legal aid are similar to those in s.21.

Section 23 amended s.2(2) of the Criminal Justice Act 1993 by increasing to 28 days the limit for the making of an application by the DPP for the review of an unduly lenient sentence. It also provided that the court may extend this period to up to 56 days.

Section 24 provides that where a person is acquitted of an offence tried on indictment the Attorney General or the DPP as appropriate may appeal an order for costs against him or her.

Considerable time was spent during the Oireachtas debate on whether "with prejudice" prosecution appeals should be introduced. The Opposition tabled amendments based on the UK Criminal Justice Act 2003, which had introduced the power of the prosecution to refer old acquittals to the Court of Appeal to determine whether a retrial could be ordered. Ultimately, the Government declined to accept these amendments. In November 2006 the Law Reform Commission published its *Report on Prosecution Appeals and Pre-trial Hearings* (LRC 82–2006) see pp. 343-4 below.. The Commission confirmed a recommendation made in its 2003 consultation paper on this topic that the extended "without prejudice" appeal actually introduced in the 2006 Act constituted a sufficient extension to facilitate the prospective correction of any errors in trial court rulings. The Commission did not recommend the introduction of any "with prejudice" form of appeal. The question subsequently became one of the matters referred to the Criminal Law Review Group, established in November 2006, whose recommendations formed the background to the Criminal Justice Act 2007, to which we will return in the *Annual Review of Irish Law 2007*.

Firearms   Part 5 of the 2006 Act (ss.25 to 67 and Schedule 1) provide for extensive amendments to the Firearms Acts 1925 to 2000. The principal amendments include increased penalties generally for offences under the Firearms Acts and the introduction, for the first time, of mandatory minimum sentences in respect of certain firearms offences. In particular, penalties for the possession of a "restricted firearm" without the necessary permit are being increased to a fine of €5,000 or 12 months' imprisonment, or both on summary conviction, and a fine of €20,000 or seven years' imprisonment, or both, on indictment. Also included were provisions setting out, for the first time, mandatory minimum sentences, of between five and ten years, for certain firearms offences, including possession of a firearm with intent to endanger life, possession of a firearm while hijacking a vehicle, use of a firearm to aid escape, possession of a firearm in suspicious circumstances, possession of a firearm with criminal intent and converting a shotgun into a sawn-off shotgun. The changes effected also amended the provisions governing the conditions attaching to the grant of a firearms certificate and the registration of firearms dealers. In so far as the new conditions governing the grant of firearms certificates are concerned, the 2006 Act specifies certain additional requirements which will have to be met by applicants for certificates, including a new requirement that all persons wishing to hold a firearm satisfy the Gardaí that they have provided secure accommodation for the firearm. In this regard, certain firearms are deemed "restricted firearms" by reference to specific criteria, including the calibre, action type and muzzle energy. Under the amendments effected by the 2006 Act, any person wishing to obtain a certificate for such a firearm will have to apply directly to the Garda Commissioner. The 2006 Act also provided for a limited "gun amnesty" during which firearms may be surrendered to the Gardaí before the new penalties and mandatory minimum sentences were introduced. The 2006 Act provided that, during the amnesty period, persons who surrender weapons will not be prosecuted for the simple illegal possession of the weapon. However, surrendered weapons will be forensically tested, where appropriate, and where found to have been used in a crime a weapon and the forensic evidence will be admissible in any proceedings subsequently brought. The details of the amnesty were set out in the Firearms Act 1925 (Surrender of Firearms and Offensive Weapons) Order 2006 (S.I. No. 451 of 2006). The 2006 Act also deals with the authorisation of rifle or pistol clubs and firing ranges, a statutory right of appeal to the District Court of decisions regarding firearms certificates and the introduction of a new type of certificate that will allow young persons to be trained in the use of firearms for sports purposes.

Explosives   Part 6 of the 2006 Act (ss. 68 to 69 and Schedule 2) provides for amendments to the Explosives Act 1875. These include new offences governing the misuse of fireworks in a public place and the possession of illegally imported fireworks with intent to supply. Increased penalties under the 1875 Act were also provided for, including significant increases in the penalties for illegal importation, sale and use of fireworks. During the Oireachtas debate, this element of the 2006 Act was stated to have been based on a survey conducted by the Department of Justice, Equality and Law Reform to determine whether those surveyed wished fireworks to be more generally available, as is the position in the United Kingdom, or whether they wished the law to remain as it is. The survey indicated that there was a strong consensus that the law should be left exactly as it is but made workable and enforceable.

Organised crime   Part 7 of the 2006 Act (ss.70 to 79) contains entirely new provisions to deal with organised crime. It was stated that Pt 7 would enable the State to give effect to commitments arising from the UN Convention on Organised Crime, as well the European Union's Joint Action on this same subject. Part 7 creates a number of new offences relating to participation in or assisting in the carrying out of criminal activities by organised gangs. It also extends the definition of "conspiracy" to cover conspiracies to carry out criminal acts, not only in Ireland or against Irish citizens but also conspiracies to carry out criminal acts abroad. A notable admission was made by the Minister for Justice, Equality and Law Reform during the Oireachtas debate on Pt 7, that it would be very difficult to bring a prosecution under its terms, given the nature of the activity and the methods used by criminal gangs. Nonetheless, the view was taken that these provisions, which were based on a Canadian analogue (as with the provisions in Pt 3 of the 2006 Act, above), should be included in order to provide law enforcement agencies with all the legal powers necessary to counteract organised crime.

Misuse of drugs   Part 8 of the 2006 Act (ss.80 to 86) amended in a number of respects, the Misuse of Drugs Act 1977, as amended. The 2006 Act created two new offences, importing drugs in excess of a certain value and supplying drugs to a prison. On importing drugs, the 2006 Act attracts the so-called "mandatory" 10-year sentence; this had been put in place by the Criminal Justice Act 1999, which inserted s.12A into the Misuse of Drugs Act 1977 in connection with the possession of drugs for sale and supply. As was pointed out during the Oireachtas debate, the 1999 Act referred to "specific and exceptional circumstances" that would lead to a mandatory minimum sentence not being imposed. The 2006 Act set out more specific provisions on the circumstances in which the 10-year sentence would apply. The background to the 2006 Act included quite pointed criticism of the judiciary as to the use of the "specific and exceptional circumstances" phrase in the 1999 Act. It was noted that the number of cases in which the 10-year sentence has been imposed had increased from 4 per cent or 5 per cent in the first few years of its operation to over 20 per cent in more recent decisions.

Drugs offender notification   Part 9 of the 2006 Act (ss.87 to 97) provides for a requirement that convicted drug offenders provide notification as to their place of residence and movements. Like the comparable provisions of the Sex Offenders Act 2001, this is often referred to, inaccurately, as a requirement involving a "register". It must be noted here that neither the 2001 or 2006 Acts involve the creation of a "sex offender register" or a "drug offenders register". Rather, their aim was to provide the Gardaí with greater intelligence and information on the movement of known sex offenders and drug dealers and traffickers. The 2006 Act states that all persons convicted on indictment of a drug trafficking offence and given a sentence of one year or more, whether fully or partially suspended, are required to provide certain notification to the Gardaí regarding their place of residence and movements, including movements in and out of the country. The duration of the notification period varies according to the level of the sentence imposed. It ranges from 12 years in the case of a person who has been given a life sentence to one year in the case of a person who has received a suspended sentence.

Adjustments are made in the case of persons who are under 18 when sentenced—generally the notification period is reduced by half for them.

Sentencing   Part 10 of the 2006 Act (ss.98 to 112) makes several changes regarding the law and practice in the area of sentencing. Broadly, Pt 10 was intended to provide some alternatives to imprisonment where the court is satisfied that the offender would benefit from an opportunity to deal with his or her offending in a non-custodial way. Part 10 contains four main elements.

First, s.99 of the 2006 Act puts on a statutory basis the power of the courts to suspend all or part of a sentence. In suspending a sentence, a court may attach conditions requiring the person to be of good behaviour and to keep the peace. Section 99(11) states that any suspended sentence which is reactivated by reference to breach of the conditions must be served in addition to the sentence for any subsequent offence which triggers the reactivation of the suspended sentence.

Secondly, s.100 provides that, where the court intends to impose a fine and a custodial sentence, the court may impose a fine but may defer any custodial sentence on condition that the person keeps the peace and is of good behaviour. This allows a monetary fine to be imposed immediately and the question of a custodial sentence to be put back. Additional conditions may be attached requiring the person to deal with certain underlying issues such as drug or alcohol abuse. In this way, the new powers give the person an incentive to address the underlying cause of the offending.

Thirdly, s.101 introduces a new form of orders, restriction on movement orders. They apply where the court is proposing a sentence of three months or more imprisonment for an offence listed in Sch.3 to the 2006 Act, primarily public order and assault-type cases. The order may impose certain conditions about, for example, being, or as the case may be, not being in a specified place at specified times.

The fourth element of Pt 10 concerns electronic monitoring, or electronic tagging. The 2006 Act provides that compliance with the terms of a restriction on movement order may be monitored electronically. It may be noted that this requires the making of ministerial Regulations before becoming operational. It was indicated that electronic tagging would not be introduced immediately but was likely to be established on a pilot basis before its introduction on a wider basis.

Anti-social behaviour: adults and children Parts 11 and 13 of the 2006 Act deal with anti-social behaviour. Part 11 deals with anti-social behaviour by adults, that is persons over 18. Part 13 deals with the arrangements for children between 12 and 18 years, and involves significant amendments to the Children Act 2001. These elements of the 2006 Act attracted major criticism outside the Oireachtas, primarily on the basis that they may lead to "net-widening", the process by which behaviour that would not otherwise have attracted attention from the criminal justice system may do so. It should equally be noted here that, while there is considerable debate on the detailed provisions of the 2006 Act, there was agreement within the Oireachtas—and the media in general—that anti-social behaviour, which is often of a relatively low-level but persistent nature, is a real source of anxiety and stress for many people, such as older or vulnerable people. The provisions also gave rise to criticism because of some adverse publicity given to the experience in the United Kingdom with the legislative introduction of Anti-Social Behaviour Orders (ASBOs). The Minister for Justice, Equality and Law Reform stated during the Oireachtas debate on the 2006 Act that its provisions took account of what he described as "the apparent excesses" of the UK experience. It was noted in particular that the power to seek ASBOs under the 2006 Act would be limited to a superintendent of the Garda Síochána (in the UK, local authorities also had this power), that significant distinctions would apply as between adults and those under 18 in this area, and that failure to comply with the terms of an ASBO would not, in itself, lead to the imposition of criminal liability.

The same definition of anti-social behaviour is used in both Pt 11 and Pt 13. In both, the process begins with a warning to desist, issued by a garda. In the case of adults, failure to observe that warning can result in an application to the District Court for an order. The order is a civil order but breach of an order once it is made can give rise, as in the case of an injunction, to a criminal offence. In the case of children, the relevant provisions of Pt 13 state that the warning will be followed by a meeting convened by a Garda superintendent. The child and parents will be required to attend. The meeting may result in a "good behaviour contract" being drawn up or in the child being placed on the Garda diversion programme, which is intended to reduce the risk of future offending behaviour. The superintendent may apply to the Children's Court (the District Court) for an order if he or she is of the view that other options are unsuitable or if the good behaviour contract has been tried but has been breached.

Children and the youth justice system   We have already noted that Pt 13, which introduced provisions on anti-social behaviour involving persons under 18 years, involved amendments to the Children Act 2001. Part 12 of the 2006 Act made other amendments to the Children Act 2001, and sought to give effect to a youth justice review carried out by the Department of Justice, Equality and Law Reform. The 2006 Act therefore provides for the establishment of a Youth Justice Service, whose main function is to provide a coordinated approach to the delivery of services to young offenders. The Youth Justice Service will assume responsibility for children's detention, community sanctions, restorative justice and the full implementation of the Children Act 2001. The amendments in this part are necessary to give effect to these proposals. Part 12 provides for the transfer of responsibility for the children detention schools from the Department of Education and Science to the Department of Justice, Equality and Law Reform, in which the Youth Justice Service is located. This will bring the children detention schools under the same service that will develop the youth justice strategy, manage the delivery and development of non-custodial sanctions and coordinate youth justice services at both national and local levels. Part 12 also removes references to "children detention centres" from the 2001 Act, effectively extending the children detention school model to all children up to 18 years of age. When these changes—and the 2001 Act—are fully brought into force, no child will be detained within the prison system.

The 2006 Act also made a number of other amendments to the Children Act 2001. Thus, a court may request the attendance in court of a representative of the Health Service Executive where the court considers that (s)he could be of assistance. More controversially, the 2006 Act amended the 2001 Act in respect of the age of criminal responsibility. As enacted, the 2001 Act provided for the age of criminal responsibility to be raised from the common law's seven years of age to 12 years for all offences. This provision in the 2001 Act had not been brought into force, and the 2006 Act amended this to provide that, three months after the enactment of the 2006 Act, the 12-year age limit would apply to almost all criminal offences, with the exception of murder and rape offences, in respect of which criminal responsibility will apply from the age of ten. It is clear that, at least in respect of murder, the changes made in the 2006 Act were greatly influenced by the murder by two under-12s of the young boy Jamie Bulger in England in the 1990s.

Criminal Law Codification Advisory Committee   Part 14 provides for the establishment of a Criminal Law Codification Advisory Committee. As we noted in the *Annual Review of Irish Law 2005*, pp.261–2, *Codifying the Criminal Law* (November 2004, available at www.justice.ie), the Report of the Expert Group on the Codification of the Criminal Law (chaired by Professor Finbarr McAuley), made a detailed and compelling case for the ultimate codification of the general principles of criminal liability and the specific legislative provisions on criminal offences. The report recommended that a statutory committee be established to oversee the codification project. The Government accepted this recommendation and Pt 14 sets out the details as they relate to the committee's functions, membership, conditions of office, meetings, programme of work, funding and its annual reports.

Miscellaneous   Part 15 of the 2006 Act (ss.176 to 196) contains a number of important miscellaneous provisions, many of which involve the implementation of recommendations from the 2003 *Report of the Expert Group on Changes to the Criminal Law*, referred to above.

Reckless endangerment of children   Section 176 of the 2006 Act sets out a new offence of reckless endangerment of children, which implements a recommendation in the 2005 *Ferns Report*, the inquiry into child sexual abuse by Roman Catholic priests in the diocese of Ferns. Section 176 provides that where a person in authority, intentionally or recklessly, fails to take steps to protect a child from harm or abuse, that person is guilty of an offence. The offence carries a penalty of up to 10 years' imprisonment.

Time limit in Petty Sessions (Ireland) Act 1851   Section 177 of the 2006 Act inserted a completely new text of s.7 of the Criminal Justice Act 1951. Section 7 of the Criminal Justice Act 1951 provides that the time limits prescribed by s.10(4) of the Petty Sessions (Ireland) Act 1851 for the making of complaints in cases of summary jurisdiction (currently six months) do not apply to an indictable offence. The new s.7 of the 1951 Act clarifies that the restriction will not apply to a scheduled offence under the 1951 Act and that it will not apply to an offence that is triable either on indictment or, subject to certain conditions including the consent of the prosecution, summarily. The effect is that the six-month time limit for prosecuting offences will apply only to offences that can only be tried as summary offences. The 2006 Act also provides that the amendment does not have retrospective effect to an offence committed before the commencement of s.177.

Jurisdiction of the District Court in criminal matters   Section 79 of the Courts of Justice Act 1924 provides that the jurisdiction of the District Court may be based on any of the following three criteria: where the crime is committed, where the accused is arrested or where the accused resides. In exceptional cases where these criteria may not apply, difficulties may arise with the jurisdiction of the District Court. Section 178 of the 2006 Act inserted a new s.79A into the 1924 Act to provide for these exceptional cases. Section 79A(1) provides that where, in respect of a crime committed in the State, the accused does not reside in the State, he or she was not arrested for and charged with the crime in the State, and either the crime was committed in more than one District Court district, or it is known that it was committed in one of not more than five District Court districts, but the particular district concerned is not known, then, for the purposes of s.79 of the Act, the crime is to be deemed to have been committed in each of the districts concerned and a judge assigned to any of the districts concerned may deal with the case. Section 79A(2) provides that where the accused does not reside in the State and he or she was not arrested for and charged with the crime in the State and the District Court district in which the crime was committed is not known, then, for the purposes of s.79 of the Act, the crime is to be deemed to have been committed in the Dublin Metropolitan District. Section 79A(3) provides that a case will not fall within the section unless it is shown that reasonable efforts have been made to ascertain the whereabouts of the accused for the purposes of arresting him or her for, and charging him or her with, the crime concerned. Section 79A(4) provides that where a judge for the time being assigned to a District Court district exercises jurisdiction in a criminal case by virtue of the section, the judge or any other judge assigned to the district will have jurisdiction in the case until its conclusion in the District Court notwithstanding that it is later established that, but for this subsection, he or she would not have jurisdiction in the case. Subsection (5) provides that a judge for the time being assigned to a District Court district, who exercises jurisdiction in a criminal case by virtue of the section, may deal with the case in any court area within his or her district. Section 179 of the 2006 Act made comparable amendments to the Courts (Supplemental Provisions) Act 1961 in connection with the jurisdiction of the Circuit Court in criminal matters.

District Court: exercise of powers by judge outside district Section 180 of the 2006 Act amends the Courts (Supplemental Provisions) Act 1961 to provide that a District Court judge may, while outside his or her assigned district, issue warrants or make certain orders where he or she would be entitled to exercise the same powers while in his or her district. In this respect, s.180 seeks to reverse the effect of the decision in *Creaven v Criminal Assets Bureau* [2004] 4 I.R. 434, in which the Supreme Court decided that a District Court judge must be present in his or her own district in order to have jurisdiction to issue a warrant. In the *Creaven* case, the District Court judge had been appointed temporarily to a number of different District Court districts outside Dublin and had issued warrants to search in relation to each district. The Supreme Court held that the legislation governing the District Court gave effect to a consistent policy for the exercise of the powers of District Court judges by reference to districts to which they are assigned. However, the Supreme Court ruled that there was no objection to a judge of the District Court being assigned simultaneously to more than one district. The court held that a District Court judge could not exercise his or her jurisdiction to issue a search warrant while he or she was physically outside his or her district. Under s.180 of the 2006 Act, a District Court judge may exercise his or her jurisdiction to issue a search warrant regardless of whether he or she is outside the district for which he or she is responsible under the law. This also complements the changes made by s.178 of the 2006 Act (see above).

Anonymity of certain witnesses Section 181 of the 2006 Act makes provision for anonymity for witnesses with a medical condition. Section 181(1) provides that in any criminal proceedings where it is proposed to call a person to give evidence, and the person has a medical condition, an application can be made for an order prohibiting the publication of anything related to the proceedings which would identify the person as a person having that condition. Section 181(2) provides that the application for the order can be made at any stage of the proceedings. Section 181(3) provides that the judge may make the order if satisfied the person concerned has a medical condition, and his or her identification as a person with that condition would be likely to cause undue distress to him or her, and that the order would not be prejudicial to the interests of justice. Section 181(8) provides that it is an offence to publish or broadcast anything in contravention of an order under the section, punishable by a fine of €25,000 or imprisonment for up to three years or both. Section 181(9) provides a defence that the person was not aware, nor did they suspect, that the publication or broadcast could identify the person as having the medical condition.

Information concerning property held in trust   Section 182 of the 2006 Act deals with information concerning property held in trust. Section 182(1) provides that in relation to an investigation into whether a person has committed an arrestable offence, a member of the Garda Síochána not below the rank of superintendent may apply to a judge of the High Court for an order for the disclosure of information regarding any trust in which the person may have an interest or with which the person may be otherwise connected. Section 182(2) provides that the judge may order the disclosure of the information if he or she is satisfied that there are reasonable grounds for suspecting that a person has committed an arrestable offence and has some interest in or other connection with the trust, that information regarding the trust is required for the purposes of such an investigation, and that there are reasonable grounds for believing that it is in the public interest that the information should be disclosed. Section 182(3) provides that an order under the section cannot interfere with legal privilege but can have effect notwithstanding other restrictions on disclosure imposed by statute or otherwise. Section 182(5) creates an offence of failing to comply with an order or giving false or misleading information which is punishable on summary conviction by a fine not exceeding €3000 or up to 12 months' imprisonment or both. On indictment the penalties are an unlimited fine or imprisonment for up to five years or both. Section 182(6) provides that information disclosed by a person is not admissible in evidence in any criminal proceedings against the person or his or her spouse, except in any proceedings for an offence under s.182(5).

Possession of article intended for use in connection with certain offences   Section 183 of the 2006 Act makes it an offence to be in possession of an article, as defined, which is intended for use in connection with certain offences and provides that a court or jury, having regard to all the circumstances and where it is reasonable to do so, may regard such possession as sufficient evidence for the purposes of the committing of the offences referred to.

Fixed charge offences: public order   Section 184 of the 2006 Act introduced a system of fixed charges for certain public order offences under the Criminal Justice (Public Order) Act 1994 by inserting two new sections, s.23A and s.23B, into the 1994 Act. Under the amendments made by the 2006 Act, a garda may issue a notice to a person in respect of two offences under the 1994 Act, disorderly conduct in a public place (s.5 of the 1994 Act) and being intoxicated in a public place (s.4 of the 1994 Act). The notice will specify the details of the offence and will indicate that if the charge is paid within a specified time, no further proceedings will arise. This was intended to allow greater flexibility to Gardaí in dealing with public order offences. As we pointed out in the *Annual Review of Irish Law 2005*, p.512, while on one view these changes may lead to less convictions under ss.4 and 5 of the 1994 Act, they may also have the ultimate effect of criminalising some homeless people who are also alcoholics.

Assault of emergency personnel Section 185 of the 2006 Act extended s.19 of the Criminal Justice (Public Order) Act 1994 to protect those, such as firemen and ambulance crews, engaged in providing emergency services and those working in the accident and emergency departments of hospitals. Section 185 creates offences of assaulting or impeding such staff and they carry a penalty of up to seven years' imprisonment.

United Nations Convention Against Torture Section 186 of the 2006 Act amended s.1 of the Criminal Justice (United Nations Convention against Torture) Act 2000 to clarify that the offence of torture is one that is done by, or with the acquiescence of, a public official and thereby bring the definition into line with that contained in the Convention.

Offences against the State Act 1939 Section 187 of the 2006 Act made two changes to the Offences against the State Act 1939. Section 187(*a*) provides that where a detention period under s.30 of the Offences against the State Act 1939 expires during the course of a hearing of an application to extend that period, the period is considered to expire when the application is determined. This change reverses the effect of the decision in *Finnegan v Member in Charge (Santry Garda Station)* [2006] I.E.H.C. 79; High Court, March 8, 2006. In *Finnegan* the applicant had been arrested at 10.55 p.m. on March 5, 2006 under s.30 of the 1939 Act. At the end of the 24-hour period of detention in the 1939 Act, his period of detention was extended for a further period of 24 hours. Just prior to the expiration of that additional period, an application was made to the District Court pursuant to s.30(4) of the 1939 Act (as inserted by s.10 of Offences Against the State (Amendment) Act 1998) for a further extension of the detention of the applicant for up to 24 hours. The order was granted at 11.20 p.m. on March 7, 2006. The applicant contended that s.30(4)(c) made clear that, if he was not charged or was not directed to be released within the period of detention, he must be released on the expiry of the detention period and it was submitted that a District Court judge had no power to extend the time period. The respondents submitted that, if there was a defect, it could be cured and that s.8(a) of the Criminal Justice Act 1984, as inserted by s.2 of the Criminal Justice (Miscellaneous Provisions) Act 1997, applied (by virtue of s.9 of the Criminal Justice Act 1984) to this situation, and that therefore the time spent on the application in the District Court was not reckonable in the 24-hour period. O'Neill J. accepted the applicant's submissions and ordered his release. He held that statutory periods of detention could not be extended by court orders and could only be extended if there was an express legislative provision to that effect (which s.187(a) of the 2006 Act has now provided). O'Neill J. noted that penal legislation had to be construed strictly and the language of the statute had to be given its natural and ordinary meaning and a purposive approach was not appropriate. He considered that it was significant that s.2(d) of the Criminal Justice (Miscellaneous Provisions) Act 1997 amended s.4(9) of the 1984 Act by including an express reference to s.8(a) of the 1984 Act, whereas the provisions of s.8(a) of the 1984 Act was not included for the purpose of an amendment of s.9 of the 1984 Act. Such an express omission could not be ignored by the court and s.8(a) of the 1984 Act was not imported into s.9 of the 1984 Act so as to affect a detention under s.30 of the 1939 Act. He concluded that the effect of the ending of lawful detention at 10.55 p.m. was that the necessary jurisdictional basis for the granting of the warrant had disappeared. While the applicant in *Finnegan* was released, we have already noted that s.187(a) of the 2006 Act has reversed the effect of the decision.

Section 187(*b*) of the 2006 Act made another change to s.30A(3) of the 1939 Act (inserted by the 1998 Act) by the substitution of "for the purpose of charging him or her with that offence forthwith or bringing him or her before a Special Criminal Court as soon as practicable so that he or she may be charged with that offence before that Court" "for the purpose of charging him with that offence forthwith". The effect is that the requirement to charge the person before the Special Criminal Court is "as soon as practicable" whereas it remains "forthwith" for other courts.

Forensic Science Laboratory   Section 188 of the 2006 Act amended s.5 of the Criminal Evidence Act 1992 to the effect that documentary evidence of the receipt, handling, transmission and storage of anything by the Forensic Science Laboratory can be admitted in court.

Proceeds of Crime Act 1996   Section 189 of the 2006 Act amended s.16B(7) of the Proceeds of Crime Act 1996 by inserting "of the Criminal Assets Bureau Act 1996" after "Sections 14 to 14C".

Search warrants   Section 190 (which amended s.14 of the Criminal Assets Bureau Act 1996), s.191 (which amended s.5 of the Prevention of Corruption (Amendment) Act 2001) and s.192 (which amended the Criminal Justice (Theft and Fraud Offences) Act 2001) each provide that a judge, in granting a search warrant, be satisfied in relation to the need for the warrant by "information on oath" as opposed to "hearing evidence on oath". This brought the relevant statutory provisions into line with the wording of the search provision in s.10 of the Criminal Justice (Miscellaneous Provisions) Act 1997 as amended by s.6 of the 2006 Act and with the language used in other statutory search provisions.

Warrants addressed to Garda Síochána   Section 193 amended s.25 of the Petty Sessions (Ireland) Act 1851 to provide that all warrants (except as otherwise provided by law) in criminal proceedings issued by the District Court are to be addressed to the superintendent or an inspector of the Garda Síochána in the Garda Síochána district within which the place where the warrant is issued is situated or the person named in the warrant resides.

Execution of arrest warrants and committal orders Section 194 provides that a warrant for the arrest of a person or an order of committal of a person may, notwithstanding s.26 of the Petty Sessions (Ireland) Act 1851, be executed by a member of the Garda Síochána in any part of the State.

Imprisonment or distress and sale of goods on conviction on indictment in default of payment of fine Section 195 provides for imprisonment or distress and sale of goods in default of payment of a fine imposed on conviction on indictment for an offence. It is similar in principle to a provision in the Courts (No.2) Act 1986 concerning the power of the District Court where there is default on payment of a fine imposed on summary conviction.

Escape from custody Section 196 of the 2006 Act increases from £500 to €3000 the maximum level of fine which may be imposed on summary conviction for an offence of aiding or facilitating any person escaping or attempting to escape from custody.

Insanity review Section 197 of the 2006 Act deleted s.13(1) of the Criminal Law (Insanity) Act 2006; this is discussed separately, below, p.338.

BREACH OF THE PEACE

In *Thorpe v DPP* [2006] I.E.H.C. 319, High Court, February 17, 2006, Murphy J. held that the offence of breach of the peace contrary to common law was an offence known to the law. The applicant had been charged in the District Court with breach of the peace contrary to common law. On a case stated, he argued that a breach of the peace contrary to common law involved a power of entry and arrest but was not of itself an offence. He also submitted that the District Court had no jurisdiction to impose a penalty as no specific penalty in respect of the charge was known, and that the law governing breach of the peace was a preventative law and that the offence was not consistent with the Constitution and could not be a criminal offence where there was no penalty specified to deal with it. The respondent argued that the offence was known to law and as a common law offence was subject to the sentencing limits of the District Court. Murphy J. answered the questions posed in the case stated by noting that *Attorney General v Cunningham* [1932] I.R. 28 and *Kelly v O'Sullivan*, High Court, July 11, 1990 (*Annual Review of Irish Law 1990*, pp.197–8) were authority in this jurisdiction for the statement that the offence of breach of the peace contrary to common law is known to the law. He held that the category of common law breach of the peace may be sub-divided into a breach of the peace which is an offence and a breach of the peace which is not. It could, therefore, also be an act for preventative justice in which a person is bound over to keep the peace. He concluded that the offence may be prosecuted in the District Court and the penalty which would be imposed on conviction was a matter for the District Court acting within the sentencing limits of that court.

DELAY

Indictable offences: child sexual abuse   In *DK v DPP*, Supreme Court, July 3, 2006, the appellant sought to challenge a decision of the High Court in judicial review proceedings refusing the appellant an order of prohibition in respect of his trial on charge of rape and indecent assault of his daughter. The appellant was clearly in a position of dominance in respect of the complainant by virtue of the father–daughter relationship. The delay in making the complaint was based on the complainant's psychiatric condition and on her fear of her father. The Supreme Court allowed the appeal, concluding that there was a real risk that the appellant would not receive a fair trial. The appellant would suffer specific prejudice if the trial was allowed to proceed on the basis that there was an absence of relevant medical notes concerning the complainant, the appellant's wife had died, another central witness had died, an unnamed and unidentified garda had interviewed the complainant in the early 1990s but had not been traced and the complainant suffered from severe psychiatric difficulties. Any of these concerns on their own might not warrant the granting of the reliefs sought but, taken together, the court concluded that the rights of the appellant would be prejudiced if the trial were allowed to proceed. The court noted that the appellant's wife, the complainant's mother, had died in 1995 and a number of witness statements would be hampered by her absence at the trial. The appellant also asserted that his wife could have given important evidence. She was a trained nurse and certainly when the complainant was young, she used to bath the complainant regularly. It seemed that if there had been regular sexual assaults on the complainant in her pre-teen years, it was likely that this would have been evident to her mother. While the court was satisfied that the delay in making the complaint was explicable and should not of itself justify the relief sought, the court was also satisfied that there was a real and serious risk of an unfair trial which could not be avoided by the giving of directions or rulings by the trial judge. The absence of relevant medical notes concerning the psychiatric history of the complainant was another significant factor. The notes were unavailable to the defence due in part to the refusal of the complainant herself to authorise the release of health board records. Given the exceptional importance of the psychiatric condition of the complainant, this would clearly disadvantage the accused.

By contrast, in *TH v DPP*, Supreme Court, July 25 2006, the respondent appealed against a decision of the High Court restraining him from prosecuting the applicant on the grounds of delay. The applicant had taken judicial review proceedings which were ultimately unsuccessful but which had delayed his criminal trial. He then sought to prohibit the trial on the grounds of delay, arguing that the respondent was responsible for much of the delay in the judicial review proceedings. He also argued that this had caused him a considerable amount of stress and anxiety. The High Court granted the relief sought. The Supreme Court reversed and allowed the appeal. The court held that the applicant was the initiator of the entire judicial review process and that those proceedings were without merit. In an appropriate case where there has been such extreme and reprehensible delay on the part of the State authorities in handling judicial review proceedings, restraint on further prosecution may be justified. But in this case, large periods of delay were the responsibility of the applicant. While there was significant delay on the part of the respondent, the principal if not the only reason for the failure to get the prosecution underway was that the applicant had brought unfounded judicial review proceedings. In the course of those proceedings the applicant had conducted a sort of war of attrition with the respondent in respect of discovery, from which he secured minimal benefit. The court concluded that the applicant was unable to point to any real risk of an unfair trial.

Indictable offences: child sexual abuse and the "dominion" issue In *H v DPP* [2006] I.E.S.C. 55; [2007] 1 I.L.R.M. 401 the Supreme Court delivered a definitive judgment on the approach to be taken in cases involving child sexual abuse. In many such cases in recent years, the courts have examined, as a preliminary question, whether the extent to which the alleged perpetrator exercised "dominion" or control over the complainant had led to the delay in making a complaint of the alleged crime. In the *H* case, the Supreme Court held that this preliminary question should be subsumed within the general question as to whether any delay, whether by the complainant leading up to the complaint or by the authorities after the complaint, would lead to prejudice and impair the defendant's right to a fair trial. This new approach was subsequently applied in a series of decisions of the court in 2006.

Thus, in *JK v DPP*, Supreme Court, October 27, 2006, the applicant appealed against a decision of the High Court (Smyth J.), refusing him an injunction prohibiting the respondent from further prosecuting him on 19 charges of sexual offences alleged to have been committed by him against three of his near relatives. Dismissing the appeal, the court held that the new test to be applied from *H v DPP* was whether there was a real or serious risk that the applicant, by reason of the delay, would not obtain a fair trial, or that a trial would be unfair as a consequence of the delay. The test was to be applied in light of the circumstances of the case. Thus, the first inquiry as to the reasons for the delay in making a complaint need no longer be made. The test of a real or serious risk of an unfair trial applied to prosecutorial delay as it did to complainant delay. The court considered that the applicant had not made out a sufficient case to establish that the items of specific prejudice would prevent him from receiving a fair trial. While the court accepted that the length of time which would have elapsed between the date of the alleged offences and the date of trial would cause difficulties to the applicant in his defence, the court considered that these difficulties could be mitigated by rulings and directions on the part of the trial judge. The delays there had been in the process of the prosecution did not amount to a denial of the applicant's right to both a fair and to an expeditious trial. Nor did the court accept that the applicant's present age and health problems amounted to such wholly exceptional circumstances that his trial should be prohibited.

In *JB v DPP*, Supreme Court, November 29, 2006, the applicant had been returned for trial on 14 charges of indecent assault on five nieces on dates between March 1971 and March 1987. It was argued that his trial should be prohibited by reason of the lapse of time in the institution and prosecution of the criminal proceedings. In the High Court, Ó Caoimh J. had granted the injunctive relief sought in respect of some charges but not all of them. On appeal, the applicant also argued that this was an exceptional case to which *H v DPP* did not apply. The first statement of complaint giving rise to the proceedings was made in September 1996, but the applicant was not returned for trial until June 2000. The High Court found that in each case, except in respect of those concerning one complainant, there was an appropriate reason for the delay in making a complaint against the applicant and that no real or serious risk of an unfair trial existed. On appeal, the Supreme Court affirmed the High Court decision. The court held that the new test in *H v DPP* did apply, namely, that in general there was no necessity to hold an inquiry into, or to establish the reasons for, delay in making a complaint; the issue for the court was whether the delay had resulted in prejudice to an accused so as to give rise to a real or serious risk of an unfair trial. Thus, a psychological analysis of complainants and the reason why they did not make a complaint as children was no longer required. In the present case, the court held that the applicant had failed to establish that there was a real or serious risk of an unfair trial or that he had suffered stress or anxiety so as to require prohibition of his trial. The fact that an application for a prohibition has not succeeded does not dispense a judge from his constitutional duty to ensure due process in the trial. By its very nature the delay in this case would be a matter for a trial judge to consider and address from several aspects. While there had been inordinate delay in this case, the court held that there was no evidence that it had jeopardised the applicant's right to a fair trial. While the delay had been inordinate the applicant had not established blameworthy prosecutorial delay.

In *SB v DPP*, Supreme Court, December 21, 2006, the High Court (Smyth J.) had granted injunctive relief to the applicant in respect of 32 charges of indecent assault. Of these, 30 alleged indecent assault on JR, a patient in a hospital in which the applicant had been a nurse between 27 and 31 years ago. The complainant alleged that he was first abused when he was awoken while sleeping on a ward and was taken to the office of the ward where he was assaulted. The complainant alleged that he had made a complaint to two nurses after the incidents occurred and that they gave him an injection and put him to sleep having told him they would talk to a doctor. All three, the doctor and the two nurses, were deceased. A formal complaint was not made until 1999. The hospital records showing the precise days that the applicant actually worked on night duty in the relevant ward were lost because they are routinely destroyed after 10 years. On appeal, the Supreme Court agreed that the charges on counts 1 to 30 should be prohibited. The court applied the test in *H v DPP*, namely, whether there was a real or serious risk that the applicant, by reason of the delay, would not obtain a fair trial, or that a trial would be unfair as a consequence of the delay. In this case the utility of the lost records was so obvious that the court found a real risk of an unfair trial to arise from their absence even if there was no further evidence. Since the two nurses and doctor to whom complaints were allegedly made were deceased, the applicant was deprived of any possibility of contradicting the making of the complaint, itself admissible to show consistency on the part of the complainant. The applicant had thus lost the real possibility of an obviously useful line of defence. Once the prosecution and the complainant had committed themselves firmly to a list of allegations, the demonstration of the impossibility of one, or certainly of any significant number, was a blow to the credibility of the prosecution case as a whole. But, in connection with the two remaining charges, the court was not convinced that the applicant had shown a real risk of unfairness in relation to these counts and therefore ordered that the trial proceed on those counts.

DURESS AND NECESSITY

In 2006 the Law Reform Commission published a *Consultation Paper on Duress and Necessity* (LRC CP 39–2006). As the paper explained, the defences of duress and necessity apply where an individual is constrained or coerced into committing a crime by reason of serious threats (duress) or dire circumstances (necessity). In many cases the defences are discussed in relation to homicide, but they also apply to other offences, ranging from receiving stolen property to unlawful possession of firearms. A common example of the defence of duress is the "do this or else" form, in which a person is faced with threats of death or serious harm, unless they commit a crime. For example, in the leading Irish case on duress, *Attorney General v Whelan* [1934] I.R. 518, the defendant was charged with receiving stolen money. He admitted that he had accepted the money but said that he had done so under duress from another man, who had been armed with a revolver. The jury found that he had been under threats of "immediate death or serious personal violence" and so duress was available as a defence.

The defence of necessity arises when a person finds themselves in a situation where their choice is constrained and they must commit an offence because of that circumstance. An example of this arose in the sinking of the ferry, the *Herald of Free Enterprise*, at Zeebrugge in 1987. As the ferry was sinking a man on the ship pushed another man to his death because he was frozen with fear and blocking the escape route for several others. Although he was not prosecuted, most commentators consider that the defence of necessity would have applied here.

On the defence of duress, the Commission provisionally recommends that its current limitations should remain. These include that the threat must be of death or serious harm; the target of the threats need not necessarily be a relative or close friend of the accused; the accused's resistance must have been overcome, and this resistance must be that of the ordinary person, with the characteristics of the accused person; the accused should have tried to seek official protection before taking the action that he did; and if the accused subjected himself to the risk of threats, for example, by joining a criminal gang, he will not be allowed to avail of the defence.

Although the defence does not apply to murder, the Commission provisionally recommends that it should be allowed as a partial defence, which would reduce it from murder to manslaughter. Moreover, while acknowledging that the plea might be made available as a partial defence to those offences, the Commission accepts that a coherent case can also be made for treating duress as a complete defence where the accused's actions can be justified on the grounds that the person chose the lesser of two evils, and invites submissions on this matter.

On the defence of necessity, the Commission provisionally recommends that it should be retained in its current form so that it would apply in certain exceptional circumstances where a person is faced with a constrained choice regarding his or her actions, the constraint arising from extraneous circumstances, and where the person, in choosing the course of action taken, breaks the law. As with duress, the Commission accepts that a coherent case can also be made for treating necessity as a complete defence where the accused's actions can be justified on the grounds of lesser evils, and invites submissions on this matter.

EUROPOL

The Europol (Amendment) Act 2006 amended the Europol Act 1997 (*Annual Review of Irish Law 1997*, pp.376–379), which gave effect to the Convention on the Establishment of the European Police Office, Europol. The 2006 Act gave effect in Irish law to three Protocols to the Europol Convention, the Protocols of November 30, 2000, November 28, 2002 and November 27, 2003.

The 2000 Protocol extended the competence of Europol to money-laundering regardless of the type of offences from which the laundered proceeds originate. The 2002 Protocol clarified certain powers in relation to participation in joint investigation teams by members of Europol and the privileges and immunity applying to members of Europol. The 2003 Protocol streamlined the internal working of Europol, particularly in relation to liaison procedures and analysis and processing of data (2003 Protocol). Section 1 of the 2006 Act amended s.1(1) of the Europol Act 1997 by adding definitions of the 2000, 2002 and 2003 Protocols. Section 2 of the 2006 Act amended s.2 of the Europol Act 1997 to give force of law in the State to the three Protocols and to provide for judicial notice to be taken of them. Section 3 of the 2006 Act amended s.6(1) of the Europol Act 1997 by providing that the Data Protection Acts 1988 and 2003 apply for the purposes of the Europol Act 1997, the Europol Convention and the five Protocols to the Convention in relation to the collection, processing, keeping, use or disclosure of certain information relating to individuals that is processed automatically at Europol.

EXTRADITION

Rule of specialty In *Attorney General v Russell*, High Court, May 23, 2006, Peart J. ordered the respondent's extradition to the United States under the Extradition Act 1965 in the following circumstances. The respondent's extradition was sought so that he could stand trial on three charges of vehicular homicide, three charges of vehicular assault, one charge of forgery and one charge of theft. The charges followed a multiple-vehicle collision in Washington state in 2001 in which three people died. The respondent was released on bail, but failed to appear at a hearing in 2001 and a bench warrant was issued for his arrest. An application was made for a warrant for the arrest of the respondent who was known to be living and working in the State under an assumed name. That warrant was issued and in October 2005 the respondent was arrested in Dublin. The respondent sought to resist his extradition arguing that the rule of specialty would be breached and its protection unavailable if his extradition was directed and that, if extradited, there was a real risk that his right to life would be imperilled and that he was likely to be exposed to inhumane and degrading punishment in breach of his constitutional rights and rights guaranteed under the European Convention on Human Rights. As indicated, Peart J. ordered his extradition.

Citing *US v Andonian* 29 F.3d. 1432 and *US v LeBaron* 156 F.3d. 621, he noted that, although the US courts had deemed that it was not a breach of the specialty rule to proceed against the respondent in respect of charges which had not been themselves the subject of the extradition requests in previous cases, this did not mean that the rule of speciality would not be observed if the respondent was extradited in the present case. Peart J. was satisfied that the provisions of the 1983 Treaty on Extradition between Ireland and the United States, to the effect that a person must not be punished in respect of any offence other than the offence for which extradition was granted, would be observed. Citing *R. (Bermingham) v Director of the Serious Fraud Office* [2006] All E.R. 268 and *Welsh v Secretary of State for the Home Department* [2006] All E.R. 289, he was also satisfied that to take into account such other conduct for the purpose of calculating or arriving at the appropriate sentence or punishment for the extradition offence, even if it could give rise to another offence if charged, did not amount to punishment for another offence; rather it was simply a process by which the appropriate sentence for the extradition offence was arrived at, and was not, therefore, a breach of the rule of specialty. Nor did he consider that there was sufficient evidence that there was a real risk, much less a likelihood, that should the respondent be returned to face trial his life would be at risk. Peart J. concluded that the treatment envisaged to be afforded to the respondent if extradited would not amount to inhumane and degrading treatment.

GENOCIDE, CRIMES AGAINST HUMANITY, WAR CRIMES AND THE INTERNATIONAL CRIMINAL COURT

The International Criminal Court Act 2006 follows from the 2001 referendum which ratified the 1998 Rome Statute of the International Criminal Court (*Annual Review of Irish Law 2001*, pp.196–199). The 2006 Act also involves significant changes to domestic criminal law, because it also provides for the prosecution in the courts in this State (and, where relevant, by courts-martial) of genocide, crimes against humanity, war crimes and other offences within the jurisdiction of the International Criminal Court. The 2006 Act also enables effect to be given to requests by the International Criminal Court for assistance in the investigation or prosecution of those offences, including requests to arrest and surrender persons, to freeze assets and to enforce any fines or forfeitures imposed by it. Finally, the 2006 Act also makes provision in relation to any sittings of the court that may be held in the State.

In terms of effect on Irish criminal law, Pt 2 has the greatest impact as it establishes domestic jurisdiction for ICC offences. Thus, s.7(1) of the 2006 Act states:

> "Any person who commits genocide, a crime against humanity or a war crime is guilty of an offence."

Each of these offences are defined in s.6 of the 2006 Act by reference to the definitions in the 1998 Rome Statute of the ICC. The definition of genocide is wider than that in the Genocide Act 1973, which is repealed by s.7(2) of the

2006 Act (but without prejudice to the need to prosecute under the 1973 Act in respect of acts committed before the 2006 Act came into force). Similarly, the definition of war crimes in the 2006 Act is wider than that under the Geneva Convention, which it also replaces. The ICC Statute—and the 2006 Act—create a completely new offence of crimes against humanity. Ancillary offences are created in s.8, while new offences against the administration of justice either before the ICC or before an Irish court considering an ICC offence are created in s.11. Sections 9 and 10 require the consent of the DPP before initiating these proceedings, while the gravity of these crimes is reflected in their applicable sentences which correspond to the penalties in the Rome Statute, that is to say, life for murder or where the seriousness of the offence justifies same and, in all other circumstances, imprisonment for up to 30 years depending on the nature of the offence. The courts may also order a fine or forfeiture in accordance with Art.77 of the 1998 Rome Statute. In such instances, the Criminal Justice Act 1994 is triggered to facilitate enforcement of the orders.

Part 3 deals with requests for arrest and surrender of persons to the ICC in connection with the investigation, prosecution of an ICC offence or, alternatively, surrender to a state of enforcement for the enforcement of an ICC sentence. This Part implements the requirement in Art.91(2)(c) of the 1998 Rome Statute that the requirements are not more burdensome than those applicable to extradition requests in treaties to which the State is a party. This Part is informed on the basis that it is a matter for the ICC and not either the Minister or the High Court to question the validity or authorisation of a warrant. The Minister may seek further information in support of a request and the High Court may consider the execution of the warrant of arrest and whether the rights of the individual have been respected during the arrest. Any matters concerning whether the warrant of arrest was properly issued are to be considered by the ICC, and Art.59 of the statute provides accordingly. If the request conflicts in any way with the State's obligations under diplomatic immunity, it is presumed that it is a matter for the ICC to resolve these issues under Art.98 of the statute in advance of making the request.

Sections 16 to 19 establish the basis for receipt of an ICC request for the arrest and surrender of the requested person. The arrangements are similar to those under the International War Crimes Tribunals Act 1998 in that once a request is received and certified by the Minister to be in order, a warrant of arrest is issued by the High Court. That court is the relevant one in so far as this Part is concerned because of the serious nature of the crimes within the remit of the ICC. This should not result in any significant increase in the work of the High Court as it is not expected that there will be a large volume of cases under this legislation. It is also appropriate that these requests are considered by a superior court because the ICC may request the surrender of a person who has not yet been charged with, much less prosecuted or convicted of, a crime. There are also safeguards from an ICC perspective in that the prosecutor must satisfy the pre-trial chamber of the ICC that there are "reasonable grounds to believe that the person has committed a crime within the jurisdiction of the ICC".

The other significant difference from domestic criminal investigation and prosecution is that, in urgent cases, a person may be detained on a provisional arrest warrant issued by the High Court for up to 60 days, as required by the statute, pending the receipt of a formal request from the ICC. While provisional arrest warrants are not unusual in extradition proceedings, this detention period is in contrast to a maximum detention of 18 days in extradition cases. Section 18 of the 2006 Act provides for a situation where there is an extradition request competing with the ICC request. If the competing request is received from another state or from a third state where no international obligation exists to comply with the request, the 2006 Act gives priority to the ICC request. Where there is an international obligation to consider, the 2006 Act lists the factors to be taken into account before any decision is reached. These factors include the dates the respective requests were received, the nationality of the requested persons, the territory of the offence and the possibility of subsequent surrender between the ICC and the requesting state. In terms of extradition within the EU, s.30(3) of the European Arrest Warrant Act 2003 provides for priority to be given to ICC requests over EU requests. Once arrested, ss.22 to 26 require that a person be shown a copy of a warrant of arrest either at the time of arrest or within 24 hours of arrest and also require that the person be brought immediately before the High Court. The court, on being satisfied that there are no outstanding issues of admissibility, may make an order for surrender to take place not earlier than 15 days after the making of the order.

INSANITY AND DIMINISHED RESPONSIBILITY

Criminal Law (Insanity) Act 2006   The Criminal Law (Insanity) Act 2006 sets out for the first time in legislative form all the rules governing the criminal responsibility of mentally ill persons who may have committed criminal offences, including fitness to plead, the plea of insanity, the introduction of a plea of diminished responsibility and related amendments of the Infanticide Act 1949. Many of the previous common law and statutory rules were based on 19th-century conceptions of mental illness and so the 2006 Act provides a modern basis for this area of the law and brings it into line with the jurisprudence of the European Convention on Human Rights. The 2006 Act repealed in full the Criminal Lunatics Act 1800 and the Trial of Lunatics Act 1883. The Criminal Law (Insanity) Act 2006 (Commencement) Order 2006 (S.I. No. 273 of 2006) brought the 2006 Act (other than s.13(1)) into force on June 1, 2006.

The 2006 Act began its legislative life as the Criminal Law (Insanity) Bill 2002 and, indeed, the main reforms it provides for can be traced to the recommendations in the 1978 *Third Report of the Interdepartmental Committee on Mentally Ill and Maladjusted Persons*, chaired by Henchy J. The establishment of that committee had been referred to in the Department of Justice's 1962 *Programme of Law Reform*, which had noted the need to modernise the rules in this area, and which had to some extent been influenced by the (then recent) introduction of the plea of diminished responsibility in the UK in the late 1950s. In summary, therefore, this aspect of reform of the criminal law could not be faulted for being precipitous.

In summary, the 2006 Act contains extensive new provisions dealing with fitness to be tried and new rules relating to appeals against such findings; a statutory definition and restatement of the test of criminal insanity as it is understood in common law; a new verdict of "not guilty by reason of insanity" and a new plea of "guilty but with diminished responsibility" in cases of murder; and the establishment of a new review body, the Mental Health (Criminal Law) Review Board. The 2006 Act thus complements the reform of the civil law aspects of mental illness in the Mental Health Act 2001, which provided for the first time a basis for the review of the involuntary detention of persons with mental illness.

Objectives of criminal law During the passage of the 2006 Act it was pointed out that it involves a number of significant policy issues. First, the social protection role of the criminal law, under which if accused persons are found to have been insane at the time the offence was committed, they will be subject to a special regime of detention, until such time as they no longer pose a danger to themselves or to society. The second policy issue is that the State also has to balance this duty of protection with its responsibility to preserve and protect the rights of the accused person who has committed no crime in law. The third consideration is the moral distinction that must be drawn between those who are "bad" and those who do not have the mental capacity to commit crimes. In this context, the Minister for Justice, Equality and Law Reform quoted with approval the following passage from McAuley and McCutcheon, *Criminal Liability* (Thomson Round Hall, 2000):

> "Legal and medical evaluations of the conditions that might properly attract the label of 'insanity' can differ profoundly. The law regards several conditions, such as epilepsy and hypoglycaemia, that medical professionals do not classify as mental disorders, as a basis for the insanity defence. This highlights the different perspectives of the relevant disciplines and it should be realised that the defence raises a legal question of responsibility, not an issue of medical diagnosis and classification. Nevertheless, it is invariably the case that medical evidence is adduced at trial and, it can be assumed, is taken into account in the determination of the defendant's sanity. Thus, while a degree of congruence between the medical and legal evaluations can be expected, the ultimate resolution of the issue is one of law, not medicine."

The Minister noted that this fundamental difference between the medical and legal perspectives on mental illness illustrated why the 2006 Act adopts two different definitions of "mental disorder", one for the purposes of the criminal law and the other for the purposes of dealing with the accused person following the court's arrival at a verdict of not guilty by reason of insanity or unfitness to be tried on the basis of the definition in the Mental Health Act 2001.

Nature of insanity defence   The Minister for Justice, Equality and Law Reform noted during the Oireachtas debate that the defence of insanity is, in fact, an acquittal but that the plea is also unique amongst the defences in criminal law in two important respects. First, the accused person bears the burden of establishing the defence. Secondly, even though a person is acquitted by reason of insanity, he or she nevertheless loses his/her liberty because the 2006 Act provides for detention in designated centres, including the Central Mental Hospital (prior to the 2006 Act, only detention in the Central Mental Hospital was provided for).

The Minister also noted that a person's state of mind is relevant in criminal law proceedings in two ways. First, the person must be mentally fit to plead to the charge. If it is shown that the person, because of insanity, is unable at the time of the trial to understand the charge against him or her, the difference between guilty and not guilty, or is unable to instruct counsel or to challenge jurors, the trial cannot proceed, essentially because its fairness cannot be guaranteed due to the person's condition. The test at common law to be followed in such instances was laid down by the Supreme Court in *State (C) v Minister for Justice* [1968] I.R. 106. This test is not limited to any particular definition of insanity; it simply assesses the person's ability to comprehend what is going on at the time of the proceedings. Prior to the 2006 Act, if the person was found to be unfit to plead, s.17 of the Lunacy (Ireland) Act 1821 provided that he or she should be detained in strict custody until the pleasure of the Government be known. Secondly, where the person is found fit to plead, the trial will proceed but the person may raise the defence of insanity. The law will presume that the person is legally sane and, if over the age of 14, is fully accountable for his or her actions. However, if the person is able to show, on a balance of probabilities as opposed to beyond reasonable doubt, that at the time the offence was committed he or she was legally insane, he or she will have a defence to the charge. In these circumstances, the person will be deemed to have lacked the necessary *mens rea* or mental capacity to commit the crime as charged and will not, therefore, be held accountable. The test applied is based on the *M'Naghten Rules*, originally set out in 1843. Prior to the 2006 Act the law required that it must be shown that a person must have suffered, at the time of his or her act, from a defect of reason due to disease of the mind so that he or she did not know what he or she was doing, or did not know that it was wrong.

Mental disorder   Turning to the detailed provisions of the 2006 Act, s.1 defines the term "mental disorder" for the purpose of findings of "fitness to be tried" (s.4), "not guilty by reason of insanity" (s.5) and "diminished responsibility" (s.6). "Mental disorder" is defined for these purposes to include "mental illness, mental disability, dementia or any disease of the mind but does not include intoxication." It was emphasised that this is for the purpose of establishing criminal liability only, so that it differs from the civil definition of "mental disorder" for the purpose of detaining somebody in or committing somebody to a mental hospital under the Mental Health Act 2001. While the definition is not fully inclusive, the essential element for the court, for example, where criminal insanity is pleaded, is whether the accused had the *mens rea* to commit the offence for which he or she is charged. The definition of mental disorder plus the criteria in s.5 are intended to be the test for the court in coming to a decision on that issue.

Designated centre   Section 3 deals with the designation of a place as a "designated centre". It provides that it is a matter for the Minister for Health and Children in consultation with the Mental Health Commission, or the Minister for Justice, Equality and Law Reform in the case of the designation of a prison as such a centre, to decide where is the most appropriate place for the treatment of persons committed to detention under the Act. This largely follows the recommendations of the Henchy Committee, but the designation of a prison as a designated centre had not been so recommended. The 2006 Act included thus to cater for what was described as rare and exceptional situations where it might be considered appropriate in all the circumstances to detain a person in a prison rather in a psychiatric hospital. Section 3 was also amended in a number of respects during its legislative passage in the Oireachtas. First, it provides that the Central Mental Hospital is a designated centre for the receiving, detaining and providing care or treatment to persons under the Act. Secondly, it covers inpatient facilities which are not necessarily hospitals. Thirdly, the section requires the Minister for Health and Children, when designating a centre other than a prison, to consult the Mental Health Commission.

Fitness to be tried   Section 4 deals with the issue of "fitness to be tried". This term was adopted instead of the term "fitness to plead" which was used in the relevant provisions of the Lunacy (Ireland) Act 1821, which the 2006 Act repealed. The section contains a new statutory definition of fitness to be tried based on the existing common law, as set out in *State (C) v Minister for Justice* [1968] I.R. 106, referred to above. It provides that the question of fitness to be tried is determined by a court, including the District Court, without a jury. It does not relate to the guilt or innocence of a person. If the person is found unfit to be tried, the proceedings are adjourned and the court then determines how the person should be dealt with until such time as he or she has recovered, if ever. As the person will not have been found guilty of any crime, he or she will only be detained if he or she is likely to be dangerous to himself or herself or to others, or is in need of inpatient treatment.

Safeguards are provided in s.4 to reduce the possibility of persons found unfit to be tried being detained unnecessarily under the criminal law. In effect, these provisions provide that where, despite the fact that the accused is unfit to be tried, the court is satisfied that there is a reasonable doubt that he or she committed the act alleged, it will acquit him or her. In other words, a person who is clearly before a court in circumstances where unfitness is an issue can nonetheless be acquitted of the offence if the court decides that on the facts the person would, if he or she were fit to plead, be entitled to acquittal in any event. It will then be a matter for the relevant authorities, under the Mental Health Act 2001, to take whatever measures they may deem necessary in the case of the person concerned. The provision was amended in the course of the debate in the Oireachtas by including a ground for unfitness based on a person's inability to elect for trial by jury in a case involving an indictable offence. It was also amended to reduce from 28 days to 14 days the initial holding period for assessment in s.4(6)(a)(i). Subsections (9) and (10) of s.4 were added during the Oireachtas debate to protect an accused person by providing for the non-publication of a report or evidence in a case where a court decides not to order their discharge in circumstances where the procedure laid down in s.4(8) is applied.

Not guilty by reason of insanity   Section 5 of the 2006 Act provides for a new verdict of not guilty by reason of insanity to replace the existing special verdict of guilty but insane and sets out the parameters of the test for insanity which is based on the pre-2006 common law position including recent Irish case law. Section 5(1) states that, for this verdict to be made, the jury (or court in the case of the District Court or the Special Criminal Court) must find that:

> "(a) the accused person was suffering at the time [of the act] from a
>   mental disorder, and
> (b)   the mental disorder was such that the accused person ought not
>   to be held responsible for the act alleged by reason of the fact
>   that he or she—
>   (i)   did not know the nature and quality of the act, or
>   (ii) did not know that what he or she was doing was wrong,
>   or
>   (iii) was unable to refrain from committing the act."

The phrase guilty but insane has always been regarded as an acquittal despite the language used prior to 2006 and in the 2006 Act itself. Section 5 also provides that after a verdict of not guilty by reason of insanity is returned, the court will then consider the mental condition of the person by reference to the Mental Health Act 2001 to determine whether he or she should be released or detained on the grounds that inpatient treatment is required or because the person may be dangerous to himself or herself or to others because of his or her mental condition. This approach is in accordance with obligations arising under the European Convention on Human Rights. Once a person is acquitted the test as to what is done with the person is dealt with on the same basis as a decision would be made as to whether to commit the person to a mental hospital under the 2001 Act.

Diminished responsibility   Section 6 introduces the concept of diminished responsibility into Irish law, and is limited to the charge of murder, which carries a mandatory sentence of life imprisonment. Section 6(1) states that this will apply where the jury (or Special Criminal Court) finds that the accused:

> "(a) did the act alleged,
> (b) was at the time suffering from a mental disorder, and
> (c) the mental disorder was not such as to justify finding him or her not guilty by reason of insanity, but was such as to diminish substantially his or her responsibility for the act."

It was pointed out that, arguably, the concept of diminished responsibility could be applied to other serious offences, but since sentence is variable in those cases, the trial judge could, prior to 2006, already take into account the mental condition of the convicted person when considering what sentence to impose. The effect of s.6 is that if diminished responsibility is successfully pleaded, a conviction for manslaughter rather than murder will be recorded, with the sentence, at the discretion of the court, being any term up to imprisonment for life. The availability of the diminished responsibility verdict provides an alternative for juries (and the Special Criminal Court) and should reduce the danger that a jury will return an insanity verdict when faced with a person whom they regard as not being completely sane, even if he or she does not meet the legal criteria for acquittal on grounds of insanity.

Appeals   Sections 7 and 8 deal, respectively, with the question of appeals to higher courts from decisions of lower courts that a person is unfit to be tried or is not guilty by reason of insanity. Prior to the 2006 Act, findings of unfitness to plead (now called fitness to be tried) or verdicts of guilty but insane were not regarded as convictions and consequently there was no provision for a person to appeal against them. Section 9 provides that appeals may be made by the defence or the prosecution against a decision of the court of trial to order or not to order the detention of a person in these cases.

Mental Health (Criminal Law) Review Board   Sections 10 to 12 of the 2006 Act provide for the establishment of an independent Mental Health (Criminal Law) Review Board. The title of the board was amended during the Oireachtas debate to include the words "(Criminal Law)" so as to distinguish it from the bodies established under the Mental Health Act 2001, namely, the Mental Health Commission and the Mental Health Tribunals. The background to these provisions is that the European Court of Human Rights has held, in cases such as *HL v United Kingdom* (2005) 40 E.H.R.R. 32 (the *Bournewood* case) that, on the detention of persons of unsound mind, whether under the civil or the criminal law, the availability of some independent system of review of the lawfulness of detention is required to comply with the provisions of the Convention on Human Rights. The Mental Health (Criminal Law) Review Board replaces an ad hoc advisory committee which had been established in recent years in response to cases such as *Re Gallagher* [1991] 1 I.R. 31 (*Annual Review of Irish Law 1990*, pp.164–6). Section 11 states that the board comprises a chairperson (who must be a practising barrister or solicitor of not less than 10 years' experience or a judge or former judge of the Circuit Court or superior courts), and such other number of members as the Minister in consultation with the Minister for Health and Children shall appoint, at least one of whom must be a consultant psychiatrist. The term of office of members is five years and provision is made for reappointment. The Minister may appoint the staff of the board under the usual conditions and such staff shall be civil servants. Section 12 sets out the various powers of the board. These include the power to hold sittings; take account of court records; assign a legal representative to the person seeking review; require the attendance of such person before it; obtain evidence and demand the production of information and documents; pay the reasonable expenses of witnesses; and administer oaths. The failure of persons to attend before the board or to comply with requests by the board for information or documents, or where a person is in contempt of the board, are offences punishable by a fine not exceeding €3,000 or imprisonment for a term not exceeding 12 months or both.

Review Section 13 deals with the various ways in which the detention of persons found not guilty by reason of insanity or unfit to be tried, whether they are in a prison or other designated centre, including persons detained under military law, may be reviewed. As originally enacted, s.13(1) had provided that, in the case of a prison, this applied to the governor who shall act on the advice of an approved medical officer, whereas in other cases s.13 provided that in the case of, for example, a psychiatric hospital, this was the chief medical officer. Section 197 of the Criminal Justice Act 2006 (discussed generally above, pp. 302-323.) deleted s.13(1) and, therefore, the reference to the role of a prison governor where the person is detained in prison.

The review board has the responsibility for ensuring that the detention of such persons is reviewed every six months or at such lesser intervals as it considers appropriate. In cases where a person who has not been acquitted is no longer unfit to be tried, the court of committal has to be so informed and shall order that the person be brought before it to be dealt with as the court thinks proper. In the case of detention under military law, the appropriate authority has to be similarly informed so that the court martial shall be reconvened.

Temporary release and transfers Section 14 provides for the temporary release and transfer of, and other matters related to, detained persons. The purpose is to arrange for such matters without the need to apply to the review board every time. It is provided that the consent of the Minister must be obtained to ensure that the public interest is safeguarded. The Minister for Health and Children might also have an interest, particularly in the case of transfers to another designated centre, and that is also covered in the section.

Sections 15, 16 and 17 were inserted in the 2006 Act during its legislative passage in the Oireachtas. Sections 15 and 16 relate to the question of transferring persons suffering from a mental disorder from places of detention to the Central Mental Hospital for treatment and back again, and matters related thereto. This is designed to deal principally with persons who have been found guilty by a court of committing a crime or who will be in the initial stages of the criminal justice process. The onset of their mental illness will have arisen during their period of imprisonment and is not a matter that will have had to be addressed during their trial. The provisions are expressed to apply to persons who are in prison on foot of a sentence of imprisonment, on committal awaiting trial, on remand or otherwise. In other words, such persons will be involved in the criminal justice process in the ordinary way, namely, on the basis that the question of their sanity, and thus their legal capacity to commit a crime, will not have been in issue. They deal with the shortcomings of the pre-2006 arrangements by streamlining administrative formalities, which had resulted in considerable delays in dealing with these issues and had been criticised by the Council of Europe's Committee for the Prevention of Torture. Section 17 provides for the mechanism by which the case of a person who develops a mental illness while in prison can be reviewed by the Mental Health (Criminal Law) Review Board. This may be requested by the Minister for Justice, Equality and Law Reform or by the person themselves or on the initiative of the review board itself. Section 18 deals with transfer back to prison.

Notice by defence Section 19 provides that evidence as to the mental condition of an accused person shall not be raised by the defence during the course of a trial unless notice of intention to do so has been given to the prosecution in accordance with the rules of court. This is designed to ensure that neither the prosecution nor the court will be ambushed by the surprise production of such evidence at a late stage in the trial process.

Persons already in detention Section 20 applies the provisions of the 2006 Act on the review of detentions to persons already in detention before the 2006 Act came into operation.

Military law   Section 21 deals with consequential changes to the relevant provisions of the Defence Act 1954 (by inserting new ss.202, 203 and 203A into the 1954 Act) to maintain consistency between courts martial and the non-military criminal law.

Infanticide   Section 22 of the 2006 Act, which was the last major amendment made to the Act during its legislative passage in the Oireachtas, amended the Infanticide Act 1949 in two significant respects. First, it replaced the faulty basis for the reduced finding of infanticide in s.1(3)(c) of the 1949 Act, namely, that the basis for it was "by reason of the effect of lactation". Section 22 of the 2006 Act has replaced these words with the following words: "by reason of a mental disorder (within the meaning of the Criminal Law (Insanity) Act 2006)". The second major change was to replace the provision in the 1949 Act which had simply stated that, on conviction, the accused would be "punished as for manslaughter". The 2006 Act replaced this with the following: "as for manslaughter and, on conviction may be dealt with under s.6(3) of the Criminal Law (Insanity) Act 2006 as if she had been found guilty of manslaughter on the grounds of diminished responsibility." These are welcome changes, particularly in terms of the replacement of the flawed premise for the finding of lesser responsibility.

PROCEDURE

Arrest by off-duty Garda   In *DPP v Warren*, High Court, May 18, 2006 the applicant sought to challenge by way of case stated the finding of a District Court judge that his arrest for the offence of drink driving under s.49 of the Road Traffic Act 1961, as amended, had been lawful. The applicant had been followed by an off-duty member of An Garda Síochána. The garda had detained the applicant until a second member of the Gardaí arrived to effect an arrest. The applicant argued that the initial detention by the off-duty garda was unlawful because no arrest had been effected. The garda who detained the applicant said in evidence that he had specifically not arrested the applicant as he was off duty at the time and that, instead of arresting him, he had detained him and called a nearby Garda station for assistance. When the second garda arrived at the scene, the applicant was again arrested and it was argued that this second arrest was invalid as the applicant had been unlawfully deprived of his liberty and/or was in unlawful detention. Dunne J. held that the arrest had been valid and that the applicant had not been in unlawful detention. She referred to *DPP v McCormack* [1999] 4 I.R. 158 and noted that, in order to effect a valid arrest, some form of words must be used and physically detaining the person is not sufficient. In this case, the applicant had been physically detained and words had been used to the effect that he was under arrest. An arrest had, therefore, been lawfully effected. As regards the argument that the second arrest was invalid, Dunne J. held that this was not the case as a person in detention may be subsequently arrested. Arrest denotes a future restriction of liberty and it is not, therefore, necessary that the person to be arrested is at liberty when the arrest takes place. Thus, a person in detention may be arrested a second time.

Summons: information based on false name   In *DPP v Thomas*, High Court, October 2, 2006, Quirke J. held that a summons issued on the basis of a false name given by an accused had been validly issued within the six-month time limit prescribed by s.10(4) of the Petty Sessions (Ireland) Act 1851, even though the complaint on which it was issued had to be re-sworn after the six-month time limit had expired. In the case, the summons had been struck out by the District Court judge on the ground that the information had been sworn out of time. The defendant had given the incorrect name "William Scurry", and an incorrect address, to Gardaí who had arrested him on suspicion of the drink-driving offence under s.49 of the Road Traffic Act 1961, as amended. By the time the summonses were issued, it was discovered that no such person existed. A fresh application for a summons was made but the six-month time limit in s.10(4) of the 1851 Act had expired by then. On a case stated, Quirke J. noted that, because of his own dishonest and unsatisfactory conduct, the name shown on the face of the summonses was not a name by which the defendant was usually known and that, similarly, the address on the summons was not where he ordinarily resided. Although they were issued in the name of "William Scurry", the relevant summonses clearly and unambiguously related to the physical person of the defendant who, on the date of the alleged offence, chose to identify himself as "William Scurry". On the evidence, therefore, there was no doubt whatsoever that a valid application was made by the Director's representative for the issue of summonses charging the respondent with the commission of the offence. Accordingly, the application was made in accordance with law and within the statutory time limit of six months.

Supreme Court appeals   In *People (DPP) v Gilligan (No.3)* [2006] I.E.S.C. 42; [2007] 1 I.L.R.M. 182 the Supreme Court declined to consider an issue of sentencing when dealing with a certificate on a point of law of exceptional public importance. The defendant had appealed to the Court of Criminal Appeal against his conviction and sentence for drug-related offences. That court, in *People (DPP) v Gilligan*, Court of Criminal Appeal, August 8, 2003 (*Annual Review of Irish Law 2003*, p.296), dismissed the appeal against conviction. In a later judgment, *People (DPP) v Gilligan (No.2)*, Court of Criminal Appeal, November 12, 2003 (*Annual Review of Irish Law 2003*, p.244), the court reduced the term of 28 years' imprisonment to 20 years. On the application of the appellant, the Court of Criminal Appeal certified, pursuant to s.29 of the Courts of Justice Act 1924, that its decision of August 8, 2003, refusing leave to appeal against conviction, involved points of law of exceptional public importance and that it was desirable, in the public interest, that an appeal be brought to the Supreme Court. The points of law certified for the appeal to the Supreme Court included whether evidence which may have been obtained from witnesses under a State Witness Protection Programme was inadmissible or inconsistent with the right to a trial in due course of law as guaranteed by Art.38.1 of the Constitution, and whether corroboration was required in respect of the testimony of accomplice witnesses who had participated in the State Witness Protection Programme. The certificate did not refer to the sentences that had been imposed and only related to the conviction. The Supreme Court heard and dismissed the appeal of the appellant against his conviction and the appellant then informed the court of his intention to pursue his appeal against the severity of his sentence. This raised the question whether the appellant could circumvent the statutorily-declared finality of the determination of the Court of Criminal Appeal regarding his sentence, by relying on the points certified by that court, which related entirely to the validity of his conviction. The court declined to hear the matter, holding that the Supreme Court did not have jurisdiction to entertain the appeal against sentence. The court noted that the Oireachtas had provided for an appeal from all decisions of the Special Criminal Court to the Court of Criminal Appeal. The Oireachtas provided for a limited right of appeal to the Supreme Court from the Court of Criminal Appeal. The appellant could not circumvent the finality of the decision of the Court of Criminal Appeal on the matter of his sentence as that court had not certified points relating to the validity of his sentence and so the Supreme Court could not interfere with the sentence imposed. The court accepted that it had long been accepted that an appellant, who has secured a certificate from the Court of Criminal Appeal that its decision involves a point of law of exceptional public importance and that it is desirable that an appeal should be taken to the Supreme Court, was entitled, on the hearing of his appeal in the Supreme Court, to argue any other appeal point which he had taken before the Court of Criminal Appeal. The court noted that this had been adopted as a result of reliance on the *obiter dicta* of Walsh J. in *People (Attorney General) v Giles* [1974] I.R. 422, but the court considered that this was not an appropriate course to take. The court noted that, as the views of Walsh J. in the *Giles* case were *obiter*, they were not binding on the Supreme Court in the determination of the scope of s.29 of the Courts of Justice Act 1924. On this basis, and expressly departing from the views of Walsh J. in *People (Attorney General) v Giles* [1974] I.R. 422, the Supreme Court (Denham J. dissenting) concluded that the appellant was not entitled to rely on the certificate of appeal granted in respect of his conviction to appeal against the severity of his sentence.

PROSECUTION APPEALS

In 2006 the Law Reform Commission published a *Report on Prosecution Appeals and Pre-Trial Hearings* (LRC 81–2006). The report follows from two consultation papers: *Consultation Paper on Prosecution Appeals in Cases brought on Indictment* (2002) (published under the Commission's *Second Programme of Law Reform 2000–2007*); and *Consultation Paper on Prosecution Appeals from Unduly Lenient Sentences in the District Court* (2004) (published in response to a request from the Attorney General under the Law Reform Commission Act 1975 to examine whether the DPP should be given the right to appeal lenient sentences in the District Court). The Commission's main recommendations were as follows.

In connection with prosecution appeals on indictment, the Commission had recommended in its 2002 consultation paper that there should be an extended "without prejudice" prosecution appeal, which would not overturn an acquittal but would correct any legal errors for future cases. The Commission noted that this has now been implemented in the Criminal Justice Act 2006 (discussed at pp. 311-312 above) which the Commission welcomed. The Commission examined whether there should be "with prejudice" prosecution appeals, which *would* involve overturning a jury verdict of acquittal and possibly involve a retrial. The Commission noted that such appeals may not be in conflict with the Constitution, but that the law on this is particularly complex. In view of the changes made in the Criminal Justice Act 2006, the Commission concluded that it would not, at this time, recommend the introduction of such appeals, and noted that this was to be examined by the Criminal Law Review Group established by the Minister for Justice, Equality and Law Reform.

In connection with prosecution appeals from the District Court, the Commission considered that, in principle, sentences imposed in the District Court that are unduly lenient should be subject to review and that there was a perception that inconsistent sentences are imposed in the District Court. However, the Commission concluded that, because there is no reliable data on this matter, it would not be appropriate to confer a power on the DPP to appeal unduly lenient sentences in the District Court. The Commission notes that this should be kept under review, especially in light of other recommendations it makes for reform. The Commission reiterated a recommendation in its *Report on Minor Offences* (2003) that when imposing a prison sentence a judge should give reasons. The Commission welcomed the phased introduction of digital recording in the District Court which would facilitate this. In related points, the Commission welcomed the proposed introduction of an Irish Sentencing Information System (ISIS), which should provide reliable data in this area for the first time. The Commission also welcomed the changes in the role of prosecution lawyers at the sentencing stage, as indicated in the DPP's new *Guidelines for Prosecutors 2006*. The Commission surveyed developments in other countries and looked at the successes and failures of those measures.

It concluded that increased case management in criminal trials in Ireland could lead to improved focus and fewer unnecessary delays in trials. The Commission recommended that consideration be given by the Courts Service to the introduction of a pre-trial questionnaire.

ROAD TRAFFIC

Refusal to provide blood specimen   In *DPP v Malone* [2006] 2 I.L.R.M. 567 the Supreme Court considered the question of the revival of the obligation to provide a blood sample where a urine sample has not been given. The defendant had been charged with refusing to permit a doctor to take a specimen of his blood at a Garda station, contrary to s.13(3) of the Road Traffic Act 1994. The defendant had opted to provide a urine sample rather than give a blood specimen but had been unable to do so having been given three opportunities to do so. He was then asked to permit the doctor to take a specimen of his blood and the Gardaí warned him of the consequences should he fail or refuse to comply with this requirement. He responded that he would give a urine sample at a later stage and he was subsequently charged under s.13(3) of the 1994 Act. It was submitted at the conclusion of the prosecution case that the defendant had not refused to provide a blood sample. The prosecution argued that where a person opts to provide a urine sample and is unable to do so, the obligation to permit the taking of a blood specimen revives. The trial judge stated a case to the Supreme Court as to whether he was entitled to hold that the defendant had not been given a reasonable time to provide a urine sample. The court (McCracken, Kearns and Macken JJ.) answered this "no", and thus indicated that the defendant should be convicted?

The court held that the requirement under s.13 of the 1994 Act must be understood in the context that the procedure must be completed within three hours of driving. Thus, any delays which may defeat the intention of the legislature cannot be imported into the 1994 Act. The court accepted that when a person opts to provide urine, he must be given an opportunity for compliance and, where he fails to actually provide urine, the obligation to provide a blood specimen immediately revives. As the court had indicated in *DPP v O'Connor* [2000] 1 I.L.R.M. 60, the opportunity for compliance consists only of the following elements: the person must forthwith be provided with an appropriate container; he must be requested to go to a specific place to provide the specimen; and that person must actually provide the specimen at the expiration of such short time as is appropriate for the normal performance of that function. The court also accepted that what is a reasonable time in one context may not be in another. The fact that the person concerned had paid a visit to the bathroom and had not brought any extenuating circumstances which he alleges could be relevant to the attention of the Gardaí was evidence in itself that he had been afforded an adequate opportunity to provide a sample.

Evidential breath test   *McGonnell v Attorney General* [2006] I.E.S.C. 64, [2007] 1 I.L.R.M. 321 was a test case in which the Supreme Court upheld the constitutional validity of evidential breath testing using an intoxilyser or intoximeter apparatus. The plaintiffs had challenged the constitutionality of procedures for evidential breath-testing under the Road Traffic Act 1994 in prosecutions for drink driving under s.49 of the Road Traffic Act 1961, as amended. Section 13(1) of the 1994 Act states that where a person is arrested under s.49 of the 1961 Act, a member of the Garda Síochána may, at his or her discretion, require the person to provide either: (a) two specimens of breath; or (b) a specimen of blood or urine, *or* both specimens of breath *and* blood or urine. Where a person is required to provide a specimen of blood or urine, s.18 of the 1994 Act requires that the specimen be divided into two parts, one of which the arrested person may retain. Section 21 of the 1994 Act states that a duly completed statement, supplied to the arrested person under s.17 of the 1994 Act, stating the concentration of alcohol in the specimen of breath, "shall, until the contrary is shown, be sufficient evidence in any proceedings under the Road Traffic Acts, 1961 to 1994, of the facts stated therein...". The plaintiffs were arrested under s.49 of the 1961 Act and required to provide breath specimens pursuant to s.13(1)(a) of the 1994 Act which in each case gave readings of alcohol concentration over the statutory limit. The plaintiffs contended that they had been denied the opportunity of an independent breath sample or blood or urine sample which could be independently tested and were, therefore, denied the possibility of an effective defence. It was argued that the procedures were a disproportionate interference with their rights as they failed to incorporate any provision which would allow an accused to request that a blood or urine sample be taken in addition to a breath test. The High Court dismissed the plaintiffs' claim finding that having regard to evidence of the general reliability of the intoxilyser/intoximeter apparatus used for taking breath specimens, it followed that the readings in each of the plaintiffs' cases were accurate. The Supreme Court dismissed the plaintiffs' appeal and affirmed the High Court decision.

The court held that the statutory procedures for the measuring and proving of breath or alcohol levels were not a disproportionate interference with the plaintiffs' rights. The court noted that it was open to the plaintiffs to adduce evidence of the amount of alcohol they had consumed in seeking to show that the relevant apparatus should be considered defective. The court referred to its decision in *Whelan v Kirby* [2005] 2 I.R. 30 (*Annual Review of Irish Law 2004*, p.245), and pointed out that the presumption under s.21 of the 1994 Act was rebuttable and the accused person was entitled to apply to conduct an inspection of the apparatus so as to investigate its reliability. It was also pointed out that an accused person was entitled to adduce evidence regarding the manner of operation of the apparatus at the relevant time of the provision of the breath specimen. The court also noted that there were various other proofs that had to be satisfied in a prosecution for an offence contrary to s.49

of the 1961 Act of which verbal evidence must be given, particularly where the admissibility of the s.17 statement is challenged. On this basis, the court concluded that a statement under s.17 of the 1994 Act was not, therefore, tantamount to "conviction by printout".

SELF DEFENCE

Self-defence and excessive self-defence: role of trial judge   In *People (DPP) v Nally* [2006] I.E.C.C.A. 128; Court of Criminal Appeal, October 12, 2006, the defendant had been convicted on a count of manslaughter in the Central Criminal Court. The defendant was a farmer and there had been a spate of thefts and burglaries near his farm which, in his mind, were sufficient to put him in constant fear and apprehension that he could at any time be a victim of such crimes. On the date in question, the defendant found two men, a father and son, on his farm who stated that they were there to enquire as to whether a car on his property was for sale. Having seen the older man approach the back door of his house the defendant retrieved a shotgun. He stated that he accidentally discharged a shot which hit the man and, thereafter, a considerable struggle ensued. During the struggle the defendant picked up a length of wood and struck the man repeatedly on the head and body. The younger man had left the farm by car and the defendant stated he was concerned that he might return with others or with a weapon. The older man attempted to leave the property but was followed by the defendant out of the property onto the public road and the defendant fired a further shot at him which proved fatal. He then threw the body into an adjoining field.

The defendant was charged with murder and pleaded not guilty on the ground that he had acted in self-defence. During the trial, counsel for the prosecution invited the court to direct that the defendant should be convicted of either murder or manslaughter and not to allow a full defence of self-defence to go to the jury. It was submitted that the defendant had used excessive force and that a complete acquittal would be perverse. The trial judge made the requested ruling and directed the jury that only a verdict of murder or manslaughter was open to them. As indicated, the jury convicted the defendant of manslaughter. On appeal, counsel for the defendant argued that, once the issue of self-defence had been raised, either by way of evidence directly provided by the defence or based on the prosecution's evidence, it then became an issue solely and exclusively for determination by the jury, and that the trial judge was not entitled to rule on the applicant's defence in the terms that he had. He was entitled to express a view in relation to the facts, but was precluded from directing that the evidence adduced was sufficient to require a particular verdict. The prosecution contended that the charge to the jury in relation to the defence of self-defence was correct on the facts and evidence in this case. To allow the option of acquitting the applicant completely would have meant that the jury would have been misdirected on the law of self-defence. The Court of Criminal Appeal allowed the appeal and quashed the conviction.

The court noted that if the prosecution had allowed the trial to proceed in the usual manner, the trial judge would have given appropriate directions to the jury in the usual form. That usual form would have enabled the trial judge to express his opinion that the amount of force could not be objectively justified in the context of the defence of self-defence, but would have left the ultimate decision on that issue to the jury. The court noted that, in the present case, the jury had been denied the opportunity to return a verdict of not guilty, even if such a verdict may have flown in the face of the evidence. The court emphasized that jurors must retain the ultimate power to determine issues of guilt or innocence which the court considered must, of necessity, include the power to return a verdict which conflicts with the opinion of the trial judge. On that basis, the court quashed the conviction. We note here that, on the defendant's re-trial, he was acquitted. Both the trial, the appeal and the re-trial attracted considerable publicity, including enormous media discussion of the scope of self-defence in the context of the private dwelling. This also arose in a different setting in *People (DPP) v Barnes* [2006] I.E.C.C.A. 165; [2007] 1 I.L.R.M. 350, below. It was also considered by the Law Reform Commission in the wider context of legitimate defence in its *Consultation Paper on Legitimate Defence* (LRC CP 41–2006), discussed below, which was published after the Court of Criminal Appeal decision in *Nally*.

Burglar: self-defence against householder In *People (DPP) v Barnes* [2006] I.E.C.C.A. 165; [2007] 1 I.L.R.M. 350, the Court of Criminal Appeal dealt with an unusual claim of self-defence and, in the process, made general observations in this area. The defendant had been charged with murder. He accepted that he had entered a house with another burglar as they believed there was a quantity of money there. They were subsequently interrupted when the householder returned. The defendant claimed that the householder challenged them and picked up a knife. He was then disarmed and stabbed, in self-defence the defendant claimed. Counsel for the defendant argued that, though he was a burglar, he was not an aggressive one and that the mere act of burglary was not in itself an act of aggression. It was contended that it would have been unlawful for the victim to respond with any force or threat of force to the defendant's intrusion into his house. If the victim did respond with any force, it was argued that the defendant was entitled to defend himself. It was not in dispute that the defendant had given several different accounts of the burglary when interviewed by the police. The trial judge did not permit the defence of self-defence to go to the jury. The defendant was convicted on the murder charge. On appeal, the Court of Criminal Appeal refused leave to appeal and affirmed the conviction. The court (whose judgment was delivered by Hardiman J.) noted that there was no modern Irish authority on the nature of the offence of burglary and the permitted response of a victim of that offence. Referring to the English decision *R v Meads and Belts* (1828), the court found that the breaking into a person's house by a trespasser with intent to steal or commit any other form of crime was, in itself, an act of aggression. Thus, the killing of a householder by a burglar, during the course of the burglary, can never be less than manslaughter by reason of the burglar's initial, grave, aggression.

Although it was not directly relevant to the case, and thus may be considered strictly *obiter*, the court made a number of comments on the position of the householder in this situation. The court considered that a burglar may be met with retaliatory force to drive him off or to immobilise or detain him and to end the threat which he offers to the personal rights of the householder. The court added that it would be inconsistent with the constitutional provisions on the inviolability of a dwelling house that a householder could ever be under a legal obligation to flee; this is a reference to the "Castle Doctrine", discussed in detail in the Law Reform Commission's *Consultation Paper on Legitimate Defence* (LRC CP 41–2006) (see below) which, although published before the decision in *Barnes*, may not have been opened to the court. In *Barnes*, the court concluded that it followed from this that the householder could never be in a worse position in law because he has decided to stand his ground in his house. The court accepted that it was impossible to lay down any formula with which the degree of force a householder in such a position could use might be calculated. Nor would it be just to lay down a wholly objective standard, to be judged by the standards of the hypothetical reasonable person. The victim of a burglary was not in the position of an ordinary reasonable man contemplating what course of action was best in particular circumstances. He might be, as the victim in *Barnes* was, ageing, alone, confronted with numerous or much younger assailants. In almost every case, the court noted, the victim of burglary will be taken by surprise. The victim will therefore be, in almost every case, shocked and surprised and may easily be terrified. To hold a person in this situation to an objective standard would be profoundly unjust.

Having entered into this detailed exploration of the position of the householder, the court of course noted that, in any event, as the defendant had been an aggressor in the sense of having burgled the victim's house, there was no basis on which the defence of self-defence was available in this case and thus it affirmed the conviction for murder.

Reform proposals   As indicated, in 2006 the Law Reform Commission published a *Consultation Paper on Legitimate Defence* (LRC CP 41-2006). The Paper covers self-defence and the use of lethal force by law enforcement officials, such as the Garda Síochána. As the Commission noted, a critical feature of legitimate defence is that it provides a complete defence—a justification—for what would otherwise be unlawful actions. Where a person who is charged with murder can show that (s)he comes within the boundaries of self-defence, the verdict is one of not guilty. Because of this, the Commission emphasised that there is a compelling need to set out clearly and precisely the extent of force—including lethal force—that may legitimately be used to repel an attack. The principle of legality requires that persons are given clear advance notice of the parameters of such a full defence. In the consultation paper, the Commission concluded that, in order to provide as much clarity as possible on the scope of legitimate defence, it should be broken down into five components: (1) a threshold requirement concerning the type of attack on the defender; (2) the imminence of the attack; (3) the unlawfulness of the attack; (4) the necessity of the defender's use of force; and (5) the proportionality of the force used. In this respect, the Commission notes that the defence should not be reduced to a single issue of whether a person acted reasonably in all the circumstances. The Commission discusses in detail the relevant requirements that apply under each of these headings and recommends that, where necessary, their precise scope should be clarified. Among the specific issues discussed under these headings are the following.

As to the threshold requirement the Commission examines in detail the leading decision of the Supreme Court in *People v Dwyer* [1972] IR 416, in which it was made clear that self-defence applies if the defender themselves or their family is under threat by the attacker. The decision in *Dwyer* is, arguably, less clear about whether it can also apply when any property of the defender is under attack, and the Commission recommends that this should be clarified in the context of codifying the law. As to the question of imminence and emerging new cases, the Commission acknowledges that the requirement of imminence has caused immense difficulty in relation to certain newly emerging cases, including those in a violent domestic setting (sometimes referred to as "battered women's syndrome"). The Commission examines various reform options in this context, which it acknowledges must be done in the wider context of other defences, including provocation. The Commission explored in detail the scope of legitimate defence in the context of law enforcement, both from the point of view of the use of lethal force by law enforcement officials and also from the perspective of resisting arrest. The consultation paper emphasises the need to clarify the type of force that may be used by the Gardaí in circumstances such as those in the Abbeylara case, which was discussed in the 2006 *Report of the Barr Tribunal of Inquiry*.

The consultation paper examined the necessity element of legitimate defence against the general background of considerable international debate of the related rules on retreat, the "castle doctrine" and the principle of self-generated necessity. The question of what force can be used by a person when they are subject to an attack in their own home is discussed in light of the decision of the Court of Criminal Appeal in *People (DPP) v Nally*, discussed above. Because the court had ordered a re-trial in that case, which was still pending at the time the paper was published, the Commission considered that it could not comment on its precise details, but it examined the nature of the special plea of excessive defence which exists in Irish law, and which allows a jury to find the defendant not guilty of murder but guilty of manslaughter where the defender has responded to an attack using disproportionate force.

SENTENCING

Bias and inflexible policy *Pudliszewski v Coughlan*, High Court, January 23, 2006 is an unusual example of where a sentence may be quashed on judicial review. The applicant sought an order of certiorari quashing the order of the respondent, a judge of the District Court, convicting and sentencing the applicant to a period of imprisonment on charges of theft and fraud. The issue which arose was a remark which the respondent apparently made regarding the penalty he usually imposed for receiving offences. Counsel for the applicant argued that the only clear and reasonable meaning which could be attached to the statement was that the respondent fettered his own discretion by unduly limiting the District Court's sentencing jurisdiction, or that he appeared to do so. The respondent denied this and argued that the sentence imposed was not excessive or disproportionate. MacMenamin J. granted the order of certiorari. He held that the essential issue was whether or not there was evidence of subjective or objective bias or inflexible policy that went to jurisdiction. The exercise of judicial discretion in sentencing a convicted person should never be formulaic in approach or subordinated to fixed-policy criteria. He referred in this context to *People (DPP) v WC* [1994] 1 I.L.R.M. 321, *People (DPP) v Kelly*, Court of Criminal Appeal, July 5, 2004 and *Orange Communications Ltd v Director of Telecommunications (No.2)* [2000] 4 I.R. 159. In the present case, he concluded that, on the balance of public interest, the matter should be remitted to the District Court for the purpose of having the sentence on the particular charge dealt with. Following the approach in *Gilmartin v Murphy*, High Court, February 23, 2001, he held that the case should not be dealt with by the District Court judge who dealt with the matter in the first instance.

Manslaughter In *People (DPP) v O'Donoghue* [2006] I.E.C.C.A. 134; Court of Criminal Appeal, October 18, 2006, the DPP appealed under s.2 of the Criminal Justice Act 1993 on the ground of undue leniency against a sentence of four years' imprisonment imposed on the defendant after conviction by a jury on a charge of (unlawful and dangerous act) manslaughter. The defendant was an adult male in his 20s who had forcefully gripped an 11-year-old boy, a neighbour who he knew very well, in a headlock. He was charged with murder, and he pleaded not guilty to murder but guilty of manslaughter. In a statement to the Gardaí, he claimed that he had grabbed the boy after the boy had thrown stones at his car, and that the death had been an accident. At his trial, he was acquitted of murder, but was found guilty of manslaughter. On appeal, counsel for the Director argued, *inter alia*, that the case could be seen as having a number of unusual, disquieting features, properly considered as aggravating factors, that warranted the imposition of a significant custodial sentence, but which, wrongly, were not so regarded by the trial judge. It was argued that the trial judge had failed to have regard to the disparity in age between the victim and the defendant, failed to have regard to the evidence concerning the injuries which the victim suffered and failed to have significant regard to the efforts of the defendant to dispose of and conceal the body of the victim, or to consider the cover up as a substantial aggravating factor in relation to the offence of which the respondent was accused. The defendant submitted that the Director was in reality seeking to revisit the evidence tendered and to reinterpret it so as to suggest that the account of the accident as described by the defendant in his statement was not true, thereby wrongly seeking to revisit the conclusions to be drawn from the evidence or its significance when, on the contrary, the jury had, on an objective basis, clearly accepted the defendant's version of what occurred. The Court of Criminal Appeal dismissed the appeal and upheld the sentence imposed.

The court held that it was difficult to see how, in the absence of evidence, a disparity in age, size or strength had a material impact of a forensic nature in the commission of the crime for which the respondent was found guilty, and if there was no such clear undisputed evidence, the court could not criticize the trial judge for failing to take such disparity into account for the purpose of constructing the sentence. The court found that unless there was an obvious and material error in the conclusions drawn by a sentencing judge from the evidence, that is to say, a "manifest error", a sentencing judge, in carrying out the exercise which he does in the course of sentencing, was not to be criticised for choosing—as in the present case—some or other of the evidence of one expert over that of another as being an appropriate basis upon which to proceed, particularly where the experts were in agreement on the vast majority of the forensic issues, and where they disagreed, the differences between them were ones of emphasis. The court concluded that the Director had not established that the trial judge committed any error in principle in the manner in which he took account of the cover-up, and this ground was, therefore, not established. Finally, the court was, equally, satisfied that the trial judge did not permit the additional material presented at the end of the notified victim impact statement (given by the victim's mother, which attracted considerable publicity at the time of the trial, and which had not been notified to any party to the trial) to affect the exercise of his discretion in the construction of an appropriate sentence in respect of the crime, as committed by the defendant. On that basis, the appeal was dismissed.

Misuse of drugs   In *People (DPP) v Dermody* [2006] I.E.C.C.A. 164; Court of Criminal Appeal, December 21, 2006 the defendant appealed against a sentence of seven years' imprisonment for possession of a controlled drug, contrary to s.15A of the Misuse of Drugs Act 1977, as inserted by the Criminal Justice Act 1999. The issue for the court was whether the "exceptional and specific circumstances" referred to in s.15A of the 1997 Act were applicable to the defendant. The trial judge had taken into account the defendant's plea of guilty under s.15A, and the "minimum" 10 years sentence had not been imposed, but his counsel contended that the trial judge had not given sufficient weight to the fact that the very early plea of guilty on being found in possession had removed the need to investigate or prove the offence and this was an act of assistance; equally he deprived himself of the possibility of relying on any form of technicality in warrants or otherwise. Counsel for the prosecution conceded that the DPP did not consider the sentence to be unduly lenient, but he also submitted that the trial judge had taken all the relevant factors into account and had extended all reasonable leniency. Equally, the Director would not contend that the circumstances of the instant case might be so open and shut as to deprive the plea of guilty of all real value as a mitigating factor, or of all value as a factor that might render it unjust to impose the minimum sentence. The Court of Criminal Appeal declined to interfere with the sentence imposed and refused the application for leave to appeal. The court held that the reduction of three years' imprisonment in the "mandatory" 10 year sentence was, in the opinion of the court, the largest possible reduction which could be justified, having regard to s.15A of the 1977 Act and it concluded that there was no feature in the case that suggested any error of principle in not further reducing the sentence.

SEXUAL OFFENCES

Sexual assault of girls under 17: "statutory rape"   As we noted in the *Annual Review of Irish Law 2005*, p.295, in *CC v Ireland (No. 2)* [2006] I.E.S.C. 33, [2006] 2 I.L.R.M. 161 the Supreme Court held that s.1(1) of the Criminal Law Amendment Act 1935 was inconsistent with the constitutional right to a trial in due course of law for failing to include a defence of "honest mistake". On that basis, the proposed trial of the applicant in that case, who was facing a charge under s.1(1) of the 1935 Act, was prohibited. But the issue then also arose as to whether the decision in *CC (No.2)* required the release of persons who had been convicted of the offence under s.1(1) of the 1935 Act and were still serving terms of imprisonment. This gave rise to enormous public controversy in 2006. In *A v Governor of Arbour Hill Prison* [2006] I.E.S.C. 45; [2006] 2 I.L.R.M. 481, the Supreme Court (Murray C.J., Denham, McGuinness, Hardiman and Geoghegan JJ.), reversing Laffoy J. (who had released the applicant pursuant to Art.40.4 of the Constitution) held that persons who were still serving sentences for offences under s.1(1) of the 1935 Act were not entitled to be released, thus in effect limiting the retrospective effect of the decision in *CC (No.2)*. On the constitutional aspects of these decisions, see the detailed discussion in the Constitutional Law chapter, pp. 174-85 above. In addition, the Oireachtas enacted the Criminal Law (Sexual Offences) Act 2006, which put in place new offences concerning sexual assaults involving persons under 17 years of age to replace those found unconstitutional in *CC (No. 2)*. The Oireachtas also established a Joint Committee on Child Protection in July 2006 to examine the many issues that arose from this series of events.

The Joint Committee's Report was published in late 2006, available at www.oireachtas.ie, and recommended, among other matters, that the defence of "honest mistake" should be reinstated in the law, even if this necessitated a constitutional amendment. In 2007, the Government published a Bill to amend the Constitution, which would include a form of "honest mistake" defence. The proposal gave rise to substantial and robust debate, particularly in connection with the proposals to include specific constitutional protection to the rights of children. Because the proposal appeared not to have cross-party support in the Oireachtas, and because there was at the time a pending general election, the proposal was not proceeded with by the Government. In the aftermath of the election, in June 2007 the Bill was reinstated on the order paper of the Dáil and it appears that the Government intends to proceed with the proposals to amend the Constitution to underpin the rights of children. At the time of writing it appears that this amendment will be put to a referendum in 2008 and we therefore postpone any further discussion until the proposed referendum has occurred.

Education

INSTITUTES OF TECHNOLOGY

The Institutes of Technology Act 2006 constitutes part of the wider Government educational, research and training policy, influenced by international developments, notably analysis by the Organisation for Economic Co-operation and Development (OECD). The key feature of the 2006 Act is to confer greater autonomy on the Institutes of Technology (ITs) to fulfil their statutory missions. The ITs were brought within the remit of the Higher Education Authority (HEA), through amendments to the Higher Education Authority Act 1971. This was intended to provide for a more integrated and cohesive strategic approach to the development of higher education in line with national priorities. The 2006 Act came into force on February 1, 2007 (Institutes of Technology Act 2006 (Commencement) Order 2007 (S.I. No. 36 of 2007)).

It was noted during the passage of the 2006 Act that the ITs were a relatively new entity in the third level education sector, having originally been established as Regional Technical Colleges (RTCs) in the 1960s, arising from a 1964 OECD study, *Technician Training in Ireland*, and the 1965 *Investment in Education* report, which had concluded that urgent attention was required in the area of advanced technical education to produce technically qualified people against a backdrop of new planning for industrial development. They were put on a statutory footing by the Regional Technical Colleges Act 1992, and the connected Dublin Institute of Technology Act 1992. The 2006 Act owes its main content to the *Review of Higher Education in Ireland* (OECD, 2004). The review supported Ireland's strategic ambition of placing its higher education system at the front rank of the OECD in the context of the wider national objective of developing a world-leading knowledge economy and society. A key recommendation was that the differentiation in mission of the university and institute of technology sectors should be retained but that both sectors should be brought within the remit of a single authority in order to achieve a unified higher education strategy. A further recommendation stated that the extent of external regulation of the institutes of technology should be eased, which would give them greater managerial freedom to respond to the opportunities and challenges of supporting regional and national social and economic development.

PRE-SCHOOLS

Detailed requirements   The Child Care (Pre-School Services) (No. 2) Regulations 2006 (S.I. No. 604 of 2006), made under the Child Care Act 1991 (*Annual Review of Irish Law 1991*, pp.232–252), set out the various requirements to be complied with by persons carrying on pre-school services for the purposes of securing the health, safety and welfare, and promoting the development of, pre-school children. They came into force on September 3, 2007 and revoked and replaced the Child Care (Pre-School Services) Regulations 1996, the Child Care (Pre-School Services) Regulations 1997 and the Child Care (Pre-School Services) Regulations 2006 (S.I. No. 505 of 2006).

TEACHING COUNCIL

The Teaching Council (Amendment) Act 2006 amended the Teaching Council Act 2001 (*Annual Review of Irish Law 2001*, p.241) in order to provide retrospective validity to the first elections to the teaching council. The 2001 Act provided that the first elections were to be held under Regulations made by the Minister for Education and Science. The Teaching Council (First Election of Members) Regulations 2004 (S.I. No. 916 of 2004) were signed by the then Minister, and elections were held under these in 2004. The teaching council began its activities on a preparatory basis after this. However, it emerged in late 2005 that the relevant provisions of the 2001 Act under which these Regulations were thought to have been made had not, in fact, been commenced at the time they were signed, thus raising a potential question about the legal basis for the elections. The 2006 Act therefore retrospectively validated the 2004 Regulations, thus removing the lack of validity in the election process, and also paving the way for the formal establishment of the teaching council in March 2006.

UNIVERSITIES

Irish language requirement amended   The University College Galway (Amendment) Act 2006 inserted a new s.3 into the University College Galway Act 1929 to remove the requirement to appoint candidates competent in the Irish language to offices or positions in the university, now renamed the National University of Ireland, Galway (under the terms of the Universities Act 1997). The general context for the 2006 Act was that higher education in Ireland is now measured against the highest standards across the world. In competing internationally, it was regarded as counter-productive to place limitations on the ability of the university to attract the best available international research or teaching talent. In that context the requirement set down by the 1929 Act was regarded as no longer relevant. More immediately, it was also noted that, in a recent competition between two applicants for a position in the university's faculty of law, the requirements of the 1929 Act appeared to involve two separate tests. One of the candidates had come first in one test and second in the second test; he was not appointed to the post. In subsequent litigation in 2005 (which had sought to challenge the manner in which the provisions of the 1929 Act had been applied), it emerged that the candidate who had initially been appointed had moved to another post and the applicant in the proceedings agreed to have the proceedings struck out on an undertaking of being appointed to the post (see *The Irish Times*, October 19, 2005).

The new s.3 of the 1929 Act, inserted by the 2006 Act, provides that the strategic development plan of the university (required by s.34 of the Universities Act 1997) contains a provision for the delivery of education through the Irish language. During the Oireachtas debate on the 2006 Act, the precise form of the new provision was altered so that the university is required to ensure that one of its principal aims in its future strategic development plans will be the provision of education through the medium of Irish. The wording in the original proposal stated simply that one of the aims of the university in its future strategic development plans will be the provision of education through the medium of Irish. Thus, the amended provision as enacted strengthened the original proposal in that it will now be a "principal" aim of the university to ensure that its strategic development plans prioritise the provision of education through the Irish language.

Electricity and Energy

ENERGY (MISCELLANEOUS PROVISIONS) ACT 2006

The Energy (Miscellaneous Provisions) Act 2006 made a number of important changes to the energy regime, including: the expansion of the functions of the Commission for Energy Regulation (CER); regulation, by CER, of the activities of electrical contractors and gas installers with respect to safety and for the appointment, by CER, of designated bodies to facilitate this; to provide for the issue of capital stock in Bord Gáis Éireann; to increase the borrowing power of Bord na Móna; and to implement a Government decision to rehabilitate lands affected by mines and former mines and to provide for the compulsory acquisition of lands for the purposes of any such rehabilitation. The discussion that follows is based on the helpful explanatory memorandum published with the 2006 Act (which took account of the changes made during its Oireachtas debate).

All-island market in electricity   Part 2 of the 2006 Act (ss.3 to 10) made a number of amendments to the Electricity Regulation Act 1999. Section 3 of the 2006 Act inserted a new s.9B into the 1999 Act and it provides that it shall be a function of the CER to participate in the development of a market in energy (electricity and natural gas) for the island of Ireland resulting from the integration of the equivalent markets in Ireland with those of Northern Ireland. The powers of the CER include a power to arrange for the establishment of an entity, to be known as a single market operator, to operate a system of contracts and arrangements for trading in electricity on the island of Ireland.

Regulation of electrical contractors   Section 4 of the 2006 Act inserted new ss.9C to 9E into the 1999 Act to provide that it shall be a function of the CER to regulate the activities of electrical contractors with regard to safety. This replaces the "self-regulation" arrangements put in place by the representative bodies, RECI and ECCSA. The CER may appoint one or more electrical safety supervisory bodies to operate in accordance with detailed criteria (the requirements of which are outlined in ss.9C to 9E of the 1999 Act) and procedures published by the CER. CER approval is needed for any fees and charges imposed by any such body, and provision is made that any such body shall be self-financing. A person who is a member of such a body is referred to as a registered electrical contractor. A comprehensive appeals mechanism is provided for, in respect of appeals against any decision by a designated body to suspend or revoke the membership of a registered electrical contractor, with the CER as final arbiter. The CER may, following consultation with any persons it considers appropriate, determine that a class or classes of electrical works be specified works which are subject to a completion certificate whether carried out by a registered electrical contractor or otherwise (and any such works not carried out by a registered electrical contractor must undergo an inspection arranged by a designated body prior to receipt of a completion certificate). The CER may, with the consent of the Minister for Communications, Marine and Natural Resources, by regulations designate a class or classes of electrical works to be designated electrical works. The CER may appoint authorised officers for the purposes of carrying out work inspections. The section also creates an offence for non-compliance with specified provisions.

Licensing of combined heat and power (CHP) sources   Section 5 of the 2006 Act amended s.14(1) of the 1999 Act to provide greater flexibility to the CER with regard to the licensing of electricity from green and combined heat and power (CHP) sources. Section 6 amended ss.2 and 7 of the 1999 Act to replace the definition of CHP by the insertion of a new definition of CHP as set out in Directive 2004/8/EC (amending Directive 92/42/EEC) on the promotion of cogeneration based on a useful heat demand in the internal energy market. It provides for the methodology on which various forms of CHP will be calculated and for the insertion of harmonised EU "efficiency reference values" on which these calculations will be based. It also provides for the appointment of a body to calculate and certify power-to-heat ratios of specific CHP units. A new Sch.3 to the 1999 Act, consequential to the amendments effect by s.6, is also provided for.

Ministerial directions to CER   Section 7 inserted a new s.10A into the 1999 Act, which provides that the Minister for Communications, Marine and Natural Resources may give general policy directions to the CER to be followed by the CER in the exercise of its functions. Before giving such a direction the Minister shall publish a draft of the proposed direction and give reasons for it. Interested parties would have at least 30 days within which to make representations for the Minister's consideration prior to the direction being given with or without amendment, and a notice of any such direction must be published in Iris Oifigiúil.

Electricity interconnector   Section 8 inserted three new sections, 2A, 16A and 34A, into the 1999 Act and also made a number of other amendments to provide for an electricity interconnector owned by an undertaking other than the Electricity Supply Board (ESB) to be subject to authorisation and licence granted by the CER. The new s.2A provides that such an interconnector shall not be part of the transmission system other than for the purposes of charges for use of the transmission system. The new s.16A provides that the CER may, with the consent of the Minister, secure the construction of an interconnector by specified means, including by competitive tender, by authorisation granted without a prior competitive tender, or directly by requesting the transmission system operator as part of its development plan. The new s.34A provides that an interconnector operator shall offer access to the interconnector on the basis of published non-discriminatory terms under the oversight and approval of the CER. It also provides a dispute appeals mechanism.

Sudden crisis in energy market Section 9 inserted a new s.40A into the 1999 Act, which provides for the taking of emergency measures in the event of a sudden crisis in the energy market threatening physical safety or security of persons, energy infrastructure or the integrity of the transmission and distribution system for natural gas or electricity. It also provides that the Minister for Communications, Marine and Natural Resources may by order direct the CER and electricity and natural gas undertakings to take such safeguard measures as the Minister considers necessary. In making such an order, the Minister is obliged to have regard to avoidance of market disturbance and to only apply measures that are strictly necessary.

Chairperson of CER Section 10 amends the Schedule to the 1999 Act by the insertion of new paragraphs and by making a number of substitutions. The new para.2A provides for an acting chairperson of the CER to be appointed by the Minister where the chairperson is unavailable to perform his or her duties. The new para.2B provides that decisions of the CER shall be determined by a majority of the votes of the members of the CER present and voting and provides for the chairperson to have a casting vote. This section also provides greater flexibility in relation to the tenure and terms of office of the chairperson. The position regarding the timing of the presentation by the CER of its annual report to the Minister and its proposed work programme for the following year is specified.

Natural gas safety Part 3 of the 2006 Act (ss.11 to 14) establishes a revised regulatory regime for natural gas safety. Section 11 amended s.2 of the 1999 Act by providing a definition of the term "natural gas fitting". Section 12 amends s.9(1) of the 1999 Act by expanding the functions of the CER to include regulating and promoting natural gas safety and consulting with the National Standards Authority of Ireland regarding gas safety standards. It also amends s.9 of the 1999 Act by setting out how the CER is to carry out these functions by establishing and implementing a natural gas safety framework and by directing natural gas undertakings to advise their customers and the public as to natural gas safety. Section 13 inserted new ss.9F to 9J into the 1999 Act. They provide for regulation of the activities of gas installers in relation to safety in a similar manner to the regulation of electrical contractors provided for in ss.9C to 9E of the 1999 Act (inserted by s.4 of the 2006 Act, above). The CER may appoint a single designated body (which may be referred to as a gas safety supervisory body) for the registration, and the monitoring of training and standards, of registered gas installers to operate in accordance with detailed criteria (the requirements of which are outlined in ss.9F to 9J of the 1999 Act) and procedures published by the CER. Provision is also made to ensure that responsibility for the ongoing maintenance of a natural gas fitting is allocated to the most appropriate person(s), and to remove any doubt as to the legal position of gas installers with regard to this. The section also provides for the CER to specify the form of completion certificates used on completion of gas works and to designate classes of gas works to be gas works as defined by the section. Provision is made for the natural gas transmission system operator and distribution system operator to appoint a gas emergency officer with powers to enter land (with force if necessary) and to take emergency measures where there is a danger to a person or property arising from natural gas. The CER may appoint a gas safety officer for the purposes of carrying out work inspections. The section also creates an offence for non-compliance with specified provisions. Section 14 inserted a new s.9K into the 1999 Act which allows the Minister for Communications, Marine and Natural Resources to make an order to extend certain of the natural gas safety provisions to include liquefied petroleum gas (LPG).

Bord Gáis Éireann Part 4 of the 2006 Act (ss.15 to 18) deals with the powers and functions of Bord Gáis Éireann (the Board) in the Gas Act 1976, as amended. Section 15 amended the definitions of "foreshore", "harbour authority" and "local authority" in s.2 of the Gas Act 1976 to bring them into line with their use in other legislation. Section 16 inserted a new section into the Gas Act 1976 which confers on the Board the power to create capital stock in amounts equal to the net assets of the Board. This was required to facilitate the introduction of an employee share ownership plan (ESOP) for employees of the Board in the absence of the introduction of legislation to privatise the Board. Sections 17 and 18 amend ss.10A and 10B of the Gas Act 1976 in order to provide for the full opening of the natural gas market. It expands the list of eligible customers to include "any person". Eligible customers are those customers who are free to switch their natural gas supplier, or on whose behalf a natural gas supplier may be granted third party access to gas pipelines or facilities. This section includes a commencement provision which ensures that the market will be fully open no later than the July 1, 2007 deadline set by Directive 2003/55/EC concerning common rules for the internal market in natural gas (the 2003 Directive repealed Directive 98/30/EC which had previously dealt with this). It also empowers the Minister by order to open the gas market in advance of this deadline.

Gas supplier of last resort Section 19 inserted new ss.21A and 21B into the

Gas (Interim) (Regulation) Act 2002 to provide for the designation, by the CER, of a licensed supplier to act as a supplier of last resort, and a licensed shipper to act as a shipper of last resort, to supply gas to final customers of another licensed supplier or shipper (as appropriate) in certain specified circumstances. The provisions of this section are required as a consequence of full gas market opening in ss.17 and 18 of the 2006 Act, above.

Turf Development Board Section 20 amended ss.22(1)(b) of the Turf Development Act 1998 and provides for an increase in the statutory borrowing limit of Bord na Móna (the Turf Development Board) from €127 million to €400 million. It was intended that this increase in the borrowing limit would give the company greater commercial ability to develop its approved future strategic direction, including waste management and electricity generation through renewable sources, into which both areas it has since diversified through a company called AER.

Electricity Supply Board Section 21 amended s.2 of the Electricity (Supply) (Amendment) Act 2001 to provide for a 10 per cent capital stock shareholding in ESB to be vested in the Minister for Communications, Marine and Natural Resources and give the Minister the same legal entitlement as other capital stock shareholders. The amended s.2 provides for the capital stock in ESB to be apportioned between the Minister for Finance (85 per cent), the Minister for Communications, Marine and Natural Resources (10 per cent) and the Employee Share Ownership Plan (ESOP) (5 per cent). The amended s.3 provides the Minister for Communications, Marine and Natural Resources with all the rights and powers that the current stockholders hold, for example, voting rights at the company's AGM. The amended s.7 provides that any dividend to be paid to the two Ministers should continue to be paid to the Exchequer and the amended s.11 ensures that any relevant expenses incurred by the Minister for Communications, Marine and Natural Resources are met by monies provided by the Oireachtas.

Planning Section 22 was intended to ensure that, on commencement of the relevant provisions of the Planning and Development (Strategic Infrastructure) Act 2006, no additional consent requirements are superimposed where an application for approval has been made, or required consents given in respect of electricity transmission lines, strategic gas infrastructure, or State developments which require an environmental impact assessment. The amendment was intended to provide a safeguard against unnecessary delays or duplication of effort for development of these types. Additionally it provides that, where an undertaker who is in receipt of the various required consents for a strategic gas infrastructure development, subsequently decides to apply for a modification of the route of a pipeline only, the developer must apply to the Strategic Infrastructure Division for approval under s.182C of the Planning and

Development Act 2000 (inserted by the 2006 Act) to make the modifications to the pipeline. However, the decision of the Strategic Infrastructure Board would relate to the proposed modifications to the route of the pipeline only. Planning permissions received in respect of any terminal (such as that in connection with the Corrib Gas Field) would stand.

Rehabilitation of mines	Part 9 of the 2006 act (ss.23 to 30) deal with the rehabilitation of land used for mining. It was explained during the Oireachtas debate that this arose primarily from the long-term impact of the former mining activity in the Silvermines area of County Tipperary, in respect of which the State has initiated an action against the principal operator of the mine, Mogul of Ireland Ltd. The Government decided on June 28, 2005 (Ref. S 180/20/10/0354) that the State would assume responsibility for rehabilitation of the former mine at an estimated cost of €10.6 million over a four-year period. Tipperary (North Riding) County Council has agreed to carry out the rehabilitation programme on behalf of the Minister, but funding and overall responsibility for the project remains with the Minister. Section 24 empowers the Minister or a local authority to prepare and implement a mine rehabilitation plan where such a plan is deemed necessary for the purpose of human or animal health, or for protection of the environment, or in the public interest. Provision is also made for consultation with relevant stakeholders, including the local community, regarding preparation of a mine rehabilitation plan. Section 25 empowers the Minister, with the consent of the Minister for Finance, to advance monies to persons, including a local authority, for mine rehabilitation projects. Projects commenced before the passing of the 2006 Act will be deemed to come within the scope of this section. Section 26 empowers the Minister to appoint a local authority as his agent to carry out and implement a mine rehabilitation plan. Section 27 gives the Minister, or his agent, power of entry to relevant lands where such entry is required for preparing, revising and implementing a mine rehabilitation plan. There is provision for payment of compensation to owners of lands affected by this section. Section 28 gives the Minister power to acquire, by agreement or compulsorily, lands considered necessary or expedient for the purpose of carrying out a mine rehabilitation plan. The consent of the Minister for Finance will also be necessary. Where compulsory acquisition is proposed, the usual public consultation procedures will be required. Section 29 provides for recovery of expenditure incurred by the Minister or a local authority on mine rehabilitation works from a person who is obliged to carry out those works. This provision is a discretionary one; there is no strict legal obligation to seek recovery of State expenditure.

INTERNAL MARKET IN ELECTRICITY

The European Communities (Internal Market in Electricity) Regulations 2006 (S.I. No. 524 of 2006) set out more detailed requirements under Directive 2003/54 concerning common rules for the internal market in electricity. They came into force on October 8, 2006.

Equality

VULNERABLE ADULTS

In 2006 the Law Reform Commission published a *Report on Vulnerable Adults and the Law* (LRC 83-2006). This report formed part of the Commission's *Second Programme of Law Reform 2000–2007*, which deals with "Vulnerable Adults and the Law" under two related headings: the law and older people; and the law concerning adults whose ability to make decisions may be limited, for example, through intellectual disability, dementia or an acquired brain injury (such as in a car crash). The report brought together these two areas and built on two consultation papers published by the Commission, a *Consultation Paper on Law and the Elderly* (LRC CP 23–2003) and a *Consultation Paper on Vulnerable Adults and the Law: Capacity* (LRC CP 37–2005). Because of this, the report is divided into two parts. The first part recommends the enactment of a new mental capacity law to create clear rules on when a person has the legal competence (capacity) to make a wide range of decisions, including making contracts such as buying groceries at a shop, transferring ownership in land or making healthcare decisions. The second part recommends that the current wards of court system should be replaced by a new guardianship system.

Empowerment and protection   In the report the Commission aims to promote the empowerment of vulnerable adults, while also recognising that some protections are still needed. In terms of empowerment, the Commission recommends that the proposed law should include a clear presumption that all people over 18 have mental capacity. The Commission also recommends that a modern "functional" approach to legal capacity should be put in place. The functional approach means assessing a person's decision-making ability in relation to a particular decision at the time the decision is made.

Protection: equity release schemes   The Commission also recognises that vulnerable adults may still need protection against abuse. For example, the Commission has recommended that all types of equity release schemes—many of which are aimed at older people—should come under the IFSRA, the Financial Regulator. Some equity release schemes have been designed so that they are not financial products, so that the IFSRA cannot currently regulate these types of schemes.

Guiding principles   The Commission recommends that the proposed capacity legislation should contain specific guiding principles which must always be taken into account. These are: no intervention can take place unless it is necessary for the person, including whether the person might regain their capacity; any intervention should be the least restrictive of the person's freedom; account must be taken of their wishes, past and present; account should be taken of the views of their relatives, carers and those who they live with; and due regard should be given to their right to dignity, bodily integrity, privacy and autonomy.

Healthcare decisions and informal authority to act The Commission also makes specific recommendations in the healthcare context. At present, many routine healthcare treatments—such as dental treatment—are carried out for adults who have limited or no capacity on the basis of "consent forms" signed by a relative. These consent forms have no legal standing, and technically they could be regarded as assaults. The Commission recommends that this should be dealt with by stating in the proposed law that such routine treatments are lawful if they are clearly in the person's best interests; this is called an informal authority to act. The Commission also recommends that the Minister for Health and Children could appoint a Working Group on Capacity to Make Healthcare Decisions to formulate a code of practice for healthcare professionals. The code of practice would provide guidelines on assessing a person's capacity to make a healthcare decision and on the situations where treatment can be carried out under the proposed informal authority to act.

Enduring powers of attorney The Enduring Powers of Attorney Act 1996 allows a person who currently has mental capacity to appoint someone (such as a spouse or partner) to make decisions on his/her behalf; the power of attorney only comes into force when the person loses capacity, for example, through dementia. The 1996 Act is currently limited to financial matters only. The Commission recommends that the 1996 Act should be extended to include minor healthcare and treatment decisions.

Guardianship system to replace wards of court The report also concludes that the current institutional framework for protecting people with limited (or no) mental capacity—the High Court wards of court system—is also in need of reform. The wards of court system is governed mainly by the Lunacy Regulation (Ireland) Act 1871, which states that a person can only be made a ward of court if he or she is deemed to be a "lunatic, idiot or person of unsound mind". As well as using objectionable and outdated language, the wards of court system uses an "all-or-nothing" approach to capacity—if the person is made a ward of court, he or she loses control over all aspects of his/her financial and personal life. The Commission recommends that this system should be replaced by a new decision-making structure, called guardianship. This would involve the creation of a guardianship board, which would make decisions about whether a person does or does not have continuing capacity to make key decisions about him/herself. This could include deciding that a personal guardian should manage a limited aspect of the person's financial affairs, but not necessarily everything. The Commission also recommends establishing a new independent public guardian.

The proposed guardianship system   The report recommends that the proposed guardianship board would be a three-person full-time multi-disciplinary board (along the lines of the Garda Síochána Ombudsman Commission), chaired by a High Court judge. The board could make guardianship orders and intervention orders. Where a guardianship order is made, a personal guardian could be appointed over the property, financial affairs and welfare of a person who lacks capacity, whether in a limited way or more generally. An intervention order would be made for a specific purpose (such as ordering a once-off service), where a guardianship order would not be required. The Commission also recommends the establishment of the Office of Public Guardian, which would have a supervisory role over personal guardians and those acting under enduring powers of attorney. The public guardian would also have the power to develop and publish suitable codes of practice and have an educational role in this area, acting in cooperation with other bodies, including the National Disability Authority and the Health Service Executive.

Mental Capacity and Guardianship Bill 2007   The 2006 report contains the Commission's final recommendations on these areas and includes a draft Scheme of a Bill to implement them. It is worth noting that a private member's Bill (sponsored by Senator Mary Henry), the Mental Capacity and Guardianship Bill 2007, which was based on this draft Scheme, received a Second Stage debate in the Seanad in early 2007, during which the Government accepted the general principles in the Bill.

Equity

INJUNCTIONS

In *Whelan Frozen Foods Ltd v Dunnes Stores* [2006] I.E.H.C. 171, Mac-Menamin J. granted an interlocutory injunction restraining the defendant from proceeding with a unilateral variation of contracts between the parties for the warehousing and distribution by the plaintiff of frozen and chilled foods and textile products. It appeared that the plaintiff was solely dependent on the defendant for its business. The defendant wished to move to a "stock ownership system" whereby it would acquire title to the goods supplied directly rather than maintaining the margin system which, it contended, left open the possibility of disproportionate profits accruing to the plaintiff. Uncontradicted evidence was given that Mr Frank Dunne, a substantial shareholder of the defendant, had stated to a director of the plaintiff company, that he was going to "halve" the plaintiff's business.

The plaintiff, in securing the interlocutory injunction, alleged economic duress; it maintained that, if the injunction was not granted, there was a real prospect that it would become insolvent. There was no dispute that, under the *Campus Oil* test, a fair issue had been established.

MacMenamin J. considered that the instant case could be distinguished from *Curust Financial Services Ltd v Loewe-Lack-Werk* [1994] 1 I.R. 450 and *Ó Murchú t/a Talknology v Eircell Ltd* [2001] I.E.S.C. 15. In the latter case, Geoghegan J. had referred to:

> "the well known principle that in general the courts will not grant an injunction which would involve ongoing supervision. A court, therefore, is very slow to grant injunctions in either service contracts or trading contracts because it is very difficult to assess at any given time thereafter as to whether such injunctions are being obeyed or not. It is also usually impractical and undesirable that two parties be compelled to trade with one another when one, for reasons which are perfectly rational, does not want to carry on such trading."

In MacMenamin J.'s view, the evidence on financial viability and quantification of loss in both *Curust* and *Ó Murchú* was very different from that in the instant case, where there was still in existence an ongoing relationship between the parties which, while imperfect, did not raise the spectre of the need for any supervision by a court of its order on an ongoing basis pending trial.

The distinctions between those two decisions and the instant case were far more fundamental than that of judicial supervision:

> "First as a principle … in the balance of convenience it is clear that as a *general* rule a court should where possible strive to maintain the *status quo*. However, this is but one element in weighing the balance of convenience. Second, the court must always have regard to the fact that as illustrated in *Curust* the onus lies upon the plaintiff to establish as a matter of probability that damages will not be an adequate remedy. There should be evidence which establishes this proposition, both as to the general position of the company, its indebtedness and net asset situation and whether a real risk exists to solvency. In the instant case I consider there is such evidence, albeit disputed, and weight can be given thereto by reason of the fact that [the accountant giving evidence on behalf of the plaintiff] has had access to a far broader range of relevant information than [the accountant giving evidence on behalf of the defendant]. It can by no means be criticised therefore as mere assertion. The balance is affected further because of the probable results of the acts of the defendant in the context of its effect upon the plaintiff. The plaintiff and his advisors say the company will become insolvent, and the jobs of many people will be put at risk. But here there is also added the uncontroverted evidence as to the intentions of Mr. Frank Dunne, to halve the plaintiff's volumes at some point undefined."

Where there was doubt as to the adequacy of damages, MacMenamin J. observed that the court should look at the question of balance of convenience:

> "Where other factors appear to be evenly balanced, it is a counsel of prudence to take such measures as are calculated to preserve the *status quo*. One of the tests which the court must apply is 'the balance of the risk of doing an injustice'".

MacMenamin J. considered that:

> "the evidence in the application points only one way, that is in favour of an injunction, even having regard to any point which might be made as to the duration of any notice period. The adequacy of damages as a remedy must be seen as predicated on the continued existence of the parties as going concern[s] to the trial of the full action. If there is credible evidence of a real risk to solvency as against mere reversion to *status quo ante* pending trial, the arguments of the defendant become unsustainable."

PRE-PURCHASE AGREEMENTS

In *Shiel v McKeon* [2006] I.E.H.C. 194, Clarke J. dismissed a claim based on a "*Pallant v Morgan* equity" (following the decision of that name, reported in [1953] 1 Ch. 43) which can arise where prospective bidders before a sale agree that one will seek to purchase the property and the other will refrain from competing on the understanding that the successful party will hold some of the property in trust for the other. In the instant case, the plaintiff was defeated on the evidence by another equitable principle—that "he who seeks equity must do equity". The decision is analysed by Fergus Ryan in the chapter on Contract Law above, pp. 259-261.

SPECIFIC PERFORMANCE

In *Fitzsimons v Value Homes Ltd* [2006] I.E.H.C. 144, Clarke J. granted specific performance of a contract for the building and sale of an apartment in an affordable housing scheme. The contract had already been varied by agreement to provide for an increased price as the defendant company had encountered financial difficulties. Clarke J. considered that specific performance should be ordered in respect of the contract as varied. The variation was, in his view, binding:

> "If, as appears to be the case, the company was not in a position to complete the development then serious consequences could, potentially, have arisen for [the plaintiff] … [S]he had paid a deposit. In the event that the company became insolvent it would, of course, be the case that the company would be in breach of its contractual obligations to her including, depending on the course of action she decided to adopt, an obligation to repay the deposit. The practicalities of the situation were such that it might well have been the case that she would not have been able to recover all, or indeed any, of the sum that might theoretically be due and owing to her. In those circumstances it seems to me that the variation offered provided a potential advantage to [the plaintiff] in the sense that she agreed to pay an increased price as a *quid pro quo* for ensuring that the development would be completed."

In the chapter on Contract Law, above p.242, Fergus Ryan analyses *Guilfoyle v Farm Development Co-operative Ltd* [2006] I.E.S.C. 18 in which the Supreme Court affirmed Smyth J.'s dismissal of a claim for specific performance of an alleged oral contract.

European and International Law

North/South implementation bodies   The 1998 Good Friday or Belfast Agreement, signed by the major political parties in Northern Ireland in 1998 (*Annual Review of Irish Law 1998*, pp. 118–127), led to the establishment of a devolved Northern Ireland Assembly and Executive, and the amendment of Arts 2 and 3 of the Constitution of Ireland. On the same day, the Governments of the United Kingdom and of Ireland signed the 1998 British–Irish Agreement, which provided for the establishment of a North/South Ministerial Council, comprising representatives of the Northern Ireland Executive and Ministers of the Irish Government, and of implementation bodies which would implement all-island policies agreed by that Council. The British–Irish Agreement Act 1999 gave legal effect to the British–Irish Agreement. The British–Irish Agreement (Amendment) Act 2006 ensured that one of those bodies, the Special EU Programmes Body (SEUPB), could continue in force. The SEUPB was established to manage the EU's PEACE and INTERREG cross-border funds. It was explained during the Oireachtas debate on the 2006 Act that in 2007 there would be changes at EU level in the funding structures for the period 2007 to 2013. While the PEACE programme would continue much as before, the policy areas and objectives covered by the INTERREG programme were to be transferred to a new EU territorial cooperation objective. As a result, some of the terms used in the 1999 Act to describe the SEUPB's remit would become out of date on January 1, 2007. It was explained that it had always been the Government's clear intention that the SEUPB should continue in its role in managing the EU funds and that the UK Government shared this intention. The two Governments confirmed this shared understanding through an exchange of letters, signed by the Minister for Foreign Affairs and the UK Government's Secretary of State for Northern Ireland. This exchange of letters constituted an international agreement and the 2006 Act gave domestic legal effect to that agreement.

EUROPEAN COMMUNITY AND EUROPEAN UNION

Accession by Bulgaria and Romania   The European Communities (Amendment) Act 2006 amended the European Communities Act 1972 to provide that certain provisions of the Treaty concerning the accession of the

Republic of Bulgaria and Romania to the European Union became part of the domestic law of the State.

Implementation of Community law by ministerial regulations Significant changes to the form by which Community law is implemented in Irish law, particularly through the use of ministerial regulations, have been evident in the legislation enacted in 2005 and 2006. These changes arise directly from the decisions of the Supreme Court in *Browne v Ireland* [2003] I.E.S.C. 43; [2003] 3 I.R. 205 and *Kennedy v Attorney General* [2005] I.E.S.C. 36; [2005] 2 I.L.R.M. 401. In the *Browne* case, the Supreme Court declared invalid a ministerial order under s.223A of the Fisheries (Consolidation) Act 1959 to penalise any breach of the EU prohibition on the use of drift nets. In the *Kennedy* case, the Supreme Court declared invalid a different ministerial order, relating to detailed discretionary national measures to give effect to the CFP, on the ground that it lacked a basis in primary legislation. Sections 14 and 15 of the Sea-Fisheries and Maritime Jurisdiction Act 2006, discussed in the Fisheries and Harbours chapter, below pp. 392-3, filled these specific gaps. Thus, s.14 of the 2006 Act amended the regulation-making power in s.224B of the Fisheries (Consolidation) Act 1959 to extend its geographical scope and to apply to all activities in breach of the common fisheries policy. A similar example from 2005 is s.58(10) of the Safety, Health and Welfare at Work Act 2005: see Byrne, *Safety, Health and Welfare at Work Act 2005* (Thomson Round Hall, 2006), p.107.

No jurisdiction of Irish courts to determine validity of administrative decisions in another Member State In *Short v Ireland* [2006] I.E.S.C. 46; [2007] 1 I.L.R.M. 161, the Supreme Court (Murray C.J., Fennelly and Macken J.J.) accepted that the Irish courts have no jurisdiction to determine the validity of administrative decisions of another European Community Member State. The plaintiff claimed that the operations of the third defendant, British Nuclear Fuels plc, which had been sanctioned by administrative decisions in the United Kingdom had been carried out without an environmental impact statement as required by European Community law. The third defendant claimed that the court had no jurisdiction to adjudicate on this claim and sought to have this issue determined as a point of law. As already indicated, the Supreme Court accepted this argument. The court noted that the decisions under which the third defendant operated were made pursuant to the applicable provisions of the laws of the United Kingdom. The courts of the United Kingdom have jurisdiction to determine the validity of those decisions, in accordance with UK law. The court accepted that, while European Community law may become relevant, in that event the courts of the United Kingdom have power to refer questions of interpretation for preliminary ruling to the Court of Justice of the European Communities. The Supreme Court concluded that it was not the function of the courts of another Member State to pronounce on the validity of such administrative decisions.

Family Law

NULLITY OF MARRIAGE

Homosexual Orientation The question of the extent to which a party's homosexual orientation should invalidate a marriage is one that has troubled the courts over the years. Homosexual orientation is not a specific ground for annulment. It can, however, fall within the generic ground, first identified by Barrington J. in *RSJ v JSJ* [1982] I.L.R.M. 263, of incapacity to form a caring or considerate marital relationship with the other partner to the marriage. The Supreme Court so held in *UF v JC* [1991] 2 I.R. 330. The court was anxious not to characterise a homosexual condition as a mental illness but identified it instead as an inherent and unalterable condition.

It is clear enough, therefore, that a person who is 100 per cent homosexual in orientation may well fall within the scope of the *RSJ* ground. It is less clear whether such a completely homosexual orientation, if established, inevitably comes within this ground. One can conceive of cases where the sexual dimension of a marriage may be of little or no importance to the parties, as where they both are very old or infirm.

More problematic are cases where the degree of homosexual orientation is less intense, as, for example, where a person is bisexual. The issue arose in *AB v NC* [2006] I.E.H.C. 127. The parties met in 1996 when the applicant was aged 29 and the respondent aged 28. The respondent had previously married when he was 18 or 19 following the pregnancy of his girlfriend. The marriage lasted only a very short time. The respondent reared the daughter of the marriage. The parties lived together from around 1997. Their relationship at that time was, in the applicant's words, "really very good". They decided to have a baby. Their daughter was born in 1998. The couple parted briefly in 2002, on account of rows relating to the presence in the home of the respondent's elder daughter. They married in July 2003. In January 2004, during a drunken row late in the night, the respondent revealed to the applicant that he had homosexual feelings. They separated three weeks later.

The applicant took nullity proceedings in the Circuit Court, invoking, *inter alia*, the *RSJ* ground. These proceedings were unsuccessful and she appealed to the High Court.

In evidence, the respondent acknowledged that he had been attracted sexually to men "a little bit" in his teenage years but said that he liked women as well. O'Higgins J. found that the report submitted to the court by the medical inspector was less than fully satisfactory. The inspector did not appear to have investigated in any detail the respondent's contention that he was bisexual rather than homosexual. First, the inspector had not mentioned the Kinsey rating scale in his report; in evidence he had referred to it as running from zero to ten rather than zero to six, which was usually the scale referred to in the courts. Secondly, the inspector had not addressed the question of the respondent's possible sexual encounters with males before the marriage, although the respondent had given evidence that no such encounters had occurred then. Thirdly, he had not referred to the sexual history of the respondent after the breakdown of the relationship in 2004. Finally, the inspector had placed at least some reliance on the breakdown of the first marriage informing his views on the inability of the respondent to maintain a marital relationship. O'Higgins J. considered that the circumstances occasioning that marriage and the respondent's young age were factors rendering it unsafe to attach any significance to the breakdown of the first marriage when assessing his homosexual orientation.

O'Higgins J. regarded the facts of the instant case as "very different" from those of *UF v JC*, where the respondent was a practising homosexual at the time of the marriage ceremony who had concealed his condition from the applicant. In the instant case there had been unchallenged evidence that the respondent had had no homosexual experiences before the marriage. Again in contrast to *UF v JC*, the respondent had not engaged in homosexual conduct during the marriage. O'Higgins J. accordingly held that this ground had not been made out.

One must retain certain doubts about this case. The respondent's orientation clearly included a significant homosexual component, albeit under the surface for many years. Must the partner of a person with such an orientation, which resurrects itself shortly after marriage, be forced to accept it or resort to divorce? And if the person with the homosexual orientation seeks an annulment, must he or she be refused? Is the existence of strong homosexual or bisexual leanings inevitably inconsistent with the capacity to form and maintain a caring and considerate relationship with one's spouse if these leanings are never acted upon? If action is decisive, is there a danger of turning the *RSJ* ground for annulment into the equivalent of the ground of adultery in proceedings for judicial separation?

Informed consent In the *Annual Review of Irish Law 2004*, pp. 278–280, we analysed the decision of *PF v G O'N (otherwise GF)*, Supreme Court, November 28, 2004, where an attempt was made to rein in the undue breadth of the ground of lack of informed consent which the court (albeit a differently constituted one) had articulated in *M O'M v B O'C* [1996] 1 I.R. 208. In its earlier decision the court had granted an annulment where the husband had failed to tell his wife before they married that he had attended a psychiatrist on several occasions over a period of six years. This was regarded as "a matter of great importance" and "a circumstance which was clearly relevant to the decision" of the wife to marry him. Moreover, the test was a subjective one in the sense that the court appeared to emphasise the extent to which the party whose consent was in issue attached significance to particular facts.

In *PF v G O'N (otherwise GF)*, McGuinness J. (Murray and Geoghegan JJ. concurring) distinguished *M O'M v B O'C*. In *PF* the question was whether the husband's ignorance of the fact that his wife had engaged in sexual relations with another man before and during the marriage could be regarded as vitiating the husband's consent. McGuinness J. thought not. She concluded that:

> "the case of *M O'M v B O'C* should be distinguished from the present case on the facts and on the particular nature of the information involved which gave rise to considerations of inherent disposition and mental stability. I respectfully agree with O'Higgins J [the High Court judge in the proceedings] that it cannot be extended to cover concealed misconduct and other forms of misrepresentation."

In *AB v NC* [2006] I.E.H.C. 127 the issue again fell for consideration. We have already set out the facts in more detail above at p.372. Briefly, the applicant alleged that the respondent had failed to disclose to her his homosexual orientation before entering into marriage with her and that accordingly she had not given her full, free and informed consent. The essence of her claim was that, six months after the marriage ceremony, the respondent, in the course of a drunken row, disclosed to her that he had had a homosexual orientation since he was a teenager and that he had thought that if he married her this would make it go away. The respondent's version was that he had not said that he was homosexual but rather that he was having difficulties with his sexuality. The parties were aged 36 and 37 respectively when they married. They had lived together for six years before marrying. Their daughter was aged five at the time of the marriage.

O'Higgins J. preferred the respondent's version. This involved an acknowledgement that he had been sexually attracted to men "a little bit" in his teenage years but that he had liked women as well. O'Higgins J. accepted his evidence that, at the time of his marriage, he did not consider that his sexual orientation was in issue. In O'Higgins J.'s view, the respondent had married the applicant in good faith. He commented:

> "It appears unlikely and implausible in circumstances where the parties had lived together in a satisfactory heterosexual relationship that the respondent would actually go through a marriage ceremony in the hope that feelings of attraction towards men would go away. I do not accept that the marriage was entered into in the hope that the respondent's attraction to men would go away or that the applicant's consent was procured by fraud or deceit in any way."

O'Higgins J. referred to the decision of *M O'M v B O'C* and *PF v G O'M (otherwise GF)* and observed:

> "I have already found that at the time of contracting the marriage the question of sexual orientation was not an issue for the respondent in circumstances where he had been living in a heterosexual relationship for a number of years. I cannot accept in the particular circumstances of the case the question of the respondent's sexual orientation was a real concern and a 'circumstance of substance' which should have been disclosed to the applicant and in default of which her consent was vitiated, and therefore I do not accept that he concealed any 'circumstance of substance'. The evidence discloses that the attraction towards another male which led to the row in January, 2004, came as a shock to the respondent as well as to the applicant. In my view, at the time of contracting the marriage, the respondent was unaware of any issue concerning his sexual orientation being of significance. I do not consider that the respondent acted dishonestly to his intended partner and I do still ask was he guilty of any deceit (although the question of intention to decei[ve] may well be of no significance in non disclosure cases in the context of nullity)."

Accordingly, O'Higgins J. declined to grant an annulment on this ground. Since the alternative ground, based on the *RSJ* ground, also failed, the nullity application was unsuccessful.

O'Higgins J.'s holding on lack of informed consent raises a number of questions. The holdings in both *M O'M v B O'C* and *PF v G O'M (otherwise GF)* appeared to accept that this ground might be made out where there had been non-disclosure of a party's *inherent disposition*. It seems clear from *UF v JC* that a homosexual orientation can constitute an inherent disposition. It would be hard to see how bisexuality or latent homosexuality which subsequently manifests itself more strongly could not be similarly described. In the instant case, the respondent had experienced some element of homosexual attraction during his teens. That he did not later attach a great deal of weight to it does not change that fact. A further fact is that he had not disclosed this attraction to the applicant before the marriage. Even if he did not regard it as important, the applicant might well have done so. In simple terms, the respondent was at least bisexual, possibly fully homosexual. He had had some intimation of this before he married. His condition was one which might be regarded by a potential heterosexual partner as ruling out marriage. It is a little curious that no nullity decree should have been granted either on this ground or on the *RSJ* ground in respect of a person whose bisexual or homosexual orientation emerged within six months of the marriage ceremony.

FINANCIAL PROVISION

In the *Annual Review of Irish Law 2005*, pp. 406–410, we analysed *RG v CG (Divorce)* [2005] 2 I.R. 418, where Finlay Geoghegan J. had to deal with the troublesome question of the extent to which an earlier "full and final settlement" clause should continue to control in subsequent proceedings for judicial separation or divorce. Her approach may be contrasted with that of Hardiman J. in *WA v MA* [2005] 1 I.R. 1, analysed in the *Annual Review of Irish Law 2004*, pp. 306–310. See further Clissmann & Hogan, "Trends in Divorce on the Ten Year Anniversary of its Introduction", (2007) 12 *Bar Review* 46, 46–47. This incisive article discusses two decisions of Abbott J. on the subject, which have not been circulated on the judgments database or on BAILII.

In *S McM v M McM*, High Court, November 29, 2006 (discussed by Clissmann and Hogan at pp.47–48), the spouses had married in 1967 and separated in 1991. The separation agreement of that time contained a "full and final settlement" clause. The husband agreed to provide £83,000 (representing 60 per cent of the proceeds of sale of the family home) to his wife as well as £25,000 per annum as maintenance for her and their three children. In divorce proceedings, Abbott J. interpreted the test emerging from the earlier case law as being:

> "whether the circumstances of the provider (the husband) have altered substantially and dramatically for the better since the making of the settlement a relatively long time ago in 1991."

In the intervening years, the husband's salary had increased from £80,000 to €420,000. The maintenance had increased only from £25,000 to €72,000. Abbott J. considered that it would be unfair to let the terms of the 1991 settlement "prevent the wife from enjoying the better standard of living experienced throughout the country in real terms, especially when they have been enjoyed ... by the husband." In his view, the settlement "should not act as a restraint in relation to providing reasonable resources to enable the [wife] to catch up with modern prosperity...".

The husband's assets were worth more than €7 million, the wife's around €800,000. Having addressed the factors set out in s.20(2) of the Family Law (Divorce) Act 1996, Abbott J. increased the maintenance to €90,000; ordered the husband to make a lump sum of €400,000 to his wife; ordered the division of the pension fund by providing the sum of €1.25 million for a retirement fund for the wife; and directed the husband to hold 10 per cent of his shares in the family company in trust for his wife so that she could hold and dispose of them by deed or will but not call for their vesting. Commenting on this latter order, Clissmann and Hogan observe (at p.48):

> "This award is a novel approach for an Irish Court to take, as the ties

between divorcing couples are more usually severed (apart from the case of maintenance awards) and it was frequently deemed inappropriate to give a spouse some shares and thus an ongoing interest in the other spouse's company. This award could represent a more imaginative approach to achieving a just solution, and the beginnings of a step-back from any tentative Irish 'clean break' strategy."

Clissman and Hogan also discuss (at pp. 48–50), Abbott J.'s decision in *SJN v PC O'D*, High Court, November 29, 2006. Here, unusually, the wife was the economically stronger party. The spouses separated in 1991. There were two children. In 2001 the High Court granted a decree of judicial separation on the terms of a settlement in which the husband agreed to pay his wife £300,000 and the wife agreed to release any interest in the family home and another premises. The husband released to the wife all his interest in her companies and agreed to pay €1,000 maintenance. A subsequent restructuring of the wife's companies revealed that her financial situation had been better than it had appeared in 2001, though Abbott J. acquitted the wife of any *mala fides* for what he described as this "information deficit". The wife's assets at the time of the divorce were well over €15 million, the husband's less than €3 million. The husband's business had not prospered in the intervening years.

Abbott J., according to Clissmann and Hogan (at p.49), summarised the interests of divorcing parties and the public in the full and final settlement clauses in family law proceedings as follows:

1. commercial and economic reasons;

2. the sharing and avoidance of risk;

3. the avoidance of personal and emotional turmoil from the uncertainty and unresolved conflict, including the risk of continued litigation; and

4. the avoidance of further costs.

As to the first of these factors, Abbott J. noted that we live in a market economy and that "relieving social litigation" should not cause the pursuit of commercial goals to be inhibited. As to the second, it was "axiomatic that those who bear the most risk should enjoy the greater reward in economic terms". (This observation is almost identical to what O'Higgins J. said in *CD v PD* [2006] I.E.H.C. 100, considered below at p.381.)

In the instant case, although the 2001 settlement was entitled to be given "considerable weight", Abbott J. considered that the husband should be protected from an embarrassing gap in wealth relative to the wife as this could cause "a loss in self-esteem, grieving or obsession with the litigation" so that he "would easily lose the capacity to celebrate, enjoy and be bubbly with his children as a father should". Taking into account the "information deficit", Abbott J. reduced the maintenance to €7,000 per annum and awarded the husband a lump sum of €2,148,800.

These two decisions provoke a couple of observations. In an era of radical changes in property values and of a large increase in wealth, distributed unevenly, should courts have a role in removing inequalities, thus created, where spouses have separated or divorced? If the answer is yes, and Abbott J.'s judgments in these cases go some way in that direction, then why should the court not have a similar role in relation to spouses whose marriages have not broken down? The poverty of analysis evident in the Supreme Court decision in *L v L* [1992] 2 I.R. 77 comes back to haunt us.

As to Abbott J.'s idea that a man whose assets are less than those of his wife needs an economic boost at the expense of his wife in order to promote his morale and consequently make him a happier and better father, suffice it to raise the question whether wives whose husbands earn more than they do must fatefully accept their lot. The deeply gendered assumptions quickly emerge.

In *FTM v CTM* [2006] I.E.H.C. 333, Abbott J. addressed the question of the court's powers under s.9(1)(c) of the Family Law Act 1995. Some of the assets which fell for consideration had been conveyed to a trust. In the earlier judgment, McKechnie J. had held that the trust might appropriately be the subject of an order under s.9(1)(c). Abbott J. observed:

> "On the basis of the tax experts' advice, it will be necessary to ensure the trustees (whether existing or new) cooperate with the solution offered by the Court by way of 'judicial encouragement' highlighted by the authorities. In the event of such cooperation not being forthcoming, then the matter would have to be considered further by the Court under the general rubric of liberty to apply to be given in the order now to be made by the Court. However, it would seem to me to be entirely premature to cross that bridge before the parties or the Court come to it."

Counsel for the applicant submitted that it was open to the court to make an order under s.9(1)(c), effectively divesting the trust of the house and land in the first instance in favour of the applicant and then making the appropriate order for the applicant to make provision for the respondent. Counsel argued that there were tax advantages in taking this approach. Abbott J. was prepared to follow this course but made no formal order until the parties indicated what course they proposed to follow as a result of considering the indicative order which he made.

In *MK v JPK* [2006] I.E.S.C. 4 the Supreme Court addressed the question of currency differences in the making of orders for financial provision, including maintenance. The spouses had married in 1963. The husband had obtained a Haitian divorce and thereafter gone through a ceremony of marriage with another woman in Massachusetts in 1985. The wife remarried in Ireland, raising their six children. The husband's career blossomed. In 2000 Lavan J. granted a decree of divorce, and ordered the husband to pay to the wife a lump sum of around 50 per cent of his assets as well as maintenance equal to about half his annual income. The husband appealed successfully to the Supreme Court ([2001] 3 I.R. 371, analysed in the *Annual Review of Irish Law 2001*, pp. 352-357. The retrial before O'Neill J. involved somewhat different orders for financial provision. These included orders for a lump sum payment by the husband to the wife of €450,000, the transfer to her of the entire beneficial interest in the family home, the payment of €40,000 maintenance per annum and the payment by him of the wife's costs in both High Court hearings.

On appeal to the Supreme Court, the husband argued that, since the dollar had decreased sharply in value subsequent to O'Neill J.'s decision, the orders should now be expressed in dollars rather than euros. As McCracken J. observed, the issue came down to the question of who should bear the risk of currency fluctuations. McCracken J. fully accepted that it was open to a trial judge in family law matters to direct payment of either lump sum or maintenance in the currency of the residence of either party. He did not think it was possible to lay down any general rules as to how that discretion should be exercised save to say that it must be exercised so as to comply with the obligations imposed on the court by s.5 of the Family Law (Divorce) Act 1996 to ensure that the court make "such provision as the court considers proper having regard to the circumstances exists or will be made for the spouses and any dependent members of the family". The reference to proper provision being made for "the spouses" emphasised that the court in exercising its discretion had to give consideration to the interests of both the husband and the wife. In the instant case the husband had clearly suffered financially through the decline in the value of the dollar between the date of the hearing and the date of the appeal, but the wife had given evidence, which had been accepted by O'Neill J., that it was her intention to use the lump sum to purchase a house in Dublin, a fact which O'Neill J. had considered to be of considerable importance.

McCracken J. observed:

> "In effect he was awarding here a sum which he considered would allow her to do so. The trial judge clearly was of the view that providing for the purchase of a house was a proper provision to be made for the wife and, were she to bear the risk of the currency fluctuations, the result might be that she would be unable to purchase the house."

McCracken J. quoted from *GW v RW* [2003] 2 F.L.R. 180, where it had been stated that, where children are living abroad, it would usually be proper for the court to express an award of child maintenance in the currency of the country of the payee in order to protect the children from exposure to the risk of currency fluctuation. McCracken J. commented:

> "I would agree with th[is] principle... And I think it applies equally to a provision for a spouse as to provision for children. The provision of

the lump sum had a specific purpose which could only be fulfilled if the award was in the currency of the country in which it was intended to expend the monies. Providing for all payments to be made to the wife to be in the currency of the country in which she resides is in my view a perfectly proper exercise of the discretion of the learned trial judge, and further I think that the amount awarded was a suitable amount in the light of the assets available to both parties."

On the question of the costs of the first High Court proceedings the wife invoked what McCracken J. himself had said in *Mangan v Independent Newspapers* [2003] 1 I.R. 442 at 447, regarding defamation proceedings:

"If the plaintiff had to bear his own costs of the abortive trial, and certainly if he had to bear both sets of costs, then the entire award of damages to him would be eaten up in paying those costs. In this case the plaintiff was seriously libelled and the jury considered the proper compensation to him was €25,000. They would have been totally unaware that the money would not go to the benefit of the plaintiff, but would be used to pay costs. This would certainly seem to me to tip the balance of any discretion in the learned trial Judge in favour of the plaintiff."

McCracken J. did not consider that these observations applied in the instant case. There was a considerable logic in a general rule that, where damages were awarded, the purpose of those damages was to compensate a plaintiff and not to be used in paying the costs of an abortive trial:

"Here the situation is very different. These are family law proceedings in which the court must have regard to the interests of both parties. This is not a case in which damages have been awarded to the wife for some wrongdoing or injury caused to her by the husband. In family law cases there is a pool of assets, comprising those of both the husband and the wife, which assets are to be used both to make proper provision for both spouses and any dependant members of the family and to pay the costs of both parties. There is no question of either party having further assets which could be used to pay costs. In my view, therefore, the general rule does not necessarily apply in family law proceedings.

It is indeed very unfortunate that the assets available to the parties have to be reduced by the amount of the costs of the first trial. In the circumstances of family law cases the court must look at the effect of the award of costs on both parties. If the husband has to bear the costs of both parties of the first trial this is going to very considerably reduce the assets available out of which an award may be made to the wife."

Accordingly, the Supreme Court modified O'Neill J.'s order by relieving the husband of the obligation to pay the costs of the first trial.

In *CD v PD* [2006] I.E.H.C. 100 O'Higgins J. threw some light on two important questions relating to financial provision: the circumstances in which a court should extinguish Succession Act rights in judicial separation proceedings and the principle of fairness when determining allocation of spousal interests in property. The spouses married in 1991 and had three children. The respondent husband was 42 years old; the applicant wife was 40. They were joint owners of the family home, another property in Dublin and a mobile home. Each share was worth over €1,760,000. The respondent also had a property in London worth over €220,000. He had "partnership/investments" of over two million euros, as well as other assets. His expenditure for securing debts was €75,000. The applicant had worked as a legal secretary before she had children. On the premise that her Succession Act rights would be extinguished, the applicant proposed that she be given a half share of certain of the respondent's investments or a one-third share of them plus a lump sum of €500,000. O'Higgins J. regarded this as unreasonable. To impose such a trust could have serious implications for the respondent's ability to borrow. Moreover, it would in his view be unfair since:

> "it would involve the applicant having a 50% or a 33% interest in investments without any exposure to the considerable risks involved in those investments. There is evidence that the respondent is jointly and severally liable for debts said to be in excess of €80 million. Although it is unlikely that he will be called on to pay any sum of that magnitude he is exposed and at risk. Furthermore there may be a call-up of certain monies in respect of some of the investments. In my view it could be seen as being unfair to the applicant that without partaking in the risk into the future she should be entitled to 50% of the benefits."

Counsel for the respondent made proposals on the basis that the applicant's Succession Act rights would be extinguished. He contended that under s.15A of the Family Law Act 1995 (inserted by s.52 of the Family Law (Divorce) Act 1996) it was possible for a spouse to apply to the court, even after Succession Act rights had been extinguished, where proper provision was not made under ss.8, 9, 10, 11 or 12 for any reason other than the conduct of an applicant referred to in s.16(2)(1). This offered sufficient protection, in his submission, for the applicant in the instant case where the respondent was willing to pay her a sum equivalent to her Succession Act rights. Only in the most exceptional circumstances would the court refuse to make an order extinguishing Succession Act rights when granting an order for judicial separation. O'Higgins J. did not agree. He stated:

> "I do not think it necessary or even desirable to attempt to enumerate the

circumstances in which Succession Act rights might not be extinguished following the making of an order for judicial separation. The extinguishing of rights under the Succession Act is one of the options open to the court on granting an application for judicial separation. It is one of a wide variety of orders available to the court in discharging its obligation to ensure that proper provision is made for the parties. Whether or not to extinguish the rights under the Succession Act is not a decision that should be taken in isolation from all the circumstances of the case or from the other orders which the court intends to make."

A relevant factor in the instant case was the extremely unpredictable financial position of the respondent into the future. It was likely that he would accumulate a great deal of wealth in the next 10 to 12 years. Although the court had to take into account the assets of the parties as they were at the time of the judicial separation hearing, it was also obliged to have regard to the income and earning capacity of the parties for the foreseeable future. The applicant had indicated that she intended to apply for a divorce in due course on the granting of which her rights under the Succession Act would be extinguished in those circumstances. It seemed to O'Higgins J. to be fair and reasonable not to make an order extinguishing the applicant's rights under the Succession Act. On the question of the distribution of assets, O'Higgins J. stated:

"It is clear that the duty of the court is to endeavour to ensure proper provision for the parties rather than equal division of the assets ... The court should strive not for equality but for fairness. In attempting to achieve that fair result the factors set out in the legislation must be taken into account, but the importance to be attached to each of the factors will widely vary from case to case and there is no hierarchy of importance to be attached to the various factors. In considering the question of proper provision the percentage of the assets to be distributed may or may not be of importance. As Denham J. stated in *T v T* [2002] 3 I.R. 334 at 384:

'The concept of one third as a check on fairness may well be useful in some cases, however, it may have no application in many cases.

In the particular circumstances of the present case and in particular having regard to the very great earning capacity of the respondent it is of little assistance in the present case.'"

O'Higgins J. quoted a passage from the speech of Lord Nicholls in *White v White* [2001] 1 A.C. 596:

"If a husband and wife by their joint efforts over many years, his directly in his business and hers indirectly at home, have build up a valuable business from scratch, why should the claimant wife be confined to the court's assessment of her reasonable requirements, and the husband left with a much larger share? Or, to put the question differently, in such a case, where the assets exceed the financial needs of both parties, why should the surplus belong solely to the husband? On the facts of a particular case there may be a good reason why the wife should be confined to her needs and the husband left with the much larger balance. But the mere absence of financial need cannot, by itself, be a sufficient reason. If it were, discrimination would be creeping in by the back door. In these cases, it should be remembered, the claimant is usually the wife. Hence the importance of the check against the yardstick of equal division."

O'Higgins J. commented:

"This passage is of but limited assistance in this jurisdiction where there is no 'yardstick of equal division.' However, it is of course correct that the proper provision must be assessed on the basis of the assets and that the concept of proper provision cannot be assessed without taking into account the assets."

O'Higgins J. went on to make a range of orders, including orders granting the applicant sole ownership of the family home and requiring the respondent to transfer his interest in the family home to the applicant, an order that the applicant transfer her interests in the other property in Dublin to the respondent and a maintenance order for the applicant and her children for €10,000 per month net.

In *LB v Ireland* [2006] I.E.H.C. 275, MacMenamin J. rejected a challenge to the constitutional validity of s.5(1)(a) of the Family Law (Maintenance of Spouses and Children) Act 1976, s.5 and ss.12 to 21 of the Family Law (Divorce) Act and s.2(1)(f) and s.3(1) of the Judicial Separation and Family Law Reform Act 1989. The gravamen of the plaintiff's claim was that orders made by a court under these provisions affected a spouse's property rights; only the State was entitled to make orders determining the property rights of the citizen; the powers which the State had vested in the courts to make such orders relating to maintenance, property and pension rights constituted "legislation" and consequently formed an unlawful derogation of the State's powers to legislate in this area. The Oireachtas had no power to delegate its legislative function to any other organ of the State, including the courts.

In the light of the Supreme Court decision of *TF v Ireland* [1995] 2 I.L.R.M., it is scarcely surprising that MacMenamin J. dismissed the claim. The fact that *TF* was concerned with judicial separation rather than divorce raised no principled basis for distinction since *TF*'s rationale was rooted in the same "no fault" philosophy as that underlying divorce. See our observations in the

Annual Review of Irish Law 1995, p.287.

A few comments are perhaps in order. First, the relationship between a person's right to property, under Arts 40.3 and 43, and a court's power to deprive him or her of that right in the context of family law, is a good deal less obvious than a casual reading of *LB v Ireland* might suggest. The issue is compounded by the problems of traditional gender role differentiation and the changes in social norms regarding sexual conduct and procreation.

If one looks to the past for guidance, one is bound for disappointment and frustration. A couple of centuries ago, marriage was regarded as an irrevocable lifelong commitment, the only socially supported way of engaging in sexual relations and procreation. Yet wives were not treated well by the law. Their husbands had control over their property without legal sanction. In the event of misconduct by their husbands, they could obtain a decree of divorce *a mensa et thoro* (judicial separation) but the court granting the decree could not make an order affecting their husband's property and was restricted to awarding alimony in the form of periodical maintenance payments. In matters of succession, husbands could effectively disinherit their wives. Fathers of children born outside marriage owed them only the most limited maintenance obligation and their children had no claim to their property either *inter vivos* or by way of succession entitlements. It is hard to discern in the traditional family law principles much of a sentiment that marriage or paternity guaranteed significant restrictions on a man's property rights. Conversely, women's property rights were affected by marriage, severely to the detriment of the women concerned.

The Married Women's Property Acts of the late 19th century, in introducing the principle of separation of property, were initially regarded as protective of women's rights. Over time, with the increasing phenomenon of wide access to mortgages and the occurrence of significant inflation, separation of property became an engine of injustice to wives who had sacrificed careers outside the home in order to rear their children.

The approach of the Irish courts over the past 30 years has been less than satisfactory. After years of failing to develop equitable principles so as to recognise in proprietary terms the value of the work of women in the home, the Supreme Court in *L v L* [1992] 2 I.R. 77 rejected Barr J.'s attempt to give practical effect to the constitutional rhetoric of support for these women, holding that courts had no power to affect men's property entitlements in this way in the absence of legislation. When the legislature responded with a mild reformist measure, the Matrimonial Home Bill 1993, the Supreme Court struck it down as violating Art.41's protection of decisions made by spouses.

The position relating to maintenance of spouses was totally unsatisfactory before the enactment of the Family Law (Maintenance of Spouses and Children) Act 1976. A wife whose husband did not maintain her had no legal protection save that of agency of necessity in the law of contract, which depended on the charity of shopkeepers. Proceedings for divorce *a mensa et thoro* were not available for failure to maintain, even where the husband had deserted his wife. (In any event these proceedings were entirely theoretical since they involved High Court proceedings which were beyond the means of most wives and certainly beyond those of wives whose husbands had not maintained them. This is one reason why the decision of *Airey v Ireland* (1979) 2 E.H.R.R. 305 was so significant.) Under the Married Women (Maintenance in case of Desertion) Act 1886, a paltry sum of maintenance could be awarded to deserted wives. It was not until 1971 that the High Court was given jurisdiction under this legislation. Wives living with husbands who did not support them could not avail themselves of any judicial remedy. The idea that the law has always been solicitous of the maintenance entitlements of married women is completely misconceived.

Undoubtedly the combined effect of the decisions in *L v L*, *Re Article 26 and the Matrimonial Home Bill 1993* and *TF v Ireland* is that legislation giving courts the power to award maintenance and make orders for financial provision may be constitutional. What is less clear is the outer boundary of such legislation. At what point, and for what reason, would a legislative provision enabling the court to make an order affecting a person's property interest become unconstitutional? Would the values underlying Arts 41 and 42 permit *any* judicial transfer of a spouse's property to another family member without entrenching or his or her right to property under Arts 40.3 or 43? It is noteworthy that the Matrimonial Home Bill 1993 was struck down out of concern, not for these constitutional provisions, but for Art.41 itself. We have also seen how, in *SJN v PC OD*, High Court, November 29, 2006 and *CD v PD* [2006] I.E.H.C. 100, two judges separately concluded that a point is reached when it becomes unfair in financial provision to award the spouse who has not engaged in capitalist risk-taking at the expense of the (usually male) risk-taking spouse. There is a subterranean value system still operating in the minds of Irish judges which could yet throw up some nasty surprises in the context of the right to property in divorce and judicial separation.

COHABITATION

The Law Reform Commission published its *Consultation Paper on the Rights and Duties of Cohabitees* (LRC CP 32–2004). A detailed, comprehensive analysis is preserved by John Mee, "A Critique of the Law Reform Commission's Consultation Paper on the Rights and Duties of Cohabitees", 39 Ir. Jur. 74 (2004). In its *Report on the Rights and Duties of Cohabitants* (LRC 82–2006), the Commission makes its final recommendations on the subject.

The cultural debate has moved on radically in the short period between publication of the consultation paper and publication of the report. Internationally, there has been a significant advance in the judicial and legislative movement towards recognising same-sex partnerships and same-sex marriage. See Eardly, "The Constitution and Marriage; the Scope of Protection", (2006) 12 *Bar Review* 137; Ferrer Riba, "Same-Sex Marriage, Express Divorce and Related Developments in Spanish Marriage Law" [2006] Int'l Fam. L. L. 139. The report reflects these developments though this dimension is not probed in any great depth.

The Commission's discussion of the various philosophies for approaching unmarried cohabitation might, on a favourable view, be described as pluralistic. A less favourable assessment would be that the Commission's recommendations, in their totality, present a conflicting set of perceptions as to society's approach towards family relationships. In advocating simultaneously "contract" and "redress" models, the Commission seeks to advance the values of autonomy and paternalism in a way that cannot easily be harmonised.

Why should society care one way or the other about people's intimate relationships? Why should it intrude into their privacy and prescribe rules of behaviour or confer entitlements to one party which impose binding responsibilities on the other? The old answer was that intimate relationships tended to lead to children and that children thrive best on the loving care and guidance of both parents who have made a permanent commitment to each other. Marriage was therefore privileged; unmarried cohabitation and parenthood were stigmatised.

All that has changed utterly over recent decades. The link between sexual conduct and procreation has been greatly weakened; no-fault divorce and unmarried parenthood have become widely accepted; and unmarried cohabitation, while still not very hugely practised in Ireland, has significantly increased. Allied to these developments has been a weakening in the social influence of religious values, a strengthening of social support for the individualist norms of privacy and autonomy and a growing view that the State has no legitimate role in telling people how best they should live their lives. Importantly, there is far greater sensitivity to gender issues and an as yet unresolved debate as to whether the law should remove gender differentiation in family relationships in areas such as maintenance, financial provision and guardianship of children or intervene more energetically to protect women from gender-based violence or financial exploitation in intimate relationships.

The Commission's proposals appear to favour both sides of the debate. The Commission recommends that "cohabitants"—couples living together in an intimate relationship, whether same-sex or opposite-sex—should have their autonomy respected by being able to enter binding "cohabitant agreements", but that a "qualified cohabitant", who has been living with his or her partner for at least three (or, where there is a child of the relationship, two) years should be able to seek redress in respect of a deceased partner's estate or, *inter vivos*, where there is economic dependency. It is hard to see how these proposals, in their totality, do not have the effect of turning unmarried cohabitation into a shadow marriage after a few years. At a time when marriage is being shorn of permanence and of ongoing mutual financial responsibilities and is likely to be modified further over time by acceptance of pre-nuptial agreements, it is culturally curious that the free choice by parties *not* to marry should be overridden by an intrusive panoply of judicial orders based on a premise of dependence and paternalism.

Let us look in more detail at a few of the Commission's proposals. On cohabitation agreements the controversial decision of Kelly J. in *Ennis v Butterly* [1996] 1 I.R. 426 might have been considered to represent an obstacle. The Commission does not maintain that the holding was wrong; instead it seeks to distinguish the case from its proposal that legal recognition be afforded to these contracts. It states (para.3.07):

> "The Commission notes that the basis of the verbal contract in *Ennis v Butterly* did not merely involve financial and property affairs but appeared to replicate a marital contract. Such a contract is unenforceable, but this should not signify that all cohabitation contracts are void. Such decisions do not operate as a bar to the enforceability of a cohabitation agreement where the agreement does not attempt to replicate the marriage contract, or does not have an immoral purpose, but restricts itself merely to regulating the financial and property affairs of the parties. In light of the uncertainty on this issue, the Commission believes the position as to the status and validity of cohabitation contracts be clarified."

With respect, such an analysis subtracts from the flesh and blood humanity of the cohabitation relationship the important element of sexual intimacy. It was this element that excited the antipathy of the Victorian judges, who stigmatised agreements to live together in unmarried cohabitation as immoral. The Commission's strategy, of turning its eyes from the sexual dimension, seems curiously prudish. The weakness of this approach may perhaps be shown by enquiring as to the content of the contractual concept of consideration in a "cohabitant contract" if it does not extend to sexual intimacy.

Let us examine the key terms of s.11 of the draft Bill. subsections (2) to (5) provide as follows:

> "(2) Where, on an application by or on behalf of a qualified cohabitant, on notice to the respondent, the court is of the opinion that the deceased failed to make adequate provision or no provision for the qualified cohabitant in accordance with his or her means, whether by his or her will or otherwise, the court may order that such provision shall be made for the qualified cohabitant out of the net estate of the deceased as the court considers just and equitable.
>
> (3) In making an order under this section, the court shall make what provision is reasonable in the circumstances, having regard to the factors set out in *section 12(5)* and also the following factors –

    (a) the interest of the beneficiaries of the estate,

    (b) any benefit received or to be received by the qualified cohabitant on, or as a result of, the deceased's death other than out of the net estate, and

    (c) the provision (if any) made for the qualified cohabitant through orders made under *sections 13, 14 or 15.*

(4) For the purposes of this section, 'net estate' means the estate as remains after provision for the satisfaction of –

    (a) capital acquisitions tax (or the equivalent of such tax however described);

    (b) other liabilities of the estate having priority over legal rights and the prior rights of a surviving spouse within the meaning of the *Succession Act 1965*, and

    (c) the legal rights and the prior rights, if any, of any surviving spouse.

(5) An order under this section shall not affect the legal right of a surviving spouse within the meaning of the Succession Act 1965, or any devise or bequest to the spouse or any share to which the spouse is entitled on intestacy."

The trigger for court intervention, therefore, is that the deceased "*failed to make adequate provision* or [*made*] *no provision* for the qualified cohabitant in accordance with his or her means…" (emphasis added). If of opinion that this is in fact the position, the court is to order such provision out of the estate as it considers "*just and equitable*". No definition of adequacy of provision is provided, yet it is the crucial test for authorising the court to act. The term is somewhat vague and contains unarticulated normative premises which place the court in a difficult position. It does not appear that adequacy is here inexorably linked to the requirement of financial need. A woman who has spent the past 30 years with a fabulously rich partner could, it seems, apply successfully under s.11 if he left her only a modest inheritance which went no further than to meet her financial needs; she could argue that this was inadequate in the sense that it failed to represent an appropriate provision, having regard to the deceased's massive wealth. The difference between "adequate" and "proper" provision is hard to draw. The Commission may well have baulked at using the latter term since it indicates social normative approval of cohabitation but, unless the Commission intended to restrict claims under s.11 to cases where the provison left the applicant in an economically parlous situation, the word "adequate" is loaded with closet normative force which helpfully could have been more clearly articulated.

    The reference to "no provision"—the word "made" is omitted—raises further difficulty. Why should the failure by the deceased to make provision for his or her partner *necessarily* trigger a judicial intervention in which the court could award what it considers just and equitable out of the deceased's estate?

Such a failure could in some circumstances not be in any sense culpable, in the same way as the failure by a parent to make provision in a will for a child does not indicate a breach of the test for intervention set out in s.117 of the Succession Act 1965. If two very rich cohabitants have lived together for several years, why should the failure by one of them to have made any provision for the other warrant judicial intervention?

Fisheries and Harbours

HARBOURS

Power of sale   In *Attorney General v Port of Waterford Company*, Supreme Court, July 12, 2005 the applicant unsuccessfully sought a declaration that a proposed sale by the respondent of a harbour was *ultra vires*. The applicant claimed that as the respondent owned the property as a public trustee it was bound to keep the harbour and use it to the public benefit and could not therefore sell it. The respondent relied on the provisions of the Harbours Act 1996 as conferring a power of sale on it. Section 15 of the 1996 Act provided that a decision by a company to acquire any land or to dispose of any of its land (whether by sale or the grant of a lease) could only be made by the directors of the company. The applicant was unsuccessful in the High Court and, on appeal, in the Supreme Court.

Dismissing the appeal, the Supreme Court (Geoghegan, Fennelly and Macken JJ.) held that, although an express power of sale is not contained in the 1996 Act, it is specifically recognised by s.15 of the 1996 Act and, in any event, the sale of property is recorded as an object of the appellant in the memorandum of association. Where the memorandum provides for such an object, the company will have the power, by necessary implication, to carry its objects into effect. In this case, that included the power to sell any of its property. The court held that, on its true construction, the 1996 Act permits a port company to buy and sell property for the purposes of performing its functions under the 1996 Act. To the extent that it is under a duty to the public in respect of the uses of its property in the harbour, that did not affect its power of sale. It was quite clear that the respondent was empowered by the 1996 Act, subject to its provisions, to sell parts of the harbour.

SEA-FISHERIES AND MARITIME JURISDICTION

Sea-Fisheries and Maritime Jurisdiction Act 2006   The Sea-Fisheries and Maritime Jurisdiction Act 2006 involved a part-consolidation, with amendments, of Pt 13 of the Fisheries (Consolidation) Act 1959, and a full consolidation, with amendments, of the Maritime Jurisdiction Act 1959, as amended. Together with the Fisheries (Amendment) Act 2003, which provides an independent licensing and appeals system for sea-fishing boats, the sea-fisheries elements of the 2006 Act thus comprehensively updated the statutory framework for sea-fisheries. Section 4 and Schedule 1 of the 2006 Act also involved an element of statute law revision by providing for the repeal of obsolete, spent or superseded provisions in 16 Fisheries Acts (the earliest four dating from 1455 to 1516) and of seven other Acts listed in Sch.1. This element of statute law revision must be seen against the general background of "regulatory reform", including the comprehensive pre-1922 statute law revision project which resulted in the enactment of the Statute Law Revision Act 2007 (setting out the first definitive "White List" of the pre-1922 Acts which remain on the statute book, and to which we will return in the *Annual Review of Irish Law 2007*).

Illegal fishing and EC law   As indicated, the 2006 Act revised and replaced with amendments Pt 13 of the Fisheries (Consolidation) Act 1959, as amended. The 2006 Act thus clarified and strengthened the previous provisions against illegal sea-fishing and safeguarded the implementation of national fisheries policy or EC common fisheries policy, notably, by remedying defects in ss.223A and 224B of the 1959 Act (ss.14 and 15 of the 2006 Act); by making it an offence to contravene certain EC Regulations which are directly applicable (s.11 of the 2006 Act); by streamlining arrangements for allocating and managing the State's sea-fishing quotas and sea-fishing effort entitlements (ss.12 and 13 of the 2006 Act); by updating penalties for a wide range of sea-fisheries offences (s.28 of the 2006 Act); and making new statutory provisions for forfeiture of proceeds from illegally caught fish (s.31 of the 2006 Act). There was considerable opposition from the fishing industry to the proposed new penal aspects of the 2006 Act as it had been originally published as a 2005 Bill. Ultimately, some significant changes in this respect were made as the 2006 Act progressed through the Oireachtas. In dealing with forfeitures arising on conviction on indictment, s.28(5) of the 2006 Act in effect maintains the *status quo ante* by providing for a standard forfeiture, as a statutory consequence of the conviction on indictment, of any fish and any fishing gear on board the sea-fishing boat concerned (except in the case of conviction on indictment under s.8 or s.9 of the 2006 Act, involving foreign seafishing boats where the court has discretion (as was the case prior to the 2006 Act) whether or not to order forfeiture of any fish and fishing gear concerned). As to fines and forfeitures on summary conviction, the 2006 Act increased the maximum fine on summary conviction to €5,000 in all cases, from €635 or €1,270, as the case may be, including cases where it is agreed to proceed summarily as regards any of the indictable offences mentioned above. Section 28(6) of the 2006 Act amended the *status quo ante* as to forfeitures in the case of persons convicted summarily for the first time of an offence (other than an offence to which s.8 or s.9 of the 2006 Act relate). Under the 2006 Act the court now has a discretion as to whether to order the forfeiture of unlawfully caught fish and any fishing gear used in the commission of the offence or to which the offence relates. Prior to the 2006 Act forfeiture arose as a statutory consequence of conviction. In the case of summary conviction for an offence under s.8 or s.9 of the 2006 Act, involving foreign fishing boats, the court retains its previous discretion whether to order forfeiture of any fish and fishing gear concerned. Where the court decides not to order forfeiture, it must say why in all cases. Where a person is convicted summarily a second or subsequent time for an offence (other than an offence under s.8 or s.9 of the 2006 Act), forfeiture of unlawfully caught fish and any fishing gear used in the commission of the offence or to which the offence relates will arise as a statutory consequence of conviction, as heretofore.

Ministerial regulation of sea-fishing   The 2006 Act also included a number of related amendments to the regulatory framework. Sections 12 and 13 streamline the arrangements for allocating and managing the State's sea-fishing quotas and sea-fishing effort entitlements. Sections 74 to 80 revise provisions which originated in the Merchant Shipping Act 1894 relating to the registration of sea-fishing boats. For convenience, s.97 of the 2006 Act contains the full up-to-date text of the law relating to sea-fishing boat licensing, incorporating the changes made by s.53 of the Maritime Safety Act 2005. Section 100 reduces unnecessary bureaucracy by exempting from compulsory registration as a ship under the Mercantile Marine Act 1955, any sea-fishing boat of less than 15m in length overall which is registered in the statutory register of fishing boats or is formally exempted from such registration. The 2006 Act clarified the scope of ministerial policy directives to the Seafishing Boat Licensing Authority or to the appeals officers, by including a specific reference to measures to control and regulate the capacity of the sea-fishing fleet and the rational management of fisheries (s.99 of the 2006 Act). The Act also updated the law relating to the registration of sea-fishing boats and miscellaneous offences involving sea-fishing boats (ss.74 to 80 of the 2006 Act). The Act also clarified and modified aquaculture licensing law, by placing on a statutory footing a longstanding arrangement under which the Minister for Communications, Marine and Natural Resources could renew an aquaculture licence, even one that had already expired, relaxing the automatic ending of a licence if the Minister is satisfied that a two-year delay in starting, or a two-year cesser of, aquaculture operations arose for bona fide reasons (for example, fish health or environmental conditions) and permitting a reduction in licensed area or production, or the use of novel or experimental equipment in licensed areas, under certain conditions (s.101 of the 2006 Act).

Significant changes to the ministerial regulatory power arose directly from the decisions of the Supreme Court in *Browne v Ireland* [2003] I.E.S.C. 43; [2003] 3 I.R. 205 and *Kennedy v Attorney General* [2005] I.E.S.C. 36; [2005] 2 I.L.R.M. 401. In the *Browne* case, the Supreme Court declared invalid a ministerial order under s.223A of the Fisheries (Consolidation) Act 1959 to penalise any breach of the EU prohibition on the use of drift nets (with provision for conviction on indictment) within the area of application of the common fisheries policy (CFP), which includes but extends beyond the 200 nautical-mile exclusive fishery limits of the State. The Supreme Court held that this prohibition should have been the subject of ministerial regulations under the European Communities Act 1972 which at that time (until the enactment of the European Communities Act 2007) only provided for summary offences. The use of ministerial regulations under s.224B of the 1959 Act (with provision for conviction on indictment) was not availed of in the order impugned in the *Browne* case because that section as it stood prior to the 2006 Act only applied to within the 200 nautical-mile exclusive fishery limits of the State. Accordingly, s.224B of the 1959 Act was amended by s.14 of the 2006 Act to extend its geographical scope and to apply to all activities in breach of the common fisheries policy, and not merely illegal fishing or attempting to fish illegally (for example, not keeping proper records or proper equipment on board). In the *Kennedy* case the Supreme Court declared invalid a different ministerial order, relating to detailed discretionary national measures to give effect to the CFP, on the ground that it lacked a basis in primary legislation. Section 15 of the 2006 Act filled that gap, in line with s.14, as regards such measures.

Prosecution of offences   The 2006 Act also provides for a significant transfer from the Attorney General to the DPP of responsibility for the prosecution of sea-fisheries offences (s.39 of the 2006 Act) and for the prosecution of offences under the Dumping at Sea Act 1996, as amended (s.103 of the 2006 Act).

Sea-Fisheries Protection Authority   The 2006 Act also provides (Pt 2, Ch.5 of the 2006 Act: ss.40 to 73 and Sch.3) for the establishment of an independent statutory Sea-Fisheries Protection Authority for improved enforcement of sea-fisheries law and food safety law in relation to fish and fishery products. The authority is responsible for enforcing the EU common fisheries policy in the State. It was designed to incorporate 38 existing departmental sea-fisheries protection officers as well as 45 new officers, and also such additional experts from other statutory bodies as may be required and available from time to time to meet particular seasonal or locational enforcement needs. The provisions in the 2006 Act were modelled on those for the Commission for Communications Regulation and the Railway Safety Commission established under the Railway Safety Act 2005 (*Annual Review of Irish Law 2005*, pp.619–624). The authority was formally established on January 1, 2007 by the Sea-Fisheries Protection Authority (Establishment Day) Order 2006 (S.I. No. 376 of 2006). The 2006 Act also provides for the establishment of a statutory Sea-fisheries Protection Consultative Committee, representative of the sea-fishing and seafood sectors and other relevant interests. This will serve as a two-way forum between the sea-fisheries protection authority and those sectors and interests, and for readily-accessible complaints procedures by which persons aggrieved by enforcement action taken by, or on behalf of, the authority can have their complaints considered by an independent third party.

Maritime jurisdiction   The maritime jurisdiction elements of the 2006 Act (Pt 3, Chap.5 of the 2006 Act: ss.81 to 94 and Sch.2) replace with amendments the Maritime Jurisdiction Act 1959, as amended. They thus set out a clear statutory basis for the exclusive economic zone of the State, which underpins the exclusive fishery limits of the State, in accordance with Pt 5 of the 1982 United Nations Convention on the Law of the Sea, as set out in Sch.2 to the 2006 Act. In this respect, s.84 of the 2006 Act provides for the first time in Irish law a definition of the "contiguous zone", that is, the area between 12 and 24 nautical miles offshore from baselines, in accordance with Art.33 of the 1982 Convention on the Law on the Sea. This was inserted to provide the foundation for further legislation, by the relevant Ministers, for enhancing the power of the State to protect archaeological objects in the contiguous zone, as well as to prevent infringements of customs, fiscal, immigration and sanitary laws within the national territory and territorial seas of the State, as specifically provided for in Arts 33 and 304(2) of the 1982 Convention on the Law of the Sea.

Licences and harbour centre charges   The 2006 Act also made provision for due payment of taxes by applicants for sea-fishing boat licences (s.98 of the 2006 Act) and of charges in respect of any vessel availing of services at any of the five state-owned Fishery Harbour Centres (Howth, Dunmore East, Castletownbere, Rossaveel and Killybegs) (s.102 of the 2006 Act).

Garda Síochána

CCTV

The Garda Síochána (CCTV) Order 2006 (S.I. No. 289 of 2006) establishes the criteria for the use of CCTV in public places by members of the Garda Síochána or other authorised persons under s.38 of the Garda Síochána Act 2005 (*Annual Review of Irish Law 2005*, p.419). The order came into force on May 30, 2006.

GARDA INSPECTORATE

The Garda Síochána Inspectorate (Establishment Day) Order 2006 (S.I. No. 401 of 2006) established the Garda Síochána Inspectorate provided for in the Garda Síochána Act 2005 (*Annual Review of Irish Law 2005*, p.423) with effect from July 28, 2006.

GARDA RESERVE

The Garda Síochána (Reserve Members) Regulations 2006 (S.I. No. 413 of 2006) set out the recruitment, training, commission and termination of the members of the Garda reserve, as provided for in the Garda Síochána Act 2005 (*Annual Review of Irish Law 2005*, p.418), with effect from July 26, 2006.

Health Services

HEPATITIS C AND HIV INFECTION FROM BLOOD PRODUCTS

Insurance indemnity scheme The Hepatitis C Compensation Tribunal (Amendment) Act 2006 is the third legislative response to the fallout from the infection with hepatitis C and HIV of a large number of people who had been given infected blood products in the 1970s and 1980s. The 2006 Act sets out an insurance support scheme for those who contracted hepatitis C and HIV from the infected blood products. The first legislative response had been to establish a compensation scheme, administered through the Hepatitis C and HIV Compensation Tribunal established under the Hepatitis C Compensation Tribunal Act 1997 (*Annual Review of Irish Law 1996*, p.408, and *Annual Review of Irish Law 1997*, p.478). It was noted during the passage of the 2006 Act that, by the end of 2005, the tribunal had made awards to approximately 2,200 people, including most of the 1,700 persons infected with hepatitis C or HIV, and a significant proportion of their spouses, partners or dependents. The total figure for awards made to the end of 2005 stood at €580 million. The second legislative response was the provision of a range of healthcare services without charge by means of a special health card issued under the Health (Amendment) Act 1996, the cost of which was noted as approximately €15 million per annum. After enactment of the 2006 Act, it was also noted that every person who received a compensation award at the tribunal under the 1997 Act, as amended by the 2006 Act, would also receive the special health card.

The 2006 Act deals with the insurance difficulties which those infected and their spouses face. It was acknowledged that, while it was relatively easy to find precedents for monetary compensation schemes (such as those set out in the 1997 Act), a scheme to address the insurance difficulties of this nature could not be found anywhere in the world. Persons to whom this scheme will apply fall into two categories with regard to insurance matters: those individuals who can get insurance but only with increased premiums; and those individuals who are deemed by the insurance industry to be uninsurable. The 2006 Act provides reasonable access to the insurance market for those for whom the cost of insurance to date has been rendered prohibitive or for whom cover is currently unavailable. The 2006 Act provides for life assurance and mortgage protection cover. Under the scheme, the State will pay the additional risk premium where the life assurer is willing to provide cover, subject to an additional premium. The State will assume the risk on the life cover where the assurer is not willing to provide this cover. The 2006 Act also allows as a matter of priority for the development of a scheme for travel insurance. The scheme will be administered under the aegis of the Health Service Executive. It was estimated that the insurance scheme under the 2006 Act would cost about €90 million over its projected life span of 30 years or more.

Turning to the detailed provisions of the 2006 Act, s.1 sets out a definition of diagnosis for the purposes of the existing compensation scheme under the 1997 Act and the insurance scheme under the 2006 Act. It was noted during the Oireachtas debate on the 2006 Act that the symptoms linked with hepatitis C include fatigue, aches and pains, depression, dry skin and rashes. Many of these symptoms are common to a number of viral and other conditions not associated with hepatitis C. To ensure that the support schemes operate in a fair and equitable manner and that those determining eligibility under the schemes use clear consistent criteria, the 2006 Act states that a hepatitis C diagnosis should be defined in terms of a scientific test or by reference to certain defined symptoms in respect of acute infection acquired within 16 weeks of the administering of the infected anti-D blood product which originally caused the infection. During the Oireachtas debate, the test to be used in this respect was subject to a significant amount of debate. It had been originally proposed that the enzyme-linked immunosorbent assay (ELISA) test would be the sole test. It was noted that the ELISA test is accepted internationally as being the standard method for diagnosing hepatitis C for the purposes of the healthcare services. In practice, the ELISA test is used as the first-line indicator that any hepatitis C sufferer has been exposed to the hepatitis C infection at some time in the past and should be further investigated for evidence of current infection. Following further consideration, the 2006 Act includes reference to two other tests, known as the RIBA test and the PCR test. The 2006 Act also empowers the Minister for Health to include by order any other relevant recognised test that may be developed in the future.

Section 2 of the 2006 Act deals with eligibility for compensation in respect of loss of consortium. It was noted that persons who were directly infected with hepatitis C or HIV are compensated at the compensation tribunal in their own right, on the evidence presented, for all the effects of hepatitis C and HIV, including its impact on their relationships in the past and into the future. Moreover, in the case of young people, the tribunal and the courts take into account the age of the claimant and recognise the consequences of infection on the future relationships of young people, particularly those who have not formed permanent or stable relationships. The Hepatitis C (Amendment) Act 2002 provided for compensation in respect of loss of consortium suffered by the spouses and partners of infected persons who entered into marriage or long-term relationships without the spectre of hepatitis C or HIV hanging over them and then found that the expectations which they had of a normal family life were severely affected by their partners' condition. The 2006 Act provides that where a new relationship is formed in the knowledge of the hepatitis C or HIV diagnosis, this particular head of claim will not apply. This is on the basis that, for a loss of consortium to exist, there must have been a committed relationship already in existence and the legitimate expectation that this would continue without the imposition of a viral illness acquired through the use of state-provided health services. Eligible partners in relationships formed after diagnosis will remain entitled to all the other relevant heads of claim under the compensation scheme, such as compensation for any actual losses incurred in looking after their partners, loss of services, loss of society, post-traumatic stress disorder, mental distress and dependency losses.

Section 3 empowers the Minister for Health to make regulations providing for the establishment, operation, administration and supervision of the insurance scheme. This will provide certain types of insurance to claimants who are: hepatitis C-infected anti-D recipients; hepatitis C-infected transfusion recipients; HIV-infected recipients of relevant products; the children or spouses of eligible persons with hepatitis C or HIV who have themselves been diagnosed positive for the virus; parents, brothers or sisters of infected persons who have themselves been diagnosed with hepatitis C or HIV infection; and certain other claimants, all of whom have been refused the relevant insurance on the grounds that they have been diagnosed positive for hepatitis C or HIV, or the administrator reasonably believes they would be refused if they applied for insurance or who are refused insurance unless they pay a higher premium than persons of similar age and gender who have not been diagnosed positive for hepatitis C or HIV. The Minister may also make regulations to specify the administrator of the scheme, his or her functions, and the conditions subject to which a benefit will be provided, not provided or ceased under the scheme. The scheme will provide life assurance of €420,000 or seven times the annual earned income to a maximum of €525,000 of the claimant or his or her spouse or partner of three years' standing at the time the application is made or their joint income. All the amounts mentioned will be index linked to the consumer price index.

The scheme will provide mortgage protection insurance for the purchase, change or improvement of the claimant's primary residence to a maximum of either €394,000, which will be index-linked, or the average Dublin house price plus 25 per cent, whichever is greater. For the first year after the scheme comes into effect, an eligible claimant will be allowed to re-mortgage any property he or she owns to a total of €100,000.

The Minister is also empowered under s.3 to make regulations to provide for annual travel insurance. The Act provides that travel insurance benefits will be covered by the scheme within six months of the establishment of its life and mortgage protection elements. A claimant who wants to avail of the full benefits of the scheme without restriction must make an application to the administrator within one year of the scheme coming into effect or three years of the date on which he or she was diagnosed positive for hepatitis C or HIV, whichever is the later. The exceptions are applications for annual travel insurance and life and mortgage cover by claimants under 30 years of age. Once the travel insurance element of the scheme is up and running, a claimant can apply for full benefits at any time.

Regarding young claimants, the 2006 Act provides that the full benefits of the scheme would apply without restriction to eligible claimants up to the age of 30 years rather than be confined to the first year of the scheme. With the exception of this group, claimants who make an application after the first year of the scheme's operation and would be deemed uninsurable will still be able to avail of insurance, but the benefits will have a phasing-in period.

Section 4 outlines the appeals procedure to apply. A person may appeal a relevant decision of the scheme within 90 days of being notified of the decision in writing. It provides that the Minister will appoint one or more solicitors or barristers of at least five years' standing to consider appeals. The decisions of the administrator that can be appealed are a refusal to consider an application; a decision that a claimant is not eligible; a decision that a benefit cannot be provided, must cease to be provided or is partially or incrementally provided; or a decision on the amount of the sum assured under the scheme. The appeals officer will be independent but will comply with any guidelines on procedure issued by the Minister. He or she will consider any oral or written submissions made by the appellant and the scheme administrator, make a decision in writing giving reasons and send the written decision to both the appellant and the administrator.

A person affected by a decision of the appeals officer may appeal to the High Court on a point of law within 28 days of receipt of the written decision. If the appeals officer's decision is not being appealed to the High Court, the administrator will carry out the decision as soon as practicable. Each appeals officer will report to the Minister in writing at intervals to be decided by the Minister, who will lay copies of the report before the Oireachtas. The appeals officer's report will not identify any claimant.

Section 4 also provides for the establishment of a special account to pay costs arising from the scheme, including the cost of administration and the payment of benefits. The special account will be an account with the paymaster general, subject to whatever terms and conditions the Minister for Finance will decide in consultation with the Minister for Health and Children and subject to audit by the Comptroller and Auditor General. The scheme administrator may specify any forms that he or she sees fit and the documents that are required to be submitted with them. These forms must be completed in full by an applicant and accompanied by the necessary documents. The administrator may require a statutory declaration to be made that the particulars contained in the forms are true. Multiple copies of forms or documents may be required or, in particular circumstances, alternative documents.

Because of the importance of confidentiality for persons infected with hepatitis C and HIV through the administration of blood and blood products within the State, s.4 also states that everyone connected with the process, including the administrator, the appeals officer or officers and the insurers, must maintain confidentiality in respect of all relevant matters and must not allow unauthorised access to any relevant documents. A person who contravenes this provision and is convicted of a summary offence will be liable to a fine of up to €3,000, six months' imprisonment or both. A person found guilty of an indictable offence will be liable to a maximum of €25,000 fine, two years' imprisonment or both.

Section 5 distinguishes between the special account previously set up to pay the costs of the compensation scheme and the separate account to be established to pay for the insurance scheme under the 2006 Act. Section 6 provides that the same definition of hepatitis C as proposed for the purposes of entitlement to compensation will apply to the Health (Amendment) Act 1996, which entitles eligible persons with hepatitis C to a range of healthcare services without charge.

IRISH MEDICINES BOARD

Introduction to 2006 Act   The Irish Medicines Board (Miscellaneous Provisions) Act 2006 amended the Irish Medicines Board Act 1995 (*Annual Review of Irish Law 1995*, pp. 339–340) and other legislation such as the Misuse of Drugs Acts 1977 to 2006, in order to confer significant new functions on the Irish Medicines Board (IMB). In general, the 2006 Act allows for the transfer of certain functions regarding controlled drugs from the Department of Health and Children to the IMB and for the improved operation and enforcement activities of the IMB in respect of medicines and the control of clinical trials. It amends the 1995 Act regarding medicinal products, cosmetic products, veterinary medicinal products, drug precursors and medical devices. It allows for the making of regulations for nurse prescribing and for information to be provided by the retail, restaurant and catering sectors on meat sold or served to consumers where this is not already a requirement. It enables customs and excise officers to exercise surveillance of medicinal products at ports, airports and land frontiers. It clarifies the legal position on eligibility for dental, aural and ophthalmic services and extends eligibility for dental, aural and ophthalmic examinations to all children.

Misuse of drugs   Part 2 of the 2006 Act provides for the IMB to act as the licensing authority for controlled drugs under the Misuse of Drugs Acts 1977 to 2006. The designation of the IMB for this purpose is consistent with the Department of Health's strategy by which executive functions that are not directly related to the mission or objective of the Department should be devolved to an appropriate executive agency. The 2006 Act formalised existing arrangements that had already been in place under which staff at the IMB carry out this work, and it amended the 1995 Act to transfer legal competence to the IMB to carry out licensing and inspectorial functions under the Misuse of Drugs Acts.

Section 4 of the 2006 Act amends s.5 of the Misuse of Drugs Act 1977 and allows regulations to be made to permit registered nurses or classes of registered nurses to prescribe certain controlled drugs in specified circumstances. There are a number of amendments throughout the 2006 Act which provide for an enabling provision for nurse prescribing: see in particular s.16 of the 2006 Act, discussed below.

Section 5 of the 2006 Act extends the powers available in the Misuse of Drugs Act 1977 to prohibit bodies corporate involved in the practice of community pharmacy and their officials from having controlled drugs following a conviction for an offence under the Misuse of Drugs Acts or the Customs Acts. These powers were already available in respect of practitioners and pharmacists convicted of such an offence.

Section 6 of the 2006 Act amended s.8(7) of the Misuse of Drugs Act 1977, as amended. Section 8 of the 1977 Act provides that the Minister may issue a special direction against a practitioner. The amendment effected by s.6 of the 2006 Act provides that where the Minister has issued a special direction against a nurse, he or she should send a copy of the report to An Bord Altranais. This is a consequential amendment to the enabling provision for nurse prescribing in s.16 of the 2006 Act.

Section 7 of the 2006 Act amended s.14 of the Misuse of Drugs Act 1977. Section 14 of the 1977 Act empowers the Minister to grant licences or issue permits or authorisations for any of the purposes of the 1977 Act, or to attach or vary conditions to such licences, permits or authorisations and to revoke any such licence, permit or authorisation. It provides for the making of regulations requiring the payment of prescribed fees in respect of the granting or issuing of such licences, permits or authorisations. Section 7 of the 2006 Act amended s.14 of the 1977 Act to transfer these functions, which were previously carried out by the Department, to the IMB. It also provides that licences, permits and authorisations issued prior to the commencement of s.7 of the 2006 Act continue to be valid.

Section 8 of the 2006 Act amended s.17 of the Misuse of Drugs Act 1977 to confine the prohibition concerning poppies to the cultivation of poppies for the purpose of producing opium. The range of poppies covered by the original definition in the 1977 Act had included many poppies grown for decorative or ornamental purposes.

Section 9 of the 2006 Act amended s.24 of the Misuse of Drugs Act 1977 to enable the IMB to authorise officers to carry out inspections under the 1977 Act and allows the Pharmaceutical Society of Ireland to authorise officers to inspect pharmacy shops. The term "practitioner" is included in this section to ensure that registered practitioners—medical and dental—fall within the remit of this section so that records held by them with regard to their prescription, possession and use of controlled drugs can be subject to inspection should the need arise.

Section 9 also provides that the appropriate warrants of authorisation are issued by the Minister, the IMB or the Pharmaceutical Society of Ireland to authorised persons carrying out inspections and that appropriate transitional arrangements are in place for those persons with existing certificates of authorisation.

Functions of IMB   Part 3 of the 2006 Act contains the amendments to the Irish Medicines Board Act 1995. In this respect, it updates and consolidates the functions carried out by the IMB under EC Directives on medicinal products, veterinary medicinal products and medical devices, many implemented in ministerial regulations. The changes ensure that the enforcement provisions for all of these regulations are now contained in the 1995 Act, as amended by the 2006 Act. Sections 10, 11 and 12 of the 2006 Act update the functions already carried out by the IMB concerning medicinal products, veterinary medicinal products and medical devices. The 2006 Act also extended the IMB's functions to include its designation as competent authority for the purposes of EC Directives relating to medical devices, cosmetic products and precursor drugs and in respect of clinical trials for medicinal products for human use. The IMB was also designated as the competent authority for Directive 2004/23/EC, which sets standards of quality and safety for the donation, procurement, testing, processing, preservation, storage and distribution of human tissues and cells for human applications. It was noted during the Oireachtas debate on the 2006 Act that the 2004 Directive does not apply to blood and blood products, organs or in vitro research.

Section 11 of the 2006 Act also empowers the IMB to issue various export certificates in respect of medicinal products, veterinary medicinal products, cosmetic products and medical devices as are required by manufacturers exporting such products to other countries. In discharging these functions, s.11 provides that the IMB is also required to have regard to the provisions of any national legislation applicable to such products.

Section 13 provides that the chairperson of the IMB Advisory Committee for Medical Devices is an *ex officio* member of the board of the IMB. This replicates provisions in the original text of the 1995 Act for the chairpersons of the advisory committee on human medicines and the advisory committee on veterinary medicines. Section 14 amended section 9 of the 1995 Act to ensure that no refusal of a licence, authorisation or certificate in respect of medicinal products, on the grounds of safety, quality or efficacy, may be made unless the appropriate advisory committee has been consulted. Section 15 amended s.13 of the 1995 Act to make broader provision for the IMB to charge fees in regard to its activities.

Section 16 of the 2006 Act amended s.32 of the 1995 Act to clarify that sale and supply will not include administration and also provides that ministerial regulations may be made to control administration if required. It also provides for the specific control of prescription medicinal products and for non-prescription medicinal products in pharmacies and, in the case of some products, for their availability in non-pharmacy outlets. As thus amended, s.32 of the 1995 Act enables the making of regulations relating to medical devices and in respect of the implementation of EC Directives relating to medicinal products, medical devices and cosmetic products. This was done in response to the decision of the Supreme Court in *Browne v Ireland* [2003] I.E.S.C. 43; [2003] 3 I.R. 205, in which the court expressed the view that specific statutory authority should be in place in the context of the creation of indictable offences which arise from the implementation of EC Directives. Section 17 inserts new ss.32A to 32F into the 1995 Act to improve enforcement powers concerning medicinal products, cosmetic products and medical devices. Section 32B provides for the appointment of authorised officers and sets out the various powers available to them for carrying out inspections in regard to the products and devices. These include additional powers to authorised officers to enable appropriate inspections to be carried out, including the effective supervision of the activities of those persons selling medicinal products by mail order, including the Internet. Section 32C provides for the taking and handling of samples of these products and devices. Section 32D provides for the certificate stating the results of any test, examination or analysis carried out on a sample to be accepted as prima facie evidence in court. Section 32E sets out the penalties for offences created by the 2006 Act and allows the IMB, where it has seized stocks under the 1995 Act (as amended), to seek orders from the courts to appropriately dispose of these stocks and where appropriate to recover the costs incurred from the offending company. Section 32F provides that summary proceedings for an offence can be instituted under the 1995 Act up to two years after the date of the offence. Sections 30 to 40 of the 2006 Act make consequential amendments to the various regulations made under the 1995 Act. These amendments, which relate to enforcement, arise out of the insertion of the new ss.32A to 32F into the 1995 Act.

Nurse prescribing Section 16(a)(iii) of the 2006 Act provides for another important insertion into s.32(2)(l) of the 1995 Act, which enabled regulations to be made providing for nurse prescribing. This was introduced at Committee Stage in the Seanad debate on the 2006 Act, and reflects the general policy of the Department of Health to expand the professional role of nurses into areas which were traditionally the reserve of medical practitioners, that is, doctors. This also reflects international developments in this area and the growing academic-based qualifications of nurses. The purpose of this amendment to the 1995 Act is to introduce prescriptive authority for nurses in circumstances where it is safe to do so, to give greater accessibility and convenience for patients and to help community services and acute services. It was noted during the Oireachtas debate that there would be consultation with all stakeholders on the implementation of this provision before regulations were drawn up to ensure that the necessary safeguards and controls are put in place. It was also noted that An Bord Altranais, the Nursing Board, would play an important role in setting the educational and clinical standards to be required of nurses who will be permitted to prescribe. In February 2007, the Department announced that draft Regulations on nurse prescribing had been notified to the European Commission with the intention of signing the Regulations later in 2007. Section 26 of the 2006 Act amended s.59(2) of the Health Act 1970 to enable prescriptions written by nurses to be reimbursable under the relevant drugs repayment schemes.

Clinical trials   Part 4 of the 2006 Act amended the Control of Clinical Trials Act 1987 in a number of respects. Section 22 provides that the 1987 Act (as amended) does not apply to clinical trials that are controlled under the European Communities (Clinical Trials on Medicinal Products for Human Use) Regulations 2004 (*Annual Review of Irish Law 2004*, p.313). The 2004 Regulations were amended by the European Communities (Clinical Trials on Medicinal Products for Human Use) (Amendment No. 2) Regulations 2006 (S.I. No. 374 of 2006) to implement Directive 2005/28, which lays down principles and detailed guidelines for good clinical practice as regards investigational medicinal products for human use. They came into force on July 12, 2006.

Section 23 of the 2006 Act permits proceedings for an offence under the Control of Clinical Trials Acts 1987 to 2006 to be instituted up to two years after the date of the offence and invests capacity in the IMB to bring summary proceedings for an offence under the 1987 Act (as amended). Section 24 inserts a new s.15A into the Control of Clinical Trials Act 1987, and enables the IMB to appoint appropriate officers to enforce and supervise clinical trials falling under the 1987 Act (as amended). This includes powers to inspect records held by practitioners in respect of clinical trials. It was noted during the Oireachtas debate on the 2006 Act that it is likely that most if not all of these records would be held for use in the course of a practitioner's professional practice and that if a warrant had to be obtained for each occasion when an inspection was required it would render the supervision of clinical trials impractical if not impossible. Therefore, warrants from the District Court are only required where a private dwelling is concerned. However, the section also provides that warrants will not be required for that part of a private dwelling that is used for a professional practice.

Beef labelling   Section 25 of the 2006 Act substituted the complete text of s.54 of the Health Act 1947, as amended. Section 25 includes provision to enable the making of regulations to extend the requirements on labelling for poultry meat, pig meat and sheep meat to provide full country of origin information on all such meat at retail and catering level. The purpose of the amendment was to enable the making of regulations to extend the EC-based beef labelling requirements that exist at retail level to include a requirement in Ireland for information on the country of origin of beef at the point of final consumption in the restaurant and catering sectors. It also provides for an increase in the maximum fines for breaches of regulations under s.54 of the 1947 Act, including those relating to meat labelling. It was noted that EC approval would be required before such Regulations could be made. The relevant Regulations are the Health (Country of Origin of Beef) regulations 2006 (S.I. No. 307 of 2006). These provide that a food business operator providing prepared beef to consumers shall not advertise the beef for sale or supply, present it for sale or supply, or sell or supply it unless the country or countries of origin of the beef are indicated at the point of advertising, presenting, sale or supply in clear legible type on the advertisement, menu or other presentation used.

Health examinations for children Sections 27 and 29 of the 2006 Act amended the Health Act 1970 and the Health (Amendment) Act 1994 to provide that all primary school or home-taught children are eligible for dental, ophthalmic and aural health examinations. Prior to the 2006 Act, these examinations were confined to children of five years and under and children who attend national schools, and did not include children who were attending private primary schools or who were home-taught.

Health service eligibility Section 28 of the 2006 Act amended s.67 of the Health Act 1970 which provides for eligibility for dental, ophthalmic and aural services. It was pointed out that when s.67 of the 1970 Act was commenced in 1972, the relevant regulations limited its application to holders of medical cards under the General Medical Services (GMS) Scheme and provision of these services had been limited to medical card-holders since that time. The Department of Health sought the advice of the Attorney General on the question as to whether this restriction complied with s.67 of the 1970 Act. His advice was that s.67 of the Health Act 1970 should be amended to provide legal clarity to the issue, and this was the purpose of s.28 of the 2006 Act.

LONG-STAY CARE REPAYMENT SCHEME

The Health (Repayment Scheme) Act 2006 was the legislative response to the decision of the Supreme Court in *Re the Health (Amendment) (No. 2) Bill 2004* [2005] I.E.S.C. 7; [2005] 1 I.L.R.M. 401 (*Annual Review of Irish Law 2005*, p.192). The Supreme Court held that the attempt in the 2004 Bill to validate restrospectively the imposition of charges on fully eligible persons for their publicly-funded long-term care was unconstitutional. The 2006 Act came into force on June 30, 2006: Health (Repayment Scheme) Act 2006 (Commencement) Order 2006 (S.I. No. 338 of 2006). The future charging for long-stay care was put on a statutory footing by the Health (Amendment) Act 2005 and the Health (Charges for In-Patient Services) Regulations 2005.

The 2006 Act provides for the legal framework for making repayments to those wrongly charged for inpatient services in publicly-funded long-stay residential care. The 2006 Act also set out an appropriate framework to regulate patient private property (PPP) accounts operated by the Health Service Executive (HSE) on behalf of such patients, in particular those with limited decision-making capacity. During the Oireachtas debate on the 2006 Act, it was estimated that approximately 20,000 people who were still alive and a further 40,000 to 50,000 estates would benefit from repayments under the scheme. The overall costs arising from the long-stay charges repayment scheme have been estimated at approximately €1 billion. It was also noted that a high proportion of those patients due a repayment have varying degrees of mental impairment, meaning that any scheme would clearly require appropriate safeguards to be put in place to prevent fraud and exploitation of those who receive repayments and are not in a position to manage their own financial affairs.

In these instances the 2006 Act enabled repayments to be placed in PPP accounts. These PPP accounts need to be regulated given the significant amount of money which may be in these accounts as a result of repayments of long-stay charges. PPP refers to money and personal possessions that patients have with them on admission to care. In the case of long-stay patients, the property also includes regular pension payments. PPP accounts are operated by the HSE (the successor of the former health boards) in supporting clients in managing their financial affairs and assisting them in dealing with various aspects of daily living. The PPP account system manages the private money of long-stay patients, which may include pension income, maintenance charges, spending money, comfort payments to patients-clients and lodgments to clients' accounts. This account provides the patients with an ability to exercise their autonomy through such activities as choice of clothing, recreational activities and so on. The account may be administered by an institution as a service to patients who are not in a position to administer the property themselves or have a relative or other person do it on their behalf. It was accepted that there was a need for clarity and consistency in the area of PPP accounts and the 2006 Act introduced a specific statutory framework for these accounts to protect patients' interests, particularly in the context of large repayments under the scheme being placed in these accounts.

The 2006 Act provides that all those fully eligible persons who were wrongly charged and are alive, and the estates of all those fully eligible persons who were wrongly charged and died since December 9, 1998 will have the charges repaid in full. The limit to estates of those who died since December 9, 1998 reflects the reference in the Supreme Court decision that "[t]he State has available to it a defence of the Statute of Limitations, that is, a six year limit". The repayments include both the actual charge paid and an amount to take account of inflation by reference to the consumer price index.

The 2006 Act also include an independent appeals process which will be independent of the HSE. The Minister is empowered to appoint suitably-qualified independent appeals officers to consider appeals and the appeals process will allow both written and oral submissions to support an appeal.

Applicants to the scheme will be advised of the outcome of their application as soon as possible and will be provided with details of their entitlement to appeal, if their application has been rejected or if they dispute the amount of the repayment. Applicants will also be informed of their right to bring a complaint to the Office of the Ombudsman.

An area of particular concern in the drafting of the 2006 Act and in the administration of the repayment scheme relates to those patients who may have mental capacity issues. The unfortunate reality is that a high proportion of patients in long-stay care have varying degrees of deteriorating mental impairment and special arrangements are required for such persons given that they will be in receipt, in certain cases, of significant amounts of money but may not have the capacity to manage their financial affairs. As part of the 2006 Act, where doubt may exist about the capacity of an individual, a certificate issued by a registered medical practitioner who has examined the relevant person in the past six months prior to the application, will be required to be submitted with the application form. In developing the framework in the 2006 Act to protect vulnerable patients, it was pointed out during the debate on the 2006 Act that consideration had been given to the work of the Law Reform Commission, which had published a *Consultation Paper on Law and the Elderly* in 2003 and a *Consultation Paper on Vulnerable Adults and the Law: Capacity* in 2005. As anticipated during the Oireachtas debate on the 2006 Act, these papers culminated in the publication by the Commission of a *Report on Vulnerable Adults and the Law* in late 2006. The report recommended the replacement of the wards of court system with a guardianship system regime. It is notable in this context that the 2006 Act did not recommend that those lacking capacity would be brought within the wards of court system. Instead, the 2006 Act provides that, where a doubt exists as to the capacity of an individual, repayments can only be made into that individual PPP account, pending a decision on the capacity of that individual. Under the 2006 Act, moneys lodged to these PPP accounts will be used specifically for the benefit of the individual patient. In order to protect these monies, in the case of persons with mental capacity issues, no monies in excess of €5,000 per year can be used for the benefit of the patient without the payment being approved by the Circuit Court. Day-to-day expenditure for personal purposes can be made without the necessity of court application, but the expenditure of large sums of money will be regulated. Moneys may also be invested by the HSE, on behalf of the patient, in financial institutions authorised by the financial regulator. The 2006 Act also provides for the appointment of an independent person to be appointed by and to report to the Minister for Health and Children on PPP accounts to ensure that these accounts are administered in an appropriate fashion and that any monies expended are for the benefit of the patient. PPP accounts will be administered in line with national guidelines, which are to be developed by the HSE, to ensure consistency in their application throughout the country.

MENTAL HEALTH

Mental health tribunals: review of involuntary detention   The Mental Health Act 2001 (Commencement) Order 2006 (S.I. No. 411 of 2006) brought into force the remaining provisions of the Mental Health Act 2001 on November 1, 2006. Notably, the 2006 Order provided for the commencement of the Mental Health Tribunals under the 2001 Act, thus putting in place for the first time in the State a regime of systematic review of the validity of involuntary committals to mental health facilities.

Habeas corpus: review of involuntary detention   The benefits of the review system now available under the Mental Health Act 2001 through the mental health tribunals is emphasised by the decision earlier in 2006 in *LK v Clinical Director of Lakeview Unit, Naas General Hospital* [2007] 2 I.L.R.M. 69. In this case, the applicant sought an inquiry under Art.40.4 of the Constitution into the lawfulness of her detention in hospital under the Mental Treatment Act 1945 (which the 2001 Act has now replaced). Clarke J. made a preliminary direction requiring the disclosure of the applicant's medical records. Clarke J. took the view that, in accordance with the views expressed by the Supreme Court in *Croke v Smith (No. 2)* [1998] 1 I.R. 101, the onus was on the applicant's custodian to show that she remained, as of the date of the inquiry, in need of care by virtue of being of unsound mind to the extent that deprivation of liberty was necessitated. He acknowledged that there was a circularity involved in such inquiry, in that the applicant required access to her medical records in order to contest the validity of her continued detention, but a person requiring to be detained under the 1945 Act might be held not to have capacity to authorise the release of such records. The minimum entitlement of the applicant was to a reasonable facility to enable her to put before the court an expert view on the factual matters material to the issues which arose. In the instant case, an expert view was relevant in relation to the applicant's capacity, the appropriateness or otherwise of the disclosure of information and whether the court should be satisfied that the test for continued detention outlined in *Croke v Smith* had been met. Accordingly, he directed, first, that a consultant psychiatrist, on the nomination of the applicant's solicitor, should have reasonable access to the applicant and to all relevant medical records; secondly, that such consultant might report to the applicant's solicitor on his views arising out of his inquiries on any of the issues relevant to the case as identified by the court; and, thirdly, that, for the time being, the applicant's solicitor should not disclose the contents of any such report, save to the applicant's counsel and for the purposes of discussion of the general conclusions of the report with the applicant.

It is notable that this apparently novel approach by Clarke J. is likely to remain largely of historical interest in view of the coming into being of the Mental Health Tribunals under the 2001 Act. Indeed, his use of the decision in *Croke v Smith* is itself of some interest, since the Supreme Court had in that case upheld the validity of the 1945 Act. It is worth noting in this respect that the applicant in *Croke* initiated proceedings under the European Convention on Human Rights, claiming that the absence of an independent review mechanism in the 1945 Act was in breach of the right to liberty in Art.5 of the Convention: *Croke v Ireland*. In 2000, the Irish Government entered into a "friendly settlement" with the applicant on its undertaking to support the enactment of what became the 2001 Act, which of course includes this review mechanism: see Byrne and McCutcheon, *The Irish Legal System* (4th ed., Butterworths, 2001), para.17.54.

Minimum standards in approved centres   The Mental Health Act 2001 (Approved Centres) Regulations 2006 (S.I. No. 551 of 2006), made under the 2001 Act, set out the minimum standards required in approved centres, for example, hospitals or other in-patient facilities for the care and treatment of persons suffering from mental illness or mental disorder that are registered with the Mental Health Commission, and for the proper conduct of such centres. They came into force on November 1, 2006.

Information Law and the Ombudsman

ESTELLE FELDMAN, Research Associate, Trinity College, Dublin

INFORMATION COMMISSIONER

All statutory references in this section are to the Freedom of Information Acts 1997 to 2003 unless otherwise stated. The Act has been previously considered in *Annual Review of Irish Law 1997*, p.2 *et seq.*; *Annual Review of Irish Law 1999*, p.1 *et seq.*; p.350 *et seq.*; *Annual Review of Irish Law 2000*, p.273 *et seq.*; *Annual Review of Irish Law 2001*, p.391 *et seq.*; *Annual Review of Irish Law 2002,* p.306 *et seq.; Annual Review of Irish Law 2003,* p.373 *et seq.*; *Annual Review of Irish Law 2004,* p.319 *et seq.*; *Annual Review of Irish Law 2005,* p.430 *et seq.* In addition to hard copy, documents referred to may be found at the Information Commissioner's website http://www.oic.gov.ie. Since the Freedom of Information Act 1997 came into force, there have been two Information Commissioners, Mr Kevin Murphy 1997–2003, and the present incumbent, Ms Emily O'Reilly, since mid–2003; hence references to publications may refer to "he" or "she" depending on the date of publication.

SUPREME AND HIGH COURT APPEALS

Section 42 of the Act governs the right to take an appeal from a decision of the Information Commissioner to the High Court on a point of law. Such decisions issue consequent on a s.34 review (*Annual Review of Irish Law 1999*, p.351 *et seq.*). The statutory barrier preventing appeals from the High Court to the Supreme Court was withdrawn by the Freedom of Information (Amendment) Act 2003 (*Annual Review of Irish Law 2003*, p.391). In 2006 the High Court issued judgments in two cases, and one appeal was struck out by order. The Supreme Court issued a judgment in early 2006 in *McK v Information*, an appeal that it had heard in 2005.

Separated parent's right of access to records of minor   The High Court judgment in *McK v Information Commissioner* [2004] I.E.H.C. 49, [2004] 2 I.R. 12 was considered in *Annual Review of Irish Law 2004*, p.321 *et seq.* (This case is also referred to as *NMcK*). The appeal concerned the refusal of a hospital to give a separated father access to his minor daughter's medical records. As noted in the *Annual Review of Irish Law 2005*, p.444, the Supreme Court appeal by the Information Commissioner against the High Court's decision was heard in November 2005 but the reserved judgment was not delivered until January 2006. The Supreme Court, *per* Denham J., McGuinness, Hardiman, Geoghegan, and Fennelly JJ. assenting, both affirmed and varied the High Court decision. The High Court's judgment was affirmed as to the correct test to be used in administering the Freedom of Information Act 1997 (Section 28 (6)) Regulations 1999, namely a presumption of parental entitlement to a minor child's medical information. However, the Supreme Court remitted the matter to the Information Commissioner for review in accordance with the correct test and in light of all of the circumstances.

McK High Court judgment As has been previously noted (*Annual Review of Irish Law 2004*, p.321 *et seq.*), the High Court judgment was rooted in the Supreme Court judgment of Hardiman J. in *North Western Health Board v HW* [2001] 3 I.R. 622 which declared that any legislation vindicating and defending the rights of children must be interpreted in the light of the Constitution, particularly Art.41 (The Family) and Art.42 (Education).

Delay when minor child involved Of most concern to the Supreme Court was the delay from the time the requester had made his initial request for his daughter's medical records to the hospital in January 2000 until the delivery of the judgment in January 2006:

> "The elapse of time has a special relevance where a minor child is involved. L was born in 1988. The hospital stay in issue was in January, 2000. At that time she was still a minor. Six years later she is in her 18th year, she was born on the 30th May 1988. This alters the circumstances, as her wishes are now most relevant. The delay is not the fault of the requester, and it is most unfortunate. However, the effects of the delay cannot be ignored in view of the necessity to balance the changed circumstances, including the attitude of L."

Parental primacy affirmed Noting that the Freedom of Information Act 1997 and the consequent Regulations must be interpreted in accordance with the Constitution, Denham J. agreed that the Commissioner erred in law in requiring tangible evidence of parental interest. This "tangible evidence" test reversed the onus of proof. "The relationship between parent and child has a special status in Ireland. Under the Constitution the family is the primary and fundamental unit group in our society: Article 41.1°. The State has guaranteed to protect the family in its constitution and authority: Article 41.1.2°." Consequently, Denham J. continued, the judicial branch of government has a duty to protect the family and its authority.

Rights of child within family Denham J. made a clear declaration that each member of the family unit also has rights, "[t]hus while the parents have duties and rights in relation to a child, and a child has rights to parental care, the child also has personal rights which the State is required to vindicate if the parent fails in his or her duty".

Parent's rights/duties caring for ill child—a rebuttable presumption   The extent of the Supreme Court's opinion on the parental care of an ill child is as follows:

> "A parent's rights and duties include the care of a child who is ill. As a consequence a parent is entitled to information about the medical care a child is receiving so that he or she may make appropriate decisions for the child, as his or her guardian. The presumption is that a parent is entitled to access such information. That position is not absolute. The circumstances may be such that the presumption may be rebutted. But the primary position is that the presumption exists. Consequently, the approach of the Commissioner was in error when he required 'tangible evidence' that the release of such information would serve the best interests of the minor. The obverse is the correct approach. The presumption is that the release of such medical information would best serve the interests of the minor. However, evidence may be produced that it would not serve her interests, and, in considering the circumstances, her welfare is paramount."

The error of the Commissioner was in not presuming that the parent was entitled to the child's medical records. Based on that presumption the Commissioner should then proceed to consider "any evidence which exists addressing the issue that it would not be in the minor's best interests that the parent should be furnished with such information".

Request remitted to Information Commissioner   Having specified the correct test that the Commissioner must use in deciding whether or not a minor child's medical records should be released to a parent, Denham J. remitted the matter for decision to the Commissioner. This remittal was consequent on three factors: the delay, the circumstances of the case, and "especially the age of the minor [nearly 18 years of age], whose views now are very relevant".

Growing autonomy of minor child   The importance of the case was signified by the number of judges sitting in judgment, a bench of five rather than three. It was not unreasonable, therefore, to anticipate some significant judicial comments on Arts 41 and 42 of the Constitution which deal with the rights of the family and the right to education. In particular it had been hoped that the court would comment on the rights of children to preserve confidentiality of information as against the rights of parents as enshrined and inferred in the Constitution and from earlier court judgments. In *Annual Review of Irish Law*

2004, p.275 *et seq.,* William Binchy was somewhat critical of the High Court judgment in *McK* as it related to the full emergence of autonomy in children. In the context of balancing the constitutional rights of parents and of children, he commented that the "presumption of parental entitlement to access to joint personal information in relation to children tilts the preference for parental rights too far." Unfortunately, the Supreme Court judgment failed to address this issue. See also elsewhere the chapter on constitutional law and *Annual Review of Irish Law 2005*, p.451.

Aftermath of McK
Commissioner requires opinion of minor child It may be noted that, on remittal, applying the correct test to the 1999 Regulations and taking account of L's opinion as instructed by the Supreme Court, the Commissioner held that the records should not be released to her father. The Commissioner notes in her *Annual Report 2006* that this was the first case of its kind in which her staff met with the young person affected to ascertain her views. In subsequent cases where parents have requested release of the personal records of a minor child, the Commissioner appears to have taken the view that the opinion of the minor child should be heard in relation to release or not, always assuming the child to be competent to form and express such an opinion. See Case Numbers 99491, 020593, and 030587, in all of which the records concerned related to a greater or lesser extent to the personal information of Mr McK's daughter and/or of his son. Mr McK had refused permission to the Commissioner for his minor son, aged 16 at the time, to be interviewed by the Commissioner's staff. As a consequence the Commissioner took the view that "as I had not been able to establish the views of the son, I was not in a position to reach any conclusion on the matter." In Case Number 050129 the *Annual Report* states: "In relation to the Supreme Court finding that the views of Miss McK were very relevant, I noted that, in this case, the child was not yet 10 years old. I therefore did not consider it appropriate to have sought his views on whether his hospital records should be released to his father" (*Annual Report of the Information Commissioner 2006,* pp. 23–24). For the constitutional implications see the chapter on Constitutional Law.

Control of records In *Minister for Enterprise, Trade and Employment v Information Commissioner* [2006] I.E.H.C. 39 the High Court found that the Department of Enterprise, Trade and Employment (the Department) did not control records held by the requester's local enterprise board (the Board) relating to his application for grant assistance. The Department had appealed the decision of the Commissioner that the Board's records are under the control of the Department and that a right of access to such records exists.

The requester had directed his request to the Department as local enterprise boards, despite being public bodies disbursing public funds, were not at that time subject to the Freedom of Information Act. The Department had refused the request, citing s.10(1)(a) of the Act which provides for refusal of a request if the record concerned does not exist or cannot be found after reasonable steps to ascertain its whereabouts have been taken. This issue was addressed in the *Annual Review of Irish Law 2003*, p.386 *et seq.* in the analysis of *Ryan v Information Commissioner*, unreported, High Court, May 20, 2003 and has been affirmed since, for example, *Holland v Information Commissioner* [2004] I.E.H.C. 176 (*Annual Review of Irish Law 2004*, p.325 *et seq.*). Murphy J. in the instant case stated that "[c]learly this was not, in the circumstances, an appropriate ground for a refusal."

The correct section which related to the Department's control or otherwise of the Board's records was s.2(5) which makes it clear that a reference to records held by a public body includes a reference to all records under its control (*Annual Review of Irish Law 2004*, p.328 and *Annual Report of the Information Commissioner 2004*, 19). The substantive issue was whether or not the relationship of the Department to the Board resulted in the Department having that control. Having examined the relevant provisions of the Industrial Development Act 1997 and the articles of association of the Board, together with the operating agreements between the Department and the Board, Murphy J. found that the Minister's role appears to be that of "financing and supervising such financing which emanates from both national and European sources". However, the responsibility for making decisions on the implementation of the enterprise plan lies with the Board. It seemed to the court that "the directions that may be given by the Minister are meant to safeguard the grant given and would appear to be prudent banking conditions rather than reservations on the powers of the Board or, indeed, control of the business and administration of the Board by the Minister". Murphy J. cited and accepted the test of control in Blaney J.'s judgment in *Ó Coindealbhain (Inspector of Taxes) v Mooney* [1990] 1 I.R. 422 and concluded that the Board is not controlled by the Minister: "The Board is in business on its own account subject to limited and defined reporting requirements that do not include the information requested."

Curial deference   Murphy J. noted that the court should have regard to the discretion of the Information Commissioner in appeals of this nature:

> "The curial deference which courts owe to deciding bodies should only be interfered with where the bases for their decisions are in any way erroneous, beyond their powers or unreasonable. In the present case it seems to this Court that the finding in relation to control while based on stateable grounds was, on balance, an extension of the meaning of control beyond that which was, on analysis, not justified by the operating agreement and the articles of association of the Board."

Legal Aid Board: information given in confidence   *Gannon v Information Commissioner* [2006] I.E.H.C. 17 was an appeal from a decision of the

Information Commissioner upholding the Legal Aid Board's refusal to provide access to records relating to a grant of legal aid to a third party. The substantive issue was whether the records concerned were exempt from release under s.26(1)(a) of the FOI Act, which protects information given to a public body in confidence, provided that certain requirements are met. This provision is subject to a public interest balancing test under s.26(3). Quirke J. in the High Court rejected the appeal finding that the Information Commissioner had acted within jurisdiction, that she was entitled to reach the conclusion which she had reached, and that there were no grounds for the court to interfere with her findings.

Section 26(1) has been considered by the Supreme Court in *Sheedy v Information Commissioner* [2004] I.E.H.C. 192; [2004] 2 I.R. 533; [2005] I.E.S.C. 35 (*Annual Review of Irish Law 2005*, p.431 *et seq.*).

Pursuing costs A third High Court appeal was struck out by order of the court, *Gibbons v Information Commissioner*, High Court, Dunne J., *ex tempore,* June 19, 2006. There is a solicitor's note extant from which this comment is derived. The relief sought by the applicant was not within the jurisdiction of the Freedom of Information Act. During the preliminaries, the "clearest indications and warnings were given to the appellant that costs would be sought by the respondent". Dunne J. so ordered with a suggestion that the respondent apply leniency in this respect. The Commissioner's policy of pursuing unsuccessful litigants for costs was outlined in the *Annual Report of the Information Commissioner 2003* (see *Annual Review of Irish Law 2003*, p.383).

FAILURE TO RESPECT OFFICE OF INFORMATION COMMISSIONER

Curial deference respected

It is interesting to note that in both High Court appeals the court paid respect to the notion of curial deference in relation to the Information Commissioner. This is a most welcome situation and a far cry from the attitude taken by the court in the first appeal heard by the High Court in which, *inter alia*, the Commissioner's right to hear an appeal *de novo* was called into question (*Minister for Agriculture and Food v Information Commissioner* [2000] I.R. 309, *Annual Review of Irish Law 1999*, p.350 *et seq.*).

This is in stark contrast to what seems to be an increasingly dismissive attitude of the Government towards the Office of the Information Commissioner and, it would seem from the conclusion of the s.32 deliberations, to the Commissioner herself.

Commissioner's views rejected in totality by politicians

Section 32 of the FOI Act refers to non-disclosure enactments that are not included under any other section of the Act. Access shall be refused to any record whose disclosure is prohibited, or whose non-disclosure is authorised in certain circumstances, by statute (including statutory instrument). In circumstances where such a statute is listed in the Third Schedule to the Act, the disclosure of records is assessed solely by reference to the other provisions of the FOI Act. Section 32 has been previously considered in *Annual Review of Irish Law 1999*, pp. 350 and 354 *et seq.*; *Annual Review of Irish Law 2001*, 398 (as part of *School League Tables* case analysis); *Annual Review of Irish Law 2003*, p.394; *Annual Review of Irish Law 2004*, p.320 (as part of *School League Tables* case analysis), p.328 *et seq*; *Annual Review of Irish Law 2005*, p.460 *et seq*.

In *Annual Review of Irish Law 2005*, the Commissioner's *Report to the Joint Oireachtas Committee on Finance and the Public Service for the Purpose of Review of Non-Disclosure Provisions in Accordance with The Freedom of Information Act 1997 [section 32]* (*S32 Report*) was considered. In her *Annual Report 2006* the Commissioner deals at some length with the Oireachtas Committee members' response to her submission. The Commissioner had already made her views known in a speech delivered at a "Public Affairs in Ireland" conference. As the Commissioner herself writes, her comments from that speech reproduced in her *Annual Report* are worth repeating here:

"In September 2006 the Joint Committee on Finance and the Public Service completed its report to the Oireachtas following a lengthy series of deliberations which included appearances before the Committee both by myself and by senior officials of the Departments of Finance and of Health and Children. In net terms, the Committee was faced with a situation in which, out of a total of 150 secrecy provisions identified, in 36 instances there was disagreement between myself and the relevant Minister as to whether the secrecy provision should be made subservient to the FOI Act or should continue to override the FOI Act. The Committee, therefore, had to choose between my recommendation—that the 36 secrecy clauses should each be made subservient to the FOI Act—and that of the relevant Minister—that the secrecy clauses should continue to override the FOI Act ...

In appearing before the Committee, I felt that my argument was understood and, broadly speaking, accepted by it. However, when the Committee presented its Report to the Oireachtas in September last its recommendation, in the case of those secrecy provisions on which I disagreed with the relevant Minister, was to support the Minister in each case.

I should add, for the sake of clarity, that possibly for the first time in its history, the Committee went to a vote on this issue. It then split, regrettably, along party political lines. I say regrettably for the following reasons. I believe and still believe in the bona fides of that

Committee and I believe that each Committee member, regardless of party affiliation, genuinely engaged with the issues at hand, many of which were complex. I also believe that the majority agreed with my views on the recommendations at issue. But, in the end, apparently, an unstated political imperative overrode everything else.

I am not so sensitive that I cannot live with the rejection of a recommendation or decision. My appeal decisions are subject to appeal to the High Court and subsequently to the Supreme Court and I am accustomed to having my decisions scrutinised, and occasionally rejected, by the Courts. What concerns me, and indeed disappoints me greatly, about this particular episode is that the Committee has given no analysis of any kind, or any explanation in its report, as to why it opted for one set of recommendations over another. Indeed, the substantive Committee Report consists of little more than one page; and the recommendation itself is conveyed in the single sentence: 'The Joint Committee supports the Ministers' recommendations.'"

The *Annual Report* continues:

"Commentators have suggested that a 'whip' was imposed on certain Committee members after, as one such member explained, they had made 'an error of judgement' in their initial assessment. Whatever the reality, the experience has been a very disheartening one both for my Office and for myself. But wider forces were at play apparently. I appreciate that it is not very usual for office holders such as myself to comment in this fashion in relation to an Oireachtas Committee. However, there is nothing to be gained from adopting the pretence that the Committee's handling of the Section 32 issue does not warrant comment. There are important issues at stake here and I believe, as an independent office holder, that I should make these comments in the interests of promoting an honest and thorough debate on what is an important aspect of our democracy" (*Annual Report of the Information Commissioner 2006*, 16–17).

RESTRICTIONS ON THIRD PARTY ACCESS TO INFORMATION

In *Minister for Enterprise* the judgment makes reference to art.17 of the articles of association of the Waterford City Enterprise Board whereby the directors "undertake to keep confidential and not to disclose to any third party any information relating to specific projects in respect of which support or assistance is sought." Thus, whilst the High Court appeal was about whether or not the Minister for Enterprise, Trade and Employment had control over the Board, a public body but one excluded at that time for the purposes of freedom of information, there was consideration given to the concept that information pertaining to third parties should be kept confidential. In *Gannon* the judgment held that although "there is a valid public interest in ensuring the proper distribution of public funds there was and is also a right vested in the third party to have his privacy and the confidential character of his private personal information respected and protected". In *Gannon* it was quite clear that a third party was seeking access to records relating to another person but in *Minister for Enterprise* the requester, Mr Michael Freyne of Waterford Braiding Ltd, was seeking access to records relating to a grant application he had made. This was not a third party request. Were county enterprise boards as public bodies included under the Freedom of Information Act there is no guarantee that Mr Freyne would have been granted access to the records he requested. As the Commissioner clearly pointed out in her decision that led to *Minister for Enterprise*:

> "I find that the Board's records are under the control of the Department and that a right of access to such records exists. I have decided that the Department must assemble all relevant records held by the Board and must decide whether any such records can be released to you having regard to the provisions of the FOI act. In the event that the Department wishes to claim an exemption in respect of any such records, it must send copies of the records in question to my Office and I will then make a supplementary decision as regards any further exemptions claimed [*Case 010147 Mr X and the Department of Enterprise, Trade and Employment*, October 10, 2004]."

Thus, the Freedom of Information Act contains very strict protections where exemptions to general access to records applies. Why then is there such reluctance from government to include all public bodies and agencies under the Act? What is to be gained by precluding Mr Freyne and others like him from the right to access information pertaining to his affairs? Murphy J. noted in *Minister for Enterprise* that "[t]here is no suggestion that the Board departed from the recommendation of the Evaluation Committee in relation to Mr. Freyne's application". In the absence of an independent review of the documentation, whether by the Information Commissioner or by the court, that is not an evidentiary statement. Moreover, and of far greater significance, had there been a suggestion that the Board had departed from the recommendation of the Evaluation Committee, could the Minister, were he willing, intervene or would it be left to the courts, a situation whereby executive functions, namely the disbursement of public funds, are under judicial rather than executive oversight (see also the constitutional law chapter). City and county enterprise boards have been included under the Act from mid-2006 but there are hugely significant public bodies which remain outside the remit of the Information Commissioner and the Ombudsman, p.423.

ACCESS TO RECORDS OF DECEASED PERSONS

In the *Annual Review of Irish Law 2005*, p.452 *et seq.* it was recorded that the Information Commissioner had called for a total review of the Freedom of Information Act 1997 (section 28 (6)) Regulations 1999 (S.I. No. 47 of 1999 (the Regulations)) as a matter of real urgency (*Annual Report of the Information Commissioner 2005*, pp. 23–27. This was with particular reference to the issue of access to the personal records of deceased persons. In her *Annual Report* the Commissioner renews her call for immediate review of this highly unsatisfactory situation: "While it has been indicated to my Office by the Department of Finance that a review of the Regulations is underway, at the time of writing my Office has not been informed of any tangible progress on the matter. This remains a real issue, as I am required to make my decisions based on the law as it stands, not as it ought to be or how it has been promised to be" (*Annual Report of the Information Commissioner 2006*, p.17). Indeed, the Commissioner has expressed the opinion that, by following a literal interpretation of the Regulations, an FOI decision-maker may well fall into the error of making a decision that is itself contrary to the Constitution. Yet, until such time as the Regulations are struck down by the courts or, preferably, repealed and replaced by the Oireachtas, they must be presumed to be constitutional.

SIGNIFICANT DECISIONS

Discovery and legal professional privilege   During 2006 the Commissioner dealt with a number of cases involving discovery and legal professional privilege. There are complex issues involved in relation to release of records in these circumstances as there is a risk of contempt of court given that discovered documents may not be used for any purpose other than the litigation concerned. Section 22(1)(b) covers the exemption of such records. However, the Commissioner notes in the *Annual Report* that the contempt of court exemption does not necessarily apply to a record simply because it has been subject to the discovery process. Several important aspects of the exemption in so far as it relates to the discovery process were addressed in these cases, namely: (1) the point at which an implied undertaking is given or received by a party to litigation; (2) the documents covered by a discovery order; (3) the parties bound by an implied undertaking given on discovery; and (4) whether the exemption applies to records refused through discovery on the grounds of relevance (Cases 050166 and 040334). Section 22(1)(a) provides a mandatory exemption that applies to records which would be exempt from production in court proceedings on the grounds of legal professional privilege (Cases 040333 and 010314). See *Annual Report of the Information Commissioner 2006*, pp.27–29.

Tribunal cases

Section 46 excludes records held by a tribunal of inquiry from the scope of the Act and s.46(1)(a)(II) provides for an exception to this exclusion for records relating to the general administration of a tribunal. Cases 010221 and 010264 are summarised in Ch.4 of the *Annual Report of the Information Commissioner.* The Commissioner found against the Department of Environment, Heritage and Local Government and the Tribunal of Inquiry into Certain Planning Matters and Payments (Mahon Tribunal) and ruled that the majority of the records sought were appropriate for release while the Tribunal was still sitting (*Annual Report of the Information Commissioner 2006*, pp.29–30 and 37–38).

STATUTORY CERTIFICATES AND NOTICES

Certificates of Exemption

Section 20 Section 20 of the Freedom of Information (Amendment) Act 2003 gives discretionary power to secretaries general of government departments to certify that a record of whatever nature relates to a deliberative process of government and is thus exempt from release. Such a certificate is not amenable to internal review and cannot be appealed to the Information Commissioner. Section 20(1)(c) states, *inter alia*, that such a certificate shall be final. Effectively this means that the decision is entirely in the hands of the senior civil servant and that *all* Ministers, not just the departmental Minister, are bound by this unreviewable decision. In 2006 the first such certificate was issued by the Secretary General of the Department of Justice, Equality and Law Reform (*Annual Report of the Information Commissioner 2006*, p.14 and Appendix 1). The grave constitutional implications of issuing a s.20 certificate are discussed in the Constitutional Law chapter.

Section 25 Under s.25(1) a Government Minister may exempt a record from the application of the Freedom of Information Act (*Annual Review of Irish Law 2000*, p.275 (two certificates issued with expiry dates of February 2, 2002 and March 29, 2002); *Annual Review of Irish Law 2001*, p.409 (one certificate issued); *Annual Review of Irish Law 2002*, p.308 (two certificates issued); *Annual Review of Irish Law 2003*, pp. 391–392 (one previously issued certificate renewed for further two years); *Annual Review of Irish Law 2004*, p.326 (two previously issued certificates renewed); *Annual Review of Irish Law 2005*, pp.467–468 (one previously issued certificate renewed)). The only Minister to have issued certificates is the Minister for Equality, Justice and Law Reform. In 2006 no new certificates were issued; however, the Minister for Justice, Equality and Law Reform renewed two previously issued certificates for a further two years. A copy of the report in respect of this certificate is included in Appendix I of the *Annual Report of the Information Commissioner 2006*.

Statutory notices of non-compliance with Information Commissioner requests

Section 37 notice The Act provides for the issue of a notification under s.37 to the head of the public body requiring the production of information and/or records.

Section 35 notice Section 35 of the Act provides that, where a statement of reasons for refusing a request is inadequate, the Commissioner may require the head concerned to furnish a further statement (*Annual Review of Irish Law 2002*, p.275; *Annual Review of Irish Law 2003,* p.393; *Annual Review of Irish Law 2004,* p.326; *Annual Review of Irish Law 2005*, p.468).

No s.35 notices were issued by the Commissioner in 2006; however, to the Commissioner's dismay, five s.37 notices were issued:

> "This reverses a trend of declining requirement to issue such notices since 2002, and I hope it does not mark a reduction in the due diligence that has marked the relations between my Office and public bodies generally. It is a matter of some concern to me that three of the five section 37 notices issued in 2006 were to the same public body, the Department of Justice, Equality and Law Reform. One of those three notices was in relation to three separate FOI requests for which records had not been provided to this Office for consideration. It is of further concern to me that my Office did not receive any substantive reply following the issue of one of these notices to that Department, a situation which required intervention at the highest official level between my Office and the Department before an appropriate response was forthcoming" (*Annual Report of the Information Commissioner 2006*, p.13).

The Commissioner promises to return to this issue in her *Annual Report 2007*.

NEW BODIES COME WITHIN FOI

The *Annual Report 2006* notes that in June 2006 the Minister for Finance announced that he had made regulations bringing over 130 additional public bodies under the scope of the FOI Act. The bodies include a substantial number of bodies in the education sector, including the education support centres; in the enterprise sector, including the city and county enterprise boards; and other bodies in whose activities the public will have a very keen interest, for example, the National Treatment Purchase Fund and the Commission for Taxi Regulation. However, the report continues by noting the significant bodies that have not been brought within the remit:

"in the area of the Department of Justice, Equality and Law Reform: An Garda Síochána, the Garda Ombudsman Commission, the Office of the Refugee Applications Commissioner, the Office of the Refugee Tribunal, and the Judicial Appointments Advisory Board;

in the area of the Department of Finance: the Central Bank and Financial Services Authority of Ireland, the Irish Financial Services Regulatory Authority, the National Treasury Management Agency, the National Pension Reserve Fund Commission, and the State Claims Agency;

in the area of the Department of Education and Science: the 33 Vocational Educational Committees, the State Examinations Commission, the Residential Institutions Redress Board, and the Central Applications Office;

other bodies include: the Adoption Board, the Irish Red Cross, the Personal Injuries Assessment Board, and the Law Society of Ireland (which might be included to the extent that it performs statutory functions under the Solicitors Acts)."

This failure to bring important public bodies within the FOI regime was discussed by the Commissioner in her report for 2005. Of particular concern is the continuing exclusion of An Garda Síochána in its totality:

"We are alone among 26 Council of Europe countries recently surveyed in excluding our police force from the ambit of the FOI Act. In the context of ongoing reform, such as establishment of the Garda Inspectorate and the Garda Ombudsman Commission, I feel that now is the correct time to make An Garda Síochána amenable to the FOI Act" (*Annual Report of the Information Commissioner 2006*, p.15; see *Annual Review of Irish Law 2005*, p.468 *et seq.*).

OMBUDSMAN

The Ombudsman is governed by the Ombudsman Act 1980. In addition to hard copy, documents referred to may be found at the Ombudsman's website http://www.ombudsman.gov.ie/en. The following is based on *Office of the Ombudsman Annual Report 2006* (*Omb Report 2006*). Mr Michael Mills was appointed first Ombudsman in 1984. He was succeeded by Mr Kevin Murphy in 1994 who was succeeded by the present incumbent, Ms Emily O'Reilly, in mid-2003; hence references to publications may refer to "he" or "she" depending on the date of publication.

Information Commissioner and Ombudsman compared   Whereas both the Information Commissioner and the Ombudsman deal with matters of administrative accountability, as has been noted previously, there are significant differences in the statutory role and responsibility of each Office (*Annual Review of Irish Law 2000*, p.276 *et seq.*; *Annual Review of Irish Law 2001*, p.409 *et seq.*; *Annual Review of Irish Law 2002*, p.310; *Annual Review of Irish Law 2003*, p.395 *et seq.*; *Annual Review of Irish Law 2004*, p.330 *et seq.*; *Annual Review of Irish Law 2005*, p.470 *et seq*).

FAILURE TO EXTEND REMIT OF OMBUDSMAN

The Ombudsman opens her *Annual Report* for 2006 by outlining the major gaps of her jurisdiction in relation to public bodies. This is of increasing concern as there has been an acceleration of creating new agencies responsible for functions which were traditionally within the remit of Ministers and their departments and the creation of new single-purpose agencies, for example, FÁS, the Environmental Protection Agency and the Health and Safety Authority:

> "There are now over 450 such bodies in existence, only a handful of which come within my remit as Ombudsman even though, paradoxically, many do come within the scope of freedom of information legislation. Other accountability mechanisms are also lacking in that they are subject to little or no parliamentary oversight and there has been a diminution in Ministerial responsibility and control over functions which formerly were part of the relevant department. The need for legislation to correct this accountability deficit and to allow users of the services of these public bodies to complain to the Ombudsman is long overdue" (*Annual Report of the Ombudsman 2006*, p.5; see also Constitutional Law chapter).

Ombudsman (Amendment) Bill The purpose of the Ombudsman (Amendment) Bill is to widen the remit of the Ombudsman's Office to a range of additional bodies including institutes of technology, universities, vocational education committees, FÁS, regional fisheries boards and the claims functions of the National Treasury Management Agency. In 2006 it failed to materialise yet again.

Moreover, the Government has failed to implement the recommendation of the Constitution Review Group in *Report of the Constitution Review Group* (Pn. 2632, May 1996) that a new Article be included in the Constitution to confirm the establishment of the Office of the Ombudsman and to ensure the independence of its function and operation (*Annual Review of Irish Law 2000*, p.276; *Annual Review of Irish Law 2005*, p.474).

STATUTORY NOTICES OF NON-COMPLIANCE
WITH OMBUDSMAN REQUESTS

Section 7   A s.7 notice is a statutory demand for the provision of information required by the Office of the Ombudsman in examining a complaint and is normally only issued as a last resort when there has been an unacceptable delay on the part of the public body in providing the requested information (*Annual Review of Irish Law 2002*, p.314; *Annual Review of Irish Law 2003*, p.396; *Annual Review of Irish Law 2004*, p.330; *Annual Review of Irish Law 2005*, p.470). 18 notices were issued in 2006, 12 against local authorities, four against regions of the Health Services Executive and two against government departments. Kildare County Council was in receipt of five s.7 notices, for the second year running the highest number issued against any public body (*Annual Report of the Ombudsman 2006*, pp. 33–34).

Kildare County Council   For the first time in any annual report the Ombudsman singles out a particular body for severe criticism. Kildare County Council has been in receipt of 17 s.7 notices over a period of two years. It is salutary to quote the Ombudsman extensively, as this section of the *Annual Report*, while delivered in the usual measured tones, is so uncharacteristic of the Office and indicative of the extraordinary frustration experienced by the Ombudsman:

"A survey of complaints received by my Office against Kildare County Council (KCC) since 2003 identified delay on the part of the Council as a very significant problem for my Office in processing complaints. These delays relate mainly to the provision of reports and responses to my Office in relation to complaints referred to the Council. In the course of 2005 it was necessary to issue a Section 7 notice to the Council on twelve occasions. (A Section 7 notice usually requires a named person to provide the report requested by a specific date, otherwise, the person would be required to attend at my Office to provide the information or report.) The twelve Section 7 notices should be viewed in the context of a total of 27 complaints received against the Council in that year. In 2006, five Section 7 notices issued in the context of 28 complaints received.

My Office does not take an inflexible approach to the difficulties that bodies within remit may have from time to time in terms of resources and staff. In the course of seminars and meetings held in various local authorities throughout the country over recent years, my Office has stressed the need for local authorities to advise my Office if difficulty and/or delay is likely to arise in relation to a request for a report on any particular complaint. My Office does not issue Section 7 notices lightly, or without first having given the body concerned ample opportunity through reminder letters and phone calls to deal with the matter" (*Annual Report of the Ombudsman 2006*, pp. 37–38).

THE OMBUDSMAN AND THE
HEALTH SERVICE SECTOR

Under the Health Act 2004 a statutory complaints procedure came into effect on January 1, 2007, bringing the major hospitals in the Dublin area, the so-called public voluntary hospitals, within the Ombudsman's jurisdiction. In addition, other similar hospitals in the rest of the country, together with institutions nationwide providing services on behalf of the Health Services Executive to the intellectually disabled, came within her jurisdiction (*Annual Report of the Ombudsman 2006*, 31; see *Annual Review of Irish Law 2005*, p. 470 *et seq.*).

Nursing homes In her *Annual Report 2006* the Ombudsman details a number of complaints handled during that year which dealt with, among other issues, an error in the assessment of means for the purposes of the payment of nursing home subvention; a decision to refuse nursing home subvention causing extreme hardship which had been caused by an overly rigid exercise of discretionary powers; and a dispute about refund of nursing home costs (*Annual Report of the Ombudsman 2006*, p.11 *et seq.*).

Nursing home charges The scheme to repay the illegally-raised health charges from fully eligible persons in publicly-funded long-term residential care is provided for by the Health (Repayment Scheme) Act 2006. The Act also regulates patient private property accounts by way of the introduction of a statutory framework to protect patients' interests:

"As with other aspects of the public health services my role in relation to decisions about these repayments is to protect individuals from unfair, unsound or unjust actions on the part of those who are entrusted to make these refunds. I have already received a number of complaints in this regard e.g. from individuals who have been refused admittance to the scheme, parents of adult children with intellectual disabilities and spouses in certain circumstances who have been refused admittance as a 'connected person' under the Act. A connected person is an individual who can make an application for a recoverable health charge under the legislation. I anticipate that I will receive many other such complaints during 2007" (*Annual Report of the Ombudsman 2006, 37;* see *Annual Review of Irish Law 2005*, p.473).

SECTORAL OMBUDSMEN

Financial Services Ombudsman The statutory provisions outlining the terms for appealing a decision of the Financial Services Ombudsman to the High Court were considered in *Ulster Bank Investment Funds v Financial Services Ombudsman* [2006] I.E.H.C. 323. The Ulster Bank was appealing a decision of the Financial Services Ombudsman directing the bank to pay significant compensation to all customers who invested in its international share portfolio. This direction effectively required the bank to make good a 15 per cent reduction in the value of the fund (€7.4m) that arose in November 2004. In addition a request was made to the financial regulator to review the practice at this bank (and any other financial service provider which may have operated a similar type investment policy) from a regulatory perspective. The issue in the case was to determine the scope of the appeal taken under s.57CL of the Central Bank Act 1942 as amended by s.16 of the Central Bank and Financial Services Authority of Ireland Act 2004. Finnegan P. held that to succeed on the appeal the plaintiff must establish as a matter of probability that, taking the adjudicative process as a whole, the decision reached was vitiated by a serious and significant error or a series of such errors. The decision has been appealed to the Supreme Court.

Ombudsman (Defence Forces) Ms Paulyn Marrinan Quinn, formerly Pensions Ombudsman, was appointed first Ombudsman for the Defence Forces in November 2005. Publications of the office can be accessed at www. odf.ie.

STATUTES AND STATUTORY INSTRUMENTS

Central Bank Act 1942 (Financial Services Ombudsman Council) Levies and Fees Regulations 2006 (S.I. No. 556 of 2006) made by the Financial Services Ombudsman Council in accordance with ss.57BE and 57BF of the Central Bank Act 1942 (as amended) amend the Central Bank Act 1942 (Financial Services Ombudsman Council) Levies and Fees Regulations (No. 3) 2006 (S.I. No. 828 of 2006) and provide for a scheme of levies on regulated entities to fund the operation of the Financial Services Ombudsman's Bureau for the year ended December 31, 2007.

Civil Service Regulation Act 1956 (Section 1a) (Office of the Ombudsman) Order 2006 (S.I. No. 447 of 2006) designates the duly-appointed Director General of the Office of the Ombudsman to be the Head of the Office of the Ombudsman for the purposes of the Civil Service Regulation Act 1956.

Companies (Auditing and Accounting) Act 2003 (Prescribed Bodies for Disclosure of Information) Regulations 2006 (S.I. No. 619 of 2006) prescribe bodies to whom the Irish auditing and accounting supervisory authority may disclose information for the purposes of s.31(3) of the Companies (Auditing and Accounting) Act 2003.

Freedom of Information Act 1997 (Prescribed Bodies) Regulations 2006 (S.I. No. 297 of 2006) prescribe each of the bodies listed in the schedule to the Regulations as a public body for the purposes of the Freedom of Information Act 1997 (No. 13 of 1997) by their inclusion in subpara.(5) of para.1 of the First Schedule to that Act. [See above and *Annual Report of the Information Commissioner 2006*, p.15.]

Employees (Provision of Information and Consultation) Act 2006 (No. 9 of 2006) implements Directive 2002/14/EC of the European Parliament and of the Council of March 11, 2002 by providing for the establishment of arrangements for informing and consulting employees in undertakings, to implement Art.3(2) of Council Directive 2001/23/EC of March 12, 2001 on the approximation of the laws of the Member States relating to the safeguarding of employees' rights in the event of transfers of undertakings, businesses or parts of undertakings or businesses and to provide for related matters.

Employees (Provision of Information and Consultation) Act 2006 (Commencement) Order 2006 (S.I. No. 382 of 2006) appoints July 24, 2006 as the date from which the provisions of the Employees (Provision of Information and Consultation) Act 2006 come into operation.

Employees (Provision of Information and Consultation) Act 2006 (Prescribed Dates) Regulations 2006 (S.I. No. 383 of 2006) prescribe September 4, 2006 as the date from which, under s.4(1)(a), the legislation will apply to undertakings with at least 150 employees. They also prescribe, for the purposes of s.9(1)(a), September 4, 2006 as the date on or before which such undertakings must put in place pre-existing agreements, if they wish to avail of this option.

Pensions Ombudsman Regulations 2006 (S.I. No. 302 of 2006) take account of changes made to redress provisions in Pt VII of the Act (Equal Pensions Treatment) whereby complaints relating to equal pension treatment are no longer submitted to the Pensions Board but rather to the Director of the Equality Tribunal and clarify that the IDR procedure is exhausted within its terms at the expiry of the three-month period from when all the particulars of the complaint have been furnished, or where the Ombudsman considers it appropriate at a later date to be specified by him.

Law Reform

2006 was a busy year for law reform proposals. The Law Reform Commission published five reports and four consultation papers.

In the Equality chapter, above p.364, we consider its *Report on Vulnerable Adults and the Law* (LRC 83–2006). In the Family Law chapter above p.385, we analyse the Commission's *Report on Rights and Duties of Cohabitants* (LRC 82–2006).

In its *Report on e-Conveyancing: Modelling of the Irish Conveyancing System* (LRC 79–2006), the Commission adds a further dimension to its grand project on e-Conveyancing. Its *Report on Reform and Modernisation of Land Law and Conveyancing Law* (LRC 74–2005), analysed in the *Annual Review of Irish Law 2005*, pp. 509–510, dealt with substantive reform. The 2006 Report deals with the administrative and procedural aspects. After public tender, the Commission appointed BearingPoint to produce a detailed "end to end" process model of the entire conveyancing process. This resulted in a "Modelling Report" which envisaged the establishment of a project board drawn from key stakeholders to come up with detailed proposals to Government regarding the implementation of the most appropriate model for e-Conveyancing in Ireland. The Commission generally supports the approach taken in the Modelling Report.

In its *Consultation Paper on Privity of Contract: Third Party Rights* (LRC CP40–2006), the Law Reform Commission provisionally recommends that the privity rule be modified to enable third parties to enforce rights under contracts made for their benefit. Such a change would reflect statutory reforms that have taken place over the past three decades in Australia, New Zealand, England and Wales, and Singapore. The United States of America has for a century and a half recognised the claim of intended non-party beneficiaries. The Supreme Court of Canada favoured the same approach in *London Drugs v Kuchne & Nagel International Ltd* [1992] 3 S.C.R. 299 and *Fraser River Pile & Dredge Ltd v Can-Dive Services Ltd*, [1999] 3 S.C.R. 108, which is reflected also in the Quebec Civil Code and a New Brunswick statutory initiative. For extended analysis, see Jason Brock, "A 'Principled' Exception to Privity of Contract: *Fraser River Pile & Dredge Ltd., v Can-Dive Services Ltd*" 58 *U. Toronto Faculty of L. Rev.* 53 (2000).

There are of course already very many exceptions to the privity rule in Irish law, some going back a considerable time, others inspired or necessitated by our membership of the European Community. The case in favour of a complete abolition of the rule is, as the Commission acknowledges, far from straightfoward; although this would place our law in line with the civil law system, it ignores such civil law restrictions on the entitlement of a non-party to sue as *cause* and good faith, which have no direct common law counterparts.

As to the compelling character of the case for reform, one may perhaps be somewhat sceptical. The Commission points to the complexity involved in large construction contracts, where ingenious lawyers have responded to the privity rule with such devices as collateral contracts and direct agreements, chains of assignments and trusts and direct payment and name-borrowing provisions. There is a good prospect that modification of the privity rule would simplify matters; but the economic magnitude and wide variety of activities involved in such contracts will continue to ensure that they need the close and expensive attention of a small army of lawyers.

The Commission's analysis of the arguments against the substantial modification to the privity rule which it proposes, based on traditional contract theory, is somewhat disappointing. As regards bargain theory, the Commission states (paras 1.141–1.143):

> "It could be argued that any reform of the privity rule would infringe this basic principle of contract law. A third party could sue on the contract, even though they have not provided anything in exchange and cannot themselves be sued under the contract. The third party would acquire all of the benefits and none of the burdens in the contract.
>
> However, the Commission considers that the law has developed, and the bargain theory of contract is not the only theory used to enforce promises. Traditionally, contracts would be enforced where the promise was written in a deed under seal. The courts have developed concepts such as unjust enrichment, detrimental reliance and legitimate expectations, and have used these concepts to enforce promises even where the parties do not have a traditional two-sided bargain or exchange of promises. Public policy has an important role to play in determining when a promise can be enforced and by whom it can be enforced.
>
> It is the Commission's view that public policy may favour the enforcement of third party rights, even though it could be argued that enforcement of such rights is not possible under traditional contract law rules. If the parties to a contract intend to benefit a third party, the third party may reasonably rely on that intention and may suffer a detriment if there is a breach of contract. Public policy may dictate that the third party should not be without a remedy in this situation."

One may question the force of this argument. At most, it goes so far as suggesting that bargain theory may have to be modified or suspended where public policy dictates otherwise. In a legal system with a privity rule one should hesitate before characterising as reasonable the reliance by the non-party beneficiary on an intention to benefit him or her when he or she should be aware that the law does not support any such reliance. It is noteworthy that the only public policy basis for abrogating the privity rule in this context which the Commission identifies is where there has been "reasonabl[e] rel[iance]" *and detriment* suffered by the intended beneficiary; yet the Commission in its later proposals expressly rejects the requirement of proof of detriment.

The Commission goes on to address (paras 1.144–1.147) the argument in favour of retention of the privity rule based on freedom of contract as follows:

> "The idea of freedom of contract means that the parties are free to enter into whatever kind of contract they like, provided it is legal. The courts will not interfere with the bargains that have been struck between the parties. If the parties freely and voluntarily entered into a contract, the courts' only function is to enforce that contract. Thus, the courts will not add to any agreement, or imply terms merely because it is reasonable to do so.
>
> One aspect of freedom of contract is that the parties should be free to agree to vary or cancel an arrangement into which they have entered. It could be argued that giving third parties rights of enforcement infringes the contracting parties' freedom to contract.
>
> However, the Commission considers that granting a third party enforceable rights need not infringe the parties' freedom of contract. It is possible to contemplate reforms which allow a third party to enforce their rights whilst protecting the right of the contracting parties to vary or cancel their agreement.
>
> The Commission assumes that contracting parties who have intentionally entered into an agreement to confer a benefit on a third party have in mind that the contract will be carried out, and that the third party will benefit. If the rule of privity operated so that this intention could not be seen through to completion, the parties' intentions would be thwarted and the contract's purpose would be nullified. It could be argued that the concept of freedom of contract supports the enforcement of third party rights in this situation, and that the contractual intention of the parties should be enforced in the most effective way possible by the courts."

As regards the Commission's speculation about the parties' thwarted intentions, this may have some basis in fact where the parties are poorly legally advised, but justice in such cases may in any event be achieved through such doctrines as the contractual trust and estoppel. The idea that allowing an intended beneficiary to sue "need not infringe the parties' freedom of contract" is hard to reconcile with the Commission's recommendation that the parties should not be able to modify or terminate the contract without the beneficiary's consent once there has been reliance or acceptance by the beneficiary.

Let us now consider the details of the Commission's provisional recommendations.

The Commission proposes (para.3.42) that the test of whether a third party may enforce terms under a contract made for his or her benefit should satisfy two criteria:

1. the parties intend that the third party is to receive the benefit of the contract or a term of the contract; and

2. the parties intend that the term benefiting the third party should be enforceable by the third party in his or her own name.

The Commission also proposes that the contracting parties should be given the opportunity to rebut any presumption in favour of enforceable third party rights. The intentions of the parties should be determined using the normal principles of interpretation in contract law.

The Commission here favours the English approach (Contract (Rights of Third Parties) Act 1999, s.1) over that of New Zealand (Contracts (Privity) Act 1982, s.4) on the question of onus of proof as to the parties' intention that the promise be enforceable by the beneficiary. It criticises New Zealand's placing the onus on the beneficiary to establish this intent, stating (para.3.39):

> "The problem with this test is that it is often difficult to gauge accurately the intentions of contracting parties if they are not expressed in the contract. As a result, the application of this kind of test could be overly restrictive."

To this it may be rejoined that, if it is hard to prove parties' "unexpressed" intentions, it is equally hard to disprove them. Parties engaging in this task may have an uphill struggle and courts, in the absence of clear evidence, will be tempted to resort to the "equities" of the particular case. The result may be a holding not based on actual intent but rather on a perceived moral entitlement. The Commission rejects such an express basis for the beneficiary's claim; but this is what is likely to follow from one based on presumed intent.

The Commission provisionally recommends (para.3.62) that the third party should be identified in the contract either by name or description. Such a description should include being a member of a class or group of persons. There would be no requirement that the third party be in existence at the time of entering into the contract.

The Commission provisionally recommends (para.3.95) that reliance and acceptance should be used as alternative methods of determining when a third party's rights have crystallised. After reliance or acceptance by the third party, the contractual parties will be unable to modify or terminate the contract without the consent of the third party. The Commission also provisionally recommends that the contracting parties should remain free to include in the contract an express provison for the variation or termination of third party rights.

The Commission provisionally recommends (para.3.119) that, in an action brought by a third party, the promisor should have available, by way of defence or set-off, all matters that arise from or in connection with the contract that are relevant to the term that the third party is seeking to enforce. In addition, the promisor should be able to rely on any other outside issues, relevant to the conduct of the third party, that would have been available had the third party been a party to the contract. The contracting parties would be free to include an express provision restricting or expanding the scope of the defences or set-off.

The Commission provisionally recommends (para.3.147) that certain types of contract should be excluded from any reforming legislation. These might include contracts between a company and its members, negotiable instruments and the carriage of goods by sea. The Commission appears less keen on completely excluding employment contracts from the purview of the legislation, noting that the English reform restricts its exclusion to the enforcement by a third party of a term of a contract of employment against any employee.

In the *Annual Review of Irish Law 2005*, pp.507–509, we analysed the Law Reform Commission's *Consultation Paper on Charitable Trust Law: General Proposals* (LRC CP 36–2005) and its *Consultation Paper on Legal Structures for Charities* (LRC CP 38–2005). In March 2006, the Department of Community, Rural and Gaeltacht Affairs published a *General Scheme for the Charities Regulation Bill 2006* (available at www.pobail.ie/en/CharitiesRegulation/). In October 2006, the Commission published its *Report on Charitable Trusts and Legal Structures for Charities* (LRC 80–2006). In its report the Commission notes the areas where the *General Scheme* reflects or differs from its provisional recommendations in its consultation paper, revisits these areas and makes final recommendations for reform.

Regarding charity trustees, the Commission reiterates its earlier recommendation that a minimum of three trustees be required to act for a charitable trust or three officers in the case of an unincorporated association where a corporate trustee acts as sole trustee; it considers that there should be at least three directors on the board of directors. If the numbers fall below three and the person with power of appointment of new trustees is unwilling or unable to do so, the Charities Regulator—a new and important office proposed in the *General Scheme*—should have power to make the appointments necessary to bring the numbers back up to the statutory minimum.

In Chapter 2 of the report, the Commission largely reiterates and expands upon its provisional proposals, made in LRC CP 38–2005, for the establishment of a new form of legal structure for charities, to be called the Charitable Incorporated Organisation (CIO). The Commission sees several advantages in this approach: it would facilitate mutual recognition of charities operating in different states; protect charities from EU harmonisation of the rules relating to company law; and, conversely, facilitate resolution of the concerns expressed at

EU level about the potential for misuse of charitable organisations, especially in terms of money laundering.

In its *Consultation Paper on Multi-Unit Developments* (LRC 42–2006), the Law Reform Commission addresses the legal implications of the huge rise in the number of residential and commercial multi-unit developments in Ireland. Of the 80,000 housing units completed in 2005, over 18,000 were apartment complexes. The Commission records an estimate that more than 10 per cent of the total population now lives in developments of this kind. What has been happening in Ireland is part of a global trend: see van der Merwe, "A Comparative Study of the Distribution of Ownership Rights in Property in an Apartment or Condominium Scheme in Common Law, Civil Law and Mixed Law Systems", 31 *Georgia J. of Int'l & Comp. L.* 101 (2002).

The paper is divided into two sections. The first focuses on matters concerning the need for regulation; the second addresses the land law implications. Because commercial multi-unit developments, such as the traditional office block and the more recent phenonema of shopping centres and industrial estates, have tended to cause less problems than residential accommodation, the consultation paper concentrates on multi-unit developments comprising largely or exclusively residential accommodation.

The unit owner of such accommodation, especially where the development is substantial, has two proprietary interests: a leasehold interest in the unit that has been purchased and an interest in the property vested in the management company. Normally, membership of the management company is tied to ownership of the unit, so that it passes automatically when the unit changes hands.

The Commission first addresses the planning dimension. It provisionally recommends (para.2.08) a review by planning authorities and the Department of the Environment, Heritage and Local Government of planning and housing policy relating to multi-unit developments. Among the problems it identifies are the ubiquity of small units which are often an attractive short-term option for young people without families before upgrading to a more permanent house. It notes (para.2.04):

> "In terms of sustainability of communities, this is undesirable as it leads to an area becoming characterised by a highly transient population. This makes it difficult to establish and develop a sense of community leading in turn to social deprivation for some residents and so-called 'ghettoisation' in an area over time."

The Commission also notes the recent controversy concerning certain local authorities' policies on taking charge of services, the operation of s.180 of the Planning and Development Act 2000, and requiring developers to establish management companies to provide services which would otherwise be taken in charge. The Commission provisionally recommends (para.2.23) that the scope of s.180 be clarified and guidelines issued thereafter. It studiously avoids venturing too far into areas of policy, which it regards as being beyond its brief.

The Commission identifies a number of problems relating to development bonds; often they are too low to have a significant deterrent effect. Nevertheless, the Commission emphasises that they have improved the accountability of builders. It provisionally recommends (para.2.34) that the bonds system be reviewed and that national guidelines be produced to facilitate efficient and efficacious use of bonds for both local authorities and developers. Such guidelines should be periodically reviewed to ensure their deterrent effect.

Turning to developers, the Commission identifies a range of concerns about the practices that have evolved on account of lack of any regulation of their role. It observes (para.3.05) that:

> "Some of these involve a failure to comply strictly with legal responsibilities and others involve practices which give rise to various problems. Much reference has already been made, for example, to the taking in charge problems arising with local authorities resulting from developers' failure to complete developments properly or punctually, and from some developers' reluctance to cede control of management companies to apartment owners."

A "worrying trend" (para.3.17) involves developers, while still in control of the management company before completion of the development, asking unit owners to pay service charges in advance for several years:

> "Developers do this as a way of raising a large lump sum of cash immediately. The developer is then, in effect, a debtor to the management company for the next few years. The money is used for the developer's immediate expenses or development costs. From a consumer perspective, this practice is unsatisfactory and clearly should not be allowed. It places a demand for a sum of money on unit owners for services which have not yet been contracted for. Furthermore, it is undesirable from the management company's point of view for the developer, who should cede any interest in the management company as early as possible once the development is completed, to have control over what is effectively the management company's money over a long term period."

The Commission therefore provisionally recommends (para.3.19) that there be a statutory prohibition on developers seeking payment of more than a year's advance on service charges. This should be subject to review on a case-by-case basis by the Regulator where the developer claims that he or she has a legitimate purpose for demanding such advance payments.

The Commission goes on to recommend provisionally (para.3.26) that service charges never be used to pay for "snagging problems" or any other expenses incurred by the developer in completing the development and that developers be under a statutory obligation to establish the management company in due time. Developers should be statutorily prohibited, while in control of the management company, to commit the company to long-term contracts with managing agents (para.3.29).

The Commission expresses particular concern about reports of developers unduly delaying the transfer of assets to the management company. It recommends (para.3.32) that this practice be prohibited. The developer should be under a clear statutory obligation to transfer the relevant interests to the management company as soon as the sale of the last unit intended to be sold is completed. Breach of the statutory regulations should constitute a criminal offence (para.3.42).

In Chapter 4 of the consultation paper, the Commission provisionally recommends a range of detailed requirements which should apply to management companies of multi-unit developments. One such recommendation (para.4.56) is that any annual accounts should be readily available to potential unit owners or their professional legal advisers.

Although there is already a substantial degree of legal protection for consumers of multi-unit developments, in terms of planning, building and fire and safety regulations and common law actions, the Commission identifies a series of problems faced by unit owners chiefly emanating from lack of supervision and regulation of the sector and from lack of understanding of the proper functions of various stakeholders involved in multi-unit developments. It provisionally recommends (para.6.16) that a guide for management company directors including a full scheme of their rights and responsibilities be compiled.

The Commission notes that all those who have studied the subject of residential multi-unit developments have concluded that there is a major "understanding deficit" which must be addressed urgently. It states (para.6.21):

> "There is far too much confusion over what is involved in owning and living in or renting an apartment or other unit in such a development. This lack of understanding relates to a wide range of matters, such as:
> (i) the nature, purpose and operation of the management company;
> (ii) the distinction between the management company and managing agents;
> (iii) the role and rights of unit owners as members of the management company;
> (iv) the extent to which local authorities are likely to take in charge

the infrastructure of the development;
(v) the nature and purpose of service charges and how they are
calculated;
(vi) the nature and purpose of a reserve or sinking fund and the need
for one."

The Commission provisionally recommends (paras 6.22–6.23) that developers
and other professionals (such as estate agents, auctioneers and solicitors) who
are involved in the sale of a unit be required to furnish all prospective owners
of apartments or other units in such developments with information clarifying
these matters before a binding contract to purchase is completed.

In Chapter 7 the Commission provisionally recommends the establishment
of a regulatory body to oversee regulation of the multi-unit development sector
in Ireland. This body's remit would cover management companies (para.7.14).
It would advise on the drafting and content of statutory regulations designed
to provide purchasers of units in multi-unit developments with consumer
advice and other protection and also monitor the operation of such regulations
(para.7.22). The Commission invites submissions on the most suitable
regulatory body to regulate multi-unit developments.

The Commission provisonally recommends (para.7.24) that legislation
be introduced to regulate multi-unit developments and this legislation should
apply primarily to multi-unit developments involving residential units and a
high degree of interdependence. Application to other residential developments
involving a lesser degree of interdependence or features such as employment of
managing agents or establishment of a managing company should be provided
for where appropriate.

In Chapter 10 the Commission concludes that there is no need in Ireland at
this stage for a statutory scheme to facilitate freehold ownership of apartments
and other units in multi-unit developments. It recommends (para.10.13) that,
if legislation on enforceability of freehold covenants is enacted, the restriction
on lessees of flats to acquire the freehold should be reviewed.

In Chapter 11 the Commission provisionally recommends (para.11.05) that
the proposed legislation should contain "rescue" provisions to enable problems
arising in respect of existing or future developments, of whatever kind and
whenever created, to be resolved. It proposes (paras 11.15 and 11.20) that an
application to the Circuit Court for a "remedial" order should be capable of
being made by any person or body interested in a multi-unit development,
including the proposed regulatory body, but not unsecured creditors. The
basis of such an application should be to solve a problem which prevents the
development from functioning effectively or denies legitimate expectations to
those interested and which cannot be solved otherwise. Notice of the application
would have to be served on any other interested person or body who would
have the right to make representations at the hearing of the application. Rules
of court should require, as appropriate, applicants to furnish the court with a

proposed solution for approval.

The court should have very wide discretion as to the remedial orders it could make. The applicant for a remedial order would have to put forward in the application a draft order or scheme for the approval of the court. In exercising its discretion, the court should be required to take into account representations made to it by any interested person or body, the interests of all interested persons or bodies taken as a whole, and the need to compensate any person who establishes that a vested interest will be adversely affected by the order.

The idea underlying the Commission's proposals is obviously a sensible, pragmatic one. Yet the circumstances in which a court should be entitled to intervene to alter rights, albeit with compensation, should not be based on amorphous concepts. The notion of "a problem which prevents the development from functioning effectively" is very broad. Problems are an inevitable characteristic of daily life; they may arise on account of misconduct or simple disagreement between people of good will or through circumstances entirely independent of human behaviour or relationships. Perhaps a more narrowly defined basis for invoking the very broad discretion of the court would be a better way for the legislation to proceed.

In the Criminal Law chapter, we consider the Law Reform Commission's *Report on Prosecution Appeals and Pre-Trial Hearings* (LRC 81–2006), above p.343, its *Consultation Paper on Duress and Necessity* (LRC CP 39–2006) , above p.327 and its *Consultation Paper on Legitimate Defence* (LRC CP 41–2006), above p.348.

Legislation

BRIAN HUNT, Mason Hayes+Curran

TABLE OF ACTS ENACTED DURING 2006

Number	Title	Date Passed
1	University College Galway (Amendment) Act 2006	February 22, 2006
2	Teaching Council (Amendment) Act 2006	March 4, 2006
3	Irish Medicines Board (Miscellaneous Provisions) Act 2006	March 4, 2006
4	Competition (Amendment) Act 2006	March 11, 2006
5	Social Welfare Law Reform and Pensions Act 2006	March 24, 2006
6	Finance Act 2006	March 31, 2006
7	Aviation Act 2006	April 4, 2006
8	Sea-Fisheries and Maritime Jurisdiction Act 2006	April 4, 2006
9	Employees (Provision of Information and Consultation) Act 2006	April 9, 2006
10	Diplomatic Relations and Immunities (Amendment) Act 2006	April 12, 2006
11	Criminal Law (Insanity) Act 2006	April 12, 2006
12	Registration of Deeds and Title Act 2006	May 7, 2006
13	Parental Leave (Amendment) Act 2006	May 18, 2006
14	Road Safety Authority Act 2006	May 31, 2006
15	Criminal Law (Sexual Offences) Act 2006	June 2, 2006
16	Employment Permits Act 2006	June 23, 2006

17	Health (Repayment Scheme) Act 2006	June 23, 2006
18	European Communities (Amendment) Act 2006	June 28, 2006
19	National Sports Campus Development Authority Act 2006	July 5, 2006
20	Defence (Amendment) Act 2006	July 12, 2006
21	National Economic and Social Development Office Act 2006	July 12, 2006
22	Hepatitis C Compensation Tribunal (Amendment) Act 2006	July 16, 2006
23	Road Traffic Act 2006	July 16, 2006
24	Building Societies (Amendment) Act 2006	July 16, 2006
25	Institutes of Technology Act 2006	July 16, 2006
26	Criminal Justice Act 2006	July 16, 2006
27	Planning and Development (Strategic Infrastructure) Act 2006	July 16, 2006
28	Road Traffic and Transport Act 2006	October 4, 2006
29	Sea Pollution (Miscellaneous Provisions) Act 2006	October 31, 2006
30	International Criminal Court Act 2006	October 31, 2006
31	Patents (Amendment) Act 2006	December 11, 2006
32	British-Irish Agreement (Amendment) Act 2006	December 11, 2006
33	Electoral (Amendment) Act 2006	December 11, 2006
34	Industrial Development Act 2006	December 18, 2006
35	Appropriation Act 2006	December 19, 2006
36	Social Welfare Act 2006	December 19, 2006
37	Europol (Amendment) Act 2006	December 23, 2006
38	Irish Film Board (Amendment) Act 2006	December 23, 2006

39	Houses of the Oireachtas Commission (Amendment) Act 2006	December 23, 2006
40	Energy (Miscellaneous Provisions) Act 2006	December 24, 2006
41	Investment Funds, Companies and Miscellaneous Provisions Act 2006	December 24, 2006
42	Local Government (Business Improvement Districts) Act 2006	December 24, 2006

ACTS AND STATUTORY INSTRUMENTS

Primary legislation   During the year, 42 Acts were enacted. This marks an increase on 2005 when 34 were enacted. 2006 was the last full calendar year of the Government's term in office and, accordingly, some of the Acts passed were significant, reforming measures.

Secondary legislation   Just over 700 statutory instruments were made during 2006. This represents a significant decrease on previous years. The number of S.I.s made in recent years peaked at over 900 in 2005. The partnership document *Towards 2016* pledged that efforts to make secondary legislation available electronically at an earlier stage would continue. It is understood that a pilot project to give effect to this commitment is currently underway.

Private members' bills   Several private members' bills were published during the year, principally by members of the opposition. Amongst those published were: Freedom of Information (Amendment) Bill 2006; Courts (Register of Sentences) Bill 2006; Health (Hospitals Inspectorate) Bill 2006; Genealogy and Heraldry Bill 2006; Criminal Law (Home Defence) Bill 2006; and the Defence of Life and Property Bill 2006 which was initiated by the Senator Morrissey of the Progressive Democrats.

IRISH STATUTE BOOK

Updating of Irish Statute Book online   The Irish Statute Book website was updated in 2006 so that it now includes all of the Acts from 2005 and 348 of the statutory instruments made during 2005. The Chronological Tables only appear to reflect amendments effected up until the end of 2004.

Errors in Irish Statute Book online   In August 2006, the Office of the Attorney General announced that it had become aware of an error in the data on the Irish Statute Book website. The error arises where, in the text of an Act or statutory instrument, there is a reference to a number of sections, for example,

"Sections 17, 18, 19 and 25"; in some instances the electronic version refers only to one section, so the earlier text becomes truncated to read "Section 17". As a consequence, the electronic version of the Irish Statute Book now contains an expanded disclaimer to warn users of the nature of the recently announced problem. In addition, the disclaimer actually encourages users to "check the official Stationery Office version of the Act or statutory instrument concerned", which does seem to give rise to legitimate questions as to the usefulness of the electronic version of the Irish Statute Book in its present form.

The Taoiseach was questioned in the Dáil on the steps the Government proposed to take in order to rectify the problems identified in the online statute book. He stated that the original contract for creating the Irish Statute Book database was valued at just over €1 million (628(3) *Dáil Debates* Col. 774). The Taoiseach also stated that the recent updates of the electronic statute book had cost €150,000. He confirmed that IT consultants to assist in the resolution of the problem had been identified and that the Office of the Attorney General was very anxious to have the matter rectified as soon as possible.

Review of Irish Statute Book   During 2006, the Office of the Attorney General, which hosts the Irish Statute Book website (www.irishstatutebook. ie), invited members of the public to participate in a survey of the website. The survey questionnaire focused on a number of areas including: frequency of use; type of user; accessibility; functionality; and frequency of updating. The consultation process has concluded, but the results have not yet been published.

INITIATIVES TO IMPROVE LEGISLATION

Statute law restatements   In May 2006 the Taoiseach infused some much-needed life into the statute law restatement process when he announced that responsibility for compiling and publishing restatements would be taken away from the Office of the Attorney General and be conferred on the Law Reform Commission. To coincide with this, the Law Reform Commission embarked on a two-month period of public consultation in order to identify which legislation required to be restated with priority. The Commission is currently devising a slightly revised, more reader-friendly format for restatements. In 2007, the Commission published a *Consultation Paper on Statute Law Restatement* (LRC CP 45-2007) which includes a number of revisions for future Restatements.

Statute law revision   In early 2006 the Office of the Attorney General embarked on a public consultation process regarding the next phase of the statute law revision project: the Statute Law Revision (Pre-Union) Bill. The approach proposed to be taken by that Bill was to repeal all legislation passed before January 1, 1801, with the exception of specific statutes identified in the Bill. As part of the consultation process, the Attorney General published a list of the statutes proposed for retention in the Bill. A further stage of consultation was embarked upon, this time focusing on Acts from the period between the coming into effect of the Act of Union on January 1, 1801 and the coming into effect of the Constitution of the Irish Free State on December 6, 1922. Following the conclusion of the consultation processes, the Statute Law Revision Act 2007 was enacted, which contains a "White List" of 364 pre-1922 Acts which represents a definitive list of such Acts now remaining on the Irish Statute book.

It is expected that further statute law revision measures will be introduced to deal with local and personal statutes, private statutes, post-independence legislation and secondary legislation.

E-consultation   The first e-consultation took place during 2006 in relation to the Broadcasting Bill 2007. The e-consultation process was led by the Joint Committee on Communications, Marine and Natural Resources and was facilitated by the establishment of a dedicated website (www.econsultation. ie) through which members of the public were invited to send their views and submissions on the general scheme (heads) of the Broadcasting Bill. The consultation process was divided up into three stages. Stage I was concerned with the invitation and receipt of submissions. Stage II consisted of the Joint Committee exploring, through oral hearings, some of the submissions that it received. Stage III enabled members of the public to post their comments on aspects of the proposed Bill on the website. The conclusion of the consultation process was marked by the publication of a Report of the Joint Committee in April 2007 which reflects the terms of the submissions which were made to it during the consultation process.

Public engagement with legislature   In May 2006, during the Order of Business in the Seanad, Senator Joanna Tuffy drew attention to a motion which her party had placed before the Seanad which would propose the establishment of a petitions committee. The motion read:

> "That Seanad Éireann will establish a petitions committee and initiate procedures for civil engagement with the Seanad through a right of individuals, community groups and organisations to petition the Seanad and make a request to the Seanad to take a view or initiate or amend legislation in relation to matters of public interest or concern." (184(3) *Seanad Debates* Col. 223).

The leader of the Seanad, Senator Mary O'Rourke, welcomed the motion and pledged not to oppose it:

> "It is a motion to establish a petitions committee and initiate procedures

for civil engagement with the Seanad. It is an excellent motion. I hope Senator Tuffy puts it forward in Private Members' time. I will seek, if I can, that we do not put forward an amendment and that this House will accept it. It is well put together and necessary." (184(3) *Seanad Debates* Col. 231).

The motion was formally debated in the Seanad in October 2006. In advocating support for the motion, Senator Tuffy pointed out that other Parliaments, such as the German Bundestag, the Scottish Parliament and the European Parliament, all have a petitions committee. She set out her views on how the committee might work:

"In that type of right to petition, members of the public would have an instigating role. They could come up with ideas for legislation and make requests. Individuals or groups could identify a gap in a particular law and seek appropriate change. They could also call for a debate on a particular issue. Under this process members of the public could have a major influence on legislation and on their legislators" (184(17) *Seanad Debates* Col. 1481).

She noted that in Scotland, individuals, community groups and organisations can make requests or petitions to the Scottish Parliament on matters of public concern or to propose or request a change to existing legislation. In the instance of Scotland, this can and has led to changes in the law. Senator Tuffy felt that the establishment of such a committee would lead to greater engagement of the public with the world of politics:

"There is a great need to re-engage the public. If an issue, local, national or international, agitates people or is not, in their opinion, being addressed with the priority it deserves, they need to be persuaded there is a process through which ... they can put it right" (184(17) *Seanad Debates* Col. 1486).

Responding to the proposal on behalf of the Government, Minister Dick Roche was largely welcoming of the motion. He raised a number of questions about the precise approach to be adopted by the committee if formed, and he pledged to have the matter raised at the Committee on Procedure and Privileges at its next meeting (October 18, 2006). At the conclusion of the Seanad debate, the motion was declared carried.

The question of the acceptance of petitions in the Seanad was previously debated in that House in 1925. Given the slow pace of Seanad reform and the failure, as of the time of writing, to give effect to the more recent motion, there are few grounds for optimism concerning the establishment of such a committee in the near future.

Towards 2016 In 2006, the Government and social partners concluded the latest social partnership agreement, entitled *Towards 2016: Ten Year Framework Social Partnership Agreement 2006–2016*. It pledged the introduction of legislation in a number of areas. In addition, the agreement also made specific commitments concerning the better regulation agenda and the improvement of access to legislation.

The Government committed itself to ensuring that Government Departments publish, within their annual reports, details of legislation and regulations published during the relevant year and how regulatory impact assessment (RIA) was applied in such cases (p.17). The agreement also records the Government's intention to conduct a wide-ranging survey to ascertain business attitudes to regulation. This, it says, will better inform Government of those regulatory areas causing most concern to business, in terms of their impacts on the effective operation of markets and/or their imposition of administrative burdens. Based on the findings of the survey, proposals to address any negative impacts of regulation on business, competitiveness and the consumer will be considered (p.18). The agreement also commits the Department of the Taoiseach to reviewing the operation of regulatory impact assessments by the end of 2007 and to using the findings of that review to refine and amend RIA requirements and processes (p.18).

Limitation of Actions

PERSONAL INJURIES

In *Egan v Midland Health Board* [2006] I.E.H.C. 227, the plaintiff, an elderly man, underwent a complete hip replacement on December 21, 1995 under the care of the second defendant, a surgeon, in a hospital owned and run by the first defendant. The result was not positive: injury to the sciatic nerve made him unable to move his right leg. The second defendant told him of the injury and the plaintiff consented to a further operation a couple of days later, which did not remove the problem. He remained in bed until well into February 1996. The plenary summons was issued on February 6, 2000, three years and six weeks after the first operation.

Johnson J. rejected a defence based on the Statute of Limitations. He referred to s.2(1)(c) of the Statute of Limitations (Amendment) Act 1991, which provides that the limitation clock starts to run only where the plaintiff could reasonably be aware "that the injury was attributable in whole or in part to the act or omission which is alleged to constitute negligence, nuisance or breach of duty."

The plaintiff had submitted that this meant that, until such time as he could reasonably have known the actual act of the second defendant which caused the injury and which was alleged to constitute negligence, the statute would not run. Johnson J. observed:

> "It is quite clear in this case that the actual replacement was not in itself negligent and it is equally quite clear that between that time of the operation on 21st December, 1995 and 6th January, 1996, that the plaintiff was in hospital in bed and whereas he may have been aware that the condition of his right leg was attributable in general terms to the hip replacement he could not possibly have been aware as to the niceties of the suggestions which were to be made on his behalf regarding the acts which were alleged to constitute negligence on the part of the defendants."

Johnson J. noted that, in *Gough v Neary* [2003] 3 I.R. 92, the law had been clearly set out and it was clear that not "until such time as the plaintiff was aware his case was based on the allegation that the damage to the sciatic nerve was caused by an instrument, either clamps or bands, could the plaintiff have been in a position to contemplate the institution of proceedings ...". What Johnson

J. was addressing here was the troublesome issue relating to the distinction between awareness of the fact of significant injury and awareness of negligence on the part of another. Patients who have undergone surgery are always aware that there has been an intrusion on their body but they do not regard it as an injury because of the therapeutic context. In the present case, as long as the plaintiff attributed the inability to move his leg to the inevitable consequences of the operation, rather than some external cause, not itself necessarily involving negligence, the limitation clock did not begin to tick.

FRAUD

In *Devrajan v KPMG* [2006] I.E.H.C. 81, Hanna J. held that the Statute of Limitations 1957 defeated a claim for fraud taken against a bank. The essence of the alleged fraud related to the bank's alleged failure to disclose to its customers the manner in which interest was calculated. Holding that the proceedings constituted an abuse of process on the basis that they could confer no benefit on the plaintiff because he had made a settlement with the bank in respect of which he had received compensation, Hanna J. concluded that the six-year period specified by s.11 of the Act had long since expired and that s.71(1), which stops the clock until a plaintiff "has discovered the fraud or could with reasonable diligence have discovered it", had no application because it was "abundantly clear" that the plaintiff had been aware of the matters of which he complained in the early 1990s; none of the matters alleged against the defendants had been "in any way concealed from him by any of the parties".

In *O'Reilly McCabe v Minister for Justice* [2006] I.E.H.C. 208 Murphy J. held that negligence claims relating to wardship in 1996–1997; to the plaintiff's marriage in 1972; to transfers of property made involving her husband; and a bank charge and discharge made in the 1970s and 1980 were defeated by the Statute of Limitations. The court had found that there was no evidence of fraud which had "not [been] pleaded with particularity (much less any found to substantiate any criminal offence)". Accordingly, Murphy J. concluded that neither s.44 nor s.71 of the 1957 Act applied.

SEXUAL ABUSE

In *TM v JJ, JM, The Minister for Education and Science, Ireland and the Attorney General* [2006] I.E.H.C. 26, Johnson J. held that the plaintiff fell within the provision of s.48(1) and (2) of the Statute of Limitations (Amendment) Act 2002. Born in 1960, he had been subjected to repeated acts of sexual abuse while a student at a national school between 1969 and 1971, by the principal teacher who was then a Franciscan brother. When he had made a complaint to his father, his father initially "sided with him" and then sided against him. When confronted by other allegations of sexual abuse, mainly of girls, the teacher had denied any wrongdoing and, when moved from the school, "was given a hero's send off by the vast majority of the parish". The plaintiff felt totally isolated, since he considered himself to have been branded a liar. He suffered great trauma and was unable to talk to anyone about the matter for many years.

In 1998 the teacher was prosecuted for sexual abuse of other children. It was only then, with great difficulty, that the plaintiff was able to disclose to the authorities what had happened to him and, ultimately, initiate legal proceedings.

Having heard the evidence of the plaintiff and the evidence of a psychiatrist and psychologist, Johnson J. held that the claim was not defeated by the Statute of Limitations. He referred to the ongoing trauma and the vilification to which the plaintiff had been subjected. This condition was "copperfastened" by the evidence of the psychiatrist and psychologist.

In *O'K v H* [2006] I.E.H.C. 13 the facts of the case were closely similar: sexual assaults inflicted by a principal teacher on a young girl in 1973 followed by a delay of 25 years before the initiation of litigation. De Valera J. held that the limitation defence should fail, not on account of the 2000 Act, but by reason of the "knowledge" requirements in the Statute of Limitations (Amendment) Act 1991. Having heard the plaintiff's evidence and that of a psychiatrist and a psychologist, de Valera J. concluded that it had not been until the teacher had been prosecuted in 1998 that the plaintiff realised that the psychiatric and psychological problems of which she complained could be attributed to the actions of the teacher in 1973.

These two decisions may be contrasted with that of *G v H, C, O'C, O'Reilly (and his Successors Provincials of the Divine Word Missionaries), the Fellows and the Board of Management of All Hallows College* [2006] I.E.H.C. 399, where the plaintiff alleged that he had been repeatedly subjected to sexual abuse between 1981 and 1988. He claimed that he had been labouring under a legal disability up to a point in time that was less than three years prior to the institution of the proceedings. He averred that he had suffered from a form of breakdown and had been diagnosed as suffering from depression in 1989; he had consulted a child psychiatrist but had not derived any benefit from this; he was then referred to a clinical psychologist whom he attended for a number of years and, as a consequence, his memories of the acts constituting abuse had become clear.

O'Neill J. evinced scepticism about these averments. He noted their lack of specificity and the fact that they had not been supported by any evidence from any of the doctors who treated the plaintiff. O'Neill J. considered this "surprising". When O'Neill J. also took into account the fact that the plaintiff had made allegations of abuse to his family from 1990 onwards, he was led to conclude, on the balance of probabilities, that the plaintiff's state of mind had not been such as could be characterised as suffering from the effects of mental disability that would prevent the limitation period from running.

Quirke J.'s decision in *O'Dwyer v McDonnell* [2006] I.E.H.C. 281 is of some interest in this context, even though it is dealing with the issue of delay rather than of limitation of actions. It again involved a claim of sexual abuse, accompanied by physical abuse, allegedly perpetrated on the plaintiff while attending a school run by religious brothers between 1953 and 1963. Section 3 of the Statute of Limitations (Amendment) Act 2000 which suspended the operation of the limitation period for some victims of sexual abuse, made it clear the court retained the power to dismiss an action on the ground of delay. An example of the exercise of this power is *Kelly v O'Leary* [2001] 2 I.R. 526, analysed in the *Annual Review of Irish Law 2001*, pp. 443-5 In the instant case, Quirke J. saw some relevance in the approach of the courts to allegations of delay in criminal prosecutions for sex offences. He noted that in *H v DPP* [2006] I.E.S.C. 55, Murray C.J. had referred to the earlier decision of *P O'C v DPP* [2000] 3 I.R. 87, where he had stated:

> "Expert evidence in a succession of cases which have come before this Court and the High Court has demonstrated that young or very young victims of sexual abuse are often very reluctant or find it impossible to come forward and disclose the abuse to others or in particular complain to Gardaí until many years later (if at all). In fact this has been so clearly demonstrated in a succession of cases that the Court would probably be entitled to take judicial notice of the fact that this is an inherent element in the nature of such offences."

In *H v DPP*, Murray C.J. commented:

> "The Court's judicial knowledge of these issues has been further expanded in the period since that particular case. Consequently there is judicial knowledge of this aspect of offending. Reasons for such delay are well established, they are no longer 'new factors'.
>
> Therefore, the Court is satisfied that it is no longer necessary to establish such reasons for the delay. The issue for the Court is whether the delay has resulted in prejudice to an accused so as to give rise to a real or serious risk of an unfair trial."

Quirke J. acknowledged the difference between criminal prosecutions and civil proceedings, but nonetheless considered that:

> "the principles which apply to applications to prohibit the criminal trial of persons accused of child sexual abuse overlap to some extent with the principles which apply to applications of the kind which is before this court. That is not just because this court is now deemed to have the judicial knowledge identified by the Supreme Court in *H v DPP*. It

is because both sets of principles required the court to investigate (a) the length of the delay and (b) the cause of the delay. In applications to dismiss civil claims on grounds of delay the court, if satisfied that the delay was 'inexcusable', went on to determine where the 'interests of justice' lay. The test identified by the Supreme Court in *H v DPP* can be said to reduce emphasis upon apparent culpability for the delay complained of and to focus upon the overriding right of an accused person to a fair trial.

In civil claims for damages arising out of torts such as negligence, breach of contract or assault and false imprisonment, Statutes of Limitations enacted by the legislature regulate the time within which proceedings may be commenced. This court may not seek to legislate or to interfere with the statutory limitation periods prescribed by the legislature. Nonetheless, the court has an inherent discretion to dismiss such claims on grounds of delay.

In the aftermath of the decision of the Supreme Court in *H v DPP*, it can reasonably be asked whether, in applications to dismiss civil claims on grounds of delay, the court should now reduce emphasis on apparent culpability for the delay complained of and focus upon the issues of potential prejudice arising from the delay, i.e. the interests of justice and the right to a fair trial in civil proceedings.

Culpable or '*inexcusable*' delay can still be a factor in the consideration by the court of the '*circumstances*' of each application made."

Quirke J. went on to hold that the plaintiff's claim should be dismissed on the ground of delay. A defendant faced with alleged wrongdoings more than half a century ago suffered presumptive prejudice, rendered more acute where the claim was one of vicarious liability. Although the plaintiff had consulted his solicitors in 1999, it had not been explained on his behalf why a plenary summons had been served only in 2002. A valid statement of claim had not been delivered until 2004. At least 13 relevant witnesses for the defence had died.

Quirke J.'s analysis is novel. One should, however, sound a note of caution about any coalescence of analysis between criminal prosecutions and civil proceedings. The goals of criminal justice do not coincide with those of civil justice; the two operate in separate areas. At a time when victim-centred concerns are reshaping the criminal justice system it is opportune that there should be a national debate on the repective aims of criminal and civil law and the relationship between them.

CONTRIBUTION

In *Kenny v Western Health Board* [2006] I.E.H.C. 370, Quirke J. held that the provisions of s.9(2) of the Civil Liability Act 1961, prescribing a two-year limitation period for proceedings against deceased persons, trumped the general rule laid down in s.31, whereby claims for contribution must be commenced within the period of two years after the liability of the claimant is ascertained or the injured person's damages are paid, whichever is the later. Since the right to contribution was expressly declared by s.30 to be a cause of action within s.9, it followed that a claim for contribution should be categorised as a "proceeding" within the meaning of s.9 and regulated by the statutory time limit which that section provided.

ESTOPPEL

An interesting question arose in *Evanson v McColgan* [2006] I.E.H.C. 47: should the estoppel principle extend to a case where the plaintiff, or his or her legal adviser, believes the limitation period to be three years when in fact it is two? If the plaintiff's failure to sue is attributable in part to this mistake and in part to a request on behalf of the defendant to hold off from suing as liability will not be contested, should the defendant be estopped from raising the limitation defence?

In this case the plaintiff resided in Northern Ireland. She was a passenger in a car involved in an accident in which the driver died. She sued the deceased driver's estate for negligence. The defendant's insurers passed the file to their Belfast office. Correspondence took place between the plaintiff's lawyer, whose office was in Northern Ireland, and the insurer's Belfast office. The fact that, under s.9(2) of the Civil Liability Act 1961, the limitation period against a deceased defendant is only two years was not appreciated.

MacMenamin J. held that the defendant was estopped from raising the limitation defence. In contrast to *Yardley v Boyd*, High Court, December 14, 2004, lack of familiarity with s.9(2) had not been the sole reason for the failure to sue within the limitation period. In the instant case, there had been "clear representations", a "clear course of negotiation and conduct" and "an abandonment of liability". In contrast to the example that Keane C.J. had mentioned in *Ryan v Connolly* [2001] 2 I.L.R.M. 174, the settlement negotiations had not become dormant.

One can understand the desire of courts to take a strongly equitable approach when addressing estoppel in the context of limitation defences. Nevertheless, it is perhaps debatable whether estoppel should apply where a mistake has been made about the limitation period. True, the plaintiff may have been induced not to proceed during the time when the limitation period ran out and, as a matter of historical fact, the plaintiff can attest convincingly that the claim would have proceeded within the period had this representation not been made. But estoppel arguably should not be established simply by showing that, in the absence of the representation, the claim would happen to have been made within the limitation period. If a plaintiff or his or her legal adviser believes mistakenly that there is a further year before the limitation period expires, there is surely something inequitable in letting that mistake deprive a defendant of a limitation defence simply because the defendant's representation has induced the plaintiff not to sue forthwith.

Murphy v Grealish [2006] I.E.H.C. 22 involved a more straightforward application of the estoppel principle. MacMenamin J. evinced little hesitation in holding that the defendant was estopped from pleading the limitation defence where there had been a clear and unambiguous assurance, "stated not once but several times within the limitation period", that liability would not be an issue in the case. This was not an instance of what Henchy J. in *Doran v Thompson* [1978] I.R. 223 had described as the practice of insurers "to dispose of unprosecuted claims [by] allow[ing] them to die of inanition". In the instant case, the prosecution of the claim had acquired significant momentum in the period running up to the expiry of the limitation period and beyond. The defendant's admission of liability and maintenance of correspondence and steps towards settlement for a period just short of a year after the expiry of the limitation period with no mention of the Statute of Limitations amounted to a representation by conduct that the Statute would not be pleaded.

ADVERSE POSSESSION

The legal principles relating to adverse possession are straightforward. In *Murphy v Murphy* [1980] I.R. 183, Kenny J. observed:

> "In section 18 of the Statute of Limitations 1957 adverse possession means possession of land which is inconsistent with the title of the true owner: this inconsistency necessarily involves an intention to exclude the true owner, and all other persons, from enjoyment of the estate or interest which is being acquired. Adverse possession requires that there should be a person in possession in whose favour time can run. Thus it cannot run in favour of a licensee or a person in possession as a servant or caretaker or a beneficiary under a trust ..."

The real difficulty lies in applying these principles to the facts of particular cases. Lord O'Hagan in *Lord Advocate v Lord Lovat* (1880) 5 App. Cas. 273 observed:

> "As to possession, it must be considered in every case with reference to the peculiar circumstances. The acts, implying possession in one case,

may be wholly inadequate to prove it in another. The character and value of the property, the suitable and natural mode of using it, the course of conduct which the proprietor might reasonably be expected to follow with a due regard to his own interests—all these things, greatly varying as they must, under various conditions, are to be taken into account in determining the sufficiency of a possession."

In cases where the parcel of land involved is for the time being of little value to the original owner, O'Hanlon J., in *Doyle v O'Neill*, High Court, January 13, 1995, warned that the adverse use had to be of a particularly definite and positive character such as to leave no doubt in the mind of the original owner that occupation adverse to his title was taking place. The plea of adverse possession failed in that case. It succeeded, however, in *Griffin v Bleithin* [1999] 2 I.L.R.M. 182.

In *Tracey Enterprises MacAdam Ltd v Drury* [2006] I.E.H.C. 381, Laffoy J. referred to all of these precedents when rejecting the defendant's plea of adverse possession. The disputed property was at the foothills of the Dublin mountains. There had been some disagreement between the parties as to the precise dimensions of their respective properties. During the period from 1983 to 2000 the defendant had cleared waste from the disputed plot and had used it from time to time for the purpose of testing machinery following repair or service in his adjoining workshop. In 2000 he erected a fence to prevent cattle straying off land which he regarded as commonage. The original owner of the disputed plot had taken little interest in it over the years.

Laffoy J. held that the defendant's use of the plot prior to his erection of the fence had not constituted possession. His clearing waste had been "in a manner akin to abating a nuisance" rather than involving an act of possession. His incursions to test machinery had been sporadic. His use of the plot "would not have sent out a signal that the defendant was occupying [it] to the exclusion of the true owner and all others". The erection of the fence did not, in Laffoy J.'s view, involve the necessary *animus possidendi*. The defendant had not asserted an exclusive possession. Moreover, his stance when challenged had been to engage in a paper title boundary dispute rather than assert adverse title. The first time he had made such a claim had been in 2004.

PROCEEDS OF CRIME

In *FJ McK v SG* [2006] I.E.H.C. 447, members of An Garda Síochána, when searching the defendant's home pursuant to a search warrant in 1997, came upon bags and bundles of money, including some counterfeit currency. They seized the money. The defendant was not subsequently charged. In November 2003 Judge Smithwick made an order, pursuant to the provisions of the Police Property Act 1897, directing the return of the monies to the defendant. In

December 2003 Finnegan P., being satisfied that these monies constituted, directly or indirectly, the proceeds of crime, made orders under ss.2 and 7 of the Proceeds of Crime Act 1996. In later proceedings before White J. for an order under s.3, the defendant argued that the Statute of Limitations barred the proceedings. White J. rejected this contention, stating:

> "The monies were seized in the course of a Garda investigation separate and distinct from the role or function of the Criminal Assets Bureau or of an 'authorised officer' within the meaning of the Proceeds of Crime Act 1996. Once this seizure took place, the monies could not be said to be in the possession of, or under the control of, the defendant. Clearly the Garda Síochána had both possession and control of the monies, and it was only when the District Court order under the Policy Property Act 1897 had been made, that the defendant could be said to be in possession or control of the monies."

Local Government

BUILDING CONTROL

Building energy performance assessment The European Communities (Energy Performance of Buildings) Regulations 2005 (S.I. No. 872 of 2005) amended the Building Control Act 1990 to enable the Minister for the Environment, Heritage and Local Government to make building Regulations implementing certain provisions of Directive 2002/91 on the energy performance of buildings. The relevant Regulations were the Building Regulations (Amendment) Regulations 2005 (S.I. No. 873 of 2005), which amended the Building Regulations 1997 (*Annual Review of Irish Law 1997,* p.557) to provide for the introduction of a building energy performance assessment methodology for new dwellings commencing on or after July 1, 2006, as required by Directive 2002/91. The Regulations also set higher thermal performance and insulation standards for non-domestic buildings where work commences on or after July 1, 2006. The Regulations were subject to the transitional exemption of construction works for which planning permission or approval was applied for on or before June 30, 2006, provided substantial work had been completed by June 30, 2006.

Air-conditioning systems European Communities (Inspection and Assessment of Certain Air-Conditioning Systems) Regulations 2006 (S.I. No. 346 of 2006) also implemented Directive 2002/91 on the energy performance of buildings, in respect of the inspection and assessment of buildings' air-conditioning systems with an effective rated output of more than 12 kW. Systems-owners must have these systems formally and independently inspected and assessed in accordance with the official manual published or approved by the Department of Communications, Marine and Natural Resources, as may be revised from time to time, with a view to ensuring efficient energy management usage by such systems. The Regulations came into force on January 1, 2007.

Planning and Development Law

GARRETT SIMONS, B.L.

PLANNING AND DEVELOPMENT (STRATEGIC INFRASTRUCTURE) ACT 2006

Introduction   The single most important event of the last 12 months was the enactment of the Planning and Development (Strategic Infrastructure) Act 2006. The 2006 Act effects numerous amendments to the Planning and Development Act 2000. The two areas of principal concern to practitioners are, first, the wholesale revision of the judicial review procedure and, secondly, the introduction of a new streamlined procedure for strategic infrastructure development. The changes to the judicial review procedure will be addressed presently under a separate heading.

Strategic infrastructure development   Generally an application for planning permission is made in the first instance to the relevant planning authority, with a right of appeal thereafter to An Bord Pleanála. In the case of specified categories of infrastructure projects, however, the planning application is made directly to An Bord Pleanála. The commencement date for this new procedure was January 31, 2007.

Development projects to which the procedure applies   The categories of infrastructure project are specified in the Seventh Schedule of the amended PDA 2000. They include energy infrastructure projects; transport infrastructure projects; and environmental infrastructure projects (including certain waste disposal installations). An analogous procedure is provided for the approval of electricity and gas infrastructure. In order for the strategic infrastructure procedure to apply, not only must the development be of a category prescribed under the Seventh Schedule, it must also meet one or more of the following criteria set out in s.37A(2):

(a) the development would be of strategic economic or social importance to the State or the region in which it would be situate;

(b) the development would contribute substantially to the fulfilment of any of the objectives in the National Spatial Strategy or in any regional planning guidelines in force in respect of the area or areas in which it would be situate;

(c) the development would have a significant effect on the area of more than one planning authority.

An applicant proposing to make an application in respect of any of the specified categories of development project must first consult with An Bord Pleanála as to whether the special procedure is to apply. In any such consultation, An Bord Pleanála may give advice to the prospective applicant regarding the proposed application and, in particular, regarding (a) whether the proposed development would, if carried out, fall within one or more of paragraphs (a) to (c) of s.37A(2); (b) the procedures involved in making a planning application and in considering such an application; and (c) what considerations, related to proper planning and sustainable development or the environment, may, in the opinion of the board, have a bearing on its decision in relation to the application. Under the Planning and Development Regulations 2006, the board is required during the course of a pre-application consultation to indicate (a) the plans, particulars or other information which the board will require for the purposes of consideration of an application; (b) the time frames and sequencing to be applied to the application process; and (c) any other matters in relation to the application process as the board considers appropriate.

Where, following consultations, An Bord Pleanála is of the opinion that the proposed development would, if carried out, fall within one or more of paragraphs (a) to (c) of s.37A(2), it shall serve a notice in writing on the prospective applicant stating that it is of that opinion.

If, conversely, the board is of the opinion that the proposed development would not fall within any of those sub-paragraphs, it shall serve a notice in writing on the prospective applicant stating that it is of that opinion. The notice shall include a statement that the prospective applicant's application for permission, if it is proceeded with, must be made to the appropriate planning authority. An application cannot be made to a planning authority in respect of a specified category of infrastructure project unless the consultation procedure has been gone through, and An Bord Pleanála has given notice that it is of opinion that the proposed development would, if carried out, fall within one or more of paragraphs (a) to (c) of s.37A(2), *i.e.* a form of negative clearance is required.

Environmental impact assessment Environmental impact assessment is mandatory in the case of all planning applications subject to the special procedure. The planning application must be accompanied by an environmental impact statement. An Bord Pleanála may refuse to deal with any application made to it where it considers that the application for permission or the environmental impact statement is inadequate or incomplete, having regard in particular to the permission regulations and any regulations made under s.177 or to any consultations held.

Removal of planning authority stage   The removal of the planning authority stage of the decision-making process has attracted much criticism. From a strictly legal viewpoint, however, the amendment in this regard is not as far-reaching as it might first appear. The fact that under the unamended PDA 2000 the decision of the planning authority was subject to a *de novo* appeal to An Bord Pleanála meant that, even before the 2006 Act, the final decision on most major infrastructural developments was already being taken by An Bord Pleanála, not by the planning authority.

Opponents of the new procedure will, of course, point to the fact that, under the previous system, in the majority of cases the decision of An Bord Pleanála whether to grant or refuse had been the same as that of the planning authority, thus suggesting that the planning authority's decision had some influence on the outcome of the appeal process. Such a suggestion probably proves too much in that, from a strictly legal viewpoint, it undermines the independence and impartiality of the appeal system to suggest that the decision of the planning authority influences the outcome. It is more satisfactory that the views of the planning authority are made known by way of the submission of a report on the application—which report is to be considered along with all other submissions—rather than by way of a formal decision which it might be suggested should enjoy some subliminal influence on the outcome of the appeal.

Is a right of appeal essential to fair procedures?   It does not appear to be a requirement of constitutional justice that decision-making take place in two stages, *i.e.* that there is an inherent right of appeal. Rather, the test is whether fair procedures have been afforded prior to a (final) decision being made, and there is no reason in principle why this should not be achieved in a one-stage process. Of course, there are many examples of decision-making where the nature of the first stage is such that, on its own, it would not be acceptable, but the shortcomings are remedied by the existence of a second stage. Indeed, the current planning process itself provides an example of this. The absence of certain of the *indicia* of a fair hearing—such as the possibility of an oral hearing or the production of documents—is probably only acceptable because of the existence of a second stage before An Bord Pleanála where such procedures are, in principle, available. It does not follow, however, that there is a freestanding right to an appeal; the significance of the procedure before An Bord Pleanála is that it supplements deficiencies at the first stage. If, conversely, the full panoply of rights were available at the first stage, then a second stage would not, strictly speaking, be necessary.

Material contravention of development plan   The role of the planning authority is attenuated in that the development plan—although it remains a material consideration—is not binding on An Bord Pleanála. In contrast to the position in respect of all other development, there are no qualifications on the circumstances in which An Bord Pleanála may decide to grant a permission for strategic infrastructure development, or any part thereof, which contravenes materially the development plan.

Prior to the 2006 Act there were qualifications imposed on the circumstances where An Bord Pleanála could override a decision of the planning authority to refuse planning permission on the basis of material contravention. The removal of these statutory qualifications in the case of strategic infrastructure downgrades the status of the development plan. An examination of the detail of the unamended legislation, however, indicates that this change in status is more apparent than real. An Bord Pleanála had been entitled—prior to the 2006 Act—to grant planning permission in material contravention of the development plan where the proposed development was of "strategic or national importance", or where planning permission should be granted having regard to regional planning guidelines. The new procedure under the 2006 Act is only applicable to developments which meet certain qualifications; these include that the development be of strategic economic or social importance, or that the development would contribute significantly to the fulfilment of any of the objectives in the National Spatial Strategy or in any regional planning guidelines. In many cases, therefore, development of the type now subject to the new procedure would not, even under the unamended legislation, have been refused where it would involve a material contravention.

JUDICIAL REVIEW PROCEDURE

Planning and Development (Strategic Infrastructure) Act 2006   The principal amendments to the judicial review procedure introduced by the 2006 Act are as follows. First, the circumstances in which the special judicial review procedure applies have been greatly extended; rather than being confined to certain categories of decisions, the procedure now applies to "any decision made or other act done" by a local authority, planning authority or An Bord Pleanála in the performance or purported performance of a function under the PDA 2000. Secondly, the express statutory requirement for prior participation has been removed. Thirdly, the time for the bringing of proceedings may now only be extended where the delay was as a result of circumstances outside the control of the applicant. Fourthly, certain non-governmental organisations ("NGOs") are exempted from the usual *locus standi* requirement.

The fact that the procedure now applies to acts occurring during the course of the processing of a planning application or planning appeal may result in an increase in the number of legal challenges. Rather than await the outcome of the planning process—which might well have produced a result favourable to them—litigants may feel obliged to move for judicial review at an early stage, lest they find themselves time-barred subsequently.

Substantial interest   An applicant for judicial review is required, under s.50 of the PDA 2000, to satisfy the High Court at the leave stage that he or she has a "substantial interest" in the matter which is the subject of the application. This requirement is more onerous than that imposed in conventional judicial review, *i.e.* sufficient interest. The question of what constitutes a "substantial interest" was examined in a number of judgments in 2006 and, in one instance, a point of law in this regard was then certified for leave to appeal to the Supreme Court.

The most detailed examination is to be found in *Harding v Cork County Council* [2006] I.E.H.C. 295. See, generally, G. Simons, "Locus standi, public interest and the EIA Directive" (2007) 14 I.P.E.L.J. 21. Clarke J. suggested that a requirement for prior participation is inherent in the concept of "substantial interest", and that an applicant for judicial review must have previously asserted his or her interest in the context of the planning process (either expressly or by implication as deriving from the case he or she makes). An exception to this requirement applies where the non-participation was caused by a breach of proper process in the planning application. The entire issue of prior participation is discussed in more detail under a separate heading.

Clarke J. went on then to suggest that the court, having identified the interest which an applicant has either expressed (or might be taken to have been prevented from having expressed), should identify the importance of the interest by reference to criteria such as:

    (a) the scale of the project and the extent to which the project might be said to give rise to a significant alteration in the amenity of the area concerned. The greater the scale and the more significant the alteration in the area, the wider the range of persons who may legitimately be able to establish a substantial interest;

    (b) the extent of the connection of the applicant concerned to the effects of the project by particular reference to the basis of the challenge which he puts forward to the planning permission and the planning process;

    (c) such other factors as may arise on the facts of an individual case.

On the facts of *Harding*, Clarke J. concluded that the applicant did not have a substantial interest. The applicant had grown up in the area of the proposed development and retained family connections with the area; he lived at Kinsale, some two to three kilometres from the headland where the proposed development was to be carried out, and visited the area on a relatively regular basis. Clarke J. accepted that Mr Harding was more than a mere bystander and that he would have had a "sufficient interest" for the purpose of conventional judicial review proceedings. In the view of the court, however, the test for "substantial grounds" required more than a familial connection with an area coupled with a pattern of visiting the area as a former native and as a seafaring person.

In *O'Brien v Dun Laoghaire Rathdown County Council* [2006] I.E.H.C. 177 a neighbouring landowner, who lived within sight of the proposed development, was held not to have a "substantial interest" because, in the opinion of the court, the proposed development would not have any "significant detrimental effect" on visual amenity. It is submitted that the judgment goes too far, and that it is quite inappropriate that a person's standing should turn on whether or not the court considers that the proposed development would have an adverse impact on that person's property. Once a person has demonstrated that their property is sufficiently proximate to the proposed development to be affected by it, he or she is entitled to insist that any decision to grant planning permission is reached in accordance with law, if necessary by bringing judicial review proceedings. The entitlement to seek judicial review should not be short-circuited simply because a judge of the High Court makes the subjective assessment that there will be no significant detrimental effect.

The High Court in *O'Brien* also rejected an argument that the applicant's membership of An Taisce gave her standing. An Taisce itself has a special status as a prescribed body and it would, in the view of the court, be nonsensical if persons who were members of An Taisce could assert a separate special status simply because of their membership.

The extent, if any, to which the principals of a limited liability company can rely on the property rights of the company was examined in *Moriarty v South Dublin County Council* [2006] I.E.H.C. 109. This case concerned a challenge to a planning permission brought by the principal of a rival retail business. The proceedings were brought in the principal's own name. At the full hearing, an objection was raised to the applicant's *locus standi* on the basis that he was not the owner of the relevant lands, which lands were instead held under a lease by a limited liability company. The applicant for judicial review was a director and principal shareholder of that company. Hanna J. ruled that the applicant had failed to demonstrate a substantial interest, indicating that the applicant could not "dip in and out of corporate status". Hanna J. went on then to consider *obiter* whether the company itself would have had a substantial interest, and suggested that in the absence of evidence of an impact on the company's business it had not established a loss such as would give rise to a special interest. This latter aspect of the judgment is controversial and, it is submitted, should not be followed. Businesses have a legitimate interest in ensuring that their commercial rivals comply with the requirements of the planning legislation: see, for example, *R. (on the application of Rockware Glass Ltd) v Chester CC* [2005] E.W.H.C. 2250; [2006] J.P.L. 699. To impose a high evidential burden on such businesses seems inappropriate, and might well involve the High Court having to adjudicate on matters such as market impact in circumstances where retail impact assessment is more properly a matter for the planning bodies.

Prior participation   Before its amendment by the Planning and Development (Strategic Infrastructure) Act 2006, the special judicial review procedure under s.50 of the PDA 2000 required that an applicant have either participated in the planning process, or be able to demonstrate "good and sufficient" reasons for his or her not having previously made objections, submissions or observations as the case may be. As a result of the amendments under the 2006 Act, there is no longer any *express* statutory requirement in this regard. However, a number of cases decided before the 2006 Act suggested that in determining whether an applicant had a "substantial interest" it was appropriate to have regard to his or her prior participation in the planning process. Thus, it seems that notwithstanding the amendment of the legislation in this regard, a requirement for prior participation may survive, albeit now in the form of one of the elements of "substantial interest".

In *O'Brien v Dun Laoghaire Rathdown County Council* [2006] I.E.H.C. 177, the applicant for judicial review had not personally participated in the planning process, although she was a member of An Taisce, which had made submissions on the application for planning permission. The applicant submitted that the reason she did not make submissions or observations was because of her membership of An Taisce, and that her objections at the time were expressed by An Taisce. The High Court rejected this argument, ruling that the applicant had not demonstrated that there were good and sufficient reasons for her failure to participate personally in the planning process:

> "If mere membership of An Taisce was to be considered a sufficient or a good excuse for not having made objections, submissions or observations, that would clearly undo the intended effect of the restriction in the subsection. In my view, for that reason alone, her membership of An Taisce cannot be considered a good or sufficiently good reason for not having made objections. Additionally of course it can be said that because of her membership of An Taisce and her keen interest in planning matters, that she was more than unusually aware of the issues involved and in a better position than most, to have, in her personal capacity, had she so wished, put in an objection. Knowing all of that, she consciously decided not to object in her personal capacity and to pursue her interest through An Taisce. Having taken that course she cannot now, as it were, step outside it, and continue a struggle which manifestly An Taisce don't wish to pursue."

With respect, this is to miss the point. The objective of a requirement for prior participation is to limit the circumstances in which it is necessary to have recourse to the courts, by ensuring that all issues are raised at the administrative stage of the decision-making process. This then affords the decision-maker an opportunity to address whatever concerns might be raised. The achievement of this objective depends on the *content* of the earlier submissions, not on the identity of the person making those submissions.

Costs   The requirement that the application for leave to apply for judicial review be on notice often results in lengthy hearings on the leave application. In the event that leave is granted, it might be argued that the leave should not have been opposed and that, irrespective of the outcome of the substantive application for judicial review, costs should be awarded against those parties unsuccessfully opposing the leave application. In *Usk and District Residents Association Ltd v Environmental Protection Agency*, unreported, High Court, Finlay Geoghegan J., October 13, 2006 it was suggested that it may be appropriate to award the applicant its costs of the leave application independently of the ultimate outcome of the judicial review proceedings. On the particular facts of the case, however, costs were reserved on the basis that it was not unreasonable to oppose the leave application in circumstances where leave was only granted on limited grounds; extensive grounds had been advanced in the statement of grounds, some of which were abandoned only at the commencement of the hearing and others of which were pursued but refused.

Alternative remedies   In principle, a person dissatisfied with a decision of the planning authority on an application for planning permission has a choice of appealing the decision to An Bord Pleanála, or of challenging same by way of judicial review proceedings. Judicial review is a discretionary remedy, however, and relief may be refused where the court considers that an adequate alternative remedy is available to the applicant. The High Court in *Harding v Cork County Council (No. 2)* [2006] I.E.H.C. 295 examined the circumstances where an appeal to An Bord Pleanála might not be an adequate remedy. The planning process is unusual in that an appeal to An Bord Pleanála consists of a *de novo* hearing, with the appeal being determined as if the application for planning permission had been made to An Bord Pleanála in the first instance. Thus, aspects of the process at first instance will not necessarily be relevant to the appeal. Clarke J. indicated that the mere fact that an issue in respect of which complaint is made relating to the first stage of a two-stage process will not be dealt with by an appellate body dealing with the second stage, does not necessarily mean that an appeal would not be an adequate remedy. The appeal is an adequate remedy if the appeal body comes to a fair and proper decision considering all appropriate matters. Clarke J. went on to say that an appeal is likely to be regarded as an adequate remedy in a two-stage administrative process unless either (a) the matters complained of in respect of the first stage of the process are such that they taint the second stage or affect overall jurisdiction, or (b) the process at the first stage is so flawed that it can reasonably be said that the person had not been afforded his or her entitlement to a proper first stage of the process in any meaningful sense.

Appeal to Supreme Court   The determination of the High Court of either an application for leave to apply for judicial review, or of a substantive application for judicial review, is final, and no appeal lies to the Supreme Court save with leave of the High Court. Leave to appeal shall only be granted where the High Court certifies that its decision involves a point of law of exceptional public importance and that it is desirable in the public interest that an appeal should be taken to the Supreme Court. In *Arklow Holidays Ltd v An Bord Pleanála (No. 3)* [2006] I.E.H.C. 280, the High Court had to consider whether a decision to refuse leave to appeal might itself be certified for appeal. It was argued that the initial decision to refuse leave to appeal was part of the "determination" of the High Court of the application for leave to apply for judicial review and, as such, was itself capable of being certified for appeal. In the alternative it was said that if the refusal of leave to appeal was not part of the "determination", then there was no express prohibition on an appeal being brought to the Supreme Court without leave. Clarke J. rejected these arguments:

> "It is clear, therefore, that the proper interpretation of this section is that it, in principle, precludes any appeal to the Supreme Court in respect of planning judicial review matters. That exclusion is subject to the limited exception which derives from the certification process. However, it is clear from those determinations of the Supreme Court that the decision as to whether to grant a certificate is a matter for the High Court and for the High Court alone. I am therefore satisfied that it is not open to the High Court to certify a question as to whether there should have been a certificate in the first place as a matter for appeal to the Supreme Court."

Clarke J. went on to say that to permit an appeal of the type sought would create the possibility of a huge multiplicity of hearings which would defeat the purpose of expedition which formed the policy behind the relevant provisions.

The *Arklow Holidays Ltd* litigation is also of interest in so far as the statutory requirement that an appeal be "desirable in the public interest" is concerned. In his judgment on the application for leave to appeal—*Arklow Holidays Ltd v An Bord Pleanála (No. 2)* [2006] I.E.H.C. 102—Clarke J. had held that it would not be in the public interest to certify an appeal by reference to the importance of the proposed development project and the consequences of the likely delay that would be incurred. Clarke J. elaborated upon this issue in his subsequent judgment in *Arklow Holidays Ltd v An Bord Pleanála (No. 3)* [2006] I.E.H.C. 280. In particular, Clarke J. rejected any suggestion that the merits of the development project had been taken into account in refusing leave to appeal:

> "Nothing in the certification judgment should be taken as indicating a view as to the merits or otherwise of the project in dispute or that such merits were or could be a factor in the exercise of the court's discretion.

However what the judgment does say is that an early resolution of legal questions concerning all projects is an important aspect of the statutory regime and, in my view, such a policy applies with particular force in respect of major public infrastructural projects. In those circumstances, without taking any view as to the merits or otherwise of the project itself, I took into account the undoubted major public infrastructural nature of the project involved in this case and the importance of bringing finality to the questions concerning the validity of it, as a factor to be properly taken into account and weighed against, on the facts of this case, the position of Arklow which sought to rely on what I described as a technical argument and one in respect of which Arklow had suffered no prejudice.

It is therefore the fact that there is a particular public interest in the early resolution of questions which have the capacity to delay major public projects that was taken into account, not any view that the project as proposed was, necessarily, meritorious."

With respect, the approach of the High Court in this regard is not entirely convincing. First, the fact that proceedings concern a major development project cuts both ways: contrary to what the judgment suggests, the scale and importance of the proposed development might actually tell in favour of allowing an appeal. Such projects are capable of having significant effects on the environment and it is important, therefore, that any decision to grant planning permission have been reached properly in accordance with law.

Secondly, in so far as Clarke J. relies on the "technical nature" of the point of law certified as justifying the refusal of leave, there is an element of begging the question. Whether the point is a good one or a bad one is ultimately a matter for the Supreme Court, and not for the High Court in deciding whether or not to certify. Clarke J. had previously ruled that the question of whether a person is excluded from challenging a planning permission on the basis of a potentially significant failure to comply with the requirements of the planning regulations, on the basis of his not having been misled, was a point of law of exceptional public importance, and was an issue which could arise in a great number of cases. It seems somewhat anomalous, therefore, for the court then to turn around and dismiss the point as a technical one.

APPEALS TO AN BORD PLEANÁLA

Content of appeal   Generally only a person who had previously made submissions or observations at the planning authority stage of the decision-making process is entitled to appeal to An Bord Pleanála. Under s.127(1)(e) of the PDA 2000, an appeal to An Bord Pleanála is to be accompanied by the acknowledgement by the planning authority of the receipt of the submissions or observations. This requirement was held to be mandatory by the High Court in *Murphy v Cobh Town Council* [2006] I.E.H.C. 324. On the unusual facts of the case, however, MacMenamin J. found that there had been substantial compliance with the requirement, and that the breach was *de minimis*. The appeal had been accompanied, not by the formal acknowledgement furnished by the planning authority at the time of the making of the submission or observation, but by a subsequent letter from the planning authority giving notice that an appeal (by different appellants) had been received by An Bord Pleanála. This letter did, however, make express mention of a previous communication with the planning authority, and thus it could be readily inferred that the appellant had made a submission or observation in respect of the planning application. Notwithstanding this, An Bord Pleanála had rejected the appeal as invalid. The appellant brought judicial review proceedings challenging this decision. MacMenamin J. ruled that the requirement that the appeal be accompanied by the formal acknowledgement was mandatory and that, absent the *de minimis* rule, non-compliance would render an appeal invalid. MacMenamin J. held that the planning authority had unwittingly created a trap for the unwary in that the various letters it had issued to the appellant—the acknowledgement, the notification of decision and the notification of an appeal—were all similar in layout and substance, and the date of each set out in miniscule print. The appellant had mistakenly submitted the third, rather than the first, in a series of three almost identical letters. The letter actually submitted included the relevant information necessary for An Bord Pleanála to proceed. No prejudice had occurred to the procedures save in the most technical, and perhaps trivial, way. MacMenamin J. accordingly ruled that there had been substantial compliance and that the appeal was valid.

Restriction on making similar applications   Section 37(5) of the PDA 2000 provides, in brief, that no application for permission for the same development or for development of the same description may be made where there is an appeal pending before An Bord Pleanála. This provision was considered in detail by the High Court in *Swords Cloghran Properties Ltd v Fingal County Council*, unreported, High Court, Herbert J., June 29, 2006. The planning authority had refused planning permission for a commercial development, and the developer sought both to appeal against this decision and to make a second application for what was described as a revised development. The developer had attempted to avoid s.37(5) by making the second application for planning permission the day before its first party appeal was lodged. The developer argued that the section did not apply on the facts as there was no appeal pending before An Bord Pleanála as of the date of the making of the second application. The developer went on to argue that the planning authority had erred in law in refusing to accept the second application, and that the failure by the planning authority to make a decision on the merits of that application within eight weeks gave rise to a default planning permission.

Herbert J. rejected this argument, holding, first, that the decision to reject the second application was sufficient to stop time running for the purposes of any default planning permission and, secondly, that the restrictive interpretation of the phrase "an application 'which is subject to an appeal to the Board'" advanced by the developer was contrary to the grammatical and therefore the literal meaning of s.37(5)(a). Herbert J. went on to indicate that even if the section was ambiguous—and he did not accept that it was—the narrow interpretation would defeat the manifest intention of the legislature, namely to assert the primacy of the decision of An Bord Pleanála as the appellate body and to prevent the altogether inappropriate circumstance of the same issue being considered simultaneously by the planning authority and An Bord Pleanála with the unacceptable possibility of divergent conclusions.

DEFAULT PLANNING PERMISSION

Material contravention of development plan   It is well established that a default planning permission cannot arise where the proposed development would involve a material contravention of the development plan. A gloss to this principle had been introduced by the High Court in *McGovern v Dublin Corporation* [1999] 2 I.L.R.M. 314 so as to restrict a default planning permission to an application which, in the normal course of events, is one which in principle is entitled to succeed. On the facts of *McGovern*, the development, in respect of which a default planning permission was claimed, was one of a type which was listed as "open for consideration" (as opposed to "normally permissible") under the relevant development plan. This approach was followed in *Abbeydrive Developments Ltd v Kildare County Council (No. 2)*, unreported, High Court, Murphy J., November 29, 2005. Murphy J. suggested that a default planning permission will only be available where an application is "within the development plan". Where the proposed development is of a type which was open for consideration only, the development will only be permissible where the planning authority has actually had an opportunity to consider the proposed development and to decide whether it is consistent with proper planning.

ENVIRONMENTAL IMPACT ASSESSMENT

Adequacy of EIS   The High Court in *Power v An Bord Pleanála (No. 1)*, unreported, High Court, Quirke J., January 17, 2006 reiterated that the adequacy of the environmental information provided by a developer is a matter for An Bord Pleanála to determine. The decision of An Bord Pleanála in this regard is only subject to merits-based review in circumstances where that decision is shown to be unreasonable or irrational. The judgment in *Power* also emphasised that the initial environmental impact statement submitted with an application for planning permission was only part of the information provided by the developer, and that further evidence and submissions on the impact of the proposed development were received at the subsequent oral hearing held by An Bord Pleanála.

Cumulative effects	In *Arklow Holidays Ltd v An Bord Pleanála (No. 1)* [2006] I.E.H.C. 16, the High Court granted leave to apply for judicial review on the ground, *inter alia*, that An Bord Pleanála may have erred in failing to assess certain aspects of a proposed development. The project consisted of a wastewater treatment plant. The inspector, and by inference An Bord Pleanála, appear to have taken the view that it was unnecessary to assess the impact of those aspects of the development outside the redline of the wastewater treatment plant itself. Clarke J. held that it was arguable, for the purposes of a leave application, that aspects of a project, which themselves might not have impacts which would be significant, when taken on a cumulative basis and added to the impacts of other aspects of the same project might have significant environmental effects.

"Carrickmines Castle" and the second development consent	Objectors to a development project will often allege that planning permission has been granted in breach of the requirements of the EIA Directive. In some cases there will have been no assessment and it will be argued that there should have been one; in others, the contention will be that the environmental impact assessment carried out prior to the grant of planning permission was inadequate. The traditional view had been that unless a formal challenge by way of judicial review was brought within time, the absence of any assessment, or the alleged inadequacy of an assessment, could not be raised subsequently. This view will have to be reconsidered now in light of two recent judgments of the ECJ, namely *Commission v United Kingdom* (Case C-508/03), May 4, 2006; and *R. (on the application of Barker) v London Bromley Borough Council* (Case C-290/03), May 4, 2006. The intriguing prospect presented by these judgments is that a deficient assessment may have to be remedied where, for whatever reason, a further consent is required in respect of the development. See, generally, G. Simons, "Development Consents and the EIA Directive" (2006) 12 *Bar Review* 129.

To put the matter another way, the happenstance of an application subsequently for some form of consent or approval might well trigger a requirement to make good the failure to carry out any, or any adequate, environmental impact assessment at an earlier stage.

This (remedial) obligation may arise even in circumstances where there is no requirement under national law, still less a prescribed procedure, for environmental impact assessment at the stage of the later decision.

The availability of this—admittedly innovative—remedy is dependent on the later decision constituting a "development consent" within the meaning of the Directive. Scannell argues that a development consent must mean an environmental consent and cannot reasonably be construed as one of the many other consents which developers may need before being entitled to proceed with projects: Y. Scannell, *Environmental and Land Use Law* (Thomson Round Hall, Dublin, 2006), para.5–30. The leading Irish case is now that of the Supreme Court in respect of "Carrickmines Castle", *Dunne v Minister for the Environment, Heritage and Local Government (No. 2)* [2005] I.E.S.C. 49; [2007] 1 I.L.R.M. 264. The Supreme Court had to consider whether ministerial directions in respect of archaeological works—given subsequent to formal Road Acts approvals—represented a form of "development consent".

The Supreme Court held that ministerial directions did not form part of the development consent for a road development. Rather, there was a single development consent, the statutory approval under the Roads Acts, and the subsequent ministerial directions merely involved the regulation of activities for which the principal consent, raising the substantial environmental issues, had already been given:

> "The Court is satisfied for the following reasons that the Ministerial directions under s.8 do not fulfil any of the requirements necessary to constitute a *'development consent'*:
>
> (a) Firstly, the Minister does not have power under s.8 to embark upon a reconsideration of the environmental issues arising for the road development, and, more importantly, does not have power to modify the road development. All that is left for the Minister is a power to regulate the manner in which the works which are necessary to allow the road to proceed are carried out.
>
> (b) Secondly, the project is prescribed for the purposes of the environmental impact assessment Directive as the road development, the subject matter of the 1998 consent. Excavation works of the type the subject matter of the Ministerial directions under s.8 are not a prescribed project."

It seems to follow from the Supreme Court judgment that in order to constitute a "development consent" the relevant decision must allow for the consideration of, and regulation of, environmental impacts.

In analysing a series of consents, therefore, it seems that a "but for" test cannot be conclusive. In other words, the mere fact that development cannot be completed without a particular consent cannot, without more, mean that that consent must be a development consent. Thus, for example, a fire safety certificate, even if a prerequisite to the carrying on of a particular activity, would not constitute a "development consent". The test is more sophisticated. The question to be asked is the extent to which, in reaching the decision on whether or not to grant the consent, the decision-maker is entitled to take into account environmental impacts. Where environmental impacts are to be taken into account in any particular decision-making process, the resulting consent probably constitutes a development consent.

Critics might argue that the above analysis is flawed in that it is based, to some extent, on a circular argument. The relevance of whether a particular decision is part of multi-stage development consent is that, if it is, then the relevant decision-maker is required to address his or her mind to environmental impacts. There is an element of begging the question, therefore, if the test to be employed in determining whether a particular decision is a development consent is whether is the decision-maker is entitled to take into account environmental impacts?

This approach may now have to be reassessed in light of the recent judgments by the ECJ. Whereas the ECJ does recognise a distinction between principal and ancillary decisions, its view of the consequences of this distinction is vastly different. The ECJ—while accepting that it will generally be appropriate to carry out the environmental impact assessment at the stage of the principal consent—regards even an ancillary decision as forming part of the development consent.

The ECJ's analysis thus makes contingency for a deficient assessment at that stage, by requiring that a proper assessment be carried out where necessary at the time of the second decision.

The judgment in *Commission v United Kingdom* concerned the application of the concept of "development consent" to outline planning permission. Under the then English legislation, outline planning permission could be granted subject to a requirement to obtain the subsequent approval of reserved matters. (Unlike the position under Irish law, it was possible to apply for outline planning permission in respect of development projects subject to the Directive.) In the case of such development, any environmental impact assessment was to be carried out at the time of the application for the outline planning permission. Screening of sub-threshold development was similarly to be performed at the time of the initial application.

The ECJ held that the two decisions together constituted a multi-stage development consent and, further, considered that the failure to provide for the possibility of assessment at the stage of the approval of reserved matters meant that the legislative scheme was not consistent with the requirements of the Directive. The fact that the development project could not proceed "but for" the approval of the reserved matters was sufficient to constitute same as part of the development consent:

> "In the present case, it is common ground that, under national law, a developer cannot commence works in implementation of his project until he has obtained reserved matters approval. Until such approval has been granted, the development in question is still not (entirely) authorised.
>
> Therefore, the two decisions provided for by the rules at issue in

the present case, namely outline planning permission and the decision approving reserved matters, must be considered to constitute, as a whole, a (multi-stage) 'development consent' within the meaning of Article 1(2) of Directive 85/337, as amended."

The ECJ has provided little guidance as to the test to be applied in this regard. It follows from the judgment in *Commission v United Kingdom*, however, that the mere fact that a decision is an implementing decision, subsidiary to a principal decision, does not preclude a finding that that decision is a development consent. The logic here seems to be that a multi-stage development consent is not complete until the last decision is in place and, accordingly, the obligation to ensure that a proper assessment has been carried out remains until the last piece of the jigsaw is in place.

Article 10a review procedure   Under Art.10a of the EIA Directive as amended by Directive 2003/35/EC, members of the public who are affected have a right to access to a review procedure before a court of law or another independent and impartial body established by law to challenge the substantive or procedural legality of decisions, acts or omissions subject to the public participation provisions of the EIA Directive. The review procedure must be fair, equitable, timely and not prohibitively expensive.

In *Friends of the Curragh Environment Ltd v An Bord Pleanála (No. 1)* [2006] I.E.H.C. 243; unreported, Kelly J., July 14, 2006 the High Court suggested that the provisions of Art.10a were not sufficiently clear, precise and unconditional as to have direct effect. In particular, Kelly J. considered that the requirement that the review procedure not be "prohibitively expensive" was imprecise:

> "Even if the Directive can be taken to apply to judicial review applications the question arises as to what the words 'prohibitively expensive' refer to. It is not clear whether this refers to court fees which are chargeable by the State or to legal costs which are not. If it is court fees then access is available to any person on paying a modest court fee. It is particularly modest in the case of judicial review proceedings in planning matters where the originating document is a notice of motion carrying a fee which is a fraction of the fee payable for the issue of a plenary summons. If the Directive is dealing only with fees then it has no application whatsoever in the case of a PCO [pre-emptive costs order]."

With respect, it must be doubtful whether the ECJ would agree that Art.10a does not have direct effect. The ECJ has previously taken a very robust attitude to the EIA Directive and has ruled that the requirement to carry out an assessment has direct effect. This was so notwithstanding the vague wording of the Directive in this regard. The introduction of a remedies element to the Directive under Art.10a was self-evidently intended to enhance the rights of the public under the Directive; it would be ironic if this aspect of the Directive alone were found not to have direct effect.

PLANNING CONDITIONS

Security The nature of security to be provided by a developer under a planning condition was considered in *Sweetman v Shell E & P Ireland Ltd* [2006] I.E.H.C. 85. The relevant condition required the developer, prior to commencement of development, to lodge with the planning authority "a cash deposit, a bond of an insurance company or other security" to secure the satisfactory reinstatement of the site upon the cessation of the permitted activity. The form and amount of security was to be agreed between the developer and the planning authority. The developer proposed to provide security by way of a guarantee from its parent company, and that the necessary arrangements be put in place within a period of six months. In the events that transpired, the formal documentation was not put in place prior to the commencement of development. Smyth J. held that there had nevertheless been substantial compliance with the condition, and refused to grant relief under s.160 of the PDA 2000. Any delay in furnishing the necessary follow-up documentation was, in the view of the court, explicable by reference to the existence of various legal proceedings challenging the planning permission; no sensible or reasonable business person would make business commitments in the absence of legal certainty as to whether the planning permission would be fully implementable. Smyth J. indicated that he would, in any event, have refused relief as a matter of discretion, by reference to factors such as the trivial or technical nature of the breach; the bona fides of the developer; the attitude of the planning authority; the public interest and hardship to third parties; and delay on the part of the applicant.

EXEMPTED DEVELOPMENT

Section 4(1)(h) Section 4(1)(h) of the PDA 2000 provides, *inter alia*, that works for the "maintenance, improvement or other alteration" of a structure are exempted development, provided that those works do not materially affect the external appearance of the structure so as to render the appearance inconsistent with the character of the structure or of neighbouring structures. In *McCabe v Coras Iompair Éireann* [2006] I.E.H.C. 356, it was held that this exemption covered the renewal and reconstruction of a railway bridge, where the extent of the renewal or reconstruction was not such to amount to the total or substantial replacement or rebuilding of the original structure. The works involved did not result in the external appearance of the bridge becoming inconsistent with its character. The only really noticeable difference in the bridge was the replacement of a semicircular arch with an opening of rectangular appearance. Herbert J. held that shape, however, is only one of the features which contribute to the character of a structure, and there was no objective basis for considering that one particular type of opening rather than another should be regarded as establishing the character of this sort of bridge.

Practice and Procedure

MELODY BUCKLEY, B.S., J.D.

AMENDMENT OF PLEADINGS

Defences and counterclaims, joinder of State   In *Shell E & P Ireland v McGrath,* High Court, Laffoy J., March 23, 2006, the second and fifth named defendants obtained an order under RSC Ord.28, r.1 allowing for the delivery of amended defences and counterclaims; and an order under RSC Ord.15 joining the Minister, Ireland and the Attorney General as defendants to the counterclaims. Laffoy J. cited *Croke v Waterford Crystal Ltd* [2005] 1 I.L.R.M. 321 as authority for exercising the court's discretion to amend the defences on the basis that the amendment was necessary for the purpose of determining the real questions in controversy in the litigation. On the same basis, and citing *Croke,* above, as authority, she also allowed the State to be joined as defendant to the counterclaims. The plaintiffs' strongest argument was that the proposed amended defences and counterclaims raising issues of public law were time-barred and should have been raised by way of judicial review within the time limited in RSC Ord.84, and that those issues of public law were not justiciable in the instant proceedings. Laffoy J. held that as the timeliness and justiciability of the issues could be raised in the plaintiff's reply and defence to the counterclaim, they did not inhibit the exercise of the court's discretion in favour of allowing the amendments. She also granted an order under RSC Ord.25, r.1 for a trial of the preliminary issue as to whether the defendants would be permitted to raise the issues of public law in the proceedings.

THE COMMERCIAL COURT

Application for judicial review in the Commercial Court   In *Mulholland and Kinsella v An Bord Pleanala, Coverfield Developments Ltd,* High Court Commercial, Kelly J., June 14, 2005, Coverfield, the notice party, first moved for leave to apply for judicial review under the Planning and Development Act 2000 to seek certiorari to quash a decision by An Bord Pleanála. About one month later, it moved to transfer the case to the Commercial Court List under RSC Ord.63A, r.4 on the basis that its claim was commercial in nature and therefore subject to that court's jurisdiction. Two applicants objected to the transfer on the basis that an application for judicial review was not of a commercial nature. Kelly J. held that the application fell squarely within the parameters of RSC Ord.63A, r.1(g):

> "... proceedings in respect of any claim ... relating to ... any appeal
> from or application for judicial review ... where the judge of the
> Commercial List considers that the appeal or application, having regard
> to the Commercial or any other aspect thereof, appropriate for entry in
> the Commercial List."

It was thus admitted to the list. *PJ Carroll v Minister for Health and Children,*
Supreme Court, Geoghegan J., May 3, 2005, was distinguished on the basis
that it concerned a constitutional claim which fitted within the ambit of the
"catch-all" category of cases under Ord.63A, r.1(b) and not RSC r.1(g).

COSTS

Wasted costs order   On February 2, 2006 the Master, in *Kennedy v Killeen
Corrugated Products Ltd and Door Fix Ltd (third party)*, High Court, February
2, 2006, and *Kennedy v Killeen Corrugated Products Ltd and Door Fix Ltd,
third party and Law Society of Ireland, Notice Party,* High Court, Finnegan,
P., November 28, 2006, in a show cause hearing granted a wasted costs order
against the plaintiff's solicitor on the basis that the plaintiff's motion for
delivery of interrogatories was wholly unjustified. Counsel had advised the
plaintiff's solicitor to first serve a notice to admit facts concerning an allegedly
defective shutter door causing injury to the plaintiff, and thereafter if necessary,
to arrange for the delivery of interrogatories. The Master based his decision
on the following grounds:

>   (1)   Under RSC Ord.99, r.7, a solicitor may be held responsible for the
>   wasted costs, as in the instant matter, when solicitor–client costs
>   are incurred after the client's solicitor brings a clearly unnecessary
>   and burdensome motion for discovery of documents. Order 99,
>   r.7 reads in relevant part:
>> "If in any case it shall appear to the Court that costs have
>> been improperly or without any reasonable cause incurred,
>> or that by reason of any undue delay in proceeding under
>> any judgement or order, or of any misconduct or default of
>> the solicitor, any costs properly incurred have nevertheless
>> proved fruitless to the person incurring the same, the Court
>> may call on the solicitor of the person by whom such costs
>> have been so incurred to show cause why such costs should
>> not be disallowed as between the solicitor and his client and
>> also (if the circumstances of the case shall require) why the
>> solicitor should not repay to his client any costs which the

client may have been ordered to pay any other person, and thereupon may make such order as the justice of the case may require ...".

(2) By virtue of RSC Ord.63, the Master has jurisdiction to order the solicitor to pay clients' costs under RSC Ord.99, r.7. The appeal to the High Court, on November 28, 2006, was granted by Finnegan P. He concluded that the facts of the case fell "far short" of the exceptional circumstances which might justify a wasted-costs-type order. The solicitor was guilty at most of negligence, but not of gross negligence. He found that the Master lacked the jurisdiction to make such an order on the basis that there was no rule, statute or allocation for this empowerment. While the Master's jurisdiction regarding costs is detailed under RSC Ord.63, only the court is empowered to make a wasted-costs-type order under RSC Ord.99, r.7. Further, the court would be most suitable to making this type of order, given that the hearing, in evaluating the conduct of a solicitor, would be lengthy and detailed.

DELAY

Delay in delivery of statement of claim   The Master, in *Crowley v Roche Products (Ireland) Ltd,* High Court, January 20, 2006, refused to grant an extension of time for delivery of the statement of claim under Ord.122, r.7, even though the plaintiff issued a plenary summons in furtherance of a tightening of standards in compliance with Art.6 of the European Convention on Human Rights Act 2003 and the litigant's right to trial within a reasonable time. In his analysis, the Master determined that the court, as it had been doing under the *Primor/Rainsford* principles derived from *Primor v Stokes, Kennedy, Crowley* [1996] 2 I.R. 459 and *Rainsford v City of Limerick* [1995] 2 I.L.R.M. 561, would no longer apportion blame. He cited as authority a line of cases evincing what he termed the new "agenda" of the court, in imposing the ultimate sanction of dismissal for delay including *Stephens v Paul Flynn Ltd,* High Court, Clarke J., April 28, 2005 where Clarke J. stated:

> "The weight to be attached to various factors in the assessment of the balance of justice may need to be significantly re-assessed and adjusted in the light of the conditions now prevailing. Delay which would have been tolerated may now be regarded as inordinate. Excuses which sufficed may no longer be accepted. The balance of justice may be tilted in favour of imposing greater obligation of expedition and against requiring the same level of prejudice as heretofore."

He also cited *Gilroy v Flynn* [2005] 1 I.L.R.M. 290 and the opinion of Hardiman

J. The Master proposed that the court establish a "reasonable" timeframe fixed by reference to a deadline irrespective of the likelihood of "prejudice". On this basis in the instant case, as well as in future cases, a delay of three years from the accrual of the cause of action would constitute a prima facie breach of the defendant's rights under the Convention, regardless of the excuse.

Delay in filing papers in appeal   Although in *McGrath v Irish Ispat (in voluntary liquidation), formerly known as Irish Steel Ltd,* Supreme Court, Denham J., July 10, 2006, the *Primor* principles as enunciated in *Primor v Stokes, Kennedy, Crowley* [1996] 2 I.R. 459 were applicable, Denham J. took notice of the developing European jurisprudence on the issue of delay, in both the European Court of Justice and pursuant to Art.6 of the European Convention on Human Rights. In the instant matter, although the delay was clearly inordinate, the court dealt with the question of whether it was inexcusable. The plaintiff also moved under Ord.58, r.8 for leave to adduce additional evidence, arguing that one of the reasons why the delay was not inordinate was that at the time of trial his witnesses were unavailable. Denham J. found the delay inexcusable on the basis that the case was 17 years old, the defendant was in voluntary liquidation and the plaintiff was given the opportunity to file papers in a timely way concerning notice of appeal on consent, which he did not do. She also did not accept that the witnesses, whom the plaintiff alleged could adduce additional evidence, had actually been unavailable at the time of trial.

Significant time lapse since events on which proceedings based   In *Kearney v McQuillan and the North Eastern Health Board*, High Court, Dunne J., May 31, 2006, the plaintiff underwent an emergency caesarean section followed by a symphysiotomy procedure in 1969. She alleged that the symphysiotomy was performed without her consent or knowledge and that as a result she suffered and continued to suffer personal injuries. She instituted suit and the defendant, the nominee for the Medical Missionaries of Mary, the owner/occupier of Our Lady of Lourdes Hospital, Drogheda, moved to dismiss the matter on the basis that it was severely prejudiced by the delay. The vital witnesses, including the doctor who performed the surgery, were deceased. The plaintiff argued that it had no personal responsibility for the delay, a number of nurses were still available to testify and that the matter could be resolved on expert evidence. Dunne J., in exercising the power of inherent jurisdiction of the court, dismissed the action on the basis that the defendant was severely prejudiced by the delay due to the deaths of its relevant witnesses and that there was a real and serious risk of an unfair trial. She did not believe that the surviving nurses could assist the defendant on the principal issues and that the case could be decided solely upon expert testimony. The principles in *Toal v Duignan (No. 1 and No. 2)* [1991] I.L.R.M.135, as enunciated in *Manning v Benson and Hedges Ltd* [2004] 3 I.R. 556 were followed. In exercising the inherent jurisdiction of the court to dismiss the plaintiff's claim, Dunne J. applied the following factors as set out in *Manning* by Finlay Geoghegan J. in assessing the effect of the lapse of time on the fairness of a trial: the court should consider whether the defendant contributed to the delay; the nature of the claim; whether the issues were factual or legal; whether oral evidence would be required; the availability of witnesses; and the length of time between the acts or omissions and the probable trial date.

Delay, inordinate but excusable, Statute of Limitations and wrongful death In the medical negligence case, *Padraic Keane (as personal representative of the late Mrs Agnes Keane) v Western Health Board and Mrs Ann Meehan*, High Court, Quirke, J., October 2, 2006, and by addendum delivered November 22, 2006, the late Mrs Agnes Keane was admitted to hospital in Galway in 1983, where as a result of pregnancy complications she became comatose after giving birth to twins. She remained in a coma for 19 years until her death in 2002. The defendants unsuccessfully moved the court to exercise its power of inherent jurisdiction to dismiss the plaintiff's claim on the grounds of inordinate and inexcusable delay. Quirke J. found that although the delay was prima facie inordinate, it was clearly excusable. He accepted that Patrick Keane was caring for a comatose wife and twins and thus could not institute this action at an earlier date and that the fact of the death of Dr Meehan in and of itself was not sufficient to sustain the contention that the claim should be dismissed. Significant documentation was also still available, including medical, nursing and possibly other notes and records. Furthermore, no evidence was adduced in support of the contention that significant prejudice would result from the absence of other relevant witnesses.

Although the delay in prosecuting the plaintiff's claim was found to be inordinate but excusable, Quirke J. found the plaintiff's claim against the estate of Dr Fergus Meehan, the consultant who treated Mrs Keane in 1983 and died in 1991, time-barred under s.9(2) of the Civil Liability Act 1961 and therefore not maintainable. A plenary summons was issued on July 14, 2000, two years before Mrs Keane's death. The matter continued with Patrick Keane named as the personal representative of Agnes Keane in the High Court on July 7, 2005. However, pursuant to s.8 of the Civil Liability Act 1961, on the death of a person "… all causes of action shall subsist against his Estate." In the instant matter, Dr Fergus Meehan died in 1991, but as required under s.9(2) of the Civil Liability Act 1961, on the date of his death, no proceedings had been commenced on behalf of the late Mrs Keane against the late Dr Meehan's estate within the period of two years after this death, or within the relevant period and were "… pending at the date of his death" for the purpose of s.9(2) of the 1961 Act. Quirke J. cited *Moynihan v Greensmyth* [1977] I.R. 55, with a similar fact pattern, as authority for the constitutionality of s.9(2) of the 1961 Civil Liability Act 1961. In *Moynihan*, the defendant was killed in an accident. However, although the 16-year-old plaintiff properly instituted the action within the statutory time period after reaching the age of 21, her suit against the defendant's estate was dismissed as time-barred under s.9(2) of the 1961 Act.

Quirke J. also dismissed the claim for contribution and indemnity by the Western Health Board against Dr Meehan's estate in an addendum delivered on November 22, 2006. In reaching his decision he dealt with a unique conflict between the applicability of two sections of the same statute to the instant situation: s.31 of the Civil Liability Act 1961 governing contribution and s.9(2) of the same Act governing causes of actions against an estate. In preferring the more precise language of s.9(2) to the more general language in s.31, and analysing the purpose of the legislation and the intention of the legislature as identified by the Supreme Court in *Moynihan v Greensmyth,* above, he reasoned that the provisions of s.9(2) of the Act applied to the Board's claim for contribution against Dr Meehan's estate.

DISCLOSURE

Preliminary expert medical report   In the medical negligence case *Payne v Shovlin,* Supreme Court, Kearns J., February 9, 2006, the plaintiff obtained a preliminary medical report from his medical expert. The expert clearly stated that his final opinion would only be given after obtaining the expert views of other specialists. He subsequently provided a more detailed final report containing the substance of the evidence intended to be adduced by him. The plaintiff moved on notice pursuant to RSC Ord.39, r.47 for directions concerning his obligation to disclose this report in addition to the final report. The defendant argued that Ord.39, r.46(1) specified the listing of "all" expert witness reports on the schedule and that both of the expert's reports should be provided to avoid surprise or trial by ambush. In the High Court, Dunne J. held that the plaintiff was obliged to disclose both of the reports under Ord.39, r.46 and that he would suffer no prejudice as a result of the disclosure. The appeal was dismissed by Kearns J. in the Supreme Court on the basis that the preliminary report submitted by the plaintiff's expert was not subject to privilege. Order 39, r.46(1) requires production of all reports of an expert intended to be called as a witness, which contain, in whole or in part, the substance of the evidence to be given. Kearns J. considered surprise an important factor in reaching his decision. It would not serve the interests of expedition and expediency to have information emerge only in cross-examination. *Galvin v Murray* [2001] 1 I.R. 331 was distinguished on the facts and *Kincaid v Aer Lingus Teoranta,* Supreme Court, Geoghegan J., May 9, 2003 was distinguished on the basis that the plaintiff's counsel did not intend to call the expert as a witness and was thus no longer obliged to furnish the report.

ISAAC WUNDER ORDER

Proceedings struck out In *Devrajan v KPMG, Price Waterhouse Coopers,* High Court, Hanna J., January 20, 2006, Hanna J. ordered that the plaintiff's proceedings should be struck out on the basis that they constituted an abuse of process of the court, were frivolous and vexatious and that the plaintiff was guilty of inordinate and inexcusable delay. He granted an Isaac Wunder order restraining the plaintiff from instituting proceedings against the defendants without prior High Court leave. The plaintiff instituted suit against all of the defendants on the basis that Permanent TSB wrongfully stopped a standing order payment.

JOINDER

Non-party insurance company In *Byrne v John S O'Connor & Co Solicitors, and by order made the 15th day of October, 1991, Admiral Underwriting Agents (Ireland) Ltd,* defendants, Supreme Court, Kearns J., May 15, 2006, the plaintiff instituted suit against the defendant firm which represented him in an action for injuries sustained in an assault in a bar. He alleged that his negligence and breach of contract actions had become time-barred due to the alleged misrepresentations of an unqualified solicitor employed at the defendant law firm. The defendant firm's insurer, Admiral, became subrogated to the firm upon receipt of notice of the claim. However, five years after Admiral's receipt of the notice of claim and having defended the firm from that time on, it advised of its intention to avoid based on non-disclosure of a material fact and a material deficiency of client funds. Admiral's solicitors subsequently gave notice of repudiation to the estate solicitors (the principal of the firm had since died and the instant matter was handled by his estate) and notified the plaintiff's solicitors that they intended to come off the record pursuant to Ord.7, r.3. On October 8 and 15, 1999, in the High Court, O'Donovan J. allowed Admiral's solicitors to come off the record but joined Admiral as a defendant under Ord.15, r.13 to ensure that the plaintiff obtained an order as to costs. Admiral appealed to the Supreme Court and, almost seven years later, the matter was heard before Kearns J. on May 15, 2006. Admiral's appeal was refused on the basis that it was a proper exercise of the court's discretion to allow its solicitors to come off the record and at the same time to join the insurer as defendant under Ord.15, r.13 to cover costs. The plaintiff successfully argued that without Admiral's involvement in the case, an injustice would result. He would be deprived a mark in damages for his claim in negligence and left with a bill of legal costs. *O'Fearail v Manus* [1994] 2 I.L.R.M. 81 was followed in that under similar facts a solicitor was allowed to come off the record, but it was also distinguished in that the joinder/costs issue did not arise because an undertaking was furnished.

JURISDICTION

Exclusive jurisdiction (Art.17 of the Lugano Convention)   In S*tryker Corp t/a Stryker Howmedica Osteonico v Sulzer Motco AG*, High Court, O'Neill, J., March 7, 2006, the plaintiff sued the defendant in the High Court for breach of contract after the machine the defendant sold to the plaintiff exploded at the plaintiff's plant in Cork. The defendant, a company with a manufacturing plant in Switzerland, unsuccessfully sought an order under RSC Ord.12, r.26 or alternatively under the exercise of the court's power of inherent jurisdiction to set aside service of the proceedings. It argued that it met the criteria for an exclusive jurisdiction agreement under Art.17 of the Lugano Convention. Article 17 provides that in an exclusive jurisdiction agreement the parties consent to submit to the jurisdiction of the courts of a Contracting State, even though the defendant is not domiciled in that state. Specifically, the defendant argued that the plaintiff consented to the exclusive jurisdiction agreement by failing to reject the written terms conferring Swiss jurisdiction attached to quotations provided by the defendant during the negotiations for the purchase of the machine. However, O'Neill J. held that the defendant had not satisfied the onus of proving it met the Art.17 criteria. There was an absence of a consensus between the parties. The plaintiff had not, in his opinion, accepted the exclusive jurisdiction agreement even though it received the defendant's written terms and made no objection to them. The plaintiff's written conditions rejecting the agreement, which it believed it had included in its faxed acceptance, were inadvertently excluded from the fax. The conditions were not, however, excluded from the hard copy of the fax, which the plaintiff posted to the defendant. The defendant admitted receiving the conditions in the post with the hard copy, but had filed them away without reading them.

The defendant also argued that the plaintiff had failed to prove that the Irish courts were the appropriate forum for hearing the dispute under Art.5(1) of the Brussels Regulations which provides: "… a person domiciled in a Contracting State, may, in another Contracting State be sued in matters relating to contract in the courts for the place of performance of the obligation in question …". O'Neill J. found that the place for the performance of the obligation for the purposes of the Article was the plaintiff's plant in Cork and that the plaintiff was therefore entitled under Art.5(1) to sue the defendants in respect of that obligation in Ireland. The principles in *Handbridge Ltd v British Aerospace Communication Ltd* [1993] 3 I.R. 342 were applied in establishing whether the plaintiff had proved that the Irish courts were the appropriate forum under Art.5(1).

Alternative jurisdiction   In *Nestorway Ltd t/a Electrographic International v Ambaflex BV*, Laffoy J., July 19, 2006, Ambiflex, the Dutch defendant, entered a conditional appearance and moved to set aside the service of the proceedings on the ground of want of jurisdiction. Although Laffoy J. set aside the service of the proceedings, the defendant failed to convince Laffoy J. that the writing containing what it argued was its choice of forum clause conferred jurisdiction on the Dutch courts under Art.23 of the Brussels Regulation because the writing containing the clause was not incorporated into the contract as a whole. In surmounting the general rule in Art.2 of the Brussels Regulation providing that a defendant should be sued in the place where he is domiciled, the plaintiff failed to sustain the onus of proof that alternative jurisdiction—that the matter should be heard in Ireland—was conferred under Art.5(1)(b). Laffoy J. found Art.5(1) (b) inapplicable to the instant facts. Article 5(1)(b), also known as the "deeming clause", provides that for the purposes of the provision the performance of the obligation in question shall be "in the case of the sale of goods, the place in a Member State where, under the contract, the goods were delivered or should have been delivered". She determined that the performance of the terms of the contract would necessarily involve separate individual contracts for the sale of goods, so that the obligations in question could not be considered a "sale of goods".

She found in favour of the defendant under Art.5(1)(a) of the Brussels Regulations: "A person domiciled in a Member State may, in another Member State be sued (a) in matters relating to a contract, in the courts for the place of performance of the obligation in question." The plaintiff submitted no evidence of Dutch law before the court. Laffoy J. thus held that in failing to establish where the place of performance of the relevant obligations would have been under Dutch law, it failed to discharge the onus of establishing jurisdiction of the Irish courts under Art.5(1)(a).

JURY TRIAL

Courts Act 1988 In *Sheridan v Kelly and McDonnell*, Supreme Court, Fennelly J., April 6, 2006, the plaintiff instituted suit against the first-named defendant, Kelly, a Christian Brother, and the second-named defendant, a representative of the Christian Brothers (representative) for assault, gross indecency and other related allegations. He also instituted suit against, and alleged that the representative was negligent and vicariously liable for the acts of Kelly. After the plaintiff served a notice of trial for a judge and jury, the representative successfully moved in the High Court to transfer the matter to the personal injuries list to be tried by a judge sitting alone on the basis that by joining the representative to the suit against Kelly, the matter was excluded under the Courts Act 1988. The plaintiff successfully appealed to the Supreme Court. Fennelly J. rejected the representative's argument that the plaintiff was not entitled to a jury trial against both Kelly and the representative because the vicarious liability and negligence claims against the representative were excluded under the relevant s.1(1)(a) and s.1(3)(b) of the Courts Act 1988. Under s.1(a), personal injuries actions due to negligence, nuisance and breach of duty are excluded from jury trials. Under s.1(3)(b), jury trials are allowed for actions for damages for false imprisonment, intentional trespass to the person or both, and also damages if they are "… claimed in addition, or as an alternative to, the other damages claimed for another cause of action in respect of the same act or omission …". On the vicarious liability claim, Fennelly J. determined that since the core of the plaintiff's claim was the sexual assault by Kelly, an action not excluded under the Act and the alleged vicarious liability of the representative, there was full correspondence between the alleged damages flowing between the two defendants. The plaintiff's negligence claim was also linked to his claim against Kelly for false imprisonment. The damages did not have to be identical, but they could be claimed, under s.1(3)(b) of the Courts Act, "… in addition, or as an alternative to the damages claimed".

MOTION TO DISMISS

Disclosed no reasonable cause of action   In *Delahunty v Player and Wills (Ireland) Ltd, Supreme Court*, Fennelly J., April 5, 2006, the plaintiff sued two tobacco manufacturers for personal injuries allegedly caused by years of smoking. She switched to Gallaher's Silk Cut Extra Mild many years later, in or about the year she was diagnosed with lung cancer. Gallaher, the second-named defendant, moved under either RSC Ord.19, r.28, that the plaintiff's claim be dismissed on the basis that it disclosed no reasonable cause of action, or that the court should exercise its inherent jurisdiction to dismiss the plaintiff's claim as it had no reasonable prospects of success or was bound to fail. Gallaher argued that the plaintiff's addiction was not caused by smoking its cigarettes as she was addicted long before she began smoking them. The plaintiff countered that Gallaher's marketing a milder brand specifically targeted people attempting to give up smoking because of the health risks. Her expert report also linked continued smoking to progressive lung damage. Fennelly J. refused to dismiss the plaintiff's claim on the basis that there were complex and disputable issues of law and fact making it not resolvable without trial under RSC Ord.19, r.28 or by the exercise of the inherent jurisdiction power of the Court. *Barry v Buckley* [1981] I.R. 306 and *O'Neill v Ryan* [1993] I.L.R.M. 557, where the court exercised its inherent jurisdiction, were distinguished on the basis that in those cases the evidence was undisputed.

RENEWAL OF SUMMONS

Renewal refused   In *Allergan Pharmaceuticals (Ireland) Ltd v Noel Deane Roofing and Cladding Ltd*, High Court, O'Sullivan J., July 6, 2006, the third-named defendant, architects Mullaly and Leonard, successfully moved pursuant to RSC Ord.8, r.2 to set aside an *ex parte* order granting to the plaintiff, pursuant to RSC Ord.8, r.1, leave to renew the summons for three months. Leave to renew was granted to the plaintiff on the basis of "other good reason" and not because efforts were made to effectuate service. If the summons were not renewed, the claim would be statute-barred. The plaintiff argued that the delay was not caused by it, but by the professionals it employed. Its solicitor could not serve the summons as he needed to ensure that a proper case could be made, another solicitor was ill for some time and, due to inadvertence, an engineer's report was not served. The defendants argued that the delay resulting from the three years' lapse from their receipt of an O'Byrne letter to when proceedings were being taken against them, and six years and eleven months having passed since the cause of action accrued, was unfair and contrary to the interests of justice, as they had inadequate notice of the action. They stated that they would suffer extreme prejudice if their order were refused as they retained no paperwork concerning the relevant matter. The court noted the authorities' trend away from the earlier, more liberal attitudes towards delay and, in particular, delay caused by a professional advisor including: *Chambers v Kennefick,* High Court, Finlay Geoghegan J., November 11, 2005, providing a three-step test for establishing whether it is in the interests of justice to renew the summons; *Gilroy v Flynn* [2005]1 I.L.R.M. 290 modifying the *Rainsford/Primor* rationale derived from *Primor v Stokes, Kennedy, Crowley* [1996] 2 I.R. 459; and *Rainsford v City of Limerick* [1995] 2 I.L.R.M. 561 in which the court would no longer apportion blame for delay. Further authority for the trend includes *McMullen v Ireland* E.C.H.R. 422 97/98, July 29, 2004 and European legislation including Art.6(1) of the European Convention on Human Rights Act 2003 and the entitlement to the right to a fair hearing within a reasonable time. Thus, in setting aside the order for renewal of the summons, O'Sullivan J. held:

(1) The defendants suffered an element of specific prejudice due to the absence of documents.

(2) The plaintiff's explanation offered for the delay in serving the summons was at best only partially adequate for a variety of reasons including the fact that because the summons was issued towards the end of the six-year limitation period, the need for expedition was greater, and the court would therefore more carefully scrutinise and weigh up the excuse of explanation for the delay.

(3) The court assigned less weight in excusing the delay attributable to the plaintiff's professional advisors. *Gilroy v Flynn*, above, was cited as authority, along with the current European legislation.

Renewal granted for "other good reason" In *Davern v Heneghan*, High Court, Peart J., October 13, 2006, the plaintiff sustained personal injuries on May 30, 2001, about two years and eleven months prior to the commencement of her personal injuries action on April 15, 2004. As the summons was not served on the defendants within the 12-month period, the plaintiff moved *ex parte* to renew the summons pursuant to RSC Ord.8, r.1 for "other good reason". Unusually, the defendants' counsel appeared and was heard on this *ex parte* motion. The plaintiff's delay was due to her solicitor's difficulty in obtaining medical reports for both the instant accident and a prior accident. Because he did not have all of the relevant reports, her solicitor disregarded repeated letters from the defendants' solicitors requesting service of the summons. The defendant argued that it was prejudiced by the delay, but Peart J. found no actual prejudice as the case concerned only assessments as opposed to liability, and the defendant had already obtained its medical report on the plaintiff. Peart J. noted that although the mere fact that the Statute of Limitations had expired would not of itself be sufficient to justify renewal of the summons as it would not constitute "for other good reason", the defendant's insurers were put on notice of the claim at an early date, and were thus not prejudiced in any real sense. He further considered that the refusal to permit the renewal would work an injustice to the plaintiff given the efforts of her solicitor to obtain medical reports on her behalf.

SECURITY FOR COSTS

Prima facie defence and costs of application In *Usk District Residents Association Ltd v Environmental Protection Agency and Greenstar Recycling Holdings Ltd (Notice Party)*, Supreme Court, Clark J., January 13, 2006, Greenstar, the notice party, sought security for costs under s.390 of the Companies Act 1963 from Usk, the applicant/appellant, a limited company operating as a residents' association, on the basis that if Greenstar prevailed, Usk would be unable to pay its costs. Usk opposed Greenstar only on the ground that Greenstar had failed to establish a prima facie defence and not on the basis that there were any other special circumstances justifying the exercise of the court's discretion to grant an order for security for costs. In the High Court Commercial, Greenstar was granted security for costs on the basis that it had established a prima facie entitlement to the security. Usk succeeded in restricting the costs referable to the leave application, as the costs awarded were based on the low amount established by Usk's cost accountants. Greenstar was also awarded the costs of the security application. Usk appealed to the Supreme Court on the issue of Greenstar's prima facie entitlement to security for costs and on Greenstar's entitlement to the costs of the security application. Clark J. found the following:

(1) Section 390 of the Companies Act 1963 is applicable to notice parties, as Greenstar was a necessary party to the proceedings.

(2) Greenstar established a prima facie defence as to the proceedings as a whole, and not only to the judicial review. In establishing its prima facie

defence to the proceedings as a whole, Greenstar was permitted to rely not only upon documents, affidavits and exhibits submitted in response to the motion, but also upon papers relevant to any factual matters properly before the court and on any open legal argument based on facts asserted by the plaintiff or on facts prima facie established in the materials before the Court.

(3) On the issue of the High Court award of the costs of the security application, Clark J., in exercising the court's discretion, varied that order by reserving the costs rather than following the general rule applicable to the commercial list, RSC Ord.63A, r.30, which provides that parties pay costs in respect of each interlocutory matter. He considered which party actually prevailed, and which may have been said to have failed in respect of the various elements of the interlocutory application. Thus, in the High Court, although Greenstar succeeded in its entitlement to security for costs, Usk succeeded in restricting the costs so that neither party actually had a true victory. He thus varied the order by reserving the issue of costs to the judge dealing with the application for leave.

Special circumstances In *West Donegal Land League Ltd v Udaras na Gaeltachta*, Supreme Court, Geogehegan J., May 15, 2006, the plaintiff, a limited company consisting of graziers and local farmers, sued the defendant over ownership rights to land in County Donegal. The second-named defendant prevailed on his motion in the High Court for security for costs pursuant to s.390 of the Companies Act 1963. He argued that he discharged all proofs required under the Act and that there were no special circumstances justifying refusal of the security. The plaintiff failed on its appeal to the Supreme Court. Geoghegan J. found that it had not established that there were special circumstances warranting the exercise of the court's discretion in refusing the motion. He surveyed the factors determinative of whether special circumstances exist, and found the list non-exhaustive and extending beyond the guidelines provided in the reference, *Civil Procedure in the Superior Courts* (H. Delany and D. McGrath, 2nd ed., Round Hall, Dublin, 2005). The plaintiff's main special circumstance was the defendant's contradictory representations concerning his ownership of land.

The plaintiff also argued for remittal of the matter to the High Court to be heard *de novo*. Due to its placement on the motions list, the time for oral argument, which plaintiff's counsel argued was necessary to thoroughly argue the issue of special circumstances, was insufficient. In the majority opinion, Geoghegan J. viewed the plaintiff's arguments, including the placing of the motion on the ordinary list, unacceptable reasons for ordering remittal. He found that remittal could only be made in unusual circumstances and that oral evidence generally on motions for security for costs would be permitted only in exceptional circumstances where there was a conflict of fact in the affidavits.

Denham J. in a strong dissent favoured remittal to the High Court.

SUMMARY SUMMONS

Jurisdiction and counterclaim   In *McGrath v O'Driscoll*, High Court
Commercial, Clarke J., June 14, 2006, the plaintiff personally guaranteed a
bank loan and other related obligations in the purchase of a fishing vessel by
the 20 defendants, who consisted of a partnership of 17 private individuals
(personal defendants) and three companies. The partnership defaulted on the
loan and the bank sued the plaintiff surety, obtaining a substantial judgment
against him including interest and costs. Rather than pay, the plaintiff instituted
suit by summary summons pursuant to RSC Ord.2 against the defendants for
payment of the judgment, interest and costs. Under RSC Ord.2, r.1, suit may
be instituted by summary summons "[i]n all actions where the plaintiff seeks
only to recover a debt or liquidated demand in money payable by the defendant,
with or without interest, arising". Although the plaintiff argued that as a surety,
he was entitled to indemnification by the primary debtors (the defendants)
for the judgment obtained by the principal creditor (the bank), the defendants
prevailed on the basis that there was no jurisdiction. Clarke J. found that despite
the apparent applicability of the language in RSC Ord.2, r.1, no order could be
made against the principle debtors (the personal defendants) because no value
or payment was given to the bank by the plaintiff surety. He declined to follow
Smith v Howell [1851] Ex Rep 730 on the basis of the injustice which would
flow from making a similar order. He also rejected the defendants' argument that
any action taken by the plaintiff prior to payment would be premature on the
basis that the plaintiff could resort to other forms of conditional or prospective
orders existing outside the ambit of RSC Ord.2.

The defendants also established an arguable counterclaim for a sum at
least equivalent to the claim such as would afford a defence. Clarke J. was
satisfied that there was a sufficient connection between the claim and the
counterclaim making it inequitable to allow the claim to be disposed of without
also considering the counterclaim.

RULES OF COURT

The following Rules of Court were made in 2006:

Rules of the Superior Courts
Rules of the Superior Courts (European Enforcement Orders) 2006 (S.I. No. 3 of 2006)
Rules of the Superior Courts (Commissions of Investigation Act 2004) 2006 (S.I. No. 23 of 2006)
Rules of Superior Courts (Arbitration) 2006 (S.I. No. 109 of 2006)
Rules of the Superior Courts (Mode of Address of Judges) 2006 (S.I. No. 196 of 2006)
Rules of the Superior Court (Proceeds of Crime and Financing of Terrorism) 2006 (S.I. No. 242 of 2006)
Rules of the Superior Courts (Competition) 2006 (S.I. No. 461 of 2006)

Circuit Court Rules
Circuit Court Rules (European Enforcement Orders) 2006 (S.I. No. 1 of 2006)
Circuit Court Rules (Jurisdiction in Matrimonial Matters and Matters of Parental Responsibility) 2006 (S.I. No. 143 of 2006)
Circuit Court Rules (Mode of Address of Judges) 2006 (S.I. No. 274 of 2006)
Circuit Court Rules (Employment Equality Acts 1998 And 2004) 2006 (S.I. No. 275 of 2006)
Circuit Court Rules (Court Seal) 2006 (S.I. No. 409 of 2006)
Circuit Court Rules (Residential Tenancies) 2006 (S.I. No. 410 of 2006)
Circuit Court Rules (National Minimum Wage Act) 2006 (S.I. No. 531 of 2006)
Circuit Court Rules (Protection of Employees (Fixed-Term Work) 2006 (S.I. No. 532 of 2006)

District Court Rules
District Court (European Enforcement Orders) Rules 2006 (S.I. No. 2 of 2006)
District Court (Children) Rules 2006 (S.I. No. 5 of 2006)
District Court (Criminal Justice Act 1994, Section 38) Rules 2006 (S.I. No. 47 of 2006)
District Court (Housing (Miscellaneous Provisions) Act 1997) Rules 2006 (S.I. No. 133 of 2006)
District Court (Order 24) Rules 2006 (S.I. No. 149 of 2006)
District Court (Equal Status Act 2000) Rules 2006 (S.I. No. 161 of 2006)
District Court (Temporary Closure Orders) Rules 2006 (S.I. No. 162 of 2006)

District Court (Safety, Health and Welfare at Work Act 2005) Rules 2006 (S.I. No. 209 of 2006)

District Court (Order 16) Rules 2006 (S.I. No. 238 of 2006)

District Court (Employment Equality Act) Rules 1998 (S.I. No. 263 of 2006)

District Court (Taxi Regulation) Rules 2006 (S.I. No. 314 of 2006)

District Court (Warrants of Execution) Rules 2006 (S.I. No. 396 of 2006)

District Court (Case Stated) Rules 2006 (S.I. No. 398 of 2006)

District Court (Probation of Offenders) Rules 2006 (S.I. No. 544 of 2006)

District Court (Public Order) Rules 2006 (S. I. No. 545 of 2006)

Probate and Succession Law

ALBERT KEATING, B.C.L., LL.B., LL.M., D.Litt., B.L.,
Senior Lecturer, Waterford Institute of Technology

COSTS IN PROBATE AND ADMINISTRATION ACTIONS

The court when awarding costs will first be guided by the principles set down in Ord.99 of the Rules of the Superior Courts 1986. Rule 1(1) of Ord.99 provides that the costs of, and incidental to, the proceedings are at the discretion of the court. Rule 1(3) of Ord.99 deals with the costs of an action, question or issue tried by a jury, and stipulates that the costs shall follow the event unless the court, for special cause, to be mentioned in the order, shall otherwise direct. Rule 1(4) of Ord.99 goes on to provide that the costs "of every issue of fact or law raised upon a claim or counterclaim shall, unless otherwise ordered, follow the event." Order 99, r.1(5) goes on to provide that where in any proceeding in the High Court or Supreme Court the costs of any party are ordered to be paid by another party, or by a fund or estate, those costs shall, if the High Court or the Supreme Court respectively so directs, include, in addition to the costs allowed on taxation as between party and party, all or any other costs, charges and expenses, reasonably incurred for the purposes of the proceedings.

The general principles set down in Ord.99 of the Rules of the Superior Courts 1986 are equally applicable to probate and administration actions, but when determining an issue of costs in probate actions the court may also consider whether they should be awarded out of a deceased testator's estate. An unsuccessful party in a probate action may be allowed costs out of the estate if it is established that there were reasonable grounds for the litigation and that it was conducted in a bona fide manner. This is Irish practice on the matter. In *Vella v Morelli* [1968] I.R. 11 Budd J. traced the Irish practice back to the time of the Prerogative Court and in particular the judgment of Dr Radcliff in *Fairtlough v Fairtlough* (1839) 1 Milw. 36 at 39; see *Kavanagh v Fegan* [1932] I.R. 566; *Murphy v Finlen* [1931] L.J. Ir. 50; *Mulligan v McKeown* [1955] I.R. 112. Budd J. found that the old Irish practice was"a very fair and reasonable one" and one that also had the result of allaying the reasonable fears of persons when faced with the decision of whether to litigate or not. He then went on to reaffirm the Irish practice emphasising the fact that before that practice can operate in any particular case two questions must be answered, *viz.* (a) Was there reasonable ground for litigation? (b) Was it conducted bona fide? This special rule or practice regarding the award of costs in probate actions will not, however, be applied in administration actions. In *Young v Cadell*, unreported, High Court, Laffoy J., February 13, 2006 it was stated by Laffoy J. that:

> "The factors which arise in a probate suit which justify the special rule in relation to costs which was reiterated in *Vella v Morelli*, the importance of ensuring that what are presented as testamentary documents are above suspicion and that legal costs are not a deterrent to pursuing *bona fide* beliefs or suspicions as to the validity of such documents, do not arise in administration suits, which, in the case of a death testate, proceed on the assumption that the testamentary document is valid, as was the case here."

In *O'Connor v Markey & Markey*, unreported, High Court, Herbert J., July 14, 2006, Herbert J., while affirming that the authorities referred to in *Vella v Morelli* dealt with probate issues regarding the due execution or revocation of wills and the testamentary capacity of a testator, stated that by contrast "the instant application bore all the hallmarks of contentious litigation between beneficiaries which did not in any way touch upon the capacity of the testator or the state in which he left his testamentary papers", and so the issue of costs was not governed by *Vella v Morelli*.

Herbert J. referred to the judgment of Kekewich J. in *Buckton v Buckton* [1907] 2 Ch. 406 at 414–415 where the issue of costs in administration actions was considered. Kekewich J. identified three types of administration action for the purposes of determining the issue of costs:

1. In administration actions where the applicants are the personal representatives or trustees seeking the court's direction in ascertaining the interests of the beneficiaries or to have some question determined which has arisen in the administration of the estate, costs of all parties as necessarily incurred for the benefit of the estate will be taxed as between solicitor and client and paid out of the estate.

2. Where the application is made by some of the beneficiaries but is made by reason of some difficulty of construction or administration that would have justified an application by the personal representatives or trustees, they will also be allowed their costs out of the estate.

3. But where a beneficiary "makes a claim adverse to other beneficiaries, and usually takes advantage of the convenient procedure by originating summons to get a question determined which, but for this procedure, would be the subject of an action commenced by writ and would strictly fall within the description of litigation", "once convinced that I am determining rights between adverse litigants I apply the rule which ought, I think, be rigidly enforced in adverse litigation, and order the unsuccessful party to pay the costs." Kekewich J. went on to state that whether "he ought to be

ordered to pay the cost of trustees, who are, of course, Respondents, or not, is sometimes open to question, but with this possible exception the unsuccessful party bears the costs of all whom he has brought before the court."

Herbert J., adopting the principles formulated by Kekewich J., found that the case before him fell into the third category even though it was the administrator who made the application, as it was made "essentially in a nominal capacity only and does not in any material way alter the situation." He thought that it would be neither fair nor reasonable that the first defendant, having failed in his claim, should be awarded costs out of the estate or exempted from paying the costs of the special administrator and of the successful second-named defendant, both of whom he caused to be involved in this litigation. He also directed that the provisions of Ord.99, r.1(5) of the Rules of the Superior Courts shall apply, so that in addition to party and party costs, all and any other costs, charges and expenses, reasonably incurred for the purpose of the application shall be allowed.

In *Young v Cadell*, unreported, High Court, Laffoy J., February 13, 2006, the testator and brother of the plaintiff and second, third, fourth and fifth defendants, died on October 28, 2000, having made his last will and testament on August 8, 2000. A grant of probate of the will was made to the first defendant, who was a solicitor and one of the executors, on November 8, 2001. The only provisions of the will of the testator which were relevant to the issues raised in the special summons issued on July 7, 2004, were the provisions contained in clauses 4 and 5 in the following terms:

> "4. I leave my dwelling house together with a garden field (which are currently used by my brother Donal) to my brother Sam for his own use and benefit.
>
> 5. I leave all the out-offices, yard, hayshed etc. and the remainder of my land situate at Barnane, formerly owned by my parents, to my brothers Pat Young, his wife Mary Young and to each of their four children in equal shares."

The lands referred to in clauses 4 and 5 were lands registered on Folio 25344, County Tipperary. Clause 5 was relevant only in so far as the lands to which it related were registered in Folio 25344.

The allegations made by the plaintiff in the special indorsement of claim in the special summons were:

(a) that the defendants had failed, refused or neglected to communicate with the plaintiff and attempted to deny him his share under the will of the testator;

(b) that the first defendant had failed, refused or neglected to execute a deed of assent transferring to the plaintiff the dwelling house together with a garden field comprising an area of 0.5 hectares at Barnane as contained in Folio 25344 to and for his own absolute use and benefit; and

(c) that the first defendant had failed to distribute the assets of the estate of Samuel Young and the estate of Josephine Young pursuant to the rules of intestacy.

When the matter came into the Chancery List on October 17, 2005, counsel for all of the defendants other than the fourth defendant applied that the proceedings against his clients should be struck out. The basis of the application was that in his replying affidavit sworn on November 8, 2004, with regard to the dwelling house and the garden field comprising 0.5 hectares, the first defendant averred, *inter alia,* that: "Neither I nor the second defendant have any difficulty with regard to executing an Assent in favour of the Plaintiff with regard to the said property." Laffoy J. thought that the "implicit offer of the first defendant to execute an assent in favour of the plaintiff of the interest of the testator in the dwelling house and land specifically devised to the plaintiff should have been taken up in November, 2004 and that should have been the end of the matter." The offer was not, however, pursued by the plaintiff. On the other hand, an assent was not executed by the defendant.

The matter came back into the list on December 12, 2005. Laffoy J. went on to deal with the issues that arose between the plaintiff and all of the defendants other than the fourth defendant. The first defendant had filed an affidavit sworn on November 2, 2005, in which he exhibited an assent sworn by him on November 2, 2005 in which he assented to the registration of the plaintiff as full owner of the lands specifically devised to him for all the right, title, estate and interest held by the testator therein. Laffoy J. stated that the execution of that assent, in her view, "renders these proceedings redundant, the only issue remaining being the issue of costs".

In relation to the issue of costs she first considered the relevance of the decision of the Supreme Court in *Vella v Morelli* [1968] I.R. 11 to the costs issues in the proceedings. Budd J., delivering the judgment of the Supreme Court in *Vella v Morelli*, referred to the "well-established Irish practice formulated in the last century" and he quoted the statement of the practice set out in Miller's *Probate Practice* (Maxwell, 1900) at p.438 which was in the following terms: "Two questions are to be considered with reference to an application for costs of the unsuccessful party: (1) Was there reasonable ground for litigation? Was it conducted bona fide? Where both these questions can be answered in the affirmative it is usual practice of the court, without having regard to the amount or the ownership of the property, to order the general costs to be paid out of the personal estate." Later, Budd J. stated that he did not think that any good reason had been shown for departing from the old practice and he then set out the rationale of the practice as follows:

"In our country the results arising from the testamentary disposition of property are of fundamental importance to most members of the community and it is vital that the circumstances surrounding the execution of testamentary documents should be open to scrutiny and be above suspicion. Accordingly, it would seem right and proper to me that persons, having real and genuine grounds for believing or even having genuine suspicions, that a purported will is not valid, should be able to have the circumstances surrounding the execution of that will investigated by the court without being completely deterred from taking that course by reason of a fear that, however genuine their case may be, they will have to bear the burden of what may be heavy costs. It would seem to me that the old Irish practice was a very fair and reasonable one and was such that, if adhered to, would allay the reasonable fears of persons faced with making a decision upon whether a will should be litigated or not. If there be any doubt about its application in modern times, these doubts should be dispelled and the practice should now be reiterated and laid down as a general guiding principle bearing in mind that, as a general rule, before the practice can be operated in any particular case the two questions posed must be answered in the affirmative."

As Budd J. made clear at the end of his judgment, when answering the two questions posed on the facts of the case before him, the principle applies when the court is "considering whether an unsuccessful party in a probate suit should be allowed costs out of the estate."

Laffoy J. stated that the:

"factors which arise in a probate suit which justify the special rule in relation to costs which was reiterated in *Vella v Morelli*, the importance of ensuring that what are presented as testamentary documents are above suspicion and that legal costs are not a deterrent to pursuing *bona fide* beliefs or suspicions as to the validity of such documents, do not arise in administration suits, which, in the case of a death testate, proceed on the assumption that the testamentary document is valid, as was the case here."

Therefore, in her view, the rule in *Vella v Morelli* had no application to the resolution of costs in the proceedings before her.

As between the plaintiff and the defendants other than the fourth defendant, Laffoy J. made no order as to costs. Although she concluded that there was a genuine dispute between the plaintiff and fourth defendant, it was a dispute the genesis of which was anterior to the death of the testator. Therefore, it was not a dispute that could be resolved by proceedings brought by special summons for the administration of the estate of the testator.

In *John O'Connor v Gerard Markey and Mary Markey*, unreported, High Court, Herbert J., July 14, 2006 an application was made by a special administrator appointed by the court for the purpose of resolving a dispute which had arisen in the course of the administration of the estate of Philip Markey between both children of the deceased and beneficiaries under his will. The first-named defendant claimed that payment of the several debts the subject-matter of the application were the sole liability of the estate and should be paid out of the residuary gift bequeathed to the second defendant. The second defendant claimed that the first defendant was obliged to personally indemnify the estate against the total amount of these debts, which in default of payment should be paid by the special administrator out of the property devised to the first defendant. In an earlier judgment in a case between the same parties, Herbert J. found that the first defendant was obliged to indemnify the estate in respect of the whole amount of these debts (see *John O'Connor v Gerard Markey and Mary Markey*, unreported, High Court, Herbert J., January 24, 2006, below). In the current case the first defendant claimed that the entire costs of all the parties to the application should be paid out of the assets of the estate. The second defendant claimed that her costs should be paid out of the estate, or in the alternative, an order of costs should be made against the first defendant personally. The special administrator claimed that he was entitled to his costs out of the estate. Counsel for the first defendant relied on *Vella v Morelli* and the special rule in that case for the payment of his costs. Herbert J., however, thought that *Vella v Morelli* was distinguishable on its facts from the application before him and that "the principles of law restated and followed by the then Supreme Court in that case have no application to the circumstances which fall to be addressed in the present application." Furthermore, the authorities referred to in *Vella v Morelli* dealt with probate issues regarding the due execution or revocation of wills and the testamentary capacity of a testator and, by contrast, "the instant application bore all the hallmarks of contentious litigation between beneficiaries which did not in any way touch upon the capacity of the testator or the state in which he left his testamentary papers." He went on to say that the application before him arose in the course of administration of the estate, and was not a probate action, and was to all intents and purposes "a hostile *lis inter partes* between two beneficiaries under the will". He also thought that the special administrator was in reality only a nominal plaintiff to enable the opinion of the court to be obtained for directions in the course of administration.

He went on to refer to *Buckton v Buckton* [1907] 2 Ch. 406 at 414–415 and found that the instant case fell within the third class of cases identified by Kekewich J. in that case. Kekewich J. stated that:

> "In a large proportion of the summonses adjourned in the Court for argument the applicants are trustees of a will or settlement who asked the Court to construe the instrument of trust for their guidance, and in

order to ascertain the interests of the beneficiaries, or else ask to have some question determined which has arisen in the administration of the trusts. In cases of this character I regard the costs of all parties as necessarily incurred for the benefit of the estate, and direct them to be taxed as between solicitor and client and paid out of the estate. It is, of course, possible that trustees may come to the Court without due cause. The question of construction or of administration may be too clear for argument or it may be the duty of trustees to inform a claimant that they must administer their trust on the footing that his claim is unfounded, and leave him to take whatever course he thinks fit. But, although I have thought it necessary sometimes to caution timid trustees against making applications which might with propriety be avoided, I act on the principle that trustees are entitled to the fullest possible protection which the Court can give them, and that I must give them credit for not applying to the Court except under advice which, though it may appear to me unsound, must not be readily treated as unwise. I cannot remember any case in which I have refused to deal with the costs of an application by trustees in the manner above mentioned. There is a second class of case differing in form, but not in substance, from the first. In this case it is admitted on all hands, or it is apparent from the proceedings, that although the application is made not by trustees (who are Respondents), but by some of the beneficiaries, yet it is made by reason of some difficulty of construction, or administration, which would have justified an application by the trustees, and it is not made by them only because, for some reason or other, a different course has been deemed more convenient. To cases of this class I extend the operation of the same rule as is observed in cases of the first class. The application is necessary for the administration of the trust, and the costs of all parties are necessarily incurred for the benefit of the estate regarded as a whole. There is yet a third class of cases differing in form and substance from the first, and in substance though not in form, from the second. In this class the application is made by a beneficiary who makes a claim adverse to other beneficiaries, and usually takes advantage of the convenient procedure by originating summons to get a question determined which, but for this procedure, would be the subject of an action commenced by writ and would strictly fall within the description of litigation. It is often difficult to discriminate between cases of the second and third classes, but when once convinced that I am determining rights between adverse litigants I apply the rule which ought, I think, to be rigidly enforced in adverse litigation, and order the unsuccessful party to pay the costs. Whether he ought to be ordered to pay the costs of the trustees, who are, of course, Respondents, or not, is sometimes open to question, but with this possible exception the unsuccessful party bears the costs of all whom he has brought before the court."

Although in the instant case the special administrator made the application, Herbert J. was satisfied that "this was essentially in a nominal capacity only and does not in any material way alter the situation". The claim made by the first defendant, who was a principal beneficiary under the will, that he was not obliged to discharge the debts in issue in the application, was totally adverse to the second defendant who was also, to a much lesser extent, a beneficiary under the will and whose residuary bequest would be substantially or entirely consumed by the payment of these debts should they be paid out of the estate. In his judgment, it would be neither fair nor reasonable that the first defendant, having failed in his claim in this application, should be awarded costs out of the estate or exempted from paying the costs of the special administrator and of the successful second defendant, both of whom he caused to be involved in this litigation. In relation to the costs of the special administrator he went on to direct that the provisions of Ord.99, r.1(5) of the Rules of the Superior Courts shall apply, so that in addition to party and party costs, all and any other costs, charges and expenses, reasonably incurred for the purpose of the application, shall be allowed. He further ordered that the costs of the special administrator should be a charge on the real estate specifically devised to the first defendant. If these costs fell to be paid out of the real and personal assets of the testator in the order provided by s.46(3) and the First Schedule, Pt II of the Succession Act 1965, "the burden would fall on the residuary bequest to the successful second defendant thereby depriving her of all or a material part of the benefit preserved to her by the judgment of this court in exoneration of the devise to the unsuccessful first-named defendant". The costs awarded to the special administrator and to the second defendant also included the costs of the application for costs.

LIABILITY OF "MANAGERIAL" AGENT TO INDEMNIFY ESTATE

A beneficiary who agrees to act as agent for the management of the testator's business during his illness and who also agrees to discharge certain debts out of the profits of the business must indemnify the estate for the payment of such debts out of the estate after the death of the testator. Such an agent will not only be viewed as a "managerial" agent of the testator's business, but will also be a constructive trustee of the money required to discharge the debts. It was stated by Herbert J. in *O'Connor v Markey and Markey*, unreported, High Court, Herbert J., January 24 2006 that such an agent:

> "was not entitled to deal with the income of the business as he considered appropriate within the scope of the usual powers implied in the case of a managerial agent running a public house business. It was an express and fundamental term of the management agreement and, a fiduciary

duty which he solemnly undertook to discharge, that so much of the money of the business would be set aside each month, after the cost of essential items as was necessary to discharge the fees due to the nursing home as they arose in priority to all other considerations."

He went on to say that an agent in such circumstances "was more than a mere debtor of his father in relation to this money and was in fact a constructive trustee of the money for his father." The son acting as "managerial" agent was consequently obliged to indemnify his father's estate for the outstanding fees paid by it to the nursing home after his father's death.

In this case, the testator, Philip Markey, died at Curragh Lawn Nursing Home on February 28, 2002, aged 87 years. His two children, Gerard Markey and Mary Markey, the defendants in the proceedings, survived him. The testator made his will on January 24, 2000, and appointed his two children to be the executors and trustees of his will. He left a residential licensed premises known as the "Stray Inn" to his son Gerard Markey absolutely but subject, however, to the payment of the sum of £150,000 (former currency) to the estate within one month of death and the same to be charged on the property until payment. He left a parcel of land adjacent to the "Stray Inn" to his daughter Mary Markey absolutely together with a legacy of IR£20,000. Mary Markey was also the residuary devisee and legatee. As a result of an application to the High Court under s.27(4) of the Succession Act 1965, the plaintiff was issued with a grant of letters of administration with the will annexed. In the inland revenue affidavit sworn by the plaintiff it was stated that the estate owed the following debts, *viz.:*

Curragh Lawn Nursing Home €41,044.28
Beechfield Healthcare Limited €2,446.98
Bernard Berney, pharmacist €1,1323.99
ACC Bank (joint account with Gerard Markey) €14,336.93

By order of the High Court dated February 2, 2004 issues were directed to be tried on oral evidence between the defendants. These issues were agreed and defined by a notice of issues filed on March 9, 2004, *viz.:*

(i) whether the outstanding account of Curragh Lawn Nursing Home in the sum of €41,004.28 at the date of death of the deceased was payable by the estate or by the first-named defendant personally;

(ii) whether the outstanding account of Beechfield Healthcare Limited in the sum of €2,446.98 at the date of death of the deceased is payable by the estate of the deceased or by the first-named defendant personally;

(iii) whether the outstanding account of Bernard Berney, pharmacist,

in the sum of €1,132.99 at the date of death of the deceased
is payable by the estate of the deceased or by the first-named
defendant personally;

(iv) whether the outstanding account of ACC Bank plc, in the sum
of €14,916.16 at the date of death of the deceased is payable
by the estate of the deceased or by the first-named defendant
personally;

(v) whether interest is payable on the sum of €190,460.71 payable
by the first-named defendant, and if so at what rate;

(vi) whether the costs and expenses to include reserved costs and
expenses of all the proceedings to date in the deceased's estate
in full or in part should be borne by:

(a) the first-named defendant personally; or

(b) the second-named defendant personally, or

(c) the estate of the deceased.

Herbert J. thought that central to the determination of the first four issues
in the case were the terms upon which the first defendant assumed the sole
management of the "Stray Inn" when his father became a resident of Curragh
Lawn Nursing Home on November 30, 1995. He found that the first defendant
agreed to manage the business on behalf of his father. He also found that the
agreement to do so was made orally between the late Philip Markey and the
first defendant without the advice, assistance or presence of any third party
either lay or expert. The first defendant, at all times during his evidence, fully
accepted that he had entered into occupation and remained in occupation of
the "Stray Inn" and ran the business as a manager for his father and in no other
capacity whatsoever. It was established by evidence that no lease, tenancy
agreement, licence or franchise was entered into between the deceased and
the first defendant in respect of the "Stray Inn".

Herbert J. also found that the first defendant did not execute the deed of
mortgage made with the ACC Bank as agent for the deceased so as to bind him.
The first defendant "was authorised by Philip Markey to carry on the business
of the 'Stray Inn' as a general agent on his behalf of the type aptly described
by Bowstead and Reynolds on Agency, (17th Edition: 2001: London, Sweet &
Maxwell), article 29 page 106 *et seq.*, as a 'managerial agent'". He held that
it was an express and fundamental term of the contract between them that the
first defendant would, out of the profits of the business, discharge all sums
due to Curragh Lawn Nursing Home in respect of his father as they became
due. The income derived from the licensed premises was the deceased's sole
income. He was satisfied that it was clearly understood between them that the
sole reason why the first defendant was given the management of the "Stray
Inn" by the deceased was to ensure that sufficient income was generated by
the business to maintain the deceased in Curragh Lawn Nursing Home. He
found that the first defendant's overriding obligation was to manage the "Stray

Inn" in such a manner as to provide sufficient income to pay the nursing home charges in respect of his father as they became due. He was satisfied that the first defendant signed the agreement with Curragh Lawn Nursing Home on November 24, 1997 as an agent for a disclosed principal and did not assume any personal liability to the nursing home on foot of that agreement. He held that the first defendant did not have either express or implied authority to improve the fabric of the "Stray Inn" or to execute works or to adopt measures designed to maintain or to increase its custom at the expense of failing to pay the fees due to Curragh Lawn Nursing Home.

In addition to the intimate and confidential nature of the relationship between the first defendant and the deceased, because of his very serious illness and his being confined to the nursing home, the deceased was obliged to repose total trust in his son to run the business for him and to pay the nursing home fees (see *Re Coomber* [1911] 1 Ch.D. 723; *Re Goldcorp Exchange* [1995] 1 A.C. 74 at 98). Herbert J. found that the first defendant was not entitled to deal with the income of the business as he considered appropriate within the scope of the usual powers implied in the case of a managerial agent running a public house business. It was an express and fundamental term of the management agreement, and a fiduciary duty which he solemnly undertook to discharge, that so much of the money of the business would be set aside each month after the cost of essential items as was necessary to discharge the fees due to the nursing home as they arose in priority to all other considerations.

Herbert J. was satisfied that the first defendant was more than a mere debtor of his father in relation to this money and was in fact a constructive trustee of the money for his father. He went on to hold that he had not only acted in breach of trust in applying that portion of the income of the business which he should have expended in paying the nursing home fees on other matters, despite the fact that such expenditure might in other circumstances possibly fall within the scope of his implied authority as manager of the licensed premises on behalf of his father. In the circumstances of this case he had also ceased to act in good faith and in the interests of his principal by failing to pay the nursing home fees and acting for his own immediate benefit, and also for his prospective benefit as heir presumptive of the business, without fully and properly informing his father of what was occurring and the actual probable consequences of it so far as the payment of the nursing home account was concerned.

Herbert J. went on to hold that the deceased's estate was entitled to be fully indemnified by the first defendant in respect of the total sums due to Curragh Lawn Nursing Home, Beechfield Healthcare Limited and Bernard Berney, pharmacist, paid by the estate. The first defendant admitted in evidence that neither Mary Markey nor the estate of his late father were liable to reimburse him for any part of the sum that was outstanding to ACC Bank. Herbert J. concluded by stating that the court would hear the issue of the costs and expenses, to include all reserved costs and expenses of the action and of the other related proceedings (the issue of costs was considered in *O'Connor v Markey & Markey*, unreported, High Court, Herbert J., July 14, 2006, above).

CONSTRUCTION OF WILLS

In a construction suit the primary duty of the court is to ascertain and give effect to the intention of the testator (*Re Curtin, Curtin v O'Mahony* [1991] 2 I.R. 562 at 573; *Williams and O'Donnell v Shuel and Barham*, unreported, High Court, Morris P., May 6, 1997; *Re Butler, Butler v Butler*, unreported, High Court, Smyth J., March 23, 2006). When attempting to do so the court will construe the words used by the testator in order to ascertain his intention. This does not mean, however, that the court will give a literal meaning to the words used, especially if such a meaning tends to frustrate the testator's intention. If, having read the will as a whole, it becomes clear that a literal meaning would defeat the intention, the court may even go so far as "to do violence" to the language in order to give effect to the testator's intention (*Re Patterson, Dunlop v Greer* [1899] 1 I.R. 324).

The language used by the testator then will be viewed as providing the evidence of his intention. In a construction suit, bearing in mind that the testator's intention is the primary concern, the court will first read the will and give an ordinary meaning to the words used by the testator unless the context of the will suggests otherwise (*Howell v Howell* [1992] 1 I.R. 290; *Heron v Ulster Bank* [1974] N. I. 44; *Bank of Ireland v Gaynor*, unreported, High Court, Macken J., June 29, 1999; *Re Butler, Butler v Butler*, unreported, High Court, Smyth J., March 23, 2006).

Extrinsic evidence may also be adduced and admitted under s.90 of the Succession Act 1965 "to show the intention of the testator and to assist in the construction of, or to explain any contradiction in the will." Such evidence showing the testator's intention only will not, however, be admitted as the conjunctive "and" in s.90 connotes "a duality of purpose as a condition for the admission under the section of extrinsic evidence" (*Rowe v Law* [1978] I.R. 55; *Re Collins, O'Connell v Bank of Ireland* [1998] 2 I.R. 596). Extrinsic evidence under s.90 will be admissible to show the intention of the testator *and* where it assists the court in the construction of a will.

Where a gift is capable of more than one interpretation the courts may resort to what might be termed the "doubt" principle in s.99 of the Succession Act 1965. Section 99 provides that "if the purport of a devise or legacy admits of more than one interpretation, then, in case of *doubt*, the interpretation according to which the devise or bequest will be operative will be preferred" (emphasis added).

In *Re Butler, Butler v Butler*, unreported, High Court, Smyth J., March 23, 2006, the plaintiff sought construction of the following clause appearing in the will of the deceased who died on May 18, 1963:

"I give, devise and bequeath the lands of Ballynunnery, purchased by
me from the representatives of the late Patrick Butler to my son Thomas
Butler for his own use and benefit absolutely. As to all the rest, residue
and remainder of my property of every kind and nature, whether real
or personal and wheresoever situated, including my licensed premises
at Raheenduff and the lands of Raheenduff and Ballynunnery, I give,
devise and bequeath the same to my son Martin Butler for and during
the term of his natural life and after his death to such of the children
of my said son Thomas Butler as he shall by deed or will appoint and
in default of appointment to all of the children of my said son Thomas
Butler as tenants in common in equal shares."

Thomas Butler died intestate on December 10, 1966. Martin Butler purported
to exercise the power of appointment in his will in favour of the plaintiff.
Martin Butler died on May 22, 2002. The plaintiff and defendants were all
children of Thomas Butler. The special summons, *inter alia*, posed the following
questions:

1. To whom did the power of appointment refer in the will of the
   deceased?

2. Further, or in the alternative, was the power granted to Martin Butler or
   Thomas Butler?

There were contradictions in the affidavits of the children of Thomas Butler
regarding to whom they believed the power of appointment was given. The
defendants and an independent witness, a solicitor who acted for the family,
contended that all parties believed that the power was conferred on Thomas
Butler. The plaintiff on the other hand contended that the power of appointment
was conferred on Martin Butler. In relation to the latter, however, Smyth J.
found as a fact on the evidence that at no time prior to the death of Martin
Butler did the plaintiff ever convey or suggest to his solicitor or his brothers
or sister that Martin Butler had the power of appointment. As there was no
extrinsic evidence available, s.90 of the Succession Act 1965, *Rowe v Law*
[1978] I.R. and *Re Collins, O'Connell v Bank of Ireland* [1998] 2 I.R. 596,
were not relevant to the issues before the court.

As regards s.99 of the Succession Act 1965, Smyth J. thought that the
section had limited application to the proceedings, and went on to state that
the case before him "is not a case where one or other construction of who the
donee was intended to be, would render the clause operative or inoperative;
it would be operative in both eventualities but with different results". In his
judgment, "the base level intention of the testator was that the objects of the
power were to take equally".

Smyth J., having referred to the Supreme Court decision in *Curtin v
O'Mahony* [1991] 2 I.R. 566 where it was stated that the task of a court on

construing a will was to give effect to the intention of the testator, found that the intention of the testator was clear "and can be given effect to, even if the donee of the power cannot be identified". He then went on to refer to *Howell v Howell* [1992] 1 I.R. 290 where Carroll J. approved the "guidelines" for the construction of wills by Lowry C.J. in *Heron v Ulster Bank* [1974] N.I. 44 at 52. He noted that this was also the approach adopted by Macken J. in *Bank of Ireland v Gaynor*, unreported, High Court, June 29, 1999. The "guidelines" devised by Lowry C.J. were as follows:

> "1. Read the immediately relevant portion of the will as a piece of English and decide, if possible, what it means.
> 2. Look at the other material parts of the will and see whether they tend to confirm the apparently plain meaning of the immediately relevant portion or whether they suggest the need for modification in order to make harmonious sense of the whole or, alternatively, whether an ambiguity in the immediately relevant portion can be resolved.
> 3. If ambiguity persists, have regard to the scheme of the will and consider what the testator was trying to do.
> 4. One may at this stage have resort to rules of construction, where applicable, and aids, such as the presumption of early vesting and the presumptions against intestacy and in favour of equality.
> 5. Then see whether any rule of law prevents a particular interpretation from being adopted.
> 6. Finally, and, I suggest, not until the disputed passage has been exhaustively studied, one may get help from the opinions of other courts and judges on similar words, rarely as binding precedents, since it has been well said that 'No will has a twin brother' (per Werner J. in *Matter of King* 200 N.Y. 189, 192 (1910), but more often as examples (sometimes of the highest authority) of how judicial minds nurtured in the same discipline have interpreted words in similar contexts."

Having regard to guideline 3 above, and to the scheme of the will of the deceased as a whole, and what the testator was trying to do, Smyth J. thought that the testator was ultimately trying to benefit the children of Thomas Butler. He went on to say that "the construction which identifies Thomas as the donee of the power does no violence to the intention of the testator". Further, it accords with guideline 4, which refers to the application of equality and against intestacy. He held that the objects of the power, *viz.* the children of Thomas Butler, were entitled to take in equal shares.

UNDUE INFLUENCE

Where a will is made as a result of pressure being exerted on the testator, it may be impugned on the grounds of undue influence. The court, when considering whether or not to impugn the will, will first determine the nature and extent of the pressure exerted, and the effect such pressure had on the testator to make a will in favour of a particular person. While a testator may be persuaded to make a will in favour of a particular person, he may not be coerced into doing so (*Hall v Hall* (1868) L.R. 1 P. & D. 481; *Wingrove v Wingrove* (1885) 11 P.D. 81). But even where persuasion is used it must not go beyond that which:

> "appeals to the affection or ties of kindred, to sentiment of gratitude for past service, or pity for future destitution, or the like—these are all legitimate, and may fairly be pressed on a testator. Even where a testator has been 'persuaded or induced by considerations' in favour of a particular person which you may condemn, really and truly to intend to give his property to another, though you may disapprove of the act, yet it is legitimate in the sense of its being legal" [*Hall v Hall* at 482 *per* Sir J.P. Wilde; see also *Wingrove v Wingrove* at 82 *per* Sir. J. Hannen].

Pressure of whatever character, "whether acting on the fears or the hopes, if so exerted as to overpower the volition without convincing the judgement, is a species of restraining under which no valid will can be made" (*Hall v Hall* at 482). The character of the testator may also be taken into account and where threats are made which the testator has not the moral courage to resist, or complies for the sake of peace and quiet, or if the pressure used "is carried to a degree in which the free play of the testator's judgement, discretion or wishes is overborne, it will constitute undue influence, though no force is either used or threatened" (*Hall v Hall* at 482). It was stated by Murphy J. in *Elliot v Stamp*, unreported, High Court, November 7, 2006, that:

> "The definition of undue influence including importunity or threats, such as the testator has not the courage to resist, moral command asserted and yielded to for the sake of peace and quiet, or for escaping from the stress of mind or social discomfort, these have carried to a degree in which the free play of the testator's judgment, discretion or wishes is overcome, will constitute undue influence such as to render it inadvisable to plead on the basis of suspicion only."

The onus of proof rests on the party alleging the undue influence.

In *Elliot v Stamp*, the plaintiffs were the sister and nephew of Nicholas Roche, the deceased testator. The second named plaintiff was the son of the first named plaintiff. Proceedings began by way of summons dated July 13, 2004, wherein the plaintiff claimed an order refusing probate of a will purportedly executed on or about February 20, 2003; a declaration that the said will was not validly executed; a declaration that the testator was not of sound disposing mind; and in the alternative, a declaration that the will was procured by acts of undue influence brought to bear upon the deceased by the defendants. The first-named defendant was the principal beneficiary and was appointed sole executor under the purported will. The second-named defendant was his mother and the sister of the deceased. The deceased, late of Ballyvalden, Blackwater, Co. Wexford, died a bachelor without issue on or about May 3, 2003. His assets included a residential farm, credit union deposits and cash.

Certain particulars were given in the statement of claim regarding alleged dominion and control, and the involvement of the defendants, and in particular the first-named defendant in the procuring of a solicitor for the purposes of preparing and executing the will which, the particulars continued, was not the product of the free and voluntary act of the deceased but rather was the result of requests and/or demands made of the deceased by the defendants. It was further stated that the deceased was in fear of not complying with the said requests.

The defence denied that the will was void. The act was a free act of the testator who made the will with full capacity, competence and understanding. The deceased testator independently drew up his will over a two-day period between February 19 and 20 with the advice and assistance of a solicitor, and without any interference, duress, or influence, undue or otherwise. The deceased was of sound disposing mind at the date of the execution of the will which was drawn up in accordance with the provisions of the Succession Act 1965. The will contained many and numerous legacies and bequests in accordance with the testator's detailed instructions to his solicitor.

By reply delivered May 31, 2005, issue was joined. It was denied that the will was the free act of the testator or that he made the will with full capacity, competence and understanding. It was further denied that he drew up his will independently with the advice and assistance of a solicitor and without any interference, duress or influence. Particulars were given that the first-named defendant was actively involved in the procuring of the execution of the said will and repeatedly liaised with the solicitor drafting same, both in relation to its drafting up and its execution. He gave information to the instructing solicitor in relation to the tax advantage of the disposition of the deceased's farm.

The main thrust of the plaintiffs' action related, however, to the question of undue influence. But in relation to that question the court found that there was no evidence to show that the first-named defendant was in a position to wield authority over an individual, particularly an elderly vulnerable individual. Neither was there evidence that the will was made at the behest and instigation of the defendants or either of them. Nor was there any evidence as to the necessity for the deceased to comply with their requests or that he would be cut off from the affection of the defendants. It was not proven that the deceased was in a vulnerable position and lacked the ability to resist the pressure and/or demands and/or requests of the defendants or both of them to execute the will in the terms thereof. There was no evidence of the deceased being in fear of not complying with the alleged requests. Moreover, the particulars given in the reply of May 31, 2005, that the documents relating to the preparation of the alleged will "demonstrate that the first-named defendant was actively involved in the procuring of the execution of the said will and repeatedly liaised with the solicitor drafting same, both in relation to the drawing up of the said will and its execution" were not proven. The evidence adduced before the court did not substantiate such an allegation. In particular, the alleged liaison was not substantiated.

During the course of his judgment Murphy J. stated that such acts as "importunity or threats, such as the testator has not the courage to resist, moral command asserted and yielded to for the sake of peace and quiet, or for escaping from the stress of mind or social discomfort, these have carried to a degree in which the free play of the testator's judgment, discretion or wishes is overcome, will constitute undue influence," but would be inadvisable to plead on the basis of a suspicion only. He referred to *Potter v Potter*, unreported, Northern Ireland High Court, Gillen J., February 5, 2003 in which Gillen J. held that he had found no evidence at all in that case to ground such a suspicion. On the contrary, all of the evidence heard relevant to the period in question pointed in the opposite direction. The burden of proving undue influence was on the person alleging it. Gillen J. referred to *Wingrove v Wingrove* (1885) 11 P.D. 81, where Sir James Hannen stated that to be undue influence in the eyes of the law there must be, to sum it up in a word, coercion: "It is only when the will of the person who becomes a testator is coerced into doing that which he or she does not desire to do that it is undue influence." Gillen J. went on to say that:

> "Proof of motive and opportunity for the exercise of undue influence is required but the existence of such coupled with the fact that the person who has such motive and opportunity has benefited by the will to the exclusion of others is not sufficient proof of undue influence. There must be positive proof of coercion overpowering the volition of the testator. I reiterate that there was absolutely no evidence of any such influence in this case. The evidence has satisfied me that the deceased was perfectly able to conduct his own affairs and was capable of resisting any undue influence if it had been brought to bear upon him. Despite all the efforts of well-intentioned people to have him change his mode of living to embrace modern facilities, he resisted this and lived exactly as he wanted to. He was not a man to succumb to blandishment or coercion. Much less influence of course will induce a person of weak mental capacity or in a weak state of health to do any act and in such circumstances the court will more readily find undue influence. I repeat that in this case I have found no evidence of weak mental capacity or a weak state of health at the time this will was made. The deceased had the benefit of

independent advice from Mr. McRoberts Solicitor."

Murphy J. thought that the circumstances in that case had some relevance to the present case. Based on the evidence and authorities referred to, he concluded that there was no evidence of undue influence disclosed; that the onus of proof in relation to undue influence was clearly on the plaintiff and had not been discharged; and, indeed, that the confluence of circumstances did not, in any event, give rise to a suspicion let alone proof of undue influence. In this regard he considered the particulars in the statement of claim and in the reply and found no evidence whatsoever of dominion and control. In the circumstances the will was not procured by undue influence.

INTRA-EU WILLS

The EU Commission presented a Green Paper to the EU Parliament on March 1, 2005 covering a wide range of private international law issues concerning testate and intestate succession to estates within the EU and identified a clear need "for the adoption of harmonised European rules". The significant differences between Member States' systems of private international law and their respective substantive law on wills and succession made harmonisation of the rules necessary. Further, as the Commission's Green Paper observed, the growing mobility of Member State nationals in an area without internal frontiers, and the increasing frequency of unions between nationals of different Member States who may acquire property in several Member States of the EU, supports the case for harmonisation of the rules. As a result the EU Parliament by resolution made recommendations to the Commission on wills and succession, first observing that the differences in private international law rules, in so far as they are capable of making it difficult and expensive for beneficiaries to take possession of estates, could create obstacles to the exercise of the freedom of movement and the freedom of establishment referred to in Arts 39 and 43 of the EU Treaty, and the enjoyment of the right to own property which is a general principle of EU law, and that these issues should be addressed accordingly (2005/2148 (INI). The EU Parliament also felt that the adoption of a legislative initiative dealing with wills and succession would be consistent with EU law which fosters social integration of all persons whose principal residence is situated in one of the Member States irrespective of the question of nationality. While the harmonisation of Member States' substantive law of wills and succession falls outside the scope of the EU's competence, the EU is competent under Art.65 (b) of the Treaty to adopt measures "promoting the compatibility of the rules applicable in the Member States concerning the conflict of laws and of jurisdiction". The EU Parliament, however, also recognised that it was essential to uphold certain fundamental tenets of public policy that impose limits on testamentary freedom for the benefit of a testator's family or other dependents, for instance, in this country, the legal right of a surviving spouse.

The EU Parliament recommended that any legislative act should:

1. Aim to regulate succession "exhaustively" in private international law and simultaneously harmonise the rules concerning jurisdiction, the applicable law, and the recognition and enforcement of judgments, but not the substantive and procedural law of the Member States.

2. Ensure that the "forum" and "jus" coincide, thus making it less difficult to apply foreign law. Therefore, the habitual place of residence of the deceased at the time of his death, provided that it was his habitual place of residence for at least two years before his death, or where it was not, the place where the deceased had his main "centre of interests" at the time of his death, should be adopted as the criterion for establishing both jurisdiction and the connecting factor.

3. Allow a testator to choose which law should govern the succession, *viz.* the law of the country of which he is a national, or the law of the country of his habitual residence at the time the choice is made, and that this choice should be expressed in his will. Specific rules concerning the law applicable to the form of testamentary clauses should be adopted and will be regarded as valid if they comply with the law of the Member State in which they were drafted, or with the law of the Member State in which the testator had a habitual residence at the time his will was drawn up or date of death, or with the law of the Member State of which the testator was a national at the time when his will was drawn up or date of death.

4. Regulate the law applicable to agreements as to future successions by providing that in the case of one individual's succession it should be regulated by the law of the Member State in which that person had his habitual residence at the time the agreement was entered into, and in the case of several persons' succession, by the law of each of the Member States in which each of those persons had his habitual residence at the time the agreement was entered into.

5. Introduce a "European Certificate of Inheritance" that would simplify the procedures to be followed by beneficiaries in order to gain possession of the property comprising the estate. Such a certificate would identify the law applicable to the succession, the beneficiaries of the estate, the personal representatives and their powers, and the property comprising the estate, and be issued by an authority empowered to issue or authenticate official documents under the relevant national legislation.

6. Ensure the coordination of the law applicable to the succession with the law of the place in which the property is situate (*lex loci rei sitae*), so as to make the latter applicable, in particular as regards the procedures of acquiring

the property comprised in the estate and any other tangible entitlements thereto, and also to ensure that the law applicable to the succession does not affect the application of any provision of the Member State where certain immoveable property is located (*lex situs*).

7.   Ensure that the ability to choose the law applicable does not contravene the fundamental principles of reserving a proportion of the estate for the deceased person's closest relatives laid down by the law objectively applicable to the succession, for instance, the legal right of a surviving spouse under the Succession Act 1965.

The foregoing recommendations purport to harmonise the private international law rules of the Member States and are confined to those rules only. They are not applicable to the domestic substantive and procedural rules of the Member States. As was said by the EU Commission in its Green Paper, a "full harmonisation of substantive law in the Member States is inconceivable" and that "action will have to focus on the conflict rules".

LAW REFORM COMMISSION REPORT ON COHABITANTS

A qualified cohabitant   While a testator may benefit a fellow cohabitant, a surviving cohabitant has no succession rights to the estate of a deceased cohabitant under the Succession Act 1965. The only form of legal redress that a surviving cohabitant may have against the estate of the deceased cohabitant is where a claim can be based on an equitable concept like proprietary estoppel or, perhaps, under a "new model" constructive trust. The Law Reform Commission in its *Report* on *Rights and Duties of Cohabitants* (LRC 82-2006) proposes, however, that a surviving cohabitant should be given a limited discretionary remedy where inadequate or no provision has been made in the deceased cohabitant's will. A surviving cohabitant must first be a qualified cohabitant and the term "qualified cohabitants" is defined in the report as a cohabitants who have been living together for at least three years, or two years if they have a child. The Commission recommends that a qualified cohabitant should be allowed to apply to the court in the same way as a child of a testator under s.117 of the Succession Act within six months of the first taking out of a grant of representation to the deceased cohabitant's estate or 12 months from the date of death of the deceased cohabitant, whichever occurs the earliest. The Commission also recommends that Ord.79 of the Rules of the Superior Courts 1986 should be amended to permit a qualified cohabitant to apply for a grant of administration to the estate of a deceased cohabitant subject to the discretion of the probate officer on the production of the necessary proofs, and for this purpose the qualified cohabitant should take priority over siblings of the deceased cohabitant when doing so.

Conflicting claims In Chapter 5 of the report the Commission recommends that an application by a qualified cohabitant be made on the net estate of the deceased. An existing spouse will retain his or her legal right share and will not be affected by a qualified cohabitant's application under the redress model in the report and, further, that a claim pursued by a former spouse be considered by the court when addressing any entitlement to the estate by a qualified cohabitant. The Commission also recommends that a claim by surviving children must also be taken into account by the court when addressing any entitlement to the estate by a qualified cohabitant. The Commission goes on to recommend that in deciding whether or not to make an order, and when considering what provision is reasonable in the circumstances, the court may take the following factors into account:

(i) the rights of any spouse;

(ii) the rights and existence of any children of a previous relationship;

(iii) the rights of any former spouse;

(iv) the nature of the relationship and duration of habitation;

(v) the size and nature of the deceased's estate;

(vi) the provision made by the deceased for the applicant during his/ her lifetime by property adjustment order/maintenance order or otherwise;

(vii) any benefit received or to be received by the applicant on, or as a result of, the deceased's death other than out of his/her net estate;

(viii) the interests of the beneficiaries of the estate;

(ix) the financial needs, obligations and responsibilities which the applicant has or is likely to have in the foreseeable future;

(x) the contributions which the applicant made or is likely to make in the foreseeable future to the welfare of the family;

(xi) the effect on the earning capacity of the applicant of the familial responsibilities assumed during the period they lived together;

(xii) any physical or mental disability;

(xiii) any other matter, which in the circumstances of the case the court may consider relevant.

There is no fixed entitlement for applicants making such claims. Any award is confined to such financial provision as would be reasonable in consideration of all the circumstances. Furthermore, when deciding whether to make an order under a provision referred to and in determining the provisions of such an order, the court shall have regard to the terms of any cohabitation agreement entered into by the cohabitants.

LAW REFORM COMMISSION REPORT ON
VULNERABLE ADULTS

Assessment of testamentary capacity In its *Report on Vulnerable Adults and the Law* (LRC 83-2006), the Commission considered that it "would be desirable for the Law Society to produce guidelines for solicitors in this area which would recommend that solicitors take the precaution of obtaining a certificate of capacity in cases where capacity is in doubt or a future challenge to testamentary capacity is likely, for example, because the will is made during a lucid interval by a person with dementia or the testator is resident in a psychiatric facility" (see also Law Reform Commission's *Consultation Paper on Law and the Elderly* (LRC–CP 23–2003)). The Commission also considered that the taking of contemporaneous notes of a consultation between solicitor and client in relation to the execution of a will would be of assistance in the event of any challenge to the testator's capacity to make a will. The Commission went on to recommend that the Law Society and the Medical Council produce guidelines on the assessment of testamentary capacity for the benefit of their members. The guidelines should also stress the importance of taking contemporaneous notes when assessing the testamentary capacity of the testator.

Statutory wills There is no statutory provision in Ireland similar to s.96 of the UK Mental Health Act 1983 which empowers the court of protection to order the execution of a will for an adult patient who is mentally disordered if the court has reason to believe that the patient is incapable of making a will for himself. The Law Reform Commission, having considered the matter in its Report on *Vulnerable Adults and the Law*, recommended that "in exceptional circumstances, the High Court should be given the discretionary power to order the alteration of a will of an adult who lacks testamentary capacity. The court, acting on its initiative or on an application being made to it by any third party including the proposed Guardianship Board (see Ch.6 of the report) would exercise these powers in exceptional circumstances where the justice of the case demands." It will be noted that the Law Reform Commission recommended that the High Court should be given the discretionary power to order the alteration of an existing will but not "to intervene where no will is in existence". Chapter 3(4), para.3.61 *et seq.* of the same report deals with the application of the doctrine of ademption where property forming the subject-matter of a specific devise is sold to fund care arrangements for the testator and recommends that:

> "if land owned by a person who is the subject of a guardianship order
> is sold to fund their long-term care, the persons who would otherwise
> have been entitled to the land on the death of the original owner will
> be deemed to have the same proportionate interest in any surplus
> monies from the proceeds of sale which remain after the relevant care

needs have been provided for. The Commission also recommends that the discretion afforded to the courts under the proposed statutory will procedure should be capable of accommodating ademption in appropriate circumstances."

Safety and Health

CHEMICAL SAFETY

Chemicals: restrictions on manufacture   The European Communities
(Dangerous Substances And Preparations) (Marketing And Use) (Amendment)
Regulations 2006 (S.I. No. 364 of 2006) amended the European Communities
(Dangerous Substances and Preparations) (Marketing and Use) Regulations
2003 (*Annual Review of Irish Law 2004*, p.434). They implemented Directive
2005/59 (which concerns restrictions on toluene and trichlorobenzene);
Directive 2005/69 (which concerns restrictions on polycyclic aromatic
hydrocarbons in extender oils and tyres); Directive 2005/84 (which concerns
restrictions on phthalates in toys and childcare articles); and Directive 2005/90
(which concerns restrictions on substances classified as carcinogenic, mutagenic
or toxic to reproduction, "c/m/r"). They came into force on July 11, 2006.

MANUFACTURING STANDARDS

Human blood and blood components   The European Communities (Human
Blood and Blood Components Traceability Requirements and Notification of
Serious Adverse Reactions and Events) Regulations 2006 (S.I. No. 547 of
2006) implemented Directive 2005/61, which sets out traceability requirements
and notification of serious adverse reactions and events in respect of human
blood and blood components, in accordance with Directive 2002/98. The
European Communities (Quality System for Blood Establishments) Regulations
2006 (S.I. No. 552 of 2006) implemented Directive 2002/98 as regards
Community standards and specifications relating to a quality system for
blood establishments. These 2006 Regulations complemented the European
Communities (Quality and Safety of Human Blood and Blood Components)
Regulations 2005 (*Annual Review of Irish Law 2005*, p.605).

Noise emission by equipment for use outdoors   The European Communities
(Noise Emission by Equipment for Use Outdoors) (Amendment) Regulations
2006 (S.I. No. 241 of 2006) implemented Directive 2005/88 on noise emission
in the environment by equipment for use outdoors. The Regulations provide for
certain types of equipment listed in Art.1 of the 2005 Directive, which would
not be able to meet the stage II limits by January 3, 2006, solely for technical
reasons, to still be placed on the market and/or put into service by that date.

Storage of human tissues and cells The European Communities (Quality and Safety of Human Tissues and Cells) Regulations 2006 (S.I. No. 158 of 2006) implemented three related Directives. First, Directive 2004/23 on standards of quality and safety for the donation, procurement, testing, processing, preservation, storage and distribution of human tissues and cells. They also implemented Directive 2004/23 and Directive 2006/17 concerning technical requirements for the donation, procurement and testing of human tissues and cells.

SAFETY, HEALTH AND WELFARE AT WORK

In 2006 a series of four sets of Regulations were made under the Safety, Health and Welfare at Work Act 2005 (*Annual Review of Irish Law 2005*, pp.604–18). They concerned work at height, vibration, noise, asbestos and construction projects.

Work at height The Safety, Health and Welfare at Work (Work at Height) Regulations 2006 (S.I. No. 318 of 2006) implemented Directive 2001/45/EC on work equipment used at height. The 2006 Regulations replace a series of regulations on working at height with a single set of Regulations that apply to all places of work and all work activities. The 2006 Regulations apply generally to work in any place where, if the measures required by the Regulations were not taken, a person could fall a distance liable to cause personal injury. In general, therefore, the 2006 Regulations include: working on a scaffold or from a mobile elevated work platform (MEWP); working on the back of a lorry; using cradles or ropes to gain access to parts of a building; climbing permanent structures, such as gantries, masts or telephone poles; painting at height; using a ladder, step ladder or kick stool for shelf-filling, window-cleaning, shop-fitting or other maintenance tasks (for example, changing a light bulb). The Regulations specifically exclude situations where a person falls on a stairs in a permanent workplace. These situations are covered by the relevant requirements of the Workplace Regulations (now contained in the Safety, Health and Welfare at Work (General Application) Regulations 2007 (S.I. No. 299 of 2007), into which the 2006 Regulations have also been incorporated and to which we will return in the *Annual Review of Irish Law 2007*. The 2006 Regulations require that, where employees are liable to be exposed to a risk of falling, an employer must carry out a risk assessment to assess and, if necessary, measure the levels of risk to which workers are exposed. The 2006 Regulations also state that if a falling object could injure someone, steps must be taken to ensure that this is prevented. The 2006 Regulations also require regular inspection of equipment for work at height to ensure that it is safe to use. We note here that the 2006 Regulations have been incorporated into the Safety, Health and Welfare at Work (General Application) Regulations 2007 (S.I. No. 299 of 2007), to which we will return in the *Annual Review of Irish Law 2007*.

Control of vibration at work The Safety, Health and Welfare at Work (Control of Vibration at Work) Regulations 2006 (S.I. No. 370 of 2006) implemented Directive 2002/44/EC on the control of vibration at work. The 2006 Regulations apply to hand-arm vibration (HAV) and whole-body vibration (WBV). HAV is caused by the use of work equipment and work processes that transmit vibration into the hands and arms of employees. WBV is caused by vibration transmitted through the seat or the feet by workplace machines and vehicles. The 2006 Regulations require that, where employees are liable to be exposed to mechanical vibration, an employer must carry out a risk assessment to assess and, if necessary, measure the levels of mechanical vibration to which workers are exposed. The risk assessment must be based on the exposure action values (EAVs) and exposure limit values (ELVs) set out in the 2006 Regulations. The EAV is the level of daily exposure to vibration for any worker which, if exceeded, requires specified action to be taken to reduce risk. The ELV is the level of daily exposure to vibration for any worker which shall not be exceeded. Separate EAVs and ELVs are listed for HAV and WBV. The 2006 Regulations require that the employer must ensure that risk to his or her employees from the exposure to mechanical vibration is either eliminated at source or, where this is not reasonably practicable, reduced to a minimum. If the risk assessment indicates that an exposure action value (EAV) is exceeded, the employer must comply with the duty to reduce exposure to a minimum by establishing and implementing a programme of organisational and technical measures appropriate to the activity and consistent with the risk assessment. It is worth noting that there has been an enormous amount of litigation in Britain concerning illnesses arising from vibration at work. A number of claims by, for example, bus drivers are also currently pending in the Irish courts. We note here that the 2006 Regulations have been incorporated into the Safety, Health and Welfare at Work (General Application) Regulations 2007 (S.I. No. 299 of 2007), to which we will return in the *Annual Review of Irish Law 2007*.

Control of noise at work The Safety, Health and Welfare at Work (Control of Noise at Work) Regulations 2006 (S.I. No. 371 of 2006) implemented Directive 2003/10/EC on noise at work. The 2006 Regulations also replaced and revoked the European Communities (Protection of Workers) (Exposure to Noise) Regulations 1990 (*Annual Review of Irish Law 1990*, pp.474–475), which had implemented the previous Directive on Noise, Directive 86/188/EEC. The 1990 Regulations had, in turn, replaced the Factories (Noise) Regulations 1975, made under the Factories Act 1955. Because the 2006 Regulations were made under the Safety, Health and Welfare at Work Act 2005 they apply to all places of work, like the 1990 Regulations. The 1975 Regulations were limited in scope to manufacturing premises and construction projects. The 2006 Regulations can be seen against the background of the recent experience in Ireland of the army deafness claims, which involved over 15,000 noise-induced hearing loss claims. These claims led to the introduction of a standardised system for the calculation of noise-induced hearing impairment in the Civil Liability (Assessment of Hearing Injury) Act 1998 (*Annual Review of Irish Law 1998*, pp.575–579), based on the 1998 Report of the Expert Hearing Group, *Hearing Disability Assessment*—usually known as the "Green Book"—available at www. dohc.ie. Many of the army deafness claims also relied on ISO 1999: 1990 as the standard on which hearing impairment should be calculated. ISO 1999 quantifies the risk to the exposed population of a given noise level and takes into account the amount of hearing loss which would be expected in a similar population not exposed to noise. The 2006 Regulations require employers to take specific action at certain exposure limit values and exposure action values. These relate to: the levels of exposure to noise of employees averaged over a working day or week; the maximum noise (peak sound pressure) to which employees are exposed in a working day. The exposure limit values are the noise levels that must not be exceeded. The exposure action values are the noise levels at which certain actions must be taken. The 2006 Regulations require the employer to make a suitable and sufficient noise risk assessment to enable the employer to make a valid decision about whether action is necessary to prevent or adequately control exposure of his or her employees to noise in the workplace. The 2006 Regulations also state that if any worker is likely to be exposed to noise at or above an upper exposure value, the employer must establish and implement a programme of technical and organisational measures, excluding the provision of personal hearing protectors, intended to reduce exposure to noise. The 2006 Regulations also state that if the noise level at the workplace is likely to exceed 85 dB(A), the employer must ensure that hearing protectors are provided and must be worn and must delimit the areas where noise levels exceed 85 dB(A) and restrict access to the delimited area where this is practicable and the risk from exposure justifies it. The relevant noise level in the 1990 Regulations for this purpose was 90dBA, which is almost four times the noise level represented by 85 dB(A) (this is because decibels are measured using a logarithmic scale). We note here that the 2006 Regulations have been incorporated into the Safety, Health and Welfare at Work (General Application) Regulations 2007 (S.I. No. 299 of 2007), to which we will return in the *Annual Review of Irish Law 2007*.

Exposure to asbestos   The Safety, Health and Welfare at Work (Exposure to Asbestos) Regulations 2006 (S.I. No. 386 of 2006) implemented Directive 83/477/EEC, as amended by Directive 91/382/EEC and Directive 2003/18/EC. The 2006 Regulations also replaced and revoked the European Communities (Protection of Workers) (Exposure to Asbestos) Regulations 1989 to 2000, which had implemented the 1983 and 1991 Directives. Asbestos is a naturally occurring mineral with excellent insulation and binding properties and takes three main forms: chrysotile, known as white asbestos; crocidolite, known as blue asbestos; and amosite, brown asbestos. White asbestos is the most commonly used asbestos, particularly as an insulation device in older buildings, including in pipework. Blue asbestos was also used well into the 1960s as a common form of insulation in ship-building and railway coaches. Blue and brown asbestos are more commonly associated with mesothelioma, the long-term cancer connected with asbestos exposure. It is estimated that, in the United Kingdom in recent years, about 1,500 people are dying each year from mesothelioma. It would appear that, in Ireland, the National Cancer Registry (NCR) has registered a very small number of deaths arising from mesothelioma in recent years, though it may be that a number of lung cancer deaths may involve mesothelioma but are recorded as smoking-related where the deceased also smoked. In addition to these "direct" diseases, many people who have been exposed to asbestos develop anxiety and depression even where they have not yet developed any physical symptoms of disease; these are sometimes known as the "worried well" or "fear of disease" cases. We have previously discussed such cases in the context of the Supreme Court decision in *Fletcher v Commissioners of Public Works in Ireland* [2003] 1 I.R. 465 (*Annual Review of Irish Law 2003*, pp.526–32). An innovation in the 2006 Regulations is the introduction of a single exposure limit value (ELV) for asbestos. Employers must ensure that no employee is exposed to an airborne concentration of asbestos in excess of the exposure limit value (ELV) of 0.1 fibres per cm^3 as an eight-hour time-weighted average. Where there is or is likely to be an exposure to asbestos dust, the employer is required to reduce the exposure to a minimum and in any case below the ELV. The 2006 Regulations also impose a duty on employers to assess the risks to employees' health and safety resulting from any activity from which an employee is or may be exposed in their place of work and to determine the nature and degree of exposure and to identify the measures necessary to ensure the safety and health of employees. Where an initial assessment shows that the amount of asbestos fibres is equal or greater than the ELV, the employer must measure the asbestos in the air regularly. The 2006 Regulations also state that, where exposure to asbestos is envisaged, the employer must not commence work until a plan of work is drawn up. A copy of the plan must be provided to the Health and Safety Authority not less than 14 days before work begins. The detailed elements of the plan of work are set out in the Regulations.

Construction projects   The Safety, Health and Welfare at Work (Construction) Regulations 2006 (S.I. No. 504 of 2006) implement Directive 92/57/EEC. They replace and, in large part, revoke the Safety, Health and Welfare at Work (Construction) Regulations 2001 and 2003. The 2006 Regulations (like the 2001 and 2003 Regulations) involve two major elements: requirements concerning the design and management of safety and health for construction work (Pts 1 to 3, regs 1 to 29); and detailed operational Regulations for construction work (Pts 4 to 14, regs 30 to 105). The 2006 Regulations apply to what would be termed the construction industry, but they go beyond this to include civil engineering works as well as extensions to and maintenance of existing buildings. Having regard to the detailed nature of the Construction Regulations 2006, we provide an outline only of the main duties imposed on the parties involved in construction projects.

Clients The client is the person who commissions the project. The 2006 Regulations require clients to:

- appoint, in writing before design work starts, a project supervisor for the design process (PSDP) who has adequate training, knowledge, experience and resources;

- appoint, in writing before construction begins, a project supervisor for the construction stage (PSCS) who has adequate training, knowledge, experience and resources;

- be satisfied that each designer and contractor appointed has adequate training, knowledge, experience and resources for the work to be performed;

- cooperate with the project supervisor and supply necessary information;

- retain and make available the safety file for the completed structure. The safety file contains information on the completed structure that will be required for future maintenance or renovation;

- provide a copy of the safety and health plan prepared by the PSDP to every person tendering for the project. The safety plan documents how health and safety on the project will be managed up to project completion;

- notify the Health and Safety Authority (HSA) of the appointment of the PSDP where construction is likely to take more than 500 person days or 30 working days.

Designers Regulation 2 of the 2006 Regulations defines a designer as a person engaged in preparing "drawings, particulars, specifications, calculations and bills of quantities in so far as they contain specifications or other expressions of purpose according to which a project, or any part or component of a project, is to be executed." The 2006 Regulations require designers to:

- identify any hazards that the design may present during construction and subsequent maintenance;

- where possible, eliminate the hazards or reduce the risk, for example, can roof-mounted equipment be placed at ground level or can guardrails be provided to protect workers from falling?

- provide in writing to the PSDP all relevant documentation necessary for the project supervisor to carry out his/her duties;

- communicate necessary control measures, design assumptions or remaining risks to the PSDP so they can be dealt with in the safety and health plan;

- cooperate with other designers and the PSDP or PSCS;

- take account of any existing safety and health plan or safety file;

- comply with directions issued by the PSDP or PSCS;

- where no PSDP has been appointed, inform the client that a PSDP must be appointed.

Project Supervisor for the Design Process (PSDP) The 2006 Regulations require that the client must appoint in writing a competent PSDP for each project. The 2006 Regulations state that the PSDP must:

- take account of the general principles of prevention during the various stages of the design and preparation of a project, in particular, (i) when either, or both, technical or organisational aspects are being decided, in order to plan the various items or stages of work which are to take place simultaneously or in succession, and (ii) when estimating the time required for completion of a project and, where appropriate, for stages of a project' (reg.11(1));

- identify hazards arising from the design or from the technical, organisational, planning or time related aspects of the project;

- where possible, eliminate the hazards or reduce the risk;

- communicate necessary control measure, design assumptions or remaining risks to the PSCS so they can be dealt with in the safety and health plan;

- ensure co-operation between designers on the same project and, so far as is reasonably practicable, co-ordinate their activities, with a view to protecting persons at work (reg.11(2));

- prepare a written safety and health plan for any project where construction will take more than 500 person days or 30 working days or there is a particular risk and deliver it to the client prior to tender;

- specify in the written preliminary safety and health plan the basis upon which the timescale in the preliminary safety and health plan was established, taking into account the General Principles of Prevention in the 2005 Act;

- specify in the written preliminary safety and health plan the conclusions drawn by designers and the project supervisor for the design process as to how they took into account the General Principles of Prevention and of any relevant safety and health plan or safety file;

- specify in the preliminary safety and health plan the location of welfare facilities, including water and sewage connections;

- keep a copy of the safety and health plan available for inspection by a HSA inspector for five years after its preparation;

- ensure that the preliminary health and safety plan is available in time to be provided to any person being considered or tendering for the role of project supervisor construction stage;

- prepare a safety file for the completed structure and give it to the client;

- notify the authority and client of non-compliance with any written directions issued.

The PSDP may issue directions to designers or contractors or others.

Project Supervisor Construction Stage (PSCS)   The 2006 Regulations require that the client must appoint in writing a competent PSCS for each project. The 2006 Regulations state that the PSCS must:

- notify the HSA before construction commences where construction is likely to take more than 500 person days or 30 working days;

- coordinate the identification of hazards, the elimination of the hazards or the reduction of risks during construction;

- develop the safety and health plan initially prepared by the PSDP before construction commences;

- include in the safety plan written rules for the execution of construction work, which are required for safety and health purposes;

- coordinate the implementation by contractors of the 2006 Regulations and other Regulations relevant to the project;

- organise cooperation between contractors and the provision of information;

- coordinate the reporting of accidents to the HSA;

- provide information to the site safety representative;

- coordinate the checking of safe working procedures;

- coordinate measures to restrict entry on to the site;

- coordinate the provision and maintenance of welfare facilities;

- coordinate arrangements to ensure that craft, general construction workers and security workers have a Safety Awareness Card (Safe Pass under the 2001 Regulations) and a Construction Skills card where required;

- coordinate the appointment of a site safety representative where there are more than 20 persons on site;

- appoint a safety adviser where there are more than 100 on site;

- provide all necessary safety file information to the PSDP;

- (may) give directions to any contractor or any other person so far as is necessary to enable the PSCS to comply with his or her duties under these Regulations;

- monitor the compliance of contractors and others and take corrective action where necessary;

- notify failure to comply with such a direction in writing to the HSA, enclosing a copy of the written direction (note that the PSDP must also notify the client of any such similar direction issued by the PSDP and include a copy in the preliminary safety and health plan);

- keep available for inspection a record of the names (as supplied by contractors under the Regulations) of persons at work on the site;

- keep "appropriate" records and copies of relevant documents for five years from their preparation.

Contractors   Contractors are persons who carry out construction projects. The 2006 Regulations state that contractors must:

- cooperate with the PSCS;

- provide a copy of its safety statement and relevant information to the PSCS;

- promptly provide the PSCS with information required for the safety file;

- comply with directions of project supervisors;

- report accidents to the HSA and to the PSCS where an employee cannot perform his normal work for more than three days;

- comply with site rules and the safety and health plan and ensure that their employees comply;

- identify hazards, eliminate the hazards or reduce risks during construction;

- facilitate the Site Safety Representative;

- ensure that relevant workers have a Safety Awareness Card (Safe Pass under the 2001 Regulations) and a construction skills card where required;

- provide workers with site specific induction;

- appoint a safety officer where there are more than 20 on site or 30 employed;

- consult workers and Safety Representatives;

• monitor compliance and take corrective action.

The 2006 Regulations impose a substantial number of other contractor duties, including a number of new duties, dealing with: safety at road works (the emphasis on road safety arises from a bus crash in County Meath in 2005 in which five schoolchildren were killed); and explosives. Transitional arrangements of between six and 18 months apply to the following new duties: new construction skills card requirements for road workers, mobile erection of mobile tower scaffold, mini-digger operation, self-erecting tower crane operation and shot-firing; and reversing aids and rear visibility for construction plant.

RADIOLOGICAL (NUCLEAR) SAFETY

Control of radioactive sources   The Radiological Protection Act 1991 (Control of High-Activity Sealed Radioactive Sources) Order 2005 (S.I. No. 875 of 2005) implemented Directive 2003/122 on the control of high-activity sealed radioactive sources and orphan sources. The purpose of the Directive is to prevent exposure of workers and the public to ionising radiation arising from the inadequate control of high-activity sealed radioactive sources and orphan sources by defining specific requirements that each source is kept under control. The Order came into effect on December 31, 2005.

RAIL SAFETY

The Railway Safety Act 2005 (Railway Incidents) Regulations 2006 (S.I. No. 585 of 2006), made under the Railway Safety Act 2005 (*Annual Review of Irish Law 2005*, pp.619–624), completed the implementation in the State (largely done by the 2005 Act) of the 2004 Railway Safety Directive, Directive 2004/49 on safety on the Community's railways, which had amended Directive 95/18 on the licensing of railway undertakings and Directive 2001/14 on the allocation of railway infrastructure capacity and the levying of charges for the use of railway infrastructure and safety certification. They came into force on November 23, 2006.

ROAD TRANSPORT

Carriage of dangerous goods by road   The Carriage of Dangerous Goods by Road Regulations 2006 (S.I. No. 504 of 2006) (the CDGR Regulations), which were made under the Carriage of Dangerous Goods by Road Act 1998, replace the Carriage of Dangerous Goods by Road Regulations 2004 (*Annual*

Review of Irish Law 2004, p.448). They set down detailed requirements for vehicles, tanks, tank containers, receptacles and packages containing dangerous goods, including petrol products, as defined in the UN's ADR Agreement on the Carriage of Dangerous Goods. The 1998 Act implemented the general principles of the ADR Agreement, while the 2006 Regulations implement its detailed requirements. The 2006 Regulations require, for example, that the drivers and others, such as the consignor, involved in the carriage of dangerous goods by road (including their packing, loading, filling, transport and unloading) be adequately trained and, in the case of drivers, hold certificates of such training. The 2006 Regulations also contain provisions on an EC harmonised approach to the road checks aspect of their enforcement. The 2006 Regulations implemented Directive 94/55/EC on the Transport of Dangerous Goods by Road, as amended, and came into force on July 31, 2006.

TOBACCO CONTROL AND WORKPLACE SMOKING BAN

Outdoor place or premises: structure containing modular walls   In *Malone Engineering Products Ltd v Health Service Executive* [2006] I.E.H.C. 307, High Court, July 21, 2006, Murphy J. held that a particular structure manufactured by the plaintiff did not constitute an "outdoor part of a place or premises" which brought it within the exclusions from the workplace smoking ban in s.47 of the Public Health (Tobacco) Act 2002, as inserted by s.16 of the Public Health (Tobacco) (Amendment) Act 2004 (*Annual Review of Irish Law 2004*, pp.443–447).

Section 47(7)(d) of the 2002 Act, as inserted by s.16 of the 2004 Act, provides that the prohibition on smoking in specified places shall not apply to "an outdoor part of a place or premises covered by a fixed or movable roof, provided that not more than 50 per cent of the perimeter of that part is surrounded by one or more walls or similar structures (inclusive of windows, doors, gates or other means of access to or egress from that part)". The plaintiff sought a declaration that a structure which it designed and manufactured ("Freshwall") complied with s.47(7)(d) of the 2002 Act. Evidence was given on behalf of the plaintiff that 50 per cent of the perimeter of the enclosed area was fully and permanently open and, therefore, complied with s.47(7). Evidence was given of open area calculations on a structure made of "Freshwall", in particular relating to openings on the panels, the number of air changes and floor area. A report prepared by the defendant, the Health Service Executive, concluded that the structure contained modular walls which surrounded 100 per cent of the structure and was not, therefore, in compliance with s.47 of the 2002 Act. The structure which had been measured also contained a floor with skirting boards, radiators, infrared heaters, a ceiling with acoustic tiles and five television sets. As indicated, Murphy J. refused to make the declaration which the plaintiff sought.

He held that the structure was not outdoors, but was, in every common sense, indoors. The structure clearly did not have 50 per cent of air space and 50 per cent of solid because of the fixtures and fittings with it and because of the positioning of the counter, the mirror and the radiators. Even dealing with the structure in the abstract on the common understanding of the words "outdoor", "perimeter" and "wall", Murphy J. held that this was a wall. It presented as a wall and was a continuous structure. In dealing with the concept of having air coming in, albeit baffled or muffled as it came in, it was a wall and it was outdoors.

WORKING TIME

Mobile staff in civil aviation European Communities (Organisation of Working Time) (Mobile Staff in Civil Aviation) Regulations 2006 (S.I. No. 507 of 2006) implemented Directive 2000/79 concerning the European Agreement on the Organisation of Working Time of Mobile Workers in Civil Aviation concluded by the Association of European Airlines (AEA); the European Transport Workers' Federation (ETF); the European Cockpit Association (ECA); the European Regions Airline Association (ERA); and the International Air Carrier Association (IACA). They came into effect on September 29, 2006.

Social Welfare Law

PRIMARY LEGISLATION

As has become commonplace in recent years, two Acts dealing with social welfare matters were enacted in 2006.

The Social Welfare Law Reform and Pensions Act 2006 provides for a number of measures announced in the Budget for 2006. These include, *inter alia*, increases in child benefit (s.3) and respite care grants (s.30), increasing the income threshold for one-parent family payment (s.27, commenced by S.I. No. 206 of 2006), an extension in the duration of carer's benefit (s.7) and an improvement in the means test applicable to the supplementary welfare allowance (s.34). The Act also provides for the establishment of a standard, non-contributory pension for everyone over the age of 66, to be known as the state pension (non-contributory)—see ss.16, 17 and 24 and Schedules 2 to 4 (with consequential changes to a number of other schemes provided for in ss.20 to 23 and s.25) —and further provides for the automatic transfer to the old age (contributory) pension for recipients of invalidity pension or retirement pension who attain the age of 66 (ss.11 and 12, both commenced by S.I. No. 334 of 2006). (Sections 16 to 25 of the Act were commenced by S.I. No. 334 of 2006.)

In an attempt to further modernise the social welfare code and to make it more accessible, s.4 (commenced by S.I. Nos 246 and 334 of 2006) and Schedule 1 provide for amending the titles of certain social welfare payments. Thus, old age (contributory) pension is renamed as state pension (contributory); retirement pension as state pension (transition); disability benefit as illness benefit; unemployment benefit and unemployment assistance as jobseeker's benefit and jobseeker's allowance respectively; orphan's (contributory) allowance and orphan's (non-contributory) pension as guardian's payment (contributory) and guardian's payment (non-contributory) respectively; and unemployability supplement as incapacity supplement. Sections 5 and 6 provide that income earned by a self-employed home childminder will be liable for a social insurance contribution of €253 p.a. while s.8 provides that a decision as to a person's status as a homemaker shall be made by a deciding officer with the consequence that it may now be subject to an appeal to an appeals officer. (These sections were commenced by S.I. No. 205 of 2006.) Sections 9 and 13 (both commenced by S.I. No. 334 of 2006) provide for the calculation of a daily rate to facilitate the payment of old age (contributory) pension and retirement pension from the date of the claimant's relevant birthday rather than the day in the week when these pensions are normally paid, while ss.10 and 14 (both commenced by S.I. No. 334 of 2006) provide for rounding cents for the purpose of calculating certain rates of old age (contributory) and retirement pension. Section 15 provides for the phasing out of pre-retirement allowance while ss.18 and 19 (both commenced by S.I. No. 334 of 2006) provide for the continued payment of the widowed parent grant to a widow or widower in receipt of the new state pension (non-contributory). Section 26 clarifies that it is the means of the orphan that are to be taken into account for the purpose of determining entitlement to the orphan's (non-contributory) pension while ss.28 and 29, together with Schedule 6, provide for the new early childcare supplement scheme. (Section 26 was commenced by S.I. No. 206 of 2006.) Section 31 provides for the disregard of the amount of any contribution to a personal retirement savings account for the purposes of the income thresholds applicable to the family income supplement (and is commenced by S.I. No. 246 of 2006); s.32 provides that a person entitled to the Irish invalidity pension under EU law shall not suffer a reduction in pension if s/he subsequently becomes entitled to a retirement or survivor's pension from another EU state; s.33, commenced by S.I. No. 246 of 2006, provides for amendments to the definition of certain terms in Schedule 3 to the Social Welfare (Consolidation) Act 2005 dealing with means tests and further excludes certain welfare payments from these means tests; s.35 adds to the list of public bodies authorised to use the Personal Public Service Number as a public service identifier and ss.36 and 37 provide for some minor technical amendments to the 2005 Act.

Part 3 of the Act provides for various changes to the Pensions Act 1990, while Pt 4 provides for miscellaneous changes to the Combat Poverty Agency Act 1986; the Freedom of Information Act 1997; the Comhairle Act 2000; the Taxes Consolidation Act 1997; and the Carer's Leave Act 2001.

The Social Welfare Act 2006 provides for, *inter alia*, increases in the rates of social welfare payments (ss.2–4), increases in the income levels above and below which PRSI is not payable by employed or optional contributors (ss.5–6) and changes in respect of the health contribution levy (s.13).

Section 7 provides for consequential changes to maternity benefit following on the extension of paid and unpaid maternity leave by four weeks each while s.8 provides for similar amendments to adoptive benefit arising from the extension of adoptive leave by four weeks. The Act also provides for an increase in the widowed parent grant (s.9) and for an increase in the weekly means disregard used in the calculation of state pension (non-contributory) (s.10). Section 11 abolishes the restriction on the payment of disability allowance to certain persons resident in medical institutions while s.12 extends self-employed social insurance cover to recipients of jobseeker's allowance or farm assist.

SECONDARY LEGISLATION

Thirty-two regulations dealing with the statutory social welfare code were promulgated during 2006. They are as follows:

Social Welfare Act 2005 (Sections 7 and 8) (Commencement) Order 2006 [S.I. No. 119 of 2006]—This Order provides for the commencement of ss.7(1)(a)(ii), 7(1)(a)(iii), 7(1)(b), 7(2) and 8(1)(a)(i) of the Social Welfare Act 2005 which provide for the extension of the duration of payment of maternity and adoptive benefit consequential on Budget 2006.

Social Welfare (Consolidated Payments Provisions) (Amendment) (Benefit and Privilege) Regulations 2006 [S.I. No. 120 of 2006] —These regulations provide for the abolition of the assessment of benefit and privilege for the purpose of unemployment assistance and pre-retirement allowance in the case of those aged 25 years and over living in the parental home with effect from February 1, 2006.

Social Welfare (Consolidated Payments Provisions) (Amendment) (No. 2) (Carer's) Regulations 2006 [S.I. No. 145 of 2006] —These regulations increase the income that may be earned by a claimant of carer's benefit from employment or self-employment outside the home to €290 per week and further provide for an increase in the income disregarded for the purposes of the means-tested carer's allowance to €580 per week for a married person and €290 per week for a single person.

Social Welfare (Consolidated Supplementary Welfare Allowance) (Amendment) (Diet Supplement) Regulations 2006 [S.I. No. 146 of 2006] —These regulations provide for revised rates of diet supplement under the supplementary welfare allowance scheme. They also streamline the range of specified diets under the scheme and extend the scope of the scheme to certain qualified child dependants aged 18 or over and under 22 in full-time education.

Social Welfare (Consolidated Payments Provisions) (Amendment) (No. 1) (Early Childcare Supplement) Regulations 2006 [S.I. No. 147 of 2006] —These regulations set out the dates on which early childcare supplement will be payable, for the period April to December 2006. They also disregard the early childcare supplement in determining the weekly family income for family income supplement purposes; include early childcare supplement in the definition of benefit, for the purposes of claims and payments provisions; determine the first day of the quarter in which a child is born as being the date from which early childcare supplement becomes payable; provide that the maximum period for which early childcare supplement may be backdated is six months; provide, in cases of shared custody of a qualified child who resides on a part-time basis with each of his or her parents, that early childcare supplement is payable to the parent with whom the child resides for the greater part of the quarter; and require recipients of early childcare supplement to return any payments not due as a result of a change in their circumstances.

Social Welfare (Consolidated Payments Provisions) (Amendment) (No. 3) (Island Allowance) Regulations 2006 [S.I. No. 199 of 2006] —These regulations provide for the addition of Fenit Island in Co. Kerry and Islandmore in Co. Mayo to the list of prescribed islands for the purposes of the island allowance payable to certain social welfare recipients who are normally resident on those islands.

Social Welfare (Consolidated Payments Provisions) (Amendment of Maintenance) Regulations 2006 [S.I. No. 200 of 2006] —These regulations provide for an increase in the income disregard for those receiving maintenance from a liable relative for the purpose of deciding entitlement to a rent or mortgage interest supplement.

Social Welfare (Consolidated Payments Provisions) (Amendment) (No. 5) (Treatment Benefit) Regulation 2006 [S.I. No. 201 of 2006] —These regulations provide for the introduction of an alternative contribution condition for entitlement to treatment benefit. A person over 21 will now be able to avail of treatment benefit where he or she has 26 qualifying contributions in each of the second and third last contribution years.

Social Welfare (Consolidated Payments Provisions) (Amendment) (No. 7) (Maternity and Adoptive Benefit) Regulations 2006 [S.I. No. 202 of 2006] —These regulations provide for a number of amendments to the regulations governing maternity benefit and adoptive benefit. They extend the period of payment of maternity benefit by four weeks and allow for adoptive benefit to be postponed in the event of the hospitalisation of the child, subject to prescribed conditions.

Social Welfare (Consolidated Supplementary Welfare Allowance) (Amendment) (No. 1) (Training Course Disregard, Benefit and Privilege) Regulations 2006 [S.I. No. 203 of 2006] —These regulations provide for an increase in the income disregard for those attending certain training courses and also provide that the assessment of benefit and privilege for those living in the parental home will now be abolished for those aged 25 years for the purpose of supplementary welfare allowance.

Social Welfare (Consolidated Contributions and Insurability) (Amendment) (No. 1) (Refunds) Regulations 2006 [S.I. No. 204 of 2006] —These regulations provide for refunds to employers of social insurance contributions relating to seagoing employees paid in respect of employees on wholly or mainly Irish-owned and registered ships, ships leased in the State or any EU-registered vessel.

Social Welfare Law Reform and Pensions Act 2006 (Sections 5 and 6) (Commencement) Order 2006 [S.I. No. 205 of 2006] —This Order provides for the commencement of ss.5 and 6 of the Social Welfare Law Reform and Pensions Act 2006.

Social Welfare Law Reform and Pensions Act 2006 (Section 26 and 27) (Commencement) Order 2006 [S.I. No. 206 of 2006] —This Order provides for the commencement of ss.26 and 27 of the Social Welfare Law Reform and Pensions Act 2006.

Social Welfare (Consolidated Contributions and Insurability) (Amendment) (Chargeable Excess) Regulations 2006 [S.I. No. 218 of 2006] —These regulations amend the Social Welfare (Consolidated Contributions and Insurability) Regulations to provide for exemption from PRSI of a chargeable excess as defined in s.787Q of the Taxes Consolidation Act 1997.

Social Welfare (Consolidated Payments Provisions) (Amendment) (No. 6) (Qualified Adults and Earnings from Rehabilitative Employment) Regulations 2006 [S.I. No. 219 of 2006] —These regulations increase the income limit for entitlement to the full rate of qualified adult allowance (€100 per week) and also increase the spouse earnings disregard for unemployment assistance, pre-retirement allowance, farm assist and disability allowance to €100 per week where the spouse works more than three days in the week, and to €50 per week where the spouse works three days or less in the week. They further provide for increases in the rates of tapered payments in respect of qualified adults and retain the income disregard for recipients of disability allowance and blind pension of €120 per week for earnings of a rehabilitative nature, introducing a new withdrawal rate thereafter of 50 per cent up to an upper maximum earnings limit of €350 per week.

Social Welfare Law Reform and Pensions Act 2006 (Sections 4(4), 4(5), 31 and 33) (Commencement) Order 2006 [S.I. No. 246 of 2006] —This Order provides for the commencement of ss.4(4), 4(5), 31 and 33 of the Social Welfare Law Reform and Pensions Act 2006.

Social Welfare (Consolidated Payments Provisions) (Amendment) (No.8) (Carers and Homemakers) Regulations 2006 [S.I. No. 288 of 2006] —These regulations provide that, for the purposes of carer's benefit, carer's allowance and respite care grant, the care-giver may engage, outside the home, in employment, self-employment or participate in training or education courses approved by the Minister, for an aggregated maximum of 15 hours per week. They also provide for the extension of the time limit within which an application to become a homemaker for the purposes of old age (contributory) pension may be made.

Social Welfare Law Reform and Pensions Act 2006 (Sections 2, 9, 10, 20, 21, 22, 23, 24 and 25) (Commencement) Order 2006 [S.I. No. 334 of 2006]
—This Order provides for the commencement of ss.4, 9, 10 to 14 and 16 to 25 of the Social Welfare Law Reform and Pensions Act 2006.

Social Welfare (Consolidated Payments Provisions) (Amendment) (No. 9) (One-Parent Family Payment) (Assessment of Earnings) Regulations 2006 [S.I. No. 486 of 2006]—These regulations provide for an annual assessment of means from employment and self-employment for the purposes of deciding entitlement to one-parent family payment and also for determining entitlement based on an alternative period where deemed appropriate by a deciding officer or an appeals officer, as the case may be.

Social Welfare (Consolidated Payments Provisions) (Amendment) (No. 10) (Treatment Benefit) Regulations 2006 [S.I. No. 487 of 2006]—These regulations provide for an amendment to the alternative contribution conditions for entitlement to treatment benefit. A person who becomes 66 on or after May 29, 2006 will now be able to avail of treatment benefit where he or she has 26 qualifying contributions in both the relevant contribution year and the year immediately before the relevant contribution year.

Social Welfare (Consolidated Payments Provisions) (Amendment) (No. 11) (Compensation Payments) Regulations 2006 [S.I. No. 497 of 2006]—These regulations extend the disregard, for the purpose of the means tests for social assistance schemes, of compensation payments made to persons who have contracted Hepatitis C or HIV, who have disabilities caused by Thalidomide or who made applications to the Residential Institutions Redress Board, to include any monies received by way of compensation awarded under the provisions of the Health (Repayment Scheme) Act 2006.

Social Welfare (Consolidated Payments Provisions) (Amendment) (No. 12) (State and Widow(er)'s Pension (Non-Contributory) Earnings Disregard) Regulations 2006 [S.I. No. 519 of 2006] —These regulations provide for the disregard of €100 per week in earnings from employment when calculating means for the purposes of the state pension (non-contributory), widow's (non-contributory) pension and widower's (non-contributory) pension. In addition, health contributions, superannuation contributions and trade union membership contributions are also disregarded for means test purposes from gross earnings.

Social Welfare (Consolidated Claims and Payments) (Amendment) (No. 13) (Miscellaneous Provisions) Regulations 2006 [S.I. No. 571 of 2006]
—These regulations provide for a number of amendments to the Social Welfare (Consolidated Claims and Payments Provisions) Regulations 1994 (as amended) in advance of further consolidation later this year. In the main, the amendments contained in these regulations replicate provisions in force in other statutory instruments. These regulations will facilitate, upon completion of consolidation, the production of a single, accessible and coherent document, containing provisions relating to scheme claims, payments and control, set out in statutory instruments, applicable to the social welfare code.

Social Welfare (Consolidated Supplementary Welfare Allowance) (Amendment) (No. 2) (Miscellaneous Provisions) Regulations 2006 [S.I. No. 572 of 2006] —These regulations provide for amendments to the conditions for entitlement to rent supplement payable under the supplementary welfare allowance scheme. They provide that rent supplement may not be payable in cases where a housing authority is not satisfied that the accommodation meets the standards for rented houses as provided for in regulations made under the Housing (Miscellaneous Provisions) Act 1992.

They also provide that equivalent payments equivalent to disability allowance, invalidity pension or blind pension made by EU Member States and countries with which Ireland has a reciprocal social security agreement will be treated as qualifying payments for the purposes of rent supplement.

The regulations further provide for two technical amendments. The first relates to the provisions governing the diet supplement provided under the supplementary welfare allowance scheme and the second inserts an article relating to the assessment of non-cash benefits previously provided for under separate regulations.

Finally, these regulations also extend the disregard, for the purpose of the means tests for supplementary welfare allowance, of compensation payments made to persons who have contracted Hepatitis C or HIV, who have disabilities caused by Thalidomide or who made applications to the Residential Institutions Redress Board, to include any monies received by way of compensation awarded under the provisions of the Health (Repayment Scheme) Act 2006.

Social Welfare (Temporary Provisions) Regulations 2006 [S.I. No. 580 of 2006] —These regulations provide for the payment of a Christmas bonus to long-term social welfare recipients, equivalent to 100 per cent of their normal weekly payments, subject to a minimum payment of €30.

Social Welfare (Consolidated Payments Provisions) (Amendment) (No. 16) (Early Childcare Supplement) Regulations 2006 [S.I. No. 681 of 2006] —These regulations set out the dates on which the early childcare supplement will be payable for 2007 and subsequent years.

Social Welfare (Consolidated Payments Provisions) (Amendment) (No. 14) (Increase in Rates) Regulations 2006 [S.I. No. 692 of 2006] —These regulations provide for increases in the reduced rates of illness benefit, jobseeker's benefit, health and safety benefit, state pension (contributory), state pension (transition), widow's and widower's (contributory) pension and deserted wife's benefit, in the rates of tapered increases in respect of qualified adults and in the minimum weekly rate of maternity benefit and adoptive benefit. They also provide for an increase in the prescribed amount of weekly income that the spouse or partner of a claimant of jobseeker's benefit, illness benefit, injury benefit and health and safety benefit is permitted to earn without affecting the claimant's entitlement to an increase in respect of a qualified child. They further provide for the disregard of €200 per week in earnings from employment when calculating means for the purposes of the state pension (non-contributory).

Social Welfare (Rent Allowance) (Amendment) Regulations 2006 [S.I. No. 693 of 2006] —These regulations provide for increases in the amount of means disregarded for people affected by the decontrol of rents and the minimum rent for the purposes of the rent allowance scheme with effect from January 2007.

Social Welfare (Occupational Injuries) (Amendment) Regulations 2006 [S.I. No. 694 of 2006]—These regulations provide for increases in the reduced rates of certain occupational injuries benefits.

Social Welfare (Occupational Injuries) (Amendment) (No. 1) (Miscellaneous Provisions) Regulations 2006 [S.I. No. 695 of 2006] —These regulations amend the regulations which govern the occupational injury benefit scheme, in advance of consolidation of occupational injury benefit regulations dating from 1967. They also effect miscellaneous amendments to the Social Welfare (Claims and Payments) Regulations 1952 (S.I. No. 374 of 1952); the Social Welfare (Occupational Injuries) Regulations 1967 (S.I. No. 77 of 1967); the Social Welfare (Claims and Payments) (Amendment) Regulations 1967 (S.I. No. 85 of 1967); and the Social Welfare (Occupational Injuries) (Medical Care) (Regulations) 1967. Article 7 further provides for the imposition of time-limited constraints when making a claim under the occupational injuries benefit scheme in respect of certain prescribed diseases contracted from prescribed occupations or established under an "individual proof" basis.

Social Welfare (Consolidated Payments Provisions) (Amendment) (No. 15) (Absence from State and Imprisonment) Regulations 2006 [S.I. No. 696 of 2006]—These regulations provide for a number of amendments to the Social Welfare (Consolidated Claims and Payments Provisions) Regulations 1994 (as amended) in advance of further consolidation which is due shortly.

Article 2 inserts a new Chapter 2B into Pt 7 of the consolidated regulations to include provision (currently contained in several regulations dating from 1953 to 1993) for instances where payment under certain schemes may be made while the claimant or beneficiary is absent from the State or detained in legal custody.

Social Welfare (Consolidated Supplementary Welfare Allowance) (Amendment) (No. 3) (Rent Supplement Means Disregards) Regulations 2006 [S.I. No. 697 of 2006] —These regulations provide that, in assessing the means of a claimant for rent supplement purposes, claimants of the state pension (contributory), state pension (transition), invalidity pension, widow's (contributory) pension, widower's (contributory) pension, state pension (non-contributory), widow's (non-contributory) pension or widower's (non-contributory) pension, aged 65 or over, will have the difference between their pension payment and the rate of supplementary welfare allowance payable (appropriate to their family circumstances) disregarded.

CASE LAW

During 2006, the High Court handed down two decisions relating to the social welfare code.

In *ESB v Minister for Social, Community and Family Affairs,* High Court, February 21, 2006; [2006] I.E.H.C. 59, an appeal under s.271 of the Social Welfare (Consolidation) Act 1993 was taken against an appeal officer's finding that meter readers working for the ESB were employed under a contract of service as distinct from a contract for services, *i.e.* were employees rather than self-employed contractors. Gilligan J. began by holding that findings of primary fact by an appeals officer should not be set aside unless there was no evidence to support them and that inferences of fact should not be disturbed unless no reasonable tribunal could draw the inference, though a conclusion could be set aside if it adopted a wrong view of the law. After reviewing the evidence and arguments considered by the appeals officer, he concluded that there were significant arguments to be made for and against the proposition that meter readers were employed pursuant to a contract of service and that, on the evidence available to her, the appeals officer was entitled to conclude that they were, in fact, employees. Accordingly he dismissed the appeal.

In the second case, *Power v Minister for Social and Family Affairs,* High Court, February 28, 2006; [2006] I.E.H.C. 170, the plaintiff successfully challenged an attempt by the Department to restrict the terms of an administrative scheme upon which he was relying to part-finance his third level education. This scheme provided payments to persons in receipt of social welfare payments who wished to go on to third level education and, when initially introduced, covered the period of the summer vacations. The plaintiff successfully applied for this allowance in 2002, but in March 2003 he was informed that payments would no longer be made to cover the summer vacations. He argued that, by entering upon the scheme, he reasonably and legitimately expected that the terms and conditions of the scheme would remain essentially unchanged while he was pursuing his course and that it would be unjust for the Minister now to resile from the representation, published in an explanatory booklet, that payments would cover the summer vacations.

According to McMenamin J., two questions arose for consideration. First, could the plaintiff rely upon the doctrine of legitimate expectation? Secondly, if he could, did he satisfy the preconditions for the application of that doctrine as set out by Fennelly J. in *Glencar Exploration plc v Mayo Co. Co.* [2002] 1 I.R. 84 at 162–3, namely:

> "that the public body must have made a statement or adopted a position amounting to a promise or representation, express or implied, as to how it will act in respect of an identifiable area of its activity... Secondly, the representation must be addressed or conveyed either directly or indirectly to an identifiable person or group of persons, affected actually or potentially, in such a way that it forms part of a transaction definitively entered into or a relationship between that person and group and the public authority or that the person or group has acted on the faith of the representation. Thirdly, it must be such as to create an expectation, reasonably entertained by the person or group that the public authority will abide by the representation to the extent that it would be unjust to permit the public authority to resile from it."

After adverting to the fact that the scheme in the instant case was an administrative, non-statutory scheme, McMenamin J. held that the representation in the explanatory booklet that payments would be made during the summer vacation was clear and unequivocal and nor was there anywhere in the booklet any indication that the terms and conditions of the scheme might be liable to change without notice especially to persons who, relying on the scheme, had already embarked upon an undergraduate course in third level education. After noting again that what was in issue here was a non-statutory discretionary power, the judge expressed the view that the proposition that a legitimate expectation will arise *only* if the court thinks that there is no good reason of public policy why it should not, certainly applied to a discretion or power derived from a statute or statutory instrument which is exercisable for the good of the public or a specific section thereof. He also stated that the court must ultimately carry out a balancing exercise between the interest to the claimant and the public interest in the unfettered exercise of the decision-maker's discretion. McMenamin J. went on to hold that the booklet could not be seen as a mere general statement of policy, particularly when taken in conjunction with the application form, and that the relationship in the instant case was more akin to an individualised promise and representation rather than the mere enunciation of a general policy. He also held that the doctrine of legitimate expectation could be relied upon in order to obtain a particular substantive benefit, as distinct from merely the application of a particular procedure, and that, in the instant case, the State had not adduced sufficient evidence to justify a departure from its representation. Summarising his findings, the judge concluded:

> "I consider that the respondent herein issued a statement or adopted a position amounting to a specific promise or representation, express or implied, as to how it would act in respect of an identifiable area of its activity. Furthermore, through the booklet and other material exhibited, the representation was conveyed to an identifiable group of persons, namely those individuals who had entered, obtained the benefit of the scheme, and who were in third level education by the time the decision challenged in these proceedings was adopted. The representation formed part of the transaction definitively entered into by persons who commenced third level education on the basis of representations contained in the booklet. It was reasonable for the first named applicant to conclude that the respondent would abide by the representation to the extent that it would be unjust to permit the respondent to resile therefrom…The first named applicant as a beneficiary of the scheme came within a category of persons who were prevented from otherwise obtaining educational benefit by reason of their socio economic status. On that basis I consider that it would be unjust to permit the respondent to alter the applicants' circumstances once he had committed himself to following a course of third level education on foot of the respondent's representations. The first named applicant has suffered detriment as a consequence of the breach of the commitment entered into by the respondent and on foot thereof he has sustained a loss."

In addition to granting a declaration that the changes made were contrary to the plaintiff's legitimate expectation, the judge also ruled that the plaintiff was entitled to restitution.

Sports Law

DOPING

The work of the Irish Sports Council anti-doping unit continued apace in 2006 as a record number of tests were undertaken. In all, 1,049 tests were carried out in 37 sports, an increase of 87 tests from 2005. Of this total, 892 tests took place under the National Programme and 157 under the Owner Pays system. In addition, 90 alcohol tests were undertaken. Of all these tests, 63 per cent were conducted on an out-of-competition basis. There were two adverse findings resulting in sanction in 2006.

One significant area in which Irish anti-doping policy hit the headlines in 2006 involved the case of track-and-field athlete Gareth Turnbull (the author was professionally involved in this case). Mr Turnbull was accused by the Athletics Association of Ireland of having the banned substance testosterone in his system.

Under the terms of the 2004 Irish anti-doping rules, where the ratio of testosterone to epitestosterone in an athlete's system is greater than 4:1, this is a trigger for further investigation. There are also further indicators of exogenous administration of testosterone, including the ratio between the level of testosterone and the level of luteinizing hormone and the simple level of testosterone in the athlete's system, although it is accepted that the two ratios mentioned are more accurate indicators than the simple level of the substance in the system. Most significantly, there is also a scientific test known as the IRMS test which will be undertaken where there is deemed to be a need for further investigation. A positive IRMS test can be regarded as categorical proof that testosterone has been exogenously administered; however, a negative test is not categorical proof that the testosterone is endogenously produced.

In any event, in order for a positive test for testosterone to be recorded, it will be necessary to determine that the level of the substance in the athlete's system is so outside the range of values normally found in humans that it is unlikely to be consistent with normal endogenous production. If the governing body proves this to the comfortable satisfaction of the relevant panel, then the athlete is entitled to adduce evidence to the effect that the high level of recorded testosterone was attributable to a physiological or pathological condition. In this respect, it should be noted that there is research indicating that a number of diverse factors can in theory lead to a temporary increase in the natural production of testosterone.

In the present case the athlete's T/E ratio was in excess of the 4:1 level, yet below the 6:1 level which, only two years previously, had been the standard used in the prohibited list. His T/LH ratio was normal, but his testosterone level was in excess of what the World Anti-Doping Agency standards classified as being normal. Two IRMS tests were performed on his sample, both of which produced negative results. Nonetheless, the Irish Sports Council Expert Advisory Group concluded that the level of testosterone in the athlete's system was unlikely to be consistent with natural production, and thus he was accused of having committed a doping offence.

A good deal of scientific and other evidence was adduced by both sides at the hearing, at which the Irish Sports Council was a notice party. In its determination, the anti-doping disciplinary panel found that whereas the Athletics Association of Ireland had satisfied its burden of showing that the level of testosterone in the athlete's system was unlikely to be consistent with natural production of the substance, equally the athlete had proved that, on the balance of probabilities, the positive testosterone test was the result of the fact that his normal and natural production of testosterone had been increased by reason of the fact that the night before his test (which had occurred early in the morning) he had consumed a considerable amount of alcohol.

Finally, in March 2007 the ISC announced that it would be reviewing the Irish anti-doping rules to consider allowing for the possibility that athletes who are unsuccessfully prosecuted under the terms of the rules might be given their costs incurred in defending themselves. Moreover, in the current case Mr Turnbull would be allowed his costs, prior to any such rule change.

EUROPEAN COURT OF JUSTICE AND DOPING

Beyond the specifically Irish dimension of the doping issue, of particular note is the decision of the European Court of Justice in *Meca-Medina v EC Commission* (Case C-519/04) [2006] I.S.L.R. 175. In this case the applicants, who had been professional long-distance swimmers, had been banned for four years by FINA (the international swimming federation) having tested positive for the banned substance nandrolone. This suspension was reduced to a two-year period by the Court of Arbitration for Sport.

Nandrolone, like testosterone, is a substance which is produced naturally, but whose exogenous administration is prohibited. In order to take account of the possibility that an apparently increased showing for nandrolone might be the result of endogenous production, the practice in laboratories was that a positive showing for nandrolone would be one where the threshold of 2ng/ml of urine was passed.

The applicants appealed their case to the European Commission and thence to the Court of First Instance and eventually the ECJ, alleging *inter alia*:

- that the rules on nandrolone were scientifically unfounded;
- that the general strict liability nature of the anti-doping rules were intrinsically unfair;
- that the bodies enforcing anti-doping rules (including CAS) were unfairly linked with the prosecuting bodies.

For these reasons it was argued that the rules as they affected the applicants were in violation of Arts 49, 81 and 82 of the EC Treaty.

The ECJ found against the applicants. In essence this was because at the time of the impugned test (1999) the level of scientific knowledge on the nandrolone issue was sufficiently undeveloped that a 2ng/ml threshold was regarded as being a reasonable one. This is in itself a significant conclusion in that it implies that the scientific standards by which people are judged must live up to the existing state of scientific knowledge—or to put it another way, it implies that the rules in question must be adequately scientifically based. Indeed it is precisely one of the criticisms that have been made of the rules in respect of testosterone (that applied in the Gareth Turnbull case) that the standards and rules that apply are not adequately scientifically based.

Even more significantly, however, the court rejected the conclusion reached by the European Commission and the Court of First Instance that anti-doping rules fell into those categories of sporting rules that were outside of the ambit of EC law. Previously it had been held (*inter alia* by the CFI in this case) that in as much as anti-doping rules were not specifically economic in nature (in the way that, for instance, ticketing or salary rules were) they were not subject to community law, but rather fell into what has been termed the "sporting exception" to EC law. The ECJ, however, emphatically concluded that anti-doping rules *were* subject to EC law. Thus it was held that:

> "In light of all of these considerations, it is apparent that the mere fact that a rule is purely sporting in nature does not have the effect of removing from the scope of the Treaty the person engaging in the activity governed by that rule or the body which has laid it down.
>
> If the sporting activity in question falls within the scope of the Treaty, the conditions for engaging in it are then subject to all the obligations which result from the various provisions of the Treaty. It follows that the rules which govern that activity must satisfy the requirements of those provisions, which, in particular, seek to ensure freedom of movement for workers, freedom of establishment, freedom to provide services, or competition.
>
> Thus, where engagement in the sporting activity must be assessed in the light of the Treaty provisions relating to freedom of movement for workers or freedom to provide services, it will be necessary to determine whether the rules which govern that activity satisfy the requirements of

Articles 39 EC and 49 EC, that is to say do not constitute restrictions prohibited by those articles (*Deliège*, paragraph 60).

Likewise, where engagement in the activity must be assessed in the light of the Treaty provisions relating to competition, it will be necessary to determine, given the specific requirements of Articles 81 EC and 82 EC, whether the rules which govern that activity emanate from an undertaking, whether the latter restricts competition or abuses its dominant position, and whether that restriction or that abuse affects trade between Member States.

Therefore, even if those rules do not constitute restrictions on freedom of movement because they concern questions of purely sporting interest and, as such, have nothing to do with economic activity (*Walrave and Koch* and *Donà*), that fact means neither that the sporting activity in question necessarily falls outside the scope of Articles 81 EC and 82 EC nor that the rules do not satisfy the specific requirements of those articles."

This is naturally a most significant conclusion as far as the whole of global anti-doping policy is concerned. After all, it had previously been the case that the sole arbiters of the legitimacy of anti-doping rules (including the legitimacy of the strict liability approach of anti-doping policy, the excessive nature of sanctions and so on) were disciplinary panels of the relevant governing body and ultimately the Court of Arbitration for Sport. It has been suggested (*inter alia* in this case), moreover, that in neither context is there likely to be a genuinely neutral approach taken to doping cases, in that CAS has consistently upheld the legitimacy of anti-doping policy by reference to the needs of that policy. (Thus, for example, it has upheld the strict liability nature of anti-doping rules on the basis that absent such strict liability it would be difficult if not impossible for anti-doping policy to function properly.) Now, however, it would appear that such rules are also subject to the jurisdiction of a body that is absolutely independent of sport and which, indeed, in *Bosman* (C-415/93, [1995] E.C.R. I 4921) completely revolutionised European sport through the use of EC law.

From the standpoint of the Irish anti-doping rules, this essentially means that the legitimacy of such rules are now to be determined by serious external standards. It is perhaps a criticism of these rules that they are created by sports authorities to ensure that anti-doping policy moves as speedily and efficiently as possible *for such authorities* and with little concern for the rights and interests of individual sportspeople who, like Gareth Turnbull, might conceivably be inaccurately accused of doping offences. It is doubtful whether this approach will sit easily with the ECJ as it comes to analyse issues such as the strict liability nature of the rules and the mandatory two-year suspension even for an accidental positive test.

CRIMINAL LAW

In July 2006 a footballer who punched a referee in the head, thereby rendering him unconscious, was sentenced to six months in jail. The defendant, Ian Buckley, was found to have assaulted the referee in the 82nd minute of a West Waterford/East Cork junior league game at Bridesbridge on October 16, 2005, when the referee refused to award a free kick for a tackle on the defendant. The defendant had paid some €1,000 in compensation to the referee and had attended anger management counselling, yet still received a significant custodial sentence despite the fact that he was a first-time offender.

Giving judgment, Patwell J. said that violence on the sports field should be treated as a criminal act. Drawing an analogy with the actions of the French soccer captain Zinedine Zidane who had earlier that month been sent off in the FIFA World Cup Final for head-butting an opponent, Patwell J. is reported to have said:

> "Whether it is you or a French man playing in the World Cup, to assault another person is reprehensible…The macho image attached to sport will not be taken out unless these incidents are treated as a criminal act. If charges are brought against players then there might be a lot less of this kind of thing."

Finally, in November 2006, Shelbourne FC Chief Executive Ollie Byrne escaped conviction and a charge of assault against him was struck out after he apologised to former Shamrock Rovers manager Roddy Collins and pleaded guilty to assaulting him at Tolka Park shortly before a Shelbourne/Shamrock Rovers match in June of 2005. According to Mr Byrne in reply to a question from Coughlan J., he (Byrne) had been listening to the radio at home and had heard Mr Collins making scurrilous remarks about the financial situation at Shelbourne. When he got to Tolka Park the first person he saw was Mr Collins and he snapped, and that was the reason why he assaulted Mr Collins. Mr Collins accepted that Mr Byrne had apologised and said that it was regrettable that the matter had come to court, in that he had known Mr Byrne for 15 years and that the latter was "a good man". Coughlan J. said that in light of Mr Collins's attitude, he would strike out the charge.

TORT LAW

In February 2006 a former soccer player (and Chairman of Donegal County Council) was awarded €9,000 in damages against the Football Association of Ireland by Donegal District Court for pain and injury suffered when caustic lime which had been used to mark a soccer pitch came in contact with his testicles and inner thighs. On the day on which the injury was suffered there had been a good deal of rain and the court concluded that as a result of the heavy rain the plaintiff had come in contact with the substance which caused serious (and, so the court concluded, embarrassing) burns. Flanagan J. held that the onus was on the defendants to ensure that players were warned to take precautions to avoid the inherent risks deriving from the state of the premises.

In 2006 the Privacy Bill was published which, if passed, would provide celebrities with something of a vehicle to be used to protect their privacy from unwarranted intrusion. This may be an important weapon in the fight used by sportspeople against what might be termed unwarranted and unwanted character merchandising.

In addition, in 2006 the Circuit Court awarded a Carlow GAA player €6,500 for breach of privacy, negligence and intentional infliction of emotional distress arising out of the publication in the sports supplement of the Carlow Nationalist Newspaper of a photograph of the plaintiff in which his private parts were visible. The decision was upheld in the High Court in January 2007 with Budd J. commenting: "Roll on the press council".

ADMINISTRATIVE LAW

In March 2007, Edward Griffin, formerly a manager of a Cork schoolboys' soccer team, lost a High Court challenge seeking leave to judicially review a decision taken by the Cork schoolboys' league (February 2005) and affirmed by the Schoolboys' Football Association of Ireland to prohibit him from all football activity for 20 years for allegedly punching a referee in the face after an under-11s' cup match. Mr Griffin strenuously denied assaulting the referee and claimed that he was denied natural justice in relation to how the ban was imposed, and also contended that the ban itself was unfair and unreasonable. Charleton J. rejected the application, saying that whereas the dispute was a serious one, the schoolboys' leagues were not statutory bodies and the source of their powers did not come from the legislature; rather, any agreement between the parties was in the contractual sphere. Moreover, whereas the league's disciplinary procedures could be seen as being unfair, they were not deliberately unfair. Finally, Charleton J. held that, whereas the consequences of the ban were serious, Mr Griffin had not lost his job.

A couple of points may, perhaps, be made about this decision. First, there is an ongoing uncertainty as to whether non-statutory sporting bodies may, nonetheless, be regarded as being sufficiently public to be the focus of judicial proceedings, and particularly since the decisions in cases like *Geoghegan v Institute of Chartered Accountants in Ireland* [1995] 3 I.R. 86, in which the courts have been prepared to allow non-statutory bodies that clearly perform public functions to be judicially reviewable. The most recent statement on this issue (albeit *obiter dicta*) was given in *Bolger v Osborne* [2000] 1 I.L.R.M. 250 in which Macken J. suggested that even non-statutory sports bodies might be judicially reviewable.

Secondly, and whereas naturally the significance of what is at stake will go to determine the level of fair procedures that must be applied in any case, nonetheless it is perhaps instructive to have regard to the comments of McMahon J. in *Barry & Rogers v Ginnity*, Circuit Court, April 13, 2005 to the effect that where sport is concerned there are interests and rights involved which may often not be measurable in economic terms and may indeed have no economic component to them. Thus, the judge commented that:

> "Clearly, if a player's livelihood is at stake, or if he/she is deprived of the opportunity of competing for a high honour which opportunity may not present itself again or will only be available at some distant date, the court might well be moved to entertain a complaint. Further, it should not be thought that the court's vigilance will be activated only when the member's right to earn a livelihood or other economic interest is threatened. 'Significant' or 'serious', should not be defined only in terms of economic values. It must be noted that there are many people involved in the management and administration of sporting organisations throughout the country who are not motivated by economic gain, but who are inspired by other ideals and by a sense of community good. Such persons may spend many years of their lives as treasurers or as secretaries of their local clubs, devoting their energies and talents to acquiring playing fields, building community halls in their localities and, generally, dedicating themselves to generation after generation of the young people in their communities. Their contribution to society is enormous, doing community work of inestimable value and contributing not only to the health of our young people, but also, in a very real sense, discouraging criminal and anti-social behaviour. Such persons may have dedicated substantial parts of their lives to these commendable endeavours, and expulsion from the association or organisation to which they belong, in such circumstances, might well have a sufficiently serious effect on the person's reputation and standing in the community, and his own self-esteem, to move the courts to intervene. It would be regrettable indeed, if the court confined its concern only to those situations where economic interests were threatened. In determining the occasions when the court will exercise its role in this regard little more can be usefully be said at this juncture."

In *JRM Sports Ltd t/a Limerick Football Club v Football Association of Ireland* [2007] I.E.H.C. 67, the applicants sought an interlocutory injunction either requiring the respondents to permit the applicants to play in the league of Ireland for the 2007 season or, in the alternative, restraining them from permitting any other team to play in their stead. The applicants had previously secured an interim order in this regard from Peart J.

The background to the case involved the concerted efforts by the FAI after it had taken control of the management of what had been the Eircom league, to ensure greater professionalism in the manner in which that league was run. This in turn involved a tightening of the administration processes within the league (to which all of the clubs in the league had signed up) whereby clubs would need to secure licences to play in the league and would also need to fulfil certain criteria in order to obtain such licences. As a result of its failure in this regard, Limerick City were refused a licence and thus faced the possibility of being denied a place in the league for the 2007 season. It was in respect of this refusal to issue them with a licence that the interlocutory relief was sought.

Clarke J. rejected the claims of the applicants. He confirmed that the new procedures were in effect a term of the contract between the FAI and the various clubs in the league. Moreover, in the present case, the procedures were not "couched in legalese, jargon or technical terms" and hence were readily understandable by persons other than lawyers involved in the running of the league. Put simply, the failure by the applicants to fulfil the procedures was essentially their own fault, nor would it be appropriate to grant injunctive relief in this regard. Moreover, and whereas there may well be an obligation of fair procedures implied into the contract, there was no doubt that the FAI had complied with such obligation, not least because it was the applicants who were at fault in the matter.

Clarke J. accepted that it was not open to him to analyse the merits of the decision to refuse the licence to Limerick FC, save by reference to the onerous test for irrationality laid down in *O'Keefe v An Bord Pleanála*. Thus he concluded that:

> "Even if that contract is taken to bring with it an obligation to act procedurally in a fair manner, the contract makes it clear that the body that is to decide on the merits as to whether a club is to receive a licence is the FAI and its appropriate committees and appeal boards and not the Court. I want to make it perfectly clear that in accordance with the long established jurisprudence of this Court it is not for the Court to consider whether the view taken by either the licensing committee or the appeal board was harsh, went too far, was harsher than perhaps had been applied in previous years. Those are matters for the FAI and its appropriately designated committees and boards. They are not for the Court. This is not an appeal to the Court. The Court has no role in deciding the merits or otherwise of who should be licensed."

Moreover, in terms of the *O'Keefe* test, Clarke J. concluded that there was ample evidence before the relevant committee that would have justified it in coming to the decision to which it came, and there was nothing in the process that was adopted by the committee that would justify the court in striking down its decision.

Most significantly, Clarke J. also looked to the basic principles that should apply where an interlocutory injunction was sought in respect of a decision of a sports governing body, and in particular to the question of where the balance of convenience in such a case would lie. It has been noted in previous editions of the *Annual Review of Irish Law* that it had become a relatively common practice for sportspeople who, as a result of disciplinary infractions, were suspended for a period of time in which a major sporting event was to take place, to seek an interlocutory injunction in respect of that suspension and, because of the comparative ease by which such relief would be obtained, it was entirely common that in such circumstances the relief would be granted, the suspension lifted and the sportsperson permitted to take part in the event in question. Naturally this was very frustrating for the governing bodies involved and, indeed, it was one of the primary reasons behind the creation by the GAA of its Disputes Resolution Authority.

In such cases there had also been something of an assumption that, provided a stateable case could be made by the applicant, the balance of convenience would favour the grant of the interlocutory injunction. After all, so it was argued, if the relief was not granted (and if the applicant was shown at full hearing to have been in the right) then s/he would have unjustly been denied the opportunity to take part in an event that might be of huge national (and commercial) significance, whereas if it was granted (and if at full hearing the governing body was shown to have been in the right), it would still be able to suspend the sportsperson at a later date.

In *JRM Sports Ltd v FAI*, however, Clarke J. took a rather more holistic and, it is submitted, a more appropriate view of what was at stake. Thus, in assessing the issue of balance of convenience, he concluded as follows:

> "Under this heading what I need to consider is the relative consequences of, on the one hand, giving Limerick an injunction and it turning out, when there has been a full hearing, that it was wrongly given, or on the other hand refusing Limerick FC an injunction and it turning out after a full hearing that the club was entitled to it. In that context I do take into account and agree with what is said in the final affidavit sworn in these proceedings by Mr. Drew of Limerick FC where he draws, legitimately in my view, attention to the fact that there is more than simple commerce involved in running a football team and that there are interests at stake which go beyond the commercial interests of a company running a football team. I think there is no doubt that that is true and it is an appropriate consideration to be taken into account by any Court that is faced with a dispute arising in a sporting context. While many sports, and certainly all professional sports, have commercial interests involved, there are also many other interests involved which go beyond the commerce. Indeed, even commercial entities in the sporting field frequently are principally there not for the purposes of

making money but because of a love of the particular sport concerned.
It seems to me that that consideration also applies to a body, such as
the FAI, which is charged with attempting to promote and manage a
sport not only for an individual club but for all other clubs and all of
those who have an interest in the sport concerned. A significant weight
has to be attached in any balancing which the Court has to engage in
under the balance of convenience to allowing major sporting bodies to
get on with the job of administering the sport with whose governance
they are charged. That is not to say that such bodies are above the law.
Clearly if they have been in breach of their legal obligations then the
Court must intervene. However in considering whether it is appropriate
to interfere, on a temporary basis, with what would otherwise be the
proper administration of the sport concerned then it seems to me that
the Court has to regard any such significant interference as a matter
of importance. This will be so particularly where the interference will
have more than a minimal short term effect. If every time a party was
able to pass the relatively low threshold of suggesting that it had a legal
case against a sporting body and was able to interfere with the way in
which that sporting body carried out the management of the sport on that
basis it is likely that the administration of major sports would grind to a
halt. Therefore, it seems to me, that the Court has to place a significant
weight in the balance of convenience on factors such as the overall
effect of the giving of the order sought on the proper administration of
the sport concerned.

In this case it seems to me clear that what is, in substance, being
sought is a mandatory order. Limerick does not have a licence. It says
that it should have a licence and it wants to persuade the Court that
the Court should direct that it get a licence. But the fact is that by
intervening at this stage the Court would be imposing on the FAI an
obligation either to let Limerick in and allow it play in the current season
contrary to what (in the FAI's view and it is, on the evidence, at least a
sustainable view) is in accordance with the best interests of the sport.
To impose that is not simply a matter of no consequence. It means that
the league has to go ahead for an entire season on a basis which those
charged with managing the league has decided is not the way in which
it should go ahead. In those circumstances, even if I had been satisfied
that there was a fair issue to be tried, I would not have been prepared
to grant an interlocutory injunction because it seems to me the balance
of convenience would have been against it."

Naturally, there was more at stake as far as the governing body was concerned
in this case than would normally be the case, for example, where a disciplinary
measure is challenged in the court. After all, as Clarke J. pointed out, to grant
an interlocutory injunction in this case would have been to throw the whole

operation of the league of Ireland into chaos for the 2007 season. Equally, in other cases, it is submitted that the comments of Clarke J. may still be apposite. A sports governing body's rules are pivotal to the successful operation of a sporting league, be they administrative or disciplinary rules. There is a danger that easy access to interlocutory relief by which the suspended sportsperson patently flaunted such rules would lead to the spirit, existence and operation of such rules being radically undermined, and this in turn would undermine the league itself. This was arguably a factor which did not register with sufficient clarity in the analysis of where the balance of convenience lay in certain cases.

GAA DISPUTES RESOLUTION AUTHORITY

In the *Annual Review 2005* we considered the significance of the coming into being of the Disputes Resolution Authority of the GAA (the DRA). Throughout 2006 this arbitral authority continued to hear a wide range of matters and thus to prevent disputes within the GAA from being determined by the civil courts. Moreover, in 2006 for the first time the authority (as it is entitled to do under its rules) approved settlements (see for example DRA 37/2006).

Naturally this authority does not create precedents; nonetheless, there is an increasing tendency on the part of persons presenting cases before the DRA to refer to previous decisions of the authority. In this respect, the following broad principles appear to have emerged from the second year of the authority's work:

- In order to avail of the DRA facility, applicants must exhaust internal remedies. Equally this requirement will only apply where there are genuinely available avenues of appeal (DRA 26/27/28/2006).

- Despite the fact that this is an arbitral process, the procedural rules that apply are to be followed. Thus, for example, a claim which, without good reason, is filed outside of the permitted deadline will not be heard (DRA 14/2006).

- One of the primary bases for challenging a decision of a unit of the association is that it has not acted in accordance with the rules of the association. Equally, minor procedural defects in application of rules will not lead to a decision being set aside (DRA 1/2006).

- The DRA has accepted that, under Irish law, it is fully permissible for the GAA authorities to have substantial discretion within its own rules in terms of how such rules are to be applied (DRA 1/2006). Indeed this is implicit in the decision of McMahon J. in the oft-cited case *Barry & Rogers v Ginnity*.

- The costs involved in such hearings follow the event (DRA 17/2006, DRA 19/2006). Moreover (and in a change from the approach in 2005 (DRA

2/2005) it would seem that costs will be awarded against unsuccessful applicants irrespective of their age or position (DRA 19/2006). On the other hand, it would seem that costs can be awarded to a claimant where the respondent's decision is unfairly made, even where the same decision could have been reached fairly and was, in fact, the correct one (DRA 4/5/2006).

Torts

DUTY OF CARE

In the *Annual Review of Irish Law 2001*, pp. 596-599, we critically analysed Morris P.'s judgment in *Wildgust v Bank of Ireland*, High Court, August 17, 2001. The claim was one for negligent misstatement. Mr and Mrs Wildgust had effected life policies on each of their lives with the second respondent, Norwich Union Life Insurance Society. Mr Wildgust's company had purchased properties with loan facilities from Hill Samuel Bank Ltd. The life policies had been assigned by mortgage to Hill Samuel. Mr. Wildgust's company held an account with the Bank of Ireland and an arrangement was made for the payment by way of direct debits from that account for the premiums on the life policies. The mortgage assignment required Mr Wildgust to keep up these premiums. When on one occasion a monthly premium was not paid, the Norwich Union notified Hill Samuel. The relevant manager (after a communication with Mr Wildgust that is not of direct significance to the holding in the case) contacted Hill Samuel. He was aware that, at this time, Mrs Wildgust was seriously ill. The manager received a clear assurance that the policy was "correct and in order". In fact it had lapsed. The manager, on the basis of this assurance, did not make a payment to restore the policy, as was the practice of banks in respect of policies mortgaged to them by way of security. When Mrs Wildgust died, Norwich Union refused to pay on the lapsed policy. Mr Wildgust's claim for negligent misstatement against Norwich Union fell for consideration by Morris P. and, an appeal, by the Supreme Court. Morris P. dismissed the claim.

The Supreme Court unanimously reversed Morris P. The reason why Morris P. had rejected the claim was that the representations made by Norwich Union to Hill Samuel's manager had not been relied upon by Mr Wildgust, who was not aware of it. (Mr. Wildgust had innocently believed that a payment he had made had resolved the problem.) Morris P. was of the view that the misstatement had 'in no way influenced or contributed towards' Mr Wildgust's conduct; it had not caused him to act to his detriment. To impose a duty on the defendant for the benefit of the plaintiff in these circumstances would constitute a "massive extension of a *prima facie* duty of care", which Brennan J. in *Sutherland Shire Council v Heyman* [1985] 157 C.L.R. 424 had deprecated.

In the Supreme Court, there was no concern that imposing a duty of care in the circumstances of the case would have unacceptably broad implications. Geoghegan J. emphasised that it must have been clear to Norwich Union that the plaintiff would suffer damage if its statement about the policy was not correct. He was a customer of Norwich Union who had a beneficial interest in the equity of redemption of the policy:

> "Put shortly, Mr. Wildgust was a 'neighbour' for the purposes of the law of negligence and a specially close one at that. There is no question here of the respondent being liable to large numbers of perhaps unknown persons."

In similar terms, Kearns J. stated:

> "It would be absurd to treat Hill Samuel as though it had in some way itself become the sole insured under the policy so as to exclude Mr. Wildgust from the very limited category of persons with an interest in the transaction. It would equally have been well within the understanding of the respondents that Hill Samuel, as a merchant bank in the business of lending money, was holding the policy by way of security subject always to Mr. Wildgust's equity of redemption. They were thus, in my view, both 'neighbours' in the legal sense to whom a duty was owed."

In these circumstances, Mr Wildgust should not be deprived of a remedy because the communication had been made to only one of two neighbours where one or other could and would have acted to prevent the loss. Kearns J found inspiration from what Lord Goff of Chieveley had said in *Spring v Guardian Insurance plc* [1995] 2 A.C. 296, in the context of an employment reference. Kearns J. observed:

> "From the foregoing it is apparent that I favour an interpretation, or adaption if needs be, of the *Hedley Byrne* principles which would include more than just the person to whom the negligent misstatement is addressed. The 'proximity' test in respect of a negligent misstatement in my view must go further than that and include persons in a limited and identifiable class when the maker of the statement can reasonably expect, in the context of a particular inquiry, that reliance will be placed thereon by such person or persons to act or not act in a particular manner in relation to that transaction. As I accept the submission of plaintiff's counsel that Mr. Wildgust and Hill Samuel had virtually an identical interest in preserving the policy and that both formed such an identifiable class, either of whom could have acted to prevent Mr. Wildgust's loss, I believe it is just and reasonable to ascribe to the respondents a duty of care with regard to Mr. Wildgust in such circumstances. In a nutshell, I would interpret *Hedley Byrne* in the light of what was stated in *Caparo* on the facts of this case.
>
> I am far from convinced that to so hold represents any major extension of the principles in *Hedley Byrne v Heller* ..."

The Supreme Court decision in *Wildgust* is to be welcomed. Justice surely cried out for an award of compensation on the facts of the case. If *Glencar* had the effect of denying compensation, it would have been an engine of serious injustice. It is interesting that Geoghegan J., in his reference to *Glencar*, characterised as *obiter dicta* Keane C.J.'s endorsement of the three-step test for determining the duty of care which the House of Lords had set out in *Caparo Industries v Dickman*. If Keane C.J.'s endorsement of *Caparo* has only the status of *obiter dicta*, where does that leave McCarthy J.'s two-step test in *Ward v McMaster*? Keane C.J. in *Glencar*, somewhat surprisingly, characterised McCarthy J.'s test as having only *obiter* status: see our analysis in the *Annual Review of Irish Law 2001*, pp. 554-574.

It would be a bold litigant who proceeded on the basis that he or she could convince the court to restore the two-step test to its former predominance on the basis that its rejection in *Glencar* had only *obiter* status. It is noteworthy that in *Wildgust* Kearns J., having quoted Keane C.J.'s rendition in *Glencar* of the three-step test, referred it as "[t]his most authoritative recent statement of the law in relation to the general duty of care in Negligence ...".

In *Gaffey v Dundalk Town Council* [2006] I.E.H.C. 436, a nine-year-old boy was injured when playing football on a grassed open space near his home. A fire hydrant was located in the grass. Its lid had been removed by an unknown person and the boy's leg caught in the hole, resulting in a fracture to his ankle. The lid has been "frequently" removed and left on the grass but the Town Council had not been notified of these occurrences.

The plaintiff's claim for negligence concentrated on the location of the hydrant rather than its design. It was argued that it should have been placed on the road. The evidence against this was to the effect that vehicles parked over it could obstruct easy access for the fire services and that the constant passing of cars over the lid, which was of lightweight design, could deform it and render it difficult to remove in an emergency.

Peart J. evinced little hesitation in dismissing the claim. He referred to *Whooley v Dublin Corporation* [1960] I.R. 60, the facts of which were similar, and to *Kavanagh v Cork Corporation*, Doyle's Personal Injuries Reports: Hilary and Easter Terms 1994, p.78) where Keane J. had stated that:

> "a fire hydrant, of its nature, has to be readily and quickly accessible to the fire brigade, or anyone else who has to make use of it rapidly in order to deal with an emergency. That is the whole point of it and, consequently, to have them locked in any way would obviously be more dangerous than the dangers caused by the sort of vandalism apparently common in parts of the city ...".

Peart J. was satisfied that the hydrant in the instant case had been designed in a way which, necessarily, facilitated easy access to emergency services. It could not reasonably and safely have been placed on the road. It was not reasonable to expect that the defendant should have anticipated and guarded against the possibility that the lid would regularly be removed from the hydrant and left on the adjoining grass, thereby exposing playing children to a hazard. If the defendant had been notified that the lid was being removed and left off the hydrant, then the court would have had to consider how that might have altered the situation.

Peart J.'s analysis is interesting in the ease with which it merges considerations relating to the standard of care with those regarding the duty of care. The standard of care is premised on the existence of a duty of care resting on the defendant relative to the plaintiff. It assesses the reasonableness or otherwise of the defendant's conduct in the light of four factors: the likelihood of injury occurring; the gravity of the threatened injury if it did occur; the social utility (or lack of social benefit) of the defendant's act and the social or economic cost of preventing the injury. This is the test that was applied in *Whooley v Dublin Corporation* and *Kavanagh v Cork Corporation*. It is well capable of addressing complex issues of a social and economic character where the arguments are finely balanced. The need for public authorities to have an effective system for access by fire fighters to water; the costs involved in monitoring 2500 fire hydrants in Dundalk; the impossibility of preventing malicious interference by vandals—all of these factors could be balanced under the rubric of the standard of care.

The duty of care presents a more formidable conceptual challenge. While it focuses on the particular factual details of the case before the court, it requires the court to approach the question in somewhat broader categorical terms. Thus, in the instant case, the fact that the defendant was a public authority assumes greater significance. The particular facts are seen as raising larger questions about the scope of the duty of care of public authorities under the restrictive test set out in *Glencar Exploration Co v Mayo County Council* [2002] 1 I.R. 84. It will be recalled that, in *Glencar*, the Supreme Court required a plaintiff seeking to establish a duty of care, to prove not only that there was a proximity of relationship between the parties and that there were no policy considerations negativing the imposition of such a duty, but also that it was just and reasonable to impose the duty. These three hurdles must be successfully negotiated by a plaintiff in order to establish *the very existence*, let alone the *breach*, of a duty of care.

In the instant case, Peart J., having referred to the *Glencar* test, concluded that the plaintiff passed the first requirement, of proximity of relationship. If, contrary to his view of the facts, the injury sustained by the plaintiff was reasonably foreseeable, the plaintiff should be considered to have passed the second requirement also, since "there might not exist such a compelling public policy consideration as should deny the plaintiff recovery of compensation". In Peart J.'s opinion, however, the plaintiff failed *Glencar's* third requirement, that it be just and reasonable to impose a duty of care:

"In this respect, the evidence that there are 2500 such hydrants in the town is important, as is the uncontested fact that neither the plaintiff's father, nor anybody else had never notified the Council of the fact that the lid of this hydrant was being removed thereby causing a danger to children playing on the grassed area.

It would also be relevant to consider the nature and purpose of the statutory power being exercised by the local authority in placing the hydrant where it is located. In the present case the Council are clearly obliged to place hydrants sufficiently close to houses in the area so that the fire services can be effective in an emergency. Such a duty is an important one, given the capacity for a fire to cause loss of life and serious injury. The design of the lid facilitates the easy access to the water supply in such an emergency. That would need to be balanced against the risk of possible injury by placing the hydrant on this grassed area.

It cannot be reasonable for the Council to have imposed upon it a duty to ensure that the lids are at all times in place on hydrants in the town—the more so in the absence of any information being given to them that lids are being removed. The Council has in place a system of inspection of hydrants on a routine basis to ensure that they are in working order, but it quite unreal to expect that they could inspect all these installations on a daily basis … [T]here is no evidence that the hydrants are inherently dangerous or dangerously located. It requires the mischievous act of an intervening party to create the hazard."

One sees here the difference between the two approaches. A duty of care analysis is broad, categorical and general in its application; a standard of care analysis involves a more delicate, individuated balancing of policies. In the instant case, Peart J. found, that a duty of care should not be imposed and that there had not been a breach of the duty of care. The defendant thus succeeded. But what of a case involving a public authority where the duty of care analysis indicates that no duty of care should be imposed but the standard of care analysis indicates that the defendant has been negligent? The duty of care question is logically anterior to that of the standard of care since no tortious sanction attaches to negligent conduct, in the sense of conduct in which a reasonable person would not engage, where the actor is under no duty of care to the plaintiff.

Lewis v Bus Éireann—Irish Bus [2006] I.E.H.C. 429 raises an issue of general principle disguised in somewhat mundane facts. The plaintiff was involved in an altercation when travelling on a bus from Dundalk to Drogheda. He sought to be left off the bus at a point between stops (as other passengers had been, on his evidence, though this was denied by the driver). The driver declined and requested the plaintiff to give him the can of beer he was carrying. The plaintiff refused and became verbally abusive as well as emptying the remaining contents of the can around the back of the driver's seat and on the floor of the bus. The driver told the plaintiff that he was calling the Gardaí to meet the bus; the plaintiff returned to his seat. When the bus arrived in Drogheda, the plaintiff ran into the depot, pursued by the driver. He sustained a very severe injury to his knee when his knee came in contact with the ground. The plaintiff claimed that two people had climbed onto his back. The driver acknowledged that he had pursued the plaintiff but said that the plaintiff had simply fallen without contact.

Peart J. rejected as unlikely the plaintiff's explanation. The plaintiff was not in good health at the time of the incident; he was about to commence recovery from an addiction to heroin, had hepatitis C and liver damage and had been drinking before and while on the bus. In Peart J.'s view, it was "improbable ... that he would have made it as far as beyond the second set of swinging doors in the depot with one man on his back, let alone two". Peart J. deprecated the absence of orthopaedic evidence which could have thrown light on whether such a serious injury as the plaintiff had sustained could have been caused by a simple fall. He continued:

> "The Court cannot resolve the conflict of evidence as to whether [the driver] was on the plaintiff's back or not. But whether he was, or not, he was undoubtedly in hot pursuit of the plaintiff when he need not have been. I do not overlook also the fact that the plaintiff was essentially fleeing not from [the driver] but from the gardaí who he had every reason to believe would be upon him very quickly. So, to that extent he may have tripped and fallen in any event, even if [the driver] was not in pursuit. But he was and need not have been in such pursuit, and in my view ought not to have been. I am prepared to find that this needless pursuit contributed significantly to the fall of the plaintiff, even though it is likely in my view that the plaintiff is inaccurate in his recollection of the events or may even be exaggerating what occurred ...
>
> I therefore find that the defendant, its servant or agent was negligent on this occasion, even if from a public spirit point of view he can be commended for unnecessarily pursuing the plaintiff so that he would be available to the arriving gardaí. He exposed even himself to some risks in these events."

Peart J. reduced the award by 50 per cent to take account of the plaintiff's contributory negligence.

The finding of liability in negligence against the driver in pursuing the plaintiff may come as a surprise. Earlier in his judgment, Peart J. had addressed this issue as follows:

> "The plaintiff was a sick man... He was a weak man through his abuse of drugs and it is beyond doubt that he was under the influence of alcohol

on this date to add to his difficulties. There can never have been any prospect of his escaping from the gardaí for any length of time. I am sure they were so near the depot when the bus arrived. Nevertheless, [the driver] decided to pursue him rather then run the risk that he might get away before the gardaí arrived. He need not have done that. He is a bus driver, and while I fully accept that he acted in the public interest and so that the gardaí would be able to interview him arising out of the behaviour on the bus, it must be remembered that the incident on the bus was relatively minor. Nobody was hurt, I am not for one moment condoning the plaintiff's behaviour on the bus; I am sure that it was a most unpleasant and threatening experience for [the driver] who was … responsible for the safety of all his passengers. But there was no obligation upon him to pursue the plaintiff into the depot, especially since the gardaí were almost at the depot themselves. I doubt if it is part of his terms of employment that he should act in that way, or that he has any training in that regard."

Wherein lay the driver's negligence? Is there a duty of care on the part of employees, or of the public generally, *not* to pursue a person seeking to evade arrest by members of the Gardaí? Peart J. did not proceed on the basis that the driver was seeking to make a false arrest, though it must be admitted that the precise circumstances in which a civilian may arrest another are somewhat complicated. Rather does Peart J.'s argument suggest that the driver's conduct was uncalled for and that it subjected the plaintiff, who was already seeking to evade the Gardaí, to a "needless pursuit". In future, on the basis of this decision, people who hear an old lady in a public place cry "Stop thief!" should calculate the proportionality of intervention before coming to her aid.

Peart J., when reducing compensation to take account of the plaintiff's contributory negligence, did not address the possibility of the application of the defence of *ex turpi causa*, presumably because it was not pleaded. Nor did he engage in any consideration of the *Glencar* test for determining the duty of care when discussing the question of the driver's negligence. One might have expected that the plaintiff would have encountered serious difficulty in establishing at least two of the three ingredients of the *Glencar* test: the absence of countervailing policy considerations and the requirement that it be just and reasonable to impose the duty of care in the circumstances.

Peart J.'s holding can perhaps best be understood in the context of the evidential conflict and lacunae. He made no finding on the question whether the driver had been on the plaintiff's back when he sustained the injury. One suspects that, if the case had involved a clear finding that the plaintiff had fallen when simply being pursued by the driver, Peart J. might have hesitated before holding the driver negligent.

STANDARD OF CARE

1. Schools   It is notoriously difficult for school pupils to succeed in negligence claims against schools where the injury of which they complain is sustained in the course of a broadly educational activity. It is one thing for a school not to provide appropriate supervision: here courts are appreciative of the tendency for unsupervised children quickly to become boisterous and engage in activities that risk causing injury. It is quite another thing for a pupil to complain about an injury in a sporting event: if thought has gone into the design of the game or competition and consideration given to the age and capacity of the players, then courts will be slow to give compensation to a pupil who is injured during the course of the event.

In *Carolan v Board of Management of St. Ciaran's National School* [2006] I.E.H.C. 416, the plaintiff sued for negligence in respect of injuries she received when playing a game of "dodgeball" which was part of the PE class at her school. She was nearly 13 years old at the time. During the course of the game, the pupils had to run the width of the room and had to avoid being hit by any of three sponge balls being thrown by three classmates, who were standing to the side. If a pupil was hit, he or she was "out", and went to sit on a bench. The plaintiff was the last successful pupil and had to make one more successful crossing to finish the game. She avoided the first ball and, in trying to avoid either the second or the third, "she was ducking or weaving and came to a stop and in moving off again to try and reach the far side, she stumbled or tripped over her own legs and fell to the ground on her left arm". The fall caused her severe injury, involving a fracture of both her ulna and radius. There was no issue as to the suitability of the premises or of the floor surface. Neither did the plaintiff complain about inadequate supervision.

The real criticism put forward on behalf of the plaintiff was that the game was unsafe because the throwers threw from a right angle position or sideways-on to the direction that the plaintiff was required to run; this caused a "conflict in the focus of attention". By having a conflict of attention between travelling forward and looking sideways to see the balls approaching, together with the added likelihood of the participant moving or jerking her or his head, there was a clear risk of a participant losing balance and tripping or falling.

Feeney J. dismissed the claim, stating:

> "The expert evidence called by the defendant is in the Court's view compelling in support of an absence of negligence on the part of the defendant. This is not a case of defective premises or equipment or lack of supervision, but rather a claim that a particular activity or game was unsuitable, likely to cause injury or, as stated by the plaintiff's counsel, inherently dangerous and ill-considered as being suitable for 12 year-olds. The Court is of the view that this contention is based upon a contrived examination and analysis of the game or activity.

The criticism from the plaintiff's expert lacks reality and disregards many activities and games requiring a conflict of focus; it disregards the simple and straightforward nature of the activity or game compared to other more complicated games suitable for and played by 12 year olds, such as football or basketball, and it also disregards 20 years of safe use of the game …

All physical activity carries some risk; the Court is satisfied that the chosen activity did not unreasonably or unsafely create a risk and that the game was properly chosen for use and appropriately considered by the teachers, both as to use and format. There is, as the expert witness called by the defendant says, a risk of falling in any moving game. The risk is incidental, not inherent. And the Court is of the view that it certainly cannot be categorised as this game being inherently dangerous. Physical activity is both an appropriate and vital part of the school curriculum and the activity chosen here was a simple and straightforward game that could be safely played."

2. Prisoners In *Howe v Governor of Mountjoy Prison* [2006] I.E.H.C. 394, the plaintiff, a prisoner in Mountjoy Prison, was viciously attacked without warning by another prisoner when they were in the exercise yard. The plaintiff claimed that the prison authorities had been negligent in failing to protect him from this attack. There had been a history of conflict between the two prisoners. The other prisoner, about a year previously, had alleged that he had been stabbed by the plaintiff when they were sharing a cell in Bridewell Garda Station. After a Garda investigation, the plaintiff had been prosecuted but, when the matter came to trial, the other prisoner failed to identify the plaintiff as the person who stabbed him and the plaintiff was acquitted.

The essence of the plaintiff's claim was that the prison authorities were, or ought to have been, aware of this history and ought to have isolated the two prisoners from each other. He had mentioned his concern to the Governor of Mountjoy Prison during his many meetings with the Governor. The prison authorities denied any knowledge of the earlier events.

O'Neill J. dismissed the claim. In his view, the enquiry that was made when prisoners were admitted to prison as to any concerns that they might have, together with the receptivity of the prison authorities to complaints by prisoners and their established policy of separating prisoners in these situations, discharged their duty of care; "[i]f the plaintiff had fears of an attack from [the other prisoner] he should have alerted the prison authorities to this but he did not."

3. Hotel security In *McShane v Ballymascanlon Hotel Ltd,* Circuit Court, May 17, 2006, McMahon J. dismissed a claim for negligence where the plaintiff, a guest at a wedding reception held at the defendant's premises, was, without provocation or prior warning, beaten up by three men when he and his wife were waiting for a taxi inside the hotel in the early morning. The transgressors had also attended the reception, but only the "afters" when the meal was over. They were strangers to the plaintiff.

The essence of the plaintiff's claim was that the defendant ought to have provided "bouncers or security men" for the event. McMahon J. thought that this was too demanding a requirement. While not ruling out the possibility that, very unusually, some weddings might indeed require this level of protection, the instant case was not one of them. The wedding had been a well-planned affair; the only people attending were those by invitation; there was no evidence of excessive consumption of alcohol: McMahon J. noted that it "was not a free bar situation". The event had been a well-run and happy affair; after it was over, the guests were dispersing in a normal fashion. The plaintiff had had no contact with his assailants inside the hotel. There had been no previous record of bad behaviour at the premises, " a quiet upmarket family run hotel … located in a rural setting …", which hosted 120 weddings a year. McMahon J. noted that the hotel "was set in well kept gardens and the management style was very much 'hands on'. In short, it was not a night club or disco in an urban context where one might expect more rowdy and more boisterous behaviour."

EMPLOYERS' LIABILITY

Work stress   Work stress has become an increasingly important subject of tort litigation in recent years. Employees who suffer psychiatric or psychological injury have sued their employers arguing that their employers were negligent in exposing them unreasonably to the risk of such injury or, more usually, in failing to respond adequately to a condition of psychological frailty of which they were or ought to have been aware. In the *Annual Review of Irish Law 2004, pp.* 482–486 we examined Laffoy J.'s decision in *McGrath v Trintech Technologies Ltd* [2004] I.E.H.C. 342 rejecting a claim on the basis that the plaintiff's workload had not been unduly demanding and there had been no warning signs of existing or impending injury. In the *Annual Review of Irish Law 2005*, pp. 705–706, we analysed Lavan J.'s decision in *Quigley v Complex Tooling and Moulding* [2005] I.E.H.C. 71, where the claim for bullying, victimisation and harassment succeeded, as well as *Maher v Jabil Global Services Ltd* [2005] I.E.H.C. 130, where Clarke J. held that the employer had responded appropriately to evidence of stress.

Laffoy J. returned to the theme in *Berber v Dunnes Stores Ltd* [2006] I.E.H.C. 327. The plaintiff, an employee of over 20 years' standing, became embroiled in conflict with his employer when the employer sought to transfer him from his work as a buyer back into store management. The plaintiff had Crohn's disease. The attempt to resolve the dispute by sending the plaintiff to work in store management at a local store resulted in his suffering from post-traumatic stress disorder.

Laffoy J.'s judgment contains a detailed record of the specific incidents on the way to the complete breakdown in the working relationship. She concluded on the evidence that the director of store operations at the relevant time had failed to have proper regard to the plaintiff's medical condition, especially during the period after the defendant had been informed by the plaintiff's solicitor of the effects of stress generated by the suspension of the plaintiff:

> "[The director of store operations] adopted an uncompromising stance with the plaintiff from the outset: the plaintiff was to attend for work in [the local store] or else he would be suspended. After the suspension was lifted [the director of store operations] remained entrenched in the position that he would not deal with the plaintiff until he returned to work in the [local] store, even though the plaintiff was on sick leave and the defendant had been warned of the effect which the situation was having on the plaintiff's health and well being and of the plaintiff's perception of the defendant's motivation. For three months the defendant did not yield despite repeated warnings that the situation was exacerbating the plaintiff's medical condition."

Laffoy J. adopted, as the relevant questions for determining the issue of liability, what Clarke J. had set out in *Maher v Jabil Global Services Ltd*:

> "(a) Has the plaintiff suffered an injury to his or her health as opposed to what might be described as ordinary occupational stress,
> (b) if so is that injury attributable to the workplace, and
> (c) if so was the harm suffered to the particular employee concerned reasonably foreseeable in all the circumstances?"

Laffoy J. considered that the evidence had established that the plaintiff had suffered an injury to his health, as opposed to mere ordinary occupational stress. This injury was diagnosed as "adjustment disorder"; it had exacerbated the plaintiff's Crohn's disease symptoms and hampered their treatment. The adjustment disorder was attributable to the manner in which the defendant had dealt with the plaintiff at the relevant period.

Laffoy J. had no doubt that the physical and psychological harm which the plaintiff had suffered on account of the stress generated by the manner in which he had been dealt with had been reasonably foreseeable; the effect of the work-related stress on the plaintiff's health had in any event been conveyed to the defendant by his solicitor.

Counsel for the defendant sought refuge in the statement by McMahon & Binchy, *Law of Torts* (3rd ed., Lexis Nexis, 2000, para.18.03) that, while the duty of an employer is to take reasonable care of the employee, the courts "have constantly stressed ... that the employer's duty is not an unlimited one and that 'the employer is not an insurer' (citing *Dalton v Frendo*, Supreme

Court, December 15, 1977, *per* O'Higgins C.J.). Laffoy J. accepted that this was a correct statement of the law; applied to the facts of the case, however, it led to the conclusion that the defendant's conduct had fallen short of what a reasonable and prudent employer would have done in the circumstances.

In *Corbett v Ireland*, High Court, April 25, 2006, de Valera J. dismissed a claim by a soldier for negligent failure to protect him from post-traumatic stress disorder when on tours to Lebanon. He had joined the army in 1990 at the age of 17. A year later he had volunteered to serve in the Lebanon. Two accidents occurred which, he said, had caused him serious disturbance. In one, an explosion had killed and mutilated a member of the South Lebanese Army in full view of the plaintiff. In the other a member of an Israeli mine-sweeping operation was, in the plaintiff's words, "blown to bits", about 50 metres from the plaintiff's lookout post. The plaintiff had returned to the Lebanon in 1993 and again in 1997, by which time he had been promoted to Corporal. On the 1997 tour, a helicopter crashed, killing all on board, including an Irish sergeant not personally known to the plaintiff. The crash was not within the plaintiff's direct view though that night he could see the glow caused by the burning wreckage.

The plaintiff's claim failed essentially because the army authorities were completely unaware of the particular effects which these incidents had had upon him, since they were not apparent and he had not brought them to the attention of the authorities. De Valera J. stressed that "soldiers must be prepared to be involved in events of the kind experienced by the plaintiff and the army cannot be held responsible for these events". The army did have a duty to its soldiers to ensure that, as far as possible in the circumstances obtaining at a given time, the soldiers had the appropriate training and support to allow them to cope with these traumatic events. The plaintiff's commanding officer had responded appropriately to the plaintiff's situation, following the killing of the Lebanese soldier, on the basis of the information available to him. His temporary removal of the plaintiff from duty was, in de Valera J.'s view, "clearly humane and precautionary". The officer had had "no reason to suspect anything more serious than the normal reaction from a young inexperienced soldier after a mere two weeks on his first tour of overseas duty". The plaintiff had not availed himself of the clear opportunity to amplify his concern. The plaintiff had similarily failed to bring his condition to the attention of the authorities with regard to the other incident in 1991. (The judgment is, incidentally, not entirely consistent in its various descriptions of the incidents in 1991 but nothing hinges on this.)

By the time the plaintiff went on the 1997 tour to the Lebanon, as a Corporal, he was aware of Critical Incident Stress Debriefing (CISD). On the basis of the evidence in the case, including the fact that the plaintiff had been examined at the end of his tour and found to be psychologically fit, de Valera J. concluded that the army could not have identified any aspect of his condition that could have led to future psychiatric and psychological problems. Accordingly, he dismissed the claim.

Contributory negligence   In *Kerr v Molloy and Sherry (Lough Eglish) Ltd*
[2006] I.E.H.C. 364, the plaintiff, working at a meat plant, received an injury
to his big toe when a box of frozen meat was dislodged when being stacked in
a manner that failed to provide sufficent cohesion and stability. The plaintiff
had brought the danger to the attention of the assistant operations manager,
whom he regarded as the person in charge in the absence of his supervisor.
The assistant operations manager had not adopted any remedial strategy and
he and the plaintiff continued to involve themselves in the stacking process
which led to the accident.

The defendant, his employer, accepted that, if the accident had happened
as the plaintiff described, which Herbert J. so found, it would be liable for
negligence and for breach of statutory duty. It put forward, however, the
defence of contributory negligence on the doomed basis that the assistant
operations manager had less experience in the packing process and that he
should be regarded as the helper to the plaintiff, who should be characterised
as the person in charge of the operation. Herbert J. held that the evidence
clearly demonstrated that the assistant operation manager had in fact ample
relevant experience. He had conceded in cross-examination that he would not
have expected the plaintiff to challenge him on any aspect of the job. Herbert
J. considered that it would have been "wholly unreasonable to expect" the
plaintiff, having pointed out to the assistant operations manager the possible
danger involved in stacking the boxes in the manner adopted, to leave the job
and go to the office to complain to the operations manager. Herbert J. applied
the principles set out by Ó Dálaigh C.J. in *Kennedy v East Cork Foods* [1973]
I.R. 244 that an employee's continuing with the work in the circumstances did
not "enter the realm of downright carelessness".

The plaintiff's claim had rested on negligence and breach of statutory duty
pursuant to s.6 and the Fifth Schedule of the Safety, Health and Welfare at
Work Act 1989. Herbert J. found that the plaintiff was not guilty of contributory
negligence in relation to his claim based upon breach of statutory duty and
was therefore entitled to succeed in full. He considered it is unnecessary in
the circumstances to go on to address the position in relation to the plaintiff's
alternative claim based upon negligence at common law.

The differing approaches of the courts to contributory negligence in claims
for negligence and claims for breach of statutory duty have given rise to
comment. The paternalistic values underlying factories and mines legislation
in the past were a response to the huge exploitation of workers which had
characterised the industrial revolution. In the era, prior to the enactment of
the Civil Liability Act 1961, when contributory negligence was an absolute
defence and where the doctrine of "last clear chance" had little application in
the context of industrial injuries, courts were driven to a restrictive application
of the defence of contributory negligence in both claims for common law
negligence and claims for breach of statutory duty, but particularly so in the
latter case where employers had breached a duty of protection for employees

specifically prescribed by statute. With the expansion of the scope of obligations under modern health and safety legislation—most obviously, the Safety, Health and Welfare at Work Act 2005—and the imposition (in s.13 of the 2005 Act) of duties on employees, relative to others and to themselves, perhaps the time has come for a reassessment of the differing approaches to contributory negligence mentioned above. In the instant case, such a reassessment could have yielded no change in outcome. Had Herbert J. addressed the question of contributory negligence in relation to the plaintiff's claim for negligence and (let us assume) possibly come to the conclusion that some reduction should be made for contributory negligence, the outcome would still have been that the plaintiff should succeed in full, on the basis of his full success in his claim for breach of statutory duty.

Medical care   In *Shuit v Mylotte* [2006] I.E.H.C. 89, the plaintiff failed in her claim for negligence where the first-named defendant, a consultant obstetrician/gynaecologist, had carried out a Wertheim-Meigs hysterectomy. Prior to the surgery, a CT scan had been carried out. The first-named defendant had not been furnished with a written report in relation to it but had received a verbal report on it. White J. in his judgment recorded that "[n]either the written... nor the verbal report referred to the plaintiff having a tumour, but for some inexplicable reason, the first-named defendant formed the impression that the CT scan had in fact revealed a tumour, and he so informed the plaintiff on the evening prior to her hysterectomy". Other tests carried out on the plaintiff had, however, raised the possibility that she had an early cancer.

There was a conflict of expert evidence in the case. The consultants called by the plaintiff considered that the plaintiff had been guilty of negligence in carrying out the particular procedure in the absence of a diagnosis of invasive cancer. The consultants called by the first defendant said that, in the same circumstances, they would have carried out the same procedure.

White J. quoted from Finlay C.J.'s judgment in *Dunne v National Maternity Hospital* [1989] I.R. 91. He was satisfied from the evidence that there were "two *bona fide* schools of thought on the issue as to whether the defendant acted appropriately in the circumstances presented to him". The plaintiff accordingly had failed to establish that no obstetrician of like skill, acting with ordinary care, would have performed the surgery carried out by the first defendant.

Counsel for the plaintiff invited the court to stigmatise the defendants' conduct as involving a practice with inherent defects which ought to be obvious to any person giving the matter due consideration. Under the third rule in *Dunne*, a practitioner charged with negligence who defends his conduct by establishing that he followed a practice which was general and approved of by his colleagues of similar specialisation and skill cannot escape liability if the plaintiff establishes that the practice had such inherent defects. Counsel for the first-named defendant replied that his defence had never been one of general and approved practice. White J. rejected the argument of counsel for the plaintiff. He stated:

> "I consider [the] submission [of counsel for the first-named defendant] to
> be well founded. On the evidence before me, the first-named defendant
> was treating, or intended to treat, a particular, individual patient, who
> had an unusual set or combination of symptoms, and a highly abnormal
> history. He considered her case history as a whole. He considered
> her symptoms and her family circumstances, and concluded that the
> appropriate treatment in her particular case was to carry out a Wertheim-
> Meigs hysterectomy.
>
> The first-named defendant has sworn, in evidence, that his mistaken
> belief as regards the C.T. Scan disclosing or revealing a tumour did
> not influence him in deciding the nature, and extent, of the surgery he
> carried out. Having regard to his pre operative correspondence with the
> third-named defendant, I consider it unlikely that his mistaken belief
> influenced his decision regarding the nature of the surgery he proposed
> carrying out, and I accept his testimony that it did not."

It may be useful here to reflect on the contours of the concept of a customary
practice. One interpretation would regard the term "practice" as being limited
to a run-of-the-mill, frequently repeated process rather than extending to an
individuated exercise of particularised medical judgment as to how to proceed,
based on the unique circumstances of the patient. The truth of the matter is
that medical practice often involves judgments of the latter kind. They are no
more exempt from the third rule in *Dunne* than they are from the first. If the
making of individuated judgments is not to be regarded as falling within the
scope of "practice", then a practitioner will not be able to seek the protection
of the first rule by showing that the approach he or she adopted was one that
finds support among a sufficient number of his or her peers to be capable of
being characterised as "general and approved".

In *H v St Vincent's Hospital Trustees Ltd* [2006] I.E.H.C. 443 (*ex tempore*),
Hanna J. held that the release from hospital of a patient who had shown some
signs of recovery, without the question of her incisional hernia being finally
checked out, constituted negligence, compounded by the earlier failure of
the medical team to tell her of the existence of the incisional hernia. Hanna
J. observed:

> "It is common case that the plaintiff began to show some signs of
> recovery over the ensuing days. However, I believe a false sense of
> security with regard to the plaintiff's condition overtook the medical
> team treating her, to the extent, to put it colloquially, that the hernia
> went off the agenda …
>
> I am satisfied that the plaintiff was not seen by any senior doctor
> either on the day of her departure or the day prior thereto. I accept her

evidence that she was seen by a junior doctor prior to her discharge. No note was made referable to the plaintiff's hernia and no consideration was given to it in the days prior to the plaintiff's discharge. I am satisfied that the plaintiff ought to have been examined by [the senior surgical registrar] or someone of his seniority prior to the discharge, having regard to the presence of the incisional hernia. I am satisfied that no medical specialist of equal skill to [the senior surgical registrar] acting with ordinary care would have disregarded the incisional hernia to the extent of failing at least to examine the plaintiff prior to her discharge. Equally, I am satisfied that the plaintiff ought to have been informed of the existence of the hernia. Failure to do so, in my view, amounted to negligence."

As a consequence of the failure to examine the plaintiff and the failure to inform her of the existence of the incisional hernia, the plaintiff was discharged from hospital unaware that she might encounter further problems, which she did within a very short period of time. She suffered significant physical and mental trauma when she became seriously ill, not knowing what was wrong with her, and was readmitted to hospital on the day she was discharged.

In *Madigan v Governor of St. Patrick's Hospital* [2006] I.E.H.C. 259, the plaintiff's wife went missing from a psychiatric hospital where she was a patient and was presumed to have died by suicide. The plaintiff's claim for negligence against the hospital authorities was not in respect of the treatment she received but rather the nature of the supervision afforded to her.

The plaintiff's wife had a history of depression, suicidal ideation and an earlier suicide attempt. After the birth of her son, she developed very serious depression, manifesting itself in suicidal ideation and intent. This led to her admission to the hospital. The nursing plan for her stipulated that she should be provided with a safe, secure environment and kept under close observation. When she visited her home for a brief period, she went to a beach, drank half a bottle of brandy and contemplated drowning herself. The plaintiff found 17 paracetamol tablets in her pocket. On her return to hospital, she was placed in a more secure ward and, for a period deprived of her "privileges"—the entitlement to wear her own clothes and have the freedom to move around the hospital. The restoration of this entitlement was the result of "consultations between the medicals and the nurses in the ... ward". Four days after she had been returned to the hospital, the plaintiff's wife got up at the usual time and walked in the gardens. At 1.55pm she left the ward, indicating that she was going to occupational therapy. She left the hospital at 2.05pm and was never seen again. Her clothes were found at Bray Head.

The focus of the plaintiff's claim was on the question of the observation of the deceased. Johnson J. evinced a certain impatience in this context, stating:

> "The words 'close observation' were used in the medical notes originally of the deceased and that matter was subject of a great deal of waste of time in the course of the case. It is quite clear that whatever one chooses to call the regime to which the deceased was subjected it was the decision of the medical profession and the nursing profession that this was the one appropriate for the treatment of the deceased at that time.
>
> It is quite clear that the nurses at any given time during the day, if they had any apprehension or misgiving, or in any way alerted to any alteration in mood or of the condition of the patient can change the regime and impose a stricter regime on the patient. Close observation with privileges meant you could walk around but the grounds would be checked four times a day."

The plaintiff's witnesses indicated that when the deceased left the ward to go to occupational therapy she should have been accompanied ther and back or that a telephone call should have been made from the ward to the occupational therapist to indicate she was on her way and that when she was on her way back a similar call should have been made by the occupational therapist back to the ward. The defendants indicated that it was not practical to do this and that, and if it was the opinion of the medical doctors that such an escort was required, they would not have sent her to occupational therapy at all.

Johnson J. observed:

> "This was all taken by way of being a therapeutic treatment and a clinical judgment at all material times by the doctors and the nurses.
>
> The doctors and nurses who dealt with the patient were the people who had been treating her [for three months], they are the ones who knew her and had had the opportunity of observing her for that period of time, in an out of the ward. It was a very stable community of nurses, they all got to know her, they all had her confidence.
>
> [The treating psychiatrist] believed that her suicidal ideation and inclination were containable and responding to the treatment being given, and he saw her on the morning of [her departure from the hospital] and did not change his opinion."

Johnson J. rejected the notion that the case should be tried under the principles laid down by *Kelly v The Board of Governors of St. Laurence's Hospital* [1988] I.R. 402. Johnson J. did not agree. In his view, this was "quite simply a case a doctor and/or doctors making a diagnosis and prescribing a treatment to which the plaintiffs disagree. Under those circumstances the appropriate principles are laid down in *Dunne v The National Maternity Hospital* ...".

Johnson J. was satisfied that the treatment provided by the defendants had not been negligent within these principles.

Johnson J.'s characterisation of the case as one relating to professional judgment and expertise under the *Dunne* principles rather than simply one of hospital management and nursing care is to be welcomed. *Kelly v St. Laurence's Hospital* can be criticised for treating a medically managed supervision regime as falling outside the distinctive principles applicable to professional negligence. It is true that the management of patients with suicidal ideation involves practical decision-making not dissimilar to that required of others who have to protect the security of vulnerable people but there is here an element of professional judgment which may be considered to warrant the application of the *Dunne* principles.

Informed consent to treatment   The law on informed consent in Ireland in Ireland is in an uncertain state. In *Walsh v Family Planning Services Ltd* [1992] 1 I.R. 505 the Supreme Court was divided as to the test for disclosure. Finlay C.J. and McCarthy J. appeared to favour a requirement that protected the doctor who had complied with a customary practice of disclosure save in cases where disclosure was obviously necessary. This, in essence, is the extension to disclosure of the test in relation to treatment set out in *Dunne v National Maternity Hospital* [1989] I.R. 91. O'Flaherty J. rejected the application of the *Dunne* test in the context of disclosure and Hederman J. concurred with him. O'Flaherty J. preferred a test, expressed in terms of "the established principles of negligence", requiring disclosure of material risks.

In *Walsh*, the plaintiff had undergone a vasectomy, carried out with due care, which resulted in very serious consequences, including impotence and severe pain. The risk of these consequences, inherent in the treatment, was very small indeed. The majority of the Supreme Court held that the warning that had been given was adequate in the circumstances.

Reading *Walsh* from a distance of 15 years, one can discern a judicial tension on the issue of disclosure of risk. McCarthy J. considered that, "in a case such as the present", the two tests, of customary practices of disclosure subject to override in cases where disclosure was obviously necessary and of disclosure of all material risks incident to the proposed treatment, respectively, were "essentially the same". McCarthy J. went on to observe:

> "In determining whether or not to have an operation in which sexual capacity is concerned, it seems to me that to supply the patient with the material facts is so obviously necessary to all informed choice on the part of the patient that no reasonably prudent medical doctor would fail to make it. What then is material? Apart from the success ratio of the operation, what could be more material than sexual capacity after the operation and its immediate sequelae. Whatever about temporary or protracted pain or discomfort, the only information given to the plaintiff and his wife on the scope of sexual capacity, upon which they placed so much emphasis, was that contained in the brief paragraph headed 'Does

it affect your sex life? No.' This is not a question of merely determining that a particular outcome is so rare as not to warrant such disclosure that might upset a patient but, rather, that those concerned, and this includes the authors of the information sheet, if they knew of such a risk, however remote, had a duty to inform those so critically concerned with that risk. Remote percentages of risk lose their significance to those unfortunate enough to be 100% involved. In my view it is inescapable that the defendants, possessed as they were of this knowledge, were in breach of their duty to the plaintiff, and to his wife, for failing to identify the risk of impotence, whether it be functional due to pain and discomfort, or mechanical due to some other cause."

O'Flaherty J.'s observations on this theme are also worth recording:

"I have no hesitation in saying that where there is a question of elective surgery which is not essential to health or bodily well-being, if there is a risk—however exceptional or remote—of grave consequences involving severe pain stretching for an appreciable time into the future and involving the possibility of further operative procedures, the exercise of the duty of care owed by the defendants requires that such possible consequences should be explained in the clearest language to the plaintiff."

Since Finlay C.J.'s judgment is generally understood as involving the most restrictive elaboration of the duty of disclosure, it may be useful to record here the language he used when holding that there had been no breach of that duty:

"The ... issue arises ... as to whether, having regard to the evidence as to what occurred to the plaintiff in addition to the ongoing pain ... consisting of various surgical interventions, the removal of one testicle and, apparently, a loss of potency as distinct from or in addition to a loss of sexual capacity due to pain were matters which were, on a standard of reasonable care, a possible consequence he should have been warned about. I am satisfied that the evidence did not establish that these consequences were a known complication of a carefully carried out operation of vasectomy, and that the furthest the evidence went was ... the existence of an ongoing indefinite pain, arising from orchialgia, in a very limited number of cases, indeed, expressed in single numbers amongst multiple thousands. For this reason, I conclude that ... the warning ... was sufficient, on the facts, to discharge [the doctor's] responsibility to exercise reasonable care".

What is interesting about these quoted passages is that they set the requirement for disclosure, at all events in respect of elective treatments, at a very high level. Even applying the *Dunne* test, disclosure of "a known complication", however infrequent its incidence, may be necessary. It was the lack of prior knowledge of the particular risk which eventuated, rather than its unlikelihood, which excused its non-disclosure. As O'Flaherty J. observed, "[t]he catalogue of misfortunes of this plaintiff, it must be said, went beyond anything previously known; his situation appears unique".

In the High Court decision of *Geoghegan v Harris* [2000] 3 I.R. 536, Kearns J. laid great emphasis on the fact that the risk of chronic neuropathic pain, albeit a very low one, had been a known complication of a dental implant operation rendered its disclosure imperative. We analyse Kearns J.'s judgment in the *Annual Review of Irish Law 2000*, pp. 434–441. Kearns J.'s approach is of particular interest in favouring the view that elective and non-elective treatment should involve the same obligation of disclosure and in applying ultimately a subjective test for causation, guided, where helpful, by reference to how a reasonable person in the plaintiff's position would have acted.

In *Winston v O'Leary* [2006] I.E.H.C. 440, the plaintiff had undergone a vasectomy procedure in 1989. The outcome had been seriously detrimental, involving long-term pain and a number of later medical interventions. The plaintiff's claim, as matters progressed, became limited to one focused on an allegation that he had not provided an informed consent to the procedure.

MacMenamin J., in his judgment, held that there had been a duty to warn the plaintiff of the risk of residual pain, since it was a known risk at the time the vasectomy was carried out:

> "It is clear that there was a duty to warn, from the evidence of the defendant. He himself had not encountered this particular risk and had not, in the course of any of the operations which he carried out, encountered such sequelae. Applying the principles identified in *Dunne v National Maternity Hospital* there was a duty to warn the plaintiff regardless of the remoteness of such risk".

It is interesting that MacMenamin J. should have invoked *Dunne*, which was concerned with treatment, rather than *Walsh*, which involved issues so close to those arising in *Winston v O'Leary*. MacMenamin J. did refer to *Walsh*, but contented himself with the observation that *Walsh* was "in some ways similar factually to the instant case". MacMenamin J.'s approach reflects that of Kearns J. in *Geoghegan v Harris*: if the risk is know, albeit rare, it should be disclosed. While *Winston v O'Leary* might be regarded as a case involving elective treatment, MacMenamin J. gave no indication that the breadth of disclosure was contingent on that factor.

Much of MacMenamin J.'s judgment is devoted to resolving the matters in evidential controversy. He concluded, on the balance of probability, that the defendant had given the plaintiff adequate information about the risks of the vasectomy operation, "having regard to known identified material risks …". Even if, contrary to this holding, there had been a culpable failure to warn the plaintiff of the risk, the claim would fail on the basis of lack of causation:

> "On balance the plaintiff's conduct and behaviour in 1989 speak more eloquently than the oral testimony now. He considered that the procedure was a simple one. He was 'anxious' to undergo it. His wife's continued health was an issue quite properly in his mind. There is nothing in the material before this court to indicate that in 1989 he was unusually cautious or the kind of man who would have backed away at the mention of a remote risk. Even after two weeks reflection between counselling and operation he had no hesitation in proceeding. For these reasons, I do not consider that a hypothetical breach of duty of the type posited by the plaintiff, no matter how formulated, would have induced the plaintiff to proceed with this operation when he would not otherwise have gone ahead with it."

ROAD TRAFFIC ACCIDENTS

Travelling in car with intoxicated driver In the section of this Chapter entitled Contributory negligence, below p.577, we analyse Peart J.'s decision in *Devlin v Cassidy* [2006] I.E.H.C. 287, reducing a passenger's compensation by 50 per cent to take account of his contributory negligence in travelling with a driver whose intoxication should have been known to him.

Seat belts The legal implications of failure to use a seat belt when in a motor vehicle can be considerable. The most obvious issue relates to contributory negligence, but the separate question of negligence can also arise, as where a driver or adult passenger fails to ensure that child passengers use their seat belts. Difficult issues regarding causation and its effect on the calculation of the reduction in compensation also fall for consideration.

McNeilis v Armstrong [2006] I.E.H.C. 269 raised a range of these issues. Peart J.'s judgment represents the most comprehensive analysis of the subject in recent years. The facts of the case were tragic. An accident occurred in which five people died. The four occupants of the car whose driver was wholly responsible for the accident were killed. The first defendant was the owner of this car. The other car was driven by the second defendant, the mother of three children who were travelling with her. The front seat passenger, the driver's sister, was the mother of two children who were also travelling in the vehicle. In all, there were five children in the back of the car. There were only three seat belts; none of the children wore belts. One child of the second defendant died in the accident. The other children were injured. The instant proceedings involved claims by two of the second defendant's children and one of the children of the front seat passenger against the first defendant, the owner of the vehicle, and the second defendant.

Peart J, in a judgment of 47 pages, dealt in detail with the conflicting evidence as to the efficancy of seat belts. Before resolving that conflict, he was able to deal with the issue of whether the failure by the plaintiffs to use the seat belts constituted contributory negligence. They were aged, respectively, almost 13, 14 and 8 at the time of the accident. Peart J. concluded that contributory negligence had not been established, having regard to their age, their level of maturity and "the nature of the somewhat unusual and complex situation which presented itself to them in relation to the number of seat belts relative to the number of rear seat passengers". There had been no evidence that any of the plaintiffs had been asked by the second-named defendant to wear a seat belt. The replies given by the two older plaintiffs during cross-examination did not, in Peart J.'s view, constitute sufficient evidence to fix them with the sort of realisation as to the desirability of wearing seat belts to render them guilty of contributory negligence.

Peart J. went on to consider whether the second-named defendant had been in breach of the Road Traffic (Construction, Equipment and Use of Vehicles) (Amendment) (No. 3) Regulations 1991 (S.I. No. 359 of 1991), art.7(3) which requires drivers not to permit passengers under the age of 17 to occupy a forward facing seat in the rear of the vehicle unless the passengers are either at least four years old and wearing a safety belt or restrained by an appropriate child restraint. This obligation is mitigated somewhat by art.8(3) which provides that, where three or more children under the age of 15 are being carried on a vehicle, art.7(3) applies "only in so far as is reasonably practicable". Peart J. held that art.8(3) relieved the second-named defendant of liability under the Regulations. There had been only three belts for five children and evidence had been adduced that it would not have been feasible for the two other belts to have been safely worn when there were three children in the middle. There would inevitably in such a situation have been a bunching of the children which would have precluded a proper application of these belts and it would have been impossible for one of the children in the centre to have applied the lap belt.

The fact that the second-named defendant was not liable under the Regulations did not, however, necessarily relieve her of liability in negligence in having the children unbuckled in the back seat. Peart J. held that she had owed her duty of care to them:

"The requirement of proximity is clearly present between her and th[e] plaintiffs. I am completely satisfied that it was foreseeable that in any collision which might occur the plaintiffs would be exposed to injury. I do not have to decide whether the particular type of impact or the particular injuries which were sustained were themselves foreseeable. Neither is there any room for any suggestion that there might be any public policy consideration which might mandate that she not be under this type of duty of care, and it is fair and reasonable that such a duty of care be upon her. In this way all the requirements for the existence of a duty of care exist in this case in relation to the second-named defendant towards the plaintiffs ..."

Peart J. left to another day the question whether the front seat passenger had had a duty to ensure that her own daughter wore a seat belt.

On the basis that the second-named defendant had owed a duty of care to the back seat passengers, Peart J. had to determine whether she had breached this duty. She had adduced no evidence of having given any consideration to the question of how to use the available three belts among five children. This meant that the children had been "simply put into the back and ... left to their own devices as to the seat-belts". Peart J. observed:

"Had she at least considered the problem, and made a reasoned decision in the light of the circumstances prevailing, I might have been able to conclude that she had not breached her duty of care, even if I might also form the view that the decision taken by her was wrong. But, in the absence of any evidence from her, I must conclude that she was in breach of the duty of care upon her."

Peart J.'s approach here reflects that of the health and safety legislative code which rewards those who have addressed safety issues and punishes those who have failed to do so: under the traditional common law principles, a defendant's position would not be improved by proof that he or she had addressed such an issue if the decision he or she reached was, in the view of the court, and unreasonable one.

The next, and crucial, issue of substance related to the causal connection between the children's failure to use seat belts and the injuries they had sustained. This was important because, if the evidence showed that they would in any event have sustained the same injuries, then the second-named defendant's negligence in failing to address their seat belt requirements would simply be irrelevant and not generative of liability since it would not have caused the injuries. Moreover, if they would have sustained different injuries as serious as, or more serious than, the injuries they actually sustained, again the claim for negligence against the second-named defendant would founder. (We address this aspect of the judgment presently.)

The children's injuries had included substantial femural damage. There was a substantial conflict of expert evidence between engineers who had been called by the first named and the second-named defendants. Orthapaedic surgeons had also given evidence on behalf of the second-named defendant. Peart J.'s judgment gives full details of this evidence. He concluded from it that, whereas there was no disagreement that seat belts were highly efficacious in head-on low impact crashes, the orthopaedic surgeons had attested that, in high or severe impact crash, "all bets [we]re off" and the extent of the injury sustained even if belted was completely unpredictable. Peart J. stated:

> "I accept of course that neither of these consultants has carried out research as such, and therefore it is not possible to take their evidence other than [as] anecdotal and as a general proposition. They have not sought, for example, to distinguish between injured persons who might have been front seat passengers, drivers, children of various ages and so on. But nevertheless it is helpful for the Court to hear their overall view in order to arrive at a view on the basis of a probability. [The] research [of the engineer called by the second-named defendant] also points to the probability that it is unpredictable as to what injury will be sustained in a high impact collision. Even with the benefit of [the] evidence [of the engineer called by the first-named defendant], which was most helpful, informed and interesting, I am left in some considerable doubt, I have to say, that these plaintiffs would have suffered significantly less serious injury had they been belted. There is too much speculation involved in determining whether the injury which would be sustained would be less than was suffered if belts had been worn, in order to reach a conclusion in that regard in favour of the first-named defendant."

Peart J. went on to make important observations on two issues that did not, in the event, require resolution in the instant case. The first was whether in circumstances where a driver knew, or ought to have known, that there were only three available seat belts, it would be negligent to carry more than three children in the back at all, regardless of whether three could use the available belts. Where an adult driver was carrying more children in the back of the car than there were belts available, it seemed to Peart J. to be "highly arguable" that, even if three of those children wore the available belts, it would be negligent to carry the remaining children where they must inevitably remain unrestrained.

Peart J. observed:

> "It seems to me arguable that the necessary 'proximity of relationship' exists, that the likelihood of injury is 'foreseeable', that there can be no possible countervailing public policy consideration, and that, given the prevalence of motor accidents and the obvious desirability of reducing the incidence of injury, that it would have be be 'fair and reasonable' that a duty of care of that scope should be imposed on such a driver ... I leave it for another case to decide whether it is negligent to carry in the back of a vehicle more persons, especially children, than there are available belts, even where the available belts are used. In the present case, if it had been necessary to do so, I would have concluded that it was no excuse for the second-named defendant to plead that, given that

she had five children in the back and only three available belts, it was impossible to decide which child should wear a belt."

The final matter was the "disturbing evidence" which Peart J. had heard during the case as to the dangers for young children who wear the lap-belt in the centre of the back seat:

> "The evidence has been that the lap-belt is singularly inappropriate for young children to wear. The reason for this has been stated to be that such belts are designed so as to fit across the iliac crest, which is the strongest part of the pelvic area. When a normal adults applies the lap-belt, it crosses across the iliac crest, and this has the effect that, in an impact where the person is thrown forwards, it is the iliac crest which impacts against the belt, and that part of the body is particularly well-suited to withstand the force generated. However, where a small child or even a lightly built young teenager is wearing a lap-belt, the belt will not, in an impact, remain over the iliac crest, but will ride up the abdomen somewhat. This has two effects at least. The first is that the person will 'submarine', as it is called. In other words, the young person will be thrown forward and under the belt with all the obvious risks of not being restrained appropriately. In addition, there is a clear and known risk that when the young person is thrown against the lap-belt, it will be positioned at the abdominal area, and the force generated into the body will cause massive internal organ damage, including catastrophic damage to the aorta and fracture of the spine, or even worse, hemicorpectomy. I do not believe that parents and others in charge of young children in vehicles are aware of the fact that in all probability the wearing of a lap-belt by a child will in relatively severe impacts render the child more likely to suffer serious injury or even death, than if they were unrestrained altogether. That is the content of some of the expert evidence which I have heard, and I believe it is appropriate that I should say so, even if the precise issue did not as it happens need to be the subject of a determination in relation to the particular plaintiffs with which the proceedings are concerned. It is perhaps a matter for legislation."

If this evidence were to receive widespread endorsement, it would surely have significant implications. Questions would arise, not merely as to whether it is not negligent for a parent to decide not to have a child use a lap-belt but also whether it would constitute negligence for a parent, informed of the dangers, to let a child use the lap-belt. Broader issues as to the possible liability of the State would also arise.

In the section of this Chapter entitled Contributory negligence, below p.577, we consider *Devlin v Cassidy* [2006] I.E.H.C. 287, in which Peart J. rejected the defendants' claim that the plaintiff passenger had not been wearing a seat belt at the time of the accident. The plaintiff's evidence on this issue did not greatly impress Peart J. but the evidence relating to his injuries did not support the defendants' claim.

PRODUCT LIABILITY

Tobacco litigation   In *Delahunty v Player & Wills (Ireland) Ltd, Gallaher (Dublin) Ltd, the Minister for Health and Children, Ireland and the Attorney General* [2006] I.E.S.C. 21, the Supreme Court addressed the issue of product liability in the context of "tobacco litigation". What it had to say is of some interest, though necessarily of a preliminary character.

The plaintiff, who was born in 1926, had been a life-long smoker. She began at the age of 12, when she smoked cigarettes manufactured by Player & Wills. She developed cancer in 1995 when she had an upper lobectomy operation. Her medical team advised her of the harm caused by cigarettes, including addiction. She changed her brand to Silk Cut Extra Mild, manufactured by Gallahers. She continued to smoke 20 a day; because of her addiction she was unable to give up smoking.

The plaintiff sued a number of defendants. Here we are concerned only with her claim against the second-named defendant, Gallaher (Dublin) Ltd, which was based on a negligence and breach of statutory duty, including breaches of the Liability for Defective Products Act 1991 and the Product Liability Directive (Council Directive 85/374/EEC of July 25, 1985).

The statement of claim did not differentiate between the first two defendants and contained the following general plea:

> "The plaintiff has smoked cigarettes produced, manufactured, promoted and/or sold by the first and second-named defendants, their respective servants and/or agents, for more than fifty years and she has now learned that the said cigarettes were defective in that they, *inter alia*, were and are addictive and did at all material times hereto contain and produce substances and additives which were inherently dangerous to the health and welfare of all those who consumed the said cigarettes, including the plaintiff. The first and second-named defendants, their respective servants and/or agents deliberately and knowingly used substances and/or chemical additives in their cigarettes to create dependency and addiction amongst those, including the plaintiff, who consumed such products."

Gallahers sought to have the proceedings dismissed on the grounds that the pleadings disclosed no reasonable cause of action or, alternatively, under the inherent jurisdiction of the court. This application failed before O'Leary J. in the High Court and the Supreme Court dismissed the appeal.

Counsel for Gallahers (Dublin) Ltd argued that there was no reasonable cause of action in respect of the alleged defects in the cigarettes manufactured and sold by it. It was not alleged that the cigarettes were in any way different from or defective by comparison with other cigarettes or any standard for cigarettes. They had been lawfully marketed and sold. In recent years their advertising, packaging, labelling and sale had been highly regulated. The cigarettes manufactured by the appellant were not defective in the sense of failing to provide "the safety which a person is entitled to expect", for the purposes of s.5 of the Liability for Defective Products Act 1991. That Act did not cover products which carried an inherent risk. It had been perfectly lawful to sell the products. In reality, Gallahers could have avoided liability only by withdrawing their cigarettes from the market. It could not be reasonable to say that a manufacturer could avoid liability only by going out of business. Moreover, the plaintiff had sustained her injury before she ever smoked a cigarette manufactured by Gallahers. It was not pleaded that she suffered any additional damage after October 1995, when she commenced smoking Gallahers' cigarettes, which could be attributed to the Gallahers. In so far as the plaintiff explained her behaviour by reference to her addiction, that was not the responsibility of Gallahers.

Counsel for the plaintiff submitted that the 1991 Act imposed "absolute" liability. In response to the argument that Gallahers were not responsible for causing the plaintiff's addiction, the plaintiff contended that Gallahers specifically aimed the marketing of its Silk Cut Extra Mild brand of cigarettes at least in part at people such as the plaintiff who, though already addicted, were concerned about the health risks.

Fennelly J. (McCracken and Macken JJ. concurring) addressed the question of the alleged defectiveness of the product as follows:

> "For the purposes of this appeal, it must be assumed … that the plaintiff suffered very serious illness as a result of smoking cigarettes. [Counsel for the plaintiff] made a very simple submission with regard to the Act of 1991. He says it imposes a strict liability. That depends on the cigarettes being regarded as defective products for the purposes of the Act. Section 5(1) of the Act provides:
>
> 'For the purposes of this Act a product is defective if it fails to provide the safety which a person is entitled to expect, taking all circumstances into account, including—
> > (a) the presentation of the product,
> > (b) the use to which it could reasonably be expected that the product would be put, and
> > (c) the time when the product was put into circulation.'
>
> I do not think a court could possibly decide, on a motion of the type before the Court on this appeal, whether cigarettes 'fail to provide the

safety which a person is entitled to expect.' That will require a great deal of evidence to be given at the trial. It is also highly material that the Act of 1991 was passed in order to transpose into Irish law the provisions of the Council Directive of 1985 mentioned above. The definition of defective product is based on Article 6 of the Directive. The Act must be interpreted in the light of the Directive. If the matter comes before this Court in circumstances where a decision on such an interpretation is necessary for the decision of the Court, it would appear that the obligation of the Court to refer this matter to the Court of Justice of the European Communities pursuant to Article 234 of the EC Treaty would arise. That will, of course, depend on whether such an interpretation is necessary for its decision. For that reason alone, it would be impossible to determine such an important issue at this stage. Furthermore, the High Court may wish to refer such questions to the Court of Justice and may do so at any stage of the proceedings.

I am also of the view that the claim based on liability for defective products at common law cannot be dismissed at this stage. In a situation where it has to be assumed that the product admittedly sold caused damage to the plaintiff's health, it would require very clear authority to convince a court that it is unarguable that the manufacturer is liable. I will say no more."

Fennelly J. was also satisfied that it had been sufficiently pleaded that the plaintiff had suffered injury as a result of smoking Gallahers' cigarettes after 1995. The statement of claim contained sufficient general and undifferentiated pleadings, for the purposes of Ord.19, r.28, that the plaintiff had suffered personal injuries as a result of the negligence and other wrongdoing of all the defendants. The particulars contained allegations of extensive health difficulties after 1995, though not making any distinction between the effects of smoking the cigarettes of the respective defendants. An expert medical report mentioned the fact that the plaintiff had smoked Player cigarettes until 1995 and then began smoking Silk Cut. It described her continuing symptoms of "progressive external dyspnoea secondary to chronic obstructive pulmonary disease *with emphysema as a consequence of her cigarette smoking in addition* to her prior lobectomy..." (emphasis added by Fennelly J). In his concluding opinion, he stated that she "has evidence of progressively severe chronic obstructive pulmonary disease *as a consequence of her continued smoking habit*" (emphasis added by Fennelly J).

Turning to the "apparently attractive argument" based on causation, Fennelly J. observed:

"On the hypothesis that the plaintiff was addicted as a result of smoking the cigarettes of the first-named defendant and that she knew smoking causes cancer when she commenced smoking the appellant's cigarettes, the appellant was neither responsible for the addiction nor for the consequences of the addiction. On the other hand, the plaintiff claims that the appellant's 'Silk Cut' cigarettes were targeted at vulnerable people such as the plaintiff. It was foreseeable that such people would consume cigarettes placed on the market by them. Issues of causation can be some of the most difficult in tort law. While the appellant has raised an arguable point, I cannot agree that it is decisive."

Finally, Fennelly J. noted that, if counsel for the plaintiff was correct in his interpretation of the Act of 1991, the liability of Gallaher might be strict.

Whether "tobacco litigation" will succeed this side of the Atlantic is not clear. The absence of juries, the lesser emphasis on exemplary damages and the less developed status of class actions suggest caution before a too facile assumption that what has happened in the United States of America will also take place here. For further consideration, see Sirabionian, "Why Tobacco Litigation has not been successful in the United Kingdom: A Comparative Analysis of Tobacco Litigation in the United States and the United Kingdom" (2005) 25 Nw J. Intl L & Business 485.

RES IPSA LOQUITUR

In *Boyle v Iarnród Éireann*, Circuit Court, January 30, 2006, the *res ipsa loquitur* doctrine was invoked, albeit unsuccessfully. The plaintiff, aged three-and-a-half, was injured by a used hypodermic syringe which pierced her hand when she was placed in a seat in a train by her father in Bray Station early one Sunday afternoon. Judge McMahon was satisfied that the *res ipsa loquitur* doctrine applied. The onus therefore fell on the defendant to displace its application.

Evidence was given that the train had been thoroughly cleaned before it left Connolly Station shortly after 1 p.m. The fleet manager attested that he had come across only three incidents involving syringes in 25 years and that, if there had been a needle in this position when the train was being cleaned at Connolly Station, it should have been obvious to the cleaners. In addition, every six months the seats were dismantled and the upholstery was removed and hoovered.

The train guard gave evidence that he had inspected the carriages before departure and had not seen any syringe.

Judge McMahon, holding that the defendant had not been negligent, stated:

"... I find that the cleaning system was adequate and sufficient in ordinary circumstances. Was there a failure to observe the system on the day in question? The answer must be no. The train was cleaned at Connolly Station immediately before it departed and five people were involved in the cleaning operation for a total of approximately one hour.

Furthermore, there were no special circumstances or danger known to the defendant that would have required greater care … In the absence of a general problem with needles, I think it would be asking too much to expect the train guard to examine every seat minutely after each station. Of course if the defendant is aware of a special problem, such as black spots where regular stone throwing occurs one may expect, and demand, more of the defendants … There was no evidence before the court here to suggest that the presence of needles on the defendant's trains had reached anything like epidemic proportions.

The plaintiff's father, as he was moving through the carriage to select an appropriate seat, did not see the needle, although his evidence was that after the incident he noticed that the needle was projecting some two inches out and that some of the barrel was also visible. Clearly, it was not obvious enough to come to his attention, before he placed his child on the seat.

Where did the needle come from? The incident occurred nearly an hour after the train departed from Connolly Station where it had been thoroughly cleaned. On the balance of probability it was deposited there by someone after the train left Connolly Station but before it arrived at Bray Station, possibly by someone who got off at an intermediary station It lay there unknown to the defendants and it would be too harsh to say that the defendants were negligent in failing to detect it during that short period."

REMOTENESS OF DAMAGE

In *Gaffey v Dundalk Town Council* [2006] I.E.H.C. 436, the facts of which are set out in greater detail above p.549, Peart J. held that it was not reasonably foreseeable that a fire hydrant, the lid of which could easily be removed, should have its lid removed by an unknown person, resulting ultimately in injury to the nine-year-old plaintiff when he was playing football in a grassed area where the fire hydrant was situated. Peart J. stated:

"One could say with confidence, I think, that the defendant should reasonably foresee that, if the hydrant was badly designed or poorly constructed so that it presented a hazard … children [playing on the grassed area] could sustain an injury. I am of the view, however, that the prospect that mischievous people would lift off the lid and leave it off and that a child such as the plaintiff would fall into the hydrant as a result, is too remote a prospect to be foreseeable. It requires an intervening act."

One can perhaps sound a note of caution. The concept of *novus actus interveniens* is generally categorised as one relating to causation rather than remoteness of damage. A more general point of interest arises in relation to remoteness of damage in the context of a prior liability analysis based on the duty, rather than the standard, of care. We have seen how Peart J. treated the case as raising a duty of care question. Prior to *Glencar*, this case would almost certainly have been considered to raise only a question relating to the standard of care. In determining the latter question, the court, according to the doctrine in *Overseas Tankship (UK) Ltd v Morts Docking & Engineering Co. (The Wagon Mound No. 1)* [1961] A.C. 388, is engaging in the same process as in addressing the issue of remoteness of damage since reasonable foresight is a common test. Whether this is actually so in practice need not here be debated. The point to note is simply that there will be no such necessary coincidence where the liability analysis is based on the duty, rather than standard, of care.

DEFENCES

Contributory negligence

1. Travelling in car with intoxicated driver In *Devlin v Cassidy* [2006] I.E.H.C. 287, Peart J. reduced by 50 per cent the compensation awarded to a passenger injured in a traffic accident in which the driver, who was intoxicated, was killed. The two young men, in the company of their friends, had been out for an evening's entertainment in which alcohol was available from 7p.m. to 3a.m. The plaintiff in evidence said that he had been "rightly drunk" though, perhaps inconsistently, he attested that he could remember wearing a seat belt. The driver had been selected to drive the car, which he did not own, on the basis that, in the plaintiff's evidence, he was the soberest member of the group. Peart J. commented: "Another way of putting it would be to say that he was the least drunk". The plaintiff gave evidence that, in the premises where they had been from midnight to 3a.m., he had seen the driver consume only one pint. A report made after the accident showed that the deceased had twice the permitted level of alcohol in his body and evidence that he had taken ecstasy.

In holding that a reduction of 50 per cent should be made to take account of the plaintiff's contributory negligence, Peart J. observed:

> "The plaintiff's evidence is unreliable. He has no real recall of anything that evening until it comes to evidence which could benefit him in these proceedings. I do not accept his evidence even of his own consumption of pints that evening. He has been at pains to say how drunk he was getting into the car. I presume that this is in order to absolve himself in some way from any culpability in the decision to allow himself to be driven home by a person he would otherwise know to be drunk. On

the balance of probability, I am satisfied that this plaintiff knew very
well that [the driver] was drunk, or to put it more appropriately for
these proceedings, unfit to drive due to the consumption of alcohol, as
was he himself and all the others who entered the vehicle. The testing
carried out on [the driver] confirms this also as a fact. By allowing
himself to be driven by [the driver] on this occasion, the plaintiff has
failed in the duty of care which he owes to himself. In fact the plaintiff
along with the others appears to have encouraged [the driver] to drive
the car. He seems to have been part of the decision that he was the
soberest of them all.

The breach of that duty has caused him to suffer foreseeably, both
in terms of the likelihood of an accident occuring in the first place, and
the injuries themselves. It is perfectly foreseeable that a drunken driver
is going to lose control of the car, and that in whatever impact occurs
that the plaintiff would suffer an injury. The plaintiff's own drunken
state is no rebuttal of the allegation of contributory negligence."

Rather than focus on a passenger's actual or presumed knowledge of a driver's
intoxication, perhaps courts in the future will adopt a simpler and tougher
approach towards those who become intoxicated on a night out with friends.
If they place themselves in the position of relying for lifts home on other
party-goers whose sobriety or intoxication they have no way of assessing,
it may be argued that this, in itself, involves a culpable failure to look after
themselves.

2. Seat Belts   In *Devlin v Cassidy* [2006] I.E.H.C. 287, Peart J. was faced with
a case where the plaintiff passenger claimed that he remembered using his seat
belt but the other evidence in the case cast doubt on the plaintiff's capacity
to remember what had occurred. The plaintiff had been out for an evening's
entertainment with his friends. The drinking began at 7p.m. The accident took
place at 3a.m. The plaintiff's estimate of his consumption was between eight
and 10 pints. In evidence, he described himself when he left the last place
where alcohol had been served is "rightly drunk". A doctor who had examined
him after the accident reported him as having stated that "his last memory was
sitting outside a disco in a car and then wakening up in hospital".

Peart J., whilst not expressly rejecting the plaintiff's evidence on this matter,
admitted to being "extremely doubtful" that he could in the court proceedings
recall putting on his seat belt, given the obviously self-serving nature of that
evidence and the amount of alcohol which the plaintiff admitted to having
consumed. The onus remained on the defendants, however, to show that the
plaintiff had not been wearing a seat belt. From a consideration of the nature of
the plaintiff's injuries, Peart J. concluded that the defendants had not discharged
that onus. The accident had involved a very severe impact between the car
and a tree; the driver had been killed yet, the plaintiff, in the front passenger

seat, had not. He had received injuries to his spleen, back and ankle and he had received a heavy knock to his head, rendering him unconscious for several hours but there was no evidence that his head had come into contact with the windscreen; he had a laceration on the back of his head and the cut to his eye was small. The spleen injury, while "consistent with other possibilities", was "certainly consistent also" with the lap part of the seat belt coming under pressure against his abdomen after the plaintiff had been thrown forward in the impact against the seatbelt.

In the sectin of this Chapter entitled Road Traffic Accidents, above p.567, we analyse the highly important decision of Peart J. in *McNeills v Armstrong* [2006] I.E.H.C. 269, dealing with a range of issues relating to the non-use of seat belts.

3. Mitigation of Damages In *Histon v Shannon Foynes Port Company* [2006] I.E.H.C. 292, where the plaintiff was applying for liberty to enter final judgment in the sum of close to €400,000 as a debt due and owing by the defendant in respect of loss of salary, the defendant sought to have the matter remitted to plenary hearing in which it would raise the defence of contributory negligence for the plaintiff's alleged failure to mitigate his loss by finding alternative employment. Finlay Geoghegan J. held that the plaintiff was entitled to summary judgment. Finding support for her approach in *McGregor on Damages* (17th ed., Sweet & Maxwell, 2006), paras 1–010, 7–002, she did not consider it "arguable that the principles applicable to a plaintiff's obligation to mitigate his or her loss are relevant to a claim for a debt due pursuant to contract or pursuant to statute. Those principles apply to claims for loss and damage suffered by reason of an alleged wrong (whether in contract or tort)."

NUISANCE

In *Larkin v Joosub* [2006] I.E.H.C. 51, Finlay Geoghegan J. imposed liability in both negligence and nuisance on the occupiers of a house in upper Leeson Street, Dublin, which had fallen into disrepair, ultimately damaging the neighbouring property. A fire had occurred in the house in 1998, which had left what initially was a small hole in the roof. This hole was not repaired until 2001. In the meantime it increased in size. Water fell through it and percolated along and through the party wall, causing damage to the plaintiffs' property. The first-named defendant had owned the property until it was vested in the second-named defendant, the Dublin County Council, in September 2000, following procedures taken by the City Council under the Derelict Sites Act 1990. The third-named defendant was representative of the estate of the uncle of the first-named defendant, who had been part-owner of the house with the first-named defendant.

The plaintiffs' first claim was for negligence. They argued that the first and third-named defendants, as owners of the adjoining property, had owed them a duty to take reasonable care of the premises to preserve the premises from becoming dangerous and a nuisance and causing damage to the plaintiff's property. They relied on the decision of Davitt P. in *Victor Weston (Eire) Ltd v Kenny* [1954] I.R. 191. This case concerned property owned by the defendant, who had let the ground floor and basement to the plaintiff and the remaining three floors to other tenants, while retaining the hall, staircases and landing under his own control. There were lavatories on these landings. A tap was left on in a top floor lavatory which led to flooding which damaged the plaintiff's stock. Complaints had previously been made about the defective character of the tap to the defendant. Davitt J. imposed liability, stating:

> "The maxim, *sic utere tuo ut alienum non laedas*, expresses in the broadest way the duty which a person, being the owner or occupier as the case may be of lands or buildings, owes to his neighbour, whether that neighbour be an adjoining owner or occupier, a person lawfully upon adjoining premises, or a member of the public using the adjoining highway. The extent of the duty varies from an absolute obligation to prevent dangerous matter from escaping, as in the case of *Fletcher v. Rylands* L.R. 1 Ex. 265 to an obligation to take reasonable care to prevent the premises from becoming dangerous and a nuisance, as in *Cunard and Wife v. Antifyre Ltd* [1933] 1 K.B. 551, *Taylor v. Liverpool Corporation* [1939] All E.R. 329 (as regards persons on adjoining premises) and *Kearney v. London and Brighton Railway Co.* L.R. 6 Q.B. 759, *Tarry v. Ashton* 1 Q.B.D. 314, *Palmer v. Bateman* [1908] 2 I.R. 393 (as regards persons on the highway)."

He expanded further on the duty of care as follows:

> "I can see no difference in principle between the position of the defendant in this case and that of the landlords in *Hargroves, Aronson and Co. v. Hartopp* [1905] 1 K.B. 472 and *Cockburn v. Smith* [1924] 2 K.B. 119. It seems to me that the same principle applies to each, and that the defendant in this case was under a legal obligation to take reasonable care to prevent any part of the premises which he retained from becoming a source of danger or damage to the adjoining occupiers, his tenants, and so to prevent the water from escaping from his top lavatory and doing damage. The next point to be decided, therefore, is whether the defendant was negligent."

In *Larkin v Joosub*, counsel for the first and third defendants sought to distinguish *Victor Weston* by reason of the fact that the defendant was a landlord. Finlay Geoghegan J. did not accept this distinction: "The principles as stated appear to me to relate to the defendant as an owner of adjoining property and

I would respectfully agree with them as such."

Accordingly, she concluded that the first and third-named defendants had been under a legal obligation to take reasonable care to prevent any part of their premises from becoming a source of danger or damage to the adjoining occupiers or owners including the plaintiffs. As a matter of common sense it was foreseeable that a hole in a roof close to a party wall in a terraced house, which permitted rain to fall down along the party wall, might cause damage by penetration of the water through the party wall into the adjoining premises. The only real issue was whether the Joosub defendants had known or ought to have known of the hole in the roof caused by the fire.

The Joosub defendants had been resident in South Africa for many years prior to the fire. The first-named defendant did not give evidence. The property was looked after on behalf of the owners by an estate agent, who did not give evidence.

On the evidence, Finlay Geoghegan J. found that the premises had already been in a derelict state prior to the fire in August 1998. Before then the property had been occupied by squatters and the subject of many complaints from the plaintiff to the estate agent and the City Council. In 1997 an official of the Derelict Sites Section of the City Council had written directly to the first-named defendant in South Africa and had later been in correspondence with the Irish solicitors of the first and third-named defendants and threatened proceedings under the Derelict Sites Act.

Finlay Geoghegan J. stated:

"In accordance with the principles set out by Davitt P., an owner of property owes a duty of care to the owners and occupiers of adjoining property to take reasonable care to prevent his property becoming dangerous or a nuisance. Such a duty of care must include an obligation to inspect the property from time to time and to carry out such repairs as appear necessary. A person who is a non-resident owner must be under a duty of care to arrange for someone to carry out such inspections and repairs on his behalf.

The fire occurred in August, 1998. The evidence is that initially the hole in the roof was small and increased in size over the following months. On the evidence given I am satisfied that the hole was such that it must have been evident upon any reasonable inspection of the property carried out in the months following the fire. I find, as a matter of probability, that Mr. Ryan, agent for the Joosub defendants, was aware of the hole in the roof of No. 16 following the fire. The evidence was that the hole was initially covered with polythene which was then blown off and the hole in time worsened.

Accordingly I am satisfied that the Joosub defendants were aware of the hole in the roof of No. 16 and failed to take any steps to repair it or, if they were not aware, such lack of knowledge was caused by their own breach of duty in failing to arrange for regular inspections of the property to be carried out on their behalf in this jurisdiction."

Counsel for the first and third-named defendants had sought to rely upon the absence of any evidence from the plaintiffs that they had made them aware of the damage. Finlay Geoghegan J. considered, however, that their liability in negligence to the plaintiffs for the damage caused by their breach of duty in failing to repair the hole in the roof was not dependent upon the plaintiffs' notifying them of the damage though it might be relevant to the issue of mitigation.

Turning to the position of the Council, Finlay Geoghegan J. considered that the duty of care owed by the Council as the owner and occupier of the house was no different from that of the first and third-named defendants. In *Glencar Exploration Plc v Mayo County Council* [2002] 1 I.R. 84, Keane C.J., in considering the liability of the defendant for the alleged negligence in the performance of a statutory function, had distinguished other situations in the following terms:

> "There are, of course, many instances in which a public authority will be liable in negligence because the duty of care imposed by the law on them is no different from that arising in private law generally. Obvious examples are the duties owed by local and other public authorities arising out of their occupation of premises or their role as employers. In such cases, the plaintiff does not have to call in aid the fact that the defendants may have been exercising a statutory function: their duty of care as occupiers, employers, etc., is no greater, but also no less, than that of their counterparts in the private sector."

The Council had become the owner of the property in September 2000, when there had been a hole in the roof for approximately two years. It had not been disputed that it was then under a duty of care to repair the hole in the roof. The roof was not repaired until February 2001.

The duty of care owed by the Council to the plaintiffs in September 2000 had to be considered in the context of communications which had taken place between the parties prior to that date and the council's knowledge of the damage being caused to the plaintiffs' property by the state of dereliction and, in particular, the hole in the roof.

The first named plaintiff had been in contact with the Derelict Sites Section since July 1997. He had met with representatives of that section prior to the fire in August 1998. At that stage the complaints related to the general state of dereliction of the property, occupation by squatters and rats in the building. An official of the Council had been inspecting the premises at least since October 1999 and had been aware of the hole in the roof. In January 2000 an express complaint had been made by the first named plaintiff that, by reason of the hole in the roof, water was entering his premises and damaging it. In February 2000 an inspection had been carried out on behalf of the Council and the hole in the roof photographed. Not surprisingly, Finlay Geoghegan J. concluded that the Council, for some time prior to the vesting order, had been aware of the damage being caused to the plaintiffs' property by reason of the water entering through the hole in the roof of the neighbouring property.

Following the vesting order in September 2000, the responsibility for the building rested with the Development Department. An inspection report prepared by an architect in the City Architect's Department, included the following statement:

> "While the building appears reasonably sound when viewed from the street it must be stated that this structure is seriously at risk. This is because fire damage at the upper level has destroyed the roof leaving the building open to the weather, causing water damage to the property and probably also damaging adjoining houses in the terrace."

The final paragraph of the report stated:

> "Immediate action is required to safeguard the property and to prevent further deterioration of the structure and adjoining properties. Works are urgently required to make the building envelope watertight, to secure the property and to take action to contain outbreaks of rot within the building. Roof works will be the major part of this operation and should include the reinstatement of the roof structure to its original profile and all other works necessary works [*sic*] to properly weather the adjoining buildings. Other works urgently required are to secure window and door openings at the rear of the property and to address the immediate outbreaks of wet and dry rot in the building."

Notwithstanding this report, which was made on October 26, 2000, the repairs to the roof did not begin until February 2001. Further significant rain damage was caused between October 2000 and February 2001.

Having regard to the history of the dealings between the plaintiffs and the Council in relation to the property and the Council's state of knowledge of both properties in September 2000, Finlay Geoghegan J. concluded that the Council had been negligent and in breach of a duty of care owed to the plaintiffs in failing to repair the roof of the building and make it weatherproof in the month of October 2000. It also appeared that the contractors engaged by the Council to carry out repairs of the roof had done so negligently, leaving it exposed and without protection over a weekend period during which there was very heavy rain causing further and particular water damage to the plaintiffs' premises. The Council did not dispute that it was responsible for such negligence.

Finlay Geoghegan J. held that the Council and the first and third-named defendants were concurrent wrongdoers in being responsible for the same damage. She based this conclusion on Hamilton J.'s decision in *Lynch v Beale,* High Court, November 23, 1974 where a building owner had sued his architect, main contractor and nominated sub-contractor for loss sustained as a result of alleged negligence and breach of contract of the three defendants in the construction of hotel premises. The premises had collapsed due to two main factors the subsidence of foundations and inadequate design in the building. The defendant submitted that there were two separate and distinct causes for the structural defects and that the defendants were not concurrent wrongdoers. Hamilton J., in considering this, stated: "The damage claimed in this case against all the defendants is the same damage, *viz.*: the loss sustained by him as a result of the internal collapse of the hotel and the subsidence thereof and the court is satisfied that the defendants are 'concurrent wrongdoers' as defined in the Civil Liability Act, 1961."

Finlay Geoghegan J., agreeing with this approach, stated:

> "The requirement of the definition is that the persons alleged to be concurrent wrongdoers are responsible to the plaintiff for the same damage. Hence it is the damage suffered by the plaintiff which is being referred to.
>
> On the facts of this case, the damage suffered by the plaintiffs is the cost to the plaintiffs of now repairing No. 17 and the rental loss past and future. Further, the acts allegedly constituting concurrent wrongs as found in this judgment took place successively as envisaged by s. 11(2)(c). It is the cumulative effect of the water during the respective periods which has necessitated the repairs to the building, which in turn has caused the damage to the plaintiffs (in sense of cost of repairs) within the meaning of s. 11(1) of the Act of 1961. Accordingly, I have concluded that all the defendants are concurrent wrongdoers within the meaning of the section."

Perhaps it could be argued that the damage in the instant case did indeed have a sequential character, in which it would have been possible to sever the earlier damage from the later.

Turning to the claim based on nuisance, Finlay Geoghegan J. noted that there was "significant overlap" between the claims in negligence and in nuisance. In *Sedleigh-Denfield v O'Callaghan* [1940] A.C. 880 Lord Wright had referred to the succinct definition by Talbot J. in *Cunard v Antifyre* [1933] 1 K.B. 551 at 557 of private nuisances "as interferences by owners or occupiers of property with the use or enjoyment of neighbouring property." Finlay Geoghegan J. considered that a hole in a roof in a terraced house close to a party wall which permitted, over a period of time, rain to fall down the party wall and to percolate into the neighbouring property came within that definition. It had not been alleged that any of the defendants caused the nuisance. Rather the claim was that each of them had continued the nuisance. In *Sedleigh-Denfield v O'Callaghan*, Viscount Maugham had stated: "In my opinion an occupier of land 'continues' a nuisance if with knowledge or presumed knowledge of its existence he fails to take any reasonable means to bring it to an end though with ample time to do so."

Sedleigh-Denfield v O'Callaghan made clear that an owner or occupier of a property would not be liable for the continuance of a nuisance unless he had knowledge of such nuisance. However, such knowledge included the knowledge of servants or agents for whom he was responsible and which must be attributed to him.

There was no dispute that the Council had been aware of the nuisance at the time it became the owner and occupier of the premises. On the evidence, the estate agent for the first and third-named defendants had been aware of the hole in the roof and ingress of water in the area of the party wall. This was knowledge which must be attributed to the first and third-named defendants.

For the same reasons as grounded the finding of negligence, Finlay Geoghegan J. concluded that each of the defendants had failed to take reasonable steps to bring the nuisance to an end during the respective periods when they were owners and occupiers of the property and in that sense had continued the nuisance.

It will be interesting in the future if a court is called on to spell out precisely how the action for nuisance differs from that of negligence. The House of Lords was clear that it did, in *Hunter v Canary Wharf Ltd* [1997] A.C. 655. Whether Irish courts will go so far is not entirely clear. O'Sullivan J.'s decision in *Molumby v Kearns* [1999] I.E.H.C. 86, suggests that they will not. If alternate claims are possible, as in the instant case, perhaps plaintiffs need have no worries.

DEFAMATION

Innuendo   In *Byrne v RTE* [2006] I.E.H.C. 71, MacMenamin J. dismissed an application for further particulars by the defendant where it had broadcast a programme alleging sharp practice by unnamed solicitors in encouraging clients to engage in false claims against Dublin Bus. In answer to a question whether, if a solicitor's name case is on headed notepaper the company would think that this could be a problem, a claims investigator of C.I.E. responded that the company had rules for dealing with particular solicitors.

The programme showed a Bus Éireann claims official perusing a file in which documents bearing the plaintiff solicitors' headed letterhead could be seen momentarily. The defendants sought particulars as to the identity of those who the plaintiffs claimed had identified them from the broadcast. They argued that the "equality of arms" principle underlying Art.6(1) of the European Convention on Human Rights and the more general guarantee of fair procedures under Art.40.3 of the Constitution guaranteed them a reasonable opportunity to present their case to court without being placed at a substantial disadvantage in not being able to weigh the question of damages.

MacMenamin J., in dismissing the defendants' application, distinguished English and Australian authorities on which the defendants had relied. A number of these had involved cases of true innuendo, in which the defendant would not in some instances be able to assess the number and identity of those who interpreted the communication as defamatory, in the absence of particulars by the plaintiff. In the instant case, though the plaintiffs had pleaded innuendo, the claim was in fact one of "false" or "popular" innuendo: see McMahon & Binchy, *Law of Torts* (3rd ed., Lexis Nexis, 2000). There had been:

> "a publication to the general public at large on matters which by the very context and circumstances of the publication, demonstrate an imputation defamatory in nature, that is, to publish allegedly of the plaintiffs that they had been guilty of sharp practice or other disreputable or dishonest or incompetent conduct in their profession."

Privilege   In *Berber v Dunnes Stores Ltd* [2006] I.E.H.C. 327, the defence of qualified privilege was held to apply to the circulation by the manager of a local store to management personnel of the store of a duty roster relating, among others, to the plaintiff, which included his name under the heading "new trainees". The plaintiff had in fact worked for nearly 21 years with the defendant. Having been a buyer, he had recently been moved to store management at this local store. The plaintiff regarded this description as defamatory. Laffoy J. held on the evidence that the manager had not been actuated by malice. The roster sheet had been fairly full when he came to insert the plaintiff's name; by inserting it, he had not been conscious of the implications and there had been no ill intent towards the plaintiff. Moreover, the other managers in the local branch had been aware of the plaintiff's status in the store.

MALICIOUS INSTITUTION OF CIVIL PROCEEDINGS

In *Independent Newspapers (Ireland) Ltd v Murphy* [2006] I.E.H.C. 276, Clarke J. threw some light on the scope of the action for malicious institution of civil proceedings. Mr Murphy had earlier sued the newspaper for defamation. This has resulted in the compromising of the proceedings on the basis of an agreement by the newspaper to pay a sum of money (inclusive of costs) and publish an apology. The proceedings were struck out by consent. The alleged defamation related to whether Mr Murphy had attended the home of the former politician Ray Burke and handed him a brown paper bag containing £50,000. This issue had previously formed the central focus of the Flood Tribunal at a certain point of its deliberations.

The newspaper later sought to have the settlement rescinded on the basis that the earlier proceedings had been a malicious abuse of the process of the court and had been based on a fraudulent misrepresentation. It also sought damages. Mr Murphy contended that the newspaper was estopped from pleading that the earlier proceedings had been an abuse of process, malicious or otherwise unlawful.

In an appeal from an order of the Master relating to discovery of documents, Clarke J. considered it appropriate to give consideration to the legal issues so to enable a reasonable estimate to be made of the factual issues that might be before the court.

Clarke J. referred to the *locus classicus, Dorene Ltd v Suedes (Ireland) Ltd* [1981] 3 I.R. 312 and acknowledged that the precise parameters of the cause of action for malicious institution of civil proceedings remained to be clearly defined. Clarke J. noted that, in *Dorene*, the reason why the civil proceedings had been considered to have been prosecuted maliciously was that, after advice of counsel that the proceedings had no sound legal basis, they had nonetheless continued to be maintained. In the instant case, it appeared that issues of fact rather than law might be in question.

Clarke J. commented:

"It is, of course, in principle open to a party to allege that the reason the court should conclude that proceedings were maliciously progressed was because of the assertion by the plaintiff of factual matters which the plaintiff knew not to be true. There seems no reason in principle why, in an inappropriate case, the pursuit of a claim in such circumstances, based on an assertion of facts which the plaintiff knew not to be true, would not equally amount to an abuse of process. However, additional difficulties arise where, unlike in *Dorene*, the proceedings have already been concluded whether by compromise or by determination by the court, without reference to the question of malicious prosecution.

In the latter case (and on the assumption that the plaintiff succeeds), there will be a binding determination by the court to the effect that the facts are as contended for by the plaintiff. Such a finding could only be gone behind in the limited circumstances identified in the jurisprudence such as a case where it can be shown that the plaintiff's success was procured by a fraud on the court (citing as an example *House of Spring Gardens Ltd v Waite* [1990] 3 WLR 347). In the absence of the defendant being in a position to have the original order set aside on such grounds, the Court could not entertain a second set of proceedings which was predicated upon the fact that the original finding of the court was incorrect."

Somewhat different considerations might well apply in respect of a case which had been compromised rather than determined by the court. In those circumstances, there was no finding of a court, binding on the parties, which could only be set aside on very limited grounds. It seemed to Clarke J. to be:

> "at the very least arguable that it could be the case that a plaintiff, in a position such as Independent, can simply not re-run on the same evidence the action which it had compromised by means of asserting that the claim made by the plaintiff in that action was false to the knowledge of the plaintiff concerned and no more.
>
> The issues which arise in litigation vary. However quite a number of cases turn largely on questions of fact where it is clear, in advance of the hearing, that the paries propose leading contradictory evidence as to key events. Where the parties compromise such an action, such settlement will be based on a view (presumably with the benefit of expert advice) as to the chances of each succeeding or failing in persuading the court that the facts are as they allege. If it were possible, in effect, to reopen such a case, notwithstanding such a settlement, by the defendant simply asserting that the plaintiff's factual contentions were, to the knowledge of the plaintiff, false, without more, then it would, in practical terms, be virtually impossible to compromise any such action. If, in such a case, the court were merely asked to hear the competing evidence which would have been presented to the court on the first action with a view to persuading the court that the plaintiff's evidence was not to be believed, then the court would, in effect, be being asked to allow the defendant to run the case which he had already settled. Without expressing any concluded view on this issue it seems to me that such a conclusion as to the state of the law would be improbable".

ECONOMIC TORTS

In *Irish Municipal Public and Civil Trade Union v Ryanair Ltd* [2006] I.E.H.C. 118, the scope of torts relating to the international infliction of economic injury fell for consideration in an application to strike out the proceedings. The plaintiffs, a union and a number of pilots, claimed that the manner in which the defendant employer had communicated with the pilots, in offering financial inducements to them "and/or threatening to impose penalties upon" them with the object of inducing them to refrain from carrying on collective bargaining through a trade union violated the plaintiff's constitutional rights and their rights under the European Convention on Human Rights, as well as amounting to the torts of conspiracy, inducement of breach of contract and intentional interference with the plaintiffs' contractual and commercial relations or their economic and commercial interests.

Laffoy J. declined to strike out the proceedings. Although Art.40.6.1 (iii) of the Constitution had not the effect of obliging an employer to negotiate with a trade union, the decision of the European Court of Human Rights in *Wilson v United Kingdom* (2002) 35 E.H.R.R. 20, relating to Art.11 of the Convention and financial incentives not to join trade unions, raised sufficent issues to defeat a strike-out application.

As to the claims in regard to the economic torts, Laffoy J. summarily dispatched two arguments by the defendant. The submission that no actionable conspiracy had been pleaded could be met by an amendment to the statement of claim alleging a conspiracy between the defendant and its executives. The defendant had cited no authority for its argument that the claim for inducement of breach of contract was unsustainable because the relationship between the union and its members lacked a contractual character. In the absence of such authority, Laffoy J. was not satisfied that the argument was correct.

In relation to other economic torts, counsel for the defendant referred the court to the observations of Murphy J. in *Bula Ltd v Tara Mines Ltd (No. 2)* [1987] I.R. 95 in respect of what he had described as "a category of innominate tort which may be referred to an unlawful interference with economic interets". In Murphy J.'s view, to seek such relief was "to press the law to the limit of its existing frontiers if not indeed to new ones". Laffoy J. did not express an opinion on what Murphy J. had to say. She contented herself with the observation that:

> "in relation to the generality of the economic torts, as I understand
> the argument advanced on behalf of the plaintiffs, it is that, whatever
> the impact of the decision of the ECHR in the *Wilson* case and the
> enactment of the Act of 2003 is, it bears on the plaintiff's legal rights
> at common law as well as their rights under the Constitution and under
> statute. Therefore, in my view, the claims based on common law must
> come under the umbrella of the conclusion that it is not clear that the
> plaintiffs' claim must fail".

It will be recalled that in *Bula Ltd v Tara Mines Ltd. (No. 2)*, the plaintiff had argued that the Irish courts should adopt the rationalisation of the law by the House of Lords in *Merkur Island Shipping Corporation v Laughton* [1982] A.C. 570 by recognising the existence of a generic economic tort of which the torts of conspiracy, intimidation and inducing a breach of contract were mere species. Recently, in *OBG Ltd v Allan* [2007] U.K.H.L. 21, the House of Lords disdained a unitary approach by distinguishing sharply between inducement of a breach of contract and intentionally causing loss by unlawful means. For practical principles, in the context of Irish law, this may not have a substantial impact since violation of constitutional rights or rights under the European Convention may be considered to amount to the adoption of unlawful means.

INFRINGEMENT OF CONSTITUTIONAL RIGHTS

In *Osbourne v Minister for Justice* [2006] I.E.H.C. 117, an action for damages
for breach of constitutional rights failed where a woman received injuries
when members of the Gardaí were searching premises where she lived, having
obtained a search warrant. The search warrant was defective. Although the
Gardaí had reasonable grounds for the search warrant which they had also
obtained for the premises next door, the belief that the plaintiff's premises
might be used as an escape route by the suspected thief from the next-door
premises did not, in Clarke J.'s view, authorise the issuing of a search warrant
in respect of the plaintiff's premises. Clarke J. was satisfied that no member of
the Gardaí had been aware of the technical deficency of the warrant and that
therefore their actions could not be described as knowingly wrongful.

Clarke J. referred to what Walsh and Kingsmill Moore JJ. had said on the
subject in the famous Supreme Court decision of *People (Attorney General)
v O'Brien* [1965] I.R. 142. While *O'Brien* had been concerned with the
admissibility of evidence, there was in Clarke J.'s view "no reason ... not to
apply the overriding principle to the question of any other consequences of
reliance upon an invalid warrant". He was:

> "therefore satisfied that no claim in damages (whether for breach of
> constitutional rights or in tort) can be brought in respect of actions taken
> on foot of a warrant which though apparently valid was technically
> infirm, but was not relied upon in circumstances which amounted to,
> as Walsh J. put it in *O'Brien*, a 'deliberate or conscious violation of
> rights' where a false basis was put forward for obtaining the warrant
> or where a basis was put forward which, while correct on the facts,
> was one which the person seeking the warrant knew did not justify the
> grant of the warrant. Furthermore it is implicit from the judgments in
> *O'Brien* that reliance on a warrant which is subject to a technical defect
> but where that defect was known, prior to the execution of the warrant,
> by those involved in its execution might also amount to a deliberate or
> conscious violation or rights.
>
> Such an overall view of the entitlement to damages arising from
> the consequences of the execution of a warrant which is technically
> defective is, in my view, consistent with the jurisprudence of the courts
> in the analogous area of breach of statutory duty by officials or others
> charged with carrying out public functions. In such circumstances it is
> now well settled that damages do not arise in the absence of a deliberate
> and knowing breach of statutory obligation."

Clarke J., emphasising the lack of awareness by members of the Gardaí of the
defect in the warrant, observed that:

"it follows from my findings in respect of the warrant that those circumstances need to be examined on the basis that no claim can be brought which stems from any invalidity in the warrant itself. Those circumstances need to be examined, therefore, on the basis that the Gardaí had in their possession an apparently valid warrant in respect of [the plaintiff's premises] and that any infirmity in respect of that warrant was not a matter which those executing it were aware of at the relevant time."

Clarke J. concluded that, whilst the plaintiff gave an account of the events as she believed them to be, she had not in fact been manhandled by the Gardaí when they were seeking to subdue the person suspected of theft. The likelihood was that, when the plaintiff was outside the property attempting to gain access to it, she had come to be injured in the course of hostile physical action being taken by others against the Gardaí as they attempted to leave with the, now arrested, person.

The decision provides some observations. First, one wonders about the application of *O'Brien* principles in this context. The truth of the matter was that the warrant was defective, however innocent of evil design the members of the Gardaí may have been. A trespass to land does not cease to be so because of innocent intent. The Gardaí, when on the plaintiff's premises, had no legal entitlement to be there and were trespassers. (If this is so, the exact location of the incident could well be of great significance since, if it was outside the plaintiff's premises, the issue of trespass would not be relevant.)

It appears that the plaintiff's claim was framed in terms of breach of constitutional rights. If it had been framed in terms of trespass to land, she would arguably have been successful (assuming that the incident could be located, at least in part, within the area under her possession). Can it be that the form of action should have such a decisive effect? If it does, it represents a startling inversion of the *Meskell* principle, as interpreted in *Hanrahan v Merck Sharp & Dohme (Ireland) Ltd* [1988] I.L.R.M. 629, which regards tort law as the normal vehicle for the delivery of protection of constitutional rights, so that a claim for damages for breach of constitutional rights should be invoked only where the particular tort is basically ineffective in providing the appropriate vindication of the constitutional right in question.

It is worth noting developments under the European Convention of Human Rights. In *Keegan v United Kingdom* [2006] All E.R. (D) 235, the European Court of Human Rights held that there had been a violation of Art.8 of the Convention where police officers obtained a search warrant for the applicant's home which they later forcibly entered. Though they were acting with good faith, they had not used sufficient care in checking the reliability of the evidence on which they formed the belief that the search was justified. Under English law the malicious obtaining of a search warrant constituted a tort. This did not constitute an appropriate calibration of the respective interests of the police and those in the home, in the view of the court:

> "The fact that the police did not act maliciously is not decisive under the Convention which is geared to protecting against abuse of power, however motivated or caused ... The Court cannot agree that a limitation of actions for damages to cases of malice is necessary to protect the police in their vital functions of investigating crimes. The exercise of powers to interfere with home and private life must be confined within reasonable bounds to minimise the impact of such measures on the personal sphere of the individual guaranteed under Article 8 which is pertinent to security and well-being (see, e.g. *Buckley v The United Kingdom*, judgment of 25 September 1996, *Reports* 1996-IV, s. 76). In a case where basic steps to verify the connection between the address and the offence under investigation were not effectively carried out, the resulting police action, which caused the applicants considerable fear and alarm, cannot be regarded as proportionate."

As regards the analogy with actions in tort of breach of statutory duty by officials or others charged with carrying out public functions, it is perhaps debatable whether it is "now well settled" that damages do not arise in the absence of a knowing breach of statutory obligation. Whether this is so will depend on the particular statutory provision. A statutory duty can range from absolute liability to liability based on a specific intent or the presence of malice. Many statutory duties imposed on those carrying out public functions require the exercise of reasonable care, which is not dependent on proof of any specific intent. Indeed, some statutory functions falling short of the character of statutory duties may require those discharging functions to exercise due care. It is true that the potential scope of negligence actions in such latter circumstances has been radically curtailed by the Supreme Court decision of *Glencar Exploration Co v Mayo County Council* [2002] 1 I.R. 84.

The tort of misfeasance in public office, which is limited to intentional rather than negligent wrongdoing by public officials, has inspired some Irish jurisprudence hostile to the notion that a claim for negligence or breach of statutory duty should be available where a claim for misfeasance in public office will fail. This is particularly notable in Geoghegan J.'s judgment in *Kennedy v Law Society of Ireland* [2004] 1 I.L.R.M. 178. See our discussion in the *Annual Review of Irish Law 2005*, pp. 665–669.

DAMAGES

Duty to mitigate damages   In *Mahon v Dawson* [2006] I.E.H.C. 331, a solicitor's negligence prevented a client, a dairy farmer, from validly exercising an option in November 2003 to purchase 65 acres of agricultural land in County

Kildare. The client sued for breach of contract and professional negligence, as was clearly his entitlement under the principles set out in *Finlay v Murtagh* [1979] I.R. 249. Both parties accepted that the appropriate test to be applied in relation to the assessment of damages was an award of damages as in a breach of contract case: to put the plaintiff in the same situation as if the contract has been performed.

A question arose as to whether the plaintiff should have mitigated his damages by purchasing other land of equal amount when he lost the option. The plaintiff contended that it was not reasonable to have expected him to do this before earlier litigation had definitively established that he had no valid option to exercise. He indicated, moreover, that he had desired to use the 65 acres in question as part of a consolidated larger holding of 100 acres, on which he would have concentrated part of his dairy farming business.

Feeney J., in an *ex tempore* judgment, stated:

> "In considering how justice can be done between the parties and the facts
> of this case the court has to have regard to the realities of the situation,
> including the availability of funds to the plaintiff, the allowance of a
> reasonable period for the ascertainment of the availability of particular
> landholdings, the apparent unavailability of a suitable unified 100-acre
> holding for use in dairy farming, the organisation and management of
> the farming business, the continuing increase in the cost of land and
> the uncertainty caused by the full defence of the defendant to the claim
> herein."

Taking those matters into account Feeney J. concluded that a period of approximately six months should be allowed from the date of clarification of the legal position concerning the option in November 2003 before it could reasonably be expected that the plaintiff might have arrived at a position where he could have bought some land and mitigated, in part, his loss. By May 2004 the cost of land had risen. The sum provided for in 1996 option would not have enabled the purchase of 65 acres. It should also have been clear by this time that the purchase of the combined 100-acre unit was unlikely to occur.

Feeney J. considered that the plaintiff ought to have mitigated his damages by purchasing a landholding in May 2004 of about half the acreage of that which had been the subject matter of the option. Feeney awarded around €150,000 on the basis of this approach. He awarded the sum of €25,000 for general damages to reflect the disruption in the plaintiff's farming activities. The relative modesty of this amount was designed to reflect the principles stated in *Doran v Delaney (No.2)* [1999] 1 I.R. 303.

Restitutionary damages   *Conneran v Corbett & Sons Ltd* [2006] I.E.H.C. 254 raised a number of interesting issues as to the calculation of damages in a claim for interference with an easement. The claim, by lessees against a lessor, had been framed in contract, trespass and nuisance. The plaintiffs held two retail units and a storage unit at a shopping mall. The first defendant, their lessor, had sold the car park and loading area to the second defendant who developed the area. The plaintiffs, in proceedings decided by Laffoy J. in 2004 ([2004] I.E.H.C. 389) successfully claimed that there had been an interference with this casement entitling them to bring in deliveries of stock and material for their retail units through the car park into a loading area which had been destroyed by the development.

In the 2006 proceedings the plaintiffs claimed that they had sustained additional wages costs and delivery costs. Laffoy J. rejected these claims on the evidence. One aspect worth noting here is that she considered that the reduction prescribed in *Reddy v Bates* [1983] I.R. 141 to take account of the contingences then affecting the labour market had an analogy with contingences that might impact on the trading capacity of lessers during the currency of a lease.

Laffoy J. was not disposed to adopt a model of restitutionary damages which might compensate the plaintiffs for the profit made by the defendants in developing the shopping centre. The plaintiffs had not pleaded this basis of damages nor had sought exemplary damages. (It is worth recalling that the second basis of an award of exemplary damages authorised in *Rookes v Barnard* [1964] A.C. 1129 is where the defendant has sought to make a profit out of committing the tort.) Laffoy J. in any event saw no merit in the restitutionary damages claim in the circumstances of the case. It was "both fanciful and lacking obvious merit", particularly as planning permission for the development had been granted before the institution of the proceedings and the plaintiffs, who had been appellants on appeal to An Bord Pleanála, had withdrawn their appeal on payment of a sum of money, albeit without prejudice to their contention that there was an inference with their property rights.

Counsel for the defendants invoked the decisions of the Supreme Court in *Vesey v Bus Eireann* [2001] 4 I.R. 193 and *Shelley-Morris v Bus Atha Cliath* [2003] 1 I.R. 232 on the basis that contradictory and confusing evidence had been adduced on behalf of the plaintiffs and that the court should not attempt to unravel the contradictions or lack of clarity. In *Shelley-Morris*, Denham J. had observed:

> "I wish to reiterate what was said by this court in *Vesey v Bus Eireann*…
> that the onus of proof in these cases lies on the plaintiff who is, of course,
> obliged to discharge it in a truthful and straightforward manner. Where
> this has not been done 'a court is not obliged, or entitled, to speculate
> in the absence of credible evidence' (*per* Hardiman J. at p. 199). To do
> so would be unfair to the defendant …"

Laffoy J. did not think that this *dictum* applied to the instant proceedings. She considered it "fair to say that the quantification of the plaintiffs' loss in this type of case is likely to give rise to more difficulty than the quantification of damages in a personal injuries action, where the approach to be adopted is well established".

Laffoy J. reviewed the decisions, in both contract and tort, which had addressed the test for determining damages for breaches analogous to that of which the plaintiffs complained. What emerged as a "cornerstone of the traditional or normal measure" was diminution in value. The plaintiffs had not addressed evidence of this type of damage. This presented a formidable difficulty to Laffoy J. who resolved the problem by noting that the matter could be addressed when the revised rents for the leased property were fixed. The plaintiffs would, she noted, "have 'another bite of the cherry' in the rent revision processes". She awarded €50,000 compensation for the loss that would not be addressed in those processes.

Actuarial evidence In *Kenny v Crowley*, Supreme Court, June 21, 2006, the exclusion of actuarial evidence by the High Court judge, on the authority of *Reddy v Bates* [1983] I.R. 141 was upheld. The plaintiff, as a result of serious problems with his kidneys, had largely ceased to work some years before the accident. He was in receipt of unemployment benefit. He "tipped around" mending engines locally for friends for which he received occasional payment. The plaintiff gave evidence, however, that about a year before the accident, he had taken steps to fit out a workshop and commence the business of marine engine servicing and repair. He was not a trained mechanic and neither the High Court nor the Supreme Court regarded the plaintiff's evidence as sufficient to provide the basis for mounting an actuarial claim.

General damages In *Kenny v Crowley,* Supreme Court, 21 June 2006, an award by the High Court of €90,000 for general damages was increased on appeal to €120,000. The plaintiff had been injured when his car collided with the defendant's cattle. Liability was not in issue. The case was treated by the High Court and Supreme Court as one falling under the eggshell skull principle, on account of the fact that, prior to the accident, the plaintiff "had a lazy left eye and … depended on his right eye". As a result of the accident he had very limited sight in his right eye, had double vision which affected his left eye and gave him dizziness. As well as this injury, he suffered soft tissue injuries to his back and neck "and a depression which followed the events". Denham J. (Hardiman and McCracken JJ. concurring) observed:

> "As to the current value of a case where an eye is lost, I sought to refer to the P.I.A.B. Valuation Book. However, I understand that it does not quantify damages for the loss of an eye, as yet. From previous experience with such cases it appears to me that a figure of Eur90,000 is significantly too low a figure for such damage and loss, especially in the circumstances of the plaintiff."

Exaggeration   In *Kenny v Crowley*, Supreme Court, June 21, 2006, the plaintiff received very serious eye injuries in an accident. The High Court judge awarded €90,000 as general damages, a sum increased to €120,000 by the Supreme Court. The High Court judge in his judgment referred to a claim for loss of earnings of €550,000, observing that the plaintiff had "chosen to hoodwink" the court. He awarded nothing under this head. This evidence was to the effect that the plaintiff had not been working for a number of years before the accident, save for "tipping around" with odd jobs mending engines. About a year before the accident, however, he had taken initial steps to fit out a workshop and commence the business of marine engine servicing and repair. This evidence was not sufficient to ground the introduction of actuarial evidence. Had the conclusion been reached that the plaintiff, although not a qualified mechanic, could have made the transition to the business that he had in mind, the sum of €550,000 would not have been unrealistic.

Denham J.'s remarks are worth recording here:

"The High Court stated that the plaintiff had chosen to hoodwink the Court with a claim for loss of earnings into the future of Eur550,000. However, on reading all the evidence, I am satisfied that the plaintiff's evidence did not advance such a claim. The figure arose from an assessor's report which was partly based on incorrect information—that the plaintiff was a mechanic. This concern by the High Court, that it was being hoodwinked, highlights the need for care by legal advisers of a plaintiff in preparation of a case. The law as to exaggerated claims is a matter which should be addressed at the preparation stage by legal advisers with a plaintiff. I am not satisfied that there was any collusion by the plaintiff so as to make an exaggerated claim. While there was absolutely no basis for a claim for Eur550,000, or indeed any significant sum of money for loss of future earnings, in the circumstances of the case that figure should not be a basis either to award the plaintiff or to penalize him. I am satisfied that this is not a concocted claim, a fraudulent claim. Nor is it a case where the injuries were exaggerated by the claimant because of a subjective belief that the injuries have had a worse effect than they have. Nor is it a case where the plaintiff has deliberately exaggerated his injuries. Thus the decision of *Shelley-Morris v Bus Atha Cliath/Dublin Bus* [2003] 1 I.R. 232 does not apply.

The evidence prepared as to future loss of earnings bore little relationship to the position of the plaintiff. However, from the evidence of the plaintiff, I do not believe he was seeking to establish a fraudulent claim. Problems arose from the preparation of the evidence for the trial. In view of the developing law on the issue of exaggerated claims it behoves legal advisers to address such issues, for, amongst other results, an unrealistic approach to expert evidence which is not relevant could give rise to an entire claim being deemed fraudulent. However, in all the circumstances, it is clear that this is not such a case."

In *Kerr v Molloy* [2006] I.E.H.C. 364 the plaintiff sustained an injury to his big toe in an industrial accident in 1999. He maintained during the hearing of his claim for negligence and breach of duty that the injury prevented him from working and that he was in constant pain. After a review of the evidence and medical reports and an inspection of the plaintiff's toe, Herbert J. was driven to conclude that the plaintiff was seriously exaggerating his injuries and that his evidence in regard to his inability to work and his constant pain was false in a material respect. Moreover, Herbert J. was satisfied that the plaintiff knew that this evidence was false. Herbert J. declined, however, to dismiss the action as he considered that this would result in an injustice being done. The plaintiff had made no claim for loss of earnings and had not pursued his claim for special damage. The plaintiff's assertion that he had constant pain, when asked about the matter, had, in Herbert J.'s view, "a certain formulaic quality about it rather than appearing to be … consciously considered repl[ies]". The court had not at any stage been misled by these replies. Herbert J. commented: "In these circumstances, I believe that it would be altogether disproportionate and therefore unjust to dismiss this plaintiff's action, though I would have done so had he made a claim for loss of earnings or loss of ability to compete in the labour market."

In *Corbett v Quinn Hotels Ltd* [2006] I.E.H.C. 222, Finnegan P. awarded €47,500 as general damages to the time of judgment and €7,500 as general damages into the future in a case where the plaintiff, aged 40 at the time of the accident in 2000, had suffered injuries mainly to her knees and shoulder. In respect of both these injuries the plaintiff's evidence was not easily corroborated by the medical evidence. Video evidence adduced by a private investigator showed her able to walk for a protracted distance briskly and without any apparent difficulty. Finnegan P. refused an application under s.26 of the Civil Liability and Courts Act 2004. He held that the plaintiff had suffered injury to her knees which had caused her considerable difficulty for perhaps a month; thereafter, a condition of mild degree chondromalacia had caused her occasional but not significant discomfort. Perhaps related to her low mood, she concentrated overly on the injury to her knees and subjectively believed her symptoms to be a great deal worse than they really were. A somewhat similar subjectivity affected the plaintiff in her response to her shoulder injury, complicated further by the fact that the accident had exacerbated a pre-existing injury to her shoulder.

Transport

AVIATION

Eurocontrol Convention   The main purpose of the Aviation Act 2006 (which began its legislative life as the Air Navigation (Eurocontrol) Bill 2005) was to implement the 1997 consolidated text of the Eurocontrol Convention, the International Convention relating to Co-operation for the Safety of Air Navigation. The original Eurocontrol Convention had been signed in 1960 and was implemented by the Air Navigation (Eurocontrol) Act 1963, as amended. The 1963 Act was subsequently repealed and replaced by the Irish Aviation Authority Act 1993, which implemented later amendments to the 1960 Convention and also provided that the Irish Aviation Authority was to implement specific provisions of the Convention.

The 1997 consolidated text of the 1960 Convention, implemented by the 2006 Act, is designed in particular to strengthen the cooperation between the Contracting States by way of joint activities in the field of air navigation. It was noted during the passage of the 2006 Act that this does not prejudice the principle that every state has complete and exclusive sovereignty over the airspace above its territory, nor the capacity of every state to exercise its perogatives with regard to security and defence in its national airspace.

The main provisions of the consolidated 1960 Convention include an updating of the objectives of Eurocontrol, commensurate with its current and possible future activities; a new institutional structure for formulating and implementing the organisation's policy; an expansion of the tasks of the organisation to achieve a European air traffic management system; more effective decision-making based on majority voting; and an enabling provision for EC membership of Eurocontrol.

At about the same time as the consolidated Convention was signed in 1997, EC Member States agreed in principle to Community membership of Eurocontrol, facilitated by the new Art.40 of the Convention, as the most appropriate way for the EC to exercise its competence in air traffic management. Negotiations between the European Commission and Eurocontrol subsequently resulted in the text of an agreed accession Protocol in 2002. The accession of the EC to Eurocontrol was the culmination of negotiations aimed at ensuring consistency between the two organisations as they work together to develop the European air traffic management system. This move was followed by the conclusion of a memorandum of cooperation between both organisations in 2003, establishing a framework for mutual cooperation and support in five areas. These were: the implementation of the single European sky; research and development; data collection and analysis in the areas of air traffic and environmental statistics; satellite navigation; and international cooperation in the field of aviation.

It was noted during the passage of the 2006 Act that air traffic management in Europe, with 73 air traffic control centres operating in the pan-European airspace, is fragmented and is facing capacity constraints in the future. An estimated 350,000 flight hours a year are wasted due to inefficient air traffic management and airport delays. In this context it was pointed out that the European Commission had proposed a regulatory approach in the area of air traffic management with the objective of achieving a harmonised approach to safety in air traffic management; the regulation of air traffic services; technical inter-operability of systems; and airspace design and management at a European level. A single sky committee chaired by the European Commission will oversee the preparation of implementing measures to establish the appropriate regulatory framework. These proposals envisage Eurocontrol acting as the technical adviser to the single sky committee and playing a significant role in defining and developing rules in accordance with mandates given by the EC. It was also noted that the single sky legislation had implications for the organisation and management of air traffic control services in Ireland, notably in terms of the role of the Irish Aviation Authority (IAA) as service provider and regulatory authority for air navigation services.

It was pointed out that, while Eurocontrol was previously almost exclusively concerned with air traffic management activities for the "en route" segment, the 1997 revised Eurocontrol Convention has considerably extended the scope of its activities to include the entire spectrum of air traffic services. The changes enable: the introduction of independent performance review and target-setting; improvements to safety regulation; strengthened policy and planning for the airport/air traffic system interface as part of the "gate-to-gate" concept; improved airspace design processes; improved standards-making; the provision for common design and procurement of systems; enhanced research, development, trials and evaluation, and more effective introduction of new technology; enhanced user consultation/ involvement; and enhanced global cooperation and influence.

Against this background, the 2006 Act amends the Irish Aviation Authority Act 1993 and also makes provision for related matters. Specifically, the 2006 Act reflects changes in the management structure of Eurocontrol and provides for the making of Regulations requiring the IAA to comply with any conditions laid down for the operation of a common European air traffic flow management system at a common international centre. The 2006 Act also provides that Eurocontrol officers may give evidence in Irish courts and also provides for such officers to carry out on-the-spot inspections.

Having regard to the largely executive nature of air navigation and safety regulatory functions, the requirement to ensure that these remain responsive to market needs and the desirability of capitalising on its potential for additional commercial and employment opportunities, the Oireachtas assigned these functions to the IAA in the 1993 Act. The Authority has responsibility for regulating the technical and safety aspects of civil aviation and for the provision of air traffic standards. In its regulatory capacity it oversees the safety standards in the operation, maintenance and airworthiness of Irish registered aircraft, Irish air navigation services, Irish airlines and aircraft maintenance organisations, the competency of Irish pilots and aircraft maintenance engineers and the operation of Irish aerodromes. In fulfilling its role, the IAA operates to international safety standards and procedures as laid down by the International Civil Aviation Organisation, the European Joint Aviation Authorities, Eurocontrol, which is the European organisation for the safety of air navigation, the European Civil Aviation Conference and the European Union.

During the debate on the 2006 Act in the Oireachtas, a number of amendments were proposed to address concerns raised by some aircraft leasing companies on the issue of detention and sale of aircraft for unpaid debts. Articles 5 to 9 of Annex IV to the revised 1960 Convention refer to the issues of attaching the "en route" charge as a lien on the aircraft, making the operator and owner jointly and severally liable and detention and sale of aircraft to enforce recovery. These provisions are not included in the 2006 Act and it was noted that, under the Convention, the State was not required to legislate for the creation of liens or joint and several liability. On this basis it was pointed out that the 2006 Act would not increase existing powers relating to detention and sale of aircraft for unpaid charges, which have been in place since the enactment of the Air Navigation and Transport Act 1988 (*Annual Review of Irish Law 1988*, p.467). It may be noted that the leasing companies had also voiced concerns about the powers contained in the 1988 Act and they have asked that they be modified in the 2006 Act. As a result, the Minister for Transport consulted the Office of the Attorney General and other interested parties, namely, the IAA, the Dublin Airport Authority and Eurocontrol. All argued against the removal or dilution of the existing powers of detention and sale. Following consideration of all the views expressed on both sides, it was decided not to make any changes to the existing powers in the 2006 Act.

The 2006 Act also incorporated the provisions of the European Communities (Compensation and Assistance to Air Passengers) (Denied Boarding, Cancellation or Long Delay of Flights) Regulations 2005 (S.I. No. 274 of 2005), under which the Commission for Aviation Regulation was appointed as the designated body for the purposes of implementing Regulation (EC) No. 261/2004 establishing common rules on compensation and assistance to passengers in the event of being denied boarding and of cancellation or long delay of flights (repealing Regulation (EEC) No. 295/91). It was pointed out that, as the 2005 Regulations had been made under the European Communities Act 1972, they only allowed for summary prosecution (and associated minor penalties) for their infringement. The opportunity was taken in the 2006 Act to re-cast the Commission's role in primary legislation, which was done explicitly for the purpose of enabling it to pursue prosecutions on indictment in the event of serious breaches of the legislation.

MERCHANT SHIPPING AND MARINE ENVIRONMENT

IMO Conventions on oil pollution The main purpose of the Sea Pollution (Miscellaneous Provisions) Act 2006 was to implement a number of International Maritime Organisation (IMO) Conventions and Protocols concerning the protection of the marine environment. These were: the Protocol to the International Convention on Oil Pollution Preparedness, Response and Co-Operation 1990 (OPRC); the International Convention on the Control of Harmful Anti-Fouling Systems 2001 (AFS Convention); Annex VI as added to the International Convention on the Prevention of Pollution from Ships (MARPOL) by the Protocol of 1997; and the International Convention on Civil Liability for Bunker Oil Pollution Damage 2001 (Bunkers Convention). The 2006 Act also amended Pt III of the Merchant Shipping Act 1992. It was noted during the Oireachtas debate on the 2006 Act that these IMO instruments owed their origin to the Erika incident off the coast of France in December 1999, because it led to a reassessment at EU and international levels of many aspects of the regulatory arrangements which apply regarding maritime safety and the protection of the marine environment. This process was given added impetus in November 2002 when the Bahamas registered tanker Prestige, laden with 77,000 tonnes of heavy fuel oil, broke in two off the coast of Galicia, Spain, spilling an unknown but substantial quantity of its cargo.

The 2006 Act thus forms part of an interlocking series of legislative enactments in this area. The Sea Pollution (Amendment) Act 1999 had given effect to OPRC. The Convention was designed to ensure that proper arrangements are in place in each Member State of the IMO to deal with emergency situations arising from spillage of oil into the sea. Resolution 10 of the 1990 conference that adopted OPRC invited the IMO to initiate work to develop an appropriate instrument to expand the scope of the OPRC Convention to apply, in whole or in part, to pollution incidents by hazardous substances other than oil and prepare a proposal to this end. The IMO in March 2000 adopted a Protocol to that effect. The 1999 Act provides for the preparation of oil pollution emergency plans by harbour authorities and operators of offshore installations and oil handling facilities, and their submission to the Minister for approval. It also provides that the Minister may direct a local authority to prepare and submit such a plan for approval. The Irish Coast Guard, formerly known as the Irish Marine Emergency Service, which was established in 1991 as part of the Department of Communications, Marine and Natural Resources, has been designated as the Irish national response agency and has made the necessary arrangements to give effect to the Convention. The Irish Coast Guard is also to be similarly designated for the purposes of the Protocol. The 2006 Act amended the 1999 Act to give effect to the terms of the Protocol.

A second aspect of the 2006 Act is to implement the International Convention on the Control of Harmful Anti-Fouling Systems for Ships 2001 (AFS Convention). The background to the 2001 Convention was the use of anti-fouling systems to keep the hulls of ships clean, smooth and free from fouling organisms, such as barnacles, algae and molluscs, so that the ships would travel faster through the water and consume less fuel. During the 1960s the chemical industry developed cost-effective anti-fouling paints using metallic compounds, in particular the organotin compound tributyltin (TBT). By the 1970s most seagoing vessels had TBT paints on their hulls. Awareness of the harmful environmental effects of organotin compounds gradually grew in the late 1980s. Scientific studies have shown that organotin compounds, in particular TBT, used as anti-fouling systems on ships, pose a substantial risk of adverse impacts on ecologically and economically important marine organisms. The 2001 Convention provides rules to ban the use of organotin-based anti-fouling systems, TBT, which are harmful to the marine environment and provides a mechanism through which other harmful anti-fouling systems may be banned or regulated in the future on a global basis.

The 2006 Act also amended the Sea Pollution Act 1991, which deals with the prevention of pollution of the sea by oil and other substances and gives effect to the International Convention for the Prevention of Pollution from Ships, done at London on November 2, 1973, as amended by the Protocol done at London on February 17, 1978 (MARPOL 73/78), also known as the MARPOL Convention. The Convention was modified by the Protocol of 1997, in which a new Annexe 6 was added relating to the prevention of air pollution from ships. The 2006 Act amended the 1991 Act to enable Regulations to be made relating to Annexe 6.

As to the Bunkers Convention, the 2006 Act complements the Oil Pollution of the Sea (Civil Liability and Compensation) (Amendment) Act 2003, which updated Irish legislation on spills from tankers. It can also be seen as complementing the Sea Pollution (Hazardous Substances) (Compensation) Act 2005, which implemented in Irish law the International Convention on Liability and Compensation for Damage in connection with the Carriage of Hazardous and Noxious Substances by Sea 1996. The Bunkers Convention implemented by the 2006 Act contains a civil liability regime for ships other than oil tankers.

ROAD TRANSPORT

Two Acts concerning Road Safety Strategy The Road Safety Authority Act 2006, discussed below, established on a statutory basis the Road Safety

Authority (RSA). The 2006 Act also amended the Road Traffic Act 2002 to facilitate the mutual recognition of driving disqualifications on a bilateral basis between the UK, Northern Ireland and the State. The Road Traffic Act 2006, also discussed below, complemented the Road Safety Authority Act 2006 by introducing mandatory (random) alcohol testing, banning the hand-held use of mobile phones, facilitating the use of speed cameras and enabling provisions to facilitate future reforms of the driver licensing system. The two Acts passed in 2006 represented a significant legislative component of the national Road Safety Strategy. Indeed, their enactment within a short space of time could be attributed, at least in part, to the much-publicised criticism of the failure to implement these elements of the strategy voiced by Mr. Eddie Shaw, the former non-executive chair of the National Safety Council (the predecessor to the RSA), who had resigned on the basis that he had failed to persuade the Government of the need for these measures. In that respect, his resignation may have accelerated, at least to some extent, the enactment of the two 2006 Acts.

Road Safety Authority   The decision to establish the RSA by the Road Safety Authority Act 2006 was intended to lead to a more focused development of initiatives to promote road safety, result in improvements in driver formation in general and lead to improved service delivery for the driving test, which will facilitate future reform of the driver licensing system. The RSA's mandate includes the development of future road safety strategies by developing programmes that will form the basis of the Government's future road safety strategies. The RSA was also mandated to deal with an exceptionally long backlog in the State in delivering driving tests. The functions assigned to the RSA are intended to bring within a single authority those activities focused on improving driver and vehicle standards and the promotion of road safety which were previously under the auspices of the Department of Transport or its agencies.

Section 4 of the 2006 Act states that the RSA's functions include driving tests, vehicle-testing and registration of driving instructors. The RSA will be the issuing authority for certificates of competency following successful completion of a driving test, and test certificates certifying that vehicles meet test standards on successful completion of a vehicle test. In this context, the authority will take over responsibility for the commercial vehicle testing scheme operated by local authorities and the NCT/"MOT" car testing scheme. As already mentioned, the RSA also takes over the road safety functions formerly carried out by the National Safety Council. The RSA is also responsible under the Road Transport Act 1986 relating to enforcement of road haulage licences, the 2002 EU Directive on Working Time in Transport and associated EU Regulation on driver hours and the EU Regulation on digital tachographs.

Section 14 of the 2006 Act provides for the appointment of a board of the RSA by the Minister. The board consists of a chairperson and not fewer than six and not more than 11 ordinary members who may serve no more than two terms. The period of membership of any member will not exceed five years. Sections 15 and 16 contain provisions on the appointment of a chairperson and ordinary board members as well as the meetings and procedures of the board. Section 17 provides for the appointment of a chief executive officer, who is responsible for the staff, administration and business of the RSA and will be the person charged with the day-to-day running of the RSA and the carrying out of its functions and will be answerable to the board. The chief executive officer will be responsible for the propriety of the authority's accounts and the economic and efficient use of its resources and will be answerable to any committee of the Houses of the Oireachtas set up to examine its affairs.

Section 38 amends s.9 of the Road Traffic Act 2002, which provides for the procedures to apply when the European Convention on Driving Disqualifications is in force. It was pointed out during the passage of the 2006 Act that, at a meeting of the British–Irish Council, it was agreed that the terms of the Convention be applied between the UK and Northern Ireland by means of a bilateral agreement between Ireland and the UK. Prior to the 2006 Act the procedures in s.9 of the 2002 Act could only apply when the Convention comes into force across the EU, which is 90 days after the last Member State which signed it has adopted it. The amendment effected by the 2006 Act provides for s.9 of the 2002 Act to apply before the Convention comes into force.

Road Traffic Act 2006   The Road Traffic Act 2006 complemented the Road Safety Authority Act 2006, discussed above, and introduced mandatory (random) alcohol testing, banned the hand-held use of mobile phones, facilitated the use of speed cameras and enabled provisions to facilitate future reforms of the driver licensing system. Indeed, as the Minister for Transport pointed out in presenting the Act, it was the sixth major legislative initiative in six years intended to underpin and promote road safety. That legislative progression had seen the introduction of penalty points, a new system for the independent licensing of taxis, hackneys and limousines, a new structure of speed limits based on metric values and, most recently, the establishment of the RSA in the Road Safety Authority Act 2006, discussed above.

Mandatory alcohol testing   Section 4 of the 2006 Act implemented, belatedly, a recommendation in the *Report of the High Level Group on Road Safety* (which was tasked with the preparation and delivery of a road safety strategy) that mandatory (random) alcohol testing be introduced. It was pointed out that the introduction of mandatory alcohol testing was the subject of lengthy consideration and consultation, which included a very significant engagement by the Office of the Attorney General, supported by independent legal advice. The aim of that consideration was to see the introduction of a system through which motorists could be made subject to a requirement to submit to a preliminary breath test without there being any prior suspicion that alcohol had been consumed or that the behaviour of the motorist warranted that a test be administered. The determination of the legislative provisions necessary to support the proposed scheme has been an extensive process in order to strike the appropriate balance between the rights of the individual and the service of the common good by the adoption of a measure that will enhance road safety. Section 4 of the 2006 Act provides that the establishment of checkpoints for mandatory alcohol tests can only be pursued on the specific written authorisation of an officer of the Garda Síochána not below the rank of inspector. That authorisation must be in writing and must clearly establish the place, date and times of day when the checkpoint may be operated. It was envisaged that the Garda Commissioner would establish guidelines to assist and inform all members of the force in the carrying out of their roles in regard to the operation of mandatory alcohol tests. The introduction of mandatory roadside testing for alcohol in the 2006 Act provided for the first time a means for the detection of drink-driving offences that is based exclusively on the level of alcohol consumption as opposed to a motorist's behaviour. A typographical error in s.4 was corrected by s.1 of the Road Traffic and Transport Act 2006, which was enacted within one day of its presentation to the Oireachtas in October 2006.

Reform of fixed charge penalties and disqualification periods It was noted that, if motorists choose to continue to drink and drive, the introduction of mandatory alcohol testing would inevitably result in further increases in the levels of detection. In recognition of this, the 2006 Act promotes an alternative option to a court hearing for those charged with the commission of certain drink-driving offences. Thus, s.5 provides for the introduction of a new system of fixed charges for certain drink-driving offences, the payment of which will lead to the imposition of a fixed period of disqualification. The section provides that where a motorist has been detected with a level of not more than 100 milligrammes of alcohol per 100 millilitres of blood, or the equivalent levels in urine or breath, he or she will have the opportunity to pay a fixed charge of €300 and accept a driving disqualification of six months. If the charge is not paid, however, criminal proceedings may be brought. The consequences of a conviction will be significantly more onerous as a result of other initiatives in the 2006 Act, discussed below. It is notable that the possibility of paying a fixed charge is only available to those who have not been convicted of a drink-driving offence in the previous five years and can only be availed of once to any motorist in any period of five years.

The advent of the new system of administrative disqualification for certain drink-driving offences places in the spotlight the range of mandatory disqualifications applied prior to the 2006 Act under the Road Traffic Acts 1961 to 2006. The immediate consequence of the decision to apply an administrative disqualification of six months to a specific group of drink-driving offences meant that the minimum periods of disqualification that apply following convictions for drink-driving offences generally required review. The result of that review is set out in s.6 of the 2006 Act. The range of offences to which this system applies had previously been set out in the Road Traffic Act 1994. Given the much higher profile that applies to road safety since 1994, and accepting that there was a broad consensus for the need for more consistent deterrents that reflect the seriousness with which society views the more serious breaches of traffic law, s.6 of the 2006 Act provides that the minimum period of disqualification for the most serious offences, which include dangerous driving causing death or serious injury, and the most serious drink-driving offences, were increased from two years to four years in respect of a first offence and from four to six years for a second or subsequent offence. Similarly, the minimum period of disqualification following a conviction for a drink-driving offence was increased from six months to one year; this period of disqualification was also applied by s.6 of the 2006 Act to the general range of offences that attract consequential disqualifications. The offences of driving when disqualified and of dangerous driving were added to that group of offences.

The review of the system of consequential disqualifications also prompted an examination of the system by which those who have been disqualified from driving may apply to the courts to have their licences returned. The pre-2006 provisions relating to such applications were regarded as cumbersome and lacking in clarity. Section 7 of the 2006 Act promotes a new system through which applications may be made to the courts for the restoration of a licence. In particular, the facility will only be applied in respect of first-time disqualifications of not less than two years. The determination of "first time" is defined by reference to a ten-year threshold from a previous disqualification. Under the 2006 Act the application for the restoration of a licence may only be made following the completion of half of the period of the disqualification and a successful application will only result in a reduction of one third in the overall period at the maximum. These new provisions mean that where a person is disqualified for any period of not more than two years, the full period of disqualification will apply and where a person is the subject of repeat disqualifications, he or she will not be able to avail of the facility to apply for the restoration of the licence.

Hand-held mobile phones and equipment   Section 3 of the 2006 Act deals with the hand-held use of mobile phones and in-vehicle equipment. It sets out a specific ban on the holding of a mobile phone by a person while driving a motor vehicle. It also enables the Minister to make Regulations for mobile phone use generally, as well as in-vehicle technologies of an information, communication or entertainment nature for the purposes of preventing driver-distraction arising from inappropriate use of such technologies by occupants of vehicles. In addition to a maximum fine of €2,000, the commission of the offence of holding a mobile phone while driving attracts the endorsement of four penalty points on conviction.

Driver licensing regime Sections 8 to 13 of the 2006 Act relate to the driver licensing system. The main object of these provisions is the introduction of a learner permit to replace the provisional licence and enabling Regulations to require learner drivers to undergo a course of instruction. Section 8 provides that the Minister may by order recognise a driving licence issued by another country for the purpose of exchanging that licence for an Irish driving licence. Driving licence exchange arrangements operate in respect of licences issued by Member States of the European Union and the European Economic Area. These arrangements replace those in the Road Traffic (Licensing of Drivers) Regulations 1999, and reflect the need to include such provisions in primary legislation: see also the discussion of the Road Traffic and Transport Act 2006, immediately below.

Road haulage licensing regime The Road Traffic and Transport Act 2006, which was enacted within one day of its presentation to the Oireachtas in October 2006, dealt with a serious gap in the road haulage licensing regime. It had emerged that s.3 of the Road Transport Act 1986, the main statutory power given to the Minister for Transport to grant licences to road haulage operators, had been inadvertently repealed in October 2005 by the Road Transport Act 1999 (Repeals) (Commencement) Order 2005, in the mistaken belief that s.3 of the 1986 Act was obsolete. The Office of the Attorney General has confirmed that a power for the Minister to grant such road haulage operator licences must be contained in primary legislation. As both passenger and haulage operators share a common regulatory framework under EU law, the Office of the Attorney General also reviewed the power of the Minister for Transport to grant passenger transport operator licences. The power to grant such licences is contained in reg.3 of the European Communities (Road Passenger Transport) Regulations 1991, which were made under s.3 of the European Communities Act 1972. The Attorney General advised that specific provisions are not contained in the relevant EC Directives that permit or oblige the issue of these licences. Accordingly, the Attorney General advised that it was beyond the Minister's power at the time to make Regulations providing for such licences and that primary legislation was therefore required. Section 2 of the 2006 Act remedied this problem. Section 2(1) empowers the Minister to grant both road haulage and road passenger transport operator licences. Section 2(2) provides that applicants must be of good repute, appropriate financial standing and have professional competence. Section 2(5) retrospectively validates any licences for both road haulage and passenger operators granted, or deemed to have been granted, under the 1991 Regulations.

Safety belts and child restraints The European Communities (Compulsory Use of Safety Belts and Child Restraint Systems in Motor Vehicles) Regulations 2006 (S.I. No. 240 of 2006) implemented Directive 2003/20, amending Directive 91/671 on the approximation of the laws of the Member States relating to compulsory use of safety belts in vehicles of less than 3.5 tonnes, and extend the existing requirements in relation to the wearing of safety belts and child restraint systems in motor vehicles. Essentially, Directive 2003/20 provides that where safety belts are fitted in a vehicle they must be worn. In particular, the Regulations afford children greater protection when travelling in cars and goods vehicles by requiring them to be restrained in an appropriate child restraint. They came into force on May 5, 2006.

Subject Index